First-Year Writing: Writing in the Disciplines

Seventh Custom Edition
Texas Tech University
2013-2014

D1402016

Taken from:
Real Texts: Reading and Writing Across the Disciplines,
Second Edition
by Dean Ward and Elizabeth Vander Lei

Reading Rhetorically, Fourth Edition
by John C. Bean, Virginia A. Chappell, and Alice M. Gillam

Style: Lessons in Clarity and Grace, Eleventh Edition
by Joseph M. Williams and Gregory G. Colomb

Cover Art: Courtesy of Texas Tech University

Taken from:

Real Texts: Reading and Writing Across the Disciplines, Second Edition
by Dean Ward and Elizabeth Vander Lei
Copyright © 2012, 2008 by Pearson Education, Inc.
Published by Longman
Glenview, IL 60025

Reading Rhetorically, Fourth Edition
by John C. Bean, Virginia A. Chappell, and Alice M. Gillam
Copyright © 2014, 2011, 2007, 2004 by Pearson Education, Inc.
Published by Longman

Style: Lessons in Clarity and Grace, Eleventh Edition
by Joseph M. Williams and Gregory G. Colomb
Copyright © 2014, 2010, 2007 by Pearson Education, Inc.
Published by Longman

Pearson Learning Solutions, 501 Boylston Street, Suite 900, Boston, MA 02116
A Pearson Education Company
www.pearsoned.com

Printed in the United States of America

1 2 3 4 5 6 7 8 9 10 V013 17 16 15 14 13

000200010271811084

JA/LC

ISBN 10: 1-269-45337-8
ISBN 13: 978-1-269-45337-0

BRIEF CONTENTS

CONTENTS

5 USING RHETORICAL READING FOR RESEARCHED WRITING PROJECTS   98

6 INCORPORATING READING INTO WRITING   114

7   ACTIONS   147

8   CHARACTERS   165

COURSE OVERVIEWS

ENGL 1301 and 1302 fulfill part of the communication requirement of the core curriculum.

All courses under the communication requirement have the following learning outcomes.

Students should:

- Demonstrate the ability to specify audience and purpose and to make appropriate communication choices.
- Demonstrate the ability to apply appropriate form and content in written, visual, and oral communication.
- Demonstrate the ability to apply basic principles of critical thinking, problem solving and technical proficiency in the development and documentation of exposition and argument.

More specific discussion of outcomes is included in each course overview.

ENGLISH 1301: ESSENTIALS OF COLLEGE RHETORIC

English 1301 helps build the foundation for each student's academic writing career. It is designed to help all students develop their writing ability at the college level. Throughout the semester, students will complete a variety of assignments in order to practice and improve their critical thinking, writing, and reading skills. Students will write summaries of texts and visuals, evaluations of academic sources, and a rhetorical analysis of a particular text. In doing so, they will learn more about planning and organizing writing, drafting and revising to improve content and coherence, and editing and proofreading to increase their understanding of conventions of grammar and mechanics. Finally, they will develop a greater understanding of the role of writing in various university courses.

1301 EXPECTED LEARNING OUTCOMES

By the end of the course, students will be able to:

- Identify, discuss, and analyze various rhetorical strategies and elements of the writing process
- Analyze text and visuals, and compose summaries and paraphrases of those works
- Synthesize ideas presented in a variety of works and present those ideas in a coherent essay
- Demonstrate a competency with conventions of Standard English

ENGLISH 1302: ADVANCED COLLEGE RHETORIC

English 1302 focuses on persuasive writing and writing from sources. Students will build on the skills learned in English 1301 as they conduct preliminary research and write a literature review, develop claims for argument, compile and evaluate evidence and support for their claims, learn to recognize and avoid fallacious reasoning, and gain a better understanding of the role of language in argument. Students will also conduct academic research using both print and electronic sources, evaluate and incorporate source material into an argument, and practice citing that material appropriately.

1302 EXPECTED LEARNING OUTCOMES

By the end of the course, students will be able to:

- Identify, discuss, and analyze various rhetorical strategies and elements of writing arguments
- Construct specific claims, supporting arguments, and rebuttals to opposing arguments
- Evaluate source material for use in a variety of rhetorical situations
- Integrate source material into arguments and cite that material appropriately according to specified style guides

METHODS FOR ASSESSING THE EXPECTED LEARNING OUTCOMES

The expected learning outcomes for the course will be assessed through:

- Weekly Writing Assignments
- In-Class Application Activities
- Class Discussions
- Grammar Diagnostics and Activities

COURSE REQUIREMENTS

- Complete assigned readings and in-class and out-of-class writing assignments and exercises, including worksheet notes, brief assignments, drafts, peer critiques, writing reviews, and grammar diagnostics and activities
- Participate actively in full-class and small group discussions
- Participate thoughtfully and respectfully online

REQUIRED MATERIALS

- *Texas Tech's English 1301/1302 Textbook (Custom Edition 2013-2014)*
- *The St. Martin's Handbook (TTU E-Custom Edition)*
- Electronic storage media to hold copies of all work completed and submitted for the course
- Access to a computer with Internet capabilities

ASSIGNMENTS

You will have one or more writing assignments due each week. The weight or value of each assignment varies, depending on the type of assignment and where each assignment falls in the curriculum. You will find specific details concerning each assignment prompt and weight online; the types of assignments you will write are described briefly below. Please note that there is no final exam in ENGL 1301 or 1302.

There are five types of assignments in this course:

- Brief assignments
- Essay drafts
- Peer critiques
- Writing reviews
- Grammar activities

Brief Assignments

In both courses, you will complete a number of targeted writing assignments. These brief assignments will enable you to focus on a particular skill, such as identifying an audience or evaluating source material.

Essay Drafts

At different points in the semester, you will write longer essays. Completing these drafts enables you to practice a number of key writing skills, including generating a substantial amount of text, revising that text, and editing the text.

Peer Critiques

To complete a peer critique, you will read another student's draft and respond to a series of questions about that draft. Peer critiques can benefit both the writer who composes the critique and the writer who receives the critique. When you write a peer critique, you will practice both your critical reading and writing skills. The student who receives your critique will then practice critical reading, thinking and writing by examining your advice and then deciding whether it should be followed in revising his or her draft.

Writing Reviews

At the end of the course, you will compose a writing review. A writing review is a first-person, reflective narrative that discusses some of the choices you made in composing various texts as well as detailing what you have learned during the course and how you can apply this knowledge in other areas.

Grammar Diagnostics and Activities

You will be asked to complete a grammar diagnostic. Throughout the semester, you will complete a series of online grammar activities that are selected for you based on your demonstrated abilities. These activities will be assigned for completion out of class.

Grading

All assignments carry specific value or weights, and your grade for each assignment will be a number of points (on a 0–100 scale) multiplied by the relative weight of the assignment. Each assignment in this course will be evaluated and assigned a numeric grade according to a scoring rubric for that assignment.

In both ENGL 1301 and 1302, your assignments will be assessed anonymously by a group of qualified instructors via the Raider Writer interface. These instructors include current M.A. and Ph.D. students in our graduate English programs, recent graduates of those programs, lecturers who hold either an M.A. or a Ph.D., or tenure-line faculty. All instructors, regardless of experience level, engage in professional development and training activities every semester.

Brief assignments, peer critiques, and writing reviews are graded by one instructor, and all major drafts in the class receive at least two reads in order to obtain an averaged score. When you submit to Raider Writer, one of the instructors assigned to your course will receive your assignment and begin the grading process.

Your final grade for the course will be calculated by dividing the number of points you have earned by the total weights of all assignments. You may check online throughout the course to see your accumulated grade totals.

Grades are awarded based on the following scale:

90 – 100 (A)

80 – 89 (B)

70 – 79 (C)

60 – 69 (D)

0 – 59 (F)

Note that grades are not rounded. A 79.6, for example, is still a 79, or a C.

If your instructor chooses to use class participation grades, he or she will provide you with a written description of those policies on the first day of class.

The following descriptions explain more about what the various grades in ENGL 1301 and 1302 indicate about your performance on each assignment. Please refer to these, the specific rubric for each assignment, and your instructor's commentary if you have questions about your grades.

A

An "A" text effectively meets the needs of the rhetorical situation by illustrating a thorough understanding of purpose, audience, and context. The topic is clearly defined and focused. The thesis is clear, supported with specific and appropriate evidence. Sources are used appropriately and cited correctly. The organization is effective. The introduction establishes a context for writing and contains a focused thesis statement; the body paragraphs are well developed and follow logically from the information that precedes them; the conclusion moves beyond restating the thesis to discussing the implications and/or significance of the topic. The language used is clear, readable, and sometimes memorable as well as appropriate in tone. The writer has followed all directions for the assignment.

B

A "B" text has a clear sense of purpose and audience. The topic is adequately defined and focused. The thesis is adequate, but could be focused more, especially given the quality of evidence the writer has used. Sources are used appropriately and cited correctly. The text has an effective introduction and conclusion. The order of information is logical, and the reader can follow the line of argument because of the transitions and topic sentences used. Paragraphs contain sufficient detail to assist the reader in understanding the argument. The language used is clear and readable. Sentence structure is appropriate for educated readers, and the writer has used subordination, emphasis, and varied sentences. Vocabulary is appropriate. The text contains few surface errors, few, if any, of which impair the readability of the assignment. The writer has followed all directions for the assignment.

C

A "C" text demonstrates some sense of purpose and audience. The topic is generally defined, and the thesis is general. It is supported with evidence; however, the essay doesn't demonstrate an understanding of the complexity of the topic or of alternative points of view. Sources are used, although there may be some minor mistakes in the in- text citation or works cited list. The organization is fairly clear; the reader can understand the structure of the text although the lack of some transitions and/or topic sentences may make the task more difficult. Paragraphs are adequately developed and divided appropriately. The language is competent. Sentence structure is simple, but generally correct, and word choice is correct, but limited. The text contains errors in spelling, usage, and punctuation. The writer has followed all directions for the assignment.

D

A "D" text demonstrates little awareness of the rhetorical situation. It might, for example, over- or underestimate or ignore the audience's prior knowledge, assumptions, or beliefs. The text may have little sense of purpose. The thesis statement may be flawed or missing, and the evidence presented irrelevant or inadequately interpreted or understood. The text might rely too much on outside sources with little or no original analysis, and the essay may contain incorrect in- text or works cited. The organization is problematic. Introductions or conclusions are not functional; paragraphs are inadequately developed, and transitions and topic sentences are dysfunctional or missing. The text has numerous and consistent errors in spelling, usage, punctuation, and sentence structure, many of which may hinder communication. The writer has attempted to follow all directions for the assignment, but may, for example, have omitted one or more parts of the assignment.

F

An "F" text is inappropriate in terms of the rhetorical situation. The text has no purpose or direction. The text is insufficiently developed, states the obvious about the topic, and falls short of the minimum length requirements because of this. The text has multiple problems with organization. The text contains numerous and consistent errors at the sentence level that seriously hinder communication. The text may be borrowed or purchased from elsewhere, recycle from another course (including a previous iteration of this course), or use sources improperly or without documentation. It may be plagiarized. The writer makes little or no attempt to follow the directions provided for the assignment.

Attendance

All sections meet once weekly; it is expected that you will arrive on time and attend all scheduled classes. If you must miss class because of an official university activity, you must notify your instructor at least one week in advance, provide documentation in the form of a letter from the sponsoring department or unit, and arrange to turn in work either before your departure or immediately upon your return.

Your instructor will take attendance each week. After your second absence, 5% of your final grade may be deducted for each additional absence. Your Dean may also be notified in accordance with University policies. Chronic attendance problems, such as tardiness, will be dealt with at the discretion of the classroom instructor.

Regular attendance is essential to your success in this course.

Due Dates and Late Penalties

All assignments must be turned in online by 11:59.59 p.m. (Central Standard or Central Daylight Time) on the date stipulated in the online syllabus. After you turn in an assignment, confirm that it has been received by checking your list of submitted assignments. Be sure you keep an electronic copy of your work.

If you have trouble submitting your work online for any reason, email your instructor and include **a copy of your completed assignment**, along with an explanation of the technical problem, **prior to** the deadline for the assignment. As soon as the technical problem has been resolved, you must submit your assignment as usual. Your instructor reserves the right to remove the late penalty if and only if he or she has proof that you completed the assignment on time. Otherwise, any assignment(s) submitted late will receive **a 10-point deduction per day** late.

Penalties for late assignments are assessed after the assignment has been evaluated.

For example, if a draft is two days late and receives an initial grade of 88, the 20 point penalty assessed will make the final grade for that draft a 68. Any exceptions to the above policies must be arranged with the instructor prior to the due date.

Turning assignments in on time is essential to your success in this course.

Classroom Behavior

As college students you are expected to behave in a courteous and respectful manner toward your instructor and the other students enrolled in the course. The following behaviors are among those viewed as unacceptable:

- Reading newspapers in class
- Using electronic devices, including but not limited to cell phones, iPods, and laptops without the instructor's permission
- Talking while others have the floor
- Interrupting others
- Acting belligerently or in a belittling manner
- Challenging the instructor's authority
- Displaying disruptive behavior

An additional note concerning correspondence: Students are expected to behave in civil and appropriate ways both in the classroom and online. Verbal harassment of instructors or fellow students orally, through email, through the writing concern box, or through the comment evaluation function will not be tolerated. Students should be especially careful of their online communication in this regard, for it sometimes encourages aggressive language (flaming) or even inappropriately informal language. Language that might be appropriate for friends is not always appropriate for academic discourse. Students must maintain a professional and courteous tone in all online correspondence.

Individual instructors may have additional policies concerning classroom behavior; these will be distributed to students in writing at the beginning of the course and kept on file in the Composition Program office.

Students who repeatedly disturb the progress of the class may be asked to leave the class and discuss their behavior with a writing program director and/or a representative from Student Judicial Programs as a result of an instructor-initiated Campus Incident Report.

Verbal harassment of instructors or fellow students orally or through email will not be tolerated. Instructors reserve the right to count absent or to drop from the course those students who repeatedly disrupt the class in ways that are unacceptable.

Academic Integrity and Plagiarism

Texas Tech University aims "to foster a spirit of complete honesty and a high standard of integrity. The attempt of students to present as their own any work that they have not honestly performed is regarded by the faculty and administration as a serious offense and renders the offenders liable to serious consequences, possibly suspension" (Undergraduate Handbook 49). The university defines several types of dishonesty. "Scholastic dishonesty" includes, but is not limited to, cheating, plagiarism, collusion, falsifying academic records, misrepresenting facts, and any act designed to give unfair academic advantage to the student (such as, but not limited to, submission of essentially the same written assignment for two courses without the prior permission of the instructor) or the attempt to commit such an act. More detailed information concerning each form of dishonesty can be viewed at the official university academic integrity website: http://www.depts.ttu.edu/student judicialprograms/academicinteg.php.

In writing courses, plagiarism is the most common form of academic dishonesty. For the purposes of this course, "plagiarism" includes, but is not limited to, the appropriation of, buying, receiving as a gift, or obtaining by any means material that is attributable in whole or in part to another source, including words, ideas, illustrations, structure, computer code, other expression and media, and presenting that material as one's own academic work being offered for credit. Any student who fails to give credit for quotations or for an essentially identical expression of material taken from books, encyclopedias, magazines, Internet documents, reference works or from the themes, reports, or other writings of a fellow student is guilty of plagiarism.

The instructor or Writing Program Director is responsible for initiating action against academic dishonesty or plagiarism. In the case of convincing evidence, the instructor should and will take appropriate action. A Campus Incident Report will be filed with Student Judicial Programs.

Note: Except on assignments where revision of past text is called for, the re-submission, or recycling, of text that has been used on previous assignments—in this course or in any other course, in this semester or any previous semester—will result in a "0" for the assignment.

Incompletes

A final grade of "Incomplete," according to the Undergraduate Catalog, "is given only when a student's work is satisfactory in quality but, due to reasons beyond his or her control, has not been completed. It is not given instead of an F. The instructor assigning the grade will stipulate, in writing, at the time the grade is given the conditions under which the 'I' may be removed" (50). To qualify for an Incomplete, students must have completed at least 60% of the work for the class with a grade of C or better. Students seeking an Incomplete must work with both the instructor and a writing program administrator to determine a proposed completion date. The Incomplete becomes an F if the proposed completion date (up to one year from the date filed) passes without the work being submitted.

Annual Essay Awards

All students in ENGL 1301 and 1302 are eligible to compete for annual awards for best rhetorical analysis, literature review, and argument. Students are nominated by their classroom instructor. The awards ceremony takes place toward the end of the spring semester. Prizes include a certificate and small cash award.

Getting Help with the Course

To get help with assignments, or grammar and mechanics, you can meet with your instructor during office hours. Some instructors prefer to meet with you during office hours to discuss your question rather than conducting the discussion via email; instructors will let you know their preferences during the first week of class.

You may also meet with a tutor at the University Writing Center (UWC). The UWC is located in room 175 of the EN/PH Building. You may also access tutors and writing resources via the UWC website at http://uwc.ttu.edu/.

When you do meet with your instructor or a tutor, make sure you come prepared with specific questions, having reviewed the assignment, the supporting material in the textbook, and the assignment description.

For assistance with other course-related issues, please visit a writing program director in room 211D in the EN/PH Building. Directors can answer questions about the program, the instruction, the assignments, and our online tools.

Software for the Course

The first-year writing program uses the Raider Writer course-management software for submission and grading of documents. Key features for student use include the following:

- 24/7 access to your essays, assignments, due dates, commentary, grades, and attendance records
- A submission box for you to turn in writing assignments, including brief assignments, drafts, peer critiques, and writing reviews

- A page in which you examine grades and comments on all assignments, as well as see your cumulative grade in the course

To begin using Raider Writer, look for an activation email, which will be sent to your **ttu.edu** email account within 24 hours of your first day of class. When you receive the email, follow the instructions in it to reset your password and begin using Raider Writer. If you do not receive this email, or if you have any other problems resetting your password and logging in, **it is your responsibility to notify your instructor immediately in order to resolve the problem. No late penalties will be waived if you have not notified your instructor of any trouble you have logging in.** All students must successfully login to RaiderWriter **no later than the last day of the add/drop period**. Failure to do so will jeopardize your progress in the course.

Also, please keep your account and password confidential. The enrolled student is responsible for all content posted under his or her name throughout the semester. Do not share your account information with anyone.

Disabilities

"Any student who, because of a disability, may require special arrangements in order to meet the course requirements should contact the instructor as soon as possible to make any necessary arrangements. Students should present appropriate verification from Student Disability Services during the instructor's office hours. Please note: instructors are not allowed to provide classroom accommodations to a student until appropriate verification from Student Disability Services has been provided. For additional information,

please contact Student Disability Services in West Hall or call 806.742.2405."
(http://www.depts.ttu.edu/opmanual/OP34.22.pdf)

Religious Holy Days

Texas law requires institutions of higher education to excuse a student from attending
classes or other required activities, including examinations, for the observance of a religious holy day.

The student shall also be excused for time necessary to travel.

An institution may not penalize the student for the absence and allows for the student
to take an exam or complete an assignment from which the student is excused.

While no prior notification of the instructor is required, OP 34.19 indicates that a student who intends to observe a religious holy day should make that intention known to the
instructor prior to the absence. The student should make up any missed work.

If the work is not made up in a timely fashion, the instructor may respond appropriately.

PART ONE

THE RHETORIC

STRATEGIES FOR COLLEGE WRITING

Academic writing, reading, and inquiry are
inseparably linked; and all three are learned by not doing
any one alone, but by doing them all at the same time.

—James Reither

In this chapter, you will learn:

- How strategies for "reading rhetorically" can enhance your academic success
- How the metaphors of "conversation" and "composing" can deepen your understanding of your reading processes
- How eight key questions for reading rhetorically can help you analyze a text

We have designed this book to help you succeed at the writing, reading, and inquiry tasks that James Reither refers to above. College students are often surprised, even overwhelmed, by the heavy reading they are assigned and by the challenge of integrating material from that reading in their own writing. Along with textbook chapters and other assigned readings in a course, your college reading will include specialized Web sites, books, articles, and abstracts that you will examine in order to prepare research papers for a wide variety of classes, not only for English but for natural science, social science, and pre-professional classes such as introductory courses in accounting or nursing. Throughout this book, we will be describing and explaining how the techniques of **reading rhetorically** will help you do all this successfully.

Imagine the following scenario: It's early evening on Thursday, and you are planning your weekend's study schedule. Besides an assignment to read a chapter in your chemistry textbook for Monday, you have some writing assignments due next week. Consider this hypothetical list of reading and writing assignments that you need to get started on over the weekend:

- Find and analyze a local newspaper editorial for your political science class according to concepts laid out in a textbook chapter titled "Interest Groups and the Media."
- Summarize and write a critical reflection on a recent *Atlantic* online Web "Dispatch" assigned for your Environmental Studies class.
- Identify points of difficulty in a Platonic dialogue for your humanities seminar and formulate questions about them for discussion.
- Begin developing a research question for a major paper for your African history class, due next month.

For many students, a list like this seems daunting simply because it lays out many different kinds of reading and writing tasks that all must be done in the same relatively short period of time. This challenge of what some people call "alla-tonceness" is what this book is designed to help you with. The techniques of reading rhetorically—the central concept of this book—will help you sort through and develop the varied reading and writing skills called for in college courses.

For each assignment on our hypothetical list, your ability to meet your instructor's goals would depend not only on your ability to craft clear, grammatical sentences, but also on your ability to read insightfully and analytically. Note that each one calls upon students to read in a particular way. This variety occurs because professors design assignments to help students learn not just the subject matter but the academic methods central to their disciplines. Thus, assignments often necessitate reading with different purposes and types of awareness. In these four cases, students need to

- Comprehend political science textbook concepts about interest groups well enough to tie them to an editorial
- Distill the key ideas in a popular Web article and reflect upon how they apply (or not) to ideas being discussed in a course
- Spot ambiguities and formulate discussion questions that zero in on them
- Scan through class notes and library databases to locate issues that will focus on an individual research question

For the most part, students adapt to these new demands and gradually learn what academic reading entails, so that by the time they are juniors and seniors within their major fields, they know how to do the reading and writing demanded in their disciplines and future professions. But the process is often slow and frustrating, marked by trial and error and the panicky feeling that reading for different purposes is like hacking through a jungle when there might be a path nearby that could make the journey easier.

We hope that learning to read rhetorically, a concept that informs every chapter of this book, will help you find that path and thus accelerate your growth as a strong academic reader and writer.

WHAT DO WE MEAN BY "READING RHETORICALLY"?

To read rhetorically is (1) to read with attention to how your purposes for reading may or may not match an author's purposes for writing and (2) to recognize the methods that authors use to try to accomplish their purposes. Remember this: All authors have designs on their readers. Authors want their readers to see things their way so that readers will adopt their point of view. But rhetorical readers know how to maintain a critical distance from a text and thus determine carefully the extent to which they will go along with the author.

As you move into your college majors, new writing assignments will ask you to write about your reading in a way that shows that you are "doing" a discipline, for example, *doing* political science or *doing* philosophy. That is why we stress throughout these chapters the importance of interacting with a text beyond just understanding what it says. In college, reporting about what you have read will be only a beginning point. You will be asked to find meaning, not merely information, in books and articles. You will be asked to respond to that meaning—to explain it, to use it, to analyze it, to critique it, to compare it to alternative meanings that other writers have created or that you create yourself as you write.

To fulfill such writing and reading assignments, you will need to analyze not just *what* texts say but how they say it. This double awareness is crucial to reading rhetorically. By analyzing both the content and the technique of a given text, a rhetorical reader critically considers the extent to which he or she will accept or question that text.

THE DEMANDS AND PLEASURES OF ACADEMIC READING

Once you become immersed in academic life—caught up in the challenge of doing your own questioning, critical thinking, analysis, and research—you'll discover that academic reading has unique demands and pleasures. If you ask an experienced academic reader engaged in a research project why she reads, her answer may be something like this: "I'm investigating a problem that requires close analysis of several primary sources. I also need to read secondary sources to see what other researchers are saying about this problem. Then I can position myself in the conversation."

This may seem a curious answer—one that you might not fully understand until you have had more experience writing papers that require analysis or research. To help you appreciate this answer—and to see how it applies to you—consider that in most college courses, you will have two underlying goals:

Goal 1. Learning conceptual knowledge. You need to learn the body of information presented in the course—to master the key concepts and ideas of the course, to memorize important facts, to learn key definitions or formulas, to understand the discipline's theories, and understand how they seek to explain certain data and observations. Cognitive psychologists sometimes call this kind of learning **conceptual knowledge**—that is, knowledge of the course's subject matter. Transmitting conceptual knowledge is the primary aim of most college textbooks. Ironically, even textbooks designed for beginners present challenging reading assignments because their pages are packed with specialized terminology that students need to know if they are to follow lectures, pass exams, and, more generally, understand how chemists (for example) think about, label, and measure the physical world.

Goal 2. Learning procedural knowledge. Most college courses are designed to help you learn the discipline's characteristic ways of applying conceptual knowledge to new problems. What questions does the discipline ask? What are its methods of analysis or research? What counts as evidence? What are the discipline's shared or disputed assumptions? How do you write arguments in this discipline, and what makes them convincing (say in literature, sociology, engineering, or accounting)? Thus, in addition to learning the basic concepts of a course, you need to learn how experts in the discipline pose problems and conduct inquiry. Cognitive psychologists call this kind of learning **procedural knowledge**—the ability to apply conceptual knowledge to new problems by using the discipline's characteristic methods of thinking.

When teachers assign readings beyond the typical textbook—newspaper or magazine articles, scholarly articles, or primary sources such as historical documents or literary texts—they are asking you to use procedural knowledge by analyzing or using these readings in discipline-specific ways. Consider the political science assignment in our opening scenario. The professor who assigned analysis of a local newspaper editorial undoubtedly wants students to learn what the textbook says about interest-group politics (conceptual knowledge), and then to apply those concepts to analyze current events (procedural knowledge). As you read a variety of editorials looking for one to analyze, you would need to read them through the lens of your political science textbook. A different kind of challenge is presented by the Platonic dialogue. Not only does it contain complex ideas, but it also demonstrates a form of discourse and a philosophical way of thinking that has had a lasting impact on European traditions. The professor's decision to start by asking students to raise questions about difficult passages provides a way for students to start exploring the text without being intimidated by it.

As you read the various kinds of texts assigned in your courses and write different kinds of papers, you will discover that academic disciplines are not inert bodies of knowledge but contested fields full of uncertainties, disagreements, and debate. You will see why college professors want you to *do* their discipline rather than simply study it. They want you not just to study chemistry or political science or history, but to *think like a chemist or a political scientist or an historian*. As you learn to read rhetorically, you will learn to recognize different authors' purposes and methods, the ways that claims are typically asserted and supported in different disciplines, and the types of evidence that are valued by those disciplines. For example, historians value primary sources such as letters and diaries, government records, and legal documents. Psychologists gather quite different kinds of research data, such as empirical observations of an animal's learning behaviors under different diet conditions, statistical data about the reduction of anxiety symptoms in humans after different kinds of therapy, or "think-aloud" transcripts of a person's problem-solving processes after varying amounts of sleep. Your accumulating knowledge about disciplinary discourses will teach you new ways of thinking, and you will learn to use those methods in your own writing.

It is important to realize that even people with considerable background knowledge and high interest in a subject will probably find course readings daunting when they are dense with new concepts, vocabulary, and information. With so much unfamiliar material, each new sentence can seem just as important as the one before, causing you to think, "I've got to know all of this—how will I ever write anything about it?" Reading rhetorically can help you separate key concepts from supporting details.

READING AND WRITING AS CONVERSATION

Consider again how our experienced researcher at the beginning of the last section answered the question, "Why do you read?" It is obvious that she is immersed in *doing* her discipline and that she sees reading as central to her work. But she also says that she is reading "to position myself in the conversation." What does she mean by that? How is reading part of a "conversation"?

To understand this metaphor of conversation, think of writers as talking to readers—and think of readers as talking back. For example, suppose our researcher's investigation leads her to new insights that she would like to share with others. If she is a professional scholar, she may write an academic article. If she is an undergraduate, she may write a research paper. In both cases, her intended audience would be academic readers interested in a particular problem or question. Motivated by the belief that she has produced something new or controversial to add to the conversation, she aims to present the results of her research and try to persuade readers to accept her argument and claims.

Thinking of yourself as joining a conversation will be helpful whenever you read or write so that you can consider not only the text you are reading, but also the conversation that it joins. Think of this conversation as multi-voiced. The first voice is that of the text's author; a second voice (actually a set of voices) is the network of other writers the author refers to—previous participants in the conversation. The third voice is yours as you respond to the text while you read, and later when you write something about it.

This broad view of readers and writers interacting via texts extends the metaphor of "conversation" to say that texts themselves are in a conversation with previous texts. Each text acts in relationship to other texts. It asserts a claim on a reader's attention by invoking certain interests and understandings, reminding readers of what has been previously written about the subject. For example, articles in scientific journals typically begin with a **literature review**; that is, a summary of important research already conducted on the question at hand. Similarly, political commentators will summarize the views of others so that they can affirm, extend, or take issue with those views. In the arts, reviewers of music, film, and books are likely to refer to (and, on the Web, perhaps link to) not just the work under review but discussions about the given artist's reputation, which, of course, was established not just by word of mouth but also by other texts or performances with which the current reader may not be familiar.

Joining the Conversation

The reasons any of us engage in conversation, oral or written, will vary widely according to the occasion and our individual needs. In academic and workplace settings, we read so that we can make informed contributions to a conversation that is already in progress. Indeed, we are expected to join in.

Entering an oral conversation can sometimes be a simple process of responding to a question. ("Have you seen the new film at the Ridgemont?") But if a conversation is already well under way, finding an opening can sometimes be a complex process of getting people's attention and staking claim to authority on a subject. ("Um, you know, I've seen all of John Woo's films, and I think. . . .") The challenge is even greater if the goal is to redirect the conversation or contradict the prevailing opinion. ("Yes, but listen! The reading I've done for my cinematography class tells me that his action films are not as innovative as the ads claim.") When we take up writing as a way of entering the conversation, we don't have to worry about interrupting, but we do have to review the conversation for our readers by laying out introductory background.

To explore the similarities between your motives for joining a conversation and your motives for reading, consider how the influential twentieth-century rhetorician and philosopher Kenneth Burke uses conversation as a metaphor for reading and writing:

> Imagine you enter a parlor. You come late. When you arrive, others have long preceded you, and they are engaged in a heated discussion, a discussion too heated for them to pause and tell you exactly what it is about. In fact, the discussion had already begun long before any of them got there, so that no one present is qualified to retrace for you all the steps that had gone before. You listen for a while, until you decide that you have caught the tenor of the argument; then you put in your oar. Someone answers; you answer him; another comes to your defense; another aligns himself against you, to either the embarrassment or gratification of your opponent, depending upon the quality of your ally's assistance. However, the discussion is interminable. The hour grows late, you must depart. And you do depart, with the discussion still vigorously in progress.[1]

For Writing and Discussion

To explore the implications of Burke's parlor metaphor for your own reading processes, consider the following questions.

On Your Own

1. In what ways does Burke's parlor metaphor fit your experience? Freewrite for a few minutes about an oral conversation in which you managed to assert your voice—or

---

[1] Kenneth Burke, *The Philosophy of Literary Form: Studies in Symbolic Action*, 3rd ed. (Berkeley: U of California P, 1973), 110–11. Print.

"put in your oar," as Burke says—after listening for a while, or about a situation where reading helped you gather a sense of the general flow of ideas so that you could have something to say about a topic.

2. Consider a community that you belong to where you feel that you can quickly catch the drift of an in-progress conversation (e.g., other triathlon athletes, or regulars on Farmville). What are some "hot topics" of conversation in these communities? What might exclude someone from these conversations? If you wanted to address a general audience about this issue, how much background information would you need to supply?

3. Now let's reverse the situation. Have you ever listened to a conversation in which you were a baffled outsider rather than an insider? Describe an experience where you had to work hard to get inside an ongoing conversation. Then consider how that experience might be an appropriate analogy for a time when you were frustrated by trying to read a book or article addressed to an insider audience rather than to someone with your background.

With Your Classmates

Share your responses with other members of your class. See if others have had experiences similar to yours. What have been the topics of conversations where they were in "insider" and "outsider" roles? Help each other appreciate the concepts of insider and outsider audiences and of reading as joining a conversation.

READING AND WRITING AS ACTS OF COMPOSING

The give and take of oral conversation connects naturally to our second metaphor, reading as an act of composing. The idea that writing is an act of composing is probably familiar to you. Indeed, the terms *writing* and *composing* are often used interchangeably. Originally associated with fine arts such as painting, music, or literary writing, the term *composing* still carries with it the idea of originality or creativity, even though it has come to mean the production of any kind of written text, from a memo to a prize-winning novel. Unlike the term *writing*, the word *composing* suggests more than the mere transcription of a preexisting meaning or idea. Instead, it suggests a creative putting together of words and ideas to make a new whole. Except for the act of literally recopying what someone else has written, all writing, even memo writing, is a matter of selecting and arranging language to accomplish a purpose that is unique to a particular situation and audience.

However, the idea that reading is an act of composing may be less familiar. The ancients thought of reading as a passive activity in which the author, via the text, deposited meaning in a reader—the text was metaphorically (or even literally) "consumed." The Old Testament prophet Ezekiel, for example, has a vision in which he is instructed by the Lord to open his mouth and literally consume a book that gives him the knowledge he needs to speak to the rebellious Israelites. Commenting on the consumption metaphors associated with reading, Alberto Manguel, in *A History of Reading*, notes the parallels between the cooking metaphors associated with writing—the author "cooks up" a plot or "spices" up her introduction—and the eating metaphors associated with reading—the reader "devours" a book, finds "nourishment" in it, then "regurgitates" what he has read.[2] Although the image of Ezekiel's eating of a text seems fantastic, the mistaken idea persists that reading is a one-way transaction: author → text → reader. To illustrate the flaws in this model of the reading process, let's try a simple experiment described by reading researcher Kathleen McCormick. Read the following passage and jot down your interpretation of its meaning:

> Tony slowly got up from the mat, planning his escape. He hesitated a moment and thought. Things were not going well. What bothered him most was being held, especially since the charge against him had been weak. He considered his present situation. The lock that held him was strong but he thought he could break it. . . . He was being ridden unmercifully. . . . He felt that he was ready to make his move.[3]

There are two common interpretations: readers assume that Tony is either in jail or in a wrestling match. Unless you are familiar with wrestling, you likely thought Tony was a prisoner planning a jailbreak. However, if this paragraph appeared in a short story about a wrestler, you would immediately assume that "mat," "escape," "charge," "being held," and "lock" referred to wrestling even if you knew very little about the sport. This experiment demonstrates two important aspects of the reading process: (1) readers use their previous experiences and knowledge to create meaning from what they read; and (2) context influences meaning.

Research such as McCormick's shows that readers make sense of a text not by passively receiving meaning from it, but by actively composing a reading of it. This composing process links the reader's existing knowledge and ideas with the new information in the text. What the reader brings to the text is as important as the text itself. In other words, reading is not a process in which an author simply transfers information to the reader. Rather, it is a dynamic process in which the reader's worldview interacts with the writer's worldview. The reader constructs meaning from the text, in effect creating a new "text" in the reader's mind. The new text is the reader's active interpretation of the text being read.

When college writing assignments ask you to explain and support your reading (or interpretation) of a text, whether verbal or visual, it is important to distinguish between *private* associations that are only loosely related to the text and interpretations that are *publicly* defensible in terms of textual evidence. Private associations are one-way responses in which a certain word, image, or idea in a text sends you off into your own world, causing you to lose track of the network of cues in the text as a whole. Although such private responses are natural, and indeed one of the pleasures of reading, if you are to offer a public interpretation, you must engage in a two-way interaction with a text, attending to

[2]Alberto Manguel, *A History of Reading* (New York: Penguin, 1997), 170–71. Print.

[3]Kathleen McCormick, *The Culture of Reading and the Teaching of English* (Manchester, England: Manchester UP, 1994), 20–21. Print.

both its network of cues and your personal responses and associations with it. In short, "good" or sound interpretations are those that are supported by textual evidence and thus are understandable as well as persuasive to other readers, whose experiences and beliefs are probably different from yours.

READING RHETORICALLY AS A STRATEGY FOR ACADEMIC WRITING

The metaphors of conversation and composing bring out the essential rhetorical nature of reading and writing. By **rhetorical**, we mean "related to an intended effect." Invoking the term "rhetoric" always draws attention to a writer's relationship to and intentions toward an audience. Consider Aristotle's definition of rhetoric as the art of discovering the available means of persuasion in a given situation. Although the word "persuasion" focuses on an audience, Aristotle's definition highlights **discovery** along with **persuasion**. From this pairing, we can understand that writers must thoroughly understand their subject in order to discover the best methods for presenting their material to others. By "best," we mean the most ethically responsible as well as the most persuasive. Rhetoric's partnership of discovery and persuasion makes it clear why reading rhetorically is a powerful academic strategy in all disciplines. When you read rhetorically, you read with awareness of both the purposes of the author whose text you are reading and your own purposes as a reader and writer.

The Purposes of the Author Whose Text You Are Reading

When we introduced the term *reading rhetorically* early in this chapter, we described authors as having designs on their readers. That phrasing underscores the fact that writers want to change readers' perceptions and thinking, and that they use both direct and indirect means to do so. Typically, a writer's goal is to change a reader's understanding of subject matter in some way. Sometimes the change might simply confirm what the reader thought beforehand—readers typically enjoy music and film reviews that affirm their own opinions and political columns that echo their views. At other times, the change might involve an increase in knowledge or in clarity of understanding (an article explaining how bluenose dolphins use whistling sounds to converse with each other might increase your awe of sea mammals). Sometimes the change might radically reconstruct a reader's whole view of a subject (an article reporting new scientific evidence might convince you to reverse your position on legalization of medical marijuana). How much change occurs as a result of reading? The reader decides.

Your Own Purposes as an Active Reader/Writer

When an assignment asks you to respond in some way to texts that you have read, you must take on the role of an active reader who composes meanings. Your responses might range from writing marginal notes on the text itself (something that expert readers do) to posting an entry on your class online discussion forum to writing a major research paper. Your decisions about the way you will read a text and think critically about it will depend upon your own purposes as a writer.

QUESTIONS RHETORICAL READERS ASK

You can begin the practice of reading rhetorically by asking the eight analytical questions that follow when you encounter new texts. Whether you are reading the abstract of a scientific article or comments posted on a forum about R&B styling, these questions will help you discover how a writer's purpose and worldview become evident in a text. These insights, in turn, will help you analyze how a given text works so that you can decide how you want to respond to it and use it in your own writing.

1. What questions does the text address, explicitly or implicitly? (Why are these significant questions? What community cares about them?)

2. Who is the intended audience? (Am I part of this audience or an outsider?)

3. How does the author support his or her thesis with reasons and evidence? (Do I find this argument convincing? What views and counterarguments are omitted from the text? What counterevidence is ignored?)

4. How does the author hook the intended reader's interest and keep the reader reading? (Do these appeals work for me? Do they make me suspicious of the author's motives?)

5. How does the author make himself or herself seem credible to the intended audience? (Is the author credible for me? Are the author's sources reliable?)

6. Are this writer's basic values, beliefs, and assumptions similar to or different from my own? (How does this writer's worldview accord with mine?)

7. How do I respond to this text? (Will I go along with or challenge what this text is presenting? How has it changed my thinking?)

8. How do this author's evident purposes for writing fit with my purposes for reading? (How will I be able to use what I have learned from the text?)

For Writing and Discussion

The Questions Rhetorical Readers Ask can be useful for analyzing visual texts as well as verbal texts. To demonstrate the power of rhetorical reading, we invite you to use the eight questions to analyze how the Web page depicted in Figure 1.1 attempts to influence the thinking of viewers/readers. (In Chapters 3 and 4, we offer some specific advice on how to do a rhetorical analysis of visual texts such as this one.)

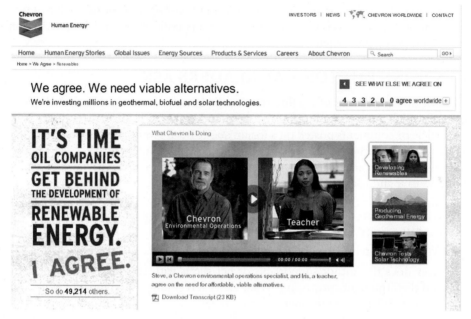

Figure 1.1 Screen capture from Chevron Web statement about developing renewable energy

Working alone or with classmates, use the eight questions to consider first, how the various visual and verbal elements work to project a corporate image for Chevron, and second, how you respond to that image.

Some background: The page shown in Figure 1.1 came up via a click on "We Agree" (depicted as a red rubber stamp) on the Chevron home page. It was part of a major advertising campaign on this theme that included both print and television. If you are not able to find the site online, here is a brief summary: The video presents 30 seconds of overlapping statements in which the young teacher in the right frame calls for speeding up the development of renewable energy ("We've got to get on this now!") while the Chevron environmental operations specialist in the left frame speaks enthusiastically about the millions of dollars Chevron is investing in solar and biofuel technologies, "Right now!"

An Extended Example: Researching the Promise of Biofuels

Imagine that your instructor in a geography or political science class assigns a major research paper that will require you to find and select your own sources. These potential sources (there may be hundreds of possibilities) will pose reading challenges different from those of your course textbooks because these sources will be written for many different audiences and purposes by authors with varied credentials on the subject. On any given topic—let's take the development of biofuels as a broad example—it's likely your research will turn up scholarly articles, popular magazine articles, news reports, a few books, and a range of politically charged editorials, op-ed columns, blogs, and Web sites. All of them will have been published in different contexts for readers with a range of different concerns: experts and nonexperts, theorists and researchers, farmers and automakers, politicians of every stripe, and ordinary citizens trying to figure out the best car to buy, or which politician to vote for. As a reader who is planning to write, you will need to determine what, among all this material, suits *your* needs and purposes.

Your purposes may grow out of personal interests and questions. Let's take as an example a first-year student we'll call "Jack," who has become interested in biofuels because holiday dinners with relatives who farm in the Midwest have produced many heated arguments about corn ethanol. One uncle produces feed corn to be sold not to cattle farmers, but to ethanol producers. Another uncle grows corn for people food. He is certain that the market for corn ethanol will disappear within a couple of years because cleaner and more efficiently produced biofuels will be developed. Both of these men support environmental causes, and each feels that his choice about what kind of corn to grow will be better for the environment. Additionally, one uncle argues that producing corn ethanol contributes to U.S. energy independence; the other argues that using good farmland to produce fuel rather than food will have negative consequences. These dinner-table conversations became even more intense after Congress ended federal tax breaks for companies that produce gasoline mixed with ethanol.

Motivated by curiosity about which of his uncles might be making the better choice, Jack decides to write a paper for his political science class about the pros and cons of growing corn for ethanol production. During class discussion, he gains and shares insights with a classmate who grew up in a big city and is writing about corn ethanol from the perspective of consumers who are environmentalists, asking whether it really is a clean fuel. They are both aware of intense debates around these issues, as reflected in the visual arguments represented in Figures 1.2 and 1.3, and they agree that their goals are to gather information for their papers, not controversial arguments.

Despite a wealth of readily available materials on the subject, both students eventually find themselves hard pressed to provide definite answers to their questions. Searches of periodicals databases uncover a wealth of materials on ethanol and other biofuels, but the conclusions seem almost contradictory. Published reports indicate that despite the end of federal tax subsidies for ethanol producers, the amount of corn grown for ethanol continues to increase. Meanwhile, university professors and oil companies receive press coverage for their research about the practicality of using other biofuels to run gasoline engines.

Web searches turn up a wide range of perspectives on ethanol, from industry groups supporting expanded corn ethanol production, to oil companies boasting of their commitment to alternative fuels, to environmental organizations opposing the use of farmland for biofuel development. Furthermore, Jack's classmate discovers that environmental groups have been arguing not only that the fuel is not particularly clean or efficient but also that ethanol production is actually bad for the environment. Between them, they discover that, as yet, there is no clear answer about the wisdom of developing corn ethanol for automotive fuel, nor about the trade-offs of using agricultural land for developing biofuels.

Figure 1.2 Illinois billboard advertising corn seed hybridized for ethanol production from Pioneer Hi-Bred International, Inc.

Figure 1.3 Editorial cartoon by Robert Ariail

In other words, Jack and his friend learn that there is not one "ethanol debate." There are many, depending on the interests and values of the debaters. Jack discovers that he must recognize and investigate the perspectives not only of farmers like his uncles, but also of environmental organizations, producers of ethanol and gasoline, investors in alternative fuels, scientists (who want hard evidence), government agencies (who rely on the scientists' research), manufacturers of gasoline engines—and ordinary consumers shopping for a car that fits their values and pocketbook. (Excerpts from Jack's research log are in Chapter 5. His paper about multiple perspectives on biofuels appears at the end of Chapter 6.)

Jack's experience illustrates our larger point that only careful reading will lead to a good academic paper on a complex subject. Reading rhetorically is a powerful academic skill that will help you recognize the persuasive strategies built into many different kinds of texts. Inevitably, no text tells the whole story. A reader needs to focus not only on what a given text says but on its rhetorical strategies for making its case. To promote an argument, some texts will distort opposing perspectives; others will make certain perspectives invisible. A headline on the Web about "Biofuels' Potential to Revolutionize the Global Economy" may primarily be a pitch to interest investors in a start-up company. The organization behind a headline announcing an article about the "Pros and Cons of Ethanol" might be a trade association that lobbies for (or against) corn ethanol, or it could be a lone environmental blogger repackaging reports of unknown reliability. Eventually, after you (like Jack) have read enough materials from sources you have learned to trust, by writers you learn to respect (in part by checking their credentials), you will be able to fill in background that you perhaps did not even notice was missing when you first started reading in a given subject area.

How can you tell whether a text seeks to give you a full picture in a fair and reliable manner or is simply making another one-sided argument about a hotly contested issue? By learning to read rhetorically. Doing so will enable you to read—and then write—successful college papers.

CHAPTER SUMMARY

In this chapter, we have defined the concept of reading rhetorically, and explained how practicing it can help you be successful with a wide variety of college writing assignments. In the preceding pages, we

- Defined rhetorical reading as paying attention to both the content of a text ("what") and the author's method of presenting that content ("how")
- Described the special demands and pleasures of academic reading, which often requires recognizing how different academic disciplines value evidence and report research
- Used the metaphors of conversation and composing to describe how both reading and writing are active processes through which readers construe a text's meaning by bringing their own values and experiences to it and articulating their own ideas in response
- Provided a list of eight questions rhetorical readers use to judge how a text works and how to respond to it
- Showed the value of rhetorical reading as an academic strategy through which a reader analyzes a text's content and strategies in order to decide how to respond— whether to assent to the writer's ideas, modify them, or resist them

In the chapters that follow, we will offer you a variety of strategies that are likely to bring you success as you respond to assignments like these by using rhetorical reading skills to work with the texts upon which your writing will be based.

2

ANALYZING YOUR READING
AND WRITING CONTEXT

It is like the rubbing of two sticks together to make a fire, the act of reading, an improbable pedestrian task that leads to heat and light.

—Anna Quindlen

In this chapter, you will learn:

- To analyze a text's original rhetorical context (purpose, audience, and genre)
- To analyze your own rhetorical context for reading
- To adapt experts' reading strategies and make your reading more efficient
  - By using genre knowledge
  - By analyzing the text's original social/historical context
- To recognize the major role reading plays in different types of college writing assignments

Here is this chapter's point in a nutshell: Writers write for a purpose to an audience within a genre. Together, these three factors—purpose, audience, and genre—create what we call **"rhetorical context."** The more aware you are of these factors, the more efficient you will be as a reader and the more effective you will be as a writer. Analyzing a text's rhetorical context as you read will enable you to frame a response in terms of your own rhetorical context: What will be your purpose, audience, and genre? Your answers will influence not only what you write but also the way you read and use additional texts.

RHETORICAL CONTEXT: PURPOSE, AUDIENCE, AND GENRE

Recognizing the influence of rhetorical context helps rhetorical readers reconstruct the strategy behind an author's choices about content (for example, what to include and exclude), structure (for example, what to say first, when to reveal the thesis, how to arrange the parts, how to format the document), and style (whether to use big words or ordinary words, complex or easy sentence structure, lots of jargon or no jargon, and so forth).

Analyzing an Author's Purpose

In Chapter 1 we noted that writers have designs on readers—that is, writers aim to change a reader's view of a subject in some way. They might aim to enlarge a reader's view of a subject, clarify that view, or restructure that view. This motive to reach out to an audience through language inevitably stems from some problem or perceived misunderstanding or gap in knowledge that an author wishes to remedy. Rhetorician Lloyd F. Bitzer used the term **exigence** for a flaw that an author believes can be altered by a text presented to an audience.[1] This flaw might be a circumstance that is other than it should be, a situation in need of attention, or perhaps an occasion in need of special recognition. Your ability as a reader to pinpoint an author's sense of a flaw, a problem, or some other situation in need of change will enable you to zero in on that author's purpose. Furthermore, when you are ready to write about what you have read, thinking of your purpose as writing in order to remedy a flaw will help you focus sharply. Such "flaws" or problems may be as simple as the need to provide information or as complex as the need to advocate for standardizing a set of medical procedures in order to reduce infections. (You will see surgeon Atul Gawande make this argument in the reading at the end of Chapter 4.) For example, you might need to inform a potential employer of your availability and qualifications for a particular job, so you submit a letter and résumé. Or you could need to demonstrate to a history professor that you do, indeed, have a good grasp of the economic system that dominated during China's Ming dynasty, so you answer an exam question with careful detail.

A set of categories for conceptualizing the ways that writers aim to change readers' minds is summarized in Table 2.1 (see pp. 18–20). Based on a scheme developed by rhetoricians to categorize types of discourse in terms of a writer's aim or purpose, the table identifies eight **rhetorical aims** or purposes that writers typically set for themselves. This framework offers a particularly powerful way of thinking about both reading and writing because each row zeroes in on how a writer might envision a purpose that connects subject matter to audience in a given rhetorical situation. In the table, we describe how texts in each category work, what they offer readers, and the response their authors typically aim to bring about. The table illustrates the differences among the aims with examples of texts that a college student might compose in response to assignments in a variety of courses.

We have labeled the table's third column "Desired Response" because we want to emphasize that a writer can only *desire* a certain response from a reader; they cannot assume

---

[1]Bitzer's concept of an exigence within a *rhetorical situation*, modified over the years, was first described in his essay, "The Rhetorical Situation," *Philosophy and Rhetoric* 1.1 (1968): 1–14. *EbscoHost*. Web. 3 June 2012.

Table 2.1   A Spectrum of Purposes

Rhetorical Aim	Focus and Features	Desired Response	Examples
Express and Reflect **Offers Readers:** Shared emotional, intellectual experience	**Focus:** Writer's own life and experience **Features:** Literary techniques such as plot, character, setting, evocative language	**Readers** can imagine and identify with writer's experience. **Success** depends on writer's ability to create scenes, dialog, and commentary that engage readers.	Nursing student reflects on her semester of Service Learning at a school for young children with developmental delays and disabilities.
Inquire and Explore **Offers Readers:** Shared intellectual experience, new information, new perspectives	**Focus:** Puzzling problem seen through narration of writer's thinking processes **Features:** Delayed thesis or no thesis; examination of subject from multiple angles; writer's thinking is foregrounded.	**Readers** will agree question or problem is significant, identify with writer's thinking, and find new insights. **Success** depends on writer's ability to engage readers with question or problem and the exploration process.	Students in an honors seminar taught by a physicist and philosopher write papers that explore the question: "What makes study of the origins of the universe significant to daily life in the twenty-first century?"
Inform and Explain (also called *expository writing*) **Offers Readers:** Significant, perhaps surprising, new information; presentation tailored to readers' interest and presumed knowledge level	**Focus:** Subject matter **Features:** Confident, authoritative stance; typically states point and purpose early; strives for clarity; provides definitions and examples; uses convincing evidence without argument	**Readers** will grant writer credibility as expert, and be satisfied with the information's scope and accuracy. **Success** depends on writer's ability to anticipate readers' information needs and ability to understand.	Economics intern is assigned to track 10 years of the rise and fall of mortgage interest rates and report on experts' current explanations of the trends.

Table 2.1 A Spectrum of Purposes (*continued*)

Rhetorical Aim	Focus and Features	Desired Response	Examples
Analyze and Interpret **Offers Readers:** New way of looking at the subject matter	**Focus:** Phenomena that are difficult to understand or explain **Features:** Relatively tentative stance; thesis supported by evidence and reasoning; new or unsettling analyses and interpretations must be convincing; doesn't assume that evidence speaks for itself	**Readers** will grant writer credibility as analyst and accept insights offered, or at least acknowledge value of approach. **Success** depends on writer's ability to explain reasoning and connect it with phenomena analyzed.	Literature student analyzes the definition of *justice* employed by various characters in Sophocles' play *Antigone* with the goal of interpreting the author's understanding of the concept.
Persuasion: Take a Stand **Offers Readers:** Reasons to make up or change their minds about a question at issue	**Focus:** Question that divides a community **Features:** States a firm position, provides clear reasons and evidence, connects with readers' values and beliefs, engages with opposing views	**Readers** will agree with writer's position and reasoning. **Success** depends on writer's ability to provide convincing support and to counter opposition without alienating readers.	For an ethics class, an architecture student decides to write an argument in favor of placing certain buildings in his community on the historic preservation register, thus preserving them from demolition or radical remodeling.
Persuasion: Evaluate and Judge **Offers Readers:** Reasons to make up or change their minds about a focal question regarding worth or value	**Focus:** Question about worth or value of a phenomenon **Features:** Organized around criteria for judgment and how phenomenon matches them	**Readers** will accept writer's view of the worth or value of the phenomenon. **Success** depends on writer's ability to connect subject to criteria that readers accept.	Political theory students are asked to evaluate and choose between the descriptions of an ideal ruler embodied in Plato's philosopher king and Machiavelli's prince.

Table 2.1   A Spectrum of Purposes (*continued*)

Rhetorical Aim	Focus and Features	Desired Response	Examples
Persuasion: **Propose a Solution** **Offers Readers:** A recommended course of action	**Focus:** Question about what action should be taken **Features:** Describes problem and |solution, then justifies solution in terms of values and consequences; level of detail depends on assumptions about readers' knowledge	**Readers** will assent to proposed action and do as writer suggests. **Success** depends on readers' agreement that a problem exists and/or that the recommended action will have good results.	A group of seniors majoring in social welfare collaborates on a grant proposal t o a community foundation interested in improving health education in a rural area.
Persuasion: **Seek Common Ground** **Offers Readers:** New perspectives and reduced intensity regarding difficult issues	**Focus:** Multiple perspectives on a vexing problem **Features:** Lays out the values and goals of the various stakeholders so that others can find commonalities to build on; does not advocate	**Readers** will discover mutuality with opponents; conflict may not be resolved; discussion could lead to cooperative action. **Success** depends on readers' discovery of mutual interests.	An environmental studies student designs a thesis project to interview advocates and stakeholders who are divided over a proposal to remove a dam from a major river; her goal is to find and highlight points of agreement.

or force that response. The reader is in charge because it is the reader who decides whether to accede to the writer's intentions or to resist them. Because writers try to persuade an intended audience to adopt their perspective, they select and arrange evidence, choose examples, include or omit material, and select words and images to best support their perspective. But readers are the ones who decide—sometimes unconsciously, sometimes deliberately—whether the presentation is convincing. Your awareness of how a text is constructed to persuade its intended audience will enable you to decide how you want to respond to that text and use it in your own writing.

For Writing and Discussion

To explore the spectrum of aims presented in Table 2.1, choose an issue or situation that interests you and fill in the grid of a similar table with sample writing scenarios and purposes for each of the table's eight rows of rhetorical aims. Working alone or with others, fill in as many cells in the example column as you can. Choose from the following hypothetical writers or another writer-reader combination that intrigues you in connection with the topic you choose.

- College students in a variety of courses
- A single writer (perhaps an entertainment columnist or a sports writer) seeking publication in a variety of venues, including the Web, about the same subject matter
- People in a variety of roles writing with different aims about the same topic (perhaps a family matter such as pets or divorce, or a public matter such as green energy or human rights)

Identifying an Author's Intended Audience

Audience plays a major role in guiding an author's choices. As you analyze a text, watch for cues in the author's language and use of detail that reveal assumptions about the intended audience.

For example, suppose a writer wants to persuade legislators to raise gasoline taxes in order to reduce fossil fuel consumption. Her strategy might be to persuade different groups of voters to pressure their congressional representatives. If she writes for a scientific audience, her article can include technical data and detailed statistical analyses. If she addresses the general public, however, her style will have to be less technical and more lively, with storylike anecdotes rather than tabular data. If she writes for an environmental publication, she can assume an audience already supportive of her pro-environment values. However, if she writes for a business publication such as the *Wall Street Journal*, she will have to be sensitive to her audience's pro-business values—perhaps by arguing that what is good for the environment will be good for business in the long run.

ANALYZING AN AUTHOR'S DESIGNS ON YOUR THINKING

One way to analyze an author's purpose is to consider the kind of change the author hopes to bring about in readers' minds. Try using this formula to quiz yourself about the author's desire to change your mind:

At the beginning of the text, the writer assumes that the reader believes _____
_____.

By the end of the text, the writer hopes that the reader believes _____
_____.

These questions will help you, as a rhetorical reader, to analyze your own response to the text—whether you are going to think or do what the writer apparently hopes you will.

Analyzing a Text's Genre

As writers respond to rhetorical situations by adapting content, structure, and style to different purposes and audiences, they must also adapt to the conventions of a text's **genre**, a term that refers to a recurring category or type of writing based on identifiable features such as structure (for example, a thesis-driven argument or an informal reflection) and document design (for example, the format of academic papers, Web pages, or promotional brochures). These genre-based decisions about format include whether to add visual images, and, if so, what kind will be appropriate and effective. Because particular textual features are expected in particular situations, a writer's effort to follow or modify genre conventions can become a valuable tool for engaging readers and moving them toward desired responses such as those indicated in Table 2.1.

You may be familiar with the concept of genre from literature classes where you studied an assortment of genres, such as plays, novels, and poems. Within each of these broad literary genres are subgenres such as the sonnet and haiku or tragedy and comedy. Similarly, workplace writing has a number of subgenres (memos, marketing proposals, financial reports, progress reports) as does academic writing (laboratory reports, field notes, article abstracts, literature reviews). As the descriptions of typical college writing assignments later in this chapter show, even familiar academic assignments have subgenres (informal response papers, essay exams, article summaries, or researched arguments that present a semester's worth of work).

Consider one commonly encountered genre: the **inverted pyramid** of a news article, in print or online. These reports begin with the key facts of a news event—*who, what, when, where, why,* and *how*—before offering background information and details. As Figure 2.1 shows, a similar structure is recommended for Web writing, where it is necessary to capture readers' attention quickly, in the limited amount of space immediately visible on a screen.

In both cases, someone in a hurry or with only a passing interest in the subject matter should be able to glean the gist of the news or of the Web site's purpose by reading just the

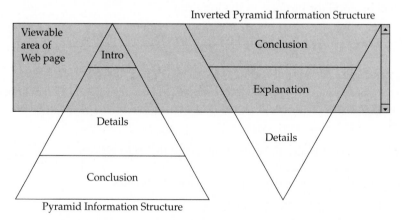

Figure 2.1 Diagram of inverted pyramid structure recommended for organizing Web content

initial sentences. Furthermore, on Web sites, putting the essential facts first makes it easier for search engines to spot and report on the page's content.

Genre differences in written texts frequently become evident through visual cues, and these cues in turn create reader expectations. The Web site of the *New York Times* uses type-faces and layout that resemble those of its paper edition, but the home page of a veterinary clinic (interested in inviting new patients) will likely be different from the home page of an advice blog about caring for exotic birds. Similarly, genre differences influence the look of print documents. If you were browsing publications in the current periodicals rack at a library, you could quickly distinguish popular magazines such as *Popular Science* and *Business Week* from scholarly journals such as the *American Journal of Human Genetics* or the *Journal of Marketing Research*. The glossy covers of the magazines, often adorned with arresting photographs, distinguish them from sober-looking scholarly journals, the covers of which typically display a table of contents of the articles within. (These genre distinctions are less apparent when you are browsing through articles in a computerized periodicals database, a challenge we address in Chapter 5.) As you develop your ability to recognize genres and the ways that their conventions shape content, you will also sharpen your ability to decide whether and how to use particular texts for your own purposes.

As illustration, consider the distinctive differences between the genres of the two articles introduced by the images in Figures 2.2 and 2.3. As the captions indicate, the first is taken from the scholarly journal *Appetite* and the second was originally published in a monthly health newsletter, the *UC Berkeley Wellness Letter*. A quick glance makes evident the differences in these texts' rhetorical contexts, from the different page layouts to the contrasts between casual language and formal vocabulary.

The article from *Appetite* depicted in Figure 2.2 is one of two studies from the October 2011 issue that were used by a staff writer for the *Wellness Letter* to produce "Chew on This"—a short, easy-to-read summary of recent research on gum-chewing (presented in full in Figure 2.3). This piece was written to catch the attention of casual readers whose curiosity might be piqued by the clever title and the questions about the effects of chewing gum placed in bold-face headings, questions that readers will discover do not have definitive answers. Contrast this informal article with the formality and detail evident on the first page of the *Appetite* article in Figure 2.2. Despite the playful wording in the title—"Cognitive Advantages of Chewing Gum. Now You See them, Now You Don't"—the overall presentation of the opening page signals that it is a scholarly research report, including the label at the upper left labeling it as such. Scholarly elements highlighted by the labels and circles in the figure include the names of four authors (with an asterisk indicating the one to whom correspondence may be sent), a history of the article's submission to the journal, an abstract, a keywords list, and an introduction reviewing the literature from previous studies on the topic. The article's remaining seven pages describe in detail the methodology of two studies about gum-chewing and test-taking behaviors, present charts and graphs of the results, and discuss the significance of those results.

Casual readers are likely to respond positively to the newsletter's brief summary of the research, but the readers of the scholarly journal are looking for more than lighthearted advice about gum-chewing. The Appetite article's intended audience is other researchers, not the general public. The keywords list will help those researchers find this article so that

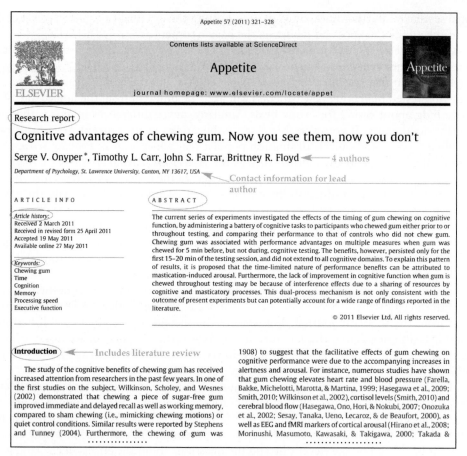

Figure 2.2 Image from page 1 of a research report the scholarly journal *Appetite* about the fleeting cognitive benefits of gum-chewing

they can read about both its findings and methodology. As is customary, the article's last page suggests what work needs to be done by subsequent researchers: "In summary, the current study demonstrates that the discrepancies in research findings of the burgeoning literature on the effect of gum chewing on cognitive function can be attributed to the timing of chewing….further studies are needed to provide a more complete picture of the relationship between physiological changes and cognitive functioning due to the chewing of gum." (Onyper et al., 327—see full citation below).[2]

From dense scientific research reports like this, the unnamed author of "Chew on This" used expert reading skills to dig out key points of information—and ambiguity—and trans-

[2]Serge V. Onyper, et al., "Cognitive Advantages of Chewing Gum. Now You See Them, Now You Don't." *Appetite* 57.2 (2011): 321–328. *Science Direct*. Web. 9 June 2012.

Chew on This ◄———————— Punning Title

Most people chew gum for pleasure or out of habit; others to freshen breath or stop a food or cigarette craving. Does gum provide any real benefits? There have been lots of studies on gum over the years, including two recent ones.

Informal language in attention-getting questions

The best evidence concerns gum's ability to prevent cavities by boosting saliva flow and neutralizing acid produced by mouth bacteria. Sugar-free gums are best for this, notably those with the sugar alcohol xylitol, which suppresses the growth of cavity-producing bacteria. Still, gum can't replace brushing and flossing.

Closes with scholarly quote followed by joking paraphrase.

Can gum make you thinner? Gum chewing burns only about 11 calories an hour. But if it keeps you from eating a candy bar, that's a big plus. Studies on whether gum reduces appetite have produced conflicting findings. The latest study, in the journal *Appetite*, found that when women chewed gum (15 minutes, once an hour, for three hours), they ate about 30 fewer calories when subsequently offered a snack compared to when they hadn't chewed gum. The women also said they felt less hungry and fuller after chewing the gum. Gum manufacturers have helped publicize these results. But each piece of gum had 5 to 10 calories, so the women didn't actually cut down on calories significantly. Would sugarless gum have had the same effect? Maybe, maybe not.

Make you smarter? Some early research found that gum chewing improved performance on memory tests, perhaps by boosting blood flow to the brain and stimulating a part of the brain where information is processed. But more recent studies have failed to find any brain benefit—or have noted that gum sometimes worsens performance.

Another recent study in *Appetite* found that gum improved performance on certain cognitive tests, but only when it was chewed before, not during, the tests. The benefit lasted just 15 to 20 minutes. According to the researchers, gum doesn't help thinking—and possibly even impairs it—during a task because of "interference due to a sharing of metabolic resources by cognitive and masticatory processes." In other words, some people can't think (or walk) and chew gum at the same time.

Figure 2.3 Text of the "Last Word" column on the last page (p. 8) of the *UC Berkeley Wellness Letter*, Feb. 2012. Note that the journal that published the original research, *Appetite*, is mentioned only briefly (as highlighted in the figure).

form them into a lively little article designed to spark a few smiles as well.[3] This reader-writer might have been trained as a journalist, or might be a graduate student in psychology or public health who will go on to build a career by publishing in journals like *Appetite*.

[3]The *Appetite* article about gum-chewing and snacking is by Marion M. Hetherington and Martin F. Regan, "Effects of Chewing Gum on Short-Term Appetite Regulation in Moderately Restrained Eaters." *Appetite* 57.2 (2011): 475–482. *Science Direct*. Web. 9 June 2012.

In the pages ahead, we suggest strategies for you as both reader and writer for developing your own abilities to work with and for a variety of audiences, purposes, and genres.

For Writing and Discussion

Both of the scholarly articles about gum-chewing from the October 2011 issue of *Appetite* (see full citations in footnotes 2 and 3) should be available through your school library, probably electronically. We invite you to explore in more detail the genre differences between them and the newsletter article in Figure 2.3. If your library also subscribes to the *UC Berkeley Wellness Letter*, you will have an opportunity to note contrasting genre features in that publication as well.

ANALYZING YOUR OWN RHETORICAL CONTEXT AS READER/WRITER

When you are assigned to read texts of any type (a textbook, a scholarly article, data on a Web site, historical documents, or other kinds of readings), think not only about the authors' rhetorical context, but also about your own.

Determining Your Purpose, Audience, and Genre

When you write about various texts or use them in your own arguments, you will be writing for a purpose to an audience within a genre. In college, your purpose will be determined by your assignment. (See the final section of this chapter, "Typical Reading-Based Writing Assignments Across the Curriculum," pp. 30–35.) Your audience may range from yourself to your professor and your classmates, to readers of a certain newspaper or blog, even to participants in an undergraduate research conference. Your assigned genre might come from a wide range of possibilities: summary, Web posting, rhetorical analysis, reader-response reflection, source-based argument, or a major research paper.

Identifying your purpose at the outset helps you set goals and plan your reading accordingly. Your purpose for reading may seem like a self-evident matter—"I'm reading Chapter 1 of this sociology book because it was assigned for tomorrow." That may be, but what we have in mind is a more strategic consideration of your purpose. Ask yourself how the reading assignment ties in with themes established in class. How does it fit with concepts laid out on the course syllabus? Is this your first course in sociology? If so, you might set a purpose for yourself of gathering definitions of the foundational concepts and specialized vocabulary used by sociologists. These basic but strategically stated goals might lead you to allow extra time for the slowed-down reading that students usually need in order to get their bearings at the beginning of introductory courses.

To illustrate the importance of establishing purposes for your reading, let's move farther into the semester and assume you are skimming articles to select some for closer reading and possible use in an annotated bibliography for this first course in sociology. Further, imagine that your assignment is to choose and summarize articles that demonstrate how sociological research can shed light on a current public controversy. As we discuss in detail in Chapter 5, an important first step in an assignment like this is to identify a clear and compelling **research question**. A strong research question will enable you to know what you're looking for, and it will guide you to read more purposefully and productively. Let's say you are interested in whether pop culture has a negative effect on family values. You want to think that it doesn't, but from sometimes intense discussions among family and friends, you realize that the answer might be "it depends." Maybe sociological research has laid out some systematic ways of thinking about this issue, and a more productive question would be "How does pop culture impact family values?" or "What is known about how pop culture impacts family values?"

Following the demands of your research question, you will need to define both "pop culture" and "family values" and narrow your focus as you find articles related to your controversy. Some sources will report research findings contrary to your own views; others will tend to confirm your views. To summarize them fairly, you will have to pay careful attention to the way these authors articulate their own research questions and present their results. Setting goals ahead of time for both your writing and your reading will help you know what to look for as you select and read articles.

Matching Your Reading Strategies to Your Purpose as Reader/Writer

Although all readers change their approach to reading according to their audience, purpose, and the genre of the text at hand, most readers do so without thought or reflection, relying on a limited set of strategies. By contrast, experienced readers vary their reading process self-consciously and strategically. To see how one accomplished undergraduate, Sheri, contrasts her "school" reading with her "reading-for-fun" process, see the box on the next page. You will no doubt notice that her strategies combine idiosyncratic habits (the blue pen and cold room) with sound, widely used academic reading habits (looking over chapter headings, checking for study guide questions, and so on).

What personal habits or rituals do you combine with your more purposeful reading behaviors? The awareness and flexibility evident in the way Sheri talks about her reading are valuable because planning as she does would enable you to work efficiently and maximize the use of your time. Furthermore, thinking about your purpose as Sheri does will help you maintain a sense of your own authority as you read, a notion that is very important for college writing.

Sheri's self-awareness and deliberate reading strategies are not typical. When we ask students to describe the behaviors of good readers, many initially say "speed" or "the ability to understand a text in a single reading." Surprisingly, most experienced readers don't aim for speed reading, nor do they report that reading is an easy, one-step process. On the contrary, experienced readers put considerable effort into reading and rereading a text, adapting their strategies and speed to its demands and to their purpose for reading. Because your purposes for reading academic assignments will vary considerably, so must your academic reading strategies. You will read much differently, for example, if your task is to

PREPARING TO READ: SHERI'S PROCESS

"When I am reading for class, for starters I make sure that I have all of my reading supplies. These include my glasses, a highlighter, pencil, blue pen, notebook paper, dictionary, and a quiet place to read, which has a desk or table. (It also has to be cold!) Before I read for class or for research purposes I always look over chapter headings or bold print words and then formulate questions based on these. When I do this it helps me to become more interested in the text I am reading because I am now looking for answers.

"Also, if there are study guide questions, I will look them over so that I have a basic idea of what to look for. I will then read the text all the way through, find the answers to my questions, and underline all of the study guide answers in pencil.

"When I read for fun, it's a whole other story! I always take off my shoes and sit on the floor/ground or in a very comfortable chair. I always prefer to read in natural light and preferably fresh air. I just read and relax and totally immerse myself in the story or article or whatever!"[4]

interpret or analyze a text than if you are simply skimming it for its potential usefulness in a research project. Contrary to popular myth, expert readers are not necessarily "speed" readers. Experienced readers pace themselves according to their purpose, taking advantage of four basic reading speeds:

- *Very fast:* Readers scan a text very quickly if they are looking only for a specific piece of information.
- *Fast:* Readers skim a text rapidly if they are trying to get just the general gist without worrying about details.
- *Slow to moderate:* Readers read carefully in order to get complete understanding of an article. The more difficult the text, the more slowly they read. Often difficult texts require rereading.
- *Very slow:* Experienced readers read very slowly if their purpose is to analyze a text. They take elaborate marginal notes and often pause to ponder over the construction of a paragraph or the meaning of an image or metaphor. Sometimes they reread the text dozens of times.

As your expertise grows within the fields you study, you will undoubtedly learn to vary your reading speed and strategies according to your purposes, even to the point of considering "efficient" reading of certain texts to involve slowing way down and rereading.

HOW EXPERT READERS USE RHETORICAL KNOWLEDGE TO READ EFFICIENTLY

This section illustrates two strategies used by expert readers to apply rhetorical knowledge to their reading processes.

---

[4]Sheri's description of her reading process is quoted in Paula Gillespie and Neal Lerner, *The Allyn and Bacon Guide to Peer Tutoring* (Boston: Allyn & Bacon, 2000), 105. Print.

Using Genre Knowledge to Read Efficiently

Besides varying reading speed to match their purpose, experienced readers also adjust their reading strategies to match the genre of a text. It is clear that the articles represented in Figures 2.2 and 2.3 (pp. 24–25) call for different kinds of reading strategies, but you may be surprised to learn that many scientists wouldn't read the scholarly article straight through from beginning to end. Instead, depending on their purpose, it is likely that they would read different sections in different order. The material in the following box describes how a group of physicists were guided both by their purpose for reading and by their familiarity with the genre conventions of scientific research reports. We invite you to read the material in the box before proceeding to the next paragraph.

Considering how scientists with different interests read specialized articles in their discipline, we can surmise that some researchers would read the results section of the *Appetite* article very carefully, whereas others would concentrate on the methodology section. Still another reader, perhaps a graduate student interested in finding a dissertation topic, might read it to see what research the authors say still needs to be accomplished. With sharply narrow interests and purposes, these readers would probably not find the article difficult to read. In contrast, nonspecialists might find it daunting to read, but as experienced readers, they would recognize that it is not necessary to understand all the details in order to understand the article's gist. They might read the abstract, then skip directly to the discussion section, where the authors analyze the meaning and the significance of their results.

Using a Text's Social/Historical Context to Make Predictions and Ask Questions

Recognizing that a text is part of a larger conversation about a particular topic, experienced readers can also use textual cues—such as format, style, and terminology—as well as their own background knowledge to speculate about the original context of a text, make predictions about it, and formulate questions.

PHYSICISTS' TECHNIQUES FOR EFFICIENT READING

Researchers who studied the way that physicists read articles in physics journals found that the physicists seldom read the article from beginning to end but instead used their knowledge of the typical structure of scientific articles to find the information most relevant to their interests. Scientific articles typically begin with an abstract or summary of their contents. The main body of these articles includes a five-part structure: (1) an introduction that describes the research problem, (2) a review of other studies related to this problem, (3) a description of the methodology used in the research, (4) a report of the results, and (5) the conclusions drawn from the results. The physicists in the study read the abstracts first to see if an article was relevant to their own research. If it was, the experimental physicists went to the methodology section to see if the article reported any new methods. By contrast, the theoretical physicists went to the results section to see if the article reported any significant new results.[5]

[5]Research reported by Cheryl Geisler, *Academic Literacy and the Nature of Expertise* (Hillsdale, NJ: Erlbaum, 1994), 20–21. Print.

These strategies for actively engaging with a text's social or historical context are illustrated in Ann Feldman's report of interviews with expert readers reading texts within their own areas of expertise. For example, Professor Lynn Weiner, a social historian, describes in detail her behind-the-scenes thinking as she prepared to read a chapter entitled "From the Medieval to the Modern Family" from Philippe Aries's *Centuries of Childhood: A Social History of Family Life*, written in 1962. Quotations from Professor Weiner's description of her thinking are shown in the box below. As Professor Weiner reads, she continues to elaborate this context, confirming and revising predictions, asking new questions, evaluating what Aries has to say in light of the evidence he can provide, and assessing the value of his ideas to her own work as a social historian. She concludes by saying, "A path-breaking book, it was credited with advancing the idea that childhood as a stage of life is historically constructed and not the same in every culture and every time. In my own work I might refer to Aries as I think and write about families as they exist today."

Professor Weiner's description of creating a context for understanding the Aries book suggests that the ability to recognize what you do not know and to raise questions about a text is as important as identifying what you do know and understand. Sometimes readers can reconstruct context from external clues such as a title and headings; from a text's visual appearance; from background notes about the author, including the date and place of publication; or from what a book's table of contents reveals about its structure and scope. But readers often have to rely on internal evidence to get a full picture. A text's context and purpose may become evident through some quick spot reading (explained in the next chapter), especially in the introduction and conclusion. Sometimes, however, the full rhetorical and social context can be reconstructed only through a great deal of puzzling as you read. It's not unusual that a whole first reading is needed to understand exactly what conversation the writer is joining and how she or he intends to affect that conversation. Once that context becomes clear, rereading of key passages will make the text easier to comprehend.

> ### BUILDING A CONTEXT FOR READING
>
> "This work isn't precisely in my field and it is a difficult text. I also know it by its reputation. But, like any student, I need to create a context in which to understand this work. When the book was written, the idea of studying the family was relatively new. Before this time historians often studied kings, presidents, and military leaders. That's why this new type of social history encouraged us to ask, 'How did ordinary people live?' Not the kings, but the families in the middle ages. Then we have to ask: 'Which families is [Aries] talking about? What causes the change that he sees? . . . For whom is the change significant?' . . . I'll want to be careful not . . . to assume the old family is bad and the new family is good. The title suggests a transition so I'll be looking for signs of it."[6]

TYPICAL READING-BASED WRITING ASSIGNMENTS ACROSS THE CURRICULUM

In college, a reading assignment is often only the first step in a complex series of activities that lead toward writing something that will be graded. In many cases, the material you are

---

[6]Ann Feldman, *Writing and Learning in the Disciplines* (New York: Harper, 1996), 16–17, 25–29. Print.

asked to read and respond to may include visual elements that demand attention, such as charts and graphs, photographs, drawings, or specific features of document or Web design. What you write will naturally vary according to the situation, ranging from a quick answer on an essay exam to an extensive source-based paper. In this section, we discuss five types of common college assignments in which reading plays a major role:

1. Writing to understand course content more fully
2. Writing to report your understanding of what a text says
3. Writing to practice the conventions of a particular type of text
4. Writing to make claims about a text
5. Writing to extend the conversation

The role that reading plays in connection with these different purposes for writing can be placed along a continuum, starting at one end with assignments in which the ideas in the texts you read predominate and moving to assignments in which the content is subordinate to your own ideas and aims. The first two assignment types ask you to write in order to learn course subject matter and to practice careful listening to texts. The last three ask you to compose your own analyses and arguments for specific audiences. Writing teachers sometimes distinguish these two categories of assignment goals by referring to them as "writing to learn" and "learning to write."

Writing to Understand Course Content More Fully

"Writing-to-learn" assignments aim to deepen your understanding of materials you read by asking you to put the author/creator's ideas into your own words or to identify points of confusion for yourself. The primary audience for writing in this category is often yourself, although teachers may sometimes ask you to submit them so that they can check on your understanding and progress. The style is informal and conversational. Organization and grammatical correctness are less important than the quality of your engagement with the content of the reading. These assignments typically take one of the following forms.

In-Class Freewriting

The point of freewriting is to think rapidly without censoring your thoughts. It is often assigned in class as a way to stimulate thinking about the day's subject. A typical in-class freewrite assignment might be this:

> Choose what for you personally is the single most important word in what we read for today. You need not speculate about which word the author or your instructor or any other classmate would choose. Just choose the word that seems most important to you, and then explore in writing why you chose it. This word may occur only once or many times.[7]

---

[7]We thank Joan Ruffino, an instructor at the University of Wisconsin–Milwaukee, for this freewriting assignment.

Reading or Learning Logs

Reading or learning logs are informal assignments, usually organized chronologically, in which you record your understanding, questions, and responses to a reading or image. Some teachers give specific prompts for entries, whereas others just ask that you write them with a certain regularity and/or of a certain length. A typical prompt might be "How would you describe the author's voice in this essay?" If a teacher asks you simply to write your own reflections in a log, you might use some of the questions rhetorical readers ask (p. 11) to examine the text's method and your response to it.

Double-Entry Journals

Double-entry journals are like reading logs but formatted so that you may conduct an ongoing dialogue with your own interpretations and reactions to a text. Once again, the audience is primarily yourself. Although the double-entry system was originally designed for lined notebook paper, it can work equally well—or even better—on screen. Here is how the system works: Divide a notebook page with a line down the middle, or set up a two-column layout in your word processing program. On the right side of the page, record reading notes—direct quotations, observations, comments, questions, objections. On the left side, record your later reflections about those notes—second thoughts, responses to quotations, reactions to earlier comments, answers to questions or new questions. Skip lines as necessary so that your dialogue on the left lines up with your original notes on the right. Another option is to use a commenting function to create a sidebar column for your responses to your original notes; but in our experience, students find the spatial alignment difficult to track. Rhetorician Ann Berthoff, who popularized the double-entry approach, says that it provides readers with a means of conducting a "continuing audit of meaning."[8] In a double-entry journal, you carry on a conversation with yourself about a text.

Short Thought Pieces or Postings to a Discussion Board

Sometimes written for an instructor, sometimes for a specified group of peers, short (250–300 words) response papers or "thought" pieces are somewhat more formal than the assignments discussed so far, but they are still much more informal than essay assignments. They call for a fuller response than the previous types of writing, but the purpose is similar—to articulate an understanding of a particular text by identifying significant points and offering a personal response or interpretation of them. Teachers will often provide a specific prompt for these assignments, sometimes as a way to generate a series of short pieces that will build to a larger paper. When the piece is written for a discussion forum, instructors may ask that you include a question or respond to a classmate's questions.

Here is a sample response piece that was posted to an online class forum. The teacher asked the students to write about the insights they gleaned regarding obsessive-compulsive disorder (OCD) from reading Lauren Slater's essay "Black Swans," in which the author narrates the onset of her ongoing battle with it.

---

[8]Ann Berthoff, *The Making of Meaning* (Montclair, NJ: Boynton Cook, 1981), 45. Print.

STUDENT POSTING TO A CLASS FORUM

Reading "Black Swans" taught me some basic information about OCD, but more importantly, it taught me how terrifying this disease can be. It begins with a single obsessive thought that leads to a cycle of anxiety, repetitive behaviors, and avoidance of situations that produce the obsessive thoughts. In severe cases, like Slater's, the person completely avoids life because the obsessive thoughts invade every aspect of life.

What impressed me most about this essay, however, was Slater's ability to put me in her shoes and make me feel some of the terror she felt. She vividly describes her experience at being stricken with this condition without warning. A single thought—"I can't concentrate"—suddenly blocked out all other thoughts. Even her own body seemed foreign to her and grotesque: "the phrase 'I can't concentrate on my hand' blocked out my hand, so all I saw was a blur of flesh giving way to the bones beneath, and inside the bones the grimy marrow, and in the grimy marrow the individual cells, all disconnected." I see why Max says it was the most terrifying aspect of the disease to him. I can't imagine being disconnected from my own body. More horrifying to me, though, was her sense of being completely unable to control her mind: "My mind was devouring my mind." I will be interested to see what others think.

Writing to Report Your Understanding of What a Text Says

Another common reading-based assignment asks you to report your understanding of what a text says. Here, your goal is to summarize the text rather than respond to it. Reports like this are necessary, for example, when essay exam questions ask students to contrast the ideas of several authors. Another example would be an **annotated bibliography** summarizing sources related to a particular topic or question, or a literature review at the beginning of a report for a science class. A summary can be as short as a single sentence (when, for example, you want to provide context for a quotation in a paper) or longer and more detailed (when, for example, you are summarizing an opposing view that you intend to refute in your own argument.) Although summaries or reports of your understanding of a text will vary in length and purpose, they are always expected to be accurate, fair, and balanced. (We offer guidelines for writing summaries for a variety of purposes, including a rhetorical précis, in Chapter 3.)

Writing to Practice the Conventions of a Particular Type of Text

Assignments that ask you to practice the conventions of a particular type of writing—its organizational format, style, ways of presenting evidence, and so on—use readings as models. Such assignments are common in college courses. In a journalism class, for example, you would learn to write a news report using the inverted pyramid structure; in a science course, you would learn to write up the results of a lab experiment in a particular scientific report format. Novices in a discipline learn to write in specialized genres by reading examples and practicing their formats and rhetorical "moves."

Generally, using readings as models of a genre or subgenre involves the following activities:

- Identifying the features that characterize a particular type of text
- Noting the ways in which a rhetorical situation affects the features identified in model texts
- Deciding on your own topic and reason for writing this particular type of text
- Using the features of the model text (or texts) and your own rhetorical situation to guide your writing

Let's say, for example, that you've been asked to write a **proposal argument**. Proposals typically include three main features: description of the problem, proposal of a solution, and justification of that solution. As you read sample proposals, you will find that in different contexts, authors deal with these features differently, depending on their audience and purpose. In some cases, for example, there is a great deal of description of the problem because the intended audience is unfamiliar with it or doesn't recognize it as a problem. In other cases, it is presumed that the intended reading audience already recognizes the problem. The key to success is to adapt a model text's structural and stylistic characteristics to your own rhetorical purpose, not to follow the model slavishly. (For more details about proposal arguments, see Table 2.1 on pp. 18–20.)

In courses across the curriculum, your ability to analyze and adopt the conventions particular to a given discipline's ways of writing will help you write successful papers. For example, when you are asked in a philosophy class to write an argument in response to Immanuel Kant's *Critique of Pure Reason*, you are primarily being asked to engage with the ideas in the text. But secondarily, you are also being asked to practice the conventions of writing a philosophical argument in which counterexamples and counterarguments are expected. Thus, in any field of study, it pays to be alert not only to the ideas presented in material you are assigned to read, but also to its structure and style.

Writing to Make Claims About a Text

Assignments in this category ask you to analyze and critique texts, including texts in which images and layout are key elements of rhetorical effect. Such papers must go beyond a summary of what a text says to make claims about that content and how it is presented. Many academic writers take as their field of study the texts produced by others. Literary critics study novels, poems, and plays; cultural critics analyze song lyrics, advertisements, cereal boxes, and television scripts; historians analyze primary source documents from the past; theologians scrutinize the sacred texts of different religions; lawyers analyze the documents entered into court proceedings, the exact wording of laws and statutes, and the decisions of appellate courts. In all these cases, the analysis and critique involve examining small parts of the whole to understand, explain, and perhaps object to, overall points and success.

Many college composition courses ask students to write rhetorical analyses of texts. To **analyze**—a word that at its root means "take apart"—a text, you need to identify specific rhetorical methods and strategies used by the author, show how these rhetorical choices contribute to the text's impact, and evaluate those elements in light of the author's evident purpose. In assignments like this, the text and your ideas about it are of equal importance. These assignments asking for analysis are not invitations for you to refer briefly to the text and then take off on your own opinions about the topic, nor are they invitations merely to summarize or rehearse what the text has said. Rather, analysis assignments expect you to engage critically with a specific text. On the one hand, you will be expected to represent what the text said accurately and fairly. On the other hand, you will be expected to offer your own analysis, interpretation, or critique in a way that enables readers to see the text differently. Further guidance about engaging with texts this way appears in Chapter 4, which includes guidelines for writing a rhetorical analysis along with a sample assignment and student paper as illustration.

Writing to Extend the Conversation

These assignments treat texts as voices in a conversation about ideas. They typically ask writers to read and synthesize material from several sources. Here, your own ideas and aims take center stage; your source texts play important but less prominent backup roles. The most familiar form this assignment takes is the research or seminar paper. A key difference between these assignments and high school research papers is that college instructors expect the paper to present your own argument, not simply to report what others have said. In other words, you are expected to articulate a significant question or problem, research what published authors have said about it in print or on the Web, and formulate your own argument. To write these multisource papers successfully, you must use your source texts primarily to position yourself in the conversation and to supply supporting data, information, or testimony. The argument—your main points—must come from you.

A helpful way to approach these assignments is to treat the texts you have read as springboards for further research and discovery. Think of the readings you encounter in your research as voices in a conversation that your essay will join. By giving you the opportunity to define your own purposes for writing in dialog with other texts, such assignments prepare you for the research assignments typical of many college courses, where your goal is to synthesize material from a number of sources and then produce your own paper, inserting another voice—your own—into the ongoing conversation. To illustrate this kind of research writing, at the end of Chapter 6 we include Jack's analysis of multiple perspectives on the potential of corn ethanol as an automobile fuel.

CHAPTER SUMMARY

This chapter has focused on the three major elements of rhetorical context—purpose, audience, and genre. In the first part of the chapter, we explained how to analyze these three factors for a text that you are reading. We then showed you how to analyze your own rhetorical context as a reader/writer. In particular, we showed you how

- To analyze a text's original rhetorical context

- To determine your own rhetorical context and to match your reading strategies to your own purposes
- To use rhetorical knowledge to make your reading more efficient
  - By using genre knowledge to read more efficiently
  - By analyzing the text's original social/historical context

Finally, we explained five different ways that assignments across the curriculum might ask you to use readings.

3

LISTENING TO A TEXT

The process of reading is not just the interpretation of a text but the interpretation of another person's worldview as presented by a text.

—Doug Brent

In this chapter, you will learn:

- Strategies that will help you attend closely to a text and give it the fairest hearing possible
- Concepts for "reading" visual elements and recognizing how they enhance, support, or extend points contained in a verbal text
- Techniques for preparing idea maps and descriptive outlines of texts (both verbal and visual)
- Guidelines for composing summaries and rhetorical précis.

In this chapter, we focus specifically on the nuts and bolts of reading the kinds of texts you will be assigned in college. You will learn to integrate the strategies used by experienced readers into your own reading repertoire. These strategies—for **preparing to read, reading initially, and rereading**—will make you both a better reader and a shrewder writer.

Our discussion in this chapter as well as the next extends the metaphor of reading as conversation by using the terms "listening" and "questioning" to describe specific reading techniques. The **listening strategies** we discuss will help you read attentively so that you can understand a text in the way the author intended and then represent the text fairly when you write about it.

To illustrate the strategies presented in the rest of this chapter and in Chapter 4, we will refer to three texts: the *UC Berkeley Wellness Letter* article, "Chew on This," found on page

25; an excerpt from art historian Kirk Savage's chapter on the Vietnam Veterans Memorial in *Monument Wars*, "The Conscience of the Nation," printed at the end of this chapter; and Atul Gawande's argument for "A Life-Saving Checklist," presented at the end of Chapter 4. We use "Chew on This" as an example of the lively popular pieces you are likely to encounter when doing research on contemporary culture. Savage's text illustrates the sophisticated scholarly reading you are likely to be assigned in a variety of disciplines. Gawande's text exemplifies the tightly argued opinion pieces you will find when you research public policy issues or when you read news and opinion articles in the ordinary course of being an informed citizen.

WRITING AS YOU READ

Rhetorical readers "listen" by reading with pen in hand in order to interact with the text and record their ideas-in-progress. When they read on screen, they use a text highlight tool or keep a second file open for note-taking. You will find that writing as you read will transform your reading process from passive receptivity into active meaning-making.

You may have heard of "active listening," a technique by which listeners use eye contact and body language to convey that they are listening carefully to someone. Writing as you read is **active reading**. Skilled rhetorical readers might write in the margins of a text (unless it is a library book), or they might keep a reading log or journal in which they record notes—on paper or in a designated "ideas" file on their computer. Sometimes they stop reading in the middle of a passage and freewrite their ideas-in-progress. When a text stimulates their own thinking, writing down those ideas captures that thinking for future reference and stimulates further thought. To put it another way, rhetorical reading strategies focus on both **comprehension** (a reader's understanding of a text) and **invention**—the ideas a reader generates in response to a text. Thus, writing while you read helps you generate ideas, as well as interact more deeply with a text.

Not surprisingly, then, most of the rhetorical reading strategies that we present in this book require you to write. To foster the reading-writing connection, we recommend that you, too, keep a reading log, paper or electronic, in which you practice the strategies described in this chapter. Doing so will help you develop powerful advanced reading skills, as well as generate a wealth of ideas for essay topics.

Depending on your purposes for reading a given text, some of the strategies described in this chapter will seem more appropriate in some situations than in others. Some are used consciously by experienced readers on a regular basis; others are designed to help you acquire the mental habits that have become second nature to experienced readers. For example, they almost always take notes as they read, and they frequently write summaries of what they have read. However, experienced readers would be less likely to write a descriptive outline (described later in this chapter; see pp. 56–59), not because the exercise isn't valuable, but because experience has allowed them to internalize the mental habit of attending to both the content and function of paragraphs as they read. By practicing descriptive outlining on a couple of readings, you too will begin to internalize this dual focus of rhetorical reading. Descriptive outlining is also a valuable tool to use in your own writing as you analyze a draft in order to make decisions about revision. In addition, it will foster your ability to talk about visuals—how they work, and how you might use them in your own writing.

PREPARING TO READ

In Chapters 1 and 2, we pointed out that strong readers manage their reading processes according to the type of text they are reading and their purpose for reading it. The strategies we present in this section encourage you to prepare to read as though you were about to join the text in a multi-voiced conversation. As we explained in Chapter 1, the text you are reading is one voice among a network of other voices. Your response to the text constitutes yet another voice in the ongoing conversation about the topic. Practicing these strategies will prepare you to read in a powerful way that will enable you to join that conversation.

Recalling Background Knowledge

By pausing to recall your prior knowledge, experience, and opinions regarding a text's subject matter, you can make your reading more purposeful. As illustration, recall for a moment the sociology assignment we imagined in Chapter 2: an annotated bibliography on a controversy over the effects of pop culture on family values (pp. 27–28). Before you begin reading, it might be helpful to narrow the scope of your research by considering what aspects of "pop culture" have, in your experience, seemed most objectionable to defenders of "family values." Still more important for careful reading would be to define for yourself the term "family values" so that you can track your ideas against the way the term is used in the materials you find. Your sociology textbook might offer a standard definition, for example, or you might find several articles with consistent definitions. On the other hand, if you found that writers are at odds about how to define the term, that controversy would be very important to note and track.

For any assignment, pausing to review your background knowledge will help you recognize the gaps in that knowledge. By jotting down some notes about what you know and need to know, you can establish benchmarks that will help you assess a text's effect on your current views or beliefs, as well as its usefulness for a writing project. The journals or reading logs that we recommend are the perfect place to brainstorm about what you already know or feel about a subject. If you have little knowledge about the subject, jot down some questions that will enable you to engage with what you read. Leave open the possibility that your ideas and purposes for writing might change as you read. Later, when you finish reading the text, the notes in your reading log will provide valuable cues for review.

> **AS YOU JOT READING NOTES AND REVIEW THEM, ASK YOURSELF QUESTIONS LIKE THESE:**
> • What did I learn from the text that is new to me?
> • What did the text prompt me to consider that I had not thought about before?

- Has the text confirmed my prior knowledge and beliefs—or has it raised some doubts?
- How might I use information and ideas from this text when I write papers or exams, or make decisions in my workplace or community?

Using Visual Elements to Plan and Predict

Visual features are one of the first things we notice about a text. They lead us to approach the reading of a poem, for example, quite differently than we do the reading of a scholarly article, résumé, or comic strip. Even tacit knowledge of genres sets up particular expectations and affects how we go about reading a text. As we point out in Chapter 2's discussion of genre, the design of a text, on paper or screen, provides important clues to its writer's and publisher's designs upon readers' attention and ideas. The color, design, and images on a book or magazine cover typically are meant to entice us to open and read inside. On Web sites, color, design, images, and animation combine to grab our attention so that we'll pause to read instead of clicking away to a new page. Textbooks capitalize on color and page design to hold and guide students' attention. Careful attention to a text's visual features can help you plan your reading of it, as well as enable you to make predictions about its purpose. It is common practice for students to leaf through a textbook chapter to spot illustrations, charts, or graphs; to note the headings on subsections; and, of course, to calculate how long it will take to read an assigned set of pages.

Although it may seem that the visual features of a text are distinct from the verbal, the print features of written texts also affect readers' attitudes and expectations about a reading. Broadly, it is inevitable that we take in the layout of pages and screens we encounter, perhaps without attending specifically to the details assembled by the page designers. Readers notice images, especially large ones, accompanying a text, and as we discuss later in this chapter and the next, these images inevitably influence our understanding and appreciation of the contents. Indeed, even the absence of images has an impact, as in the text-heavy page of the scholarly journal seen in Figure 2.2 (p. 24). At a more fine-grained level, the choice of typeface and font size can affect not only readability, but the way a text conveys a mood and tone. Consider the different levels of seriousness and informality conveyed by the fonts in Figure 3.1. These differences are significant for your choices as a writer because just as they help you recognize context and purpose when you read various textual genres, they provide the same signals to your own readers. For example, we have all been cautioned against using ALL CAPS in emails because they give the effect of SHOUTING. Similarly, it is wise to submit academic papers printed in a typeface, or font, that has serifs, those little strokes at the tops and bottoms of letters. Doing so will make your paper easier for your professors to read and will convey the message that you are aware of appropriate academic conventions.

Consider the visual features of this chapter: frequent subheadings, boldfaced terms, bulleted lists, annotated examples. What do these features suggest about its genre? About how to go about reading it? Even if you were reading a copy of this chapter on screen or on paper separately from the book, you would easily recognize that it came from a textbook because its instructional features emphasize important points and break up information for ease of reading and review. Because you are quite familiar with textbooks, you have undoubt-

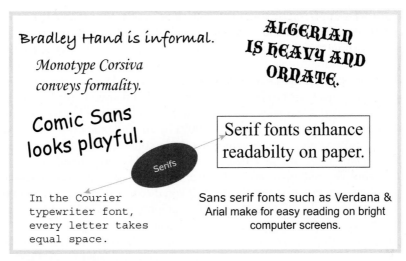

Figure 3.1 Typeface varieties

edly developed strategies for reading texts like this one—skimming the headings before reading, noting words in bold, using the bulleted information for review.

Spot Reading

Spot reading is a process that gives you a quick overview of a text's content and structure and thus helps you (a) determine the fit of the text's rhetorical context and purpose with your own purposes for reading; and (b) predict content and formulate questions. For example, when your purpose for reading is to acquaint yourself with the vocabulary and concepts of a new field, spot reading will help you determine whether a book or article is written at an introductory level. If it is, then you can expect textual cues to point to important new vocabulary and concepts. If it is not, then you may decide to find a more basic introductory text to read first, or you may decide to look up unfamiliar terms and to allot extra time to reread passages that seem dense initially.

If an article or book that interests you has an abstract or introduction, you might begin spot reading there. Other places for productive spot reading are the opening and concluding paragraphs or sections of an article. The opening usually introduces subject matter and announces a purpose, and the conclusion often sums up the text's major ideas. If you are working with a textbook that provides summaries and study questions, it is a good idea to read through these before beginning to read the section they describe. If the text is short, you might try reading the opening sentences of each paragraph. With a book, consider what the chapter titles in the table of contents reveal. Sometimes, particularly in textbooks, the table of contents will provide subheadings that reveal valuable detail about content. Spot reading there can help you determine what will be covered and whether the book, or particular parts of it, will help you address a research question. Furthermore, the organizational strategy revealed through a table of contents can provide important information about an author's method, perhaps guiding you to choose certain sections as essential reading.

An Extended Example: Spot Reading in Kirk Savage's *Monument Wars*

Suppose you are enrolled in a Humanities seminar focused on public art and are part of a small group putting together a print- and Web-based research project related to Vietnam and other war memorials in your group members' various hometowns as well as in Washington, D.C. (A photo of the Vietnam Veterans Memorial in Washington is presented in Figure 3.2.) Imagine that your professor has recommended that you "read around" in a book by Kirk Savage called *Monument Wars*. When you look up the library call number, you learn that it was published fairly recently (2009) by an academic press (University of California Press), and you glean valuable insights about content from its subtitle: *Washington, D.C., the National Mall, and the Transformation of the Memorial Landscape*. These signs of the book's scholarly credentials give substance to your professor's recommendation. Furthermore, when you find it on the library shelf you discover that it is heavy and thick—390 pages—many of them devoted to notes, a bibliography, and an index. A serious book. Will it be difficult to read? Are you part of its intended audience?

Flipping through the pages on your way to the circulation desk, you would see that the book has many photographs and other illustrations directly related to the Vietnam Veterans Memorial (VVM), including the one reproduced in Figure 3.3. Back at the front of the book, you might notice the author's dedication of the book to his family and, curiously, "to all the people of this earth who may never have a monument to call their own." Thus the author sets a tone that runs counter to the book's many images of ornate buildings and heroes on horseback. Although details about the author are scarce in the book itself, a quick Web search later will reveal that Kirk Savage holds a high academic position at the University of Pittsburgh and writes frequently in a personal blog about war memorials and monuments. "A great potential resource," you might think as you sit down to examine the book itself.

Figure 3.2 Visitors at the national Vietnam Veterans Memorial in Washington, D.C. Visitors often pause to create rubbings of names engraved into the reflective black stone. The two intersecting walls memorialize more than 58,000 members of the U.S. Armed Forces who were killed or missing in action in Southeast Asia between 1959 and 1975, or who died later from injuries directly related to combat in the Vietnam War.

Figure 3.3 Illustration of Maya Lin's winning design for the Vietnam Veterans Memorial, by Paul Oles, 1981

Consider the list of chapter titles on the Contents page:

1. A Monument to a Deceased Project

2. Covering Ground

3. The Mechanic Monster

4. Inventing Public Space

5. The Monument Transformed

6. The Conscience of the Nation[1]

7. An End to War, an End to Monuments?[2]

While the term "public space" in the title of Chapter 4 would echo concepts discussed in your class, the idea of "the monument transformed" or a monument serving as the "conscience of the nation" would be highly intriguing. A closer look at the illustrations during another flip through the pages reveals that the book is organized chronologically. A quick skim of the introduction confirms the dedication's hint that Savage is interested in the human side of memorials. He begins by quoting a congressman from 1800 to the effect that the invention of the printing press has made monuments "good for nothing" (1), something Savage obviously intends to dispute. Spot reading of the opening sentences of the paragraphs that follow underscores the subtitle's suggestion that the history of monuments on the National Mall is one of disputes and conflicts. Savage begins the final paragraph of the

[1] An excerpt from this chapter appears on pages 65–68.

[2] Kirk Savage, *Monument Wars* (Berkeley, CA: U California P, 2009). N. pag.

introduction this way: "All this means that monuments will still be subject to dispute and change before and after they are built, and the landscape of national memory will never cease to evolve" (22).

A quick check of the index reveals quite a few pages listed under "Vietnam Veterans Memorial," so you would likely leave the library confident that you have an excellent resource, one you can not only "read around" in but use for ideas directly relevant to your project. You might even decide to buy your own copy so that you can mark it up as you read.

As this example shows, spot reading can provide a framework for making predictions and posing questions about content that will help you make sense of ideas and information once you begin reading. It can also help you anticipate and tolerate difficult-to-understand passages, confident that, even though you don't understand every bit of the text on the first reading, you nevertheless have some sense of its overall purpose. In short, spot reading helps you stay in control of your reading process by helping you confirm and revise your predictions and look for answers to your questions. It takes little time and offers a worthwhile payoff in increased understanding.

LISTENING AS YOU READ INITIALLY

Just as good listeners attend carefully to what their conversational partners say, trying to give them a fair hearing, so, too, do good readers "listen" carefully to what a text says, trying to consider its ideas carefully and accurately before rushing to judgment. College reading assignments put a particular premium on giving an impartial hearing to ideas and positions that are new and sometimes radically different from your own. Moreover, in class discussions, examinations, and paper assignments, you will frequently be asked to demonstrate that you have listened well to assigned texts. Professors want to know that you have comprehended these texts with reasonable accuracy before you proceed to analyze, apply, or critique the ideas in them. In the language of Kenneth Burke's metaphor of the conversational parlor, you might think of this listening phase of the reading process as the phase where you try to catch the drift of the conversation and give it the fullest and fairest hearing before "putting in your oar."

Listening strategies help you understand what to listen for, how to hear what the text is saying, and how to track your evolving understanding of the text. The first time through a text, reading with its grain, you are trying to understand a text's overall gist and compose a "rough-draft interpretation" of its meaning and your own response. As we discuss later in this chapter, after you have a sense of the gist, a second reading will enable you to confirm and deepen your understanding, and revise it if necessary.

We have urged you to read with a pen or pencil in hand, to adopt experienced readers' practice of marking passages, drawing arrows, and making notes. (You can do this with electronic highlighting and annotating, too.) Active use of your hands as well as your eyes will be necessary to undertake the four strategies for an efficient initial reading that we recommend in the next four sections.

Note Organizational Signals

Headings and transition words serve as organizational signals that help you anticipate and then track a text's overall structure of ideas. Experienced readers use these signals to identify the text's central ideas, to distinguish major ideas from minor ones, to anticipate what is coming next, and to determine the relationship among the text's major ideas. Organizational signals and forecasting statements (which directly tell you what to expect) function like road signs, giving you information about direction, upcoming turns, and the distance yet to go. For example, experienced readers note words that signal a change in the direction of thought, such as *however, in contrast, or on the other hand*. Likewise, they take advantage of the guidance provided by words such as *first, second*, and *third* that signal a series of parallel points or ideas; words such as *therefore, consequently*, or *as a result* that signal logical relationships; and words such as *similarly, also*, or *likewise* that signal additional support for the current point. Circling or otherwise marking these terms will make it possible for a quick glance back to remind you of the structure of ideas.

Mark Unfamiliar Terms and References

As you read, it is important to mark unfamiliar terms and references because they offer contextual clues about the intended audience and the conversation of which a given text is a part. The very unfamiliarity of these terms and references may tell you that the text is written for an insider audience whose members share a particular kind of knowledge and concerns. To become part of the conversation, you need to learn such terms. We suggest that you mark them with a question mark or write them in the margins and return to them after you finish your initial reading. Stopping to look them up as you read will break your concentration. By looking them up later, after you have that "rough-draft" sense of the text's overall purpose, you will gain insight into how key terms function and how they represent major concerns of a particular field or area of study.

"Read as though it made sense and perhaps it will."

—I. A. Richards

Identify Points of Difficulty

One of the most important traits of experienced readers is probably their *tolerance for ambiguity and initial confusion*. They have learned to read through points of difficulty, trusting that confusing points will become clear as they continue to read. When you are reading about new and difficult subject matter, you will inevitably encounter passages that you simply do not understand. A valuable reading strategy is to identify explicitly what you don't understand. We recommend that you bracket puzzling passages and keep reading. Later, you can come back to them and try to translate them into your own words or to frame questions about them to ask your classmates and professor.

Annotate

When you annotate a text, you underline, highlight, draw arrows, and make marginal comments. Annotating is a way of making the text your own, of literally putting your mark on it—noting its key passages and ideas. Experienced readers rely on this common but powerful strategy to note reactions and questions, thereby recording their in-process understanding of a text. By marking the page, they are able to monitor their evolving construction of a text's meaning.

Annotations also serve a useful purpose when you return to a text to reread or review it. Not only can they remind you of your first impressions of the text's meaning, but they also can help you identify main points and come to new levels of understanding—clearer answers to earlier questions, new insights, and new questions. Indeed, we recommend that you annotate each time you read a text, perhaps using different colors so that you have a record of the new layers of meaning you discover. Of course, you would not do this in a library book, and there's one additional caveat: annotating can become counterproductive if you underline or highlight too enthusiastically. A completely underlined paragraph tells you nothing about its key point. To be useful, underlining must be selective, based both on your own purposes for reading and on what you think the writer's main points are. In general, when it is time to review the text and recall its main ideas, notes in the margin about main ideas, questions, objections, and connections will be far more useful than underlining or highlighting.

To illustrate this listening strategy, at the end of this chapter, we have annotated part of the excerpt from Kirk Savage's *Monument Wars* about the Vietnam Veterans Memorial on pages 65–68. The annotations were made from the perspective of the student we asked you to imagine who is working on a project about public art and memorials and who decided to buy a personal copy of the book in order to make annotations like these. These notes demonstrate one student's efforts to understand Savage's points about the memorial as an "antimonument." We invite you to turn to the selection now and read carefully through both the passage and the annotations. Consider how these or other annotations would help you understand the passage more fully—and think about what uses you or another student might make of these annotations.

CONNECTING THE VISUAL TO THE VERBAL

Visual images frequently accompany the verbal texts we encounter in periodicals and on the Web. They **enhance, support, and extend** a text's meaning, all in ways undoubtedly intended to increase rhetorical effectiveness. A number of factors work together to make the use of images particularly powerful. For one thing, we live in a highly visual culture where information is often transmitted through images. Our attention is more readily attracted and engaged by verbal texts that include visual elements. For another, the general beliefs persist not only that "a picture is worth a thousand words" but also that "pictures don't lie" and "seeing is believing," all despite widespread knowledge that images can easily be doctored or manipulated. (Indeed, puzzle quizzes about exactly how a photo has been changed have become popular in college newspapers.) For all of these reasons, careful readers must be alert to the subtle and indirect messages conveyed through visuals.

The importance of visual elements, particularly images, in relation to a text can vary considerably. At one end of the continuum are visual elements that are clearly incidental to the verbal message—for example, generic clip art added to a poster publicizing a meeting. At the other end are texts in which the visual message predominates and verbal elements play only a minor role, a phenomenon frequently seen in advertisements. Perhaps more significant at this end of the continuum are photographs of certain historical moments, images that have become iconic in that they have come to represent far more than the event recorded by the camera. Images of the planes ramming into the twin towers on September 11, 2001, come to mind as examples. An iconic historical image with a positive connotation features Dr. Martin Luther King, Jr., at the 1963 March on Washington. Photos from this event often show King at the Lincoln Memorial or the crowds stretching before him from the Reflecting Pool to the Washington Monument. They have come to stand not just for the event, or even progress toward the 1964 Civil Rights Act, but for Americans' freedom to peaceful assembly and protest.

Somewhere between incidental decorations and iconic historical images is the special case of cartoons, especially political cartoons. Here the visual and verbal are tightly intertwined, with the visual sometimes leading, sometimes carrying the verbal.

In academic writing, visual elements are usually subordinate to the verbal content, with their importance depending on their function. Nonetheless, it is very important that as an academic reader you stay alert to the way that visual elements function in relation to a verbal message and thus play into the rhetorical effect of a text.

Visuals That Enhance Verbal Content

Photographs, drawings, and other images often function to attract readers' attention, set a tone, and frame responses. In these ways, they **enhance** the text's verbal content by augmenting it with the vividness and immediacy of an image. The images of the Vietnam Veterans Memorial in Figures 3.2 and 3.3 here in this book on pages 42 and 43 function that way. Or consider the example of the colorful animated graphics that typically introduce television news programs, heralding station or network slogans about "late-breaking" or "leading-edge" news and "on-your-side" newscasters.

A survey of just a few campus bulletin boards will likely reveal multiple examples of visuals used primarily to enhance a textual message. A good example is prominently displayed in a classroom where one of us teaches. A photo of a young man's eyes and broad forehead take up almost all of an 11- by 17-inch poster. From across the room, the whites of his eyes and a jumble of print draw attention. The eyes are rolled way up, as if he is reading what is printed in several different sizes of type on his forehead. The largest print reads "62%," "regret," and "under." Walking closer, one can make out smaller type that reads, "the influence." (Are you guessing the topic at hand?) One must get very close to read the words in smallest print and thus put together the full message: "62% of students regret something they did under the influence of drugs and alcohol." Drawing us in to read that message is what that poster is all about. The big eyes and big forehead, while they might be read as symbolic of deep thought (or a headache), serve primarily as attention-getting enhancements of the message, which is part of a campaign against binge drinking designed to change ideas about what constitutes "normal" alcohol use on campus.

Visuals That Support Verbal Content

A second way in which the visual relates to the verbal, common especially in academic writing for technical and pre-professional fields, is to support the verbal message. In our everyday lives, news photographs offer a common example of how visual elements provide evidence for claims. The contrasting photographs in Figure 3.4, for example, document the destruction caused by Hurricane Sandy on a well-known amusement pier in Seaside Heights on the Jersey Shore. They thus provide dramatic background images for the Associated Press (AP) story they accompanied. The story, which the AP headlined "Will Jersey Shore ever be the same after Sandy?", celebrated the former iconic status of the boardwalk and the shoreline itself in American culture, and quoted local residents and celebrities lamenting the damage done and cherishing memories of the time spent at places like this.

Thanks to advances in computer software and printing technology, even student authors can provide evidence for their claims by referring readers directly to visual images in photographs and other graphics. Prominent among visual elements that support verbal content are **information graphics**, which are typically used to promote readers' comprehension of discrete and detailed points of information, especially in workplace settings. Table 3.1 above—itself an information graphic—provides a quick list of visuals commonly used for specific explanatory and informative purposes. Most of these are fairly easy to create with standard desktop software, and are increasingly common in both print and Web materials.

Understanding the purpose and function of information graphics will help you develop your rhetorical reading skills and prepare you to incorporate graphic elements into your texts in college and on the job. Notice that the list of graphics in the right-hand column of Table 3.1 includes photographs and drawings, which become information graphics when they are used to support verbal material by providing illustration, typically with added captions. Similarly, elements of page design such as checklists, shaded boxes, and bulleted lists merge into this category when they are used to help readers efficiently find, use, and understand information.

Visuals That Extend Verbal Content

A third function visual elements can serve is to **extend** the meaning of a verbal text by enlarging or highlighting a particular dimension of it. Visual elements that function in this way can suggest new interpretations, provoke particular responses, or create links to other ideas. In many of these cases, a reader might initially puzzle over the connection between an image and the verbal text it accompanies, not knowing quite how to interpret it until after reading the text. Visuals that work this way often accompany advertisements, by implication connecting the product being sold with physical attractiveness, romantic success, improved economic status, or any number of other desirable attributes.

In some cases, a reader may not know quite how to interpret an image until after reading the text. Consider, for example, the drawing by Randy Mack Bishop in Figure 3.5. Bishop is an illustrator for the *Dallas Morning News* whose work is available to newspapers nationwide through NewsArt.com. Before we describe the context in which an editor at the *Milwaukee Journal Sentinel* placed it, take a moment to consider what ideas or issues Bishop's image evokes for you.

Figure 3.4 Contrasting photographs of the Funtown Pier in Seaside Heights, New Jersey, before and after Hurricane Sandy in late October, 2012. The top photo was taken August 10, 2010, and the bottom on October 31, 2012.

Table 3.1   Common Uses of Information Graphics

Purpose	Graphic to Use
Present detailed or complex data	Table
Bring an object or process to life	Drawing, photograph, flowchart
Show change over time	Line graph
Show relation of parts to the whole	Pie chart
Contrast quantities and phenomena	Table, bar graph
Locate and show distribution of phenomena	Map
Highlight key points	Shaded boxes, bulleted lists

Figure 3.5 Editorial art drawing by Randy Mack Bishop

The drawing came to our attention when it appeared on the *Journal Sentinel*'s op-ed page alongside a reprinted opinion piece by *New York Times* columnist Maureen Dowd with the headline "Scarred for Life: Courage Begets Courage."[3] Puzzled? We were. In the column, Dowd writes admiringly about her niece's courage in donating part of her liver to her uncle (Dowd's brother). By the end of the piece, Dowd has resolved to become an organ donor herself. Implicit in the column is an argument urging others to do the same. Because Bishop's drawing does not connect directly to the text, readers might interpret its meaning variously. However, most would probably agree that it extends Dowd's abstract idea of support, perhaps suggesting that the support of others enables us to be courageous and to rise above selfish concerns.

For Writing and Discussion

To explore the many different ways that visual elements of a text can connect to its verbal elements, work with a partner or group to examine how the editors of a current print magazine have used various visual elements to engage readers. Prepare your findings for presentation to your classmates.

1. Focus on editorial content, not advertisements, to find examples of each role for visuals that we outline in this chapter.
2. Look for visuals that may serve more than one function. How do captions, if supplied, guide readers to connect them to verbal content?
3. Are there visuals that defy categorization? Explain.

For this assignment, we recommend examining both Web and paper issues of magazines available in most libraries that cover a variety of content for a broad, general audience, and that thus use many types of visuals, such as *Time, Bloomberg Business Week,* or *The New Yorker.* When you examine online editions of these periodicals, consider how various Web images compete with each other, then analyze how images function to draw the eye on the screen in contrast to on a print page.

LISTENING AS YOU REREAD

Rhetorical reading often requires careful rereading. Of course, not every text requires rereading; however, whenever detailed analysis is required or whenever a text is particularly difficult, a careful second (and sometimes a third) reading is needed. Experienced academic readers will often use the techniques we lay out in this section as a way of keeping track of complex texts that they will need to use as a basis for their own writing, perhaps as foundational evidence for their own assertions, perhaps as a taking-off point for a critique.

In the remainder of this chapter, to help you acquire the mental habits of strong academic readers and to give you practice with the types of writing you will use frequently as part of college-level analysis and research, we offer strategies for approaching texts in ways

---

[3]Maureen Dowd, "Scarred for Life: Courage Begets Courage," *Milwaukee Journal Sentinel* 3 June 2003: 11A. Published originally as "Our Own Warrior Princess," *New York Times* 1 June 2003: 4.13. Print.

that go beyond skimming for content: idea maps, descriptive outlines, summaries, and rhetorical précis.

Mapping the Idea Structure

Idea maps provide a visual representation of a text's major ideas and the relationships among those ideas. In many college courses, it is important to get a sense of how an assigned text works as a whole, not just pieces of its concepts or data. An excellent way to establish this sense of the whole is to reread the text with the goal of creating an idea map. This process will enable you to distinguish main points from subordinate ones; then, as you connect them in a visual diagram, the process will help you understand how the text establishes relationships among those primary and secondary ideas. These relationships are akin to a hierarchy in a power structure: particular explanations and sets of details chunk together to support particular overarching points that in turn flesh out a thesis. You might think of idea maps as X-rays of the text's idea structure.

The time to map a text's idea structure is after you have finished reading it and are sitting back to review its main ideas. To create a map, draw a circle in the center of a page and write the text's main idea inside the circle. Then record the text's supporting ideas on

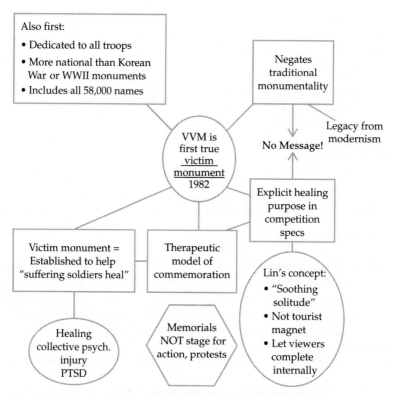

Figure 3.6 Idea map for Kirk Savage's discussion of the Vietnam Veterans Memorial in Chapter 6 of *Monument Wars*, reprinted at the end of this chapter

branches and subbranches that extend from the center circle. In Figure 3.6, we offer a sample idea map of the excerpt from Savage's "The Conscience of the Nation," found on pages 65–68. If you tend not to be a visual thinker, creating an idea map can be challenging because it forces you to think about the text's main ideas in a new way; indeed, that is the advantage of doing an idea map. You may even find that creating a map reveals inconsistencies in the text's organizational structure or puzzling relationships among ideas. This, too, is important information and may be an issue you should bring up in class discussion or in your written responses to the text. In any case, creating an idea map is a way to understand a text at a deeper level and thus to understand and evaluate its importance in relation to course content or to a writing project of your own.

Describing What Verbal Texts Say and Do

Descriptive outlining enables you to extend your understanding of what a text or visual image says into how it is working rhetorically (what it *does*).[4] Some people call these *"says/does outlines."* In them, a *says statement* summarizes the content of a stretch of text (a sentence, a paragraph, a group of paragraphs), and a *does* **statement** sums up how that particular piece of text functions within the whole. It might *describe* or *explain* or *argue*, for example. For help with conceptualizing what texts can *do*, see the list of Verbs That Describe What Texts Do on the next page.

   Does statements should not repeat content but should focus instead on the purpose or function of that content in relation to the overall purpose of the larger text. Here are some sample *does* statements:

   * Offers an anecdote to illustrate previous point
   * Introduces a new reason for adopting policy
   * Provides statistical evidence
   * Summarizes the previous section

Using *does* and *says* statements to create a descriptive outline will help you see how a text works at the micro level, paragraph by paragraph, section by section. This kind of analysis is particularly useful as a way to begin a summary as well as to focus an analysis or critique of an author's rhetorical methods.

Sample Does-Says Statements

To illustrate, we offer the following sample *does* and *says* statements for the three opening paragraphs of the Savage selection printed at the end of this chapter. We begin each set with a does statement to keep the focus on the function of a given paragraph within the unfolding structure of the larger text. Notice that the implicit subject of the *does* and *says* verbs is the text itself.

---

[4]We first learned about descriptive outlining from Kenneth Bruffee's work in *A Short Course in Writing*, 3rd ed. (Boston: Little Brown, 1985), 103. Print.

Paragraph 1
Does: Announces a new way of understanding Maya Lin's accomplishment with the Vietnam Veterans Memorial (VVM)
Says: VVM is first true victim monument, designed to help soldiers heal

Paragraph 2
Does: Places VVM in context with other war memorials
Says: VVM is "first" in a number of categories

Paragraph 3
Does: Discusses VVM in relation to monument traditions preceding it
Says: VVM is "fundamental" break with tradition because it delivers no message

VERBS THAT DESCRIBE WHAT TEXTS DO

Each of these verbs might be used to complete a phrase such as "this paragraph [or section] _____."

adds (e.g., adds detail)	explains	qualifies
analyzes	expresses	questions
argues	extends	quotes
asks	generalizes	reasons
cites	illustrates	rebuts
compares	informs	reflects
connects	interprets	repeats
continues	introduces	states
contradicts	lists	speculates
contrasts	narrates	suggests
demonstrates	offers	summarizes
describes	opposes	supports
details	predicts	synthesizes
dramatizes	presents	traces
elaborates	projects	uses
evaluates	proposes	

Descriptive outlining will give you analytical distance that will prove to be not only a powerful tool for rhetorical analysis, but also a valuable aid for your own writing. When you are revising, asking yourself what specific sections of your text are doing and saying—and what you want them to do and say—will help you focus on both content and organization as you compose or revise. Even during composing, asking yourself what you want your text to *do* next will often help you figure out what to *say* next.

At first you may find that creating a descriptive outline is more difficult than you expect because it forces a slow rereading of a text's distinct parts. But that slowed-down analysis is the purpose of the technique. It is designed to prompt thought that goes beyond scooping up surface meaning. Rereading this way will take you to a clearer understanding of the argument and structure of the text you are examining. Trust us!

For Writing and Discussion

On Your Own

Make a paragraph-by-paragraph descriptive outline of a book chapter or article that you have been assigned to read in one of your other courses (or of another text as your teacher directs), providing one *does* sentence and one *says* sentence for each paragraph. Then, from the set of *does* and *says* statements, create an idea map that represents visually the relationship or hierarchy of ideas in the article or chapter. For models, use Figure 3.6 and the sample descriptive outline based on the opening paragraphs of the Savage excerpt at the end of this chapter.

With Your Classmates

Working in small groups, compare your idea maps and descriptive outlines. Each group can then draw revised idea maps and put them on the board or an overhead for discussion.

Describing What Visual Texts Do

The strategies of descriptive outlining can also help you understand more deeply the role and significance of a text's visual features in relation to its verbal content. Again, such analysis can go beyond deepening your understanding of texts and help with your own writing. How? It will help you articulate what kind of a visual you need for a given project; furthermore, in collaborative situations in both school and the workplace it can help you clarify what to ask someone else—a group or team member—to help you find.

With visual images, we typically reverse the analysis process and start with a *says* statement. (If it helps, you might think of it as a "depicts" or "shows" statement.) You will want this visual *says* statement to present the image on its own terms, describing it as if it stood alone, without the text accompanying it. Make it a literal description of the visual image itself.

For example, consider the image from the Peace Corps Web site that we reproduce in Chapter 4 (p. 85). For now, let's ignore both the overall screen layout and the links on the left and instead focus on what we would need to include in a says-statement description of the photograph and the text box inside it: "Ready to make a difference in 2013?" To capture what we see as we study the image, this says-statement needs to mention the delighted smiles on the faces of the young girl and her mentor/teacher (no doubt a Peace Corps volunteer), the direction of their gazes, and the juxtaposition of this happy scene with the recruiting message in the box on the right.

In contrast, a *does* statement about an image needs to consider its context and purpose. Why is this image there? What work does it do, or lead our eyes to do? A good way to start is to consider the enhancing, supporting, and extending categories we discussed earlier. For Figure 4.3, a good *does* statement might note that the photograph *enhances* the recruiting message by suggesting the volunteer is making a difference in the life of the girl, and by implication, so may "you," the viewer of the site. (The small print answers a presumed "yes" to the "ready?" question by saying: "The Peace Corps has a position for for you," and a link to "Learn more."

The following list provides sample *does-says* statements about two images presented earlier in this chapter: the shocking evidence of the destruction caused by Hurricane Sandy in Figure 3.4, and the more abstract image in Figure 3.5, for which numerous interpretations are possible. Notice again that the subject of the verb in the *does* statement is understood to be the text itself—in these cases, the images.

Figure 3.4

Does: Provides "before-and-after" images that support the validity of the headline's question about the future and document the destruction to which the people quoted in the article are reacting.

Says/Depicts: contrasting scenes of the Funtime Pier show children at play in the sand during the summer and the amusement pier's owner walking among the remnants of destroyed buildings and rides.

For the next example, we combine *says* and *does* statements into one sentence that could be used in a discussion of the combined text and image:

The drawing by Randy Mack Bishop in Figure 3.5, which depicts three figures headed away from us with their arms around each other and seeming to rise off the ground together as they head away from us, their arms around each other, extends Maureen Dowd's text about organ donation with an inspirational image representing an abstract idea of mutual support.

WRITING ABOUT HOW TEXTS WORK: GUIDELINES AND TWO EXAMPLES

Probably the best way to demonstrate that you have "listened" carefully to a text is to compose a **summary**—a condensed version of a text's main points written in your own words, conveying the author's main ideas but eliminating supporting details. When your goal is to describe not only the content of a text but *how* that text makes its points, a still more powerful technique is to write a **rhetorical précis**.

How Summaries Are Used in Academic and Workplace Settings

Composing a summary requires you to articulate the gist of a text. Summaries take many forms and fulfill a variety of functions in the workplace as well as academic courses. In research papers, you will often present brief summaries of sources to give readers an overview of another writer's perspective or argument, thus bringing another voice into the conversation. If the source is particularly important to your project, you might write a longer summary—perhaps even a full paragraph. The ability to write a good summary will be valuable for any number of academic assignments that ask you to report your understanding of what a text says (see p. 34), particularly for the literature reviews typically required in science classes. Summaries are also likely to be useful in a persuasive "take-a-stand" paper: first, to provide evidence that supports your view, and second, to present fully and accurately any arguments that oppose your view (after which you will try to counter these arguments). Furthermore, for a paper in the social or physical sciences, you will often be expected to write an **abstract** of your own work (a summary), because it is conventional in these fields to begin a published work with a highly condensed overview in case busy readers don't have time to read the whole text. In business and professional life, the equivalent of an abstract is an **executive summary**, a section that appears at the front of any major business report or proposal. Summary writing, in other words, is one of the most frequently used forms of writing that you will encounter in your academic and professional life.

Summaries will vary in length according to purpose. At times, you may summarize a text in one or two sentences as a way of invoking the authority of another voice (probably an expert) to support your points. For example, suppose you wanted to use Savage's concept of the therapeutic model of commemoration to contrast the Vietnam Veteran's Memorial with a statue of a nineteenth-century general mounted on a horse. You might write something like the following:

> Unlike the statue of the general on his horse, which is intended to commemorate the general's heroism, the Vietnam Veterans Memorial (VVM) has what Kirk Savage calls a "therapeutic" purpose. In his book Monument Wars, Savage lays out the advantages of the "therapeutic model of commemoration" that is embodied in Maya Lin's design for the VVM. Elements of this model include a healing purpose, absence of a "message," and an overall setting that will allow viewers to explore the meaning of the monument internally.

After this brief summary introducing the concept, you could go on describe the extent to which the heroic monument you are considering possesses these or contrasting qualities, perhaps calling upon Savage's discussion of hero monuments elsewhere in his book. (Its index has multiple references to the topic.)

At other times, summaries may be one of your main purposes for writing. A typical college assignment might ask you to summarize the arguments of two writers and then analyze the differences in their views. In the summary part of such an assignment, your professor will expect you to demonstrate your understanding of what might be quite complex arguments. The guidelines that follow will help you do so.

Guidelines for Writing a Summary

Writing a fair and accurate summary requires that you (1) identify a text's main ideas, (2) state them in your own words, and (3) omit supporting details. For efficiency and thoroughness, the best first step is to create a descriptive outline of the text you need to summarize, using *does* statements to clarify its structure and *says* statements to put in your own words the main point of each paragraph. (A first draft of your summary could be simply your sequencing of all your *says* statements.) Making a descriptive outline will help you see the

---

Box 3.1 Composing a Summary

Step 1: Read the text first for its main points.

Step 2: Reread carefully and make a descriptive outline.

Step 3: Write out the text's thesis or main point. (Suppose you had to summarize the whole argument in one sentence.)

Step 4: Identify the text's major divisions or chunks. Each division develops one of the stages needed to make the whole main point. Typically, these stages or parts might function as background, review of the conversation, summary of opposing views, or subpoints in support of the thesis.

Step 5: Try summarizing each part in one or two sentences.

Step 6: Now combine your summaries of the parts into a coherent whole, creating a condensed version of the text's main ideas in your own words.

---

text's different sections and organizational strategies. Almost all texts—even very short ones—can be divided into a sequence of sections in which groups of paragraphs chunk together to form distinctive parts of the argument or discussion. Identifying these parts or chunks and how they function within the whole text is particularly helpful because you can write a summary of each chunk, then combine the chunks.

We present a step-by-step process for summary writing in Box 3.1. To illustrate the process, we present a summary written by a student we'll call "Jaime" of the *UC Berkeley Wellness Letter's* "Chew on This" article (p. 25). Because this article is so brief, it may at first seem that it would be difficult to summarize, but that shortness makes it a good example of the process of omitting details in order to boil a text down to its essence.

Sample Summary with Attributive Tags

In the following summary of "Chew on This," notice that Jaime regularly refers back to the article itself by using what are called "attributive tags" or "signal phrases," such as, "the author reports," "it presents," "the article suggests," and so forth. These phrases serve as signals that Jaime is summarizing someone else's ideas rather than stating his own. Using phrases like these will help you avoid one of the big mistakes that novice writers make when summarizing: making the original author invisible. (For more detailed suggestions about using phrases like these, see Chapter 6, pp. 139–142.)

We invite you to read over Jaime's summary and evaluate it against the checklist in Box 3.2. What might you say or do differently to make this a better summary? Could you make it shorter still, perhaps by just one line, without cutting important information?

Box 3.2   Checklist for Evaluating Summaries

Good summaries must be fair, accurate, and complete. Use this checklist to evaluate drafts of a summary.

- Is the summary economical and precise?
- Is the summary neutral in its representation of the original author's ideas, omitting the current writer's own opinions?
- Does the summary reflect the proportionate coverage given various points in the original text?
- Are the original author's ideas expressed in the summary writer's own words?
- Does the summary use attributive tags (also called "signal phrases"), such as "Savage describes," to remind readers whose ideas are being presented?
- Does the summary quote sparingly (usually only key ideas or phrases that cannot be said precisely except in the original author's own words)?
- Will the summary stand alone as a unified and coherent piece of writing?
- Is the original source cited so that readers can locate it?

Jaime's Summary of "Chew on This"

[1]"Chew on This," published as a Last Word feature in the February 2012 UC Berkeley Wellness Letter, briefly updates readers about recent research regarding whether gum-chewing is beneficial and suggests that any benefits are minor or do not last for long. [2]The article's unnamed author reports that the most likely benefit of gum chewing is increased saliva flow, which prevents cavities, especially with sugar-free gum containing xylitol. [3]But regular brushing and flossing are more important. [4]The article reports in somewhat more detail about studies published recently in the scholarly journal Appetite. [5]Regarding the possibility that gum-chewing helps prevent weight gain, one study found that the main weight-control benefit comes not from burning calories but from chewing gum instead of snacking on something with higher calories. [6]Another study published in Appetite focused on the possibility of improved cognitive performance from gum-chewing and reported that recent studies show that the benefits are brief and that not everyone experiences them.

Guidelines for Writing a Rhetorical Précis

A **rhetorical précis** (pronounced *pray-SEE*) provides a structured model for describing the rhetorical strategies of a text, as well as for capturing the gist of its content. It differs from a summary in that it is less neutral, more analytical, and comments directly on the method of the original text. ("Précis" means "concise summary.") Highly structured, it is designed for presentation of insights about a text from the perspective of a rhetorical reader. If you think of a summary as primarily a brief representation of what a text says, then you might think of a rhetorical précis as a brief representation of what a text both says and does. Although less common than a summary, a rhetorical précis is a particularly useful way to sum up your understanding of how a text works rhetorically.

Part summary and part analysis, the rhetorical précis is also a powerful skill-building exercise often assigned as a highly structured four-sentence paragraph (see Box 3.3).[5] As explained in the box, these sentences provide a condensed statement of a text's main point (the summary part), followed by brief statements about its essential rhetorical elements: the methods, purpose, and intended audience (the analytical part). Note the ways in which Jaime's four-sentence rhetorical précis of the *Wellness Letter* article is similar to and different from his six-sentence summary of the article.

Jaime's Rhetorical Précis

[1]A UC Berkeley Wellness Letter article, "Chew on This" (Feb. 2012), summarizes recent research on the possible benefits of gum-chewing and reports that so far, this research shows only small or brief benefits. [2]The author notes first that gum-chewing may increase saliva flow that prevents cavities (but should not replace brushing and flossing), but then takes a "maybe" approach when reporting that gum-chewing's possible benefits for both weight maintenance and brain stimulation are limited and short-lived. [3]The fact that this article fills the newsletter's customary spot for brief research reports establishes the author's purpose as informative, but its informal tone suggests that it is written to amuse as well as to inform. [4]The

---

Box 3.3 How to Structure a Rhetorical Précis

Sentence 1: Name of author, genre, and title of work, date in parentheses; a rhetorically accurate verb (such as claims, argues, asserts, suggests); and a "that" clause containing the major assertion or thesis statement in the work

Sentence 2: An explanation of how the author develops and supports the thesis, usually in chronological order

Sentence 3: A statement of the author's apparent purpose

Sentence 4: A description of the intended audience and/or the relationship the author establishes with the audience

---

[5]Our rhetorical précis assignment and illustration are based on the work of Margaret K. Woodworth, "The Rhetorical Précis," *Rhetoric Review* 7 (1988): 156–65. Print.

author assumes an audience of well-educated readers who have high interest in health and wellness issues but a cautious attitude toward research findings, and thus is able to use a humorous tone as well as a clever, punning title that implicitly warns that what is being reported is something to "chew on" but not to be taken as certain.

A BRIEF WRITING PROJECT

This assignment asks you to apply what you've learned about reading rhetorically in this chapter by listening carefully to a text and writing about what you "hear." Working with a text identified by your instructor, use the strategies suggested in this chapter to prepare three short assignments, each of which will help you move on to the next.

1. A descriptive outline of the text
2. A 150- to 200-word summary of the text
3. A four-sentence rhetorical précis of the text

CHAPTER SUMMARY

Building on Chapter 2's recommendations about analyzing the rhetorical contexts of the texts you are reading in relation to your own purposes for writing, this chapter has focused on the nuts and bolts of preparing to read, of "listening" carefully to a text, and of writing to describe a text's content and technique.

- To read effectively, you need to read with pen in hand or a keyboard at the ready, interacting with texts by making annotations as you read.
- Before reading, practice specific preparatory strategies such as recalling background knowledge, using visual features to plan and predict, and spot reading.
- While reading, note organizational signals, and mark unfamiliar terms and references, using marginal comments and queries to identify points of difficulty.
- Read visuals carefully as well, noting how—and how well—they enhance, support, or extend the points contained in the text.
- To deepen your understanding of a text, reread carefully, employing such strategies as idea maps and descriptive outlines.
- To compose accurate descriptive accounts of content and rhetorical strategy, use the systematic guidelines we present for summaries and rhetorical précis.

The Conscience of the Nation
Kirk Savage

Kirk Savage is professor of the History of Art and Architecture at the University of Pittsburgh and active in public discussions about monuments and memorials, including the planned Eisenhower Memorial in Washington, D.C., and the 9-11 Memorial in New York City. *Monument Wars* (2009), from which the following selection has been excerpted, received rave reviews in both the popular and scholarly press and was awarded the 2010 Charles C. Eldredge Prize for Distinguished Scholarship in American Art from the Smithsonian American Art Museum. *Washington Post* commentator Philip Kennicott describes Savage as "a monument optimist."[6] His first book, *Standing Soldiers, Kneeling Slaves: Race, War, and Monument in Nineteenth-Century America*, published by Princeton University Press in 1997, examined the representation of race and slavery in monuments. In his faculty biography Savage describes himself as interested generally in the concepts of "traumatic memory" and "therapeutic memorial," concepts he discusses regarding the VVM, the Oklahoma City National Memorial, and plans for the World Trade Center memorial(s) in an essay in *Terror, Culture, Politics: Rethinking 9/11*, ed. Daniel Sherman and Terry Nardin (2006). His blog can be found on his University of Pittsburgh Web page.

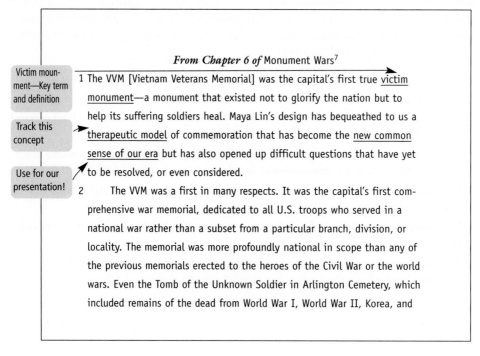

From Chapter 6 of Monument Wars[7]

Victim monu-
ment—Key term
and definition

1 The VVM [Vietnam Veterans Memorial] was the capital's first true victim monument—a monument that existed not to glorify the nation but to help its suffering soldiers heal. Maya Lin's design has bequeathed to us a

Track this
concept

therapeutic model of commemoration that has become the new common sense of our era but has also opened up difficult questions that have yet

Use for our
presentation!

to be resolved, or even considered.

2   The VVM was a first in many respects. It was the capital's first comprehensive war memorial, dedicated to all U.S. troops who served in a national war rather than a subset from a particular branch, division, or locality. The memorial was more profoundly national in scope than any of the previous memorials erected to the heroes of the Civil War or the world wars. Even the Tomb of the Unknown Soldier in Arlington Cemetery, which included remains of the dead from World War I, World War II, Korea, and

[6]"'Monument Wars' Puts Eisenhower Memorial Controversy in Context." *Washington Post*. Washington Post Co., 18 June 2012. Web. 29 June 2012.
[7]Kirk Savage, *Monument Wars*. (Berkeley, CA: U California P, 2009), 266–70. Print. Note: Our footnotes to this excerpt summarize rather than repeat Savage's footnotes.

Vietnam and served as a national focal point for ritual services on Memorial Day and Veterans Day, did not satisfy the felt need for comprehensive recognition of the nation's servicemen.[8] The VVM was the first—and is still the only—war memorial in the capital and the nation that claims to include the names of all the U.S. dead. Maya Lin's sunken black granite walls were designed, first and foremost, with this intention—to carry the names of the fifty-eight thousand U.S. servicemen who lost their lives in the war. The explicit healing purpose of the monument drove this logic of comprehensiveness. Once born, though, the new type could be adapted to other purposes. The Korean War Veterans Memorial and the World War II memorial are also comprehensive, though quite different in tone and content from Lin's prototype; neither one attempts the reproduction of individual names at the heart of her design.

[Margin note: Note: "explicit healing purpose"]

3   Dedicated in 1982, Lin's walls have since become the most talked-about, most written-about monument in American history. The memorial is now so popular a fixture on the Mall that we can forget how radical her proposal once was and how close her critics came to stopping it altogether. Lin herself has called her work an antimonument—a negation of traditional monumentality. She brought into material form an attitude that had long been articulated in modernist circles. The British art historian Herbert Read, writing in the late 1930s in the aftermath of the catastrophes of World War I and the Spanish Civil War, had declared that in the modern world "the only logical monument would be some sort of negative monument." A negative monument, he assumed, would have to be "a monument to disillusion, to despair, to destruction."[9] Lin, however, found a way to break this logic that conflated negation and disillusion. She did not intend her memorial to deliver a message of protest against war (as did Picasso's huge mural *Guernica*, about which Read was writing). The break with tradition was more fundamental: her memorial avoided delivering *any* message. The meaning was to be generated by the viewers themselves, in their experience of the place.

[Margin note: "modernist circles"?]

[Margin note: No message in the VVM ++ Import! NOT a protest [Find Guernica online—just curious]]

---

[8]Savage's footnote here notes an author who has also made this point.
[9]Savage inserts a footnote here indicating the sources of both Lin's and Read's remarks.

4   If this sounds vaguely familiar, that is because the "antimonument" idea tapped into an old American tradition of iconoclasm that long pre-dated modernist ideas of negation. After all, it was in 1800 that John Nicholas had proposed a "blank tablet" for Washington on which "every man could write what his heart dictated." Like the blank tablet, Lin's simple wall of names awaits completion by individual viewers and indeed the notes and other memorabilia visitors have left at the wall make manifest that internal process, like the act of writing Nicholas contemplated. On the one hand, Lin's design was a work of high conceptual art totally alien to the veterans who sponsored the monument; on the other, it represented an aspiration toward "living memory" that must have resonated with the antiauthoritarian, democratic impulses of many in their constituency.

Uh-oh. Not familiar to me! Ask Prof. R. re using this background Look up iconoclasm

Connects to the above ☆

Maybe find article or video about memorabilia —maybe 30-year anniversary

5   As many have already pointed out, the idea of a nontraditional, non-didactic war memorial was not Lin's alone. She submitted a design in response to an open competition, whose program specified that the memorial must list the names of all the American war dead; must avoid political interpretations of the war, pro or con; and must harmonize with its tranquil park setting in the new Constitution Gardens. The memorial's statement of purpose, while affirming that it would "provide a symbol of acknowledgment of the [soldiers'] courage, sacrifice, and devotion to duty," ended in this way: "The Memorial will make no political statement regarding the war or its conduct. It will transcend those issues. The hope is that the creation of the Memorial will begin a healing process."[10] Lin's genius lay in her ability to create a simple and beautiful solution to this novel and difficult program.

"nondidactic"?

Healing explicitly in statement of purpose

Note: "Lin's genius"!

6   Thus the nation's first "therapeutic" memorial was born—a memorial made expressly to heal a collective psychological injury. It is surely no coincidence that the monument campaign that led to Lin's selection began at about the time that "posttraumatic stress disorder" entered the official psychiatric diagnostic manual.[11] The man who hatched the cam-

[10]Savage's lengthy footnote here cites the source of the quote and refers to other references to the VVM as "therapeutic" and "healing," including a book published after his was in production.
[11]Savage's footnote here refers readers to discussions about veterans and trauma.

paign, Jan Scruggs, was a Vietwtraumatic stress. Scruggs wanted the monument to serve a dual healing function: for the veterans themselves, who had endured not only the trauma of combat but a crushing rejection from society afterward, and for the nation that had been so bitterly divided over the justice of the cause. The last thing he and his fellow veterans in charge of the monument campaign wanted was to reignite the political conflicts that were still fresh in everyone's mind, in part because they had been so dramatized in protests on the Mall itself. The monument was intended to rally Americans around the simple idea that the veterans of the war needed recognition and support[.]...

7   ... Lin had ... soothing solitude in mind when she designed her entry for the west end of Constitutional Gardens. Her proposal did not envision the memorial as a crowded tourist magnet like the Lincoln Memorial. Whereas that memorial was sited conspicuously on a high platform at the end of the east-west axis [of the Mall], the VVM site was screened by trees, and Lin hid the memorial even further by situating the walls below grade. The approach through Constitution Gardens created a moment of surprise: visitors would happen upon the walls unfolding in front of them, a revelation reminiscent of those [that 19th century landscape designer Andrew Jackson] Downing had had in mind for the Mall.[12]

8   This quiet, secluded experience seemed the opposite of the collective marches and assemblies held out in the open, which had defined the image of the Mall in the period from the civil rights movement to the antiwar struggle. Nevertheless, Lin's design was an outgrowth of that recent history. The experience she wanted to create developed organically from the Mall's twentieth-century psychology with its introspective quality already evident in the Lincoln Memorial and the axis to the Capitol. Lin wanted to turn that introspective experience further inward. "I thought the experience of visiting the memorial," she said later, "should be a private awakening, a private awareness of [individual] loss." For her, memo-

---

[12]Savage's footnote here refers readers to another author's discussion of Lin's intentions when she entered the competition.

rial spaces were not "stages where you act out, but rather places where something happens within the viewer."[13] Although her emphasis on the subjectivity of viewer response was already inherent in the spatial turn public monuments began to take in the early twentieth century, her understanding of that subjective process as fundamentally private belonged to a more recent cultural turn away from political activism and ritual and toward self-exploration.

[13]Savage uses a footnote here to source the quote in comments from Lin at a 1995 symposium.

QUESTIONING A TEXT

A good question is never answered. It is not a bolt to be tightened into place but a seed to be planted and to bear more seed toward the hope of greening the landscape of idea.

—John Ciardi

In this chapter, you will learn:

A repertoire of useful strategies that will help you question a text, explore your responses to it, and prepare a rhetorica

- An author's use of the three classical rhetorical appeals identified by Aristotle: *ethos, logos,* and *pathos*
- An author's use of language to create a persona, connect with the audience, and represent ideas as reasonable and compelling
- The ideology or worldview of a text; that is, the set of values and beliefs invoked by it
- The impact of visual elements that may be used to enhance, support, and extend rhetorical appeals

To demonstrate how such strategies can enable you to write critical analyses that will be valued by college professors, the chapter closes with

- Activities for exploring your responses to a text
- Guidelines for writing a rhetorical analysis
- A sample rhetorical analysis paper based on Atul Gawande's op-ed, "A Lifesaving Checklist," reprinted at the end of this chapter (pp. 95–97).

Whereas the previous chapter focused on listening to a text *with the grain* in order to understand it as fully as possible, in this chapter we focus on questioning a text, which involves reading it analytically and skeptically, *against the grain*. If you think of listening to a text as letting the author take a turn in a conversation, then you might think of questioning the text as your opportunity to respond to the text by interrogating it, raising points of agreement and disagreement, thinking critically about its argument and methods, and then talking back.

WHAT IT MEANS TO QUESTION A TEXT

Learning to question a text is central to your academic success in college. Your professors will ask you to engage with texts in ways that you may not be used to. They expect you to do more than just "bank" the knowledge you glean from reading; they expect you to use this knowledge to do various kinds of intellectual work—to offer your own interpretations or evaluations, to launch a research project of your own, to synthesize ideas from a number of readings, and to draw independent conclusions. Such thoughtful reading of texts begins with your questions addressed to the text and its author. Academics sometimes refer to the questioning process as interrogation of a text, an apt metaphor that likely brings to mind scenes from television shows where police officers or attorneys grill suspects and witnesses (metaphoric stand-ins here for a text that requires examination).

Importantly, questioning does not necessarily mean fault-finding, and it certainly doesn't mean dismissing an author's ideas wholesale. Rather, it entails carefully interrogating a text's claims and evidence and its subtle forms of persuasion so that you can make sound judgments and offer thoughtful responses. Your job in critiquing a text is to be "critical." However, the meanings of the term *critical* include "characterized by careful and exact evaluation and judgment," not simply "disagreement" or "harsh judgment." In questioning a text, you bring your critical faculties to bear on it along with your experience, knowledge, and opinion. But you must do so in a way that treats the author's ideas fairly and makes judgments that can be supported by textual evidence.

The close, even-handed examination of a text's content and persuasive strategies is greatly facilitated by using the three classical rhetorical appeals identified by Aristotle:

- *Ethos*: the persuasive power of the author's credibility or character
- *Logos*: the persuasive power of the author's reasons, evidence, and logic
- *Pathos*: the persuasive power of the author's appeal to the interests, emotions, and imagination of the audience

Although these three appeals interconnect and sometimes overlap—for example, a writer may use a touching anecdote both to establish credibility as an empathetic person (*ethos*) and to play on the reader's emotions (*pathos*)—we introduce them separately to emphasize their distinct functions as means of persuasion.

"I don't just record ideas when I read, I contend with the ideas the book presents; I work with them, engage in combat with them, synthesize them into concepts I already know, and then come up with my own ideas. I engage with the world and develop an original vision. This is the process that writers use."[1]

—Maxine Hong-Kingston

EXAMINING A WRITER'S CREDIBILITY AND APPEALS TO *ETHOS*

To change readers' minds about something, writers must make themselves credible by projecting an image of themselves that will gain their readers' confidence. In most cases, writers want to come across as knowledgeable, fair-minded, and trustworthy. To examine a writer's credibility, ask yourself, "Do I find this author believable and trustworthy? Why or why not?"

Strong academic readers always try to find out as much as possible about an author's background, interests, political leanings, and general worldview. Sometimes they have independent knowledge of the writer, either because the writer is well known or has been discussed in class, or because an article has a headnote or footnote describing the author's credentials. Often, though, readers must discern a writer's personality and views from the text itself by examining content, tone, word choice, figurative language, organization, and other cues that help create an image of the writer in their minds. Explicit questions to ask might include these:

1. Does this writer seem knowledgeable?
2. What does the writer like and dislike?
3. What are this writer's biases and values?
4. What seems to be the writer's mood? (Angry? Questioning? Meditative? Upset? Jovial?)
5. What is the writer's approach to the topic? (Formal or informal? Logical or emotional? Distant and factual, or personal? Mixed in attitude?)
6. What would it be like to spend time in this writer's company?

For Writing and Discussion

On Your Own

1. To help you consider an author's image and credibility, try these activities the next time you are assigned a reading. Describe in words your image of the author as a person (or draw a sketch of this person). Then try to figure out what cues in the text

[1] Maxine Hong-Kingston, in *Speaking of Reading*, ed. Nadine Rosenthal (Portsmouth, NH: Heinemann, 1995), 178. Print.

produced this image for you. Finally, consider how this image of the writer leads you to ask more questions about the text. You might ask, for example, "Why is this writer angry? Why does this writer use emotionally laden anecdotes rather than statistics to support his or her case? What is this writer afraid of?"

2. Try these activities with the **op-ed article** by Atul Gawande at the end of this chapter. What kind of an image does he create for himself in this text? How would you describe him in words or portray him in a drawing? Take a few minutes to find and jot down the cues in the text that create this image for you.

With Your Classmates

Compare your impressions of Gawande with those of your classmates. Do any contradictory impressions come up? That is, do some people in the group interpret the textual cues differently? Some people, for example, might see a comment as "forthright" and "frank" while others might see it as "antagonistic" or "hyperbolic." What aspects of his character (as represented in the text) do you as a group agree on? What aspects do you disagree about?

EXAMINING A WRITER'S APPEALS TO REASON OR *LOGOS*

Perhaps the most direct way that writers try to persuade readers is through logic or reason. To convince readers that their perspective is reasonable, skilled writers work to anticipate what their intended readers already believe and then use those beliefs as a bridge to the writer's way of thinking. These writers seek to support their claims through a combination of reasons and evidence.

For example, imagine a writer arguing for stricter gun control laws. This writer wants to root his argument in a belief or value that he and his readers already share, so he focuses on concerns for the safety of schoolchildren. The line of reasoning might go something like this: Because the easy availability of guns makes children no longer safe at school, we must pass strict gun control laws to limit access to guns. Of course, readers may or may not go along with this argument. Some readers, although they share the writer's concern for the safety of schoolchildren, might disagree at several points with the writer's logic: Is the availability of guns the main cause of gun violence at schools or are there other, more compelling causes? Will stricter gun control laws really limit the availability of guns? If this same writer wished to use evidence to strengthen this argument, he might use statistics showing a correlation between the rise in the availability of guns and the rise in gun violence in

EXPLANATION OF OP-ED ARTICLES

Gawande was writing as a guest columnist for the *New York Times*. Such articles are called "**op-eds**," or "op-ed articles," referring to newspapers' traditional placement of signed opinion columns on the page opposite the editorial page, which presents unsigned editorials approved by an editorial board, editorial cartoons, and letters to the editor.

schools. Here, the writer would be operating on the assumption that readers believe in facts and can be persuaded by these statistics that increased gun violence in schools is linked to the availability of firearms.

Experienced readers are alert to the logical strategies used by authors, and they have learned not to take what may appear as a "reasonable" argument at face value. In other words, they have learned to question or test this reasoning before assenting to the position the author wants them to take. To examine a writer's reasoning, you need to be able to identify and examine carefully the basic elements of an argument—claims, reasons, evidence, and assumptions. The following questions will help you examine a writer's reasoning:

1. What perspective or position does the writer want me to take toward the topic?
2. Do the writer's claims, reasons, and evidence convince me to take this perspective or position?
3. Do I share the assumptions, stated or unstated, that authorize the writer's reasoning and connect the evidence to the claim?

Claims

The key points that a writer wants readers to accept are referred to as **claims**. For example, Kirk Savage's initial claim in the selection at the end of Chapter 3 is that the Vietnam Veterans Memorial was Washington, D.C.'s "first true victim's monument," a term that he immediately defines as "a monument that existed not to glorify the nation but to help its suffering soldiers heal." Or take another example: In the reading at the end of this chapter, Atul Gawande begins his fourth paragraph by calling a decision of the federal Office for Human Research Protections "bizarre and dangerous." Both of these assertions seem contestable, so readers are smart to raise questions, especially about the wording and scope. Is the meaning of key words in the claims clear? Can particular words be interpreted in more than one way? Is the claim overstated? One might ask of Gawande, "Bizarre? How so?" "Dangerous? In what way?" Likewise, one might ask Savage why he does not consider earlier monuments, such as the Tomb of the Unknown Soldier, to be victim monuments.

Reasons

To support a main claim, writers must provide **reasons**. A reason can usually be linked to a claim with the subordinate conjunction "because." Consider the gun control argument mentioned earlier, which we can now restate as a claim with a reason: "We must pass gun control laws that limit access to guns [claim] because doing so will make children safer at school [reason]." This argument has initial appeal because it ties into the audience's likely belief that it is good to make children safe at school. However, as we discussed earlier, the causal links in the argument are open to question. Thus, we see that the "reason" that "doing so will make children safer at school" is a subclaim that itself needs to be supported with reasons and evidence.

Once you've identified the reasons that an author offers for various claims, then you can proceed to examine the adequacy of these reasons. Do they really support the claim? Is the assertion in the reason in need of further support and argument? Do the reasons tie into values, assumptions, and beliefs that the audience shares?

Evidence

The facts, examples, statistics, personal experience, and expert testimony that an author offers to support his or her view of the topic are referred to as **evidence**. To examine an author's use of evidence, consider whether the supporting material is reliable, timely, and adequate to make the case. Ask also whether there is more than one way the evidence can be interpreted.

For example, Gawande is quite convincing as he recounts what he calls the government's "blinkered" reasoning, arguing that although the reasoning may be logical, it is shortsighted. But he does not offer direct statements from the officials with whom he disagrees so that readers can judge for themselves whether the reasoning is "blinkered" or led to a "bizarre" decision. Readers skeptical of his argument might question his rendition of the rationale behind the government ruling. Similarly, in our gun control example, skeptics could question whether the statistical correlation between rising availability of guns and rising gun violence in schools is in fact a causal relationship. The fact that A and B happened at the same time does not mean that A caused B.

Assumptions

In an argument, the often unstated values or beliefs that the writer expects readers to accept without question are referred to as **assumptions**. You can interrogate an argument by questioning, even casting doubt upon, those assumptions. For example, in paragraphs 5 and 6 of his op-ed, Gawande attacks the assumptions underlying the Office for Human Research 's reasoning that the checklist for inserting IV lines and the use of an experimental drug are comparable interventions in medical care. Similarly, part of the hypothetical gun control argument presented earlier is based on an assumption that the proposed legislation will in fact limit the availability of guns. You can question this assumption by pointing to the existence of black markets.

For Writing and Discussion

Find a newspaper or magazine opinion piece (an editorial or an individual opinion piece) and identify its claims, reasons, evidence, and assumptions. You may find that some of these elements are missing or only implied. Then analyze the writer's reasoning in the piece by answering the three questions we listed on page 71 as fundamental to examining a writer's reasoning.

With Your Classmates

1. Briefly summarize the opinion piece you found and explain your analysis of it to a small group of classmates.

2. After each group member has presented his or her editorial, discuss which group member's editorial involves the most persuasive reasoning and why. Try to focus on

the writer's reasoning rather than your own opinions about the matter. Present the results of your group discussion to the rest of the class. If there is disagreement about which piece uses the best reasoning, present more than one to the class and explain the differences in your evaluation.

EXAMINING A WRITER'S STRATEGIES FOR ENGAGING READERS, OR *PATHOS*

The third of the classical rhetorical appeals is to an audience's interests and emotions—the process of engaging readers. How does a writer hook and keep your interest? How does a writer make you care about the subject? How does a writer tweak your emotions or connect an argument with ideas or beliefs that you value?

Rhetoricians have identified four basic ways that writers engage readers at an emotional or imaginative level—by influencing the reader to identify (1) with the writer; (2) with the topic or issue, including people mentioned in the text; (3) with a certain group of fellow readers; or (4) with particular interests, values, beliefs, and emotions. Let's look at each in turn.

In the first approach, writers wanting readers to identify with them might use an informal conversational tone to make a reader feel like the writer's buddy. Writers wanting to inspire respect and admiration might adopt a formal scholarly tone, choose intellectual words, or avoid "I" altogether by using the passive voice—"it was discovered that... ." In the second approach, writers wanting readers to identify with the topic or issue might explain the importance of the issue or try to engage readers' emotions. In urging community action against homelessness, for example, an author might present a wrenching anecdote about a homeless child. Other methods might be the use of vivid details, striking facts, emotion-laden terms and examples, or analogies that explain the unfamiliar in terms of the familiar. In the third approach, writers try to get readers to identify with a certain in-group of people—fellow environmentalists or feminists or Republicans or even fellow intellectuals. Some writers seek to engage readers by creating a role for the reader to play in the text. For example, the author of "Chew on This" puts readers in the role of wondering if there are benefits to chewing gum, and Savage invites readers to consider the appeal of Maya Lin's "antimonument" concept to Vietnam veterans' experiences of alienation from American society. In the fourth approach, writers appeal to readers' interests by getting them to identify with certain values and beliefs. For example, a politician arguing for radical Social Security reform might appeal to young voters' belief that there will be no Social Security available to them when they retire. Awareness of how all of these appeals work will enable you to distance yourself from arguments sufficiently to examine them critically.

For Writing and Discussion

Examine in detail the ways in which Gawande works to engage readers in his opinion piece at the end of this chapter. On what basis do his opening sentences engage your attention? What kind of a relationship does he try to establish with readers? How does he try to make you care about his topic? What interests and values does he assume his audience shares? Do you consider yourself part of his intended audience? Why or why not?

EXAMINING A WRITER'S LANGUAGE

Besides looking at a text's classical appeals, you can examine it rhetorically by paying careful attention to its language and style. **Diction**, an umbrella term referring to speakers' and writers' selection and expression of words (including matters of tone and formality), is an important rhetorical tool. So, too, are figurative language, sentence structure and length, and even punctuation. All are techniques through which a writer tries to influence the reader's view of a subject. Consider, for example, the connotation of words. It makes a difference whether a writer calls a person "decisive" rather than "bossy," or an act "bold" rather than "rash." Words like "decisive" and "rash" are not facts; rather, they present the writer's interpretation of behavior. You can question a text by recognizing how the writer makes interpretive words seem like facts.

At times, you might overlook features of the writer's language because they seem natural rather than chosen. You probably seldom stop to think about the significance of, say, the use of italics or a series of short sentences or a particular metaphor. Readers rarely ask what's gained or lost by a writer saying something one way rather than another—for example, calling clear-cut logging in the Northwest a "rape" rather than a "timber extraction process."

Consider, for example, the care that Savage takes to define the concepts of a "victim monument" (par. 1) and "therapeutic monument" (par. 6), as he carefully moves to differentiating the Vietnam Veterans Memorial from other, relatively recent, war memorials in the nation's capital. These definitions provide a necessary foundation to his claim in the Chapter 3 selection's final paragraph that the privacy and subjectivity of experiencing the monument are connected to a cultural turn toward self-exploration. With subject matter so sensitive and emotionally laden with controversy, his prose must move slowly, gently to this abstract point.

For contrast, consider the lighthearted use of language in "Chew on This" (Figure 2.3, p. 25), from the title's almost jokey comparison of literal chewing and thinking to its author's explicit attempt at humor at the end of the article about the limited findings in the cognitive research: "In other words, some people can't think (or walk) and chew gum at the same time." Relaxed language is also evident in the title of the *Appetite* research study that the newsletter has been summarizing: "Cognitive Advantages of Chewing Gum. Now You See Them, Now You Don't" (Figure 2.2, p. 24). Both titles seem to be acknowledging that the research being reported, although seriously undertaken, does not have dire consequences.

However, humorous language can be used with other intentions. Consider the attitude conveyed by Gawande's description of Michigan doctors' behaviors when they followed the checklist he advocates: "they actually wash their hands" (par. 2). Because doctors' hand-washing is something generally assumed to be standard operating procedure,

Gawande's insertion of the adverb "actually" not only is likely to catch attention but also to convey an ironic jab of sarcasm. More explicitly sarcastic, but on a far less serious subject, is Garry Trudeau's skewering of the language at high-end coffee shops, shown in Figure 4.1 (below). Here, verbal language and cartooned body language combine to critique the product labeling.

Experienced academic readers develop antennae for recognizing uses of language—some subtle, some less so—to manipulate responses. One way to develop this sensitivity is to ask why a writer makes certain choices rather than others. To what extent do particular word choices suggest calm, reasoned logic, or, conversely, stir emotions? Do the writer's word choices establish her or him as someone on "our" side? Or, if not, on whose side? How does the author establish "our" side? There will always be other ways to say X or Y. As a rhetorical reader, you need to be alert to how a writer's sentences emphasize certain points over others and how word choices may shape your view of the topic at hand. In other words, it is important to consider how the language itself seems designed to win your agreement with that writer's views.

Figure 4.1 Doonesbury

For Writing and Discussion

On Your Own

Returning to the opinion article that you worked with to analyze assumptions for the exercise on page 73 (or another article as your instructor directs), find two or three striking instances of diction (defined on p. 74) that call up specific responses in you in terms of the *language* used. Perhaps you can find interpretive words asserted as facts, or adjectives that seem more intense in attitude than what a neutral author would use. How could these sentences be rephrased to convey a different attitude toward the subject matter?

With Your Classmates

Share and compare your analyses. See if you can reach consensus on the ways that the various writers use special language features for persuasive intent.

EXAMINING A TEXT'S IDEOLOGY

Another approach to questioning a text is to identify its **ideology**, a technical term for the notion of a worldview. An ideology is a belief system—a coherent set of values and concepts through which we interpret the world. We sometimes think that ideology applies only to other people's worldviews, perhaps those of zealots blinded by a certain rigid set of beliefs. In fact, the term *ideology* applies to all of us. Each of us has our own beliefs, values, and particular ways of looking at the world. Our perspectives are inevitably shaped by family background, religion, personal experience, race, class, gender, sexual orientation, and so on. As you continue with your education, you may even discover that your perspective is influenced by the types of courses you are taking—science majors are sometimes skeptical about the ambiguities of literary texts, for example, and humanities students can similarly resist the details required in laboratory reports. Moreover, each of us is to some extent "blinded" by our worldview, by our own way of seeing. For instance, middle-class persons in the United States, by and large, share a variety of common beliefs: "Hard work leads to success." "Owning your own home is an important good." "Punctuality, cleanliness, and respect for the privacy of others are important values." "All persons are created equal." If we are among the privileged in this country, we literally may not be able to see the existing inequities and barriers to success faced by less privileged Americans.

Yet, to become astute readers, we must look for signals that reveal the ideology informing a text. One way to begin doing so is to look for patterns of opposites or contrasts in a text (sometimes called "binaries") and see which of the opposing terms the writer values more. We generally understand things through contrast with their opposites. We would have no concept of the term *masculine*, for example, without the contrasting term *feminine*. To understand *light*, we have to understand *dark* (or *heavy*). Our concept of *liberal* depends on its contrast with *conservative*. We could list hundreds of these opposites or binaries: civilized is that which is not primitive; free is that which is not enslaved; abnormal is that which

Table 4.1 Binary Patterns in the Savage Excerpt in Chapter 3

Words, Concepts, and Ideas Valued by This Text	Words, Concepts, and Ideas Not Valued by This Text
Vietnam Veterans Memorial	Heroes monuments
Victim monument, therapeutic monument	Traditional monuments
Monument as transcending political issues	Political statements on monuments
Tranquil setting for reflection	Monument as setting for protest
Private self-exploration	Activism and ritual

is not normal; people of color are those who are not Caucasian. When binaries occur as patterns in a text, one term is generally valued above the other. When you examine the pattern of those values, you can begin to uncover the text's ideology. Sometimes the opposite or devalued terms are only implied, not even appearing in the text. Their absence helps mark the text's ideology.

It is not always immediately evident which terms are valued by a text and which ones are devalued. In such cases, you can often identify a major contrast or binary elsewhere in the text—for example, loggers versus tree huggers, school vouchers versus neighborhood schools, old ways versus new ways, traditional Western medicine versus alternative medicine. You can then determine which of the opposed terms is more valued. Once you can identify the controlling binary, you can often line up other opposites or contrasts appropriately.

If you were to use these oppositions to draw conclusions about the ideology informing Savage's text (see Table 4.1 above), you might say something like the following: "Savage's text gradually builds a case for valuing monuments that honor all soldiers rather than a particular war hero, and that invite subjective interpretations rather than a single, prescribed message. He seems to value the collective sacrifices of war above the traditional emphasis on individual heroes."

For Writing and Discussion

On Your Own

Return again to the opinion piece in which you analyzed assumptions and language, this time to make a two-column chart of the binaries you find in that text. Put the words, concepts, or ideas that the author values in the left column. Place the opposing words, concepts, or ideas that the author doesn't value in the right column. (Remember, the nonvalued terms may only be implied; they may not actually appear in the text.) Then write a short analysis of the author's ideology, following the model we provided based on Savage's text.

With Your Classmates

Share your list of binaries with the classmates with whom you have been analyzing editorials. It will be interesting to discover for which texts tracking binaries proved more and less easy or difficult. Again, try to reach consensus to explain these differences.

EXAMINING A TEXT'S USE OF VISUAL ELEMENTS

Images, like words, are often selected and constructed to create particular emotional responses. Photographs, drawings, information graphs, and other images that accompany a text are typically added by the editor of the publication, electronic or print, where the text appears. Nonetheless, these images are another vehicle for rhetorical appeals and thus merit close attention when you analyze any text. The common belief that pictures are more truthful and compelling than words is often true: Visual images are often powerfully persuasive devices. Moreover, images can shape perceptions, emotions, and values without a reader's conscious awareness, thus making their influence particularly seductive. Questioning the ways in which visual elements make a text more persuasive allows you to step back and avoid the automatic consent implied in the cliché that "seeing is believing."

In Chapter 3, we discussed how consideration of a text's visual elements can help you understand a text's message more fully. We turn now to examining how analysis of these visual elements can help you recognize and question the rhetorical effects of the images themselves. To analyze the ways in which visual elements interact with a textual message, you need to "listen" to the image (what it says or depicts), determine its function (what it does), and analyze the types of appeals it is making (*ethos, logos, pathos*). As we have seen before, these categories may, of course, overlap. We suggest that you begin your analysis of visual elements with the following general questions:

1. How does the visual element relate to the writer's overall point or argument? Is this relationship explicit or implied?

2. How important is this visual element to the author's argument?

3. What kinds of rhetorical appeals does the visual element employ? How does it work rhetorically to influence the intended audience?

Visual Elements and Ethical Appeals

Visual elements frequently enhance a writer's credibility and authority. Thus, an article by a yoga teacher might include a picture of him in an advanced yoga position; an alumni magazine's article about a scientist who has made a scientific breakthrough might include a picture of the scientist working in her lab. Similarly, newspapers and magazines include head shots of syndicated columnists whom they regularly publish. These usually flattering photographs typically offer an image of the writer as smiling and approachable or, perhaps, as intellectual, sophisticated, or down to earth. Head shots also offer information about the author's age, ethnicity, and gender (if not evident from the writer's name), information that is likely to affect our reading of the text, sometimes without our being aware of it.

When the subject is affirmative action or racial profiling, for example, the race and perhaps gender of the author are likely to affect readers' perceptions of his or her credibility on the issue.

Of course, these photographs can be misleading. Many writers use the same picture for years, thus preserving the image and credibility of a younger person. The late Ann Landers's column still pictured her as a woman in her mid-forties when she was well into her seventies. Consider the difference it would have made if readers pictured the advice she offered as coming from an elderly, white-haired woman. In short, rhetorical readers need to question even these apparently straightforward visual appeals based on a writer's *ethos* as part of considering their implications. For example, the yoga teacher pictured in an advanced pose may be an expert practitioner of yoga, but does it follow logically, as the picture (and article) implies, that he is a good teacher of yoga?

The key questions to ask in analyzing how visual elements establish a writer's *ethos* are the following:

1. How does the visual element contribute to the writer's image, credibility, and/or authority?
2. How does the image of the author created by the visual element influence your reading of the text?
3. To what extent does the visual image fit the image created by the text?

Visual Elements and Logical Appeals

Drawing on the idea that "seeing is believing," writers often support their claims with visual evidence. Thus, the most common use of visual elements as logical appeals is to supply evidence to verify or support a writer's argument. Whether the visual element is a pie chart, a table of data, or a picture, these elements appear to add concreteness and factuality to an author's claims. Indeed, the genre conventions of scholarly journals dictate that authors provide information graphics to help readers understand and evaluate the strength of the research. Graphics of all sorts are, of course, very important on the Web, where readers with a wide range of literacy skills and experience may access material. Consider, for example, the graphic in Figure 4.2, from TheMint.org, a Web site designed to educate children about financial literacy. It works by using a familiar shape to illustrate an unfamiliar concept. The triangular outline of a pyramid is likely to be recognized across age groups and education levels as a means of contrasting the desirability of goods and behaviors with their advisability, usefulness, or cost. Here, the shape is used to illustrate the financial world's concept of "risk and rewards," contrasting safer, more solid investments at the base with the more risky, but potentially higher-yielding investments at the top.

Visual illustrations are a staple of educational materials, especially for beginners who are new to various subjects and tasks, and they naturally play a central role in academic and journalistic writing that analyzes and critiques the use and quality of the images themselves. In our increasingly visual culture, it is important to question whether images themselves are reliable. The fact is, technology makes it easy for almost anyone to doctor a photo. Consider, for example, the difficulty of solving the popular puzzles in print magazines and

Figure 4.2 "Risk and Rewards" graphic from TheMint.org. As the text accompanying the diagram explains, "Investments with lower risks and lower returns are at the bottom of the pyramid—where the large base makes it stable." The Web site notes that investing for a higher return at the top of the pyramid is tempting, but "there is no guarantee that higher-risk investments will actually give you higher returns."

newspapers (and on the Web) that invite readers to see how many differences they can find in two seemingly identical photographs. Furthermore, even ordinary photographs can be misleading when they omit the larger context or are published or posted without information about who took the picture or why. Intentional distortion is yet another concern. In the summer of 2006, altered photographs of war-torn Lebanon that a freelancer sold to Reuters caused something of a sensation, less because of the photos' content than because of how readily the news service had been duped. Reuters suspended the photographer, retracted the photos, and issued an apology.[2] Shortly afterward, the online magazine *Slate* published a critique of news photography in general under the headline "Don't Believe What You See in the Papers," in which writer Jim Lewis points to multiple examples of doctored and misleading photographs. His conclusion offers good advice for rhetorical readers: "Realism is a special effect like any other, and the sooner we realize as much, the better off we'll be . . . . Someday we will approach each photograph we look at with the condign [appropriate] skepticism we bring to each story we read."[3]

[2]One photo doubled the amount of smoke rising over Beirut after an Israeli attack; another increased the number of flares dropping from an Israeli plane from one to three and mislabeled them as missiles. See Donald R. Winslow, "Reuters Apologizes over Altered Lebanon War Photos; Suspends Photographer," National Press Photographers Association, 7 Aug. 2006. Web. 27 Mar. 2009.

[3]*Slate*, 10 Aug. 2006. Web. 27 Mar. 2009.

The following questions will help you analyze how visuals interact with logical appeals:

1. Does the writer make explicit the relationship between the visual element and his or her argument? If not, chances are good that the visual element was added by an editor who may have interests other than documenting the writer's claims, probably a matter of attracting readership.

2. How would you define the relationship between the visual and the text? Is it the focal point of the argument? Or does it provide additional support or evidence for the author's claims? Does it seem added primarily as decoration, perhaps to gain readers' attention?

3. Is the visual element providing evidence that is reliable, timely, and adequate to make the case?

4. Does the visual itself make an argument, and if so, is it convincing?

Visual Elements and Audience Appeals

Probably the most powerful rhetorical use of visual elements is to appeal to an audience's emotions, values, and interests—to *pathos*. Three common and often overlapping ways in which visual elements create audience appeals are by setting a tone, fostering identification between reader and content, and evoking emotions and values.

To see how graphic elements can set a tone or context that frames a reader's response, consider your expectations of an article accompanied by an image of Dr. Martin Luther King Jr., delivering his "I Have a Dream" speech in front of the Lincoln Memorial. It seems likely that you would anticipate that the article deals with a serious issue, perhaps civil rights, racial justice, or the role of social protest movements. Similarly, the drawing of the three embracing figures discussed in Chapter 3 (Figure 3.5, p. 50) combined with the headline "Scarred for Life: Courage Begets Courage" may prepare readers for an inspirational article—although, interestingly, neither the drawing nor the headline gives any hint of the specific content of Maureen Dowd's column about organ donation. To discover the meaning of this rather ambiguous image and decidedly dramatic title, readers had to stop their perusal of the newspaper to read the article. Undoubtedly, you can think of many occasions when a striking image caught your attention and triggered an emotional reaction that, in turn, prompted you to read something (or click on a link) that you might otherwise have ignored. Because photographs and drawings are frequently the first thing we notice about a text, it is important to pause both before and after reading to consider how they frame your attitude toward the subject matter.

Visual elements can also create identification with a person, situation, or topic. As we noted in Chapter 3, the smiling faces in the photograph from the Peace Corps Web site in Figure 4.3 convey an enthusiasm that, in context, invites viewers to consider how they might "make a difference" in what was then the year ahead. Even though neither person in the photograph is looking at the camera (or by implication, at us), the contagious quality of their smiles appeals to *pathos* by promoting identification, drawing viewers into the scene. The young girl's body language and facial expression communicate such delight regarding the task that engages her (with pen in her hand), and her teacher looks so pleased,

Figure 4.3 Screen capture from Peace Corps home page

that it is easy to start thinking about how to "make a difference" like the one the blond woman (by implication a Peace Corps volunteer) evidently is making. The accompanying digital text then makes it easy to click and "learn more" about how to make a difference. The clickable phrases in the list to the left of the photograph make it still easier to follow up. The links themselves tell potential volunteers exactly what to do—"learn," "connect," "start," and so forth.

As the smiles in Figure 4.3 suggest, closely tied to identification are the emotions and values elicited by visual images. News stories about natural disasters, for example, are frequently accompanied by photographs of distressed children, as are the Web sites of international aid agencies. These images prompt us not only to identify more readily with the human toll but also to feel sadness and compassion, and these emotional responses in turn shape our reading of the news or appeals for funds. Recall the power of the now iconic photograph of the soot-covered New York City firefighters raising the American flag in the aftermath of the 9/11 terrorist attacks, evoking admiration and gratitude for their bravery as well as a sense of patriotic pride. The use of this image, even on a postage stamp, automatically associates whatever text it accompanies with these emotions and values. No matter how compelling the image, however, we still need to ask for what purpose our emotions and values are being evoked. Is the topic at hand really analogous to the heroism of the firefighters on 9/11? Although we cannot avoid "gut" responses to visual images, it is important to stop to consider their intended effect and to question their appropriateness.

The key questions to ask in relation to the use of visuals that appeal to emotions, interests, and values are the following:

1. What purpose does the visual element seem to serve in relation to the text?
2. To which emotions, interests, and values does the visual element appeal? What assumptions are being made about readers' values, interests, and emotions?

3. How do specific parts of the visual element work to elicit a response? How do the parts work together as a whole?

4. Are there other ways of reading or interpreting these elements?

Visual Arguments

The juxtaposition of visual images with verbal text has been a key element in our discussion of visual elements so far. As we have pointed out, rhetorical readers must be alert to the designs that the composers of these texts may have on their audience's thinking. We must examine carefully the claims and assumptions that are implicit within the images as well as perhaps implied in the connections between images and text. We turn now to **visual arguments**, which are combinations of image, text, and layout in which the forwarding of a claim with reasons depends primarily upon the image, even when it is accompanied by verbal text.

First, let's look back at the visual arguments in Figures 1.2 and 1.3 (pp. 14, which accompanied our discussion in Chapter 1 of Jack's paper about corn ethanol. This billboard and editorial cartoon typify the way that an image dominates in a visual argument. Words serve to guide readers' quick "reading" of the case being made. However, the underlying structure of the argument—reasons, evidence, assumptions, perhaps even the claim itself—is left for readers to interpret and infer. These two visual arguments focus on a desired or undesired outcome of a chain of causal events entirely implied. Both make an appeal to *pathos* based on assumptions about an audience's emotions and values, and may be successful at invoking in readers the intended positive or negative response, at least initially. Nonetheless, it is very important for a rhetorical reader to pause to take apart not only the explicit claims in such images but the network of implied causes and effects, goods and ills that may or may not factually and logically support those claims. After all, cartoons and billboards are excellent ways to highlight a cause in the interest of building support, but as an academic reader, your interest should be in understanding the complexities behind claims that rely on condensed and implied reasoning.

An audience's willingness and ability to fill in reasons and assumptions to complete a claim is particularly evident in the visual arguments presented in Figures 4.4 and 4.5. These print advertisements are part of the Canadian paper company Domtar's "Paper because" campaign, which is designed to assert paper's value for various business and personal uses. (The campaign extends to videos as well, many of them mocking efforts to "go paperless"). Interestingly, in these advertisements, the actual product being championed is present only by implication. Depending on where the advertisements are placed, the targeted readers might be individual consumers or decision-makers at large corporations. Regardless of their roles, all are invited to fill in the blank ("I should choose paper for ___*what?*___") at the same time that they mentally fill in the reason for doing so ("because…___*why?*___"). The small print in each ad prompts a line of reasoning, one connecting to a place where many consumers literally touch paper in their everyday lives, the other promoting the company's commitment to the environment.

The For Writing and Discussion activity that follows invites you to fill in the blanks of these visual arguments by imagining yourself in a decision-making process about whether

Figure 4.4 Advertisement advocating the value of paper products, from Domtar, a major North American paper and pulp company.

to use paper for something, as an individual, a family, a student group, or a business. As you attempt to compose an argument leading in one direction or the other, consider what reasoning Domtar's advertising strategies invite. What assumptions do the strategies seem to call for? Are they assumptions that you accept, or do they need to be argued? Overall, does the implied chain of reasoning lead you to choose paper? Why or why not?

For Writing and Discussion

On Your Own

Try translating one of the visual arguments in this chapter or in Chapter 1 into a paragraph-long written argument. To do so, you will need to identify the central claims made by the figure's

"sustainability is the only business model that will survive."

"Domtar is committed to sustainable environmental policies and business practices because successful businesses recognize those are actually the same thing. Learn more at PAPERbecause.com."

Figure 4.5 Advertisement advocating the value of paper products, from Domtar, a major North American paper and pulp company.

combination of verbal and visual elements, the evidence used (or implied) in support of those claims, and the assumptions that connect the claims and evidence.

With Your Classmates

Share your written version of the visual argument with a group of classmates and together apply the questioning strategies suggested throughout this chapter to analyze and assess the argument's persuasiveness.

EXPLORING YOUR RESPONSES TO A TEXT

In this section, instead of suggesting questioning strategies, we explain approaches to interrogating a text that ask you simply to explore your own reactions to it. These approaches encourage you to record your first reactions to a text and then, after reflection, your more sustained and considered responses.

Before/After Reflections

To consider how much a text has influenced your thinking, try writing out some before and after reflections by freewriting your responses to the following statements. These questions hearken back to the questions for rhetorical reading we posed in Chapter 1 (pp. 10–11), where we suggested that before reading a text, you should consider what its author seems to assume readers think about the subject at hand and how that author works to change such thinking by the time you finish reading. To illustrate, after the following list of before/after questions, we provide Abby's responses to the first two questions in connection with the Gawande article.

1. What effect is this text trying to have on me? What kind of change does the writer hope to make in my view of the subject?

2. Before reading this text, I believed this about the topic: _____ _____. But after reading the text, my view has changed in these ways: _____.

3. Although the text has persuaded me that_____ _____, I still have the following doubts:_____.

4. The most significant questions this text raises for me are these: _____ _____.

5. The most important insights I have gotten from reading this text are these: _____ _____.

Abby's Initial Before/After Reflections About Gawande's Argument
Concerning Medical Checklists

1. Gawande wants his readers to be aware of a serious problem with medical procedures. I don't think I'm part of the primary intended audience, which is probably medical doctors and members of Congress, but I am certainly someone who could send emails to Washington to ask about this—an action that his last sentence calls for by implication.

2. Before reading this text, I knew nothing about the issue, and certainly assumed that doctors always wash their hands. But now I am worried!

The Believing and Doubting Game

Playing the believing and doubting game with a text is a powerful strategy both for recording your reactions to it and for stimulating further thinking. Developed by writing theorist Peter Elbow, the believing and doubting game will stretch your thinking in surprising ways. Elbow called it a "game" because its purpose is not to commit to ideas, but to try them out. Begin on the positive side by freewriting all the reasons why you believe the writer's argument. Then freewrite all the reasons why you doubt the same argument. In the "believe" portion, try to look at the world through the text's perspective, adopting its ideology, actively supporting its ideas and values. Search your mind for any life experiences or memories of reading and research that help you sympathize with and support the author's point of view or ideas. If you find the author's ideas upsetting, dangerous, or threatening, the believing game may challenge—even disturb—you. It takes courage to try to believe views that you feel are dead wrong or contrary to your most deeply held beliefs. Nevertheless, to be a strong rhetorical reader, you need to look at the world through perspectives different from your own.

According to Elbow, the believing game helps you grow intellectually by letting you take in new and challenging ideas. In contrast, the doubting game helps you solidify your present identity by protecting you from outside ideas. Like an antiballistic missile, the doubting game lets you shoot down ideas that you don't like. The "doubt" portion of this game thus reverses the believing process. Here, you try to think of all of the problems, limitations, or weaknesses in the author's argument. You brainstorm for personal experiences or memories that refute or call into question the author's view. Of course, in turn, the doubting game can be unsettling if you already agree with the author's views because it asks you to articulate arguments that take a stand against your own beliefs.

In the following example, Abby works on developing ideas for her rhetorical analysis of the Gawande op-ed by playing the believing and doubting game. She followed her writing instructor's advice to write rapidly, using bullet points as needed to speed things up. She allowed herself no more than ten minutes each for believing and doubting. (She set the timer on her cell phone.) Note how this exercise promotes critical thinking that goes beyond just expressing subjective opinions. The results of playing the believing and doubting game are nearly always a bit surprising.

Abby's Believing-Doubting Game Freewrite

Believe Wow. This guy's claims scare me to death. How could a bureaucracy make something this good stop? He seems to have good facts behind him, and I know he's a reputable writer because of his affiliation with the *New Yorker* as a staff writer. And I'm sure the *NYTimes* wouldn't publish something so accusatory out of the blue without some fact-checking.

What he's saying fits with what I've heard about friends' parents and grandparents getting hospital-borne infections—people say that a hospital is one of the most unhealthy places to be! So a procedure that reduces infections to the extent that Gawande says the checklist does, or did, has to be a good thing.

His argument that the checklist study should not have been stopped because it wasn't an experimental procedure makes a lot of sense to me.

Doubt Can this really be right? Here are my questions and doubts:

* Can government bureaucrats really be this unreasonable?
* Even more important, can it be true that so many doctors don't wash their hands and put on sterile gowns and gloves before inserting IVs? Enough to reduce infections from IV lines by 2/3 when they do?

Other issues:

* His attitude bothers me a little—he's so *sure*! Is his language covering something up? He's a little too blustery for my taste when he calls the gov't reasoning "blinkered" and "bizarre." I'm more inclined to believe arguments from people who are calm and methodical.
* I also wonder if an act of Congress is needed to let the research about the checklist resume. It IS research, I notice—he says so. So maybe it does need to have special oversight. I know that when we volunteered to participate in "experiments" in psych class we had to sign consent forms, even though all we were doing was answering questions. So maybe it does need to have special oversight?

Also, is the situation really as dire as he says? Can't doctors and hospitals use checklists to ensure good procedures anyway, without the research studies? Are lives really at risk

INTERVIEWING THE AUTHOR

Another strategy for exploring your reactions to a text is to imagine interviewing the author and brainstorm the questions you might ask. This strategy enables you to identify the text's hot spots for you. These might be places where you want the author to clarify something, expand on something, or respond to your own objections or counterviews. Here are some questions Abby listed for Gawande.

Abby's Interview Questions

1. I am interested to know what has happened with the checklist studies since your op-ed was published. Has there been progress since the presidential administration changed? Or are you still trying to get Congress to take action?

2. You mentioned that you are working with the World Health Organization on the checklist. They can move forward with it despite the U.S. order to stop the research, can't they?

3. Can't individual doctors and hospitals develop their own checklists and procedures to safeguard patients from these infections?

4. You said that infections from IV lines were reduced by two-thirds when the checklist was in use. What proportion of hospital-borne infections overall does that represent? What are some other causes of people getting sicker while they are in the hospital than they were when they went in? What else can we do, as patients or as citizens asking Congress to act, to make hospitals safer?

WRITING A RHETORICAL ANALYSIS PAPER: GUIDELINES AND AN EXAMPLE

A rhetorical analysis paper is the written counterpart of rhetorical reading. Writing this kind of paper gives you the opportunity to draw together and apply all the listening and questioning strategies discussed in this and the previous chapter for a twofold purpose: (1) articulating your own insights about how a text seeks to influence its readers, and (2) communicating those critical insights to other readers. Here, we offer general guidelines for writing a rhetorical analysis paper, followed by a student example. Abby's assignment is in the box on page 90.

Guidelines for Writing a Rhetorical Analysis

Getting Started
We suggest you prepare for your rhetorical analysis by undertaking at least two of the following preliminary activities:

1. Write a summary of the text you are going to analyze to make sure that you understand it well enough to represent its meaning accurately and fairly.

2. Make a descriptive outline as a way of scrutinizing distinctions between what the text says and what it does to develop those ideas.

3. Write a rhetorical précis of the text. (See pp. 59–60 for instructions.)

4. To identify a strong response or significant effect the text had on you as a reader, try one of the three activities on pages 86–88 for exploring your responses.

Selecting a Focus for Your Analysis

To write an effective rhetorical analysis, you will need to focus on some aspect of the text's rhetorical methods, an aspect that merits close examination or critique. We suggest one of two approaches. You can start deductively with the effect the text had on you as a reader—a strong positive or negative response, a tension or contradiction you found in the text, or some aspect of the text that confused or surprised you. If you begin with your response, you will need to analyze the text to discover the rhetorical features that account for this response. How do they work? Why are these features effective or ineffective? Alternatively, you can start inductively by identifying and then analyzing particularly striking rhetorical features. If you begin inductively, you will need to consider how these features work and to what effect. What new understanding of the text does your analysis reveal?

Whether you begin deductively or inductively, you will need to select specific rhetorical features to write about. Choose features that you consider particularly effective or ineffective, or in which you detect inconsistencies or tensions between two different appeals. To frame your analysis, choose among the questions about texts' rhetorical methods suggested throughout this chapter.

Drafting Your Paper

Once you have determined a focus, reread the text carefully to find specific examples of these features, taking notes on how they contribute to the effect you have identified. Use these notes to draft a working thesis that states the gist of the insights your rhetorical analysis will offer about the text's meaning and methods. You can revise and refine this working thesis after you draft the whole paper. In your final draft, the thesis should clearly introduce the new understanding that results from your analysis and indicate what that analysis says about the text's effectiveness or ineffectiveness.

ABBY'S ASSIGNMENT

Write an essay of approximately 750 words (3 pages) in which you examine the key rhetorical strategies used by Atul Gawande in "A Lifesaving Checklist" to engage readers and convince them to adopt his perspective. Assume that members of your own **audience** are familiar with the rhetorical concepts discussed in this and earlier chapters, and that they have read the text you are analyzing, but have not thought carefully about it. Your **purpose** is to offer these readers insights about how the text works rhetorically. Present a perspective that might not be obvious upon someone's first reading of the piece but that you have gleaned from your analysis of the text.

The full draft of your paper should have the following elements:

1. An introduction that includes (a) a brief summary of the text, (b) contextual information about the text, and (c) your thesis about the text's rhetorical effect
2. A series of body paragraphs that develop the thesis by (a) discussing specific rhetorical features that produce the rhetorical effect and (b) providing specific textual evidence to back up your points
3. A conclusion that makes clear (a) why the new understanding that your paper presents is important, and (b) why the insights of your analysis are significant to other readers

An Annotated Rhetorical Analysis of "A Lifesaving Checklist"

Earlier in this chapter, we presented some of Abby's early writing as she explored how she would approach analysis of Atul Gawande's 2007 *New York Times* op-ed column calling for federal rule changes that would permit resumption of research on the effectiveness of medical checklists designed to regularize anti-infection procedures. We now present the paper in which she applies many of the questioning techniques presented in this chapter. In addition, we have annotated the paper to highlight her analytical and organizational strategies.

A Surprising Checklist

Abby begins with brief information about the article and asserts her response of "surprise." Abby has chosen a deductive focus (p. 90) for her analysis.

1   For many *New York Times* readers, it must have been somewhat surprising to encounter Atul Gawande's December 30, 2007, op-ed article criticizing a little known U.S. government office for endangering lives when it ordered a halt to research on the effectiveness of a medical checklist. We expect *Times* op-eds to be about urgent aspects of politics and foreign policy, not checklists. But this article presents the surprising information that medical doctors need to be reminded to wash their hands before they put intravenous lines into patients, something that might be urgent after all. Gawande uses clear reasoning and direct language to convince readers that it is. The combination creates an effective argument that is full of energy and difficult to argue against.

Details here support her point about surprise, and forecast the other two major points she will develop: clear reasoning and direct language. Asserts thesis about why the argument is effective.

First body paragraph provides foundation for her analysis, with a factual summary of the argument and background about the checklist.

2   The medical checklist, which has five steps, was designed by researchers who wanted to see if using it on a regular basis would reduce infection. Gawande's primary claim is that the federal Office for Human Research Protections (OHRP) made a bad decision when it ordered doctors in Michigan to stop researching the effectiveness of the checklist. He wants the research resumed, and ultimately suggests that Congress may need to step in.

3   Gawande comes across with a strong *ethos*, partly because of the biographical note indicating that he's a surgeon, a *New Yorker* staff writer, and a book author. Appearing on the *New York Times* op-ed page lends him plenty of credibility, too. This authority grows through the concise, down-to-earth way that he presents facts, including lots of statistics. He starts out almost casually, setting the scene as if to tell a story. He mentions an obscure building where OHRP does its assigned work to protect people. "But lately you have to wonder," the doctor calmly notes (par. 1).[4] It may not seem like a serious life-or-death matter is coming up, but it is.

Second body paragraph examines Gawande's credibility as author and his establishment of a "down-to-earth" *ethos*.

Abby's organization follows the flow of the op-ed, pointing out the strength of the reasoning within Gawande's unfolding argument.

4   Gawande gains momentum when he reports the "stunning" (positive) results of using the checklist: a large decrease in infections and thus a big increase in saved lives and saved money (par. 3). Then, the beginning of the next paragraph is just as stunning. We learn that OHRP stopped the study. The problem, it said, was that any research project involving humans requires everyone involved (patients and health care providers alike) to sign a consent form. But not everyone had, or could.

5   Here is the core of both the government's argument and Gawande's rebuttal. OHRP says that doing research without informed consent violates scientific ethics. Gawande suggests, but never quite says exactly, that stopping the research on the checklist's usefulness violates scientific ethics. In his final paragraph, he almost says it when he asserts that the OHRP authorities are "in danger of putting ethics bureaucracy in the way of actual ethical medical care" (par. 11). His next assertions are even more direct. First, he calls for the research to continue "unencumbered." Then, in his final sentence, he says that if the agency won't allow this to happen, "Then Congress will have to" (par. 11). It almost sounds like a threat of punishment.

Abby pinpoints Gawande's central claim as a rebuttal of the government claim.

[4] Instead of using page references in her parenthetical citations of quotations, Abby is following her teacher's request to use the paragraph numbers in the reprint at the end of this chapter.

Having worked through the article, Abby briefly states her understanding of Gawande's purpose and audience, points 3 and 4 in the rhetorical précis structure (p. 60).

6   Gawande's rhetorical purpose is to inform the general public and draw it to his cause. His target audience seems to be a combination of experts (and policymakers) with different levels of awareness and concern about the stopped research, and ordinary readers who want hospitals to be safer places.

7   Gawande reaches out to the interests and values of both groups in this audience not only through reasoning, or *logos*, but by grabbing our attention through casual, conversational language. He got my nonexpert attention in the second paragraph with the surprising information that the checklist leads doctors to "actually wash their hands." It's shocking, yet it clicks with common knowledge that hospitals can make you sicker because they are home to so many dangerous germs. Soon the reader comes upon colloquial zingers such as "the results were stunning" (par. 3) and Gawande calling OHRP's decision "bizarre and dangerous" (par. 5). At first, this strong language may seem easy for a reader to resist. After all, we are taught in school to be suspicious of arguments that come on too strong. But the clarity of Gawande's reasoning is convincing.

Abby now steps back to analyze the way Gawande uses pathos to draw in the audience. Here, she analyzes the impact of Gawande's language on readers, especially nonexperts.

Based on her analysis of ethos, pathos, and language, Abby unpacks Gawande's key moves in countering the OHRP position.

8   Labeling as "blinkered logic" the government's claim that informed consent was needed for research about the checklist (par. 5), Gawande proceeds to take apart the OHRP reasoning. (The phrase "blinkered logic" brought to my mind the image of big draft horses wearing those big leather contraptions that keep them from seeing sideways. They can only see in one direction.) Gawande shows that the reasoning by analogy that considers testing a checklist to be ethically the same as testing a drug is just wrong. According to him, testing a checklist falls into the category of establishing minimum standards for the sake of safety, not the risky category of developing something new. The research on checklists is important, he continues, "not merely because it poses lower risks [than experimental drugs], but because a failure to carry it out poses a vastly greater risk to people's lives" (par. 6).

Abby points to "reasoning by analogy" as the core of Gawande's argument.

Much of Abby's analysis has been based on the flow of reading the essay, preparing her own readers to

9   Gawande's careful rebuttal is all the more effective because he places it between strong assertions about the improvements that occurred when checklist standards were followed (par. 2–3) and the dire consequences of doctors not following minimum standards (par. 7–9). Early in the article, he uses everyday language to describe results: "they actually wash their hands and don a sterile gown and gloves" (par. 2). After he presents his argument that the government's reasoning is wrong, the language is much stronger: "a large

see the strategic importance of organization in Gawande's argument, which she brings up explicitly in this paragraph.

body of evidence ... has revealed a profound failure by health care professionals to follow basic steps proven to stop infection" (par. 7). Paragraph 2 takes readers into the reality of a hospital room; paragraph 7 passes judgment on what goes wrong

10   10. By the end of this short article, a matter that seemed unlikely to concern an <u>ordinary college student</u> like me became <u>surprisingly urgent</u>, something that perhaps I <u>should email Congress</u> about. <u>Gawande's success</u> in the piece illustrates how effective an argument can be when it speaks in plain language directly to the interests of an audience, even an initially unconcerned audience. After all, evidence of "profound failure" in the health care system is difficult for anyone to brush away as insignificant.

Concluding paragraph ties the analytic threads together by commenting on how Gawande convinced this writer of his argument's importance.

CHAPTER SUMMARY

This chapter has laid out for you a variety of strategies for questioning texts and composing your response to them, processes that involve carefully interrogating a text's argument and methods in order to critique it and join its conversation. We explained questioning strategies for examining

* A writer's credibility
* An argument's reasoning and logic
* A writer's strategies for engaging an audience and appealing to its interests and emotions
* A writer's language
* A text's ideology
* A text's use of visual elements

The discussion of visual images as elements of argument described how visuals could enhance a verbal text's appeal to *ethos*, *logos*, and *pathos*, as well as stand alone as visual arguments.

We then explained three easy-to-use methods for exploring your own reactions to a text: (1) writing out before/after responses, (2) playing the believing and doubting game, and (3) imagining an interview with the author.

Finally, along with a sample rhetorical analysis paper, we offered guidelines for writing such papers, including stipulations about audience and purpose in an analysis assignment, along with tips for getting started, selecting a focus, and drafting. Abby's rhetorical analysis of Gawande's op-ed argument then illustrates how the questioning strategies described in this chapter can help you write a college-level rhetorical analysis.

A Lifesaving Checklist
Atul Gawande

Surgeon and writer Atul Gawande is a widely known advocate of using checklists for complex projects in a wide variety of fields. He is Professor of Surgery at Harvard Medical School and Professor in the Department of Health Policy and Management at the Harvard School of Public Health. He serves as director of the World Health Organization's (WHO) Global Challenge for Safer Surgical Care, and in that capacity guided development of a safe surgery checklist that was published by WHO in June 2008. It was modeled on the checklist designed to reduce hospital infections that he discusses in the article below that was modeled after aviation procedures. The surgical protocol, distributed as a laminated card, was featured in a celebrated reunion episode of the television show *ER* in March 2009. Dr. Gawande served as a consultant to the script writers.

Dr. Gawande is also a staff writer for the *New Yorker* and the author of three acclaimed books: *Complications: A Surgeon's Notes on an Imperfect Science* (2002); *Better: A Surgeon's Notes on Performance* (2007), a *New York Times* bestseller; and *The Checklist Manifesto: How to Get Things Right* (2010), also a major bestseller. The son of two medical doctors, Dr. Gawande was born in 1965 in Brooklyn, New York. This op-ed piece was published in the *New York Times* on Sunday, December 30, 2007.

1   In Bethesda, Md., in a squat building off a suburban parkway, sits a small federal agency called the Office for Human Research Protections. Its aim is to protect people. But lately you have to wonder. Consider this recent case.

2   A year ago, researchers at Johns Hopkins University published the results of a program that instituted in nearly every intensive care unit in Michigan a simple five-step checklist designed to prevent certain hospital infections. It reminds doctors to make sure, for example, that before putting large intravenous lines into patients, they actually wash their hands and don a sterile gown and gloves.

3   The results were stunning. Within three months, the rate of bloodstream infections from these I.V. lines fell by two-thirds. The average I.C.U. cut its infection rate from 4 percent to zero. Over 18 months, the program saved more than 1,500 lives and nearly $200 million.

4   Yet this past month, the Office for Human Research Protections shut the program down. The agency issued notice to the researchers and the Michigan Health and

Hospital Association that, by introducing a checklist and tracking the results without written, informed consent from each patient and health-care provider, they had violated scientific ethics regulations. Johns Hopkins had to halt not only the program in Michigan but also its plans to extend it to hospitals in New Jersey and Rhode Island.

5   The government's decision was bizarre and dangerous. But there was a certain blinkered logic to it, which went like this: A checklist is an alteration in medical care no less than an experimental drug is. Studying an experimental drug in people without federal monitoring and explicit written permission from each patient is unethical and illegal. Therefore it is no less unethical and illegal to do the same with a checklist. Indeed, a checklist may require even more stringent oversight, the administration ruled, because the data gathered in testing it could put not only the patients but also the doctors at risk—by exposing how poorly some of them follow basic infection-prevention procedures.

6   The need for safeguards in medical experimentation has been evident since before the Nazi physician trials at Nuremberg. Testing a checklist for infection prevention, however, is not the same as testing an experimental drug—and neither are like-minded efforts now under way to reduce pneumonia in hospitals, improve the consistency of stroke and heart attack treatment and increase flu vaccination rates. Such organizational research work, new to medicine, aims to cement minimum standards and ensure they are followed, not to discover new therapies. This work is different from drug testing not merely because it poses lower risks, but because a failure to carry it out poses a vastly greater risk to people's lives.

7   A large body of evidence gathered in recent years has revealed a profound failure by health-care professionals to follow basic steps proven to stop infection and other major complications. We now know that hundreds of thousands of Americans suffer serious complications or die as a result. It's not for lack of effort. People in health care work long, hard hours. They are struggling, however, to provide increasingly complex care in the absence of effective systematization.

8   Excellent clinical care is no longer possible without doctors and nurses routinely using checklists and other organizational strategies and studying their results. There need to be as few barriers to such efforts as possible. Instead, the endeavor itself is treated as the danger.

9   If the government's ruling were applied more widely, whole swaths of critical work to ensure safe and effective care would either halt or shrink: efforts by the Centers for Disease Control and Prevention to examine responses to outbreaks of infectious disease; the military's program to track the care of wounded soldiers; the Five Million Lives campaign, by the nonprofit Institute for Healthcare Improvement, to reduce avoidable complications in 3,700 hospitals nationwide.

10   I work with the World Health Organization on a new effort to introduce surgical safety checklists worldwide. It aims to ensure that a dozen basic safety steps are actually followed in operating rooms here and abroad—that the operating team gives an antibiotic before making an incision, for example, and reviews how much blood loss to prepare for. A critical component of the program involves tracking successes and failures and learning from them. If each of the hundreds of hospitals we're trying

to draw into the program were required to obtain permissions for this, even just from research regulators, few could join.

11   Scientific research regulations had previously exempted efforts to improve medical quality and public health—because they hadn't been scientific. Now that the work is becoming more systematic (and effective), the authorities have stepped in. And they're in danger of putting ethics bureaucracy in the way of actual ethical medical care. The agency should allow this research to continue unencumbered. If it won't, then Congress will have to.

5

Using Rhetorical Reading for Researched Writing Projects

The only way in which a human being can make some approach to knowing the whole of a subject is by hearing what can be said about it by persons of every variety of opinion and studying all modes in which it can be looked at by every character of mind.

—John Stuart Mill

This chapter will show you systematic and efficient techniques for using rhetorical reading strategies to find reliable sources within the twenty-first century's deluge of information. Specifically, you will learn:

- The definition of **information literacy** and skills for developing it
- A process called Question Analysis that will make your research more productive
- Important differences in publication and editing processes for different kinds of sources
- Distinctions between library databases and Web search engines
- Tips for finding and evaluating reliable sources by examining
  - Publication type
  - Relevance
  - Currency and scope
  - Credentials of authors, experts, publishers, and sponsors

To illustrate these processes, we include excerpts from the research log that the student Jack prepared while working on the paper about ethanol in Chapter 6.

As the opening epigraph suggests, wisdom emerges only through careful examination of many differing perspectives. Given the wonders of twenty-first-century digital technology, it is probably not literally possible to consider "every variety of opinion," but this same technology does make it easier to examine a wide range of perspectives and "characters of mind" than was possible even a decade ago. What remains applicable in Mill's admonition is the goal of forging new understandings and new knowledge through thoughtful interactions with the thinking and writing of others, including—perhaps, especially—those with whom we do not expect to agree. With that goal in mind, this chapter will show you how to apply the techniques of reading rhetorically to find and select materials for rhetorically effective academic papers in which you can extend the conversation about topics that are important to you.

RHETORICAL READING AND INFORMATION LITERACY

To meet the challenge of finding relevant, reliable sources for research projects, you can incorporate techniques for rhetorical reading into the productive techniques that fall under the conceptual umbrella of **information literacy**. Doing so will equip you well for making sense out of the glut of information available to us all in the twenty-first century.

Librarians define *information literacy* in terms of the following five skills, which provide a map of research activities that will lead to successful college papers:

1. Determine what kind of information is needed and how much
2. Access the information efficiently
3. Evaluate critically the information and its sources
4. Use the information effectively for a specific purpose
5. Access and use the information ethically and legally in light of economic, social, and legal issues about information use and sources

These techniques will help you work efficiently and leave you plenty of time for thoughtful writing about the information and ideas that you uncover. We cover the first three in this chapter, and the remaining two in Chapter 6. That chapter demonstrates practical techniques for incorporating source materials into your own writing so that your papers synthesize new meaning from your diverse sources, as well as credit those sources in accordance with academic conventions. We illustrate both discussions by following the work of Jack, the Midwesterner we first met in Chapter 1, who is interested in corn ethanol. His final paper, "Arguing on the Basis of Wishful Thinking: An Analysis of Multiple Perspectives on Corn-Based Ethanol," which appears at the end of Chapter 6, was written in response to the assignment in the following box.

Notice that the definition of *information literacy* begins not with retrieving information, or even searching for it, but with careful consideration of what information is needed to accomplish a writer's purposes. In other words, writers who are information literate are writers who undertake their actual research with more in mind than a generalized "topic." They begin by carefully working out a research question and a set of expectations about how they will recognize relevant, valuable answers. You need to do the same.

Of course, it is likely that as your research progresses you will need to revise your original question, narrowing or broadening it as you catch the drift of the ongoing conversation about it. (Many researchers—not only students!—find that they must narrow their initial questions significantly just to make their project feasible for the amount of time available and the number of pages allotted for an assignment.) Eventually, your modified question will become part of your paper's introduction. Combined with the answers you find, it will be the basis of your thesis statement that announces your paper's purpose.

But first you need the question. How else will you recognize good answers?

JACK'S ASSIGNMENT TO ANALYZE MULTIPLE PERSPECTIVES

For this paper, you are to extend the conversation about environmental problems and solutions by (1) **analyzing** (taking apart and examining) several different perspectives on some aspect of the public discussion, then (2) **using synthesis** (putting together) to assert **your** understanding of the connections and differences among these perspectives. Choose a topic that particularly interests you and that is complex enough to include more than two "pro-con" perspectives.

Your audience: People like your classmates and instructor, who have heard of the issue but haven't looked into it enough to understand its dynamics.

Your purpose: Fill in our lack of understanding so that we can see what makes this issue so difficult to resolve. Instead of trying to convince us who is right, provide us with insights and information that will allow us to follow the unfolding conversation.

Length: 4–6 pages. Use MLA in-text citations and a works cited list.

FORMULATING AND ANALYZING QUESTIONS

Knowing what you are looking for is an essential first step to successful research-based writing. Whether you are fulfilling an assignment for a first-year writing class or for a capstone seminar in your major, the initial step in your research process—the step before you begin searching for sources—must be articulating your purpose. What question do you want to find answers to and write about?

Think of research-based writing assignments this way: Your job is to conduct an inquiry, not to shop around for sources. We offer a cautionary tale. Consider what went wrong when a student we'll call Phoebe treated a research assignment as a hunt for bargains instead of an inquiry. She was assigned to examine the potentially negative consequences of something that interested her. She had heard that Barbie dolls were being redesigned to have more natural proportions, so she thought Barbies would be an interesting "topic." She skipped the assigned step of writing out an initial question because, as she wrote in a later reflection, she thought that because Barbie was in the news, it would be faster just to search a periodicals database and see "what there was to say." She found so many articles that she felt overwhelmed, so she just chose the first three for which full text was available. This was not a good idea.

The resulting paper amounted to a patchwork of quotes and paraphrases from source materials stitched together by Phoebe's engaging descriptions of her own dolls. But it didn't synthesize her research sources, make a point, or reveal any conclusions that Phoebe had reached through research. To meet a page limit, Phoebe had merely interspersed stories about her own Barbies among three long summaries, first of a feminist's reflections about her childhood dolls, then of a psychological report about connections between gender stereotypes and eating disorders, and finally a commentary about the negative impact of Teen Talk Barbie's dislike for math class. She provided no analysis of Barbie's proposed new figure, the original topic, nor did she synthesize perspectives from her sources. Phoebe had been working without a sense of purpose during her research reading, with the result that her paper provided no new insights for readers.

Establishing Your Purpose

In our discussion of authors' purposes in Chapter 2, we stressed the importance of reading in a way that weighs your purpose as a reader against a given author's purpose for writing. Authors seek to change their readers' thinking in some way, we said, and we stressed that you, the reader, are the one who decides how much your thinking will change (p. 10).

The same dynamic applies when you undertake a research-based writing project. In an academic setting, the audience and genre are given: you are to write for an instructor according to the conventions of that discipline, very likely in response to an assignment prompt that narrows your range of subject matter. But beyond the need to satisfy a certain assignment, your real purpose, the question you seek to answer in your paper, is yours to determine. Your need for an answer is where the work on your paper begins. That need for an answer is what we called an "exigence" back in Chapter 2, the rhetorical term for a flaw or gap in knowledge that your efforts at research and writing will seek to remedy.

In the past, you may have encountered research assignments that expected you to do little more than report on a topic by gathering information and funneling it into paragraphs (like Phoebe did for the Barbie paper). However, the expectations and standards of your college teachers who assign papers with research components will be quite different—even in first-year writing courses. Your instructors will expect you to pose questions and provide not only answers but, in the language of our service economy, "value-added" content that demonstrates your own thinking. The value that you add will result from your work analyzing, organizing, and generally making sense out of the disconnected array of available information that you initially encounter.

Using Question Analysis to Plan a Research Strategy

A helpful strategy for conducting the multilayered process of researching, reading, and writing is a technique called **Question Analysis (QA)**, which offers a series of analytical prompts as a start-up routine for a research project.[1] These prompts, presented in Table 5.1, will not only help you recognize what you already know about possible answers to your research

---

[1]The term *Question Analysis* comes from the work of academic librarian Cerise Oberman, who first broached it in "Question Analysis and the Learning Cycle," *Research Strategies* 1 (1983): 22–30. Print.

question, but will also suggest in advance what you need to "listen" for when you begin examining sources. The QA process of freewriting in response to these prompts will enable you (1) to make a preliminary map of the terrain you need to cover in your search for relevant source materials, and (2) to consider in advance what kinds of sources are going to be most useful for you to retrieve, read, and eventually integrate into your paper.

Table 5.1   Prompts for Question Analysis

Freewrite responses to these questions *before* you begin searching for sources.

Questions to Ask	Details for Follow-Up
1. What question do you plan to investigate—and hope to answer—in this paper?	Avoid questions with obvious or simple answers.
2. What makes this question worth pursuing—to you and to others?	What benefits will come from answering the question, or from discovering why it is so difficult to answer?
3. What kind of expert would be able to provide good answers or the current best thinking about possible answers?	Perhaps a physician? Wildlife biologist? Water resource engineer? Journalist who has reported extensively on the subject?
4. Where do you expect to find particularly good information about this matter?	General interest publications? Specialized publications? Are you aware of a specific source with relevant material?
5. How recent must materials be to be relevant? What factors might make information outdated?	Defining a particular timeframe will help you search more efficiently. You may need information recorded before or after a particular event, such as an election or announcement of important medical findings. For situations that change rapidly, even a few months could make a difference.
6. What individuals or interest groups have a major stake in answering your question in a particular way?	For example, players' unions and sports team owners look at salary caps from different perspectives; lumber companies and environmental activists evaluate the effectiveness of the Endangered Species Act differently.
7. What kinds of bias do you need to be especially alert for on this particular question?	Bias of some kind is unavoidable, so it's important to recognize how it is operating in your sources so that you can compensate by consulting additional sources.
8. What words or phrases might be useful for some initial searching?	Different library databases often favor different search terms, so be prepared to consult with a librarian if you are not finding what you expect.

QUESTION ANALYSIS WORK EXCERPTED FROM JACK'S RESEARCH LOG

QUESTION ANALYSIS

1. My question: What are the advantages and disadvantages of developing corn-based ethanol? Will it become a clean substitute fuel for gasoline? (Uncle Johnny) Or is it too resource-intensive to produce to be profitable? (Uncle Clyde) I don't want to get into the "food v. fuel" debate—or energy independence. I just want to focus on what the current thinking is about corn and ethanol.

2. Why my question is worth pursuing: Because finding clean alternatives to gasoline is a high priority in the U.S. and around the world!

3. Experts I need: Scientists (chemists) in this field, journalists with a good overview, automakers, maybe economists.

4. Sources I think will have good info: Special issue of news magazine (?), Web sites for ethanol producers and environmentalists (Sierra Club, Concerned Scientists—get right name, automakers, *NY Times* or *Wall Street Journal*)

5. Time frame: Sources have to be pretty current for both political and scientific reasons, especially since January 2012, when the federal subsidies ended.

6. People with a stake in this: ethanol producers, environmentalists, automakers, farmers (pro and con), politicians (maybe not so much anymore—I have to see).

7. Bias to watch for: Some people are going to make money and some are going to lose. Probably every "expert" has a stake in it one way or the other.

8. Search terms: ethanol, biofuels (what are other types of biofuel?)

The QA process takes you out of a passive role (waiting to see what you can find) and puts you in charge of your research. Taking a small bit of time to prepare for research by using Question Analysis is similar to pausing to assess your background knowledge, an important part of preparing to read, as we described in Chapter 3 (pp. 39–40). The time spent planning and predicting will help you read more powerfully and thus choose potential sources more efficiently. Whatever your purpose for research, if you clarify your questions for yourself in advance, you will greatly reduce the risk of losing sight of your purpose once you dive into the search process. In fact, students who use QA for the first time are often surprised to discover how much they already know about where they are likely to find relevant sources and what issues those sources will raise. For additional insights into the QA process, we invite you to examine the excerpts from Jack's research log on the previous page.

TIPS FOR FINDING RELIABLE SOURCES

One of the great advantages of digital library resources is that they allow you to answer many questions about a source's reliability before you retrieve the actual source. That is, the same catalog and database screens that help you locate materials will likely also help you quickly evaluate the reliability and relevance of a potential source. That evaluation will in turn help you make good decisions about how far you want to pursue retrieval of that source. (Will you look at full text? Bookmark the source for later? Skim it online? Print it? Take notes? And so forth.)

The tips we provide in this section will help you use the QA questions efficiently to choose the sources you want to look at more closely. In the next section, we provide tips for evaluating the sources you choose to examine further. To illustrate how one student's research process unfolded, we include more excerpts from Jack's research log on pages 111 and 112.

Tip #1. Prefer Sources That Have Undergone Solid Editorial Review and Fact-Checking

Whether you access sources on paper in the library stacks or electronically through a library database or Web search engine, you must scrutinize their contexts and purposes for relevance and reliability. We recommend searching your library's online catalog and periodicals databases before jumping on the Web, which contains garbage as well as gold. The abundance and immediacy of information now available through the Internet make careful scrutiny crucial to your research work, especially during the early stages of your research, when your main goal is to catch the drift of the published conversation relevant to your research question. It can be difficult to assess the credibility of Web authors or the motives of a site sponsor, but here is a valuable rule of thumb: Whether you are reading in print or online, the more that you feel like someone is shouting and the more that ads interfere with your reading, the more cautious you need to be. For academic papers, you need sources with a calm, even-handed approach.

After filling out his Question Analysis log, Jack started his search the way librarians recommend, by looking for current magazine and journal articles in a periodicals database. The materials found through these databases are easy to access, efficient to use, and more current than books, which take a long time to write and manufacture. Furthermore, the editorial processes at the newspapers, magazines, and journals indexed in the databases are typically rigorous. Such editing represents major investments of time and money. It involves multiple readers, fact-checking, quote-checking, and even background-checking of quoted sources. With so many people not only checking content but staking their professional reputations on quality and credibility, such materials clearly deserve preference.

Jack knew that his research about ethanol would have to include advocacy sites on the Web, from both ethanol producers and ethanol skeptics. But he also knew that the diversity of opinion made it all the more important that he find reliable, edited sources that could provide recent discussions. He knew that although even reputable journalists might favor one perspective over another, if they want to get their stories in print and if they want to have continued access to their sources, they need to report all points of view fairly. In the end, he brought in pro-ethanol advocates primarily through news sources and used just one anti-ethanol source directly from the Web site of an organization referred to in a *New York Times* article. (See paragraph 6 of Jack's paper.)

Library Databases and Web Search Engines

Library databases (such as ProQuest or Lexis-Nexis) and Web search engines (such as Google, Yahoo!, and Bing) will lead you to significantly different types of material because they search different parts of the Internet.[2] Libraries pay substantial subscription fees for the password-protected database services that give you access to electronic archives of print periodicals—magazines, trade journals, scholarly journals, and major newspapers. "We pay for quality," librarians at public and university libraries commonly stress. In contrast, Web search engines access the free-access part of the Internet. You can use these search engines without charge because their revenue comes from advertisers. Within seconds they will accumulate for you an overwhelming number of potential sources, many of them unreliable, unrelated to your purposes, and probably redundant. Indeed, even those links that do appear helpful might no longer be working, or might take you to a Web site where that promising article or report is no longer available. Remember this: the search engine algorithms that measure popularity are not good measures of reliability.

In contrast, initiating a search in a library subscription database sets off a search of the indexes and archives of sources recommended by experienced researchers and experts in a wide variety of fields. The focus is primarily on print sources, but some databases now index materials from radio and TV broadcasts and reputable blogs. See, for example, the "source types" in Figure 5.1, the "Easy Search" screen of the LexisNexis database. In addition, audio and video materials are frequently archived and indexed through the Web sites of

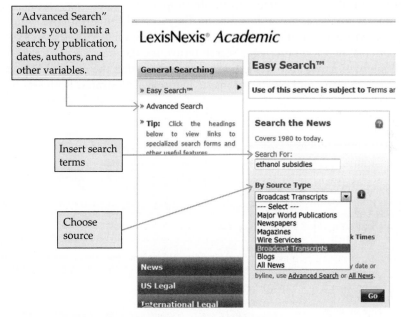

Figure 5.1 Close-up view of a LexisNexis "Easy Search" screen showing types of sources available

---

[2]We follow the practice of using "Internet" to refer to the entire network of linked computers around the world and "Web" to refer to material available through the graphical interface used by browsers such as Firefox, Internet Explorer, Safari, Chrome, and so forth.

television and radio networks, most notably National Public Radio and the PBS *NewsHour* (sources that Jack found helpful).

As our last point about TV and radio resources should confirm, we are not recommending that you shun material published on the Web. Doing so would be a big mistake. Jack needed to know what was being said on the Web sites of ethanol advocates as well as environmental activists. Many Web materials have undergone rigorous editorial processes; furthermore, highly reputable print periodicals often publish major articles on the Web. Some sites, such as nytimes.com, have far more resources available on the Web than in print editions. Nonetheless, for consistent reliability as well as for the sake of efficiency in searching and evaluating, we recommend starting with periodicals to which your library subscribes through a database.

Some specialized databases are available only on CD-ROM in the library itself, but the extensive databases of general interest materials are stored on computers that may be miles away from the library. While these computers are conducting your search, they might also be conducting a search on behalf of your best friend from home, who is attending school in another state. When you use these databases from campus, they may seem to be as free of cost as a Web search engine; however, be assured that libraries do pay substantial subscription fees to the database companies. That is why access to them is password-protected and why access is typically restricted from off campus.

Periodicals databases are indexed according to traditional bibliographic categories (author, article title, publication title, etc.) as well as by specialized key words connected to subject matter. When you enter your search terms, the database checks these indexed categories along with article abstracts and key word lists so that the results screen can suggest additional search terms and combinations, as Figure 5.2 illustrates. Both sets of results are

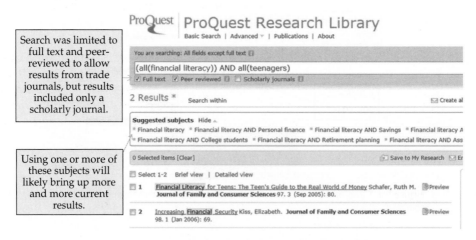

Figure 5.2 Close-up view of a screen showing results from a ProQuest Research Library search for "financial literacy AND teenagers" and providing alternate subject terms

usually much smaller and more manageable than those produced by Web searches. Furthermore, as you will see in the section on evaluating sources beginning on page 108, rhetorical readers can pick up important evaluative cues from search results. One note of caution: manipulating subject terms and doing advanced searches can become complex and frustrating. If you are not getting the results you expect, ask a librarian for help.

Tip #2. Appreciate the Value of Specialized Periodicals for General Audiences

Your ability to understand your sources will be important to the success of your project, so finding material written at a suitable level of expertise must be a priority. You can count on being able to read general interest publications comfortably, but if they seem oversimplified (perhaps even sensationalized), or if they don't provide the depth of information you are looking for, consider searching within a newsstand periodical that provides in-depth discussion for the general public on more specialized topics, for example, *American Health, Money, Psychology Today, Consumer Reports* (very useful to Jack), or one of our favorites, the *Chronicle of Higher Education*. These can be good places for a student researcher to find extended but readily understood material. Be forewarned, however: The more specialized the publication, the greater the likelihood that you will find it difficult to understand, either because the material is too technical or because the author assumes readers are more familiar with the subject than you happen to be. If you find that your question has been addressed only at high levels of scholarship, you will probably need to revise it.

Tip #3. Weigh Questions About Relevance

You can often determine the relevance of a source to your project just by examining the bibliographic information provided in library catalogs (for books) and databases (for periodicals).[3] Use the bibliographic information to answer the following three basic questions about a source's purpose and method:

1. **What ideas and information does this text offer?** Examine the title, subtitle, and abstract. Does the information indicate what kind of source it is (scholarly, trade, etc.)? You can make good guesses about an article's approach and intended audience on the basis of what you already know or can discern from the periodical and article titles. For books, a table of contents may be available in the online catalog along with the name of the publisher.

2. **Can I trust the source of information?** Again consider what you know or can gather about the credentials and reputation of the author, publisher, or Web sponsor. Remember that university presses are particularly reliable. On the Web, click the Home and About Us tabs for information about the site sponsor (now required information for Modern Language Association [MLA] citations). If there is no evi-

---

[3]For Web sources, it is important that you examine the actual source, not just the link supplied by the search engine.

dence of a reputable site sponsor, do not use the source.[4] (Note: Material from an individual's home page is not usually acceptable for academic papers, no matter how impressive it may appear. Links from such pages may uncover useful and reliable sources, however).

3. **Will I be able to understand what the source says—was it written for someone at my level of expertise?** Draw inferences about the intended readers from the title, publisher's reputation, and an abstract or table of contents, then spot read as needed. If the article is full of technical material, concentrate on making sense of the abstract and conclusions sections.

Tip #4. Ask a Librarian

Librarians know where to find things and how to narrow searches. They can tell you which database to look in to find local news coverage of the effects of the emerald ash borer beetle, for example, and they usually know which database offers full-text articles from a certain journal and which offers only abstracts. Some journals and magazines are selective about the databases to which they provide access, or full-text access, and librarians will know which database is the best to consult for different types of subject matter. They also can offer good suggestions for trade publications related to something that interests you, or for alternate subject/search terms, such as "capital punishment" versus "death penalty," including which database uses which term.

TIPS FOR EVALUATING SOURCES

Once you have narrowed down a list of potential sources, the tips and questions in this section will guide your evaluation of texts you are considering as possible sources and will help you use your rhetorical reading skills to infer the original context and purpose of potential sources. The two over-reaching issues are these:

- How will a given source help you answer your research question?
- How can you use the source in your own writing?

Tip #5. Read the Abstracts and Conclusions Sections of Scholarly Articles

In the academic world, the most highly regarded periodicals are **peer-reviewed journals**, also known as **refereed journals** and **scholarly journals**.[5] These journals only publish articles that have been approved by several experts as meeting high scholarly standards and contributing to new knowledge. They rarely publish advertisements. These high levels of

---

[4]By "site sponsor" we mean the organization behind the Web page, not advertisers on it.
[5]The glossary for the library subscription database ProQuest distinguishes between "peer-reviewed" journals and "scholarly" journals, limiting *scholarly* to journals written by and for academics and published by professional associations or university presses. Most articles (but not all) in scholarly publications are peer-reviewed, as are articles in many trade publications.

credibility make such journals excellent sources for college papers. Their drawback is that material written for experts and scholars may be difficult for readers outside the field to understand. However, even if you cannot understand all the details in material from scientific journals such as the *New England Journal of Medicine* or *JAMA*, reading the abstract, background, and conclusions sections of a given study may provide you with better insights about the complexities of the findings than will a short news report.

Tip #6. Examine a Text's Currency and Scope

Take your initial evaluation further by using bibliographic information about date of publication and length to judge how usable the material may be for your purposes. Abstracts may help you catch a publication's tone and scope, but you can get better information by spot reading in the full text, which will help you judge the intended audience. In library databases, examining a PDF version of the article, if available, is ideal because the images of actual pages from the periodical will reveal layout, illustrations, and advertisements, all cues to the publication's genre and audience. If PDF is not available in the database you are using, try another of your library's periodicals databases. In some cases, you may have to go to the stacks to find paper copy to skim in order to determine whether a source that seems promising will actually be valuable for your purposes. (Note: We caution you not to rely solely on any database's abstract in place of the source itself. They are often written by nonexperts who may leave out important facts and context, or who may be sloppy about indicating when they are quoting or the extent to which they are paraphrasing. Any of these factors could lead to embarrassment for you, or worse.)

Use the following questions as a guide:

1. **How current is the source in relation to your research question?** You will usually want the most recent information available, but if you are researching a historical phenomenon, "current" must be balanced with "relevant," and thus does not necessarily mean "recent."

2. **How extensive is the source? How much detail is present? What kind of evidence is used?** A twenty-page article contrasting American and Japanese management styles might be just what you need, or it might be far too detailed for your purposes. A cheery three-paragraph piece in *Glamour* or *GQ* about the value of regular dental checkups might enable you to make a point about the treatment of dental hygiene in popular magazines, but it won't tell you much about the affordability of dental care.

Tip #7. Check Authors' and Experts' Basis of Authority

Your background knowledge about subject matter and sources will often help you answer questions about an author or expert's trustworthiness. When you need more information, skim the source for information, look for a biographical note about the author (possibly elsewhere in the publication or on the Web site), or try other available search tools. Once you have selected certain materials to read in depth for your project, use them to consider the following questions about credibility:

1. **What are the author's credentials and qualifications regarding the subject?** See what you can learn about this person's professional expertise. (You may start recognizing names that come up regularly.) Is the writer an expert in the field? A journalist who writes about the subject frequently? An abstract or a note at the end of a full-text article may supply biographical information. A quick search by author (perhaps via a click on the name) will show you what this person has written recently for the same periodical. You might discover, for example, that the author of a piece on rap music is not an expert on rap or hip-hop but does regularly write about the business side of the entertainment industry. This discovery may signal that the article is not likely to help you if you want to write about rap music's roots in the African-American folk tradition, but if you are interested in how rap has been marketed over the years or how it fits into the larger entertainment market, additional articles by this author may lead to just what you need.

2. **What are the credentials and qualifications of experts who are cited?** In general-circulation periodicals (newspapers and newsmagazines), the writer's expertise is probably less important than is the expertise of the sources interviewed. Gathering information about the people quoted in an article usually requires skimming to see what background information is supplied. Using a database to look for material written by those experts can lead to more in-depth sources and confirm their reputations.

3. **What can you tell about the writer's or expert's political views or affiliations that might affect his or her credibility?** You are more likely to uncover this information in the text than in the citation. (Much of the time you will have to use your rhetorical reading skills to infer the writer's ideology—see Chapter 4.) If the purpose of your paper dictates that you need to find out more about a writer's ideological biases, a quick search in *Books in Print*, in a biography database, or on the Web will probably tell you what you need to know. You might learn, for example, that a particular writer recently received an award from the American Civil Liberties Union (on the left) or the Heritage Foundation (on the right), or you might discover that a medical expert interviewed about the dangers of plastic surgery is a well-known celebrity doctor. It will be up to you to determine the extent to which this information adds or detracts from the person's credibility in relation to your research questions and purposes.

Tip #8. Consider the Reputation of Publishers and Sponsors

Crucial information for evaluating a source can become apparent when you examine the purposes and motives of its publisher. Regardless of whether you access the source on paper or on the Web, it is important to consider how and why the material has become available in the first place. The following questions about audience, review process, and reputation will help round out your process of evaluating potential sources.

1. **What is the periodical's target audience—the general public or a specialized audience? Is it known for providing good information about the subject that interests you?** If you are researching antidepressants, for example, you will find that articles in popular magazines are often upbeat about their value. You'll probably find more reliable information about the side effects of drugs in specialized magazines or medically oriented journals.

2. **How extensive a review process did the article have to undergo before the text was published? Is it from a scholarly journal?** Increasing numbers of print periodicals, particularly newspapers, post material on the Web, and you can rely on their editorial processes regarding material found on their sites. Nevertheless, it's also important to remember that general circulation publications and news sites are driven by marketplace concerns. Editors choose articles that will help sell copies (or draw eyeballs) because increases in circulation and clicks will increase advertising revenue. Beware of overstatement.

3. **Is the publisher or site sponsor known to have a viewpoint that might influence its coverage of material that is relevant to your question?** We have previously noted that books published by university presses can be assumed to be reliable, for example. Nonetheless, do be alert for political biases, not because you can avoid bias but because you may want to be sure to consult sources with different leanings. A wide variety of nonprofit, public service, and governmental entities have extensive and useful Web sites. Consider how an organization's mission may influence its Web presentations. If you use material from an organization known for supporting certain causes or positions, scrutinize it carefully for the effects of bias. If you let your own readers know relevant information about a source's reputation (something that might not be obvious), you will be demonstrating that you are knowledgeable about that reputation.

MORE EXCERPTS FROM JACK'S RESEARCH LOG

To illustrate how a student might apply these evaluation strategies to a research project, we conclude this chapter with more items from Jack's research log.

Evaluating Sources

1. **Update on My Searches**

   Searched for "ethanol" in ProQuest, the Web, and in "Times Topics" at *nytimes.com*. I found 100's of articles, and by spot reading or skimming them, I have discovered that my question is too simple. Uncle Clyde and Uncle Johnny are both right, but by going all out with corn hybridized for ethanol, Johnny is taking the bigger risk if the bottom falls out of the ethanol market because of oil prices or a bad economy. I had no idea there were so many organizations (lobbies, I guess) with a stake in this.

2. Best Sources So Far

**Archive of a *Chronicle of Higher Education* online discussion with an Iowa State engineering professor about biofuels—his answers to questions give good information, but it's the questions themselves that are helping me focus. (Bookmarked—may print it so I can see it better.)

Relevance? Provides great overview—I'm learning a lot from it that fits into the more news-based articles. Trustworthy, yes.

Currency and Scope? Covers many bases, which is why I like it. It's from 2007, but I haven't found anything since that is as clear from the scientific POV. (Did talk to a librarian.)

Author and experts quoted? Good—it's all from one academic expert, not an advocate. He seems cautious. Important quote: "<u>Ultimately, we cannot achieve our goals through corn grain ethanol alone</u>." (I am underlining quotes to keep track of them.)

Publishers and Sponsors? The CHE is one of the sources the librarian mentioned when I asked for help after realizing that what was coming up online was very "inside update" stuff about green business—I could understand the words, but not the context. (Too many details!) The CHE target audience is professors, but ones who are NOT experts in whatever topic. I can understand this guy, AND the people asking him questions.

**Consumer Reports*, "The Ethanol Myth." Found in Ebscohost.

Relevance? Good perspective because it's written for consumers. The "myth" aspect is that ethanol will solve everything. It's not anti-ethanol, just cautious and a good explainer.

Currency and Scope? Good-ish. 2006. Focuses on flex fuel vehicles. (They use E85, 85% ethanol, 15% gasoline; ordinary gasoline these days is 10% ethanol.)

Author and experts quoted? Based on their testing and research, so absolutely reliable—everybody knows that CR is a reliable source!

Economist, "Plagued by Politics." Linked from PBS page.

More recent (2011) than the CR piece, and the subtitle tells the story: "Biofuels are an example of what not to do." I know they tend to be lefties, but this has an international perspective and some good data.

3. Worst Source So Far

You asked for it! The headline on the home page for *www.ethanolfacts.com* says "Ethanol is the answer to many of America's challenges. This is the place for the answers about ethanol." Great reasoning, eh? Do you think there will be anything negative about ethanol on this site? On the other hand, I guess I can learn from it how they spin the bad news. It's sponsored by the National Corn Growers Association, so they must mean "corn ethanol is the answer to America's challenges."

***

Still to Do

- I need to watch a news video online about alternate sources of ethanol that my professor recommended from the PBS NewsHour.

- Search NPR. Mom said she heard something there not long ago that corn for ethanol for fuel has gone beyond corn for food.

- MUST find an update about the impact of the subsidy ending. I found a great op-ed and letters responding to it, but it turned out it was all from before Congress finally voted the subsidies out.

- Keep checking the *NY Times* Green, Inc., bloggers for updates, and go back to Times Topics for the "ethanol" entry to check my details.

CHAPTER SUMMARY

This chapter has described how rhetorical reading skills will help you succeed in two of your key tasks as a researcher: formulating questions and evaluating resources. Because college teachers expect students to demonstrate their own thinking about a given research question, successful academic papers are those in which the student's claims and commentary are more prominent than material from research sources.

To assist your pre-research and research processes, we discussed the following:

- The importance of approaching a research project with a clear sense of purpose and careful planning
- The skills needed to develop information literacy
- Question analysis (QA) prompts to use before you begin an active search for sources
- The differences between searching for sources through library subscription databases and through Web search engines
- The differences in publication and editing processes for different kinds of both print and Web sources

We offered tips for finding and using reliable sources, including consulting with a librarian, and recommended that you evaluate potential sources by asking specific questions about a potential source concerning its relevance to your project, its currency and scope, the background and reputation of authors and experts, and the credibility and likely biases of publishers and Web page sponsors.

To illustrate these processes, we provided excerpts from Jack's research log.

INCORPORATING READING INTO WRITING

The mind in action selects and orders, matches and balances, sorting and generating as it shapes meanings and controls their interdependencies.

—Ann E. Berthoff

In this chapter, you will learn:

- How to use material from your reading to extend and develop your own points
- How to make the distinction between your ideas (and words) and your sources' ideas (and words) absolutely clear to your readers
- How to manage your writing process
- How to avoid any hint of plagiarism by following guidelines for integrating summaries, paraphrases, and quotations into your work
- How to give credit where credit is due by using attributive tags and by following the Modern Language Association (MLA) guidelines for in-text citations. (The Appendix offers model citation formats.)

To illustratce many of these principles, we present at the end of the chapter Jack's MLA-formatted paper about corn-based ethanol.

In this chapter we address one of the biggest challenges in college writing: incorporating other writers' texts into your own without letting them take over. The techniques we present here will help you foreground your sense of purpose and thus help you author strong, rhetorically effective texts. As we have stressed in the preceding chapters, composing a text is an opportunity to add your voice to the ongoing conversation about a particular topic. Your readers, whether your peers or your professors, want to read what *you* have to say, not a rehash of what others have said.

ASSERTING YOUR AUTHORITY AS A READER AND WRITER

"I have nothing to say! It's all been said!" This lament is a familiar one. In the midst of a complicated reading and writing project, it is not unusual for any of us—students, teachers, or professional writers—to lose sight of our original goals and thus lose confidence that we have ideas worth writing about.

Throughout this book, we have argued that reading is an active, constructive process. We don't need to convince you that writing, too, is an active process; after all, to write, one must actually make words appear on a page or screen. Nevertheless, as we turn to the subject of connecting reading and writing, we need to warn you against **passive writing**, writing that just translates what is on someone else's page onto your page. Passive writing is packed full of summaries, paraphrases, and quotes (sometimes very lengthy quotes) but contains very little content from the writer. Writing that simply assembles other people's ideas but does not assert its author's reason for writing is not likely to give its audience a reason for reading.

Passive writing occurs when students get so immersed in reading published sources that they find it difficult to maintain their own sense of purpose as authors: they lose track of their **author-ity**, the state of being an **author**. Still worse, writers who are uncertain about a source text's content or purposes may begin to insert quotations or paraphrases into their own texts without clear purpose. Perhaps awed by the rush of facts and abstractions in materials they are reading, they yield their authority as both readers and writers to the previously published texts. They begin writing sentences that mouth the words of their sources, almost as a ventriloquist casts a voice into a dummy—but in this case, onto an inert page. In effect, these writers let themselves be silenced by the experts. Thus, they not only fail to gain their readers' confidence but they lose the opportunity to make their own contribution to the discussion.

As you work with the advice in this chapter, you will begin to discover a powerful truth: rhetorical reading leads to rhetorically powerful writing. Just as rhetorical reading involves analyzing and critiquing an author's method as well as content, rhetorically effective writing asserts its purpose and method along with its content. Strong writers use the knowledge and understanding gained from their reading to build their own authority so that they can, in turn, *author* their own texts. These strong texts will engage readers because they not only "say" clearly what they mean, but "do" what they intend: extend the conversation by providing information in a new way and asserting ideas that will alter their readers' view of the subject.

MANAGING YOUR WRITING PROCESS

To assert your authority as a writer, you need to think of writing as an active process of making new meaning, of adding your voice to an ongoing conversation about a subject. It is not just a matter of retrieving something that is fully formed in your own head or someone else's, nor is it a matter of finding other people's ideas to cobble together. Rather, it is a matter of finding a compelling reason to write—most often, a question worth exploring—then actively constructing a text that accomplishes that purpose.

Recognizing that the process of creating a text will vary from writer to writer and from situation to situation, we offer in this section a variety of strategies that will help you claim your own authority as a writer. Then, after we discuss different phases of developing a paper, we offer a number of highly practical tips in Table 6.1, "Strategies for Managing Your Writing Processes," on pages 118–122. The table follows the organization of our discussion in this section, from getting started and generating ideas to editing and polishing, including a section on "What to Do When You Get Stuck." We hope you will find the suggestions helpful. The table is designed so that you can refer to it whenever you want to nudge your writing or thinking processes forward as you are developing a paper.

Think of the strategies and processes we describe not as a series of steps to go through in a strictly linear fashion, but as a set of methods that is **recursive**—that is, these methods will enable you to curve back to revise and adjust earlier parts of a draft when you discover new angles or see a new way to refine how you stated important ideas.

Strategies for Getting Started

As a college writer, you are more likely to succeed when you can make an assignment your own. Instead of writing just to fulfill an assignment, you need to construct your own "take" on the subject. Imagine yourself writing to a real audience for a real purpose. To do this, create your own **exigence**—a term we first referred to back in Chapter 2 (p. 17) as part of explaining how important it is for rhetorical readers to analyze an author's purpose. When you take on the role of *writing* rhetorically, you must similarly focus on a purpose, this time your own intention to bring about some kind of change in your audience. Such changes can have a wide range—to correct a misunderstanding, to talk back to something someone else has said, to propose a solution to a problem, to explore and shed new light on an issue, to change your audience's thinking or attitudes, to make your audience appreciate something or value it differently, to call for action. Whether you are writing something long or short, thinking about how you want your readers to respond to your writing—your rhetorical aim—will help you come across more clearly.

Whatever kind of writing assignment you are given, the starting point of the writing process should be a problematic question or a risky claim. Although it might be tempting to start with ideas that are familiar or safe, that you are already firmly committed to or that are already settled in your mind, that approach usually leads to flat, perfunctory writing that fails to engage readers. The better approach is instead to start with a question that is genuinely puzzling to you, or with a tentative claim that provokes multiple perspectives and invites audience resistance or skepticism.

Strategies for Generating Ideas

Once you have identified a starting point, you will need to develop your ideas by analyzing more fully the single text you are writing about or by finding additional texts that can expand, deepen, and challenge your understanding of your research question. In either case, the rhetorical reading strategies in Chapters 3 and 4 should help you generate ideas. Remember that when you are writing to make a claim about a particular text (whether it is an assigned text or a research source you have found), it is important to re-read the text with your paper's starting point and purpose in mind. Be sure to note all the textual details you might use to support your own claim. Likewise, look for counterevidence that you may have missed on your first time through the text and that you will need to address in some way. Perhaps this counterevidence will cause you to qualify or soften your claim.

Conferencing with your teacher, peer group, or a writing center tutor is another good way to generate ideas for writing. When you try to explain your rough plans to someone else, it's likely you will discover new ideas along with connections that you didn't see before. Moreover, your conferencing partners will probably ask you questions that will trigger new lines of thinking or enable you to see gaps in your current thinking that may require further analysis or research. The questions listed in the first part of Table 6.1 (p. 118) are designed to help you discover such new approaches.

Strategies for Writing a First Draft

Good first drafts are usually messy, confusing, and imperfect. Fear of this messiness, or fear of the blank screen or page, often prevents writers from producing idea-generating early drafts and thus reduces the time available for multiple revisions. To get past such fears, think of your first draft as a **discovery draft**. Its purpose, in other words, is to extend the process of figuring out what you have to say and how to say it. You can work out some of the details later. A writer's most original ideas often appear in the final paragraph of these drafts, at the

STRUCTURE OF A CLASSICAL ARGUMENT

  I. Introduction or *Exordium*
       Explains the significance of the issue
 II. Narrative or *Narratio*
       Provides background information
       States the writer's thesis or claim
III. Partition or *Partitio*
       Maps the issues to be discussed
 IV. Confirmation or *Confirmatio*
       Supports the claim through a sequence of reasons and evidence
  V. Refutation or *Refutatio*
       Summarizes and responds to opposing views
 VI. Conclusion or *Peroration*
       Calls for action and relates the argument to larger issues

point where the writer finally recognized them. This is not a problem at the rough draft stage because your goal is simply to start working out ideas. On the next draft, you can move those ideas to a more prominent position in the paper as you reshape and refine your ideas.

If your paper assignment calls for a particular organizational format—such as a classical argument, a technical report, an evaluative review of literature—use that format as an idea-generating template for producing various parts of your text. The box above, for example, presents an outline for a classical argument. This kind of structure can help you build your first draft section by section. The specific requirements for each section will provide you with implicit questions to address in that section. When you write out the answers, you will have a discovery draft. You'll find good tips about drafting, including a helpful list of strategies for getting "unstuck," in Table 6.1 (see below).

Strategies for Evaluating Your Draft for Revision

Producing an initial draft is only the first step in producing a successful, polished paper. For most college assignments, success requires substantial revision through multiple drafts. Effective revision is not just minor repair or sentence correction but a matter of literally re-seeing a draft. This kind of re-seeing requires a critical distance that is not easy to achieve, so Table 6.1 offers specific techniques to help you see your text the way a reader might. As you gain experience as a writer, you will find that the urge to revise begins when you discover confusing passages, points that need more support or development, contradictions or flaws in thinking, gaps in your argument, places where the text fails to anticipate audience questions or objections, and so forth. Sometimes you will even decide to reword your thesis and reorganize.

Table 6.1 Strategies for Managing Your Writing Processes

Strategies for Getting Started

When responding to a text	When exploring your own research question:
Establish your own response using key questions.	Brainstorm a list of questions or problems that intrigue you.
• Is the author credible? What proves her credibility?	• Why does this question or problem matter? To whom?
• How is the author appealing to reason? What evidence does she provide?	• Do you expect to find agreement about answers? Uncertainty? Controversy?
• How is the author appealing to the reader's emotions, values, and interests? How can you tell?	• What do you expect to find as points of disagreement or uncertainty?
• What language is the author using? What does that say about her intent?	• What kinds of experts will have good answers?
• What visuals are included? How do they interact with the text?	• Where will you find good information?

Table 6.1 Strategies for Managing Your Writing Processes (*continued*)

• What does the text reveal about the author's ideology?	• Who (individuals or interest groups) has a major stake in answering your question in certain ways?

What change do you want to bring about in your readers' thinking?

- What is your broad aim in this text you will write? Informing? Interpreting? Persuading? (See Table 2.1.)
- Why is this change in your audience's thinking important?
- Do you want readers to see an inconsistency or contradiction?
- Do you want to ensure readers aren't fooled by a ploy or faulty reasoning?
- Do you want to highlight the broad significance of a claim?

Strategies for Getting Ideas

When responding to a text	When exploring your own research question:
Develop your ideas by analyzing the text you're writing about.	Develop your ideas by finding texts that will deepen and challenge your understanding of your question.
• Whose minds is the text trying to change, about what, and why?	• How will a given source advance your purpose for writing?
• Whose minds are you trying to change, about what, and why?	• Does it provide background information?
• What information will help you establish your credibility?	• Does it provide a perspective on framing the discussion?
• How can you make your readers concerned about your topic?	• Does it provide support for your claims?
	• Does it provide a new perspective?

(*continued*)

Table 6.1 Strategies for Managing Your Writing Processes (*continued*)

Strategies for Generating Ideas (*Continued*)

- What kind of supporting evidence will be persuasive to your readers?
- What values or interests do you share with your readers?
- What differences in opinions or values might you need to try to overcome?

- Does the source provide a compelling example or illustration of a point?
- Does it provide solid evidence you can refer to?

Remember: Conferencing with your teacher, peer reviewers, or a writing center tutor can be a great way to generate ideas.

Strategies for Writing a First Draft

- Try to produce a complete first draft without worrying about perfection.
- Use formats for specific genres (e.g., a classical argument, lab report, literature review, etc.) to establish sections you can fill in.
- Create an outline with a bulleted list of important points you want to make.
- Use color, lines, and arrows to connect related ideas and source texts.
- If you have trouble with introductions, start somewhere else with a point you feel strongly about.
- Plan on rewriting your opening paragraph once you have a nearly complete draft.
- Turn off spelling and grammar checkers while you are drafting.

What to Do When You Get Stuck

- Make notes to yourself in caps about the problem ("NEED TRANSITION") and move on.
- If you have a vague idea but can't figure out how to say it, freewrite in caps or color, "WHAT I REALLY WANT TO SAY IS… ."
- Open a second file and complain there about why you are stuck. Moving away from your text is likely to help you figure out a solution.
- Silence your internal critic by turning off your computer monitor so you can't see what you're writing, then spill out your unpolished ideas. When you turn the screen back on, fill in gaps and straighten out the sentences.
- Try talking out your draft with someone who will take notes or record you. You can often discover what you have to say better by talking than by writing.

Table 6.1 Strategies for Managing Your Writing Processes (*continued*)

Strategies for Evaluating Your Drafts for Revision

Techniques to Help You Adopt a Reader's Perspective

- Print your draft and read it from hard copy, annotating for problems and ideas for revision.
- Try to "listen" to your own text in some of the ways outlined in Chapter 3.
  - Make a descriptive outline of its major chunks.
  - Draw an idea map.
  - Write a rhetorical précis.
- For papers that call for a thesis-support structure, make sure your support paragraphs connect back to your thesis statement clearly and directly.

Strategies for Peer Response and Revision

Tips for Offering Feedback to Others

Respond honestly and productively.

- Address the writer's specific requests for feedback.
- Offer comments from a *reader's* perspective.
- Make sure that your comments are text-specific, not general.
- Identify specific points that were unclear and try to explain the questions they raised for you.
- Be selective. Choose only two or three major concerns to comment on in detail.
- Respond at the level of ideas, not "grammar" issues or punctuation.
- Ask questions to help the writer generate ideas for clarification and support, and to help the writer extend and complicate her thinking.
- Play devil's advocate: introduce objections or other points of view to help the writer make a more convincing argument.

Get a sense of the whole before formulating your responses.

- If someone is reading a draft aloud, listen to the whole draft before taking notes.
- Listen twice, making notes during the second reading so you can confirm or rethink your first impressions.
- Record your responses in three columns: positive comments, negative comments, and questions.
- If you are reading silently, read the paper through completely, using lines or marginal notes to mark passages you want to look at again or comment on.
- Use a second reading to fill out a peer-response form or decide on the most constructive feedback you might offer.

Table 6.1 Strategies for Managing Your Writing Processes (*continued*)

Strategies for Evaluating Your Drafts for Revision

Tips for Using Peer Feedback to Revise

Let your peer responders know what concerns you about the draft—your goal is to learn how it comes across to readers.

- Ask for feedback in terms of your rhetorical aim.
- Ask your peer responders whether your text accomplished your intended purpose.
- Ask specific questions about passages that you have already identified as problematic.
- Keep an open mind as you listen to peer responses.
- Don't waste time by trying to defend what you've written.
- Expect some contradictory feedback. "Try on" any differing perspectives to determine what in the text is causing them.

Use peer feedback to develop a revision plan.

- Weigh the feedback and decide for yourself where and how to revise.
- What does the feedback tell you about the draft's successes and failures?
- Which responses are the most important to address first?
- Attend to higher-order concerns (focus, organization, development of ideas, logic) before lower-order concerns (sentence-level, grammatical, and mechanical problems).

Strategies for Editing and Polishing the Final Draft

See what's really on the page, not what you hope is there.

- Read your text aloud to yourself or someone else to catch missing words, wrong words, and other kinds of errors.
- Have someone else read your paper back to you. Listen for unclear sentences and awkward wording.
- To slow down your reading, read your paper line by line. Use another sheet of paper to cover the text you have not yet read.
- Keep track of the kinds of errors you habitually make, and be on the lookout for these errors as you proofread.
- Use computerized spelling, grammar, or style aids as only *one* of several steps in your editing process.
- Have a friend or classmate read over your final paper because no matter how careful you are, you may miss some errors.

Strategies for Peer Response and Revision

One of the best ways to see your text differently is through another reader's eyes. Because you know what you meant to write, it is often difficult to see any gaps or confusing points in what is actually on the page. Other readers, not privy to your inner thoughts, can spot these issues much more readily. Peer-response groups allow you to receive feedback from a "live" audience, whether this feedback comes in the form of written or face-to-face oral comments.

The benefits of working in a peer-response group go beyond the insights you gain about your own draft; you also benefit from the experience of offering feedback to others. For one thing, you can learn to recognize and understand various kinds of writing problems by seeing them in someone else's writing. This understanding, with practice, helps you detect those problems when they crop up in your own writing. In addition, offering constructive feedback helps you develop a language for talking about what's working in a text and what's not. This language, in turn, helps you analyze your own writing. Put simply, receiving and giving peer response enables you to achieve the kind of critical distance on your own writing that is so crucial to effective revision.

Perhaps the most frequent complaint we hear from student writers about peer-response groups is that the responders didn't offer any real feedback but instead offered vague, polite comments. To help you make the most of suggestions from peer reviewers and to help you help others with their drafts, Table 6.1 offers a number of suggestions for listening, reading, and responding specifically and productively.

Strategies for Editing and Polishing Your Final Draft

College professors expect final drafts that are carefully edited and proofread. Editing can be difficult, however, because most of us have trouble recognizing the surface errors in our own writing—omitted words, spelling and punctuation errors, wrong or repeated words. We literally fail to see what is on the page; instead, we substitute what we intended to write for what is there. Consequently, you must train yourself to detect and correct errors in sentence structure, word choice, spelling, punctuation, citation conventions, and grammar or usage.

Cautionary advice about computerized proofreading aids: Do not rely solely on grammar and spell checkers to detect the errors in your paper. Spelling checkers, for example, do not detect homonym errors—*its* when you need *it's*—and they don't flag misspellings that turn out to be correctly spelled words that are not what you meant—*cant* for *want*. Similarly, grammar checkers mechanically mark things like passive voice or repeated words that may actually be appropriate in a particular context. For example, the computer highlighted the second *that* in the following sentence: "I believe that that is wrong." But this sentence might be perfectly appropriate in a context where it is clear what the second *that* refers to. Remember that grammar checkers do not actually understand language. To check on word choices, punctuation, grammar, and usage rules as well as citation conventions, keep at hand a recently published handbook. In addition, use an online or paper dictionary to *be sure* a word that you do not often use means what you think it does. Researchers are finding that this kind of error is becoming more frequent. Thus, avoid embarrassment by *never* using a word you find through a thesaurus unless you first double-check its meaning in a separate dictionary.

Finally, because grammar software can flag so many items that don't really need your attention, if you are going to use it, we strongly advise you to wait until you have an almost final draft before you do so. Table 6.1 offers additional tips for focusing on specifics as you polish your final drafts.

INTEGRATING MATERIAL FROM READINGS INTO YOUR WRITING

The effective use of sources in your papers will enable you to position your ideas in relation to those of others and will establish your credibility as an informed writer. Success in this aspect of your writing will be measured by your ability to incorporate the words and ideas of others judiciously (keeping readers' attention on *your* points), smoothly (using clear, grammatically correct sentences), and correctly (representing the points and language of your sources without distortion). Our detailed advice for accomplishing this is summarized with a list of "Do's and Don'ts" in Table 6.2 on page 125. Because each technique serves a useful and distinct purpose, you should become adept at all three so that you can choose the one that best suits a specific purpose within a paper. How you use sources in your texts should result from careful rhetorical choices.

Using Summary

Probably the most common way of incorporating a source into your own writing is through **summary**. As we described in Chapter 3, the reason for summarizing all or part of another writer's text is to present in your own words a condensed version of that writer's points in a way that connects to your own ongoing discussion.

It is best to introduce a summary of others' work with a phrase that alerts the reader to the fact that what follows comes from an outside source, and you must provide an accurate reference that pinpoints where others can find that source. Summarizing is an especially effective rhetorical strategy in the following situations:

- When the source directly supports your thesis, presents ideas you will analyze, or offers a position you wish to argue against
- When the source offers important background information for your ideas
- When you need to provide readers with an overview of a source's whole argument before analyzing particular ideas from it
- When you want to condense and clarify information from a source

The length of your summary will depend on its location and function in your paper. Your goals for your paper will dictate how much of a source you need to summarize. Consider what you want the summary to *do* to move your own points forward. (See pp. 56–60 in Chapter 3 for more details about preparing summaries. You may also want to consult the discussion of the differences between what texts *do* and *say* on pp. 53–55.)

To illustrate how length can vary with purpose, let's examine two summaries of different lengths in Abby's rhetorical analysis of Atul Gawande's op-ed argument, "A Lifesaving

Table 6.2 Do's and Don'ts with Summaries, Paraphrases, and Quotation

When You Summarize	Do	Don't
	• Make your summary as concise as possible • Represent your source's meaning accurately and fairly	• Distract readers by including points not directly relevant to your purpose
When You Paraphrase	**Do**	**Don't**
	• Paraphrase only what you need to develop your points • Be sure you understand the l anguage you are paraphrasing • Recast sentences to create a genuine paraphrase	• Merely change a few words • Distort the original's meaning or intention
When You Quote	**Do**	**Don't**
	• Keep the actual quotation as short as possible • Fit the quotation naturally into your own sentence structure • Verify the absolute accuracy of the quotation	• Use quotes as a shortcut around difficult ideas • Distract readers with long quotes

When You Summarize

- Link your text to your sources with clear attributive tags and appropriate citations.
- Represent the source fairly and accurately.

Checklist." (Abby's paper, "A Surprising Checklist," is located at the end of Chapter 4, pp. 91–94.) Abby sets the context for her analysis essay with a very brief summary in her opening sentence. Notice how Abby's nutshell version of Gawande's piece echoes her own title theme of "surprise."

Summary Example 1

For many *New York Times* readers, it must have been somewhat surprising to encounter Atul Gawande's December 30, 2007, op-ed article criticizing a little known U.S. government office for endangering lives when it ordered a halt to research on the effectiveness of a medical checklist.

In the second example, Abby uses a longer, detailed summary of Gawande's final paragraph to comment on how his reasoning unfolds overall. She includes brief quotes for further illustration.

Summary Example 2

Gawande suggests, but never quite says exactly, that stopping the research on the checklist's usefulness violates scientific ethics. In his final paragraph, he almost says it when he asserts that the OHRP authorities are "in danger of putting ethics bureaucracy in the way of actual ethical medical care" (par. 11). His next assertions are even more direct. First, he calls for the research to continue "unencumbered." Then, in his final sentence, he says that if the agency won't allow this to happen, "Congress will have to" (par. 11). It sounds almost like a threat of punishment.

Cautionary advice: We offer two cautions about writing summaries. First, you should summarize only the points that are essential to your purpose. Summaries that are too long or that cover too many points will distract readers from the main flow of your text. Second, make sure that your summary fairly and accurately represents the original text's meaning. Be on guard against distorting the original to make it fit your argument.

In the second example, Abby uses a longer, detailed summary of Gawande's final paragraph to comment on how his reasoning unfolds overall. She includes brief quotes for further illustration.

Here's the ultimate take-away about a good summary: Ask yourself whether the original author would consider your summary to be fair and accurate.

Using Paraphrase

Unlike a summary, in which you condense the original text's ideas, a **paraphrase** restates in your own words the entirety of the original passage's point. Because paraphrases follow the original wording closely, you must cite the source by page number, if one is available. Often, paraphrases are as long as or even longer than the original, so it is best to paraphrase only short passages.

Paraphrasing is a particularly valuable rhetorical strategy in the following situations:

- When you want to emphasize especially significant ideas by retaining all of the points or details from the original
- When you want to clarify ideas that are complex or language that is dense, technical, or hard to understand

---

Box 6.1 Guidelines for Effective Paraphrase

☐ Avoid mirroring the sentence structure or organization of the original.

☐ Simplify complex ideas by pulling them apart and explaining each smaller component of the larger idea.

☐ Use synonyms for key words in the original and replace unfamiliar or technical vocabulary with more familiar terms.

☐ As a check, try paraphrasing the passage twice, the second time paraphrasing your own paraphrase; then compare your second paraphrase with the original to make sure that you have sufficiently recast it into your own language.

Because paraphrase involves closely re-presenting the original text, you must take care not to give the impression that these are your ideas. Refer to the source at the beginning of the paraphrase. Putting someone else's ideas into your own words does not make these ideas your own. To paraphrase effectively and ethically, you must translate the writer's wording entirely into your own words and acknowledge the source with an attributive tag and a citation. In the guidelines Box 6.1 above, we recommend paraphrasing twice: once from the source, then again from your own paraphrase.

To illustrate the process and rhetorical effects of paraphrasing, we invite you to consider the parallels and variations between a passage from Jack's paper about multiple perspectives on corn-based ethanol, located at the end of this chapter (pp. 140–146), and one of his sources.

Dialog from the Online Transcript of a *NewsHour* Video[1]

[IOWA] SEN. TOM HARKIN: You're going to see a lot of marginal land that's not suitable for row crop production, because it's hilly, or it's not very productive for corn or soybeans, things like that, but it can be very productive for grasses, like miscanthus, or switchgrass, and you can use that to make the cellulose ethanol.

HEIDI CULLEN: And using such land for growing fuel can help with the carbon dioxide problem, for in turning these kinds of plant materials into ethanol, you eliminate the need to use land suitable for food, feed for animals, and fiber for paper.

---

[1] Heidi Cullen, "In Iowa, Questions Arise About the Impact of Ethanol Production." *Online NewsHour*. PBS, 28 Jan. 2009. Web.

Jack recognized this exchange as important to the issue of "food-versus-fuel" land use, but knew that trying to introduce Senator Harkin and quote him would take up too much space and throw off his organizational strategy. The information about where these crops could be grown was more important than the fact that Senator Harkin provided the information. So Jack decided to paraphrase and cite the Cullen video, knowing that anyone who wanted to follow up could find more detail simply by searching in the transcript for "switchgrass." Notice that he has been able to boil down the points to a concise paraphrase and thus use this paraphrase to elaborate on the point that moves his paper from his third major issue to his fourth.

Jack's Paraphrase

For people concerned about the fourth issue, using food crop acreage to grow fuel crops, the prospect of cellulosic ethanol offers great hope. For one thing, using products other than corn kernels for ethanol production has the advantage that many of these alternative crops, such as switchgrass (ordinarily grown for hay), can be grown on "marginal" or hilly land where food crops cannot be grown (Cullen).

Cautionary advice: Paraphrasing difficult ideas or dense passages is a good way not only to help your readers understand material but also to demonstrate your own understanding of it. However, recasting scholarly or technical language can be difficult. We offer advice on three points. (1) Take care to avoid the problem of inadequate paraphrase. If your paraphrase is too close to the original wording, you may open yourself to a charge of plagiarism. (2) To avoid the potential problem of inaccurate presentation, be sure you fully understand any passage you are paraphrasing. One valuable technique is to imagine how you would convey the gist of the source's point conversationally. If you can't move beyond the words of the original, it's likely that you need to obtain a better understanding of the ideas before you use them in your paper. Quoting is not the way to solve this problem. In fact, quoting an entire passage can actually make matters worse. Long quotations suggest that you find the original points so daunting that you cannot put them into your own words. (3) As with summary, be concise: Paraphrase from the original only what you need to develop your points in detail. A long paraphrase can draw so much attention to itself that it distracts the reader. Instead, keep readers focused on your ideas about how the source material fits your points.

Using Direct Quotation

Direct quotation inserts the words of someone else into your own text. Whenever you use another writer's exact wording, you must mark the beginning and end of the passage with quotation marks and provide as precise a reference to the original source as possible. Used selectively and sparingly, quotations strengthen your credibility by showing that you have consulted appropriate authorities on a particular subject. However, quoting too frequently or using unnecessarily long quotations can actually undermine your credibility. Overreliance on direct quotations weakens your authority and suggests that you have no ideas of your own to contribute to the conversation.

Direct quotations are most effective in enhancing your credibility in the following situations:

- When the language of the source is vivid, distinctive, or memorable
- When the quotation directly supports a key point in your paper
- When the person quoted is such a well-known authority on the matter that even a few well-chosen words will carry considerable weight

To illustrate the value of keeping quotations short, we present two versions of a passage from Jack's ethanol paper. In his first draft, Jack wanted to develop his first major point, that production of corn ethanol uses extensive petroleum resources, by including an exchange from an online discussion. In a draft, he tried out the long quotation in the following passage.

Ineffective Long Quotation from Jack's First Draft

Responding to a questioner who asked whether "the EROEI [energy return on energy investment] on corn ethanol [is] such that it is a feasible candidate to replace petroleum for some of our energy needs," Robert P. Anex, associate director of the Office of Biorenewables Programs at Iowa State University, said, "The energy return on energy investment (EROEI) of corn grain ethanol is positive (the 'ethanol fuel energy out to fossil energy in' ratio is about 1.3), but ethanol is not the goal of a biofuels program. The goals are things like enhanced national security, improved environmental quality, and local economic development. For example, [a 2006 article published in *Science*] *Farrell* et al., found that corn grain ethanol does much better at displacing petroleum use than at displacing fossil energy but really excels at reducing greenhouse gas emissions. Ultimately, we cannot achieve our goals through corn grain ethanol alone, but corn ethanol has developed a biofuel market and has thereby made possible corporate investment in cellulosic ethanol that can have a much larger positive impact on the multiple goals associated with biofuels development" (Brainard).[2]

---

[2]Jeffrey Brainard, "The Race to Harvest Energy." *Chronicle of Higher Education: Live Discussions.* Chronicle of Higher Education, 24 Apr. 2007. Web. 30 Mar. 2009. Transcript.

As you can see, by quoting the dialog, especially with the necessary bracketed explanations, Jack risked losing control of his paper. He recognized Anex's response as highly important to his ultimate points—here was an expert indicating both the usefulness and limits of corn ethanol in the evolving story of clean biofuels. But the phrasing was unique to the context of the discussion, and, as he recognized, it was too long to quote. He had to decide which was the most important of Anex's several points, then help his readers understand that point and its importance. Here is Jack's revision, which cuts the original version (184 words) by two-thirds, to 62 words. More important still is that the way in which he establishes context for the quote within his own paper prevents his source from taking over the paragraph.

Jack's Revised Use of Quotation

A University of Iowa scientist explains away the problem of corn ethanol's resource intensity as "just a step along the way" (Brainard). In a Web discussion sponsored by the *Chronicle of Higher Education*, Robert P. Anex, associate director of the Office of Biorenewables Programs at Iowa State, said the real goals are "enhanced national security, improved environmental quality, and local economic development."[3]

The guidelines in Box 6.2 on page 131 will help you quote accurately and effectively.

Cautionary advice: First, not only is absolute accuracy in quotations important ethically, but any inaccuracies will undermine your credibility. Second, be sure that you are not quoting someone out of context. Doing so is a surprisingly common mistake because complex texts or unfamiliar subject matter can make it difficult to recognize changes in tone or references to opposing views. Be sure that the way you use a quotation does not misconstrue or misinterpret its original meaning.

For Writing and Discussion

One way to develop skill at incorporating the ideas of others into your own papers is to see how other writers do it. To try this out, track the use of direct quotations in Jack's paper at the end of this chapter.

---

[3]Jack does not need to include a parenthetical cite after the second sentence in which he quotes Anex because it can only be understood as from the same original passage. Providing the parenthetical citation after the first quote-containing sentence lets the reader know the source right away.

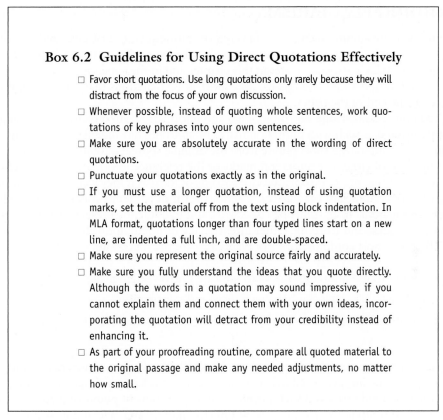

Box 6.2 Guidelines for Using Direct Quotations Effectively

☐ Favor short quotations. Use long quotations only rarely because they will distract from the focus of your own discussion.

☐ Whenever possible, instead of quoting whole sentences, work quotations of key phrases into your own sentences.

☐ Make sure you are absolutely accurate in the wording of direct quotations.

☐ Punctuate your quotations exactly as in the original.

☐ If you must use a longer quotation, instead of using quotation marks, set the material off from the text using block indentation. In MLA format, quotations longer than four typed lines start on a new line, are indented a full inch, and are double-spaced.

☐ Make sure you represent the original source fairly and accurately.

☐ Make sure you fully understand the ideas that you quote directly. Although the words in a quotation may sound impressive, if you cannot explain them and connect them with your own ideas, incorporating the quotation will detract from your credibility instead of enhancing it.

☐ As part of your proofreading routine, compare all quoted material to the original passage and make any needed adjustments, no matter how small.

On Your Own

Note all the places where Jack uses direct quotations, and describe how each quotation is used—what it *does*. Find places, for example, where he uses sources to support or illustrate one of his points, to represent an opinion he admires, to increase his credibility, or to capture vivid or distinctive language from a source. Some of his direct quotations may serve more than one function.

With Your Classmates

Compare your lists and descriptions. Are there differences or disagreements about how a particular direct quotation is being used? How effectively does Jack use quotations? Are there any quotations that might have been eliminated or shortened? Are there any places where you think his paper might have been strengthened by the use of a direct quotation where there isn't one?

AVOIDING PLAGIARISM

Whether you are summarizing, paraphrasing, or quoting, you must give credit to others' words and ideas by using a recognized system for referring readers to your sources. One such system is the MLA's, explained later in this chapter and in the appendix. The MLA system, widely used in undergraduate classes, uses short in-text citations that refer to a full list of sources at the end of the paper.

You must acknowledge borrowed ideas and information. All directly quoted language must be marked as such with quotation marks or appropriately indented formatting. Even if you are quoting only a short phrase from the original source, quotation marks are essential. Omission of either the quotation marks or the reference information has the effect of creating a text that presents someone else's words or ideas as if they were your own. In that case, you are committing **plagiarism**, a serious form of academic misconduct in which a writer takes material from someone else's work and fraudulently presents it as if it were the writer's own ideas and wording, either intentionally or unintentionally.

The three most common forms of plagiarism are the following:

- Failure to use quotation marks to indicate borrowed language
- Failure to acknowledge borrowed ideas and information
- Failure to change the language of the source text sufficiently in a paraphrase

Student writers sometimes have problems managing the details of quotations because they neglect to take careful notes that clearly mark all directly quoted material. During their revision processes, inexperienced writers sometimes lose track of which sentences and phrases are directly quoted. To avoid such problems and symptoms of potential plagiarism, make sure you take scrupulous care to mark all directly quoted language and its source in your notes and drafts. **Write down all relevant bibliographic information even before you begin reading and taking notes.** This is especially important if you are "taking notes" by copying and pasting material from an electronic source into a notes file. Some writers use color highlighting for this process, or put directly quoted language in a different font so that, as they move passages around during drafting and revision, they can keep track of which words are directly quoted even if the quotation marks disappear when changes are made. Other writers keep full original quotations at the end of the paper file or in a separate electronic file so that they can check for accuracy and proper citation as part of their final preparations before submission.

You must acknowledge borrowed ideas and information through appropriate citation. That is, all ideas and information that are not your own—including statistics—require citation through attributive tags, internal citation, and the list of sources at the end of the paper. The only exception is common knowledge. Common knowledge, as the phrase suggests, refers to information and knowledge that is widely known. (For example: George Washington was the first U.S. president, or thunderstorms are more likely in hot weather.) You can verify that certain information is common knowledge by consulting general information sources such as encyclopedias. If you are in doubt about whether something is common knowledge, or if you are concerned that your readers might credit an idea to you that is not yours, refer to and cite the source.

Perhaps the most difficult aspect of incorporating sources in a way that avoids plagiarism is sufficiently rewording the language of a source when you paraphrase. (This is why we recommend paraphrasing source material twice.) As we noted in the section on paraphrase, using the same sentence pattern as the original source and changing only a few words does not create an acceptable paraphrase, even if the writer includes a reference to the source. In the following examples, compare the acceptable and unacceptable paraphrases with the original passage from the *Consumer Reports* article "The Ethanol Myth," a major source for Jack's paper.

Original Passage From Source

The FFV surge is being motivated by generous fuel-economy credits that automakers get for every FFV they build, even if it never runs on E85. This allows them to pump out more gas-guzzling large SUVs and pickups, which is resulting in the consumption of many times more gallons of gasoline than E85 now replaces.[4]

Unacceptable Paraphrase—Too Close to the Original
Syntax and Word Choices

The increase in FFV production is caused by big fuel-economy credits that automakers get for every FFV, which are gas-guzzling large SUVs and pickups, which results in consuming many more gallons of gasoline than E85 replaces ("Ethanol Myth" 16).

Acceptable Paraphrase

...the article strongly criticizes federal tax breaks for FFV manufacturers, arguing that the tax breaks have encouraged automakers to overproduce FFVs, most of which happen to be large, inefficient SUVs and pickups. Because of the shortage of E85 gas stations, FFVs run most of the time on regular gasoline, making advertisements about their being innovative "an empty promise," the writers say (16). The result, according to *CR*, is "the consumption of many times more gallons of gasoline than E85 now replaces" (16).

---

[4]"The Ethanol Myth." *Consumer Reports* Oct. 2006: 15–19. EbscoHost. Web. 3 Apr. 2009.

Jack's revision serves as a model of what to do when paraphrasing is difficult:

1. He added phrasing that links the key point to his source's overall point.
2. He combined the points in the passage that he had trouble paraphrasing with relevant information elsewhere in the source, including direct quotes of two powerful phrases.

By following the guidelines we present for quoting and paraphrasing, you can avoid plagiarism. We close this section by passing along a final bit of advice: when you are incorporating materials from outside sources, write with your eyes on your own text, not on your source's sentences.[5] Your unfolding text should come from your mind, not someone else's text.

USING ATTRIBUTIVE TAGS TO FRAME SOURCES RHETORICALLY

All three of the techniques we have described for incorporating source material—summary, paraphrase, and quotation—work best with **attributive tags**. These are short phrases or tags that connect or attribute material to its source, for example, "Ariel Jones says …" or "According to Ariel Jones…."In the process of acknowledging the source, the tags can also enhance the rhetorical effect of your text by giving readers valuable information about the credibility of your sources, shaping your readers' response to it, and demonstrating that you, not your sources, are in charge. The following discussion explains how these phrases can do all this.[6] Specific guidelines for composing tags are provided in Box 6.3.

1. Attributive tags help readers distinguish your sentences and ideas from those in your sources (whether summarized, paraphrased, or quoted). In fact, a lack of attributive tags is often symptomatic of the passive writing we have been warning against. As illustration, let's consider the difference between two versions of a sentence from Jack's paper.

Confusion Caused by Lack of Attributive Tag

The ethanol boom has led farmers to give up subsidies that the Conservation Reserve Program had previously paid them to keep land out of production. "When this land is planted with corn, all of the carbon that's stored in these prairie grasses and in these trees is released back into the atmosphere" (Cullen)

---

[5]This advice comes from *The Craft of Research* by Wayne Booth, Gregory Colomb, and Joseph Williams, who say, "If your eyes are on your source at the same moment your fingers are flying across the keyboard, you risk doing something that weeks, months, even years later could result in your public humiliation" (Chicago: U Chicago P, 1995), 170. Print.

[6]We are grateful to freelance writer Robert McGuire, formerly a writing instructor at Marquette University, for his valuable insights and advice about attributive tags.

In the above passage, the reader expects a citation for the information in the first sentence. The reader is likely to be confused, therefore, when the next sentence opens with a quotation, signaling that another voice has entered the text. The reader doesn't know where the quoted material comes from and may not recall the name cited at the end from earlier in the paper. If curious, one would have to go to the works cited list.

But the following revised version is much better because the attributive tag in the introductory prepositional phrase refers back to the source ("Cullen") identified earlier in the paragraph. Now the reader knows that Cullen is the source for the information in the first sentence and is also the person quoted in the second sentence:

Sentence Revised with Attributive Tag

As Cullen explains in her video, the ethanol boom has led farmers to give up subsidies that the federal government had previously paid them in order to preserve land by keeping it out of production. "When this land is planted with corn," she notes, "all of the carbon that's stored in these prairie grasses and in these trees is released back into the atmosphere."

Box 6.3 Guidelines for Using Attributive Tags Effectively

☐ Make the tag part of your own sentence.

☐ The first time you bring in a particular source, put the tag before the quotation or summary so that readers will have the background they need when they reach the borrowed source material.

☐ Vary the format and vocabulary of your tags. You want to avoid a long string of phrases that repeat "according to" or "he says."

☐ Provide just enough background to help readers understand the significance of the material you are bringing in, not everything there is to say about the source.

☐ Base your decisions about attributive tags on what you are confident readers will recognize and what will help them understand the relevance of the source you are using. For example, *Time* is a well-known magazine and the *Journal of Urban History* has a self-explanatory title, so using those titles in a tag would probably provide more context than an author's name would. However, stating that an article appeared in a journal with an ambiguous title—we are aware of at least three periodicals named *Dialogue*, for example—would prob-

> ably be pointless without further explanation. In many cases, rather than use space explaining the audience for and purpose of the journal, it would be preferable to supply a brief context-setting phrase about the author's background or about how the material you are using fits the larger published conversation.

2. Attributive tags enhance your credibility by showing readers that you are careful with source materials and remain in charge of the paper. You are the one lining up and tying together source materials to fit your purposes for writing.

3. Attributive tags can enhance your text's credibility by indicating the credentials or reputation of an expert you are using as a source. For example, you might say "high school teacher Sam Delaney," "Molly Smith, an avid fan of romance literature," or "Josephine DeLoria, a controversial defense lawyer." Sometimes, credentials will convey more information than a name will: "the Justice Department's main espionage prosecutor for over twenty years."

4. Attributive tags provide a quick method of showing readers the published context of your source material. This context will help you show how the text you are writing fits within a published conversation. Here are some examples: "In her review of Victoria M. Johnson's book, Martha Smith argues…," "Kim Ochimuru, in an article detailing the results of the Harvard study, contends… ," or "A letter to the editor objecting to the paper's editorial stance outlines the following complaint."

5. Attributive tags give you the opportunity to shape readers' responses to the material you are presenting. The verb you choose to describe the source's influence is important because it will suggest your attitude toward the source. Some verbs suggest that you agree with the source; others suggest doubt about what the source says. For example, the first of the following examples conveys the writer's positive attitude toward the source material being introduced; the second conveys a skeptical attitude, leading the reader to expect that the writer will counter the source's point:

> A July 2009 *Time* magazine article verifies this claim.
>
> Some literary critics claim that the books depend too much on magic.

Attributive tags work best near the beginning of a sentence, but can be placed after other introductory phrases at any natural break. Here are some examples of tags placed at different points in sentences:

> Published as a *Newsweek* online exclusive, Kliff's article...
>
> The result of the automakers' tax breaks and the difficulty of finding E85 fuel,
> *Consumer Reports* says, is...
>
> The Union of Concerned Scientists (UCS) notes, for example,...

Your first attributive tag about a source is likely to be longer than subsequent ones, as illustrated by these contrasting examples from Jack's paper:

> As reporter Heidi Cullen explains in a PBS *NewsHour* video,...
>
> As Cullen explains in her video...
>
> Here's the explanation that an Iowa farmer gave Cullen...

In some instances, an author's name may not be as interesting or important to your readers as the place where an article appeared. For example, the reference to the *NewsHour* in the first example tells readers much more than Cullen's name alone would have, either in the sentence or in the parenthetical citation. The same kind of informativeness comes from the periodical title in the following example:

> A July 2000 *Time* magazine article verifies this claim and reports that over
> 50% of all paperbacks sold in the United States each year are romance
> novels (Gray and Sachs 76).

As the preceding examples illustrate, attributive tags can offer a variety of information in accordance with a writer's purpose and sense of the intended audience's background knowledge. The possibilities range from facts that appear in citations (e.g., author's name, work's title, publisher, or date) to supplementary details about the author (e.g., credentials or purpose) or about the work (e.g., its context or reputation since publication). Of course, if you used all this information in one tag, the sentence would have hardly any room left for your own ideas. You do not want to overwhelm your readers with details that do not immediately convey significance. Readers can always find complete titles and publication information on your works cited list. If you decide readers need a lot of background, you may want to provide it in a separate sentence, as Jack does when he introduces the *Consumer Reports* article that he will refer back to frequently in his paper:

> A careful, consumer-focused exploration of both the negatives and posi-
> tives of corn ethanol as fuel was published by *Consumer Reports* (*CR*) in
> 2006, during the war in Iraq, a time when alternative fuels and vehicles
> that could use them were being widely discussed. This magazine is known
> as a watchdog, a guide to help consumers make wise purchases, especially
> on big budget items such as automobiles. The article focuses primarily on
> road tests of flex fuel vehicles (FFVs)....

USING PARENTHETICAL CITATIONS

Clear, accurate **citations** of outside sources are an essential element of academic writing. Designed to help readers locate source materials, citations present a formalized statement of a work's author, title, publication date, publisher, medium of publication, and exact location—that is, page numbers and/or an Internet address. As we explained in the section on avoiding plagiarism, citations are required for statistics, quotations, paraphrases, and summaries of other writers' work and ideas—any information that is not common knowledge.

Although discussions of citations tend to focus on their formal properties, it is important to recognize that they have rhetorical functions as well. Citations enhance your own credibility because they reveal the quality of the sources you have used. By positioning your ideas within a published conversation, they help guide your reader's response to your text. When handled well, they enhance a text's readability as well as your own credentials as an academic writer.

Understanding Academic Citation Conventions[7]

All academic disciplines require that you cite sources, but different disciplines use different formats, known as **citation conventions**. These conventions specify particular formats for presenting information that refers readers to a source. In this book, we discuss the Modern Language Association (MLA) format, used widely in the humanities. The MLA system, updated in 2009, relies on brief **in-text** or **parenthetical citations** in the body of the paper to signal that material has come from an outside source. The full citation for that source is found readily via an alphabetical list of authors' last names from all citations in the paper placed at the paper's end and entitled "Works Cited." These complete citations convey two important pieces of information to readers: (1) what kinds of materials the writer used as a basis for the current text, and (2) exactly where the material used in the paper can be found.

In-text citations are placed in parentheses to minimize the intrusion of bibliographic information on the reading experience. If a writer has followed citation conventions care-

---

[7]Our discussion here and in the appendix is based on the *MLA Handbook for Writers of Research Papers*, 7th ed. (New York: MLA, 2009). Print.

fully, readers hardly notice the cites as they read but can return to use them to find additional information efficiently. Here's an example from Jack's paper.

MLA In-Text Citation

... called for expansion of research on emissions "to include a broad array of environmental quality dimensions" (Hill et al. 1081).

Authors' names inside the parentheses tell readers where to find the full citation of the work on the alphabetized works cited list at the end of the paper.

Corresponding Full Citation on MLA Works Cited List

Hill, Jason, et al. "Climate Change and Health Costs of Air Emissions from Biofuels and Gasoline." *Proceedings of the National Academy of Science* 106.6 (2009): 1077–1082. *PubMed Central*. Web. 6 Apr. 2009.

The specific page number in the parenthetical in-text citation allows the reader to pinpoint the cited material.

Before we go any further, we want to assure you that the details of citation conventions are not something to memorize. Scholars regularly consult models and guidelines such as those in this chapter and the appendix. You should do the same.

The content of citations communicates important information about the context and purpose of sources, and thus about the reliability and authority of the source materials. When you read scholarly articles in specialized courses for your major, you will discover that citations are also an invaluable source of information about where you can find additional resources for research projects.

In some courses, particularly history, instead of in-text citations you may be asked to use footnotes that follow the format laid out in the *Chicago Manual of Style* (also called Turabian format, after the author whose handbooks popularized it). Furthermore, professors in the social sciences might ask you to follow specialized conventions for their discipline, particularly the parenthetical author-date format of the American Psychological Association. Professors in natural science and technical classes, where it is common to refer repeatedly to many sources, may ask you to use a citation-sequence method for in-text references such as that laid out in the Council of Science (formerly Biology) Editors' *CBE Manual* or a numbering system based on the overall alphabetical order of the sources in a list at the end

---

[8]Online writing centers usually have helpful information that is easy to access. Try the Web sites for the centers at Purdue <http://owl.english.purdue.edu/owl/resource/585/01/> or the University of Wisconsin <http://writing.wisc.edu/Handbook/DocMLA.html>.

of the paper. These and other formats are described in many composition handbooks; furthermore, specialized guides are readily available online or at library reference desks.[8] Whenever you are not sure what is expected regarding citations, check with your instructor.

CHAPTER SUMMARY

In this chapter we offered tips for managing your writing process and discussed the importance of the following:

- Asserting your own authority when you use readings; that is, making your points in your own voice rather than patching together quotes and paraphrases from sources
- Claiming and maintaining your authority as you generate ideas and draft your paper
- Reading and analyzing your own drafts rhetorically so that you attend to both your content ("what") and your methods ("how") as you revise through multiple drafts

We then described when and how to use summary, paraphrase, and direct quotation, and explained that skillful incorporation of source materials into your own texts enhances your credibility and clarifies how your ideas fit into the larger published conversation about a topic. Throughout the discussion we emphasized the importance of subordinating source materials to your own purposes, ideas, and organization. We stressed the importance of careful note-taking as a means of avoiding even inadvertent plagiarism. The guidelines we provided show how to

- Incorporate brief summaries, paraphrases, and direct quotations into your work
- Avoid plagiarism by using genuine paraphrases, taking careful notes, and attending to the details of bibliographic information
- Use attributive tags to help shape the response you desire from readers
- Provide clear and correct in-text citations using MLA formatting

In the sample student paper that follows, you will find numerous examples of these techniques. The appendix to this book provides details about using MLA format for both parenthetical citations and the full citations used in lists of works cited, including model citations for many types of materials you will be likely to use in your own papers.

Incorporating Reading into Writing: An Example in MLA Format

Here is Jack's analysis of multiple perspectives on corn ethanol, written in response to the assignment at the beginning of Chapter 5 (p. 100).

Arguing on the Basis of Wishful Thinking:

1   An Analysis of Multiple Perspectives

on Corn-Based Ethanol

Where I'm from in Iowa, just about everything is about corn: growing it, harvesting it, selling it, driving it. Driving it? Yes. Many Iowans think that corn-based ethanol is the best thing since gasoline; they consider it the answer to America's worries over energy security because it will make us less reliant on imported oil. Other people think that corn-based ethanol is a terrible thing, that increasing its production is stealing land otherwise used for growing food with the result of not only raising food prices around the world but destroying rain forests (because of trees cut down for farmland), which in turn increases the rate of global warming. These extreme attitudes are just two of many varying perspectives about the extent to which corn-based ethanol either offers hope for cleaner, safer energy along a path that will reduce global warming or threatens economic destruction for farmers and increases the threat of climate change.

2   Although the discussion about ethanol, specifically ethanol distilled from corn, is often framed by both the press and activists as a "food v. fuel debate," it is far more complex than over-simplified headlines or protest banners suggest. The real problem is that nobody has enough information yet to know the best way to produce ethanol—from corn or from some other plant crop. "Clean energy" seems like a good idea, but so far, nobody has demonstrated that ethanol promises a good future for any of us, for farmers who just want to make a good living, or for consumers who just want to drive a safe, economical car without feeling guilty about harming the environment.

3   Of course, farmers and consumers alike have to make decisions before they know what the outcomes will be. They take a risk and make a choice, hoping that oil prices and the overall economy will work out for that choice to be a good one. But people who claim to be certain about the wisdom of investing in ethanol, or in cars fueled by it, are basing their arguments primarily on hope and wishful thinking. We won't know the answers for many years to come.

Annotations (margin notes):

Title echoes assignment.

Intro paragraph with personal flavor lays out extreme attitudes re subject matter.

Intro closes with implicit promise of what is to come, providing rationale for analysis paper. Purely descriptive sentence is not a thesis.

Thesis statement changes focus of the issue away from "food v. fuel"—this is the point that paper will develop.

Third paragraph elaborates on and restates the thesis, clarifying what to expect in paper.

First of two paragraphs relating important background facts.

Detailed tags provide valuable details about background of material cited—journalist and spokesman for RFA (supports increased ethanol production).

4   Important recent news about corn-based ethanol is that as of January 1, 2012, Congress ended tax credits for companies that blend ethanol into gasoline. What is surprising about this news is that, according to *New York Times* reporter Robert Pear, the gasoline refiners (the big users of the ethanol) are not worried about it. In fact, Pear reported, "Ethanol proponents eventually accepted expiration of the tax credit without putting up a big fight." To explain this phenomenon, a spokesman for the Renewable Fuels Association (RFA) told Pear that "The marketplace has evolved. The tax incentive is less necessary now than it was just two years ago. Ethanol is 10 percent of the nation's gasoline supply." He expects both the price of corn and the amount of ethanol produced in the coming year to be unchanged—good news for both farmers and the ethanol industry.

No parenthetical citations needed in the summary and quotations from Pear's article because his name is in sentence and no page numbers available on Web.

5   Many sources report that corn ethanol production has been growing in recent years. In 2011, 40% of the U.S. corn crop was used for ethanol, a larger percentage than went to livestock feed, according to National Public Radio's Dustin Dwyer. He points out that even though the tax break has gone away, government policies still mandate that gas refineries blend corn ethanol into gasoline, a huge support for the industry. The current standard for the blend is 10% ethanol, but 15% is a major goal for the ethanol industry, which also promotes 85% ethanol fuel for flex-fuel engines. (The 10% ethanol, 90% gasoline mix is generally recognized as reducing emissions without a significant decrease in power or miles per gallon.)

Fifth paragraph broadens context and provides definitions.

Controversy is introduced and documented.

6   Use of the 15% fuel blend, known as E15, was authorized by the Environmental Protection Agency for use in vehicles made since 2001, but it is highly controversial because of decreases in power and efficiency as well as reported damage to small engines such as those on chainsaws and lawn mowers. According to the *DesMoines Register*, research by a group called the Coordinating Research Council (CRC) showed that the higher blend could also damage car engines (Piller). The CRC is run by a coalition of the Petroleum Institute and an international group of automakers. Unstated is the likely fact that to accommodate E15, car engines would need to be redesigned. The CRC's claims were denounced within the article

Newspaper's title used in sentence because city's name has more significance than author's name. Citation with author's name is essential connection to works cited page.

by a spokesman from the Iowa RFA, who called the research "just bad sci-ence" (Piller).

New paragraph for perspective from environmental lists.

7   Environmentalists are not enthusiastic about the increased use of corn ethanol in gasoline, either, but for different reasons. Friends of the Earth celebrated the end of the ethanol tax subsidy with a blog posting that said, "Good riddance to a terrible policy that supported corporate polluters at the expense of environmental and social sustainability" (Rosenoer). According to the blogger, this subsidy, which had been in place since 1979, had "wreaked havoc on our natural resources, raised food prices, increased world hunger, and diverted federal funding from truly renewable energy technologies like wind, solar, and electric vehicles" (Rosenoer).

Jack turns to outside analysts for in-depth background.

8   As the "Times Topics" section of the *New York Times* explains, the basic problem is that while ethanol is a clean-burning fuel, "ethanol pro-duction consumes prodigious quantities of natural gas, diesel fuel and other inputs that lead to carbon dioxide emissions" ("Ethanol"). A careful, consumer-focused exploration of both the negatives and positives of corn ethanol as fuel was published by *Consumer Reports* (*CR*) in 2006, during the war in Iraq, a time when alternative fuels and vehicles that could use them were being widely discussed. This magazine is known as a watchdog, a guide to help consumers make wise purchases, especially on big budget items such as automobiles. The article focuses primarily on road tests of flex fuel vehicles (FFVs) that can run on either gasoline or E85, a fuel that is 85% ethanol and 15% gasoline. The article's title, "The Ethanol Myth," announces right away that *CR* considers FFVs not to be particularly good choices both because very few gas stations supply E85 and because vehicles operating on E85 "get cleaner emissions but poorer fuel econ-omy" (15).

Citation uses short title to connect with works cited.

Next two paragraphs provide extended summary and response regarding *CR* article.

9   The *CR* writers want to debunk the myth that ethanol will somehow become the answer to U.S. energy independence. After reporting their test results, the article strongly criticizes federal tax breaks for FFV manufac-turers, arguing that the tax breaks have encouraged automakers to over-produce FFVs, most of which happen to be large, inefficient SUVs and pickups. Because there is a shortage of E85 gas stations, FFVs run most of the time on regular gasoline, making advertisements about their being

innovative "an empty promise," the writers say (16). The result, according to *CR*, is "the consumption of many times more gallons of gasoline than E85 now replaces" (16). Consumers Union, the organization that publishes *CR*, proposes that federal funds instead be used to stimulate the development of cars that are more fuel efficient overall.

10   The *CR* article supplies excellent background about the many issues that make ethanol production such a hot topic. Reading it might turn someone who was shopping for an FFV into a skeptic about ethanol as automobile fuel. Four major issues mentioned in the article have come up over and over in discussions about ethanol published since the *CR* article first came out. They include (1) the great amount of petroleum-based resources that are used in the production and transport of ethanol, (2) the question of whether corn ethanol actually adds to or reduces the balance of greenhouse gases in comparison to either gasoline or ethanol from sources other than corn kernels, (3) the need to develop ethanol from other crops, such as switch grass, cornstalks, and sugar cane, into what is called cellulosic ethanol, considered more efficient because its production consumes less fossil fuel, and (4) whether it is wise, or dangerous, to devote agricultural land to fuel crops rather than food crops.

11   The first issue, the fact that corn ethanol production is highly energy intensive, concerns many people. Petroleum-based resources are used across the life cycle of the product, from fertilizer and pesticides, to mechanical tilling and harvesting, to distillation and then transport to stations where consumers can pump it into their cars. As reporter Heidi Cullen explains in a PBS *News-Hour* video, while 10 gallons of ethanol may look like 10 gallons of renewable energy, "when you account for the eight gallons of fossil fuel used to grow, harvest, and convert the crop to ethanol, you end up with only two gallons of green renewable energy." Nonetheless, she goes on to point out, the 20 percent gain does represent "an improvement over gasoline from the standpoint of both energy and greenhouse gas emissions." Another problem comes from the strain of corn production on the land itself. As Cullen explains in her video, the ethanol boom has led many farmers to give up payments from the federal Conservation Reserve Program to keep some of their land out of production. "When this land is planted with corn," she notes, "all of the carbon

Summary's concluding sentence forecasts what follows.

Note Jack's use of transitions.

Brief paragraph adds emphasis to the expert opinion countering that in previous paragraph.

that's stored in these prairie grasses and in these trees is released back into the atmosphere."

12   A University of Iowa scientist explains away the problem of corn ethanol's resource intensity as "just a step along the way" (Brainard). In a Web discussion sponsored by the *Chronicle of Higher Education*, Robert P. Anex, associate director of the Office of Biorenewables Programs at Iowa State, said the real goals are "enhanced national security, improved environmental quality, and local economic development."

Citation names author who wrote up the Web chat with Anex, the expert quoted.

Research reported from another set of experts.

13   The second major issue, the emissions impact of corn ethanol, leads directly to the third, development of cellulosic ethanol from new crops. Researchers at the University of Minnesota have found that cellulosic ethanol can have a greater positive impact than was previously thought and have called for expansion of research on emissions "to include a broad array of environmental quality dimensions" (Hill et al. 1081). They, like *Consumer Reports*, call for conservation, specifically, "improved emissions controls[,] ... increases in fuel efficiency[,] and fuel conservation ... that would reduce the need for increased fuel supplies" (1081). But here's the catch: economical ways of producing cellulosic ethanol have yet to be found.

Paragraph's closing sentence and colloquial tone pave the way for Jack's closing points, which link back to the thesis.

Voices from paragraphs #11 and 12 brought back for Jack's elaboration on *CR* article's fourth point.

14   For people concerned about the fourth issue, using food crop acreage to grow fuel crops, the prospect of cellulosic ethanol offers great hope. For one thing, products such as switchgrass (ordinarily grown for hay) can be grown on "marginal" or hilly land where food crops cannot be grown (Cullen). Professor Anex from Iowa State told an online questioner that decisions about "food v. fuel" are ultimately moral decisions, which, he hopes, will be based on "the best science possible" (Brainard).

15   The biofuels story is ever-changing as research continues and the world economic situation fluctuates. It seems inevitable that the current flow of corn ethanol will ebb away because, as everyone knows at some level, we do live in a world of limited resources. *Consumer Reports* tells us straight out: "Even with the most optimistic estimates, ethanol on its own will never be able to provide Americans with energy independence" (19). It's more than likely, they go on to say, that "ethanol will be one in a portfolio of choices" for clean transportation energy. In the words of one of my favorite TV ads a few years back, from the oil company Chevron, no

Jack again uses a personal tone in concluding commentary, leaning on the *CR* article for authority and bringing in the irony of the oil company's conservation ad before his final comment, which echoes his title.

less: "The world is changing. And how we use energy today cannot be how we'll use it tomorrow. There is no one solution. It's not simply more oil, more renewables, or being more efficient. It's all of it."

16   Let's hope THAT is not wishful thinking.

Works Cited

Brainard, Jeffrey. "The Race to Harvest Energy." *Chronicle of Higher Education: Live Discussions*. Chronicle of Higher Education, 24 Apr. 2007. Web.30 Mar. 2009. <http://chronicle.com/live/2007/04/anex>. Transcript.

Chevron Corporation. "Tomorrow." *Chevron Television and Print Advertising*. You Tube, n.d. Web. 10 June 2012. <http://www.youtube.com/watch?v=CSkScYdlpuw>.

Cullen, Heidi. "In Iowa, Questions Arise About the Impact of Ethanol Production." *Online NewsHour*. PBS, 28 Jan. 2009. Web. 3 July 2012. <http://www.pbs.org/newshour/bb/environment/jan-june09/mixedyield_01-28.html>. Transcript.

Dwyer, Dustin. "After Backlash, Ethanol Industry Is Thriving." *Morning Edition*. National Public Radio, 26 Apr. 2012. Web. 28 May 2012. <http://www.npr.org/2012/04/26/151417943/checking-in-on-eurozone-economies>. Transcript.

"Ethanol." *Times Topics*. New York Times, 3 Jan. 2012.Web. 26 May 2012. <http://topics.nytimes.com/top/reference/timestopics/subjects/e/ethanol/index.html>.

"The Ethanol Myth." *Consumer Reports*. Oct. 2006: 15–19. *EbscoHost*. Web. 28 May 2012.

Hill, Jason, et al. "Climate Change and Health Costs of Air Emissions from Biofuels and Gasoline." *Proceedings of the National Academy of Science* 106.6 (2009): 1077–1082. *PubMed Central*. Web. 6 Apr. 2009.

Pear, Robert. "After Three Decades, Tax Credit for Ethanol Expires." New York Times. *New York Times*, 1 Jan. 2012. Web. 10 June 2012. <http://www.nytimes.com/2012/01/02/business/energy-environment/after-three-decades-federal-tax-credit-for-ethanol-expires.html?_r=1>.

Piller, Dan. "Oil Companies Say E15 Ethanol Damages Engines." *Des Moines Register*. Des Moines Register, 16 May 2012. Web. 10 June 2012.<http://blogs.desmoinesregister.com/dmr/index.php/2012/05/16/oil-companies-say-e15-ethanol-damages-engines/>.

Rosenoer, Michal. "Celebrating the New Year with a Victory Against Corn Ethanol." *Blog: Friends of the Earth*. Friends of the Earth, 6 Jan. 2012. Web. 28 May 2012. <http://www.foe.org/news/blog/2012-01-celebrating-the-new-year-with-a-victory-against-corn>.

[Margin note, left:] Works cited list would start on new page in actual paper.

List continues the double-spacing in the paper and is formatted with hanging indents.

"n.d." = "no date"

[Margin note, left:] No URLs for database citations because each search is unique.

[Margin note, right:] Instructor requires URLs be included for Web items. Compare formats for different types of sources to models in Appendix.

When URLs wrap across lines, they should break only at slash marks.

[Margin note, right:] Inclusive pagination for print publication from library database.

ACTIONS

Suit the action to the word, the word to the action.

—William Shakespeare, *Hamlet*, 3.2

I am unlikely to trust a sentence that comes easily.

—William Gass

UNDERSTANDING HOW WE EXPRESS JUDGMENTS

We have words enough to praise writing we like—*clear, direct, concise*—and more than enough to abuse writing we don't: *unclear, indirect, abstract, dense, complex.* We can use those words to distinguish these two sentences:

1a. The cause of our schools' failure at teaching basic skills is not understanding the influence of cultural background on learning.

1b. Our schools have failed to teach basic skills because they do not understand how cultural background influences the way a child learns.

Most of us would call (1a) too complex, (1b) clearer and more direct. But those words don't refer to anything *in* those sentences; they describe how those sentences make us *feel.* When we say that (1a) is *unclear,* we mean that we have a hard time understanding it; we say it's *dense* when *we* struggle to read it.

The problem is to understand what is *in* those two sentences that makes readers feel as they do. Only then can you rise above your too-good understanding of your own writing to know when your readers will think it needs revising. To do that, you have to know what counts as a well-told story. (To profit from this lesson and the next three, you must be able to identify verbs, simple subjects, and whole subjects.)

TELLING STORIES ABOUT CHARACTERS AND THEIR ACTIONS

This story has a problem:

> 2a. Once upon a time, as a walk through the woods was taking place on the part of Little Red Riding Hood, the Wolf's jump out from behind a tree occurred, causing her fright.

We prefer something closer to this:

> ✓ 2b. Once upon a time, Little Red Riding Hood was walking through the woods, when the Wolf jumped out from behind a tree and frightened her.

Most readers think (2b) tells its story more clearly than (2a), because it follows two principles:

- Its main characters are subjects of verbs.
- Those verbs express specific actions.

Principle of Clarity 1: Make Main Characters Subjects

Look at the subjects in (2a). The simple subjects (underlined) are *not* the main characters (italicized):

> 2a. Once upon a time, as a <u>walk</u> through the woods was taking place on the part of *Little Red Riding Hood, the Wolf's* <u>jump</u> out from behind a tree occurred, causing *her* fright.

Those subjects do not name characters; they name actions expressed in abstract nouns, walk and jump:

SUBJECT	VERB
a <u>walk</u> through the woods	was taking place
the Wolf's <u>jump</u> out from behind a tree	occurred

The whole subject of *occurred* does have a character *in* it: *the **Wolf's** jump*. But *the Wolf* is not *the* subject. It is only attached to the simple subject *jump*.

Contrast those abstract subjects with these, where the characters (italicized) are also the simple subjects (underlined):

> 2b. Once upon a time, <u>*Little Red Riding Hood*</u> was walking through the woods, when <u>*the Wolf*</u> jumped out from behind a tree and frightened *her*.

The subjects and the main characters are now the same words:

SUBJECT/CHARACTER	VERB
Little Red Riding Hood	was walking
the Wolf	jumped

Principle of Clarity 2: Make Important Actions Verbs

Now look at how the actions and verbs differ in (2a): its actions are not expressed in verbs but in abstract nouns (actions are boldfaced; verbs are capitalized):

> 2a. Once upon a time, as a **walk** through the woods WAS TAKING place on the part of Little Red Riding Hood, the Wolf's **jump** out from behind a tree OCCURRED, causing her **fright**.

Note how vague the verbs are: was *taking, occurred*. In (2b), the clearer sentence, the verbs name specific actions:

> ✓ 2b. Once upon a time, Little Red Riding Hood WAS WALKING through the woods, when the Wolf JUMPED out from behind a tree and FRIGHTENED her.

Here's the point: In (2a), the sentence that seems wordy and indirect, the two main characters, Little Red Riding Hood and the Wolf, are not subjects, and their actions—*walk, jump,* and *fright*—are *not* verbs. In (2b), the more direct sentence, those two main characters *are* subjects and their main actions *are* verbs. That's why we prefer (2b).

FAIRY TALES AND ACADEMIC OR PROFESSIONAL WRITING

Fairy tales may seem distant from writing in collegewcters doing things. Compare these two:

> 3a. The Federalists' argument in regard to the destabilization of government by popular democracy was based on their belief in the tendency of factions to further their self-interest at the expense of the common good.

✓ 3b. The Federalists argued that popular democracy destabilized government, because they believed that factions tended to further their self-interest at the expense of the common good.

We can analyze those sentences as we did the ones about Little Red Riding Hood.

Sentence (3a) feels dense for two reasons. First, its characters are not subjects. Its simple subject (underlined) is *argument*, but the characters (italicized) are *Federalists, popular democracy, government,* and *factions:*

3a. The *Federalists'* <u>argument</u> in regard to the destabilization of *government* by *popular democracy* was based on *their* belief in the tendency of *factions* to further *their* self-interest at the expense of the common good.

Second, most of the actions (boldfaced) are not verbs (capitalized), but abstract nouns:

3a. The Federalists' **argument** in regard to the **destabilization** of government by popular democracy WAS BASED on their **belief** in the **tendency** of factions to FURTHER their self-interest at the expense of the common good.

Notice how long and complex is the whole subject of (3a) and how little meaning is expressed by its main verb *was based*:

WHOLE SUBJECT	VERB
The Federalists' argument in regard to the destabilization of government by popular democracy	was based

Readers think (3b) is clearer for two reasons: the characters (italicized) are subjects (underlined), and the actions (boldfaced) are verbs (capitalized):

3b. The *Federalists* ARGUED that *popular democracy* DESTABILIZED government, because *they* BELIEVED that *factions* TENDED TO FURTHER *their* self-interest at the expense of the common good.

Note as well that all those whole subjects are short, specific, and concrete:

WHOLE SUBJECT/CHARACTER	VERB/ACTION
the Federalists	argued
popular democracy	destabilized
they	believed
factions	tended to further

In the rest of this lesson, we look at actions and verbs; in the next, at characters and subjects.

VERBS AND ACTIONS

Our principle is this: *A sentence seems clear when its important actions are in verbs.*

Look at how sentences (4a) and (4b) express their actions. In (4a), actions (boldfaced) are not verbs (capitalized); they are nouns:

> 4a. Our **lack** of data PREVENTED **evaluation** of UN **actions** in **targeting** funds to areas most in **need** of **assistance**.

In (4b), on the other hand, the actions are almost all verbs:

> ✓ 4b. Because we LACKED data, we could not EVALUATE whether the UN HAD TARGETED funds to areas that most NEEDED assistance.

Readers will think your writing is dense if you use lots of abstract nouns, especially those derived from verbs and ADJECTIVES, nouns ending in *-tion, -ment, -ence,* and so on, *especially when you make those abstract nouns the subjects of verbs.*

A noun derived from a verb or adjective has a technical name: NOMINALIZATION. The word illustrates its meaning: When we nominalize *nominalize,* we create the *nominalization* nominalization. Here are a few examples:

VERB	→	NOMINALIZATION	ADJECTIVE	→	NOMINALIZATION
discover	→	discovery	careless	→	carelessness
resist	→	resistance	different	→	difference
react	→	reaction	proficient	→	proficiency

We can also nominalize a verb by adding *-ing* (making it a gerund):

She flies → her flying   We sang → our singing

Some nominalizations and verbs are identical:

hope → hope   result → result   repair → repair

We REQUEST that you REVIEW the data.

Our **request** IS that you DO a **review** of the data.

(Some actions also hide out in adjectives: *It is applicable → it applies.* Some others: *indicative, dubious, argumentative, deserving.*)

No element of style more characterizes turgid writing, writing that feels abstract, indirect, and difficult, than lots of nominalizations, especially as the subjects of verbs.

Here's the point: In grade school, we learned that subjects are characters (or "doers") and that verbs are actions. That's often true:

subject   verb   object
We   discussed   the problem.
doer   action

But it is not true for this almost synonymous sentence:

subject   verb
The problem   was   the topic   of our discussion.
                                        doer   action

We can move characters and actions around in a sentence, and subjects and verbs don't have to name any particular kind of thing at all. But when you match characters to subjects and actions to verbs in most of your sentences, readers are likely to think your prose is clear, direct, and readable.

Exercise 7.1

If you aren't sure whether you can distinguish verbs, adjectives, and nominalizations, practice on the list below. Turn verbs and adjectives into nominalizations, and nominalizations into adjectives and verbs. Remember that some verbs and nominalizations have the same form:

Poverty predictably CAUSES social problems.
Poverty is a predictable CAUSE of social problems.

analysis	believe	attempt	conclusion	evaluate
suggest	approach	comparison	define	discuss
expression	failure	intelligent	thorough	appearance
decrease	improve	increase	accuracy	careful
emphasize	explanation	description	clear	examine

Exercise 7.2

Identify the subject, character, verb, and action in these pairs of sentences. The unclear sentence is first; the improved sentence follows. What do you notice about how characters and subjects, and actions and verbs, are aligned in each?

1a. There is opposition among many voters to nuclear power plants based on a belief in their threat to human health.

1b. Many voters oppose nuclear power plants because they believe that such plants threaten human health.

2a. There has been growth in the market for electronic books because of the frequent preference among customers for their convenience and portability.

2b. The market for electronic books has grown because customers frequently prefer their convenience and portability.

3a. There is a belief among some researchers that consumers' choices in fast food restaurants would be healthier if there were postings of nutrition information in their menus.

3b. Some researchers believe that consumers would choose healthier foods if fast food companies posted nutrition information in their menus.

4a. The design of the new roller coaster was more of a struggle for the engineers than had been their expectation.

4b. The engineers struggled more than they expected when designing the new roller coaster.

5a. Because the student's preparation for the exam was thorough, none of the questions on it were a surprise.

5b. Because the student prepared thoroughly for the exam, she was not surprised by any of the questions on it.

Exercise 7.3

Create three sentences using verbs and adjectives from Exercise 7.1. Then rewrite them using the corresponding nominalizations (keep the meaning the same). For example, using *suggest, discuss,* and *careful,* write:

I SUGGEST that we DISCUSS the issue CAREFULLY.

Then rewrite that sentence into its nominalized form:

My **suggestion** is that our **discussion** of the issue be done with **care**.

Only when you see how a clear sentence can be made unclear will you understand why it seemed clear in the first place.

DIAGNOSIS AND REVISION: CHARACTERS AND ACTIONS

You can use the principles of verbs as actions and subjects as characters to explain why your readers judge your prose as they do. But more important, you can also use them to identify and revise sentences that seem clear to you but not to your readers. Revision is a three-step process: diagnose, analyze, rewrite.

1. **Diagnose**

   a. Ignoring short (four- or five-word) introductory phrases, underline the first seven or eight words in each sentence.

      <u>The outsourcing of high-tech work to Asia</u> by corporations means the loss of jobs for many American workers.

   b. Then look for two results:

      • You underlined abstract nouns as simple subjects (boldfaced).

         <u>The **outsourcing** of high-tech work to Asia</u> by corporations means the loss of jobs for many American workers.

      • You underlined seven or eight words before getting to a verb.

         <u>The outsourcing of high-tech work to Asia</u> by corporations (10 words) **means** the loss of jobs for many American workers.

2. **Analyze**

   a. Decide who your main characters are, particularly the flesh-and-blood ones (more about this in the next lesson).

      The outsourcing of high-tech work to Asia by **corporations** means the loss of jobs for **many American workers**.

   b. Then look for the actions that those characters perform, especially actions in nominalizations, those abstract nouns derived from verbs.

      The **outsourcing** of high-tech work to Asia by corporations means the **loss** of jobs for many American workers.

3. **Rewrite**

   a. If the actions are nominalizations, make them verbs.

      outsourcing → outsource   loss → lose

   b. Make the characters the subjects of those verbs.

      corporations outsource   American workers lose

   c. Rewrite the sentence with subordinating conjunctions such as *because, if, when, although, why, how, whether,* or *that.*

      ✓ Many middle-class American workers are losing their jobs, **because** corporations are outsourcing their high-tech work to Asia.

SOME COMMON PATTERNS

You can quickly spot and revise five common patterns of nominalizations.

1. **The nominalization is the subject of an empty verb such as** *be, seems, has,* **etc.:**

   The **intention** of the committee is to audit the records.

   a. Change the nominalization to a verb:

   intention → intend

   b. Find a character that would be the subject of that verb:

   The intention of *the committee* is to audit the records.

   c. Make that character the subject of the new verb:

   ✓ *The committee* INTENDS to audit the records.

2. **The nominalization follows an empty verb:**

   The *agency* CONDUCTED an **investigation** into the matter.

   a. Change the nominalization to a verb:

   investigation → investigate

   b. Replace the empty verb with the new verb:

   conducted → investigated

   ✓ The *agency* INVESTIGATED the matter.

3. **One nominalization is the subject of an empty verb and a second nominalization follows it:**

   Our **loss** in sales WAS a result of their **expansion** of outlets.

   a. Revise the nominalizations into verbs:

   loss → lose   expansion → expand

   b. Identify the characters that would be the subjects of those verbs:

   Our **loss** in sales was a result of *their* **expansion** of outlets.

   c. Make those characters subjects of those verbs:

   we lose   they expand

   d. Link the new CLAUSES with a logical connection:

   - To express simple cause: *because, since, when*
   - To express conditional cause: *if, provided that, so long as*
   - To contradict expected causes: *though, although, unless*

Our **loss** in sales	→	*We* LOST sales
was the result of	→	**because**
their **expansion** of outlets	→	*they* EXPANDED outlets

4. **A nominalization follows *there is* or *there are*:**

   There is no **need** for *our* further **study** of this problem.

   a. Change the nominalization to a verb:

   need → need   study → study

   b. Identify the character that should be the subject of the verb:

   There is no **need** for *our* further **study** of this problem.

   c. Make that character the subject of the verb:

   no need → we need not   our study → we study

   ✓ <u>*We*</u> NEED not STUDY this problem further.

5. **Two or three nominalizations in a row are joined by prepositions:**

   We did a **review** of the **evolution** of the brain.

   a. Turn the first nominalization into a verb:

   review → review

   b. Either leave the second nominalization as it is, or turn it into a verb in a clause beginning with *how* or *why*:

   evolution of the brain → how the brain evolved

   ✓ First, <u>*we*</u> REVIEWED the **evolution** of the *brain*.

   ✓ First, <u>*we*</u> REVIEWED how <u>*the brain*</u> EVOLVED.

✓ Quick Tip

When you revise a complicated sentence, you will have more than one character-action clause. Decide how the clauses fit together, then try out these patterns: *X because Y; Since X, Y; If X, then Y; Although X, Y; X and/but/so Y.*

SOME HAPPY CONSEQUENCES

When you consistently rely on verbs to express key actions, your readers benefit in many ways:

1. Your sentences are more concrete, because they will have concrete subjects and verbs. Compare:

   There WAS an affirmative **decision** for **expansion**.

   ✓ *The Director* DECIDED to EXPAND the program.

2. Your sentences are more concise. When you use nominalizations, you have to add articles like *a* and *the* and prepositions such as *of, by,* and *in*. You don't need them when you use verbs and conjunctions:

> A **revision** *of* the program WILL RESULT *in* **increases** *in* our **efficiency** *in the* **servicing** *of* clients.
>
> ✓ *If* we REVISE the program, we CAN SERVE clients more EFFICIENTLY.

3. The logic of your sentences is clearer. When you nominalize verbs, you link actions with fuzzy prepositions and PHRASES such as *of, by,* and *on the part of*. But when you use verbs, you link clauses with precise subordinating conjunctions such as because, *although,* and *if*:

> Our more effective presentation of our study resulted in our success, despite an earlier start by others.
>
> ✓ **Although** others started earlier, we succeeded **because** we presented our study more effectively.

4. Your sentence tells a more coherent story. Nominalizations let you distort the sequence of actions. (The numbers refer to the real sequence of events.)

> Decisions[4] in regard to administration[5] of medication despite inability[2] of an irrational patient appearing[1] in a Trauma Center to provide legal consent[3] rest with the attending physician alone.

When we revise those actions into verbs and reorder them, you get a more coherent narrative:

> ✓ When a patient appears[1] in a Trauma Center and behaves[2] so irrationally that he cannot legally consent[3] to treatment, only the attending physician can decide[4] whether to medicate[5] him.

A COMMON PROBLEM SOLVED

You've probably had this experience: you think you've written something good, but your reader thinks otherwise. You wonder whether that person is just being difficult, but you bite your tongue and try to fix it, even though you think it should already be clear to anyone who can read Dr. Seuss. When that happens to me (regularly, I might add), I almost always realize—eventually—that my readers are right, that they see where my writing needs work better than I do.

Why are we so often right about the writing of others and so often wrong about our own? It is because we all read into our own writing what we want readers to get out of it. That explains why two readers can disagree about the clarity of the same piece of writing: the reader who is most familiar with its content will likely find it clearest. Both are right. Clarity is in the eye of more or less informed beholders.

That is why we need to look at our own writing in a way that is almost mechanical, that sidesteps our too-good understanding of it. The quickest way is to underline the first seven or eight words of every sentence. If you don't see in those words a character as a subject and a verb as a specific action, you have a candidate for revision.

✓ Quick Tip

When you revise a longer piece of work, look first at those passages that were hard to write because you didn't fully understand your ideas. We all tend to write badly when we're unsure about what we want to say or how to say it.

Exercise 7.4

One sentence in each of these pairs is clear, expressing characters as subjects and actions as verbs; the other is less clear, with actions in nominalizations and characters often not in subjects. First, identify which is which. Then circle nominalizations, bracket verbs, and underline subjects. Then put a "c" over characters that seem to perform actions.

1a. Some people argue that atmospheric carbon dioxide does not elevate global temperature.

1b. There has been speculation by educators about the role of the family in improving educational achievement.

2a. The store's price increases led to frustration among its customers.

2b. When we write concisely, readers understand easily.

3a. Researchers have identified the AIDS virus but have failed to develop a vaccine to immunize those at risk.

3b. Attempts by economists at defining full employment have been met with failure.

4a. Complaints by editorial writers about voter apathy rarely offer suggestions about dispelling it.

4b. Although critics claim that children who watch a lot of television tend to become less able readers, no one has demonstrated that to be true.

5a. The loss of market share to Japan by domestic automakers resulted in the disappearance of hundreds of thousands of jobs.

5b. When educators embrace new-media technology, our schools will teach complex subjects more effectively.

6a. We need to know which parts of our national forests are being logged most extensively so that we can save virgin stands at greatest risk.

6b. There is a need for an analysis of library use to provide a reliable base for the projection of needed resources.

7a. Many professional athletes fail to realize that they are unprepared for life after stardom because their teams protect them from the problems that the rest of us face every day.

7b. Colleges now have an understanding that yearly tuition increases are impossible because of strong parental resistance to the soaring cost of higher education.

Exercise 7.5

Now revise the nominalized sentences in Exercise 7.4 into sentences in which the actions are verbs. Use its paired verbal version as a model. For example, if the verbal sentence begins with *when*, begin your revision with *when*:

Sentence to revise: 2a. The store's price **increases** led to **frustration** among its customers.

Model: 2b. When we WRITE concisely, readers UNDERSTAND more easily.

Your revision: 2a. When the store INCREASED prices, . . .

Exercise 7.6

Revise these next sentences so that the nominalizations are verbs and characters are their subjects. In (1) through (5), characters are italicized and nominalizations are boldfaced.

1. *Lincoln's* **hope** was for the **preservation** of the Union without war, but the *South's* **attack** on Fort Sumter made war an **inevitability**.

2. **Attempts** were made on the part of the *president's aides* to assert *his* **immunity** from a *congressional* subpoena.

3. There were **predictions** by *business executives* that the *economy* would experience a quick **revival.**

4. *Your* **analysis** of *my* report omits any data in **support** of *your* **criticism** of *my* **findings.**

5. The *health care industry's* **inability** to exert cost **controls** could lead to the *public's* **decision** that *congressional* **action** is needed.

In sentences 6 through 10, the characters are italicized; find the actions and revise.

6. A *papal* appeal was made to the world's rich *nations* for assistance to those facing the threat of *African* starvation.

7. Attempts at explaining increases in *voter* participation in this year's elections were made by *several candidates*.

8. The agreement by the *class* on the reading list was based on the assumption that there would be tests on only certain selections.

9. There was no independent *business-sector* study of the cause of the sudden increase in the trade surplus.

10. An understanding as to the need for controls over drinking on campus was recognized by *fraternities*.

Exercise 7.7

Revise these sentences. At the end of each is a hint. For example:

Congress's **reduction** of the deficit resulted in the **decline** of interest rates. [because]

✓ Interest rates DECLINED because Congress REDUCED the deficit.

1. The use of models in teaching prose style does not result in improvements of clarity and directness in student writing. [Although we use . . .]

2. Precision in plotting the location of building foundations enhances the possibility of its accurate reconstruction. [When we precisely plot . . .]

3. Any departures by the members from established procedures may cause termination of membership by the Board. [If members . . .]

4. A student's lack of socialization into a field may lead to writing problems because of his insufficient understanding about arguments by professionals in that field. [When . . ., . . ., because . . .]

5. The successful implementation of a new curriculum depends on the cooperation of faculty with students in setting achievable goals within a reasonable time. [To implement . . ., . . .]

A QUALIFICATION: USEFUL NOMINALIZATIONS

I have so relentlessly urged you to turn nominalizations into verbs that you might think you should never use one. But in fact, you can't write well without them. The trick is to know which to keep and which to revise. Keep these:

1. **A nominalization that is a short subject that refers to a previous sentence:**

    ✓ **These arguments** all depend on a single unproven claim.

    ✓ **This decision** can lead to positive outcomes.

    Those nominalizations link one sentence to another in a cohesive flow, an issue I'll discuss in more detail in Chapter 5.

2. **A short nominalization that replaces an awkward *The fact that*:**

    The fact that she ADMITTED guilt impressed me.

    ✓ Her admission of guilt impressed me.

    But then, why not this:

    ✓ *She* IMPRESSED me when *she* ADMITTED her guilt.

3. **A nominalization that names what would be the object of the verb:**

    I accepted *what she* REQUESTED [that is, *She requested **something***].

    ✓ I accepted her **request**.

    This kind of nominalization feels more concrete than an abstract one. However, contrast *request* above with this next sentence, where *request* is more of an action:

    Her **request** for **assistance** CAME after the deadline.

    ✓ She **request assistance** after the deadline.

4. **A nominalization that refers to a concept so familiar to your readers that to them, it is a virtual character (more about this in the next lesson):**

    ✓ Few problems have so divided us as **abortion** on **demand**.

    ✓ The Equal Rights **Amendment** was an issue in past **elections**.

    ✓ **Taxation** without **representation** did not spark the American **Revolution**.

    Those nominalizations name familiar concepts: *abortion* on *demand, amendment, election, taxation, representation, revolution.* You must develop an eye for distinguishing nominalizations expressing common ideas from those you can revise into verbs:

    There is a **demand** for a **repeal** of the **inheritance** tax.

    ✓ We DEMAND that Congress REPEAL the **inheritance** tax.

CLARITY, NOT SIMPLEMINDEDNESS

Your readers want you to write clearly, but not in Dick-and-Jane sentences. Some argue that all sentences should be short, no more than fifteen or twenty words. But many mature ideas are too complicated to express so compactly. In Lessons 10 and 11 we look at ways to revise too-short, too-simple sentences into a style that is readable but still complex enough to communicate complex ideas.

IN YOUR OWN WORDS

Exercise 7.8

Go through a page of your own writing. Underline whole subjects and bracket verbs. Now, think about the story you are telling. Circle the main characters and box their actions, wherever they appear. Look especially for actions hidden in nominalizations. What do you notice? How clear will a reader likely find your writing? If necessary, revise to align characters with subjects and specific actions with verbs.

Exercise 7.9

Writers tend to think their writing is clearer than their readers do. Select a page of your writing and share it with a reader. Both of you rate its clarity on a scale of 1–10, with 10 being perfectly clear and 1 being incomprehensible. Use the procedures for diagnosing and analyzing sentences on page 154–156 to explain any difference in your rating. Revise your writing if necessary.

SUMMING UP

The two most general principles for clear sentences are these: make main characters the subjects of your verbs; make those characters' important actions your verbs.

We can represent these principles graphically. Readers must mentally integrate two levels of sentence structure. One, the grammatical level, is the relatively fixed sequence of subject and verb (the empty box is for everything that follows the verb):

| Fixed | Subject | Verb | _____ |

The other, the story level, is based on characters and their actions and has no fixed order. Readers prefer these levels to match, for characters to be subjects and their actions to be verbs. We can graphically combine those principles:

Fixed	Subject	Verb	_____
Variable	Subject	Action	_____

Keep in mind that readers want to see characters not just in a subject, as in these two:

The _president's_ veto of the bill infuriated Congress.
The veto of the bill by the _president_ infuriated Congress.

Instead, they want to see the character as the subject, like this:

✓ When _the president_ subject VETOED verb the bill, _he_ subject INFURIATED verb Congress.

When you frustrate those expectations, you make readers work harder than necessary. So keep these principles in mind as you revise:

1. Express actions in verbs:

    The **intention** of the committee is improvement of morale.
    ✓ The committee **INTENDS** to improve morale.

2. Make the subjects of those verbs the characters associated with those actions:

    A decision by _the dean_ in regard to the funding of the program by _the department_ is necessary for adequate _staff_ preparation.
    ✓ _The staff_ CAN PREPARE adequately, only after _the dean_ DECIDES whether _the department_ WILL FUND the program.

3. Don't revise nominalizations when:
    a. they refer to a previous sentence:
        ✓ **These arguments** all depend on a single unproven claim.
    b. they replace an awkward _The fact that_:
        The fact that she strenuously objected impressed me.
        ✓ **Her strenuous objections** impressed me.

    c. they name what would be the object of a verb:

        I do not know **what she** INTENDS.

      ✓ I do not know **her intentions.**

    d. they name a concept so familiar to your readers that it is a virtual character:

      ✓ Few problems have so divided us as **abortion** on **demand**.

      ✓ The Equal Rights **Amendment** was an issue in past **elections**.

CHARACTERS

Whatever is translatable in other and simpler words of the same language, without loss of sense or dignity, is bad.

—Samuel Taylor Coleridge

When character is lost, all is lost.

—Anonymous

UNDERSTANDING THE IMPORTANCE OF CHARACTERS

Readers think sentences are clear and direct when they see key actions in their verbs. Compare (1a) with (1b):

1a. The CIA feared the president would recommend to Congress that it reduce its budget.

1b. The CIA had fears that the president would send a recommendation to Congress that it make a reduction in its budget.

Most readers think (1a) is clearer than (1b), but not much. Now compare (1b) and (1c):

1b. The CIA had fears that the president would send a recommendation to Congress that it make a reduction in its budget.

1c. The fear of the CIA was that a recommendation from the president to Congress would be for a reduction in its budget.

Most readers think that (1c) is much less clear than either (1a) or (1b).

The reason is this: In both (1a) and (1b), important characters (italicized) are short, specific subjects (underlined) of verbs:

1a. *The CIA* FEARED *the president* WOULD RECOMMEND to *Congress* that it REDUCE its budget.

1b. *The CIA* HAD fears that *the president* WOULD SEND a recommendation to Congress that *it* MAKE a reduction in its budget.

But in (1c) the two subjects (underlined) are not concrete characters but abstractions (boldfaced):

1c. The *fear* of the *CIA* was that a *recommendation* from the *president* to *Congress* WOULD BE for a **reduction** in its budget.

The different verbs in (1a) and (1b) make some difference, but the abstract subjects in (1c) make a bigger one. Even worse, characters can be deleted entirely, like this:

1d. There WAS **fear** that there WOULD BE a **recommendation** for a budget **reduction**.

Who fears? Who recommends? The sentence's context may help readers guess correctly, but if the context is ambiguous, you risk them guessing wrongly.

> **Here's the point:**   Readers want actions in verbs, but they want characters as subjects even more. We create a problem for readers when for no good reason we do not name characters in subjects or, worse, delete them entirely. It is important to express actions in verbs, but the *first* principle of a clear style is this: Make the subjects of most of your verbs the main characters in your story.

DIAGNOSIS AND REVISION: CHARACTERS

To get characters into subjects, you have to know three things:

1. when your subjects are not characters

2. if they aren't, where you should look for characters

3. what you should do when you find them (or don't)

For example, this sentence feels indirect and impersonal:

> Governmental intervention in fast-changing technologies has led to the distortion of market evolution and interference in new product development.

We can diagnose that sentence:

1. **Underline the first seven or eight words:**

> Governmental intervention in fast-changing technologies has led to the distortion of market evolution and interference in new product development.

In those first words, readers want to see characters not just *in* the whole subjects of verbs, as *government* is implied in *governmental*, but as their simple subjects. In that example, however, they aren't.

2. **Find the main characters.** They may be POSSESSIVE PRONOUNS attached to nominalizations, objects of prepositions (particularly *by* and *of*), or only implied. In that sentence, one main character is in the adjective *governmental*; the other, *market*, is in the object of a preposition: *of market evolution.*

3. **Skim the passage for actions involving those characters, particularly actions buried in nominalizations.** Ask *Who is doing what?*

governmental **intervention**	→ ✓	*government* **intervention**
distortion	→ ✓	*[government]* **distorts**
market **evolution**	→ ✓	*markets* **evolve**
interference	→ ✓	*[government]* **interferes**
development	→ ✓	*[market]* **develops**

To revise, reassemble those new subjects and verbs into a sentence, using conjunctions such as *if, although, because, when, how,* and *why:*

✓ **When** a *government* INTERVENES in fast-changing technologies, *it* DISTORTS how *markets* EVOLVE and INTERFERES with their ability to DEVELOP new products.

Be aware that just as actions can be in adjectives (*reliable*→ *rely*), so can characters:

Medieval *theological* debates often addressed issues considered trivial by modern *philosophical* thought.

When you find a character implied in an adjective, revise in the same way:

✓ *Medieval theologians* often debated issues that *modern philosophers* consider trivial.

✓ Quick Tip

The first step in diagnosing a dense style is to look at subjects. If you do not see main characters there expressed in a few short, concrete words, you have to look for them. They can be in objects of prepositions, in possessive pronouns, or in adjectives. Once you find them, look for actions they are involved in.

When you are revising your writing:

Make those characters the subjects of verbs naming those actions. Then string together those character-action pairs into complete sentences.

> *When you are reading:*
> Focusing on the characters, try to retell the story in the sentences, one action at a time. If that
> fails, list character-action pairs and rewrite the sentences yourself.

RECONSTRUCTING ABSENT CHARACTERS

Readers have the biggest problem with sentences devoid of *all* characters:

> A decision was made in favor of doing a study of the disagreements.

That sentence could mean either of these, and more:

> We decided that I should study why they disagreed.

> I decided that you should study why he disagreed.

The writer may know who is doing what, but readers might not and so usually need help.

Sometimes we omit characters to make a general statement:

> Research strategies that look for more than one variable are of more use in under-
> standing factors in psychiatric disorder than strategies based on the assumption that
> the presence of psychopathology is dependent on a single gene or on strategies in
> which only one biological variable is studied.

But when we try to revise that into something clearer, we have to invent characters, then
decide what to call them. Do we use one or we, or name a generic "doer"?

> ✓ If *one/we/researchers* are to understand what causes psychiatric disorder, *one/we/they*
> should use research strategies that look for more than one variable rather than assume
> that a single gene is responsible for a psychopathology or adopt a strategy in which
> *one/we/they* study only one biological variable.

To most of us, *one* feels stiff, but *we* may be ambiguous because it can refer just to the
writer, or to the writer and others but not the reader, or to the reader and writer but not
others, or to everyone. And if you are not directly naming your reader, *you* is usually inappropriate.

But if you avoid both nominalizations and vague pronouns, you can slide into PASSIVE
verbs (I'll discuss them in a moment):

> To understand what makes patients vulnerable to psychiatric disorders, strategies
> that look for more than one variable SHOULD BE USED rather than strategies in which
> a gene IS ASSUMED a gene causes psychopathology or only one biological variable IS
> STUDIED.

✓ Quick Tip

When you are explaining a complicated issue to someone involved in it, imagine sitting across
the table from that person, saying *you* as often as you can:

Taxable intangible property includes financial notes and municipal bonds. A one-time tax of 2% on its value applies to this property.

✓ **You** have to pay tax on **your** intangible property, including **your** financial notes and municipal bonds. On this property, **you** pay a one-time tax of 2%.

If *you* seems not appropriate, change it to a character that is:

Taxpayers have to pay tax on their intangible property, including **their** financial notes and municipal bonds. **They** pay . . .

ABSTRACTIONS AS CHARACTERS

So far, I've discussed characters as if they must be flesh-and-blood people. But you can tell stories whose main characters are abstractions, including nominalizations, so long as you make them the subjects of a series of sentences that tell a story. We might have solved the problem of the previous example with a different kind of character, the abstraction *study:*

✓ To understand what causes psychiatric disorder, *studies* should look for more than one variable rather than adopt a strategy in which *they* test only one biological variable or assume that a single gene is responsible for a psychopathology.

The term *studies* names a virtual character because we are so familiar with it and because it is the subject of a series of actions: *understand, should look, adopt, test,* and *assume.*

But when you do use abstractions as characters, you can create a problem. A story about an abstraction as familiar as *studies* is clear enough, but if you surround a less familiar abstract character with a lot of other abstractions, readers may feel that your writing is unnecessarily dense and complex.

For example, few of us are familiar with the terms prospective and *immediate intention,* so most of us are likely to struggle with a story about them, especially when they are surrounded by other abstractions (actions are boldfaced; human characters are italicized):

The **argument** is this. The cognitive component of **intention** exhibits a high degree of **complexity**. **Intention** is temporally divisible into two: prospective **intention** and immediate **intention**. The cognitive function of prospective **intention** is the **representation** of a *subject's* similar past **actions**, *his* current situation, and *his* course of future **actions**. That is, the cognitive component of prospective **intention** is a **plan**. The cognitive function of immediate **intention** is the **monitoring** and **guidance** of ongoing bodily **movement**.

—Myles Brand, *Intending and Acting*

We can make that passage clearer if we tell it from the point of view of flesh-and-blood characters (italicized; actions are boldfaced; verbs are capitalized):

✓ *I* ARGUE this about **intention**. **It** *has* a complex cognitive component of two temporal kinds: prospective and immediate. *We* USE prospective **intention** to REPRE-

SENT how *we* HAVE ACTED in our past and present and how *we* WILL ACT in the future. That is, *we* **use** the cognitive component of prospective **intention** to HELP *us* PLAN. *We* USE immediate **intention** to MONITOR and GUIDE *our* bodies as *we* MOVE them.

But have I made this passage say something that the writer didn't mean? Some argue that any change in form changes meaning. In this case, the writer might offer an opinion, but only his readers could decide whether the two passages have different meanings, because at the end of the day, a passage means only what careful and competent readers think it does.

Here's the point: Most readers want the subjects of verbs to name flesh-and-blood characters. But often, you must write about abstractions. When you do, turn them into virtual characters by making them the subjects of verbs that tell a story. If readers are familiar with your abstractions, no problem. But when they are not, avoid using lots of other abstract nominalizations around them. When you revise an abstract passage, you may have a problem if the hidden characters are "people in general." Try a general term for whoever is doing the action, such as *researchers, social critics, one,* and so on. If not, try we. But the fact is, unlike many other languages, English has no good solution for naming a generic "doer."

Exercise 8.1

Diagnose and revise these next sentences. Look at the first six or seven words (ignore short introductory phrases). Then revise so that each has a specific character as subject of a specific verb. To revise, you may have to invent characters. Use *we, I,* or any other word that seems appropriate.

1. Contradictions among the data require an explanation. [we]

2. Having their research taken seriously by professionals in the field was hard work for the students. [student researchers]

3. In recent years, the appearance of new interpretations about the meaning of the discovery of America has led to a reassessment of Columbus's place in Western history. [historians]

4. Resistance has been growing against building mental health facilities in residential areas because of a belief that the few examples of improper management are typical. [residents]

5. A decision about forcibly administering medication in an emergency room setting despite the inability of an irrational patient to provide legal consent is usually an on-scene medical decision. [medical professionals]

6. The performance of the play was marked by enthusiasm, but there was a lack of intelligent staging.

7. Despite the critical panning of the latest installment of the series, the love of the loyal fans was not affected.

8. Tracing transitions in a well-written article provides help in efforts at improving coherence in writing.

9. The rejection of the proposal was a disappointment but not a surprise because our expectation was that a political decision had been made.

10. With the decline in network television viewing in favor of online streaming video, awareness is growing at the networks of a need to revise programming.

CHARACTERS AND PASSIVE VERBS

More than any other advice, you probably remember *Write in the active voice, not in the passive*. That's not bad advice, but it has exceptions.

When you write in the ACTIVE voice, you typically put

- the AGENT or source of an action in the subject
- the GOAL or receiver of an action in a DIRECT OBJECT:

	subject	verb	object
Active:	I	lost	the money
	character/agent	action	goal

A verb is in the passive voice when its PAST PARTICIPLE is preceded by a form of *be* (as it is here). The passive differs from the active in two ways:

1. The subject names the goal of the action.

2. The agent or source of the action is after the verb in a *by*-phrase or dropped entirely:

	subject	be + verb	prepositional phrase
Passive:	The money	was lost	[by me].
	goal	action	character/agent

The terms *active* and *passive*, however, are ambiguous, because they can refer not only to those two grammatical constructions but also to how a sentence makes you *feel*. We call a sentence *passive* if it feels flat, regardless of whether its verb is grammatically in the passive voice. For example, compare these two sentences.

We can manage the problem if we control costs.

Problem management requires cost control.

Grammatically, both sentences are in the active voice, but the second *feels* passive, for three reasons:

- Neither of its actions—*management* and *control*—are verbs; both are nominalizations.
- The subject is *problem management*, an abstraction.
- The sentence lacks flesh-and-blood characters.

To understand why we respond to those two sentences as we do, we have to distinguish the technical, grammatical meanings of *active* and *passive* from their figurative, impressionistic meanings. In what follows, I discuss grammatical passives.

CHOOSING BETWEEN ACTIVE AND PASSIVE

Some critics tell us to avoid the passive everywhere because it adds words and often deletes the agent, the "doer" of the action. But the passive is often the better choice. To choose between active and passive, you have to answer three questions:

1. **Must your readers know who is responsible for the action?** Often, we don't say who does an action because we don't know or readers won't care. For example, we naturally choose the passive in these sentences:

   ✓ The president WAS RUMORED to have considered resigning.

   ✓ Those who ARE FOUND guilty can BE FINED.

   ✓ Valuable records should always BE KEPT in a safe.

   If we do not know who spreads rumors, we cannot say, and no one doubts who finds people guilty or fines them or who should keep records safe. So those passives are the right choice.

   Sometimes, of course, writers use the passive when they don't want readers to know who is responsible for an action, especially when the doer is the writer. For example,

   Because the test was not completed, the flaw was uncorrected.

2. **Would the active or passive verb help your readers move more smoothly from one sentence to the next?** We depend on the beginning of a sentence to give us a context of what we know before we read what's new. A sentence confuses us when it opens with information that is new and unexpected. For example, in this next passage, the subject of the second sentence gives us new and complex information (boldfaced), before we read more familiar information that we recall from the previous sentence (italicized):

   We must decide whether to improve education in the sciences alone or to raise the level of education across the whole curriculum. **The weight given to industrial competitiveness as opposed to the value we attach to the liberal arts** new information WILL DETERMINE active verb *our decision*. familiar information

In the second sentence, the verb determine is in the active voice. But we could read the sentence more easily if it were passive, because the passive would put the short, familiar information (our decision) first and the newer, more complex information last, the order we prefer:

✓ We must decide whether to improve education in the sciences alone or raise the level of education across the whole curriculum. *Our decision*_{familiar information} WILL BE DETERMINED_{passive verb} **by the weight we give to industrial competiveness as opposed to the value we attach to the liberal arts.** _{new information}

3. **Would the active or passive give readers a more consistent and appropriate point of view?** The writer of this next passage reports the end of World War II in Europe from the point of view of the Allies. To do so, she uses active verbs to make the Allies a consistent sequence of subjects:

✓ By early 1945, *the Allies* HAD essentially DEFEATED _{active} Germany; all that remained was a bloody climax. *American, French, British, and Russian forces* HAD BREACHED _{active} its borders and WERE BOMBING _{active} it around the clock. But *they* HAD not yet SO DEVASTATED _{active} Germany as to destroy its ability to resist.

Had she wanted to explain history from the German point of view, she would have used passive verbs to make Germany the subject/character:

✓ By early 1945, *Germany* HAD essentially BEEN DEFEATED;_{passive} all that remained was a bloody climax. *Its borders* HAD BEEN BREACHED,_{passive} and *it* was BEING BOMBED_{passive} around the clock. *It* HAD not BEEN SO DEVASTATED,_{passive} however, that *it* could not RESIST._{active}

Some writers switch from one character to another for no apparent reason. Avoid this:

By early 1945, *the Allies* had essentially defeated Germany. *Its borders* had been breached, and *they* were bombing it around the clock. *Germany* was not so devastated, however, that *the Allies* would meet with no resistance. Though *Germany's population* was demoralized, *the Allies* still attacked German cities from the air.

Pick a point of view and stick to it.

Here's the point: Many writers use the passive too often, but it has important uses. Use it in these contexts:

- You don't know who did an action, readers don't care, or you don't want them to know.
- You want to shift a long and complex bundle of information to the end of a sentence, especially when doing so also lets you begin with a chunk of information that is shorter, more familiar, and therefore easier to understand.
- You want to focus your readers' attention on one or another character.

Exercise 8.2

In the following, change all active verbs into passives, and all passives into actives. Which sentences improve? Which do not? (In the first two, active verbs that could be passive are italicized; verbs already passive are boldfaced.)

1. Independence is **gained** by those on welfare when skills are **learned** that the marketplace *values*.

2. Different planes of the painting are **noticed**, because their colors are **set** against a background of shades of gray that are **laid** on in layers that cannot be seen unless the surface is **examined** closely.

3. In this article, it is argued that the Vietnam War was fought to extend influence in Southeast Asia and was not ended until it was made clear that the United States could not defeat North Vietnam unless atomic weapons were used.

4. Science education will not be improved in this nation to a level sufficient to ensure that American industry will be supplied with skilled workers and researchers until more money is provided to primary and secondary schools.

THE "OBJECTIVE" PASSIVE vs. *I/WE*

Some scholarly writers claim that they should not use a first-person subject, because they must create an objective point of view, something like this:

> Based on the writers' verbal intelligence, prior knowledge, and essay scores, their essays **were analyzed** for structure and evaluated for richness of concepts. The subjects **were** then **divided** into a high- or low-ability group. Half of each group **was** randomly **assigned** to a treatment group or to a placebo group.

Contrary to that claim, academic and scientific writers use the active voice and the first-person *I* and *we* regularly. These next passages come from articles in respected journals:

✓ This paper is concerned with two problems. How can **we** best handle in a transformational grammar certain restrictions that . . ., To illustrate, **we** may cite . . ., **we** shall show . . .

✓ Since the pituitary-adrenal axis is activated during the acute phase response, **we** have investigated the potential role . . . Specifically, **we** have studied the effects of interleukin-1 . . .

Here are the first few words from several consecutive sentences from Science, a journal of great prestige:

✓ **We** examine . . ., **We** compare . . ., **We** have used . . ., Each has been weighted . . ., **We** merely take . . ., They are subject . . ., **We** use . . ., Efron and Morris describe . . ., **We** observed . . ., **We** might find . . .

> —John P. Gilbert, Bucknam McPeek, and Frederick Mosteller,
> "Statistics and Ethics in Surgery and Anesthesia," *Science*

It is not true that academic writers always avoid the first person *I* or *we*.

PASSIVES, CHARACTERS, AND METADISCOURSE

When academic writers do use the first person, however, they use it in certain ways. Look at the verbs in the passages above. They fall into two groups:

- Some refer to research activities: *examine, observe, measure, record, use.* Those verbs are usually in the passive voice: *The subjects were observed . . .*
- Others refer not to the subject matter or the research, but to the writer's own writing and thinking: *cite, show, inquire.* These verbs are often active and in the first person: *We will show . . .* They are examples of what is called METADISCOURSE.

Metadiscourse is language that refers not to the substance of your ideas, but to yourself, your reader, or your writing:

- your thinking and act of writing: *We/I will explain, show, argue, claim, deny, suggest, contrast, add, expand, summarize . . .*
- your readers' actions: *consider now, as you recall, look at the next example . . .*
- the logic and form of what you have written: *first, second; to begin; therefore, however, consequently . . .*

Metadiscourse appears most often in introductions, where writers announce their intentions: *I claim that . . ., I will show . . ., We begin by . . .,* and again at the end, when they summarize: *I have argued . . ., I have shown . . .* What distinguishes those actions is that only the writer can lay claim to them.

On the other hand, scholarly writers generally do not use the first person to describe specific actions they performed as part of their research, actions that anyone can perform: *measure, record, examine, observe, use.* Those verbs are usually in the passive voice: *The subjects were observed . . . .* We rarely find passages like this:

> To determine if monokines elicited an adrenal steroidogenic response, **I** ADDED preparations of . . .

Most writers would use a passive verb, *were added*, to name an action that anyone, not just the writer, can perform:

> To determine if monokines elicited a response, **preparations** . . . WERE ADDED.

A passive sentence like that, however, can create a problem: its writer dangled a modifier. You dangle a modifier when an introductory phrase has an implied subject that differs from the explicit subject in the following or preceding clause. In that example, the *implied subject* of the infinitive verb determine is I or we: I determine or we determine.

> [So that **I** could] determine if monokines elicited a response, preparations WERE ADDED.

But that implied subject, *I*, differs from the *explicit* subject of the clause it introduces—***preparations*** *were added*. When the two differ, the modifier dangles. Writers of scientific prose use this pattern so often, though, that it has become standard usage in their community.

I might note that this impersonal "scientific" style is a modern development. In his "New Theory of Light and Colors" (1672), Sir Isaac Newton wrote this charming first-person account of an experiment:

> I procured a triangular glass prism, to try therewith the celebrated phenomena of colors. And for that purpose, having darkened my laboratory, and made a small hole in my window shade, to let in a convenient quantity of the sun's light, I placed my prism at the entrance, that the light might be thereby refracted to the opposite wall. It was at first a very pleasing diversion to view the vivid and intense colors produced thereby.

✓ Quick Tip

Some teachers prohibit the use of *I* everywhere in the writing of their students not because it is wrong, but because inexperienced writers begin too many sentences with *I think . . ., I believe . . .*, and so on. Others forbid *I* because they want to discourage students from writing a narrative account of their thinking: *First I read . . ., Then I considered . . .* On those two occasions, follow their advice.

Here's the point: Some writers and editors avoid the first person by using the passive everywhere, but deleting an *I* or *we* doesn't make a researcher's thinking more objective. We know that behind those impersonal sentences are still flesh-and-blood people doing, thinking, and writing. In fact, the first-person *I* and *we* are common in scholarly prose when used with verbs that name actions unique to the writer.

Exercise 8.3

The verbs in 1 through 4 below are passive, but two could be active because they are metadiscourse verbs that would take first-person subjects. Revise the passive verbs that should be changed into active verbs. Then go through each sentence again and revise nominalizations into verbs as needed.

1. It is believed that a lack of understanding about the risks of alcohol is a cause of student bingeing.

2. The model has been subjected to extensive statistical analysis.

3. Success in exporting more crude oil for hard currency is suggested here as the cause of the improvement of the Russian economy.

4. The creation of a database is being considered, but no estimate has been made in regard to the potential of its usefulness.

The verbs in 5 through 8 are active, but some of them should be passive because they are not metadiscourse verbs. Revise the active verbs that should be changed into passive verbs, and revise in other ways as needed.

5. In Section IV, I argue that the indigenous peoples engaged in overcultivation of the land, leading to its exhaustion as a food-producing area.

6. Our intention in this book is to help readers achieve an understanding not only of the differences in grammar between Arabic and English but also the differences in worldview as reflected by Arabic vocabulary.

7. To make an evaluation of changes in the flow rate, I made a comparison of the current rate with the original rate on the basis of figures I had compiled with figures that Jordan had collected.

8. We performed the tissue rejection study on the basis of methods developed with our discovery of increases in dermal sloughing as a result of cellular regeneration.

Exercise 8.4

In these sentences, change passive verbs into actives and active verbs into passives only where you think it will improve the sentence. Invent characters where necessary. (Different answers are correct for this one.)

1. The author's impassioned narrative style is abandoned and a cautious treatment of theories of conspiracy is presented. But when the narrative line is picked up again, he invests his prose with the same vigor and force.

2. These directives are written in a style of maximum simplicity as a result of an attempt at more effective communication with employees with limited reading skills.

3. The ability of the human brain to arrive at solutions to human problems has been undervalued because studies have not been done that would be considered to have scientific reliability.

4. Many arguments were advanced against Darwinian evolution in the nineteenth century because basic assumptions about our place in the world were challenged by it. No longer were humans defined as privileged creatures but rather as a product of natural forces.

Exercise 8.5

The excerpt below is from an actual letter from the chancellor of a state university to parents of students. Except for the second word, you, why is the first part so impersonal? Why is the last part more personal? Change the first part so that you name in subjects whoever performs an action. Then change the second part to eliminate all characters. How do the two parts now differ? Have you improved the letter? This exercise raises the question of deliberate misdirection.

> As you probably have heard, the U of X campus has been the scene of a number of incidents of racial and sexual harassment over the last several weeks. The fact that similar incidents have occurred on campuses around the country does not make them any less offensive when they take place here. Of the ten to twelve incidents that have been reported since early October, most have involved graffiti or spoken insults. In only two cases was any physical contact made, and in neither case was anyone injured.
>
> U of X is committed to providing its students with an environment where they can live, work, and study without fear of being taunted or harassed because of their race, gender, religion, or ethnicity. I have made it clear that bigotry and intolerance will not be permitted and that the U of X's commitment to diversity is unequivocal. We are also taking steps to improve security in campus housing. We at the U of X are proud of this university's tradition of diversity . . .

NOUN + NOUN + NOUN

One more stylistic choice does not directly involve characters and actions, but I discuss it here because it can distort the match that readers expect between the form of an idea and the grammar of its expression. It is the long COMPOUND NOUN phrase:

> Early *childhood thought disorder misdiagnosis* often results from unfamiliarity with recent *research literature* describing such conditions. This paper is a review of seven recent studies in which are findings of particular relevance to *pre-adolescent hyperactivity diagnosis* and to *treatment modalities* involving *medication maintenance level evaluation procedures.*

It is fine to modify one noun with another, as common phrases such as stone wall, student center, space shuttle, and many others show.

But strings of nouns feel lumpy, so avoid them, especially ones you invent. Revise compound nouns of your own invention; revise, especially when they include nominalizations. just reverse the order of words and find prepositions to connect them:

1	2	3	4	5
early	childhood	thought	disorder	misdiagnosis
misdiagnose	disordered	thought	in early	childhood
1	2	3	4	5

Re-assembled, it looks like this:

Physicians misdiagnose[5] disordered[4] thought[3] in young[1] children[2] because they are unfamiliar with recent literature on the subject.

If, however, a long compound noun includes a technical term in your field, keep that part of the compound and unpack the rest:

Physicians misdiagnose[5] **thought disorders**[3,4] in young[1] children[2] because they are unfamiliar with recent literature on the subject.

Exercise 8.6

Revise the compound noun phrases in these sentences:

1. Diabetic patient blood pressure reduction may be brought about by renal depressor application.

2. The goal of this article is to describe text comprehension processes and recall protocol production.

3. On the basis of these principles, we may now attempt to formulate narrative information extraction rules.

4. This paper is an investigation into information processing behavior involved in computer human cognition simulation.

5. Enforcement of guidelines for new automobile tire durability must be a Federal Trade Commission responsibility.

6. The Social Security program is a monthly income floor guarantee based on a lifelong contribution schedule.

CLARITY AND THE PROFESSIONAL VOICE

Every group expects its members to show that they accept its values by adopting its distinctive voice. The apprentice banker must learn not only to think and look like a banker, but also to speak and write like one. Too often, though, aspiring professionals try to join the club by writing in its most complex technical language. When they do, they adopt an exclusionary style that erodes the trust a civil society depends on, especially in a world where information and expertise are now the means to power and control.

It is true that some research can never be made clear to intelligent lay readers—but less often than many researchers think. Here is an excerpt from Talcott Parsons, a social scientist who was as revered for his influence on his field as he was ridiculed for the opacity of his prose.

> Apart from theoretical conceptualization there would appear to be no method of selecting among the indefinite number of varying kinds of factual observation which can be made about a concrete phenomenon or field so that the various descriptive statements about it articulate into a coherent whole, which constitutes an "adequate," a "determinate" description. Adequacy in description is secured insofar as determinate and verifiable answers can be given to all the scientifically important questions involved. What questions are important is largely determined by the logical structure of the generalized conceptual scheme which, implicitly or explicitly, is employed.

We can make that clearer to moderately well-educated readers:

> Without a theory, scientists have no way to select from everything they could say about a subject only that which they can fit into a coherent whole that would be an "adequate" or "determinate" description. Scientists describe something "adequately" only when they can verify answers to all the questions they think are important. They decide what questions are important based on their implicit or explicit theories.

And we could make even it more concise:

> Whatever you describe, you need a theory to fit its parts into a whole. You need a theory to decide even what questions to ask and to verify their answers.

My versions lose the nuances of Parsons's passage and the last one loses some of its content, but his excruciating density numbs all but his most masochistically dedicated readers. Most readers would accept the tradeoff.

Here's the point: When you read or write a style that seems complex, you must determine whether it needs to be so complex to express complex ideas precisely. A difficult style can needlessly complicate complex ideas as easily as simple ones. Einstein said that everything should be made as simple as possible, but no simpler. Accordingly, a style should be as complex as necessary, *but no more*.

If you detect a needlessly complex style *when you read*, look for characters and actions so that you can unravel for yourself the complexity the writer needlessly inflicted on you.

When you write, use the same tools to detect when you are guilty of gratuitous complexity and, if you are, revise. When you do, you follow the Writer's Golden Rule: *Write to others as you would have others write to you*.

IN YOUR OWN WORDS

Exercise 8.7

Go through a page of your own writing. Circle all of the nominalizations and label all of the verbs as active or passive. For each nominalization and for each passive verb, state the specific reason you used it. If you cannot give a reason, revise it.

Exercise 8.8

Select a passage from a major work in your field. With a colleague, analyze its professional voice. What sorts of characters does it use? What is the balance between active and passive verbs? How are nominalizations used? How, and how extensively, does it use metadiscourse? Try to distinguish traits specific to this work from those that characterize the *field's* professional voice. Now, revise a passage of your own writing so that it imitates that voice. What did you have to change?

SUMMING UP

1. Readers judge prose to be clear when subjects of sentences name characters and verbs name actions.

Fixed	Subject	Verb	_____
Variable	Character	Action	_____

2. If you tell a story in which you make abstract nominalizations its main characters and subjects, use as few other nominalizations as you can:

    A nominalization is a **replacement** of a verb by a noun, often resulting in **displacement** of characters from subjects by nouns.

    ✓ When *a nominalization* REPLACES a verb with a noun, *it* often DISPLACES characters from subjects.

3. Use a passive if the agent of an action is self-evident:

    The voters REELECTED the president with 54% of the vote.

    ✓ *The president* WAS REELECTED with 54% of the vote.

4. Use a passive if it lets you replace a long subject with a short one:

    Research demonstrating the soundness of our reasoning and the need for action SUPPORTED *this decision.*

    ✓ *This decision* WAS SUPPORTED BY research demonstrating the soundness of our reasoning and the need for action.

5. Use a passive if it gives your readers a coherent sequence of subjects:

    ✓ By early 1945, *the Axis nations* had BEEN essentially DEFEATED; all that remained was a bloody climax. *The German borders* had BEEN BREACHED, and both *Germany and Japan* were being bombed around the clock. *Neither country*, though, had BEEN SO DEVASTATED that *it* could not RESIST.

6. Use an active verb if it is a metadiscourse verb:

    The terms of the analysis must BE DEFINED.

    ✓ We must DEFINE the terms of the analysis.

7. When possible, rewrite long compound noun phrases:

    We discussed the **board**[1] **candidate**[2] **review**[3] **meeting**[4] **schedule**.[5]

    ✓ We discussed the **schedule**[5] of **meetings**[4] to **review**[3] **candidates**[2] for the **board**.[1]

9

MOTIVATION

A problem well-put is half solved.

—John Dewey

Looking back, I think it was more difficult to see what the problems were than to solve them.

—Charles Darwin

The formulation of a problem is often more essential than its solution, which may be merely a matter of mathematical or experimental skill. To raise new questions, new possibilities, to regard old questions from a new angle, requires creative imagination and marks real advance in science.

—Albert Einstein

UNDERSTANDING MOTIVATION

I focused on features of sentences and passages that lead readers to see them as clear and coherent and to understand them more easily. But features of longer units of discourse—paragraphs, sections, and whole documents—also affect readers' sense of clarity, coherence, and understanding. In Part Three, I turn to those. The first is your introduction. Getting that right helps readers see everything that follows as clear and coherent.

If we are deeply engaged in a topic, we will read anything about it we can get our hands on, even if we must work hard to understand it. Not only will we struggle through clotted sentences, but we'll use our prior knowledge to fill in gaps, correct lapses in logic, and make sense of a tangled organization. A writer with that kind of reader has a big advantage.

But most writers are not so lucky. Most writers face readers who are not so deeply engaged or knowledgeable. Accordingly, they have to prepare their readers in two ways:

- They have to motivate readers so that they want to read carefully.
- They have to let readers know what to expect so that they can read more knowledgeably.

We read most attentively when we read not just about an interesting *topic*, but about a *problem* that is important to us—from finding a good job to knowing the origins of life.

Stating Problems in Introductions

From the moment you begin to plan a writing project, don't imagine your task as just writing about a topic, passing on information that interests *you*. See yourself as posing a problem that *your readers* want to see solved. That problem might, however, be one that your readers don't yet care—or even know—about. If so, you face a challenge: you must overcome their inclination to ask, *So what?* And you get just one shot at answering that question: in your introduction. That's where you must motivate readers to see your problem as theirs.

For example, read this introduction (all these examples are much shorter than typical ones).

1a. When college students go out to relax on the weekend, many now "binge," downing several alcoholic drinks quickly until they are drunk or even pass out. It is a behavior that has been spreading through colleges and universities across the country, especially at large state universities. It once was done mostly by men, but now even women binge. It has drawn the attention of parents, college administrators, and researchers.

That introduction offers only a topic: it does not motivate us to care about it. Unless a reader is already interested in the issue, she may shrug and ask, *So what? Who cares that college students drink a lot?*

Contrast that introduction with this one: it tells us why bingeing is not just an interesting topic but a problem worth our attention:

1b. Alcohol has been a big part of college life for hundreds of years. From football weekends to fraternity parties, college students drink and often drink hard. But a new kind of drinking known as "binge" drinking is spreading through our colleges and universities. Bingers drink quickly not to be sociable but to get drunk or even to pass out. Bingeing is far from the harmless fun long associated with college life. In the last six months, it has been cited in at least six deaths, many injuries, and considerable destruction of property. It crosses the line from fun to reckless behavior that kills and injures not just drinkers but those around them. We may not be able to stop bingeing entirely, but we must try to control its worst costs by educating students in how to manage its risks.

As short as that is, (1b) has the three parts that appear in most introductions. Each part has a role in motivating a reader to read on. The parts are these:

Shared Context—Problem—Solution/Main Point/Claim

Alcohol has been a big part of college life . . . drink hard. _{shared context} But a new kind of drinking known as "binge" drinking is spreading . . . kills and injures not just drinkers but those around them. problem We may not be able to stop bingeing entirely, but we must try to control its worst costs by educating students in how to manage its risks.

solution/main point/claim

Part 1: Establishing a Shared Context

Most pieces of writing open with a shared context, as does (1b):

Alcohol has been a big part of college life for hundreds of years. From football weekends to fraternity parties, college students drink and often drink hard. _{shared context} But a new kind of drinking known as "binge" . . .

That shared context offers historical background, but it might have been a recent event, a common belief, or anything else that reminds readers of what they know, have experienced, or readily accept.

Event: A recent State U survey showed that 80% of first-year students engaged in underage drinking in their first month on campus, a fact that should surprise no one. _{shared context} But what is worrisome is the spread among first-year students of a new kind of drinking known as "binge" . . .

Belief: Most students believe that college is a safe place to drink for those who live on or near campus. And for the most part they are right. _{shared context} But for those students who get caught up in the new trend of "binge" drinking, . . .

These forms of shared context play a special role in motivating readers to read on: In (1b), I wanted you to accept that context as a seemingly unproblematic base for thinking about binge drinking *just so that I could then challenge it.* I set you up so that I could say, in effect, *you may think you know the whole story, **but** you don't.* That but signals the coming qualification:

... drink and often drink hard. _{shared context} **BUT a new kind of drinking known as "binge" drinking is spreading ...**

In other words, college drinking seems unproblematic, *but it turns out not to be*. I wanted that small surprise to motivate you to go on reading.

No opening move is more common among experienced writers: open with a seeming truth, then qualify or even reject it. You can find countless examples in newspapers, magazines, and especially professional journals. This opening context can be a sentence or two, as here; in a journal, it can be paragraphs long, where it is called a *literature review*, a survey of what researchers have said that the writer will qualify or correct.

Not every piece of writing opens with this move. Some jump directly to the second element of an introduction: the statement of a problem.

Part 2: Stating the Problem

If the writer opens with a shared context, she will typically introduce the problem with a word such as *but* or *however*:

> Alcohol has been a big part of college life for hundreds of years. From football weekends to fraternity parties, college students drink and often drink hard. _{shared context} **But** a kind of drinking known as "binge" drinking is spreading through our colleges and universities. Bingers drink quickly not to be sociable but to get drunk or even to pass out. Bingeing is far from the harmless fun long associated with college life. In the last six months, it has been cited in at least six deaths, many injuries, and considerable destruction of property. It crosses the line from fun to reckless behavior that kills and injures not just drinkers but those around them. _{problem} We may not be able to ...

The Two Parts of a Problem.   For readers to think that something is a problem, it must have two parts:

- The first part is some *condition* or *situation*: terrorism, rising tuition, binge drinking, anything that has the potential to cause trouble.
- The second part is the *intolerable consequence* of that condition, a cost that readers don't want to pay.

That cost is what motivates readers. They want to eliminate or at least ameliorate it, because it makes them unhappy. The cost of terrorism is injury and death; the cost of rising tuition is more money out of their pockets. If rising tuition did not make parents and students unhappy, it would not be a problem.

You can identify the cost of a problem if you imagine someone asking *So what?* after you state its condition. Answer *So what?* and you have found the cost:

> But a kind of drinking known as "binge" drinking is spreading through our colleges and universities. Bingers drink quickly not to be sociable but to get drunk or even to

^{pass out. condition} *So what?* **Bingeing is far from the harmless fun long associated with college life. In the last six months, it has been cited in at least six deaths, many injuries, and considerable destruction of property. It crosses the line from fun to reckless behavior that kills and injures not just drinkers but those around them.** _{cost of the condition}

The condition part of the problem is binge drinking; the cost is death and injury. If bingeing had no cost, it would not be a problem. Readers have to see the condition and cost together before they recognize a problem.

Two Kinds of Problems: Practical and Conceptual.   There are two kinds of problems and each motivates readers in a different way. You have to write about them differently.

- A *practical* problem concerns a condition or situation in the world and demands an action as its solution. That students binge drink and harm themselves is a practical problem.
- A *conceptual* problem concerns what we think about something and demands a *change in understanding* as a solution. That we don't know why students binge is a conceptual problem.

Writers outside the academic world most often address practical problems; writers inside it most often address conceptual ones.

Practical Problems: What We Should Do.   Binge drinking is an example of a practical problem for two reasons. First, it involves something that has a palpable cost that should make readers unhappy. Second, to solve it, someone must *act* differently. If we can't avoid a practical problem, we must *do* something in the world to change the condition, to ameliorate or eliminate its costs.

We usually name a practical problem in a word or two: *cancer, unemployment, binge drinking*. But that's a shorthand. Those terms name only the condition: they say nothing about costs. Most conditions sound like trouble, but anything can be the condition of a problem if its palpable costs make you unhappy. If winning the lottery made you suffer the loss of friends and family, it would be a practical problem.

You may think that the costs of a problem like bingeing are too obvious to state, but you cannot count on readers to see the problem as you do. Some readers may see different costs: where you see death and injury, a university publicist might see only bad press: *Those binge drinking students make us look like a party school, which hurts our image with parents.* More callous readers might see no costs at all: *So what if college students injure or kill themselves? What's that to me?* If so, you have to figure out how to make such readers see that those costs affect them. If you can't describe the costs you see so that they matter *to your readers*, they have no reason to care about what you've written.

Conceptual Problems: What We Should Think.   A conceptual problem has the same two parts as a practical one, a condition and its costs. But beyond that, the two sorts of problem are very different.

- The condition of a conceptual problem is always *something that we do not know or understand*.

We can express this condition as a question: *How much does the universe weigh? Why does the hair on your head keep growing, but the hair on your legs doesn't?*

- The cost of a conceptual problem is not the palpable unhappiness we feel from pain, suffering, and loss; it is the dissatisfaction we feel because we don't understand something important to us.

We can express this cost as something *more important* that readers don't know, as *another, larger question*:

Cosmologists do not know how much the universe weighs. _{condition} *So what?* Well, if they knew, they might figure out something more important: Will time and space go on forever, or end, and if they do, when and how? _{cost/larger question}

Biologists don't know why some hair keeps growing and other hair stops. _{condition} *So what?* If they knew, they might understand something more important: What turns growth on and off? _{cost/larger question}

Administrators do not know why students underestimate the risks of binge drinking. _{condition} *So what?* If they knew, they might figure out something more important: Would better information at orientation help students make safer decisions about drinking? _{cost/larger question}

Sometimes, as in the last example, the larger question is about something readers do not know how to do. But that is still a conceptual problem, because it concerns our ignorance and because its solution is not an action but information.

Think of it like this: for a conceptual problem, you answer a small question so that your answer contributes to answering a larger, more important one. Readers are motivated because your small question inherits its importance from that larger one.

If you can't imagine a way in which the answer to your small question helps to address a larger, more important question, your question may not be worth asking. It seems unlikely that this question would help us understand anything important: *What color were Lincoln's socks when he delivered the Gettysburg Address?* But this one might: How did Lincoln plan the Address? If we knew that, we might learn about something more important: the nature of his creative process.

Here's the point: Like your readers, you will usually be more motivated by large questions. But limited resources—time, funding, knowledge, skill, pages—may keep you from addressing a large question satisfactorily. So you have to find a question you *can* answer. When you plan your paper, look for a question that is small enough to answer but is also connected to another question large enough for you *and your readers* to care about.

✓ Quick Tip:

Some students think that they don't need a problem statement when their teacher assigns a specific topic, but they are wrong. If your assignment includes words like *discuss, explain,* or *analyze,* your job is to find a question behind that assignment. If your assignment states a question but not its significance, your job is to find a good answer to *So what?* Your paper will be both better written and better received if you begin it with a complete problem statement.

✓ Quick Tip:

When you read an academic book or essay, look first for the implied question in its problem statement and then for its main claim, which answers that question. They will help focus your reading. If you don't find a question in the introduction, look for one in the conclusion. If that fails, find the main claim and ask yourself, *What question does this answer?* The more you understand why a writer is telling you something, the better you will understand what she writes.

Part 3: Stating the Solution

The solution is your main point or claim. Practical and conceptual problems differ in their solutions. We solve practical problems with action: readers (or someone) must *change what they do.* We solve conceptual problems with information: readers (or someone) must change what they think. Your answer to a small question then helps readers understand a larger one.

Practical Problems.   To solve a practical problem, you must propose that the reader (or someone) *do* something to change a condition in the world:

> . . . behavior that crosses the line from fun to recklessness that kills and injures not just drinkers but those around them. _{problem} **We may not be able to stop bingeing entirely, but we must try to control its worst costs by educating students in how to manage its risks.** _{solution/point}

Conceptual Problems.   To solve a conceptual problem, you must state something the writer wants readers to *understand* or *believe*:

> . . . we can better understand not only the causes of this dangerous behavior but also the nature of risk-taking behavior in general. _{problem} **This study reports on our analysis of the beliefs of 300 first-year college students. We found that students were more likely to binge if they knew more stories of other students bingeing, so that they believed that bingeing is far more common than it actually is.** _{solution/point}

As Darwin and Einstein said, nothing is more difficult than finding a good question, because without one, you don't have an answer worth supporting.

Another Part: Prelude

You may recall being told to "catch your readers' attention" by opening with a snappy quotation, fact, or anecdote. What best catches attention is a problem in need of a solution, but a catchy opening can vividly introduce themes central to your problem. To name this device, we can use a musical term: *prelude*. Writers in the natural and social sciences rarely use preludes. They are more common in the humanities and most common in writing for the general public.

Here are three preludes that could establish key themes in a paper about binge drinking.

1. **A Quotation**

   "If you're old enough to fight for your country, you're old enough to drink to it."

2. **A Startling Fact**

   A recent study reports that at most colleges three out of four students "binged" at least once in the previous thirty days, consuming more than five drinks at a sitting. Almost half binge once a week, and those who binge most are not just members of fraternities but their officers.

3. **An Illustrative Anecdote**

   When Jim S., president of Omega Alpha, accepted a dare from his fraternity brothers to down a pint of whiskey in one long swallow, he didn't plan to become this year's eighth college fatality from alcohol poisoning.

We can combine all three:

> It is often said that "if you're old enough to fight for your country, you're old enough to drink to it." _{quotation} Tragically, Jim S., president of Omega Alpha, no longer has a chance to do either. When he accepted a dare from his fraternity brothers to down a pint of whiskey in one long swallow, he didn't expect to become this year's eighth college fatality from alcohol poisoning. _{anecdote} According to a recent study, at most colleges, three out of four students have, like Jim, drunk five drinks at a sitting in the last thirty days. And those who drink the most are not just members of fraternities but—like Jim S. —officers. _{striking fact}

> Drinking, of course, has been a part of American college life since the first college opened . . . _{shared context} But in recent years . . . _{problem}

Here, then, is a general plan for your introductions:

Prelude
Shared Context
Problem [Condition + Cost]
Solution/Main Point/Claim

DIAGNOSIS AND REVISION: INTRODUCTIONS

To diagnose how well your readers will be motivated by your introduction, do this:

1. **Determine whether you are posing a practical or conceptual problem.** Do you want readers to *do* something or to *think* something?

2. **Draw a line after your introduction.** If you cannot quickly locate the end of your introduction, neither will your readers, who might then miss both your problem and its solution, the main point of your paper.

3. **Divide the introduction into its three parts: shared context + problem + solution/main point/claim.** If you cannot quickly make those divisions, your introduction is likely to seem unfocused.

4. **Make sure the first word of the first sentence after the shared context is *but, however,* or some other word indicating that you will challenge that shared context.** If you don't explicitly signal the contrast between the shared context and the problem, readers may miss it.

5. **Divide the problem into two parts: condition and cost.**

   5a. **Is the condition the right kind for the problem?**
      * If you are addressing a practical problem, the condition must be something that exacts a palpable cost.
      * If you are addressing a conceptual problem, the condition must be something not known or understood. This should be stated not as a direct question, *What causes bingeing?,* but as a statement of what we do not know: *But we do not know why bingers ignore known risks.*

   5b. **Does the cost appropriately answer *So what?***
      * If you are addressing a practical problem, the answer to So what? must state some palpable consequence of the condition that causes unhappiness.
      * If you are addressing a conceptual problem, the answer to So what? must state some more significant issue that is not known or understood.

6. **Underline your solution/main point/claim.** This should appear at the end of the introduction in its stress position, and should state the key themes that the rest of your paper will develop (more on that in Chapter 10).

CONCLUSIONS

A good introduction motivates your readers, introduces your key themes, and states your main point, the solution to your motivating problem. Get your introduction straight, and readers can read the rest more quickly and understand it better. A good conclusion serves a different end: as the last thing your reader reads, it should bring together your point, its significance, and its implications for thinking further about your problem. Conclusions vary more than introductions, but in a pinch, you can map the parts of your introduction onto your conclusion. Just reverse their order:

1. **Open your conclusion by stating (or restating) the gist of your point, the main claim of your paper, the solution to your problem:**

   Though we can come at the problem of bingeing from several directions, the most important is education, especially in the first week of a student's college life. But that means each university must devote time and resources to it.

2. **Explain its significance by answering So what? in a new way, if you can; if not, restate what you offered in the introduction, now as a benefit:**

   If we do not start to control bingeing soon, many more students will die.

   If we start to control bingeing now, we will save many lives.

3. **Suggest a further question or problem to be resolved, something still not known. Answer** *Now what?:*

   Of course, even if we can control bingeing, the larger issue of risk-taking in general will remain a serious problem.

4. **End with an anecdote, quotation, or fact that echoes your prelude. We'll call this by another musical term, your coda (again, used most often in popular writing, rarely in the natural and social sciences):**

   We should not underestimate how deeply entrenched bingeing is: We might have hoped that after Jim S.'s death from alcohol poisoning, his university would have taken steps to prevent more such tragedies. Sad to say, it reported another death from bingeing this month.

There are other ways to conclude, but this one works when nothing better comes to mind.

IN YOUR OWN WORDS

Exercise 9.1

For this exercise, you can use pieces of writing that are finished or still in progress. For each, draw a line between the problem and the solution. Underline the condition and bracket the cost. Classify the problem of each as conceptual or practical. Then rewrite the conceptual problems as practical ones and the practical problems as conceptual ones. What did you have to change? Were some problems easier to rewrite in this way than others? Why?

Exercise 9.2

Writers, especially in academic contexts, can struggle more with problem statements than with other parts of their introductions. They know what they want to say, but they don't know why other people should care. Or worse, they just assume that others will care because they do. (Students sometimes think they don't need problem statements because the teacher assigned them a topic, but that's a mistake.) It makes sense that writers would have this struggle. To state a problem, writers need to understand not only their own ideas but also the motives of their readers. This exercise will help you do that. For a project you are just beginning, do the following:

1. In a sentence, state your topic: In this paper I am writing about _____ (e.g., science in Tennyson's *In Memoriam*, the effects of Citizens United v. Federal Election Commission on election financing, the space shuttle *Columbia* accident).

2. In a sentence, state why *you* selected this particular topic out of the many you could have chosen: I care about my topic because _____. (If you cannot complete this sentence, you need to do more thinking about your topic or choose another. You cannot expect your readers to care if you can't say why you do.)

3. In a sentence, state your *main point or claim*: The point I want to make about [topic] is that _____.

4. In a paragraph, describe one person (real or imagined) who would care deeply about your ideas. What does she (or he) look like? What does she do for a living? What are her personal interests? What books has she read in the past two months?

5. Now write a short letter to the person you have described, explaining to her why she should care about your paper.

You will probably find phrases and ideas in this letter that you can use in your problem statement.

Exercise 9.3

Have a reader diagnose an introduction you have written using the procedure on p. 191–192:

1. Determine whether the problem is practical or conceptual.
2. Draw a line at the introduction's end.
3. Divide the introduction into its three parts: shared context, the problem, and the solution/main point/claim. Do these three parts appear? Are they in the right order?
4. Circle the word or phrase (usually *but* or *however*) that indicates that you are challenging the shared context.
5. Divide the problem into its two parts: condition and cost. Does the cost answer the question *So what?*
6. Underline your solution/main point/claim.

If your reader struggled with any of these steps, revise accordingly.

SUMMING UP

You motivate purposeful reading with an introduction that states a problem readers want to see solved.

For a practical problem the key is to state its costs so clearly that readers will ask not *So what?* but *What do we do?* Here is a plan for introducing a practical problem:

Alcohol has been a part of college life for hundreds of years. From football weekends to fraternity parties, college students drink and often drink hard. shared context

Open the introduction with 1, a *brief statement* of what you will go on to qualify or even contradict.

But a kind of drinking known as "binge" drinking is spreading through our colleges and universities. Bingers drink quickly not to be sociable but to get drunk or even to pass out. [*So what?*] condition

Follow that with a statement of the condition of the problem. Introduce it with a *but, however, on the other hand,* etc. Imagine a *So what?* after it.

Bingeing is far from harmless. In the last six months, it has been cited in six deaths, many injuries, and considerable destruction of property. It crosses the line from fun to reckless behavior that kills and injures not just drinkers but those around them. costs

Answer that imagined *So what?* with a statement of the consequences of that condition, its costs *to your readers* that they do not want to pay.

We may not be able to stop bingeing entirely, but we must try to control its worst costs by educating students in how to manage its risks. solution

Conclude with a statement of the solution to the problem, an *action* that will eliminate or at least ameliorate the costs.

For conceptual problems, the key is to state a small question worth answering because it helps to answer a larger, more significant one. Here is a plan for introducing conceptual problems:

Colleges are reporting that binge drinking is increasing. We know its practical risks. We also know that bingers ignore those risks, even after they have learned about them.·shared context

Open the introduction with *shared context*, a brief statement of what you will go on to qualify or even contradict.

But we don't know what causes bingers to ignore the known risks: social influences, a personality attracted to risk, or a failure to understand the nature of the risks. [*So what?*] condition / first, small question

Follow that with a statement of the condition of the problem. Introduce it with a *but, however, on the other hand*, etc. State something that is not known or well understood. Imagine a *So what?* after it.

If we can determine why bingers ignore known risks of their actions, we can better understand not only the causes of this dangerous behavior but also the nature of risk-taking behavior in general. cost/second, larger question

Answer that imagined *So what?* with the cost of the condition, a larger and more important issue that is not known or understood but that might be answered if we know the answer to the first question.

In this study, we analyzed the beliefs of 300 first-year college students to determine . . . We found that . . .

solution

Conclude your introduction with a statement of the solution to the problem, an answer to the first question that helps answer the second one, as well.

GLOBAL COHERENCE

One of the most difficult things [to write] is the first paragraph. I have spent many months on a first paragraph, and once I get it, the rest just comes out very easily. In the first paragraph you solve most of the problems with your book. The theme is defined, the style, the tone.

—Gabriel García Márquez

UNDERSTANDING HOW FRAMEWORKS SHAPE READING

In the last lesson, I explained how you must create an introduction that does two things:

- Motivate your readers by stating a problem that they care about.
- Frame the rest of your document by stating the point and key concepts that you will develop in what follows.

In this lesson, I explain how that second point applies to all the parts of your document—its sections, subsections, and even paragraphs. Like the term *clear*, the term *coherent* doesn't refer to anything we find on the page. Coherence is an experience we create for ourselves as we make our own sense out of what we read.

What we look for on the page are signals that help us know what parts of our prior knowledge to bring to the text and how we can integrate what we read with the knowledge we have. You help your readers do that by building those signals into your writing deliberately. This lesson explains how to do that.

FORECASTING THEMES TO CREATE COHERENCE

We looked at those features that help readers create "local" coherence in short passages, but readers need more to grasp the coherence of a whole document. To help them achieve that coherence, you can use a by-now-familiar principle: begin each document, its sections, and subsections with a short, easily grasped segment that states the point and introduces the themes that readers use to organize the rest. Then, in the body, support, develop, or explain the point and themes stated in the first part.

To help readers grasp the coherence of a document and its sections, follow these six principles:

For the document:

1. Readers must know where the introduction ends and the body begins, as well as where each section ends and the next begins. Identify the start of each new section with a heading that includes the key themes for that section (see 5 below). If your field does not use headings, delete them for the final draft.

2. At the end of the introduction, readers look for the document's main point/solution to the problem, which should state the main themes developed in the rest. If you have good reason to save your main point for the conclusion, put a sentence at the end of the introduction that promises the point to come *and* states the main themes.

3. In the body, readers look for the concepts announced as themes at the end of the introduction, using them to organize their understanding of the whole. Be sure that you repeat those themes regularly.

For each section and subsection:

4. Readers look for a short segment that introduces the section or subsection.

5. At the end of that introductory segment, readers look for a sentence that states both the *point* of the section and the specific concepts you will develop as distinctive themes for that section.

6. In the body of the section, readers look for the concepts announced as themes at the end of the introductory segment, using them to organize their understanding of that section. Be sure that you repeat them regularly.

Quick Tip

You can use these six principles to prepare yourself to read a difficult document. First, highlight the question in the problem statement and the main claim that answers it (see pp. 186–189). Next, for each section, highlight its introduction, point, and key concepts. If you don't find them in the introduction to a section, look for them at the end of the section. Finally, read through just the parts that you highlighted. When you then begin reading in detail, you will have in mind an overview that will help you better understand and remember the rest.

In the limited space we have here, I can't illustrate these principles with entire documents or even long sections. So I will use paragraphs and ask you to relate their structure to that of a whole section of a document.

For example, read this:

1a. Thirty sixth-grade students wrote essays that were analyzed to determine the effectiveness of eight weeks of training to distinguish fact from opinion. That ability is an important aspect of making sound arguments of any kind. In an essay written before instruction began, the writers failed almost completely to distinguish fact from opinion. In an essay written after four weeks of instruction, the students visibly attempted to distinguish fact from opinion, but did so inconsistently. In three more essays, they distinguished fact from opinion more consistently, but never achieved the predicted level of performance. In a final essay written six months after instruction ended, they did no better than they did in their pre-instruction essays. Their training had some effect on their writing during the instruction period, but it was inconsistent, and six months after instruction it had no measurable effect.

The first few sentences introduce the rest, but we don't see in them the key concepts that follow: *inconsistently, never achieved, no better, no measurable effect;* those terms are crucial to the *point* of the whole passage. Worse, we don't get to that point until we get to the end of the passage: training had no long-term effect. And so as we read, the passage seems to ramble, until the end, when we learn what we need to know to make sense of it retrospectively. But that takes more effort than we should have to expend.

Compare this version:

1b. In this study, thirty sixth-grade students were taught to distinguish fact from opinion. They did so successfully during the instruction period, but the effect was inconsistent and less than predicted, and six months after instruction ended, the instruction had no measurable effect. In an essay written before instruction began, the writers failed almost completely to distinguish fact from opinion. In an essay written after four weeks of instruction, the students visibly attempted to distinguish fact from opinion, but did so inconsistently. In three more essays, they distinguished fact from opinion more consistently, but never achieved the predicted level of performance. In a final essay written six months after instruction ended, they did no better than they did in their pre-instruction essay. We thus conclude that short-term training to distinguish fact from opinion has no consistent or long-term effect.

In (1b), we quickly grasp that the first two sentences introduce what follows. And in the second sentence, we see two things: both the point of the passage (underlined) and its key terms (boldfaced):

1b. In this study, thirty sixth-grade students were taught to distinguish fact from opinion. <u>They did so successfully during the instruction period, but the **effect was inconsistent and less than predicted,** and six months after instruction ended, the instruction had **no measurable effect.**</u> point of the passage

Consequently, we feel the passage hangs together better, and we read it with more understanding.

Now imagine two documents: in one, the point of each section and of the whole appears at its *end* (as in 1a) and what openings there are do not introduce the key terms that follow; in the other, each point appears in an *introductory* segment to every paragraph, section, and of the whole (as in 1b). Which would be easier to read and understand? The second, of course. Keep in mind this principle:

Put the point sentence at the *end* of the short opening segment; make it the *last* sentence that your reader reads before starting the longer, more complex segment that follows.

- In a paragraph, the introductory segment might be just a single sentence, so by default, it will be the last sentence readers read before they read what follows. If the passage has a *two*-sentence introduction (as did 1b), be sure the point of the paragraph is the *second* sentence, still making it the last thing readers read before they read the rest.

- For sections, your introduction might be a paragraph or more. For a whole document, you might need several paragraphs. Even in those cases, put your point sentence at the end of that introductory segment, no matter how long it is. Make your point the last thing readers read before they begin reading the longer, more complex segments that follow.

Some inexperienced writers think that if they tip off their main point in their introduction, readers will be bored and not read on. Not true. If you motivate readers with an interesting problem, they will want to see how you address it.

> ***Here's the point:***   To write a document that readers will think is coherent, open every unit—section, subsection, and the whole—with a short, easily grasped introductory segment. At the end of that opening segment, put a sentence that states both the point of the unit and the key concepts that follow. Such "point" sentences constitute the outline of your document, its logical structure. If readers miss them, they may judge your writing to be incoherent.

TWO MORE REQUIREMENTS FOR COHERENCE

We can make sense of almost anything we read if we know its points. But to make full coherent sense of a passage, we must see two more things.

1. **Readers must see how everything in a section or whole is *relevant* to its point.** Consider this passage:

   We analyzed essays written by sixth-grade students to determine the effectiveness of training in distinguishing fact from opinion. In an essay written before training, the students failed almost completely to distinguish fact and opinion. These essays were also badly organized in several ways. In the first two essays after training began, the students attempted to distinguish fact from opinion, but did so inconsistently. They also produced fewer spelling and punctuation errors. In the essays four through seven, they distinguished fact from opinion more consistently, but in their final essay, written six months after completion of instruction, they did no better than they did in their first essay. Their last essay was significantly longer than their first one, however. Their training thus had some effect on their writing during the training period, but it was inconsistent and transient.

What are those sentences about spelling, organization, and length doing there? When readers can't see the relevance of sentences to a point, they are likely to judge what they read as being incoherent.

I am sorry to say that I can't give you a simple rule of relevance, because it's so abstract a quality. I can only list its most important kinds. Sentences are relevant to a point when they offer these:

- background or context
- points of sections and the whole
- reasons supporting a point
- evidence, facts, or data supporting a reason
- an explanation of reasoning or methods
- consideration of other points of view

2. **Readers must see how the parts of your document are ordered.** Readers want to see not just how everything they read is relevant to a point, but what principle is behind the order of its parts. We look for three kinds of order: chronological, coordinate, and logical.

- **Chronological** This is the simplest order, from earlier to later (or vice versa), as a narrative or as cause and effect. Signal time with *first, then, finally;* signal cause and effect with *as a result, because of that,* and so on. The passage about the essay research was chronologically organized.

- **Coordinate** Two or more sections are coordinate when they are like pillars equally supporting a common roof. *There are three reasons why* . . . Order those sections so that their sequence makes sense to your reader—by importance, complexity, and so on—then signal that order with words and phrases such as *first, second,* . . . or *also, another, more important, in addition,* and so on. That's how this section on order is organized.

- **Logical** This is the most complex order: by example and generalization (or vice versa), premise and conclusion (or vice versa), or by assertion and contradiction. Signal logic with *for example, on the other hand, it follows that* . . .

Quick Tip

Writers often order their documents chronologically because that is easiest for them. Once you have drafted a paper, read it through to see whether you have organized it simply as a narrative of your thinking. If you have, consider revising. Most readers aren't interested in how you thought through an issue; they want to see the results of your having done it.

On Paragraphs

It would be easy to say that all paragraphs should follow these principles:

- Begin with one or two short, easily grasped sentences that frame what follows.
- State the point of the paragraph (in traditional terms its *topic sentence*) in the last sentence of its introduction. If the introduction is just one sentence, it will be its point, by default.
- Toward the end of that point sentence, name the key themes that thread through what follows.

The problem is, not all paragraphs follow that tidy structure, and we get through most of the ones that don't just fine. We can ignore short paragraphs that serve special functions, such as providing a transition or an aside, because we have no problem reading (or writing) them. But many substantial paragraphs of six or seven sentences or more seem to have no evident principle of design. Even so, we can see in most of them some kind of opening segment that frames the rest of the paragraph. It might not include its *point*—that may come later, usually at its end. But the first sentence or two will set up what follows, introducing its key terms. And that is usually enough to help us make sense of what is to come.

For example, compare these two paragraphs:

2a. The team obtained exact sequences of fossils—new lines of antelopes, giraffes, and elephants developing out of old and appearing in younger strata, then dying out as they were replaced by others in still later strata. The most specific sequences they reconstructed were several lines of pigs that had been common at the site and had developed rapidly. The team produced family trees that dated types of pigs so accurately that when they found pigs next to fossils of questionable age, they could use the pigs to date the fossils. By mapping every fossil precisely, the team was able to recreate exactly how and when the animals in a whole ecosystem evolved.

2b. By precisely mapping every fossil they found, the team was able to recreate exactly how and when the animals in a whole ecosystem evolved. They charted new lines of antelopes, giraffes, and elephants developing out of old and appearing in younger strata, then dying out as they were replaced by others in still later strata. The most exact sequences they reconstructed were several lines of pigs that had been common at the site and had developed rapidly. The team produced family trees that dated types of pigs so accurately that when they found pigs next to fossils of questionable age, they could use the pigs to date the fossils.

Paragraph (2a) makes its point in the last sentence; paragraph (2b) in its first sentence. But in the context of an otherwise coherent text about fossil hunters and their work, we wouldn't have a big problem understanding (2a).

And that only emphasizes why it is so important to introduce the sections and subsections of your document clearly, accurately, and helpfully. If your readers begin a section knowing its point, they can make their way through a few paragraphs that are less than perfect. But if they don't know what your paragraphs add up to, then no matter how well written they are individually, your readers may well feel lost.

A BASIC PRINCIPLE OF CLARITY

This basic principle applies to individual sentences, to substantive paragraphs, to sections and subsections, and to wholes:

> Readers are more likely to judge as clear any unit of writing that opens with a short segment that they can easily grasp and that frames the longer and more complex segment that follows.

- In a simple sentence, that short, easily grasped segment is a subject/topic. Compare these two:

  1a. <u>Resistance in Nevada against its use as a waste disposal site</u> has been heated.
  1b. <u>Nevada</u> HAS heatedly RESISTED its use as a waste disposal site.

- In a complex sentence, that short, easily grasped segment is a MAIN CLAUSE that expresses the *point* of its sentence. Compare these two:

  2a. Greater knowledge of pre-Columbian civilizations and the effect of European colonization destroying their societies by inflicting on them devastating diseases has led to a historical reassessment of Columbus' role in world history.
  2b. <u>Historians are reassessing Columbus' role in world history,</u> because they know more about pre-Columbian civilizations and how European colonization destroyed their societies by inflicting on them devastating diseases.

The point of sentence (2a) is buried at its end. In (2b), the opening clause states the main point of the sentence, its most important claim: *Historians are reassessing Columbus' role . . .* That claim is then supported by the longer and more complex clause that follows.

- In a paragraph, that short, easily grasped unit is an introductory sentence or two that both expresses the point of the paragraph and introduces its key concepts. Compare these two paragraphs:

3a. Thirty sixth-grade students wrote essays that were analyzed to determine the effectiveness of eight weeks of training to distinguish fact from opinion. That ability is an important aspect of making sound arguments of any kind. In an essay written before instruction began, the writers failed almost completely to distinguish fact from opinion. In an essay written after four weeks of instruction, the students visibly attempted to distinguish fact from opinion, but did so inconsistently. In three more essays, they distinguished fact from opinion more consistently, but never achieved the predicted level. In a final essay written six months after instruction ended, they did no better than they did in their pre-instruction essay. Their training had some effect on their writing during the instruction period, but it was inconsistent, and six months after instruction it had no measurable effect.

3b. <u>In this study, thirty sixth-grade students were taught to distinguish fact from opinion. They did so **successfully** during the instruction period, but the effect was **inconsistent** and **less than predicted**, and six months after instruction ended, the instruction had **no measurable effect.**</u> _{opening segment/point} In an essay written before instruction began, the writers failed almost completely to distinguish fact from opinion. In an essay written after four weeks of instruction, the students visibly attempted to distinguish fact from opinion, but did so inconsistently. In three more essays, they distinguished fact from opinion more consistently, but never achieved the predicted level. In a final essay written six months after instruction ended, they did no better than they did in their pre-instruction essay. We thus conclude that short-term training to distinguish fact from opinion has no consistent or long term effect.

Paragraph (3a) has no clearly distinguished opening unit, and it does not announce the key themes of the paragraph. Paragraph (3b) has a clearly marked opening unit that states the point, and it clearly announces the key themes of the paragraph.

- In a section or subsection, that short, easily grasped unit may be just a paragraph; in longer units, it will be proportionally longer. Even so, at its end it expresses the point of its unit and introduces the key concepts that follow. There is not enough space here to illustrate how that principle applies to a passage several paragraphs long, but it is easy to imagine.

- In a whole document, that introductory unit might be one or more paragraphs long, perhaps even a few pages. Even so, it should be substantially shorter than the rest, and in a sentence at its end, it states the point of the whole document and introduces its key concepts.

Quick Tip

Budget your time for both drafting and revision so that you spend most of it on beginnings: the introduction to the whole, then the introductions to major sections, then introductions to subsections, and long paragraphs, then the beginnings of sentences. Get beginnings straight, and the rest is likely to take care of itself.

The Costs and Benefits of Cookie-Cutter Writing

Some writers fear that patterns like these will inhibit their creativity and bore their readers. That's a reasonable concern, if you are writing a literary essay that explores your own thoughts as you have them, for readers who have the time and patience to follow the twists and turns of your thinking. If you are writing that kind of essay for that kind of reader, go to it. Don't tie yourself to what I've said here.

On most occasions, however, most of us read less for aesthetic pleasures than to understand what we need to know. You help readers toward this end when you follow the principles of clarity and coherence we've looked at in Parts Two and Three of this book.

Such writing may seem cut and dried—to *you*, because *you* will be so conscious of the forms you followed. But it earns the gratitude of readers who have too little time to read, understand, and remember everything they must and who will, in any event, focus more on understanding the substance of your writing than on critiquing its form.

IN YOUR OWN WORDS

Exercise 10.1

A basic principle of clarity is that any unit of discourse—a sentence, a paragraph, a section, a whole document—should begin with a short segment that introduces and frames the longer and more complex segment that follows. Go through a piece of your writing section by section. Draw a line after that short segment and circle words in that segment that signal key themes in what follows. If you cannot, revise. Then repeat this exercise paragraph by paragraph.

Exercise 10.2

To feel a document (or a section of one) is coherent, a reader needs to understand how it is organized (review pp. 201-202). But writers, especially in early drafts, often organize their documents in the way that is easiest for them, not the way that is best for their readers. Specifically, writers often adopt a chronological or narrative structure by default. You can see why this is so. When getting ideas down on paper, it is easiest for writers simply to narrate their thinking or research. But most often, what readers do not want to hear a story of discovery but to understand a writer's points. Revising for global coherence, therefore, often involves translating a document from a chronological or narrative structure to a coordinate or logical one. A reader can help you do this.

Go through a document or section that you have organized chronologically. Highlight your points, paragraph by paragraph, and copy them onto index cards. Shuffle the cards and give them to a reader. Have a reader put the cards into what seems like their right order. Reorganize your document or section so that it follows that order. What did you have to change?

SUMMING UP

Plan your paragraphs, sections, and the whole on this model:

<u>Researchers</u> have made strides in the **early and accurate diagnosis** of *Alzheimer's*, [but <u>those</u> **diagnoses** have raised A NEW HUMAN PROBLEM about **informing** those at risk before they show any *symptoms of it*.] point

Open each unit with a relatively short segment introducing it.

End that segment with a sentence stating the point of that unit.

Toward the end of that point sentence, use key themes that the rest of the unit develops.

Not too long ago, when <u>physicians</u> examined an older patient who seemed *out of touch with reality*, they had to **guess** whether that person had *Alzheimer's* or was *only senile*. In the past few years, however, they have been able to use **new and more reliable tests** focusing on genetic clues. But in <u>**the accuracy of these new tests**</u> lies the risk of ANOTHER KIND OF HUMAN TRAGEDY: Physicians may be able to **predict** *Alzheimer's* long before its overt appearance, but such an <u>**early diagnosis**</u> could PSYCHOLOGICALLY DEVASTATE AN APPARENTLY HEALTHY PERSON.

In the longer segment that follows, use consistent topics (underlined).

Repeat key terms introduced toward the end of the opening segment (boldfaced, italicized, and capitalized).

Make every sentence follow the old-new principle.

Order sentences, paragraphs, and sections in a way that readers understand.

Make all sentences relevant to the point of the unit that they constitute.

CONCISION

Often I think writing is sheer paring away of oneself leaving always something thinner, barer, more meager.

—F. Scott Fitzgerald

The ability to simplify means to eliminate the unnecessary so that the necessary may speak.

—Hans Hofmann

To a Snail: If "compression is the first grace of style," you have it.

—Marianne Moore

UNDERSTANDING CONCISION

You write more clearly when you match your characters and actions to your subjects and verbs, when you get the right characters into topics and the right words under stress, when you motivate readers with well-crafted introductions, and when you frame your paragraphs, sections, and documents to help readers grasp their global coherence. But readers may still think your prose a long way from graceful if it's anything like this:

> In my personal opinion, it is necessary that we should not ignore the opportunity to think over each and every suggestion offered.

That writer matched characters with subjects, and actions with verbs, but in too many words: opinion is always personal, so we don't need *personal*, and since this statement is *opinion*, we don't need *in my opinion*. *Think over* and *not ignore* both mean *consider*. *Each and every* is redundant. And suggestion is by definition offered. In fewer words:

✓ We should consider each suggestion.

Though not elegant, that sentence at least has style's first grace—compression, or as we'll call it, concision.

DIAGNOSIS AND REVISION

Six Principles of Concision

When I edited that sentence about suggestions, I followed six principles:

1. Delete words that mean little or nothing.
2. Delete words that repeat the meaning of other words.
3. Delete words implied by other words.
4. Replace a phrase with a word.
5. Change negatives to affirmatives.
6. Delete useless adjectives and adverbs.

Those principles are easy to state but hard to follow, because you have to inch your way through every sentence you write, cutting here, compressing there, and that's labor intensive. Those six principles, though, can guide you in that work.

1. **Delete meaningless words.** Some words are verbal tics that we use as unconsciously as we clear our throats:

kind of	actually	particular	really	certain	various
virtually	individual	basically	generally	given	practically

   Productivity **actually** depends on **certain** factors that **basically** involve psychology more than **any particular** technology.

   ✓ Productivity depends on psychology more than on technology.

2. **Delete doubled words**. Early in the history of English, writers got into the habit of pairing a French or Latin word with a native English one, because foreign words sounded more learned. Most paired words today are just redundant. Among the common ones:

full and complete	hope and trust	any and all
true and accurate	each and every	basic and fundamental
hopes and desires	first and foremost	various and sundry

3. **Delete what readers can infer.** This redundancy is common but hard to identify, because it comes in so many forms.

Redundant Modifiers Often, the meaning of a word implies others, especially its modifier (boldfaced):

Do not try to *predict* **future** events that will **completely** *revolutionize* society, because **past** *history* shows that it is the **final** *outcome* of minor events that **unexpectedly** *surprises* us more.

✓ Do not try to predict revolutionary events, because history shows that the outcome of minor events surprises us more.

Some common redundancies:

terrible tragedy	various different	free gift
basic fundamentals	future plans	each individual
final outcome	true facts	consensus of opinion

Redundant Categories Every word implies its general category, so you can usually cut a word that names it (boldfaced):

During that *period* **of time**, the *membrane* **area** became *pink* **in color** and *shiny* **in appearance**.

✓ During that period, the membrane became pink and shiny.

In doing that, you may have to change an adjective into an ADVERB:

The holes must be aligned in an *accurate* **manner**.

✓ The holes must be aligned *accurately*.

Sometimes you change an adjective into a noun:

The county manages the *educational* **system** and *public recreational* **activities**.

✓ The county manages education and *public recreation*.

Here are some general nouns (boldfaced) often used redundantly:

large in **size**	round in **shape**	honest in **character**
unusual in **nature**	of a strange **type**	**area** of mathematics
of a bright **color**	at an early **time**	in a confused **state**

General Implications This kind of wordiness is even harder to spot because it can be so diffuse:

Imagine someone trying to learn the rules for playing the game of chess.

Learn implies *trying, rules* implies *playing the game, chess* is a *game*. So more concisely,

Imagine learning the rules of chess.

4. **Replace a phrase with a word.** This redundancy is especially difficult to fix, because you need a big vocabulary and the wit to use it. For example:

As you carefully read what you have written to improve wording and catch errors of spelling and punctuation, the thing to do before anything else is to see whether you could use sequences of subjects and verbs instead of the same ideas expressed in nouns.

That is,

✓   As you edit, first replace nominalizations with clauses.

I compressed five phrases into five words:

carefully read what you have written	→	edit
the thing to do before anything else	→	first
use X instead of Y	→	replace
nouns instead of verbs	→	nominalizations
sequences of subjects and verbs	→	clauses

I can offer no principle that tells you when to replace a phrase with a word, much less give you the word. I can point out only that you often can, and that you should be alert for opportunities to do so—which is to say, try.

Here are some common phrases (boldfaced) to watch for. Note that some of these let you turn a nominalization into a verb (both italicized):

We must explain **the reason for** the *delay* in the meeting.

✓   We must explain **why** the meeting is *delayed*.

Despite the fact that the data were checked, errors occurred.

✓   **Even though** the data were checked, errors occurred.

In the event that you finish early, contact this office.

✓   **If** you finish early, contact this office.

In a situation where a class closes, you may petition to get in.

✓   **When** a class closes, you may petition to get in.

I want to say a few words **concerning the matter of** money.

✓   I want to say a few words **about** money.

There is a need for more careful *inspection* of all welds.

✓　You **must** *inspect* all welds more carefully.

We **are in a position** to make you an offer.

✓　We **can** make you an offer.

It is possible that nothing will come of this.

✓　Nothing **may** come of this.

Prior to the *end* of the training, apply for your license.

✓　**Before** training *ends*, apply for your license.

We have noted a **decrease/increase in the number of** errors.

✓　We have noted **fewer/more** errors.

5. **Change negatives to affirmatives**. When you express an idea in a negative form, not only must you use an extra word: *same not different*, but you also force readers to do a kind of algebraic calculation. These two sentences, for example, mean much the same thing, but the affirmative is more direct:

　　Do not write in the negative.　　　　Write in the affirmative.

You can rewrite most negatives:

not careful	→	careless	not many	→	few
not the same	→	different	not often	→	rarely
not allow	→	prevent	not stop	→	continue
not notice	→	overlook	not include	→	omit

Do not translate a negative into an affirmative if you want to emphasize the negative. (Is that such a sentence? I could have written, *Keep a negative sentence when . . .*)

Some verbs, prepositions, and conjunctions are implicitly negative:

Verbs	*preclude, prevent, lack, fail, doubt, reject, avoid, deny, refuse, exclude, contradict, prohibit, bar*
Prepositions	*without, against, lacking, but for, except*
Conjunctions	*unless, except when*

You can baffle readers if you combine not with these negative words. Compare these:

Except when you have **failed** to submit applications **without** documentation, benefits will **not** be **denied.**

✓　You will receive benefits only if you submit your documents.

✓　To receive benefits, submit your documents.

And you baffle readers completely when you combine explicitly and implicitly negative words with passives and nominalizations:

There should be **no** submission of payments **without** notification of this office, **unless** the payment does **not** exceed $100.

Do not **submit** payments if you have not **notified** this office, unless you are **paying** less than $100.

Now revise the negatives into affirmatives:

✓   If you pay more than $100, notify this office first.

6.   **Delete adjectives and adverbs.** Many writers can't resist adding useless adjectives and adverbs. Try deleting every adverb and every adjective before a noun, then restore only those that readers need to understand the passage. In this passage, which ones should be restored?

At the heart of the argument culture is our habit of seeing issues and ideas as ~~absolute and irreconcilable~~ principles ~~continually~~ at war. To move beyond this ~~static and limiting~~ view, we can remember the ~~Chinese~~ approach to yin and yang. They are two principles, yes, but they are conceived not as ~~irreconcilable polar~~ opposites but as elements that coexist and should be brought into balance as much ~~as possible.~~ As sociolinguist Suzanne Wong Scollon notes, "Yin is always present in and changing into yang and vice versa." How can we translate this ~~abstract~~ idea into ~~daily~~ practice?

—Deborah Tannen, *The Argument Culture*

Here's the point: Readers think you write concisely when you use only enough words to say what you mean.

1. Delete words that mean little or nothing.
2. Delete words that repeat the meaning of other words.
3. Delete words implied by other words.
4. Replace a phrase with a word.
5. Change negatives to affirmatives.
6. Delete useless adjectives and adverbs.

Exercise 11.1

Prune the redundancy from these sentences.

1. Critics cannot avoid employing complex and abstract technical terms if they are to successfully analyze literary texts and discuss them in a meaningful way.

2. Scientific research generally depends on fully accurate data if it is to offer theories that will allow us to predict the future in a plausible way.

3. In regard to desirable employment in teaching jobs, prospects for those engaged in graduate-school-level studies are at best not certain.

4. Notwithstanding the fact that all legal restrictions on the use of firearms are the subject of heated debate and argument, it is necessary that the general public not stop carrying on discussions pro and con in regard to them.

5. Most likely, a majority of all patients who appear at a public medical clinical facility do not expect special medical attention or treatment, because their particular health problems and concerns are often not major and for the most part can usually be adequately treated without much time, effort, and attention.

Where appropriate, change the following negatives to affirmatives, and do any more editing you think useful.

6. Except when expenses do not exceed $250, the Insured may not refuse to provide the Insurer with receipts, checks, or other evidence of costs.

7. There is no possibility in regard to a reduction in the size of the federal deficit if reductions in federal spending are not introduced.

8. Do not discontinue medication unless symptoms of dizziness and nausea are not present for six hours.

9. No one should be prevented from participating in cost-sharing educational programs without a full hearing into the reasons for his or her not being accepted.

10. No agreement exists on the question of an open or closed universe, a dispute about which no resolution is likely as long as a computation of the total mass of the universe has not been done.

11. long as taxpayers do not engage in widespread refusal to pay taxes, the government will have no difficulty in paying its debts.

12. No alternative exists in this country to the eventual development of tar sand, oil shale, and coal as sources of fuel, if we wish to stop being energy dependent on imported oil.

13. Not until a resolution between Catholics and Protestants in regard to the authority of papal supremacy is reached will there be a start to a reconciliation between these two Christian religions.

Exercise 11.2

Here are two actual sentences from two "free" offers.

> You will not be charged our first monthly fee unless you don't cancel within the first thirty days.

> To avoid being charged your first monthly fee, cancel your membership before your free trial ends.

Which is less clear? Why might it have been written like that? Revise it.

REDUNDANT METADISCOURSE

Chapter 8 described metadiscourse as language that refers to the following:

- the writer's intentions: *to sum up, candidly, I believe*
- directions to the reader: *note that, consider now, as you see*
- the structure of the text: *first, second, finally, therefore, however*

Everything you write needs metadiscourse, but too much buries your ideas:

> The last point I would like to make is that in regard to men-women relationships, it is important to keep in mind that the greatest changes have occurred in how they work together.

Only nine of those thirty-four words address men-women relationships:

> men-women relationships . . . greatest changes . . . how they work together.

The rest is metadiscourse. When we prune it, we tighten the sentence:

> The greatest changes in men-women relationships have occurred in how they work together.

Now that we see what the sentence says, we can make it still more direct:

✓ Men and women have changed their relationships most in how they work together.

How writers use metadiscourse varies by field, but you can usually cut these two types:

1. **Metadiscourse That Attributes Your Ideas to a Source** Don't announce that something has been *observed, noticed, noted,* and so on; just state the fact:

> High divorce rates **have been observed** to occur in areas that **have been determined to have** low population density.

✓   High divorce rates occur in areas with low population density.

2. **Metadiscourse That Announces Your Topic** The boldface phrases tell your reader what your sentence is "about":

> **This section introduces another** problem, that of noise pollution. **The first thing to say about it is** that noise pollution exists not only . . .

Readers catch the topic more easily if you reduce the metadiscourse:

✓   **Another** problem is noise pollution. **First**, it exists not only . . .

Two other constructions call attention to a topic, usually mentioned at least once in the text previous to it:

> **In regard to** a vigorous style, the most important feature is a short, concrete subject followed by a forceful verb.

> **So far as** China's industrial development **is concerned**, it has long surpassed that of Japan.

But you can usually work those topics into a subject:

✓   **The most important feature of a vigorous style** is a short, concrete subject followed by a forceful verb.

✓   **China** has long surpassed Japan's industrial development.

HEDGES AND INTENSIFIERS

Another kind of metadiscourse reflects the writer's certainty about what she is claiming. *Hedges* qualify your certainty; *intensifiers* increase it. Both can be redundant when used excessively. But they can also be useful, because they signal how well you balance caution and confidence and therefore influence how readers judge your character.

Hedges

These are common hedges:

Adverbs	*usually, often, sometimes, almost, virtually, possibly, allegedly, arguably, perhaps, apparently, in some ways, to a certain extent, somewhat, in some/certain respects*
Adjectives	*most, many, some, a certain number of*
Verbs	*may, might, can, could, seem, tend, appear, suggest, indicate*

Too much hedging sounds mealy-mouthed, like this:

> There **seems to be some** evidence to **suggest** that **certain** differences between Japanese and Western rhetoric **could** derive from historical influences **possibly** traceable to Japan's cultural isolation and Europe's history of cross-cultural contacts.

On the other hand, only a fool or someone with massive historical evidence would make an assertion as flatly certain as this:

> This evidence **proves** that Japanese and Western rhetorics differ because of Japan's cultural isolation and Europe's history of cross-cultural contacts.

In most academic writing, we more often state claims closer to this (note my own hedging; compare the more assertive, *In academic writing, we state claims like this*):

> ✓ This evidence **suggests** that **aspects** of Japanese and Western rhetoric differ because of Japan's cultural isolation and Europe's history of cross-cultural contacts.

The verbs *suggest* and *indicate* let you state a claim about which you are less than 100-percent certain, but confident enough to propose:

> ✓ The evidence **indicates** that some of these questions remain unresolved.
> ✓ These data **suggest** that further studies are necessary.

Even confident scientists hedge. This next paragraph introduced the most significant breakthrough in the history of genetics, the discovery of the double helix of DNA. If anyone was entitled to be assertive, it was Crick and Watson. But they chose to be diffident (note, too, the first person we; hedges are boldfaced):

> We **wish to suggest a** [not *the*] structure for the salt of deoxyribose nucleic acid (D.N.A.) . . . A structure for nucleic acid has already been proposed by Pauling and Corey . . . **In our opinion,** this structure is unsatisfactory for two reasons: (1) **We believe** that the material which gives the X-ray diagrams is the salt, not the free acid.. . (2) **Some** of the van der Waals distances appear to be too small.
>
> —J. D. Watson and F. H. C. Crick,
> "Molecular Structure of Nucleic Acids"

Intensifiers

These are common INTENSIFIERS:

Adverbs   *very, pretty, quite, rather, clearly, obviously, undoubtedly, certainly, of course, indeed, inevitably, invariably, always, literally*

Adjectives *key, central, crucial, basic, fundamental, major, principal, essential*
Verbs   *show, prove, establish, as you/we/everyone knows/can see, it is clear/obvious that*

The most common intensifier, however, is the absence of a hedge.

Without the hedges, Crick and Watson's claim would be more concise but more aggressive. Compare this (I boldface the stronger words, but most of the aggressive tone comes from the absence of hedges):

> We ~~wish to suggest~~ **state here** ~~a~~ **the** structure for the salt of deoxyribose nucleic acid (D.N.A.) . . . A structure for nucleic acid has already been proposed by Pauling and Corey . . . ~~In our opinion,~~ [T]his structure is unsatisfactory for two reasons: (1) ~~We believe that~~ [T]he material which gives the X-ray diagrams is the salt, not the free acid . . . (2) ~~Some of~~ [T]he van der Waals distances ~~appear to be~~ **are** too small.

Confident writers use intensifiers less often than they use hedges because they want to avoid sounding as assertive as this:

> For a century now, **all** liberals have argued against **any** censorship of art, and **every** court has found their arguments so **completely** persuasive that **not** a person **any** longer remembers how they were countered. As a result, today, censorship is **totally** a thing of the past.

Some writers think that kind of aggressive style is persuasive. Quite the opposite. If you state a claim moderately, readers are more likely to consider it thoughtfully:

> For **about** a century now, **many** liberals have argued against censorship of art, and **most** courts have found their arguments persuasive **enough** that **few** people **may** remember **exactly** how they were countered. As a result, today, censorship is **virtually** a thing of the past.

Some claim that a passage hedged that much is wordy and weak. Perhaps. But it does not come on like a bulldozer. It leaves room for a reasoned and equally moderate response.

Quick Tip

When most readers read a sentence that begins with something like *obviously, undoubtedly, it is clear that, there is no question that,* and so on, they reflexively think the opposite.

Here's the point: You need some metadiscourse in everything you write, especially metadiscourse that guides readers through your text, words such as *first, second, therefore, on the other hand,* and so on. You also need some metadiscourse that hedges your certainty, words such as *perhaps, seems, could,* and so on. The risk is in using too many.

Quick Tip

In Chapter 9, we noted that problems demand solutions expressed as points or claims. But be careful about using metadiscourse when stating your solution, because it can allow you merely to announce a topic instead of advancing a claim. To avoid this pitfall, delete the metadiscourse (boldfaced) and rewrite what remains as a sentence:

> **In this study, I examine** the history of Congressional legislation to protect children in the workplace.
>
> Congress has legislated to protect children in the workplace.

If the resulting claim seems self-evident, like this one, you need to say more, or to do more thinking about what you want to say.

Exercise 11.3

Edit these for both unnecessary metadiscourse and redundancy.

1. But, on the other hand, we can perhaps point out that there may always be TV programming to appeal to our most prurient and, therefore, lowest interests.

2. In this particular section, I intend to discuss my position about the possible need to dispense with the standard approach to plea bargaining. I believe this for two reasons. The first reason is that there is the possibility of letting hardened criminals avoid receiving their just punishment. The second reason is the following: plea bargaining seems to encourage a growing lack of respect for the judicial system.

3. Turning now to the next question, there is in regard to wilderness area preservation activities one basic principle when attempting to formulate a way of approaching decisions about unspoiled areas to be set aside as not open to development for commercial exploitation.

4. It is my belief that in regard to terrestrial-type snakes, an assumption can be made that there are probably none in unmapped areas of the world surpassing the size of those we already have knowledge of.

5. Depending on the particular position that one takes on this question, the educational system has taken on a degree of importance that may be equal to or perhaps even exceed the family as a major source of transmission of social values.

CONCISE, NOT TERSE

Having stressed concision so strongly, I must now step back. Readers don't like flab, but neither do they like a style so terse that it's all gristle and bone. Here is some amiable advice from the most widely read book on style, Strunk and White's *The Elements of Style:*

> Revising is part of writing. Few writers are so expert that they can produce what they are after on the first try. Quite often you will discover, on examining the completed work, that there are serious flaws in the arrangement of the material, calling for transpositions. When this is the case, a word processor can save you time and labor as you rearrange the manuscript. You can select material on the screen and move it to a more appropriate spot, or, if you cannot find the right spot, you can move the material to the end of the manuscript until you decide whether to delete it. Some writers find that working with a printed copy of the manuscript helps them to visualize the process of change; others prefer to revise entirely on screen. Above all, do not be afraid to experiment with what you have written. Save both the original and the revised versions; you can always use the computer to restore the manuscript to its original condition, should that course seem best. Remember, it is no sign of weakness or defeat that your manuscript ends up in need of major surgery. This is a common occurrence in all writing, and among the best writers. (205 words)

We can shorten that paragraph just by erasing its redundancy:

> Revising is part of writing. Few writers ~~are so expert that they can~~ produce what they are after on the first try. ~~Quite~~ Often you will discover ~~on examining the completed work, that there are serious~~ flaws in the arrangement of the material. ~~calling for transpositions.~~ When this is the case, a word processor can save ~~you~~ time ~~and labor~~ as you rearrange the manuscript. You can ~~select material on the screen and move~~ [material] to a more appropriate spot, or, if you cannot find the right spot, you can move the material to the end of the manuscript until you decide whether to delete it. Some writers find that working with a printed ~~copy of the~~ manuscript helps them ~~to~~ visualize ~~the process of~~ change; others prefer to revise ~~entirely~~ on screen. Above all, ~~do not be afraid~~ to experiment ~~with what you have written~~. Save ~~both~~ the original and the revised versions; you can always ~~use the computer to~~ restore the manuscript to its original condition, ~~should that course seem best~~. ~~Remember,~~ It is no sign of weakness ~~or defeat~~ that your manuscript ~~ends up in~~ need[s] ~~of major~~ surgery. This is a common ~~occurrence~~ in all writing, and among the best writers. (139 words)

With some rewording, we can cut that version by another third (revisions are italicized):

> Revising is part of writing, *because* few writers ~~produce what they are after on the first try~~ *write perfect first drafts. If you use a word processor and find* ~~Often you will discover serious~~ flaws in your arrangement, ~~of the material. When this is the case, a word processor can save time as you rearrange the manuscript.~~ you can ~~select material on the screen~~

and move material to a more appropriate spot, or, if you cannot find *one*, ~~the right spot~~, to the end ~~of the manuscript~~ until you decide whether to delete it. Some writers find ~~that working with~~ a printed manuscript helps them visualize change; others revise on screen. Above all, experiment. Save ~~both the original and the revised~~ version; you can always *go back to it* ~~restore the manuscript its original condition. Remember,~~ It is no sign of weakness that your manuscript needs surgery. This is common in all writing, and among the best writers. (99 words)

And if we cut to the bone, we can reduce that in half:

Most writers revise because few write a perfect first draft. If you work on a computer, you can rearrange the parts by moving them around. If you save the original, you can always go back to it. Even great writers revise, so if your manuscript needs surgery, it signals no weakness. (51 words)

But in boiling down that original paragraph to a quarter of its original length, I've bleached out its garrulous charm, a tradeoff that many readers would reject.

I can't tell you when you've written so concisely that your readers think you are terse, even abrupt. That's why you should listen to what readers say about your writing. They know what you never can: how it feels to be your reader.

IN YOUR OWN WORDS

Exercise 11.4

Revise a passage of your own writing as I did the passage from Strunk and White's *Elements of Style* (pp. 139–140). Pick a long paragraph or section from your own writing (about 200 words). Now, shorten it to about 150 words, 100 words, 50 words. What do you gain or lose with each of these revisions?

Exercise 11.5

Every piece of writing needs some metadiscourse, but too much buries your ideas. Have a reader go through several pages of your writing and highlight all the metadiscourse. With your reader, address the following questions: Which instances of metadiscourse are useful, and which are redundant or unnecessary? Are there places without metadiscourse where some would be helpful? Revise as necessary.

SUMMING UP

You need more than concision to guarantee grace, but when you clear away deadwood, you can see the shape of a sentence more clearly.

1. Meaningless words

> Some polling sites reported various technical problems, but these did not really affect the election's actual result.
>
> ✓ Some polling sites reported technical problems, but these did not affect the election's result.

2. Redundant pairs

> If and when we can define our final aims and goals, each and every member of our group will be ready and willing to offer aid and assistance.
>
> ✓ If we define our goals, we will all be ready to help.

3. Redundant modifiers

> In the business world of today, official governmental red tape seriously destroys initiative among individual businesses.
>
> ✓ Government red tape destroys business initiative.

4. Redundant categories

> In the area of education, tight financial conditions are forcing school boards to cut nonessential expenses.
>
> ✓ Tight finances are forcing school boards to cut nonessentials.

5. Obvious implications

> Energy used to power industries and homes will in years to come cost more money.
>
> ✓ Energy will eventually cost more.

6. A phrase for a word

> A sail-powered craft that has turned on its side or completely over must remain buoyant enough so that it will bear the weight of those individuals who were aboard.
>
> ✓ A capsized sailboat must support those on it.

7. Indirect negatives

> There is no reason not to believe that engineering malfunctions in nuclear energy systems cannot be anticipated.

✓ Malfunctions in nuclear energy systems will surprise us.

8. Excessive metadiscourse

> It is almost certainly the case that totalitarian systems cannot allow a society to have what we would define as stable social relationships.

✓ Totalitarianism prevents stable social relationships.

9. Hedges and intensifiers

The only principle here is the Goldilocks rule: not too much, not too little, but just right. That's little help, but this is a matter where you have to develop and then trust your ear.

Too certain:	In my research, **I prove** that people with a gun in their home use it to kill themselves or a family member instead of to protect themselves from an intruder.
Too uncertain:	**Some** of my recent research **seems** to **imply** that there **may** be a **risk** that certain people with a gun in their homes **could** be **more prone** to use it to kill themselves or a family member than to protect themselves from **possible** intruders.
Just right?	My research indicates that people with a gun in their homes are more likely to use it to kill themselves or a family member than they are to protect themselves from an intruder.

PART TWO

AN ANTHOLOGY OF READINGS

(handwritten margin notes: "LIMIT THE AUDIENCE", "WHEN IT WAS PUBLISHED", "JARGON", "THE WAY THE ARTICLE WAS WRITTEN", "A LOT OF STATS")

ENGLISH

Into the Electronic Millennium

Sven Birkerts

Sven Birkerts (1951–) was born in Pontiac, Michigan. He attended the University of Michigan, then went on to teach at Amherst College, Emerson College, and at Harvard. He currently directs the Writing Seminars at Bennington College and continues to be Briggs-Copeland Lecturer in Nonfiction at Harvard. His books include The Gutenberg Elegies: The Fate of Reading in an Electronic Age *(1994) and* Reading Life: Books for the Ages *(2007). His honors and awards include a Citation for Excellence in Reviewing from the National Book Critics Circle (1985) and a Guggenheim Fellowship (1994). In the following essay Bikerts sounds the alarm as he faces the world of technology. His perspectives give a surprising "no" to much that is now assumed to be the norm.*

1   The order of print is linear, and is bound to logic by the imperatives of syntax. Syntax is the substructure of discourse, a mapping of the ways that the mind makes sense through language. Print communication requires the active engagement of the reader's attention, for reading is fundamentally an act of translation. Symbols are turned into their verbal referents and these are in turn interpreted. The print engagement is essentially private. While it does represent an act of communication, the contents pass from the privacy of the sender to the privacy of the receiver. Print also

Reprinted from *The Gutenberg Elegies: The Fate of Reading in an Electronic Age* (1994), by permission of Farrar, Straus and Giroux.

posits a time axis; the turning of pages, not to mention the vertical descent down the page, is a forward-moving succession, with earlier contents at every point serving as a ground for what follows. Moreover, the printed material is static—it is the reader, not the book, that moves forward. The physical arrangements of print are in accord with our traditional sense of history. Materials are layered; they lend themselves to rereading and to sustained attention. The pace of reading is variable, with progress determined by the reader's focus and comprehension.

The electronic order is in most ways opposite. Information and contents do not simply move from one private space to another, but they travel along a network. Engagement is intrinsically public, taking place within a circuit of larger connectedness. The vast resources of the network are always there, potential, even if they do not impinge on the immediate communication. Electronic communication can be passive, as with television watching, or interactive, as with computers. Contents, unless they are printed out (at which point they become part of the static order of print) are felt to be evanescent. They can be changed or deleted with the stroke of a key. With visual media (television, projected graphs, highlighted "bullets") impression and image take precedence over logic and concept, and detail and linear sequentiality are sacrificed. The pace is rapid, driven by jump-cut increments, and the basic movement is laterally associative rather than vertically cumulative. The presentation structures the reception and, in time, the expectation about how information is organized.

Further, the visual and nonvisual technology in every way encourages in the user a heightened and ever-changing awareness of the present. It works against historical perception, which must depend on the inimical notions of logic and sequential succession. If the print medium exalts the word, fixing it into permanence, the electronic counterpart reduces it to a signal, a means to an end.

Transitions like the one from print to electronic media do not take place without rippling or, more likely, *reweaving* the entire social and cultural web. The tendencies outlined above are already at work. We don't need to look far to find their effects. We can begin with the newspaper headlines and the millennial lamentations sounded in the op-ed pages: that our educational systems are in decline; that our students are less and less able to read and comprehend their required texts, and that their aptitude scores have leveled off well below those of previous generations. Tag-line communication, called "bite-speak" by some, is destroying the last remnants of political discourse; spin doctors and media consultants are our new shamans. As communications empires fight for control of all information outlets, including publishers, the latter have succumbed to the tyranny of the bottom line; they are less and less willing to publish work, however worthy, that will not make a tidy profit. And, on every front, funding for the arts is being cut while the arts themselves appear to be suffering a deep crisis of relevance. And so on.

5   Every one of these developments is, of course, overdetermined, but there   5
can be no doubt that they are connected, perhaps profoundly, to the transition that is underway.

Certain other trends bear watching. One could argue, for instance, that the entire movement of postmodernism in the arts is a consequence of this same macroscopic shift. For what is postmodernism at root but an aesthetic that rebukes the idea of an historical time line, as well as previously uncontested assumptions of cultural hierarchy. The postmodern artifact manipulates its stylistic signatures like Lego blocks and makes free with combinations from the formerly sequestered spheres of high and popular art. Its combinatory momentum and relentless referencing of the surrounding culture mirror perfectly the associative dynamics of electronic media.

ANTICIPATING AN OBJECTION

One might argue likewise, that the virulent debate within academia over the canon and multiculturalism may not be a simple struggle between the entrenched ideologies of white male elites and the forces of formerly disenfranchised gender, racial, and cultural groups. Many of those who would revise the canon (or end it altogether) are trying to outflank the assumption of historical tradition itself. The underlying question, avoided by many, may be not only whether the tradition is relevant, but whether it might not be too taxing a system for students to comprehend. Both the traditionalists and the progressives have valid arguments, and we must certainly have sympathy for those who would try to expose and eradicate the hidden assumptions of bias in the Western tradition. But it also seems clear that this debate could only have taken the form it has in a society that has begun to come loose from its textual moorings. To challenge repression is salutary. To challenge history itself, proclaiming it to be simply an archive of repressions and justifications, is idiotic.*

Then there are the more specific sorts of developments. Consider the multibillion-dollar initiative by Whittle Communications to bring commercially sponsored education packages into the classroom. The underlying premise is staggeringly simple: If electronic media are the one thing that the young are at ease with, why not exploit the fact? Why not stop bucking television and use it instead, with corporate America picking up the tab in exchange for a few minutes of valuable airtime for commercials? As the *Boston Globe* reports:

Here's how it would work:

Participating schools would receive, free of charge, $50,000 worth of electronic paraphernalia, including a satellite dish and classroom video monitors. In return, the schools would agree to air the show.

---

* The outcry against the modification of the canon can be seen as a plea for old reflexes and routines. And the cry for multicultural representation may be a last-ditch bid for connection to the fading legacy of print. The logic is simple. When a resource is threatened—made scarce—people fight over it. In this case the struggle is over textual power in an increasingly nontextual age. The future of books and reading is what is at stake, and a dim intuition of this drives the contending factions.

As Katha Pollitt argued so shrewdly in her much-cited article in *The Nation:* If we were a nation of readers, there would be no issue. No one would be arguing about whether to put Toni Morrison on the syllabus because her work would be a staple of the reader's regular diet anyway. These lists are suddenly so important because they represent, very often, the only serious works that the student is ever likely to be exposed to. Whoever controls the lists comes out ahead in the struggle for the hearts and minds of the young.

The show would resemble a network news program, but with 18- to 24-year-old anchors.

A prototype includes a report on a United Nations Security Council meeting on terrorism, a space shuttle update, a U2 music video tribute to Martin Luther King, a feature on the environment, a "fast fact" ('Arachibutyrophobia is the fear of peanut butter sticking to the roof of your mouth') and two minutes of commercial advertising.

"You have to remember that the children of today have grown up with the visual media," said Robert Calabrese [Billerica School Superintendent]. "They know no other way and we're simply capitalizing on that to enhance learning."

Calabrese's observation on the preconditioning of a whole generation of students raises troubling questions: Should we suppose that American education will begin to tailor itself to the aptitudes of its students, presenting more and more of its materials in newly packaged forms? And what will happen when educators find that not very many of the old materials will "play"—that is, capture student enthusiasm? Is the *what* of learning to be determined by the *how*? And at what point do vicious cycles begin to reveal their viciousness?

A collective change of sensibility may already be upon us. We need to take seriously the possibility that the young truly "know no other way," that they are not made of the same stuff that their elders are. In her *Harper's* magazine debate with Neil Postman, Camille Paglia observed:

Some people have more developed sensoriums than others. I've found that most people born before World War II are turned off by the modern media. They can't understand how we who were born after the war can read and watch TV at the same time. But we *can*. When I wrote my book, I had earphones on, blasting rock music or Puccini and Brahms. The soap operas—with the sound turned down—flickered on my TV. I'd be talking on the phone at the same time. Baby boomers have a multilayered, multitrack ability to deal with the world.

I don't know whether to be impressed or depressed by Paglia's ability to disperse her focus in so many directions. Nor can I say, not having read her book, in what ways her multitrack sensibility has informed her prose. But I'm baffled by what she means when she talks about an ability to "deal with the world." From the context, "dealing" sounds more like a matter of incessantly repositioning the self within a barrage of onrushing stimuli.

Paglia's is hardly the only testimony in this matter. A *New York Times* article on the cult success of Mark Leyner (author of *I Smell Esther Williams* and *My Cousin, My Gastroenterologist*) reports suggestively:

His fans say, variously, that his writing is like MTV, or rap music, or rock music, or simply like everything in the world put together: fast and furious and intense, full of illusion and allusion and fantasy and science and excrement.

Larry McCaffery, a professor of literature at San Diego State University and co-editor of *Fiction International*, a literary journal, said his students get excited about Mr. Leyner's writing, which he considers important and unique: "It speaks to them, somehow, about this weird milieu they're swimming through. It's this dissolving, discontinuous world." While older people might find Mr. Leyner's world bizarre or unreal, Professor McCaffery said, it doesn't seem so to people who grew up with Walkmen and computers and VCR's, with so many choices, so much bombardment, that they have never experienced a sensation singly.

The article continues:

There is no traditional narrative, although the book is called a novel. And there is much use of facts, though it is called fiction. Seldom does the end of a sentence have any obvious relation to the beginning. "You don't know where you're going, but you don't mind taking the leap," said R. J. Cutler, the producer of "Heat," who invited Mr. Leyner to be on the show after he picked up the galleys of his book and found it mesmerizing. "He taps into a specific cultural perspective where thoughtful literary world view meets pop culture and the TV generation."

My final exhibit—I don't know if it qualifies as a morbid symptom as such—is drawn from a *Washington Post Magazine* essay on the future of the Library of Congress, our national shrine to the printed word. One of the individuals interviewed in the piece is Robert Zich, so-called "special projects czar" of the institution. Zich, too, has seen the future, and he is surprisingly candid with his interlocutor. Before long, Zich maintains, people will be able to get what information they want directly off their terminals. The function of the Library of Congress (and perhaps libraries in general) will change. He envisions his library becoming more like a museum: "Just as you go to the National Gallery to see its Leonardo or go to the Smithsonian to see the Spirit of St. Louis and so on, you will want to go to libraries to see the Gutenberg or the original printing of Shakespeare's plays or to see Lincoln's hand-written version of the Gettysburg Address."

Zich is outspoken, voicing what other administrators must be thinking privately. The big research libraries, he says, "and the great national libraries and their buildings will go the way of the railroad stations and the movie palaces of an earlier era which were really vital institutions in their time . . . Somehow folks moved away from that when the technology changed."

15   And books? Zich expresses excitement about Sony's hand-held electronic book, and a miniature encyclopedia coming from Franklin Electronic Publishers. "Slip it in your pocket," he says. "Little keyboard, punch in your words and it will   15

do the full text searching and all the rest of it. Its limitation, of course, is that it's devoted just to that one book." Zich is likewise interested in the possibility of memory cards. What he likes about the Sony product is the portability: one machine, a screen that will display the contents of whatever electronic card you feed it.

I cite Zich's views at some length here because he is not some Silicon Valley research and development visionary, but a highly placed executive at what might be called, in a very literal sense, our most conservative public institution. When men like Zich embrace the electronic future, we can be sure it's well on its way.

Others might argue that the technologies cited by Zich merely represent a modification in the "form" of reading, and that reading itself will be unaffected, as there is little difference between following words on a pocket screen or a printed page. Here I have to hold my line. The context cannot but condition the process. Screen and book may exhibit the same string of words, but the assumptions that underlie their significance are entirely different depending on whether we are staring at a book or a circuit-generated text. As the nature of looking—at the natural world, at paintings—changed with the arrival of photography and mechanical reproduction, so will the collective relation to language alter as new modes of dissemination prevail.

Whether all of this sounds dire or merely "different" will depend upon the reader's own values and priorities. I find these portents of change depressing, but also exhilarating—at least to speculate about. On the one hand, I have a great feeling of loss and a fear about what habitations will exist for self and soul in the future. But there is also a quickening, a sense that important things are on the line. As Heraclitus once observed, "The mixture that is not shaken soon stagnates." Well, the mixture is being shaken, no doubt about it. And here are some of the kinds of developments we might watch for as our "proto-electronic" era yields to an all-electronic future:

1. *Language erosion.* There is no question but that the transition from the culture of the book to the culture of electronic communication will radically alter the ways in which we use language on every societal level. The complexity and distinctiveness of spoken and written expression, which are deeply bound to traditions of print literacy, will gradually be replaced by a more telegraphic sort of "plainspeak." Syntactic masonry is already a dying art. Neil Postman and others have already suggested what losses have been incurred by the advent of telegraphy and television—how the complex discourse patterns of the nineteenth century were flattened by the requirements of communication over distances. That tendency runs riot as the layers of mediation thicken. Simple linguistic prefab is now the norm, while ambiguity, paradox, irony, subtlety, and wit are fast disappearing. In their place, the simple "vision thing" and myriad other "things." Verbal intelligence, which has long been viewed as suspect as the act of reading, will come to seem positively conspiratorial. The greater part of any articulate person's energy will be deployed in dumbing-down her discourse.

Language will grow increasingly impoverished through a series of vicious cycles. For, of course, the usages of literature and scholarship are connected in fundamental ways to the general speech of the tribe. We can expect that curricula will be further streamlined, and difficult texts in the humanities will be pruned and glossed. One need only compare a college textbook from twenty years ago to its contemporary version. A poem by Milton, a play by Shakespeare—one can hardly find the text among the explanatory notes nowadays. Fewer and fewer people will be able to contend with the so-called masterworks of literature or ideas. Joyce, Woolf, Soyinka, not to mention the masters who preceded them, will go unread, and the civilizing energies of their prose will circulate aimlessly between closed covers.

2. *Flattening of historical perspectives.* As the circuit supplants the printed page, and as more and more of our communications involve us in network processes—which of their nature plant us in a perpetual present—our perception of history will inevitably alter. Changes in information storage and access are bound to impinge on our historical memory. The depth of field that is our sense of the past is not only a linguistic construct, but is in some essential way represented by the book and the physical accumulation of books in library spaces. In the contemplation of the single volume, or mass of volumes, we form a picture of time past as a growing deposit of sediment; we capture a sense of its depth and dimensionality. Moreover, we meet the past as much in the presentation of words in books of specific vintage as we do in any isolated fact or statistic. The database, useful as it is, expunges this context, this sense of chronology, and admits us to a weightless order in which all information is equally accessible.

If we take the etymological tack, history (cognate with "story") is affiliated in complex ways with its texts. Once the materials of the past are unhoused from their pages, they will surely *mean* differently. The printed page is itself a link, at least along the imaginative continuum, and when that link is broken, the past can only start to recede. At the same time it will become a body of disjunct data available for retrieval and, in the hands of our canny dream merchants, a mythology. The more we grow rooted in the consciousness of the now, the more it will seem utterly extraordinary that things were ever any different. The idea of a farmer plowing a field—an historical constant for millennia—will be something for a theme park. For, naturally, the entertainment industry, which reads the collective unconscious unerringly, will seize the advantage. The past that has slipped away will be rendered ever more glorious, ever more a fantasy play with heroes, villains, and quaint settings and props. Small-town American life returns as "Andy of Mayberry"—at first enjoyed with recognition, later accepted as a faithful portrait of how things used to be.

3. *The waning of the private self.* We may even now be in the first stages of a process of social collectivization that will over time all but vanquish the ideal of the isolated individual. For some decades now we have been edging away from the perception of private life as something opaque, closed off to the world; we increasingly accept the transparency of a life lived within a set of systems, electronic or otherwise. Our technologies are not bound by season or light—it's always the same time in the circuit. And so long as time is money and money

matters, those circuits will keep humming. The doors and walls of our habitations matter less and less—the world sweeps through the wires as it needs to, or as we need it to. The monitor light is always blinking; we are always potentially on-line.

I am not suggesting that we are all about to become mindless, soulless robots, or that personality will disappear altogether into an oceanic homogeneity. But certainly the idea of what it means to be a person living a life will be much changed. The figure-ground model, which has always featured a solitary self before a background that is the society of other selves, is romantic in the extreme. It is ever less tenable in the world as it is becoming. There are no more wildernesses, no more lonely homesteads, and, outside of cinema, no more emblems of the exalted individual.

25   The self must change as the nature of subjective space changes. And one of the many incremental transformations of our age has been the slow but steady destruction of subjective space. The physical and psychological distance between individuals has been shrinking for at least a century. In the process, the figure-ground image has begun to blur its boundary distinctions. One day we will conduct our public and private lives within networks so dense, among so many channels of instantaneous information, that it will make almost no sense to speak of the differentiations of subjective individualism.

We are already captive in our webs. Our slight solitudes are transected by codes, wires, and pulsations. We punch a number to check in with the answering machine, another to tape a show that we are too busy to watch. The strands of the web grow finer and finer—this is obvious. What is no less obvious is the fact that they will continue to proliferate, gaining in sophistication, merging functions so that one can bank by phone, shop via television, and so on. The natural tendency is toward streamlining: The smart dollar keeps finding ways to shorten the path, double-up the function. We might think in terms of a circuit-board model, picturing ourselves as the contact points. The expansion of electronic options is always at the cost of contractions in the private sphere. We will soon be navigating with ease among cataracts of organized pulsations, putting out and taking in signals. We will bring our terminals, our modems, and menus further and further into our former privacies; we will implicate ourselves by degrees in the unitary life, and there may come a day when we no longer remember that there was any other life.

The Poetry of Genetics
Johannes Borgstein

Johannes Borgstein, a German professor at the University Hospital Rotterdam, writes frequent articles on the aesthetic and philosophical implications of medical research. His essays appear frequently in prestigious medical journals such as The Lancet. *In this essay he questions the possibility that the human genome will ever be completely understood. He uses an analogy to the way that language works to show how complex the genome research and application will actually be.*

1   The human-genome project makes the subtle promise that once all the human chromosomes are mapped we will be in a position to determine the genetic makeup of each individual, and, as a natural consequence, be able to "correct" many of the genetic errors encountered (while carefully avoiding any allusion to the possibilities of misuse).

However, the human genome, as the infinite variety and expression of characteristics demonstrates, is vastly more complex than the sequence of codons would imply, for they can be read in different sequences depending on where the reading starts, which sequences are read, and which ones are suppressed—as a book that has several stories intermingled. To follow only one story, words or passages must be skipped in different places, whereas in other parts, continuous sequences are read.

We may conveniently make an analogy with a sequence of letters, rather than of words, which are followed in variable order, with variable starting sequence. A complex code is thus required to interpret it.

Most classic literary works, furthermore, may be read at multiple levels; generally speaking, the better the book, the more levels may be read in it. A Shakespeare play, for example, may be interpreted as a simple story, suitable for children; a complex story, interpreted by adults; a collection of aphorisms and sayings; or a source of life's wisdom. Similarly, by analogy, there are multiple levels to the human genome, whose expression varies in response to environmental factors, so as to weave a complex fabric of life at a number of levels and layers which make it extremely complex to interpret.

How the Genetic Sequences May be Read

5   Through a simple model or analogy, we can explore how a series of genetic sequences may be read in the cell. It is likely that, in reality, it is far more complex at all levels, with a larger number of intertwined "messages," and that fur-

Reprinted from *The Lancet* 351, no. 9112 (May 2, 1998), by permission of Elsevier Science Ltd.

ther higher levels of complexity exist in the expression within the cell, leaving aside for now all the possible extracellular effects of the proteins formed. Nevertheless, the analogy gives us some idea of what we are dealing with, and how difficult an interference or "correction" would be at *any* of these levels.

Let us take the following sequence of letters:

Ikeeptoseeaworldsixhonestservingmen (theytaughtmeallIknew)inagrai nofsandtheirnamesarewhatandHeaveninawildflowerwhyandholdinfinity wheninthepalmofyourhandandhowandwhereandwhoeternityinanhour (level 1)

Summary

Level 1 – letter sequence in Latin script (genetic sequence)

Level 2 – language (English)

Level 3 – separate words

Level 4 – indication of sequence in which mixed messages should be read

Level 5 – separate poems (or proteins?)

Level 6 – meaning: elementary

Level 7 – complex, abstract concepts

With the knowledge that the sequence is written in the English language (level 2), I may begin, with some difficulty, to make out the words:

I keep to see a world six honest serving men (they taught me all I knew) in a grain of sand their names are what and a Heaven in a wild flower why and hold infinity when in the palm of your hand and how and where and who eternity in an hour (level 3)

I then need some knowledge of literature and poetry to be able to separate the phrases, which belong together and are to be read sequentially:

I keep *to see a world* six honest serving men (they taught me all I knew) *in a grain of sand* their names are what **and** *a Heaven in a wild flower* why and *hold infinity* when *in the palm of your hand* and how **and** where and who *eternity in an hour* (level 4)

Until, finally, the two quatrains are set down separately:

To see a world in a grain of sand
and a Heaven in a wild flower
hold infinity in the palm of your hand
and eternity in an hour. (William Blake)[1]

I keep six honest serving men
(they taught me all I knew)
their names are What and Why and When
and How and Where and Who. (Rudyard Kipling)[2]

10   It is then largely a matter of maturity, education, and environment that   10
determines what these poems mean to me, and how I capture the different levels and use or transmit the implied concepts.

Thus, at least seven levels (panel) may be distinguished in this very simple
model of a DNA sequence. The first level is the interpretation of the individual
sequence of Latin letters or bases. (One could conceive, perhaps, of one lower
level in which the signs need to be interpreted as letters.) The second level
requires us to be conversant with the language in which the letters are written, so
that the third level permits identification of whole words out of the continuous
sequence of letters; from this sequence, in the fourth level, we attempt to make
out the phrases that under certain circumstances belong together, but which have
been intermingled (some knowledge of the authors involved is probably necessary, and the genetic code must carry instructions as to which sequences should
be read and which ones are suppressed). The fifth level of interpretation is to
select the separate poems or protein instructions, which then go through a number of subsequent steps, just as a poem may be read on various levels. The purely
visual imagery that a child might capture of sand and flowers and the rhythm of
the language, and the adult interpretation of the complex abstract ideas, sensations, and emotions that the poem induces, makes them different for everybody—though with adequate emotional similarities for us to identify with the
poet and with our fellow reader.

The actual DNA contains a large number of intermingled messages that not
only control protein synthesis but also the expression or suppression of other
messages.

With our present knowledge, we are only just beginning to interpret the letter sequence. To extrapolate from our model to human genetic engineering (as
is too readily assumed and, at times, probably even practiced) has further implications.

To insert a viral-linked sequence of genetic material into the correct section
of the right chromosome—as has been suggested and attempted for "correction"
of genetic defects encountered—is tantamount to throwing a dart at a small distant target, blindfolded. Moreover, it raises questions such as: How can we be
sure the sequence will be accommodated into the right place? How do we know
it will be expressed correctly? How can we be certain it will not have undesirable
side effects? And how can we be sure the viral "carrier" does not affect the
sequence or have other side effects?

15   A virus will merge into the genetic sequence at a predestined site (for the   15
virus), which is unlikely to coincide with our chosen site. It will be a matter
of chance that it is expressed at all, and even if not expressed, it may interfere

with the expression or suppression of other sequences with unpredictable results. Then, we should enquire what the function of the virus is in the first place, and what its other sequences are able to affect.

In theory, astonishing results may be obtained, but there are too many uncertainties, too many unanswered questions and variables, and probably hazardous consequences that are inadequately considered. To trust to chance is perhaps too simplistic, and even then it may work against us with unforeseen complications (and how can we foresee all the possible complications of a process so little understood?).

The expression of the genetic code may thus be viewed as a language with almost limitless possibilities of expression within the framework of a fixed alphabet (four base pairs and a zero making five possible symbols?) and a structured grammar. Were it otherwise, physical expression would repeat and duplicate itself rather than giving rise to circumstances in which, despite overpopulation, there are not two people alike in the world; or two leaves of a tree for that matter.

Genetic expression is modulated, as a language, by the environment (a language only developed in a social context). The surrounding cells somehow determine the expression and differentiation initally, followed by the addition of neural and more centralised humoural mechanisms as the organism grows in complexity, and, finally, by external environmental factors (think only of the calusses on the hands of a gymnast, where a purely mechanical stimulus induces thickened skin layers). Some environmental stimuli induce a whole series of "programmed" changes, as occurs in the developing embryo, whereas others may induce only minor modulations. All these factors contribute to a unique physical expression—even among identical twins, despite a variable resemblance at some levels. Although the leaves are all different, they are similar enough for us to identify the tree they came from. One of the striking conditions of living systems is that nothing is ever exactly the same; nothing can be static or in equilibrium. To state that evolution is the result of random mutations is akin to assuming that random typing by a monkey will produce the complete works of Shakespeare if we wait long enough—an overly simplistic concept that takes no account of grammar and language, let alone of meaning at its different levels. The poetry of genetics runs a lot deeper than we suspect; perhaps deeper than we *can* suspect.

Endnotes

1. Blake W. *Auguries of Innocence*. London: Penguin, 1968.
2. Kipling R. *Just So Stories (The Elephant's Child)*. London: Penguin, 1987.

Lost in Translation
Stephen Budiansky

Born in Boston, Stephen Budiansky (1957-) now lives on a farm in Virginia outside of Washington, D.C. He earned his B.S. from Yale University in 1978 and his M.S. from Harvard in 1979, after which he served as Washington editor of the magazine Nature *and as a Congressional fellow in the Office of Technology Assessment. He has served as senior writer for* U.S. News & World Report *and is currently a correspondent for* The Atlantic Monthly. *Budiansky's books include* The Covenant of the Wild *(1992),* Nature's Keepers *(1995),* The Nature of Horses *(1997), and* If a Lion Could Talk: Animal Intelligence and the Evolution of Consciousness *(1998). In this 1998 essay from* The Atlantic Monthly, *Budiansky uses interesting and sometimes humorous examples to illustrate the limitations of language translation software.*

1   In one famous episode in the British comedy series *Monty Python* a foreign-looking tourist clad in an outmoded leather trenchcoat appears at the entrance to a London shop. He marches up to the man behind the counter, solemnly consults a phrase book, and in a thick Middle European accent declares, "My hovercraft . . . is full of *eels*!"

Eventually the scene shifts to the Old Bailey courthouse, where the prisoner at the bar stands accused of intent to cause a breach of the peace for having published an English-Hungarian phrase book full of spurious translations. For example, the Hungarian phrase "Can you direct me to the railway station" is translated as "Please fondle my buttocks."

This episode is brought to mind by some recently available computer programs that claim to provide automatic translation between English and a number of other languages. Translation software that runs on mainframe computers has been used by government agencies for several decades, but with the advent of the Pentium chip, which packs the power of a mainframe into a desktop, such software can now easily be run on a personal computer. You can buy a program for translating in one direction between English and a major European language of your choice for as little as $29.95. But what has really brought machine translation, or MT, into the mainstream lately is two Internet sites that offer Spanish, French, German, Italian, and Portuguese translations free. Systran, a company that three decades ago pioneered the field under contracts from the U.S. government, provides its translator at babelfish.altavista.digital.com as part of AltaVista's Web site. ("Babelfish" is an allusion to a diminutive piscine character

Reprinted from *The Atlantic Monthly*, December 1998, by permission of the author.

in *The Hitchhiker's Guide to the Galaxy* that, when inserted in the ear, provides instant translation of any language.) Babelfish the Web site lets you type in a block of text up to fifty words long, click on a button, and watch as, seconds later, a translation appears above your words.

The second company to offer its services free (at least for now) is Globalink, a major retailer of translation software that as this article went to press had just been acquired by Lernout & Hauspie. Globalink's online translator, Comprende, will exist in a different form under the new ownership. At www.lhs.com you can send E-mail or participate in a live multinational "chat" with translations to and from English.

5 When faced with criticism of their products' translations, MT vendors tend to invoke the "talking dog"—as in, Don't be picky; it's amazing that a dog can talk at all. And in fairness, the outright breaches of the peace that these programs cause are far fewer than one might expect. When the field was still in its infancy, in the early 1960s, an apocryphal tale went around about a computer that the CIA had built to translate between English and Russian: to test the machine, the programmers decided to have it translate a phrase into Russian and then translate the result back into English, to see if they'd get the same words they started with. The director of the CIA was invited to do the honors; the programmers all gathered expectantly around the console to watch as the director typed in the test words: "Out of sight, out of mind." The computer silently ground through its calculations. Hours passed. Then, suddenly, magnetic tapes whirred, lights blinked, and a printer clattered out the result: "Invisible insanity."

When I tried out Systran's Babelfish and Globalink's Comprende, Babelfish handled that highly figurative phrase with aplomb, rendering it in idiomatic, even nuanced, French as "*Hors de la vue, hors de l'esprit.*" Both systems also translated "My hovercraft is full of eels" into French and back and into Italian and back without a glitch. Competent performances were turned in on "We have nothing to fear but fear itself," "Don't bank on it," "I fought the law and the law won," "Wild thing, you make my heart sing" ("*La chose sauvage, vous faites mon coeur chanter*"), "I shot an elephant in my pajamas," "Can you recommend a good, inexpensive restaurant?," and "The komodo dragon is the world's largest living lizard" ("*Le dragon du komodo est le plus grand lézard vivant du monde*").

But the Pythonesque possibilities were all too manifest in what Babelfish did to "I have lost my passport." After a trip into French it came back as "I have destroyed my passport"—arguably better than "I have means pass lost," by way of German. "All's well that ends well" by way of Portuguese became "All gush out that the extremities gush out," and "Would you like to come back to my place?" returned from German as "Did you become to like my workstation to return?"

Most translations fell somewhere between impressive and nonsensical; in general they were surprisingly understandable, if odd and stilted. Particularly fetching was the tendency of both Babelfish and Comprende to finish English-to-French round trips having picked up a diction vaguely reminiscent of Inspecteur Clouseau's: "Where is the room of the men?" "Do you like to return to my hotel?" All that was missing was an occasional substitution of "zee" for "the." And some uncannily Teutonic cadences emerged from excursions into German and back. "A penny, which becomes secured, is an acquired penny" has a stolidly Germanic pedantry about it. "Pepsi-Cola strikes the point, twelve full ounces, those is much" was perfect stage German.

The computer talks this way for very much the same reason that Inspecteur Clousseau does—both use literal renderings of foreign idiom. Corny imitations of a French accent abound with the likes of "And now, would madame care for the dinner?" and "The car, she is magnificent" because they more or less follow the syntactical peculiarities of the original. In French one eats "the dinner," not "dinner," and all nouns are assigned to either the masculine or the feminine gender.

10   The earliest computer translators were even more literal; they were "direct systems," which means they looked up each word or phrase in a lexicon and substituted an equivalent word or phrase in the target language. It ought to have been obvious that this approach had serious shortcomings. But such was the "naive optimism"—as Eduard Hovy, a researcher at the University of Southern California and the president of the Association for Machine Translation in the Americas, puts it—that it took a surprisingly long time for practitioners to realize that they had a lot of hard work ahead of them to produce even passable translations. In the 1950s the surging Cold War demand for translations of thousands of pages of Russian technical articles figured into the exciting belief, held by many computer scientists, that the new, programmable computers could duplicate the human mind through "artificial intelligence." Andrew Booth, an early MT researcher, recalls that right after the Second World War he tried to get the Rockefeller Foundation to fund the development of a computer that would perform the tedious calculations required to deduce a chemical compound's three-dimensional structure from the pattern of x-rays it diffracted. That was a task perfectly suited to a computer, but the foundation was not interested. It wanted a machine that would explore how people think. Booth obligingly switched gears, proposed to build a language translator, and got his funding.

Compounding the naiveté was a simplistic analogy advanced by Norbert Wiener, a brilliant and eccentric mathematician at the Massachusetts Institute of Technology who was at the forefront of computer theory: computers were used during the war to help break enemy codes; decoding is a matter of transforming a set of symbols; language translation could be the same.

Of course, it isn't. One huge snag is word order. Forty to 50 percent of the words in a typical English sentence end up in a different position in the corresponding French sentence. In French, adjectives often appear after the nouns they modify; objects of a verb often appear before the verb. In going from English to Japanese, the rearrangement rate hits almost 100 percent, partly because in Japanese—as in most languages, with the notable exceptions of English and the Romance languages—verbs regularly come at the end of the sentence. Getting the word order wrong not only makes for horrible-sounding sentences but also can change meaning, often in comic ways.

Another problem with the direct approach is the sheer amount of computational resources required. To carry out direct substitution effectively, a lexicon must include every inflected form of every verb and every plural of every noun: separate translations have to be provided for "walk," "walks," "walking," "walked," and so on. Idioms can be handled as chunks (for instance, "got out," "got by," and "got even," each of which is expressed by a different verb in French). But if other words interrupt those phrases ("I got the eels out of my hovercraft"), a direct system is helpless—there is just no way to anticipate every possible combination of words.

Like all modern translation systems, the latest products from Globalink and Systran seek to overcome these limitations by incorporating at least some grammatical rules for figuring out what words are performing what functions in a sentence. The programs literally construct a parse tree, just as students used to do in school. The computers' lexicons specify the parts of speech that might apply to each word; the parser then looks up grammatical rules that describe how different parts of speech can be combined, and tries to identify noun phrases, modifiers, auxiliary verbs, and so on. Once the sentence is parsed, the resulting syntax tree is "transferred" to the target language with the aid of a second set of rules governing grammatical combinations in that language.

15   Much of what is impressive about these programs lies in such "transfer"   15
algorithms. The komodo-dragon sentence, for example, required a substantial amount of word rearrangement to come out in even passable French. To say "the world's largest living lizard" in French, one says literally "the most big lizard living in the world": the sequence ABCD becomes BDCA—a 75 percent rearrangement.

Parsing carries with it a certain amount of clarification as a bonus. Words that in the source language can be both verbs and nouns ("Book him, Danno" versus "Give me the book, Danno"; "Fight the good fight") are distinguished automatically by a computer that recognizes valid sentence structures, and a certain number of semantically absurd translations are weeded out in this manner too. For example, Babelfish botched Groucho Marx's punch line "What an elephant was doing in my pajamas, I'll never know" by translating the first three words as "*Quel éléphant*," a construction bearing the meaning embodied in a phrase like "What a pity" ("*Quel dommage*"); but Comprende recognized that such a rendering produced a grammatically unfeasible sequence in the sentence as a whole, and instead came up with "*Ce qu'un éléphant*"—"That which an elephant."

One thing demonstrated by all of this effort is that language is far more complex than even linguists ever imagined. Yorick Wilks, of Sheffield University, in England, is one of a number of MT researchers who have been developing automated programs that comb through a corpus of text to derive grammatical rules empirically. The best known of these corpora is the Penn Tree Bank, which contains millions of words of text to which parse trees have been attached; the computer sifts through thousands upon thousands of sentences and "reads" the rules implied by those trees. This whole approach flies in the face of the tradition of Noam Chomsky, which, Wilks says, led linguists to believe that "they know language through intuition and introspection and don't need 'evidence.'" Wilks's lab has developed an English grammar that so far contains 18,000 rules—many times the number that linguists ever dreamed would be necessary.

The entire exercise of machine translation has been sobering—even "depressing," Hovy says—because the best MT systems so far appear to have less to do with linguistic breakthroughs at a conceptual level than with simple doggedness. "It doesn't matter how brain-damaged the approach," Hovy says. "The older the system, the better"—because the programs need repeated and extensive fine-tuning lexicon building, and tweaking of the rules.

Even more galling is the impressive performance turned in a few years ago by a system that made a total mockery of the theoretical excursions of linguists. This system was designed by a group of physicists at IBM who got the idea of treating translation as a problem of simple probability. Rather than working out grammatical rules themselves, they created a program to exploit the expert knowledge built into actual translated texts. The idea was brilliant stupidity: a huge corpus of bilingual text—a chunk of proceedings of the Canadian Parliament, which by law must be published in both French and English—was fed into the machine. The computer then began tallying coincidences in the crudest fashion possible: if the word "dog" appeared in an English sentence, what words appeared in the corresponding French sentence? After tallying the French words in thousands of sentences that corresponded to "dog"-bearing English sentences, the computer had in hand a table of probabilities: "*chien*" might appear, say, 99 percent of the time; much less frequent would be "*veinard*" ("lucky dog!") or "*talonner*" ("to dog one's footsteps"); least frequent of all would be every other word that had happened to appear in one "dog" sentence or another—everything from "*anticonstitutionnel*" to "*biscuiterie*" to "*pamplemousse*." Whenever the machine subsequently encountered "dog" in an English text it was given to translate, it substituted the most probable translation—"*chien*." With enough computing power it's possible to create probability tables for combinations of two or even three words, which can distinguish, for instance, "lucky dog" from "bird dog." (Beyond about three words the number of permutations grows too enormous for any existing computer to handle.)

20   The IBM system then tossed all the words in its translated sentence into a bag and let the laws of probability decide what order to put them in. Let's say the words in the bag were "*chien*," "*maison*," "*est*," "*la*," "*le*," and "*dans*." Although it is unlikely that any Canadian parliamentarians ever uttered the words "*Le chien est dans la maison*," the millions of sentences they have uttered provide plenty of statistics on how often in a French sentence each of these words directly follows another of them. The words "*la*" and "*le*" almost never follow each other; "*chien*" almost always follows "*le*" (the masculine) rather than "*la*" (the feminine); "*dans*" almost never precedes "*est*" but often follows it; and so on. The computer would simply string the words together in different combinations   20

until it came up with the one that contained the most statistically probable sequence of word pairs.

The embarrassing thing is that the IBM system performed almost as well as systems that incorporated the latest in high-falutin linguistic theory. With no programmed intelligence, no rules about meaning or grammar or word order, statistical systems got as many as 50 percent of their translated sentences correct, whereas the rate is about 65 percent for systems like Babelfish. Hovy says that developers of statistical systems were going around bragging, "Every time I fire a linguist, my system gets better."

The real failings of MT have less to do with the state of linguistic theory than with the fact that computers don't have any common sense. Language is full of ambiguity and multiple meanings that a correct reading of syntax goes only a short way toward sorting out. For example, Babelfish and Comprende missed both the meanings in Groucho's line "We took some pictures of the native girls, but they're not developed yet," translating "they" into the default masculine form—even though both girls and pictures are feminine in French. Is a "bank" a place to put money, the edge of a riverbed, or the side-to-side slope of a race-track? A five-year-old child can grasp the differences in meaning, but getting a computer to do so is another matter. Thanks to the grammatical structure of the sentence, Babelfish correctly established that "book" in "Book him, Danno" was a verb rather than a noun. But lacking common sense, it went on to translate the phrase as "*Réservez-le, Danno*"—in the sense of "Book a table" or "Book a hotel room."

In other words, semantics is the key to MT, and semantics is a matter of a lot more than linguistics—it requires real-world knowledge. Indeed, one can get near-perfect translations with just about any system by limiting its lexicon to a narrow, specialized area in which there is no semantic ambiguity. Canadian radio stations translate weather bulletins from English to French every fifteen minutes. In 1974, because the professional translators were getting bored (how many times can one translate "fog this morning"?), Richard Kittredge, at the University of Montreal's machine-translation unit, was asked to develop a program to handle the task. With a lexicon of just a few hundred words, his program achieves an accuracy rate of more than 90 percent.

A major effort now under way in MT circles is to come up with elaborate taxonomies of meaning that will in effect duplicate the real-world knowledge that allows human beings effortlessly to know which words relate to which in a sentence and which of various meanings the speaker intends. This, of course, is virtually equivalent to the challenge of artificial intelligence in toto—creating a computer that thinks, or at least comes close enough to thinking that we can't tell the difference. Hovy and colleagues at the University of Southern California have developed an "ontology" (available on the Web at a site dubbed Ontosaurus), which sorts 90,000 concepts into a branching hierarchy according to their fundamental meaning and the way they are treated in language. The universe is divided into qualities, processes, objects, and interpersonal things; an object can in turn be a social object, a physical object, or a conscious being; and so on through multiple hierarchical layers.

25   The holy grail for many people in machine translation is to use a tree like this to reduce any sentence to a pure description of meaning in an "interlingua." This can then be reassembled into a sentence in any language using a grammar-driven generator peculiar to that target language. But no one seems to be holding his breath.

Except, perhaps, professional translators. "I have people here who still feel threatened, definitely," say Dale Bostad, who works in the translation branch of the National Air Intelligence Center, at Wright-Patterson Air Force Base, in Ohio. Translators are, not unexpectedly, scornful of MT, but they are also undeniably nervous about it. Babelfish's 65 percent accuracy rate on general text is terrible, but not quite so terrible that it doesn't pay to use it in many situations. A professional translator gets about ten to fifteen cents a word, and one who works in a tough language like Chinese can charge three times as much. So if a person's aim is to take a quick look at what a document is about (the bread and butter of intelligence work and, for that matter, commerce), MT can be invaluable. Brian Garr, Globalink's chief technology officer, told me, "Our biggest challenge is setting people's expectations properly. I wouldn't use [our products] to write a manual on nuclear devices." But few applications are so demanding. About 20 percent of communication on the Internet takes place in languages other than English, and to companies that sell their wares on the Web, translation—even bad translation—can make the difference between getting an order and not. Globalink offered a gizmo for $100 a month that allowed whatever material was posted on a company's Web site to be read in five languages; its new owner will offer something similar.

Another major growth area for MT is the European Union, which employs about 2,000 translators to handle eleven languages. Only about 10 percent of its translations are done with Systran systems, but the figure is growing rapidly, as nontranslator bureaucrats realize that they can use the program directly on the EU computer network when they want a quick translation.

Dale Bostad thinks the biggest payoff may come from combining computers and people in a way that exploits the natural talents of each. A document can be given a once-over by MT, and a professional translator can then clean up the glitches. Bostad is developing software that will automatically flag the iffy sentences generated by machine translators' output (such as those containing acronyms, unfamiliar words, or improbable word sequences), so that the human beings can focus effort where it is needed most. Working in tandem with an MT system, Bostad finds, some people can produce eighteen pages an hour, whereas the standard quota for a professional government translator is five to six pages a day. Younger translators in particular have embraced this approach, Bostad says. Their attitude toward computers is, If you can't beat them, join them.

Or, in the words of Babelfish: "If you cannot strike it, connect them."

Advertising's Fifteen Basic Appeals
Jib Fowles

Jib Fowles (1940–) was born in Hartford, Connecticut and attended Wesleyan University, Columbia University, and New York University, where he received a Ph.D. in 1974. Currently he is professor of communication at the University of Houston. A Fulbright Scholar, he has published extensively on the subject of mass culture, advertising, media, and their effects on the public. His most recent works include Starstruck: Celebrity Performers and the American Public *(1992);* Why Viewers Watch: A Reappraisal of Television's Effects *(1992);* Advertising and Popular Culture *(1996); and* The Case for Television Violence *(1999). The following selection is excerpted from the article "Mass Advertising as Social Forecast."*

Emotional Appeals

1   The nature of effective advertisements was recognized full well by the late media philosopher Marshall McLuhan. In his *Understanding Media,* the first sentence of the section on advertising reads, "The continuous pressure is to create ads more and more in the image of audience motives and desires."

By giving form to people's deep-lying desires, and picturing states of being that individuals privately yearn for, advertisers have the best chance of arresting attention and affecting communication. And that is the immediate goal of advertising: to tug at our psychological shirtsleeves and slow us down long enough for a word or two about whatever is being sold. We glance at a picture of a solitary rancher at work, and "Marlboro" slips into our minds.

Advertisers (I'm using the term as a shorthand for both the products' manufacturers, who bring the ambition and money to the process, and the advertising agencies, who supply the know-how) are ever more compelled to invoke consumers' drives and longings; this is the "continuous pressure" McLuhan refers to. Over the past century, the American marketplace has grown increasingly congested as more and more products have entered into the frenzied competition after the public's dollars. The economies of other nations are quieter than ours since the volume of goods being hawked does not so greatly exceed demand. In some economies, consumer wares are scarce enough that no advertising at all is necessary. But in the United States, we go to the other extreme. In order to stay in business, an advertiser must strive to cut through the considerable commercial

Reprinted from *Advertising and Popular Culture* (1996), by permission of Sage Publications, Ltd.

hub-bub by any means available—including the emotional appeals that some observers have held to be abhorrent and underhanded.

The use of subconscious appeals is a comment not only on conditions among sellers. As time has gone by, buyers have become stoutly resistant to advertisements. We live in a blizzard of these messages and have learned to turn up our collars and ward off most of them. A study done a few years ago at Harvard University's Graduate School of Business Administration ventured that the average American is exposed to some 500 ads daily from television, newspapers, magazines, radio, billboards, direct mail, and so on. If for no other reason than to preserve one's sanity, a filter must be developed in every mind to lower the number of ads a person is actually aware of—a number this particular study estimated at about seventy-five ads per day. (Of these, only twelve typically produced a reaction—nine positive and three negative, on the average.) To be among the few messages that do manage to gain access to minds, advertisers must be strategic, perhaps even a little underhanded at times.

5   There are assumptions about personality underlying advertisers' efforts to communicate via emotional appeals, and while these assumptions have stood the test of time, they still deserve to be aired. Human beings, it is presumed, walk around with a variety of unfulfilled urges and motives swirling in the bottom half of their minds. Lusts, ambitions, tendernesses, vulnerabilities—they are constantly bubbling up, seeking resolution. These mental forces energize people, but they are too crude and irregular to be given excessive play in the real world. They must be capped with the competent, sensible behavior that permits individuals to get along well in society. However, this upper layer of mental activity, shot through with caution and rationality, is not receptive to advertising's pitches. Advertisers want to circumvent this shell of consciousness if they can, and latch on to one of the lurching, subconscious drives.

In effect, advertisers over the years have blindly felt their way around the underside of the American psyche, and by trial and error have discovered the softest points of entree, the places where their messages have the greatest likelihood of getting by consumers' defenses. As McLuhan says elsewhere, "Gouging away at the surface of public sales resistance, the ad men are constantly breaking through into the *Alice in Wonderland* territory behind the looking glass, which is the world of subrational impulses and appetites."

An advertisement communicates by making use of a specially selected image (of a supine female, say, or a curly-haired child, or a celebrity) which is designed to stimulate "subrational impulses and desires" even when they are at ebb, even if they are unacknowledged by their possessor. Some few ads have their emotional appeal in the text, but for the greater number by far the appeal is contained in the artwork. This makes sense, since visual communication better suits more primal levels of the brain. If the viewer of an advertisement actually has the importuned motive, and if the appeal is sufficiently well fashioned to call it up, then the person can be hooked. The product in the ad may then appear to take on the semblance of gratification for the summoned motive. Many ads seem to be saying, "If you have this need, then this product will help satisfy it." It is a primitive equation, but not an ineffective one for selling.

Thus, most advertisements appearing in national media can be understood as having two orders of content. The first is the appeal to deep-running drives in the minds of consumers. The second is information regarding the good[s] or service being sold: its name, its manufacturer, its picture, its packaging, its objective attributes, its functions. For example, the reader of a brassiere advertisement sees a partially undraped but blandly unperturbed woman standing in an otherwise commonplace public setting, and may experience certain sensations; the reader also sees the name "Maidenform," a particular brassiere style, and, in tiny print, words about the material, colors, price. Or, the viewer of a television commercial sees a demonstration with four small boxes labeled 650, 650, 650, and 800; something in the viewer's mind catches hold of this, as trivial as thoughtful consideration might reveal it to be. The viewer is also exposed to the name "Anacin," its bottle, and its purpose.

Sometimes there is an apparently logical link between an ad's emotional appeal and its product information. It does not violate common sense that Cadillac automobiles be photographed at country clubs, or that Japan Air Lines be associated with Orientalia. But there is no real need for the linkage to have a bit of reason behind it. Is there anything inherent to the connection between Salem cigarettes and mountains, Coke and a smile, Miller Beer and comradeship? The link being forged in minds between product and appeal is a pre-logical one.

10   People involved in the advertising industry do not necessarily talk in the   10 terms being used here. They are stationed at the sending end of this communications channel, and may think they are up to any number of things—Unique Selling Propositions, explosive copywriting, the optimal use of demographics or psychographics, ideal media buys, high recall ratings, or whatever. But when attention shifts to the receiving end of the channel, and focuses on the instant of reception, then commentary becomes much more elemental: an advertising message contains something primary and primitive, an emotional appeal, that in effect is the thin end of the wedge, trying to find its way into a mind. Should this occur, the product information comes along behind.

When enough advertisements are examined in this light, it becomes clear that the emotional appeals fall into several distinguishable categories, and that every ad is a variation on one of a limited number of basic appeals. While there may be several ways of classifying these appeals, one particular list of fifteen has proven to be especially valuable.

Advertisements can appeal to:

1. The need for sex
2. The need for affiliation
3. The need to nurture
4. The need for guidance
5. The need to aggress

6. The need to achieve
7. The need to dominate
8. The need for prominence
9. The need for attention
10. The need for autonomy
11. The need to escape
12. The need to feel safe
13. The need for aesthetic sensations
14. The need to satisfy curiosity
15. Physiological needs: food, drink, sleep, etc.

Murray's List

Where does this list of advertising's fifteen basic appeals come from? Several years ago, I was involved in a research project which was to have as one segment an objective analysis of the changing appeals made in post-World War II American advertising. A sample of magazine ads would have their appeals coded into the categories of psychological needs they seemed aimed at. For this content analysis to happen, a complete roster of human motives would have to be found.

The first thing that came to mind was Abraham Maslow's famous four-part hierarchy of needs. But the briefest look at the range of appeals made in advertising was enough to reveal that they are more varied, and more profane, than Maslow had cared to account for. The search led on to the work of psychologist Henry A. Murray, who together with his colleagues at the Harvard Psychological Clinic has constructed a full taxonomy of needs. As described in *Explorations in Personality*, Murray's team had conducted a lengthy series of in-depth interviews with a number of subjects in order to derive from scratch what they felt to be the essential variables of personality. Forty-four variables were distinguished by the Harvard group, of which twenty were motives. The need for achievement ("to overcome obstacles and obtain a high standard") was one, for instance; the need to defer was another; the need to aggress was a third; and so forth.

Murray's list had served as the groundwork for a number of subsequent projects. Perhaps the best-known of these was David C. McClelland's extensive study of the need for achievement, reported in his *The Achieving Society*. In the process of demonstrating that a people's high need for achievement is predictive of later economic growth, McClelland coded achievement imagery and references out of a nation's folklore, songs, legends, and children's tales.

15   Following McClelland, I too wanted to cull the motivational appeals from a   15
culture's imaginative product—in this case, advertising. To develop categories expressly for this purpose, I took Murray's twenty motives and added to them others he had mentioned in passing in *Explorations in Personality* but not included on the final list. The extended list was tried out on a sample of advertisements, and motives which never seemed to be invoked were dropped. I ended up with eighteen of Murrays' motives, into which 770 print ads were coded. The

resulting distribution is included in the 1976 book *Mass Advertising as Social Forecast.*

Since that time, the list of appeals has undergone refinements as a result of using it to analyze television commercials. A few more adjustments stemmed from the efforts of students in my advertising classes to decode appeals; tens of term papers surveying thousands of advertisements have caused some inconsistencies in the list to be hammered out. Fundamentally, though, the list remains the creation of Henry Murray. In developing a comprehensive, parsimonious inventory of human motives, he pinpointed the subsurface mental forces that are the least quiescent and most susceptible to advertising's entreaties.

Fifteen Appeals

1. Need for Sex.   Let's start with sex, because this is the appeal which seems to pop up first whenever the topic of advertising is raised. Whole books have been written about this one alone, to find a large audience of mildly titillated readers. Lately, due to campaigns to sell blue jeans, concern with sex in ads has redoubled.

The fascinating thing is not how much sex there is in advertising, but how little. Contrary to impressions, unambiguous sex is rare in these messages. Some of this surprising observation may be a matter of definition: the Jordache ads with the lithe, blouse-less female astride a similarly clad male is clearly an appeal to the audience's sexual drives, but the same cannot be said about Brooke Shields[1] in the Calvin Klein commercials. Directed at young women and their credit-card carrying mothers, the image of Miss Shields instead invokes the need to be looked at. Buy Calvins and you'll be the center of much attention, just as Brooke is, the ads imply; they do not primarily inveigle their target audience's need for sexual intercourse.

In the content analysis reported in *Mass Advertising as Social Forecast* only two percent of ads were found to pander to this motive. Even *Playboy* ads shy away from sexual appeals: a recent issue contained eighty-three full-page ads, and just four of them (or less than five percent) could be said to have sex on their minds.

The reason this appeal is so little used is that it is too blaring and tends to obliterate the product information. Nudity in advertising has the effect of reducing brand recall. The people who do remember the product may do so because they have been made indignant by the ad; this is not the response most advertisers seek.

To the extent that sexual imagery is used, it conventionally works better on men than women; typically a female figure is offered up to the male reader. A Black Velvet liquor advertisement displays an attractive woman wearing a tight black outfit, recumbent under the legend, "Feel the Velvet." The figure does not have to be horizontal, however, for the appeal to be present as National Airlines revealed in its "Fly me" campaign. Indeed, there does not even have to be a female in the ad; "Flick my Bic"[2] was sufficient to convey the idea to many.

As a rule, though, advertisers have found sex to be a tricky appeal, to be used sparingly. Less controversial and equally fetching are the appeals to our need for affectionate human contact.

2. Need for Affiliation.   American mythology upholds auto-nomous indi-viduals, and social statistics suggest that people are ever more going it alone in their lives, yet the high frequency of affiliative appeals in ads belies this. Or maybe it does not: maybe all the images of companionship are compensation for what Americans privately lack. In any case, the need to associate with others is widely invoked in advertising and is probably the most prevalent appeal. All sorts of goods and services are sold by linking them to our unfulfilled desires to be in good company.

According to Henry Murray, the need for affiliation consists of desires "to draw near and enjoyably cooperate or reciprocate with another; to please and win affection of another; to adhere and remain loyal to a friend." The manifestations of this motive can be segmented into several different types of affiliation, begin-ning with romance.

25   Courtship may be swifter nowadays, but the desire for pair-bonding is far from   25
satiated. Ads reaching for this need commonly depict a youngish male and female engrossed in each other. The head of the male is usually higher than the female's, even at this late date; she may be sitting or leaning while he is standing. They are not touching in the Smirnoff vodka ads, but obviously there is an intimacy, sometimes frolicsome, between them. The couple does touch for Martell Cognac when "The moment was Martell." For Wind Song perfume they have touched, and "Your Wind Song stays on his mind."

Depending on the audience, the pair does not absolutely have to be young–just together. He gives her a DeBeers diamond, and there is a tear in her laugh lines. She takes Geritol[3] and preserves herself for him. And numbers of consumers, wanting affection too, follow suit.

Warm family feelings are fanned in ads when another generation is added to the pair. Hallmark Cards brings grandparents into the picture, and Johnson and Johnson Baby Powder has Dad, Mom, and baby, all fresh from the bath, encir-cled in arms and emblazoned with "Share the Feeling." A talc has been fused to familial love.

Friendship is yet another form of affiliation pursued by advertisers. Two women confide and drink Maxwell House coffee together; two men walk through the woods smoking Salem cigarettes. Miller Beer promises that after-noon "Miller Time" will be staffed with three or four good buddies. Drink Dr. Pepper, as Mickey Rooney[4] is coaxed to do, and join in with all the other Peppers. Coca-Cola does not even need to portray the friendliness; it has reduced this appeal to "a Coke and a smile."

The warmth can be toned down and disguised, but it is the same affiliative need that is being fished for. The blonde has a direct gaze and her friends are firm businessmen in appearance, but with a glass of Old Bushmill you can sit down and fit right in. Or, for something more upbeat, sing along with the Pontiac choirboys.

30   As well as presenting positive images, advertisers can play to the need for affiliation in negative ways, by invoking the fear of rejection. If we don't use Scope, we'll have the "Ugh! Morning Breath" that causes the male and female models to avert their faces. Unless we apply Ultra Brite or Close-Up to our teeth, it's good-bye romance. Our family will be cursed with "House-a-tosis" if we don't take care. Without Dr. Scholl's antiperspirant foot spray, the bowling team will keel over. There go all the guests when the supply of Dorito's nacho cheese chips is exhausted. Still more rejection if our shirts have ring-around-the-collar, if our car needs to be Midasized. But make a few purchases, and we are back in the bosom of human contact.

As self-directed as Americans pretend to be, in the last analysis we remain social animals, hungering for the positive, endorsing feelings that only those around us can supply. Advertisers respond, urging us to "Reach out and touch someone," in the hopes our monthly [phone] bills will rise.

3. Need to Nurture.   Akin to affiliative needs is the need to take care of small, defenseless creatures—children and pets, largely. Reciprocity is of less consequence here, though; it is the giving that counts. Murray uses synonyms like "to feed, help, support, console, protect, comfort, nurse, heal." A strong need it is, woven deep into our genetic fabric, for if it did not exist we could not successfully raise up our replacements. When advertisers put forth the image of something diminutive and furry, something that elicits the word "cute" or "precious," then they are trying to trigger this motive. We listen to the childish voice singing the Oscar Mayer weiner song, and our next hot-dog purchase is prescribed. Aren't those darling kittens something, and how did this Meow Mix get into our shopping cart?

This pitch is often directed at women, as Mother Nature's chief nurturers. "Make me some Kraft macaroni and cheese, please," says the elfin preschooler just in from the snowstorm, and mothers' hearts go out, and Kraft's sales go up. "We're cold, wet, and hungry," whine the husband and kids, and the little woman gets the Manwiches ready. A facsimile of this need can be hit without children or pets: the husband is ill and sleepless in the television commercial, and the wife grudgingly fetches the NyQuil.

But it is not women alone who can be touched by this appeal. The father nurses his son Eddie through adolescence while the John Deere lawn tractor survives the years. Another father counts pennies with his young son as the subject of New York Life Insurance comes up. And all over America are businessmen who don't know why they dial Qantas Airlines[5] when they have to take a trans-Pacific trip; the koala bear knows.

35   **4. Need for Guidance.** The opposite of the need to nurture is the need to be nurtured: to be protected, shielded, guided. We may be loath to admit it, but the child lingers on inside every adult—and a good thing it does, or we would

not be instructable in our advancing years. Who wants a nation of nothing but flinty personalities?

Parent-like figures can successfully call up this need. Robert Young[6] recommends Sanka coffee, and since we have experienced him for twenty-five years as television father and doctor, we take his word for it. Florence Henderson[7] as the expert mom knows a lot about the advantages of Wesson oil.

The parent-ness of the spokesperson need not be so salient; sometimes pure authoritativeness is better. When Orson Welles[8] scowls and intones, "Paul Masson will sell no wine before its time," we may not know exactly what he means, but we still take direction from him. There is little maternal about Brenda Vaccaro[9] when she speaks up for Tampax, but there is a certainty to her that many accept.

A celebrity is not a necessity in making a pitch to the need for guidance, since a fantasy figure can serve just as well. People accede to the Green Giant, or Betty Crocker, or Mr. Goodwrench.[10] Some advertisers can get by with no figure at all: "When E. F. Hutton[11] talks, people listen."

Often it is tradition or custom that advertisers point to and con-sumers take guidance from. Bits and pieces of American history are used to sell whiskeys like Old Crow, Southern Comfort, Jack Daniel's. We conform to traditional male/female roles and age-old social norms when we purchase Barclay cigarettes, which informs us "The pleasure is back."

40   The product itself, if it has been around for a long time, can constitute a tradition. All those old labels in the ad for Morton salt convince us that we should continue to buy it. Kool-Aid says "You loved it as a kid. You trust it as a mother," hoping to get yet more consumers to go along.   40

Even when the product has no history at all, our need to conform to tradition and to be guided are strong enough that they can be invoked through bogus nostalgia and older actors. Country-Time lemonade sells because consumers want to believe it has a past they can defer to.

So far the needs and the ways they can be invoked which have been looked at are largely warm and affiliative; they stand in contrast to the next set of needs, which are much more egoistic and assertive.

5. Need to Aggress. The pressures of the real world create strong retaliatory feelings in every functioning human being. Since these impulses can come forth as bursts of anger and violence, their display is normally tabooed. Existing as harbored energy, aggressive drives present a large, tempting target for advertisers. It is not a target to be aimed at thoughtlessly, though, for few manufacturers want their products associated with destructive motives. There is always the danger that, as in the case of sex, if the appeal is too blatant, public opinion will turn against what is being sold.

Jack-in-the-Box sought to abruptly alter its marketing by going after older customers and forgetting the younger ones. Their television commercials had a seventy-ish lady command, "Waste him," and the Jack-in-the-Box clown exploded before our eyes. So did public reaction until the commercials were toned down. Print ads for Club cocktails carried the faces of octogenarians under the headline,

"Hit me with a Club"; response was contrary enough to bring the campaign to a stop.

Better disguised aggressive appeals are less likely to backfire: Triumph cigarettes has models making a lewd gesture with their uplifted cigarettes, but the individuals are often laughing and usually in close company of others. When Exxon said, "There's a Tiger in your tank," the implausibility of it concealed the invocation of aggressive feelings.

Depicted arguments are a common way for advertisers to tap the audience's needs to aggress. Don Rickles[12] and Lynda Carter[13] trade gibes, and consumers take sides as the name of Seven-Up is stitched on minds. The Parkay [margarine] tub has a difference of opinion with the user; who can forget it, or who (or what) got the last word in?

6. Need to Achieve. This is the drive that energizes people, causing them to strive in their lives and careers. According to Murray, the need for achievement is signalled by the desires "to accomplish something difficult. To overcome obstacles and attain a high standard. To excel one's self. To rival and surpass others." A prominent American trait, it is one that advertisers like to hook on to because it identifies their product with winning and success.

The Cutty Sark ad does not disclose that Ted Turner failed at his latest attempt at yachting's America Cup; here he is represented as a champion on the water as well as off in his television enterprises. If we drink this whiskey, we will be victorious alongside Turner. We can also succeed with O. J. Simpson[14] by renting Hertz cars, or with Reggie Jackson[15] by bringing home some Panasonic equipment. Cathy Rigby[16] and Stayfree maxipads will put people out front.

Sports heroes are the most convenient means to snare consumers' needs to achieve, but they are not the only one. Role models can be established, ones which invite emulation, as with the profiles put forth by Dewar's scotch. Successful, tweedy individuals relate they have "graduated to the flavor of Myer's rum." Or the advertiser can establish a prize: two neighbors play one-on-one basketball for a Michelob beer in a television commercial, while in a print ad a bottle of Johnnie Walker Black Label has been gilded like a trophy.

Any product that advertises itself in superlatives—the best, the first, the finest—is trying to make contact with our needs to succeed. For many consumers, sales and bargains belong in this category of appeals, too; the person who manages to buy something at fifty percent off is seizing an opportunity and coming out ahead of others.

7. Need to Dominate. This fundamental need is the craving to be powerful—perhaps omnipotent, as in the Xerox ad where Brother Dominic exhibits heavenly powers and creates miraculous copies. Most of us will settle for being just a regular potentate, though. We drink Budweiser because it is the King of Beers, and here comes the powerful Clydesdales to prove it. A taste of Wolfschmidt vodka and "The spirit of the Czar lives on."

The need to dominate and control one's environment is often thought of as being masculine, but as close students of human nature advertisers know, it is not so circumscribed. Women's aspirations for control are suggested in the campaign theme, "I like my men in English Leather, or nothing at all." The females in the Chanel No. 19 ads are "outspoken" and wrestle their men around.

Male and female, what we long for is clout; what we get in its place is Mastercard.

8. Need for Prominence. Here comes the need to be admired and respected, to enjoy prestige and high social status. These times, it appears, are not so egalitarian after all. Many ads picture the trappings of high position; the Oldsmobile stands before a manorial doorway, the Volvo is parked beside a stee-plechase. A book-lined study is the setting for Dewar's 12, and Lenox China is displayed in a dining room chock full of antiques.

55   Beefeater gin represents itself as "The Crown Jewel of England" and uses   55
no illustrations of jewels or things British, for the words are sufficient indicators of distinction. Buy that gin and you will rise up the prestige hierarchy, or achieve the same effect on yourself with Seagram's 7 Crown, which ambiguously describes itself as "classy."

Being respected does not have to entail the usual accoutrements of wealth: "Do you know who I am?" the commercials ask, and we learn that the promi-nent person is not so prominent without his American Express card.

9. Need for Attention. The previous need involved being *looked up to,* while this is the need to be *looked at.* The desire to exhibit ourselves in such a way as to make others look at us is a primitive, insuppressible instinct. The cloth-ing and cosmetic industries exist just to serve this need, and this is the way they pitch their wares. Some of this effort is aimed at males, as the ads for Hathaway shirts and Jockey underclothes. But the greater bulk of such appeals is targeted singlemindedly at women.

To come back to Brooke Shields: this is where she fits into American mar-keting. If I buy Calvin Klein jeans, consumers infer, I'll be the object of fascina-tion. The desire for exhibition has been most strikingly played to in a print cam-paign of many years' duration, that of Maidenform lingerie. The woman exposes herself, and sales surge. "Gentlemen prefer Hanes" the ads dissemble, and women who want eyes upon them know what they should do. Peggy Fleming[17] flutters her legs for L'eggs, encouraging females who want to be the star in their own lives to purchase this product.

The same appeal works for cosmetics and lotions. For years, the little girl with the exposed backside sold gobs of Coppertone, but now the company has picked up the pace a little: as a female, you are supposed to "Flash 'em a Coppertone tan." Food can be sold the same way, especially to the diet-conscious; Angie Dickinson poses for California avocados and says, "Would this body lie to you?" Our eyes are too fixed on her for us to think to ask if she got that way by eating mounds of gua-comole.

60   **10. Need for Autonomy.** There are several ways to sell credit card services,   60
as has been noted: Mastercard appeals to the need to dominate, and American Express to the need for prominence. When Visa claims, "You can have it the way

you want it," yet another primary motive is being beckoned forward—the need to endorse the self. The focus here is upon the independence and integrity of the individual; this need is the antithesis of the need for guidance and is unlike any of the social needs. "If running with the herd isn't your style, try ours," says Rotan-Mosle, and many Americans feel they have finally found the right broker-age firm.

The photo is of a red-coated Mountie on his horse, posed on a snow-covered ledge; the copy reads, "Windsor—One Canadian stands alone." This epitome of the solitary and proud individual may work best with male customers as may Winston's man in the red cap. But one-figure advertisements also strike the strong need for autonomy among American women. As Shelly Hack[18] strides for Charlie perfume, females respond to her obvious pride and flair; she is her own person. The Virginia Slims tale is of people who have come a long way from subservience to independ-ence. Cachet perfume feels it does not need a solo figure to work this appeal, and uses three different faces in its ads; it insists though, "It's different on every woman who wears it."

Like many psychological needs, this one can also be appealed to in a nega-tive fashion, by invoking the loss of independence or self-regard. Guilt and regrets can be stimulated: "Gee, I could have had a V-8." Next time, get one and be good to yourself.

11. Need to Escape. An appeal to the need for autonomy often co-occurs with one for the need to escape, since the desire to duck out of our social oblications, to seek rest or adventure, frequently takes the form of one-person flight. The dashing image of a pilot, in fact, is a standard way of quickening this need to get away from it all.

Freedom is the pitch here, the freedom that every individual yearns for when-ever life becomes too oppressive. Many advertisers like appealing to the need for escape because the sensation of pleasure often accompanies escape, and what nicer emotional nimbus could there be for a product? "You deserve a break today," says McDonald's, and Stouffer's frozen foods chime in, "Set yourself free."

For decades men have imaginatively bonded themselves to the Marlboro cowboy who dwells untarnished and unencumbered in Marlboro Country some distance from modern life; smokers' aching needs for autonomy and escape are personified by that cowpoke. Many women can identify with the lady ambling through the woods behind the words, "Benson and Hedges and mornings and me."

But escape does not have to be solitary. Other Benson and Hedges ads, part of the same campaign, contain two strolling figures. In Salem cigarette advertise-ments, it can be several people who escape together into the mountaintops. A commercial for Levi's pictured a cloudbank above a city through which ran a whole chain of young people.

There are varieties of escape, some wistful like the Boeing "Someday" cam-paign of dream vacations, some kinetic like the play and parties in soft drink ads. But in every instance, the consumer exposed to the advertisement is invited to momentarily depart his everyday life for a more carefree experience, preferably with the product in hand.

12. Need to Feel Safe. Nobody in their right mind wants to be intimidated, menaced, battered, poisoned. We naturally want to do whatever it takes to stave off threats to our well-being, and to our families'. It is the instinct of self-preservation that makes us responsive to the ad of the St. Bernard with the keg of Chivas Regal. We pay attention to the stern talk of Karl Malden[19] and the plight of the vacationing couples who have lost all their funds in the American Express travelers cheques commercials. We want the omnipresent stag from Hartford Insurance to watch over us too.

In the interest of keeping failure and calamity from our lives, we like to see the durability of products demonstrated. Can we ever forget that Timex takes a licking and keeps on ticking? When the American Tourister suitcase bounces all over the highway and the egg inside doesn't break, the need to feel safe has been adroitly plucked.

70   We take precautions to diminish future threats. We buy Volkswagen Rabbits for   70
the extraordinary mileage, and MONY insurance policies to avoid the tragedies depicted in their black-and-white ads of widows and orphans.

We are careful about our health. We consume Mazola margarine because it has "corn goodness" backed by the natural food traditions of the American Indians. In the medicine cabinet is Alka-Seltzer, the "home remedy"; having it, we are snug in our little cottage.

We want to be safe and secure; buy these products, advertisers are saying, and you'll be safer than you are without them.

13. Need for Aesthetic Sensations. There is an undeniable aesthetic component to virtually every ad run in the national media: the photography or filming or drawing is near-perfect, the type style is well chosen, the layout could scarcely be improved upon. Advertisers know there is little chance of good communication occurring if an ad is not visually pleasing. Consumers may not be aware of the extent of their own sensitivity to artwork, but it is undeniably large.

Sometimes the aesthetic element is expanded and made into an ad's primary appeal. Charles Jordan shoes may or may not appear in the accompanying avant-grade photographs; Kohler plumbing fixtures catch attention through the high style of their desert settings. Beneath the slightly out of focus photograph, languid and sensuous in tone, General Electric feels called upon to explain, "This is an ad for the hair dryer."

75   This appeal is not limited to female consumers: J&B scotch says "It whispers" and shows a bucolic scene of lake and castle.   75

14. Need to Satisfy Curiosity. It may seem odd to list a need for information among basic motives, but this need can be as primal and compelling as any of the others. Human beings are curious by nature, interested in the world around them, and intrigued by tidbits of knowledge and new developments Trivia, percentages, observations counter to conventional wisdom—these items all help sell products. Any advertisement in a question-and-answer format is strumming this need.

A dog groomer has a question about long distance rates, and Bell Telephone has a chart with all the figures. An ad for Porsche 911 is replete with diagrams and schematics, numbers and arrows. Lo and behold, Anacin pills have 150 more milligrams than its competitors; should we wonder if this is better of worse for us?

15. Physiological Needs. To the extent that sex is solely a biological need, we are now coming around full circle, back toward the start of the list. In this final category are clustered appeals to sleeping, eating, drinking. The art of photographing food and drink is so advanced, sometimes these temptations are wondrously caught in the camera's lens: the crab meat in the Red Lobster restaurant ads can start us salivating, the Quarterpounder can almost be smelled, the liquor in the glass glows invitingly. Imbibe, these ads scream.

Styles

Some common ingredients of advertisements were not singled out for separate mention in the list of fifteen because they are not appeals in and of themselves. They are stylistic features, influencing the way a basic appeal is presented. The use of humor is one, and the use of celebrities is another. A third is time imagery, past and future, which goes to several purposes.

80 For all of its employment in advertising, humor can be treacherous, because 80 it can get out of hand and smother the product information. Supposedly, this is what Alka-Seltzer discovered with its comic commercials of the late sixties; "I can't believe I ate the whole thing," the sad-faced husband lamented, and the audience cackled so much it forgot the antacid. Or, did not take it seriously.

But used carefully, humor can punctuate some of the softer appeals and soften some of the harsher ones. When Emma says to the Fruit-of-the-Loom fruits, "Hi, cuties. Whatcha doing in my laundry basket?" we smile as our curiosity is assuaged along with hers. Bill Cosby gets consumers tickled about the children in his Jell-O commercials, and strokes the need to nurture.

An insurance company wants to invoke the need to feel safe, but does not want to leave readers with an unpleasant aftertaste; cartoonist Rowland Wilson creates an avalanche about to crush a gentleman who is saying to another, "My insurance company? New England Life, of course. Why?" The same tactic of humor undercutting threat is used in the cartoon commercials for Safeco when the Pink Panther wanders from one disaster to another. Often humor masks aggression: comedian Bob Hope in the outfit of a boxer promises to knock out the knock-knocks with Texaco; Rodney Dangerfield, who "can't get no respect," invites aggression as the comic relief in Miller Lite commercials.

Roughly fifteen percent of all advertisements incorporate a celebrity, almost always from the fields of entertainment or sports. The approach can also prove troublesome for advertisers, for celebrities are human beings too, and fully capable of the most remarkable behavior. If anything distasteful about them emerges, it is likely to reflect on the product. The advertisers making use of Anita Bryant[20] and Billy Jean King[21] suffered several anxious moments. An untimely death can also react poorly on a product. But advertisers are willing to take risks because celebrities can be such a good link between producers and consumers, performing the social role of introducer.

There are several psychological needs these middlemen can play upon. Let's take the product class of cameras and see how different celebrities can hit different needs. The need for guidance can be invoked by Michael Landon, who plays such a wonderful dad on "Little House on the Prairie"; when he says to buy Kodak equipment, many people listen. James Garner for Polaroid cameras is put in a similar authoritative role, so defined by a mocking spouse. The need to achieve is summoned up by Tracy Austin and other tennis stars for Canon AE-1; the advertiser first makes sure we see these athletes playing to win. When Cheryl Tiegs[22] speaks up for Olympus cameras, it is the need for attention that is being targeted.

85   The past and future, being outside our grasp, are exploited by advertisers as   85
locales for the projection of needs. History can offer up heroes (and call up the need to achieve) or traditions (need for guidance) as well as art objects (need for aesthetic sensations). Nostalgia is a kindly version of personal history and is deployed by advertisers to rouse needs for affiliation and for guidance; the need to escape can come in here, too. The same need to escape is sometimes the point of futuristic appeals but picturing the avant-garde can also be a way to get at the need to achieve.

Analyzing Advertisements

When analyzing ads yourself for their emotional appeals, it takes a bit of practice to learn to ignore the product information (as well as one's own experience and feelings about the product). But that skill comes soon enough, as does the ability to quickly sort out from all the non-product aspects of an ad the chief element which is the most striking, the most likely to snag attention first and penetrate brains farthest. The key to the appeal, this element usually presents itself centrally and forwardly to the reader or viewer.

Another clue: the viewing angle which the audience has on the ad's subjects is informative. If the subjects are photographed or filmed from below and thus are looking down at you much as the Green Giant does, then the need to be guided is a good candidate for the ad's emotional appeal. If, on the other hand, the subjects are shot from above and appear deferential, as is often the case with children or female models, then other needs are being appealed to.

To figure out an ad's emotional appeal, it is wise to know (or have a good hunch about) who the targeted consumers are; this can often be inferred from the magazine or television show it appears in. This piece of information is a great help in determining the appeal and in deciding between two different interpretations. For example, if an ad features a partially undressed female, this would typically signal one appeal for readers of *Penthouse* (need for sex) and another for readers of *Cosmopolitan* (need for attention).

It would be convenient if every ad made just one appeal, were aimed at just one need. Unfortunately, things are often not that simple. A cigarette ad with a couple at the edge of a polo field is trying to hit both the need for affiliation and the need for prominence; depending on the attitude of the male, dominance could also be an ingredient in this. An ad for Chimere perfume incorporates two photos: in the top one the lady is being commanding at a business luncheon (need to dominate), but in the lower one she is being bussed (need for affiliation). Better ads, however, seem to avoid being too diffused; in the study of post-World War II advertising described earlier, appeals grew more focused as the decades passed. As a rule of thumb, about sixty percent have two conspicuous appeals; the last twenty percent have three or more. Rather than looking for the greatest number of appeals, decoding ads is most productive when the loudest one or two appeals are discerned, since those are the appeals with the best chance of grabbing people's attention.

90   Finally, analyzing ads does not have to be a solo activity and probably should   90
not be. The greater number of people there are involved, the better chance there is of transcending individual biases and discerning the essential emotional lure built into an advertisement.

Do They or Don't They?

Do the emotional appeals made in advertisements add up to the sinister manipulation of consumers?

It is clear that these ads work. Attention is caught, communication occurs between producers and consumers, and sales result. It turns out to be difficult to detail the exact relationship between a specific ad and a specific purchase, or even between a campaign and subsequent sales figures, because advertising is only one of a host of influences upon consumption. Yet no one is fooled by this lack of perfect proof; everyone knows that advertising sells. If this were not the case, then tight-fisted American businesses would not spend a total of fifty billion dollars annually on these messages.

But before anyone despairs that advertisers have our number to the extent that they can marshal us at will and march us like automatons to the check-out counters, we should recall the resiliency and obduracy of the American consumer. Advertisers may have uncovered the softest spots in minds, but that does not mean they have found truly gaping apertures. There is no evidence that advertising can get people to do things contrary to their self-interests. Despite all the finesse of advertisements, and all the subtle emotional tugs, the public resists the vast majority of the petitions. According to the marketing division of the A. C. Nielsen Company, a whopping seventy-five percent of all new products die within a year in the marketplace, the victims of consumer disinterest which no amount of advertising could overcome. The appeals in advertising may be the most captivating there are to be had, but they are not enough to entrap the wily consumer.

The key to understanding the discrepancy between, on the one hand, the fact that advertising truly works, and, on the other, the fact that it hardly works, is to take into account the enormous numbers of people exposed to an ad. Modern-day communications permit an ad to be displayed to millions upon millions of individuals; if the smallest fraction of that audience can be moved to buy the product, then the ad has been successful. When one percent of the people exposed to a television advertising campaign reach for their wallets, that could be one million sales, which may be enough to keep the product in production and the advertisements coming.

95   In arriving at an evenhanded judgment about advertisements and their emotional appeals, it is good to keep in mind that many of the purchases which might be credited to these ads are experienced as genuinely gratifying to the consumer. We sincerely like the goods or service we have bought, and we may even like some of the emotional drapery that an ad suggests comes with it. It has sometimes been noted that the most avid students of advertisements are the people who have just bought the product; they want to steep themselves in the associated imagery. This may be the reason that Americans, when polled, are not negative about advertising and do not disclose any sense of being misused. The volume of advertising may be an irritant, but the product information as well as the imaginative material in ads are partial compensation.   95

A productive understanding is that advertising messages involve costs and benefits at both ends of the communications channel. For those few ads which do make contact, the consumer surrenders a moment of time, has the lower brain curried, and receives notice of a product; the advertiser has given up money and has increased the chance of sales. In this sort of communications activity, neither party can be said to be the loser.

Endnotes

1. Brooke Shields was still a minor when she did the ads for Calvin Klein jeans. The ad was made more provocative with the tag line, "Nothing can get between me and my Calvins."
2. "Flick my Bic" was the slogan for a cigarette lighter.
3. Geritol was a product marketed to older people as a tonic for increasing energy.
4. Mickey Rooney was once a child actor and a versatile entertainer.
5. Quantas Airlines is an Australian airline that once used a koala bear in its marketing campaign.
6. Robert Young was a movie and television star. His most well-known television roles cast him as a confident and kind authority figure.
7. Florence Henderson was the mother on *The Brady Bunch*.
8. Orson Welles was a movie director and actor. Paul Masson wines used him as the spokesperson because of his cultural cache.
9. Brenda Vaccaro is a movie and television actress with a particularly smoky, sexy voice.
10. Mr. Goodwrench was the persona for an ad campaign intended to instill trust in auto mechanics.
11. E. F. Hutton was at one time one of the most respected brokerage firms in the U. S.
12. Don Rickles is a comedian known for using insult as a form of humor.
13. Lynda Carter played Wonder Woman on a television series.

14. O. J. Simpson at one time had a very appealing image as an athlete.
15. Reggie Jackson was one of the greatest home run hitters for the New York Yankees.
16. Cathy Rigby had twice been an Olympian and also World Champion in gymnastics. Her wholesome image took her to the Broadway stage.
17. Peggy Fleming had a great career as an elegant figure skater.
18. Shelly Hack was in the cast of the television show *Charlie's Angels.*
19. Karl Malden is a well-known actor who played a stern cop in the television show *The Streets of San Francisco.*
20. Anita Bryant, a former beauty queen, was known for her conservative, wholesome image.
21. Billy Jean King is one of the greatest tennis players of all time and was also a social activist.
22. Cheryl Tiegs was once a popular supermodel associated with *Sports Illustrated.*

Winning Hearts and Minds in War on Plagiarism

Scott Jaschik

Scott Jaschik grew up in Rochester, New York and graduated from Cornell University in 1985. His articles have appeared in numerous publications, such as The New York Times, The Washington Post, The Boston Globe, Campus Watch, *and* Salon. *From 1999 to 2003 he was an editor for* The Chronicle of Higher Education. *Jaschik is a co-founder of* Inside Higher Ed, *an online source for news, commentary, and jobs pertaining to higher education. He is a mentor in the community college fellowship program for the Hechinger Institute on Education and Media. He has received honors for his reporting from* The Washington Monthly *and from Investigative Reporters and Editors, a non-profit organization dedicated to improving the quality of investigative reporting. Jaschik currently lives in Washington, DC. In the following article from* Inside Higher Ed, *he profiles one professor's unique approach to teaching students about plagiarism and how to avoid it.*

1   It's come to this: Writing professors are so desperate for new ways to teach undergraduates about academic integrity that they are assigning them to plagiarize.

That's what Kate Hagopian, an instructor in the first-year writing program at North Carolina State University, does. For one assignment, she gives her students a short writing passage and then a prompt for a standard student short essay. She asks her students to turn in two versions. In one they are told that they must plagiarize. In the second, they are told not to. The prior night, the students

Reprinted by permission from *Inside Higher Ed*, April 7, 2008.

were given an online tutorial on plagiarism and Hagopian said she has become skeptical that having the students "parrot back what we've told them" accomplishes anything. Her hope is that this unusual assignment might change that.

After the students turn in their two responses to the essay prompt, Hagopian shares some with the class. Not surprisingly, the students do know how to plagiarize—but were uncomfortable admitting as much. Hagopian said that the assignment is always greeted with "uncomfortable laughter" as the students must pretend that they never would have thought of plagiarizing on their own. Given the right to do so, they turn in essays with many direct quotes without attribution. Of course in their essays that are supposed to be done without plagiarism, she still finds problems—not so much with passages repeated verbatim, but with paraphrasing or using syntax in ways that were so similar to the original that they required attribution.

When she started giving the assignment, she sort of hoped, Hagopian said, to see students turn in "nuanced tricky demonstrations" of plagiarism, but she mostly gets garden variety copying. But what she is doing is having detailed conversations with her students about what is and isn't plagiarism—and by turning everyone into a plagiarist (at least temporarily), she makes the conversation something that can take place openly.

5   "Students know I am listening," she said. And by having the conversation in this way—as opposed to reading the riot act—she said she is demonstrating that all plagiarism is not the same, whether in technique, motivation or level of sophistication. There is a difference between "deliberate fraud" and "failed apprenticeship," she said.

Hagopian's approach was among many described at various sessions last week at the *annual meeting of the Conference of College Composition and Communication,* in New Orleans. Writing instructors—especially those tasked with teaching freshmen—are very much on the front lines of the war against plagiarism. As much as other faculty members, they resent plagiarism by their students—and in fact several of the talks featured frank discussion of how betrayed writing instructors feel when someone turns in plagiarized work.

That anger does motivate some to use the software that detects plagiarism as part of an effort to scare students and weed out plagiarists, and there was some discussion along those lines. But by and large, the instructors at the meeting said that they didn't have any confidence that these services were attacking the roots of the problem or finding all of the plagiarism. Several people quipped that if the software really detected all plagiarism, plenty of campuses would be unable to hold classes, what with all of the sessions needed for academic integrity boards.

While there was a group therapy element to some of the discussions, there was also a strong focus on trying new solutions. Freshmen writing instructors after all don't have the option available to other faculty members of just blaming the problem on the failures of those who teach first-year comp.

What to do? New books being displayed in the exhibit hall included several trying to shift the plagiarism debate beyond a matter of pure enforcement.

Among them were *Originality, Imitation, and Plagiarism: Teaching Writing in the Digital Age,* just published by the University of Michigan (and *profiled on Inside Higher Ed*), and *Pluralizing Plagiarism: Identities, Contexts, Pedagogies,* released in February by Boynton/Cook.

10   Like Hagopian, many of those at the meeting said that they are focused on   10
trying to better understand their students, what makes them plagiarize, and what might make them better understand academic integrity. There wasn't much talk of magic bullets, but lots of ideas about ways to better see the issue from a student perspective—and to find ways to use that perspective to promote integrity.

What Students Are Saying

Roy Stamper, associate director of the writing program at N.C. State, gave a presentation about a discussion he followed (for purposes of understanding, not enforcement) on *the Wolf Web*, a student discussion board. Students at N.C. State post anonymously, and while Stamper said he didn't know if all of the students were posting with accuracy about their situations, he still found plenty of truth in what they had to say.

The discussion was kicked off by a student asking for advice about certain term paper companies and whether they sold good work. The student, apparently fearful of how this would make him look, talked about how he was "completely and utterly fried and overloaded" and didn't have enough time. But he also said he didn't want to get caught plagiarizing.

While some of the responses rated various term paper sites, there was also a strong, intense reaction from other students—much of it critical. "The less time you spend posting on here the more time u get to work on your paper," wrote one student. Another student wrote: "It's called college. Grow up and get your shit done."

As other students joined in, offering suggestions on time management, Stamper said he was struck that the argument being put forth against plagiarism wasn't honesty, but efficiency, and that has its dangers too, as was brought home to him by this posting: "I say that if you can get away with doing 30 minutes worth of plagiarism as opposed to a few days of work . . . then you my friend are efficient, and not necessarily a bad person."

15   Yet another student argued that term paper mills could promote efficiency   15
without turning one into a plagiarist. This student said that he used term papers obtained online to gain ideas, but that because he then rewrites these ideas himself, it's not plagiarism. "My work, with a little help," is how he characterized it.

This prompted an angry outcry from another student, who wrote: "This shit is plagiarism by any definition. If you were caught and turned over to the office of student conduct, your ass would be nailed to the cross."

Stamper said that he shared the anger of that final student (if not the idea that the plagiarist deserved to be compared to Jesus), but that once he got past the anger, he found that his lurking online raised many questions. For instance, Stamper said that while he does not believe being overworked justifies plagiarism, he has found himself wondering about whether an intense workload puts an emphasis for students on efficiency as opposed to quality. "Good writing takes a lot of time and thought. I'm not sure I'm always giving them enough time," he said.

The other thing that the online discussion demonstrated, he said, was that many students do have a strong sense of right and wrong when it comes to plagiarism and the idea that every student born in the last 30 years believes everything online is fair to use is a stereotype. Students clearly are educable, he said, and perhaps the best approach may be peer pressure—the plagiarists on the N.C. State site were clearly embarrassed and looked to justify themselves. Should writing instructors be looking to peer teaching—and specifically peer pressure—as a new tool to promote integrity, Stamper asked.

"Patchwriting" vs. Plagiarism

Several of the speakers discussed ideas related to differentiating plagiarism of the sort that involves buying a term paper or submitting another student's work with more common, and not always intentional, writing behaviors used by many students that meet textbook definitions of plagiarism but that may raise different moral and educational issues. Many cite the work of Rebecca Moore Howard (co-editor of one of the new books on plagiarism and a contributor to another), who is an associate professor of writing and rhetoric at Syracuse University.

20   Howard talks about "patchwriting" as a common undergraduate technique   20
of grouping together various sources of information, frequently with only minor changes in wording and without appropriate attribution. For her own classes, she uses *a policy* that says such writing will generally lead to a poor grade, but not to sanctions that would go to someone who bought a term paper.

Along these lines, R. Gerald Nelms, an associate professor of composition and rhetoric at Southern Illinois University at Carbondale, spoke of how plagiarism must be seen as "an educational problem that requires an educational response." Much student plagiarism, he said, is unintentional, as students don't know how to take notes, how to summarize ideas, how to attribute ideas or quotes, and what paraphrasing means (and doesn't) with regard to plagiarism.

In a handout, Nelms wrote that patchwriting is "developmental plagiarism," or "behavior that is caused by the effort of the writer not fully integrated into the community for which she or he is trying to write to imitate the behavior of that community." Such plagiarism, he said, shouldn't be viewed as acceptable, but also shouldn't draw punishment. Students who engage in patchwriting need to be taught, he said, not brought up on charges. Nelms recommended a series of teaching subjects for instructors trying to show students how to write original work.

Students need to be taught to take notes, he said in his handout—so notes aren't just direct quotes or synopses, but also include students' reactions or potential use of information. In this way, students are starting to learn how to use information, not just how to repackage it. Similarly, he said in the handout, "integration involves more than citation," and must include efforts to show students how to mix various sources, how to attribute, and how to include original ideas.

"Restorative Justice" for Plagiarists

Christy Zink, an assistant professor of writing at George Washington University, used the controversy over the play *Frozen* to teach her first-year students about plagiarism. The play—about a psychiatrist who examines serial killers—was a Broadway hit, but also led to *charges of plagiarism* against its author by a psychiatrist who said that writings about her career were used without her permission for the drama.

Zink is an advocate of using "restorative justice" to deal with plagiarism. *"Restorative justice"* is an approach to criminal behavior that involves repairing the harm done by an act, but not focusing on punishment for the sake of punishment.

One of Zink's students—even though the course was focused on a discussion of plagiarism issues—plagiarized her work for an assignment. Zink said she was a bit stunned that in such a context, a student would engage in blatant plagiarism (she stressed that this wasn't a borderline case). But the student appealed to Zink's commitment to restorative justice, and said "isn't that why I'm here? To learn from my mistakes?"

While Zink worked out a punishment herself with the student—involving new work and a grade punishment—she also decided to try to apply the restorative justice ideal to the situation by talking to all three sections of the class about the situation (without identifying the student) and seeking their views on what to do. Zink's announcement to her clases that "we have a plagiarist among us" prompted a range of reactions from students.

Zink said that her students were angry at first, but that they then argued that many other considerations should go into consideration of sanctions. To most students, "intentionality matters," Zink said. Students wanted to know if the plagiarism was "an honest mistake" or deliberate. At the same time, given that the class was so focused on plagiarism, the students were doubtful that the student couldn't have known what she was doing was wrong. So the students were both interested in motivation, and not willing to accept any excuse.

The lesson, Zink said, is that while "we need the law," we also need to make decisions on more than just legalistic approaches. As another example, she described very much not wanting to like the play *Frozen,* in part because of the plagiarism issues. But she found herself deeply moved nonetheless.

An Unusual Sort-of Plagiarized Essay About Plagiarism

Catherine Savini, director of the Undergraduate Writing Center at Columbia University, described using an unusual essay to prod students to think in new ways. The essay, *"The Ecstasy of Influence: A Plagiarism,"* appeared in *Harper's* last year. In the work, Jonathan Lethem makes an impassioned plea against traditional concepts of copyright and plagiarism, and he does so with words and phrases that are almost entirely plagiarized—with no credit while making the argument, but a key at the end fessing up to his writing thefts. His technique drew attention and controversy.

Even Lawrence Lessig, the Stanford University law professor who is a prominent critic of copyright restrictions, wrote in to express his discomfort at finding one of his own sentences used in the essay. "The freedom that Lethem depends upon—the freedom to integrate and build upon the work of others—does not need the license the plagiarist takes," Lessig wrote in a letter to the magazine. "The rules against plagiarism, after all, require only that words borrowed be acknowledged as borrowed." (Lessig also applauded the essay's creativity and expressed hope that it would prompt further thought by those who seek to regulate the use of others' works.)

Savini said that this text is at once "dangerous" and provocative for students because it appears to glorify plagiarism and yet goes so far—and copies the work of such noted authors—that students are taken aback. "Is it a model? Is it fodder?"

When she assigned students to write about the essay, many were afraid of a plagiarism trap. "How do I cite Lethem?" was the question she received from many students, anxious about whether citations should go to Lethem, to those whose works he borrowed, both or neither. Students were so puzzled by the situation, Savini said, that many went to unusual lengths to avoid quoting from the essay they were writing about.

Then Savini told the students she wanted them to consider sharing their writing with Lethem. This further challenged students, she said, because they normally don't think about audience in writing, placing their instructors in some other category. Thinking about people as being affected by their writing was another step in viewing writing as more than completing an assignment, Savini said, but as something with ethical issues involved. "It's a difficult leap of the imagination" for many students to think about anyone other than their instructors reading their work, but they need to, she said.

35   "Suddenly, students were asking questions without easy answers," Savini said, about fairness, about the obligations of authors, and the relationship between authors and readers. "It's a morass I want my students to be in," she said.

Everyone Speaks Text Message
Tina Rosenberg

*Born in Brooklyn, New York, Tina Rosenberg (1960–) is formerly a
Visiting Fellow at the National Security Archive, and a Senior Fellow at
the World Policy Institute. She has written articles for several publications,
including* The New Republic, *the* New Yorker, Harper's, The
Washington Post, *and* The New York Times Magazine. *She is the author
of* The Haunted Land: Facing Europe's Ghosts after Communism
(1996), for which she received a Pulitzer Prize, and Children of Cain:
Violence and the Violent in Latin America *(1992). She is a recipient of
a MacArthur Foundation award, the first freelance journalist to receive
this honor. In this article from the* New York Times *Rosenberg reports on
how "digital technology has become a lifeline" for people from various cultures where the indigenous languages are in danger of extinction.*

1   When Ibrahima Traore takes his sons to a park in Montclair, N.J., he often sits
on a bench and reads. He reads English, French and Arabic, but most of the time
he reads N'Ko, a language few speakers of those languages would recognize.
N'Ko is the standardized writing system for Mande languages, a family of closely
related tongues—among them Traore's language of Mandinka, but also Jula,
Bamana, Koyaga, Marka—spoken, for the most part, in eight West African countries, by some 35 million people. N'Ko looks like a cross between Arabic and
ancient Norse runes, written from right to left in a blocky script with the letters
connected underneath. Traore types e-mail to his family on his laptop in N'Ko,
works on his Web site in N'Ko, tweets in N'Ko on his iPhone and iPad and reads
books and newspapers written in N'Ko to prepare for the N'Ko classes he teaches
in the Bronx and for his appearances on an Internet radio program to discuss cultural issues around the use of N'Ko.

For years, the Web's lingua franca was English. Speakers of French, Hindi
and Urdu, Arabic, Chinese and Russian chafed at the advantage the Internet
gave not only American pop culture but also its language. For those who lived
at the intersection of modern technology and traditional cultures, the problem
was even worse. "For a long time, technology was the enemy," says Inée
Slaughter, executive director of the New Mexico-based Indigenous Language
Institute, which teaches Native Americans and other indigenous peoples how to
use digital technologies to keep their languages vital. Heritage languages were
being killed off by increasing urbanization, the spread of formal education and
the shift to cash crops, which ended the isolation of indigenous communities.

Reprinted by permission from the *New York Times*, December, 11, 2011.

Advances in technology seemed to intensify the decline. "Even in 1999 or 2000, people were saying technology killed their language," Slaughter says. "Community elders worried about it. As television came into homes, English became pervasive 24/7. Mainstream culture infiltrated, and young kids want to be like that. It was a huge, huge problem, and it's still there. But now we know ways technology can be helpful."

For many tiny, endangered languages, digital technology has become a lifeline.

When Traore was born, N'Ko had already been in use for several years. But growing up, he did not know it existed. At 6, he was sent from his village of Kiniebakoro in rural Guinea to live with a brother in Ivory Coast, where he learned to read and write in French, the language taught in school in both countries. He never saw a book, newspaper, medicine label, store name or street sign in N'Ko.

5   And yet, N'Ko was invented to allow Mande speakers like Traore to read and write in the languages they spoke at home. In 1943, Solomana Kante, a teacher's son who worked as a merchant in Ivory Coast, resolved to develop a written form for the Mande language family. (N'Ko means "I say" in Manden languages; speakers of Manden languages can typically understand one another even if they don't use all the same words for the same things.) He tried using the Arabic alphabet, then the Roman alphabet, but found that neither one could express the tonal variations of spoken Manden languages. So in 1949, he invented his own script—one flexible enough to capture any Manden language in writing. Among the first books he translated into N'Ko was the Koran. He later compiled a history of Manden languages and culture.

At the time, Guinea had a close relationship with the Soviet Union, and Kante managed to have two typewriters made in Eastern Europe with N'Ko letters. (He was given another one by the president of Guinea, according to a Guinean newspaper.) "If there was a typewriter, ink and ribbons were hard to find," says Baba Mamadi Diané, a student of Kante's who now teaches N'Ko at Cairo University. Almost all of the books and papers in N'Ko in Guinea were copied by hand by Kante's students, like medieval monks, but with several sheets of carbon paper below.

Designed as a language for the common man, N'Ko seemed destined to remain a code used by an elite. Then came the digital revolution.

Heritage languages like N'Ko are taking on new life thanks to technology. An Internet discussion group, Indigenous Languages and Technology, is full of announcements for new software to build sound dictionaries and a project to collect tweets in Tok Pisin, a creole language spoken throughout Papua New Guinea, or Pipil, an indigenous language of El Salvador. "It's the amplification of Grandma's voice," Slaughter says.

Whether a language lives or dies, says K. David Harrison, an associate professor of linguistics at Swarthmore College, is a choice made by 6-year-olds. And what makes a 6-year-old want to learn a language is being able to use it in everyday life. "Language is driven from the ground up," says Don Thornton, a software developer in Las Vegas who specializes in making video games and mobile apps in Native American languages. "It doesn't matter if you have a million speakers—if your kids aren't learning, you're in big trouble."

10   Of 6,909 catalogued languages, hundreds are unlikely to be passed on to   10
the next generation. Thornton, who has worked with more than 100 Native American tribes, says that some are already using sophisticated programs to preserve their languages. "Other groups," he says, "we ask about their language program, and they say, 'You're it.' We look at it from their standpoint—what are the coolest technologies out there? We start programming for that."

For the vast majority of the world, the cellphone, not the Internet, is the coolest available technology. And they are using those phones to text rather than to talk. Though most of the world's languages have no written form, people are beginning to transliterate their mother tongues into the alphabet of a national language. Now they can text in the language they grew up speaking. Harrison tells of traveling in Siberia, where he met a truck driver who devised his own system for writing the endangered Chulym language, using the Cyrillic alphabet. "You find people like him everywhere," Harrison said. "We are getting languages where the first writing is not the translation of the Bible—as it has often happened—but text messages."

Traore, who left Guinea for New York in November 1988, did not discover N'Ko until a 2007 trip to visit his parents in his native village. When his wife, Greta, a software developer, went into his brother's room, she noticed books in N'Ko on his shelves. Puzzled, she called her husband in. "You said your language was not written. So what are these books?" Traore was shocked. (He and Traore did not grow up together.) When he came back to New York, he googled N'Ko. "That was the big wow," he said. He found a teacher in Queens. "When I listened to the alphabet, I listened to our history. Now I can read the same words my mother would say to me."

N'Ko first moved from hand-copied manuscripts into the digital age two decades ago. In the early 1990s, Diané, the teacher of N'Ko at Cairo University, was collating an N'Ko text in a copy shop when he was approached by an employee. "Why are you killing yourself?" the man asked him. "Don't you know about DOS?" The employee explained to Diané that using computer software, he could write a new script and generate as many copies as he wished. Together with information-technology experts at Cairo University, Diané developed a rudimentary font to use on his own computer. But creating a font that *anyone* could use was a much more complicated task.

First, it meant getting N'Ko into Unicode—the international standard that assigns a unique number to each character in a given writing system. Then

Microsoft picked up N'Ko for its local language program—sort of. N'Ko was included in Windows 7, but the ligatures were misaligned, and the letters were not linked from below as they should have been. "The original plan was to fully support it, but we just didn't have the resources," said Peter Constable, a senior program manager at Microsoft. For Windows 8, which is still being tested, Microsoft has fixed the problem. Most writers of N'Ko download the font for use with Open Office's Graphite program, developed by SIL International, a Christian group with an interest in seeing the Bible reach every hut and yurt on the planet.

15   Digital technology has already transformed how Traore communicates with   15
his family. When his father died in 1994, his family in Kiniebakoro sent news of the death to cousins in Ivory Coast by going to the bus station and looking for a passenger heading toward their city; the cousins then mailed a letter to Traore in New York. It took two months. Now communication with Kiniebakoro takes a day: Traore sends an e-mail in N'Ko. His nephew, who works in the nearby town of Siguiri, checks his e-mail at the town's Internet cafe, prints Traore's letter and then goes down to the dock where canoes ferry people across the Niger River to Kiniebakoro. He asks someone on the boat to take the letter to Traore's family's house.

For Traore and others, the most pressing reason for making N'Ko available to Mande speakers is that only a small percentage of Guineans can read and write. The United Nations puts the rate of adult literacy at 39 percent, but that figure counts mostly those who live in major cities—in rural areas, it is much lower. Schooling in rural Guinea is often conducted in the open air, with no chairs, perhaps a blackboard, maybe one book. But most discouraging to students, it takes place in French, a language they don't speak at home.

"The only hope for literacy in Guinea is N'Ko literacy," Traore says. For Mande speakers, he says, N'Ko is extremely simple to learn. He and his fellow N'Ko advocates have sponsored hundreds of informal schools throughout Guinea that teach in Manden languages and N'Ko. This year, for the first time, N'Ko will be taught side by side with French in an official school—the pilot program will be in Kiniebakoro, Traore's hometown.

People had been working on breathing life into N'Ko for years, but they found out about one another only when they began to put up N'Ko Web sites. There is Traore's site, kouroussaba.com, Diané's kanjamadi.com and fakoli.net, the project of Mamady Doumbouya, a Guinean who worked as a software engineer in Philadelphia and is devoting his retirement to N'Ko. He also runs a small organization called the N'Ko Institute of America. Diané's students in Cairo are subtitling DVDs for West Africa in N'Ko. Among the first was a season of the TV show "24."

If you have an iPhone, tweeting and e-mailing in N'Ko is now easy. Eatoni, a company based in Manhattan that has created software for cellphone keyboards in some 300 languages, released an N'Ko app earlier this year. The iPhone keyboard app works on the iPad too. Eatoni's C.E.O., Howard Gutowitz, developed it after months of tests and advice from Traore, Diané and other N'Ko users. But iPhones are too expensive to be widely used in rural Africa. Almost every African villager owns or aspires to own a conventional cellphone (equipped with only a number pad)—even if he or she has to travel to town to charge it.

20 Africa is the world's fastest-growing cellphone market. Texting allows farmers to check crop prices. Nurses can send health information. People can do their banking. With airtime prohibitively expensive, texting is the preferred mode of communication. "Text messages would be a lifesaving tool for us in Guinea," Traore said. He also says he believes that the ability to text in their own language would give people a powerful reason to learn to read. "Before, men in my village used to brag about their wristwatches," Traore said. "Now they brag about their cellphones." When he shows N'Ko speakers his iPhone and tells them, "This is your language," they are dumbstruck. An N'Ko newspaper published in Conakry, Guinea's capital, recently crowed: "Don't look for N'Ko under a cabbage leaf any more. It's on the iPhone now."   20

  Those old cellphones don't have apps, of course. You use the language the phone comes with; in West Africa, that is French. The market for an N'Ko phone would be, potentially, tens of millions of people. But getting manufacturers to add new alphabets to cellphones isn't easy. Gutowitz has had a long and frustrating experience trying to do so. "Most manufacturers roll their eyes," he said. "I spent a decade running around the world talking to cellphone manufacturers—everyone I could think of—saying, 'Look, we can support 100 languages, it's a big market.' They didn't care. People say, 'Why don't you go talk to Nokia?' I have talked to Nokia. Again and again and again."

  Lamine Dabo and Nouhan Sano, Guineans who live in Bangkok, where there is a prosperous and close-knit Guinean community, have had a similar experience. They have been trying to persuade manufacturers to develop an N'Ko cellphone since 2007. Dabo and Sano's gem-importing businesses take them all over Asia, and all over Asia they bring their list of more than 17,000 N'Ko words. Dabo says it's possible to build a cheap cellphone with N'Ko as its language, a camera and slots for two SIM cards—a necessity in Africa, where reception is often spotty. When he went to Guinea and Mali to discuss the phone with distributors, he said, he was mobbed with interest. But his briefcase was filled with rejections from manufacturers. Some asked him to put up the money himself. "Everyone says it's possible, but the money is not enough for them to make it a priority," he said.

  Dabo and Sano are still trying. It might seem strange that the fortunes of N'Ko and of indigenous languages around the world should depend on the ability to subtitle "24," to write with Windows and, above all, to text. But for hundreds of heritage languages, a four-inch bar of plastic and battery and motherboard is the future of the past.

13

SPEECH

June 2, 2010. Armando Galarraga was in his first baseball season as a pitcher for the Detroit Tigers. As he racked up inning after inning of perfect pitching, people began to alert their friends, and ESPN cut away from its usual programming to cover the end of the game. Few players had ever pitched a perfect game—only twenty in professional baseball at that time. An easy throw to first base looked to be the final play. It was obvious to everyone watching that the runner was out, that Galarraga had pitched the twenty-first perfect game in baseball history. And then the umpire, Jim Joyce, called the runner safe, ending Galarraga's bid for a perfect game. As viewers watched replays that confirmed the umpire's error, they got angry.

After the game, Joyce watched a replay of the play. And then he amazed everyone: in a postgame news conference he admitted his mistake. "No, I did not get the call correct. . . . I missed the damn call. I missed it. . . . There's nobody that feels worse than I do. I take pride in this job . . . and I took a perfect game away from that kid over there who worked his ass off all night. This is probably the most important call in my career, and I missed it." Joyce later apologized in person to Galarraga.

And then Jim Joyce had a chance to be amazed himself. From across the nation, he heard praise for his apology, some calling it the perfect response to human imperfection.

- Have you ever had to apologize in public? If you had to craft a public apology, what would you be sure to include?

- Reread Joyce's words above (you can hear the full six minutes of the news conference at http://www.youtube.com/watch?v=5P1oMy4WIf0). He admits that he made a mistake, but does he ever apologize? What is the difference between admitting to a mistake and apologizing for that mistake? Does that difference matter? What made Joyce's words effective for most people?

PORTABLE RHETORICAL LESSON: WRITING FOR MULTIPLE AUDIENCES

The exercise of thinking about apologies poses a straightforward challenge: How do you respond—in words—when people you can't ignore blame you for mistakes that may or may not be your fault? You always write for an audience and try to establish a positive relationship between yourself and your readers or listeners; a crisis management situation dramatizes the need to pay careful attention to that relationship.

Two rhetorical concepts jump to attention as you imagine facing the challenge of responding to blame and managing a crisis: **audience** and **author.** Audience: Who are the people to whom you need to aim your apology? If the audience is a single person, someone you know well, you can more easily judge what you need to say. If your audience is public, less predictable, made up of people of different opinions, keeping the audience on your side becomes much harder. Author: What are your character and values—and are they consistent with the image of yourself (the persona) you need to communicate? And what's your motivation for communicating? Why do you care about what your audience thinks and does?

Any situation in which you have to keep a crisis from blowing up is difficult, but the readings in this chapter give you a chance to see writers responding to audiences at a much harder level—thus giving you the chapter's **Portable Rhetorical Lesson** of analyzing and writing for multiple audiences. Presidents Obama, Clinton, and Bush (whose speeches you either read or read analyses of in this chapter) each faced public relations nightmares—national crises for which they were being blamed. And their audiences were as varied as is possible: supporters, opponents, people whose health and livelihood would be directly affected by the presidents' words, people across the globe who would pass judgment.

To influence audiences, and to do so in the high-stakes situation of restoring the public faith, a speaker must carefully analyze those different audiences, studying their:

- Background (age? gender? class?)
- Attitudes and assumptions (beliefs? opinions? concerns?)
- Knowledge (expertise? common knowledge?)
- Needs from and expectations of the speaker

Beyond those basic elements of audience analysis, consider how you might encourage your readers to be receptive to your ideas, to remember what you wrote, and to be willing to consider new options.

In a future profession, you may need to address multiple audiences about crisis situations using means like those used by the presidents in this chapter. Even as a student, though, you face multiple audiences. You write for different teachers—in different disciplines, with different expectations and ways of grading. Many schools use teams of teachers (some of whom you may not know) to grade essays or written portfolios. And you will probably make presentations to your classmates, some of whom you won't know and who think very differently than you.

In these situations:

- Gauge the controversy of your topic for your audience (the more controversial your topic for your audience, the more careful you will have to be—something like presidents in crisis-management mode).

- Study the grading criteria for the assignment. They should help you determine what the teacher expects and considers most important; if your teacher doesn't supply criteria, ask for them. Do *not* assume that each teacher wants the same thing.

- Get audience feedback (that is, talk with your teacher about papers and presentations as you are working on them and after they are graded).

These strategies are all versions of the audience analysis that presidents and other professionals conduct as they seek to satisfy their audiences.

WRITING IN THE DISCIPLINE

INTRODUCTION

by Kathi Groenendyk,
Professor of Rhetoric

Scholars studying communication and rhetoric examine a range of texts—presidential speeches, popular television shows, newspapers, and propaganda posters, to name a few. What's in common? Communication scholars try to understand how the person creating the message (the rhetor) communicates certain meanings to an audience in a particular situation. Some of the most interesting studies examine the multiple audiences a rhetor may face and how speaking to that audience may actually *change* the audience's perception of the situation.

Political communication scholars (as well as news commentators) frequently note the strong political divisions in our country: politicians face an almost impossible task of presenting policy plans or uniting citizens on a certain issue. If the politician identifies too narrow an audience, she will, most likely, be speaking only to those who already agree with her. If she thinks of too broad an audience, her speech will be vague and will not be emotionally moving or persuasive. The politician, then, needs to both engage her critics and energize her supporters.

Communication theorists have developed various definitions of "audience" to help achieve this goal. Instead of only thinking of "audience" as those people who are sitting in front of the podium, the speaker can consider the "universal" audience—the speaker imagines what a rational group would want to know and what questions they would ask. When the speaker prepares his speech, he critiques his speech with this audience in mind. This will help the speaker avoid regional biases and help him think carefully about competing arguments. In political settings, the speaker also will benefit from thinking of his audience as those who are able to act to change the situation, for example, when a politician is looking for support on a piece of legislation. If the politician considers what is important to this audience—the one who can act to make a change—the politician can determine which information and emotional appeals should be in the speech.

With the Gulf of Mexico oil spill, President Barak Obama had to respond to a complex situation: an increasingly harmful oil spill that defied the usual technological solutions as well as growing public criticism first of BP and then of the presidential administration. The Deepwater Horizon oil rig, operated for the oil company BP, sank into the Gulf on April 20, 2010, killing eleven workers. With the collapse of the rig, oil from the well flowed directly into the waters, with scientists and BP officials debating the actual amount of oil gushing from the well. Throughout May, BP engineers and various outside experts (including even Hollywood connections—James Cameron and Kevin Costner) consulted about the best means to stop the flow. On May 28, with oil still flowing, President Obama spoke at a press conference, which was televised and reprinted in various news sources.

Who was Obama's audience? Gulf coast residents, local politicians, BP executives, and the larger American public (many of whom were distrustful of governmental bureaucracies) were a few of the audiences Obama faced, and these groups held different values and goals. Obama had to acknowledge the criticism he was facing yet change the audience's perception of his administration (that they were doing little to solve the problem) and of the crisis (that it could be fixed quickly). Obama's remarks, then, are a blend of rational explanations of current and proposed actions and appeals to shared values with Gulf coast residents and the "regular folks" of the American public. These elements make it more likely that his audiences will take action helping the effected environment, holding BP accountable, and supporting new legislation to prevent future disasters.

✓ Reading Tips

Read President Obama's speech just as you would *listen* to a speech—straight through, at a normal speaking pace. Pay attention to the main ideas and language choices to imagine how the president was writing for his audiences.

- Try to imagine how President Obama would have delivered the speech: Where would he pause, when would his voice get softer or stronger?
- Track your emotions and thoughts as you read, and mark places where you think the speech is more or less persuasive.
- Identify places in the speech that seem intended to appeal to a particular segment of the audience.

Remarks by the President after Briefing on BP Oil Spill, May 28, 2010

President Barack Obama

The White House, Office of the Press Secretary May 28, 2010

U.S. Coast Guard Station Grande Isle, Grande Isle, Louisiana

In most speeches, the speaker usually attempts to build identification with the audience—create a bond with the audience and establish the common interests. Other speakers often try to capture the audience's attention with the beginning comments. Obama takes a different approach: he provides a "news update" on the latest spill conditions. He summarizes the situation—the crisis—to which this speech responds.

Good afternoon, everybody. I know it's a little warm out here so want to get started. I've just had a meeting with these governors, members of Congress, local officials, as well as Admiral Thad Allen, the National Incident Commander in charge of response efforts to the BP oil spill. Admiral Allen gave us an update, the latest information on both the efforts to plug the well, as well as giving us an update on arrangements and coordination that's being made with respect to mitigating this damage that's been done.

He updated us on these latest efforts to stop the leak, mitigate the damage to the great beaches of the Gulf coast, and I had the chance to visit with—Charlotte—a beach like Port Fourchon that gives you a sense of what extraordinary efforts are being made at the local level, but also the damage that we're already starting to see as a consequence of this spill.

In this third paragraph, Obama builds his ethos (credibility), summarizing the actions the administration wants to take.

Now, our mission remains the same as it has since this disaster began, since the day I visited Louisiana nearly four weeks ago: We want to stop the leak; we want to contain and clean up the oil; and we want to help the people of this region return to their lives and their livelihoods as soon as possible.

When Obama gave these remarks, certain American audiences were questioning the administration's efforts. Obama acknowledges those concerns in an effort to build common ground with the audience.

And our response treats this event for what it is: It's an assault on our shores, on our people, on the regional economy, and on communities like this one. This isn't just a mess that we've got to mop up. People are watching their livelihoods wash up on the beach. Parents are worried about the implications for their children's health. Every resident of this community has watched this nightmare threaten the dreams that they've worked so hard to build. And they want it made right, and they want to make it right now.

I just had a chance to listen to Mayor David Carmadelle of Grande Isle, our host here, telling us heartbreaking stories about fishermen who are trying to figure out where the next paycheck is going to come from, how are they going to pay a mortgage or a note on their boat. And he is having to dig into his pocket at this point to make sure that some of them are able to deal with the economic impact. So this is something that has to be dealt with immediately, not sometime later. And that's everybody's driving focus—everybody who is standing behind me. This is our highest priority and it deserves a response that is equal to the task.

Obama states what work has already been done as a way to answer the administration's critics. Obama seems to imply that his audience does not know the complete situation; his administration has begun work.

That's why this has already been the largest cleanup effort in U.S. history. On the day this disaster began, even as we launched a search and rescue effort for workers on the drilling rig, we were already staging equipment in the event of a larger-scale spill. By the time we discovered the third breach, a week after the Deepwater Horizon platform sank, we had already stationed more than 70 vessels and hundreds of thousands of feet of protective boom on site.

Today, there are more than 20,000 people in the region working around the clock to contain and clean up this spill. We've activated about 1,400 members of the National Guard across four states. Nearly 1,400 vessels are aiding in the containment and cleanup effort. And we deployed more than 3 million feet of hard and sorbent boom, including an additional 100,000 just yesterday for these parishes in Louisiana that face the greatest threat.

In most environmental disasters, the American public believes that technology will solve the problem. Obama implicitly refers to that belief.

Now, I've made clear to Admiral Allen and I did so again today that he should get whatever he needs to deal with this crisis. Whatever he needs, he will get. . . .

We have ordered BP to pay economic injury claims, and we will make sure they deliver. And the parish presidents and governors here in Louisiana were already giving us some sense of some of the bureaucratic problems that we're going to have to cut through, but we are going to cut through them. And for those who are in economic distress, if you've already filed a claim and you're not satisfied with the resolution, then whitehouse.gov will point you in the right direction.

Obama makes a populist claim: much like most of his audience, Obama blames a giant corporation and governmental bureaucracy, which means that Obama does not see himself as part of that bureaucracy.

As I said yesterday, the Small Business Administration has stepped in to help businesses by approving loans, but also as important, allowing many to defer existing loan payments. A lot of folks are still loaded up with loans that they had from Katrina and other natural disasters down here, so they may need some additional help.

If you're a small business owner and you weren't aware of some of the programs that have been put in place or haven't participated, then, again, the White House website will connect you to the resources you need. And we are making sure that all the parish presidents know, and folks like the mayor, other local officials are going to be aware of how they can get immediate help from us.

What's more, we've stationed doctors and scientists across the five Gulf States to look out for people's health and then to monitor any ill effects felt by cleanup workers and local residents. And we've begun setting up a system to track these efforts—excuse me, to track these effects—and ensure folks get the care that they need. And we've told BP that we expect them to pay for that, too.

As I've said before, BP is the responsible party for this disaster. What that means is they're legally responsible for stopping the leak and they're financially responsible for the enormous damage that they've created. And we're going to hold them accountable, along with any other party responsible for the initial explosion and loss of life on that platform.

In this situation, the administration has little control—they cannot control the oil spill into the waters, they cannot control the technology being used, and they have to assert control over BP. Obama, by saying "the buck stops here," implies that his administration is responsible, and therefore capable of finding a solution. Obama is changing the audience's perception of the situation (crisis). Using these words will also remind some American citizens of President Truman, who many now view favorably. Obama is borrowing ethos, then, from Truman.

But as I said yesterday, and as I repeated in the meeting that we just left, I ultimately take responsibility for solving this crisis. I'm the President and the buck stops with me. So I give the people of this community and the entire Gulf my word that we're going to hold ourselves accountable to do whatever it takes for as long as it takes to stop this catastrophe, to defend our natural resources, to repair the damage, and to keep this region on its feet. Justice will be done for those whose lives have been upended by this disaster, for the families of those whose lives have been lost—that is a solemn pledge that I am making.

I think I can speak for anybody here, and for anybody who has been involved in the response and the cleanup effort, and for most Americans, when I say that I would gladly do whatever it takes to end this disaster today. But I want to also repeat something that I said to the group as a whole while we were meeting. This is a manmade catastrophe that's still evolving and we face a long-term recovery and restoration effort.

America has never experienced an event like this before. And that means that as we respond to it, not every judgment we make is going to be right the first time out. Sometimes, there are going to be disagreements between experts, or between federal and state and local officials, or among state officials, or between states, about what the most effective measures will be.

Obama attempts to caution his audience against expecting a quick fix. This is an important element when many Americans want immediate results.

Sometimes, there are going to be risks and unintended consequences associated with a particular mitigation strategy that we consider. In other words, there are going to be a lot of judgment calls involved here. There are not going to be silver bullets or a lot of perfect answers for some of the challenges that we face.

Understandably, the feelings of frustration and anger, the sense that any response is inadequate—we expect that frustration and anger to continue until we actually solve this problem. But in the meantime, we've got to make sure that everybody is working in concert, that everybody is moving in the same direction. And I want everybody to know that everybody here—at every level—is working night and day to end this crisis. We're considering every single idea out there, especially from folks who know these communities best. . . .

The bottom line is this: Every decision we make is based on a single criterion—what's going to best protect and make whole the people and the ecosystems of the Gulf.

And I want to thank everybody in this region who's rolled up their sleeves and pitched in to help—from the National Guard putting their experience to the task, to the local officials and every citizen who loves this area and calls it home, every American who's traveled to the region to lend a hand. If any American is looking for ways to volunteer and help, then we've put links to that information on our website, as well—that's whitehouse.gov. . . .

To the people of the Gulf Coast: I know that you've weathered your fair share of trials and tragedy. I know there have been times where you've wondered if you were being asked to face them alone. I am here to tell you that you're not alone. You will not be abandoned. You will not be left behind. The cameras at some point may leave; the media may get tired of the story; but we will not. We are on your side and we will see this through. We're going to keep at this every day until the leak has stopped, until this coastline is clean, and your communities are made whole again. That's my promise to you. And that is a promise on behalf of a nation. It is one that we will keep.

> In this paragraph Obama is appealing to the audience's emotions (pathos) and refers to shared values. This is a memorable ending to his remarks and makes his earlier statements about cleanup strategy less impersonal.

And I will make one last point—and I said this to every leader who is here: If something is not going right down here, then they need to talk to Thad Allen. And if they're not getting satisfaction from Thad Allen, then they can talk to me. There's nobody here who can't get in touch with me directly if there is an idea, a suggestion, or a logjam that needs to be dealt with.

> Obama ends with a call to action and stresses his personal connection.

So we're in this together. And it's going to be a difficult time, and obviously the folks down here are going to be feeling the brunt of it, but we're going to make sure that we're doing everything we can to get this solved as quickly as possible.

And I want to again thank everybody here for the extraordinary work that they're putting in. You shouldn't underestimate how hard these folks are working, day in, day out, on behalf of their constituencies.

So thank you very much. Thank you, everybody.

Reading Responses

1. List the actions that President Obama draws his audience's attention to in his speech. How does this emphasis on action affect different audiences for Obama's speech? Concentrate on Gulf Coast residents, local politicians, Americans who know only a little about the crisis, and political pundits who were criticizing the president.

2. Imagine a different speech, one in which Obama admitted that the federal government had acted too slowly and apologized for this slow response. What effect would such a speech have on some of the audiences for Obama's speech? In your answer, concentrate on Democrats running for reelection, BP oil executives, and the engineers who were working to stop the oil spill.

3. Who do you think was Obama's primary audience? Give evidence from the speech and reasons to support your answer.

NOTES ON GRAMMAR, STYLE, AND RHETORIC:
SENTENCE SUBJECTS

One part of the sentence that writers and speakers should pay special attention to is the subject. The subject names who or what acts, experiences something, is described, is identified further, or is acted upon.

Examining the sentence subjects in a speech or written text can reveal much about what the speaker or writer is most concerned to focus on. You might guess that he would focus on BP and how this corporation must stop the spill and pay for the damages, or on the extent of the damage of the oil spill to the environment, or on the economic toll that the oil spill was taking on people along the Gulf Coast. And President Obama does focus some attention on all of these topics. But he mainly uses sentence subjects to focus attention on himself and those under his command in the battle against the oil spill.

Not including the introductory "Good morning, everybody" and the closing "So thank you very much. Thank you everybody," there are one hundred independent clauses in the president's selected remarks. Among those one hundred independent clauses, twenty-six have as their subject the pronoun *we* (sometimes included in the contracted forms *we've* or *we're*). And there are as many as ten additional independent-clause subjects that connect closely to the people whom the *we* refers to (these are phrases such as *our mission* and *our response*).

Toward the end of his remarks, the president uses one *we* to refer to all the people of the United States. And he uses another *we* apparently to refer to himself and the people of the Gulf Coast. But overwhelmingly these *we*'s refer to himself and the people that he as president can bring into the fight against the oil. It is easy to sense while reading these remarks that these *we*'s refer to a great many people. These people have will and determination, expertise, and vast resources. And they are all under the president's command.

Beyond the sentence subjects in which *we* or some closely related term appears, there are nineteen sentence subjects in which the pronoun *I* appears. If you bring the twenty-six appearances of *we* together with the roughly ten appearances of phrases closely related to *we,* and then if you add to that number the nineteen appearances of *I,* you find that over half of the sentence subjects in this speech refer to the president or to people under his command. On the basis of those figures, it is possible to argue that this speech is mainly about the president's response to the oil-spill disaster.

Why might President Obama have decided to craft so many of his sentences in this way? At the time immediately preceding President Obama's remarks, some people were starting to write and say things about him that were similar to the things written and said about President Bush after Hurricane Katrina. And no politician could overlook the devastating effects if he or she were to come to be perceived as a slow responder to a crisis and as uncaring about some of his constituents. Thus it could be argued that President Obama crafted his remarks to present himself as very much in charge. Further, he works to show that he cares about the health and well-being of the residents of the Gulf states. As Obama says and implies, he is the president; the buck stops with him. This is the message he seems most intent on conveying.

This strategy does not come without some risks. By insisting that he is in charge, that he is responsible, President Obama sets himself up to take the brunt of blame if efforts to stop the flow of oil and to clean up the mess that the oil has made do not go well or take longer than people expect or allow.

Of course, he works hard in his speech to counter current and possible future criticism. He stresses how complex the problems are, he points out that intelligent people might not agree on possible solutions, and he notes that there might be unintended consequences of some relief efforts. But through it all President Obama and his speechwriters chose sentence subjects that kept listeners' attention fixed on the president and the people he commands. At the time and place of his remarks, his choice to focus so much attention on himself and the forces he could muster looks like rhetorical and political wisdom.

In Your Own Writing . . .

- Decide what you want your readers to focus on, and then refer to that in the subject position of your sentences.
- Consider gradually adjusting the subjects of your sentences to introduce your readers to ideas that they might otherwise oppose.
- Put information at or near the end of your sentence (in the predicate) that will shape your readers' attitude toward what you've chosen for the subjects of your sentences.

STUDENT WRITING

INTRODUCTION

by Laura McGiness,
communication arts and sciences major

The Assignment.   In a class called "American Voices," we devoted the entire semester to studying and discussing speeches throughout American history. The final assignment asked us to critically interpret an American rhetorical text by using analytical tools we had learned in class. We had to identify a significant issue or set of issues related to the text's rhetoric that we would like to explore, develop a central claim for our papers about these issues, and support our theses with a logical and clear argument. We could focus on a variety of issues, such as these: What is the meaning of the text, and how is it revealed? How does the structure of the text relate to its message? What narratives or myths are developed in the speech, and how do they relate to cultural ideals?

The Content.   Because understanding the audience is an integral part of effective public speaking, my analysis focused on strategies that President Bill Clinton used to reach a diverse audience in his public address at the Presidential Prayer Breakfast in September of 1998, when he apologized for his affair with White House intern Monica Lewinsky. Particularly, I explored how Clinton fit the content of his speech within the genre of a personal apology and how this allowed him to present a likeable persona that could appeal to both his immediate audience of clergymen and his broader audience of the American public. I also wrote about the way that the historical context and audience's values affected Clinton's potential for rhetorical success in this speech.

Learning to Write in Speech Communication.   Oratory is only considered effective communication when the speaker, audience, and text interact; therefore, communications students must appreciate these important relationships. To successfully communicate, speakers must suit both the content and style of the speech to their audience. They must speak about a pertinent topic that the audience can understand and deliver the speech in a way that makes the audience willing to listen. Likewise, if the content and style of the speech are appropriate but speakers damage their credibility (either before or during the speech), they are not likely to persuade the audience.

Therefore, good public speakers intentionally choose various rhetorical strategies to persuade their audiences, and writers in the communications discipline must be able to identify these strategies. But analyzing oratory goes beyond simple identification. When I analyzed Clinton's speech, I had to explain how and why his rhetorical strategies either worked or didn't work; I also had to speculate about why Clinton may have chosen particular strategies in his speech. I considered a variety of issues related to my speech text before deciding on my central claim. I asked myself some questions: What is the purpose of the speech and how is that revealed? What is the structure of the text and how does that relate to its message? How does the speaker relate to his audience? I then had to decide which topics would most effectively support my main point and how I could best explain these ideas in my paper. After that analysis, I was able to develop a clear central claim and support that thesis with logical evidence.

Apologizing to Friends, Enemies, and Everyone in Between: Analyzing Clinton's Rhetoric

Laura McGiness

I intentionally began with an anecdote that my readers could relate to, but I tried to present it in such a way that focused readers on the nature of an audience.

We all get plenty of practice apologizing for our mistakes. And the more we apologize, the more we appreciate how our audience influences the way we ask for forgiveness. For instance, an apology for being late would sound different if I were speaking to my boss as opposed to one of my friends. When we know what our audience expects to hear, we can adjust our apology accordingly. However, apologizing to a group of people rather than an individual suddenly makes the task much more challenging. When President Bill Clinton spoke at the Presidential Prayer Breakfast on September 11, 1998, at the height of the Monica Lewinsky sex scandal, he faced the daunting task of crafting an apology that would be appropriate and meaningful to multiple audiences: the clergymen in attendance at the prayer breakfast, who heard it live, and the American public, who would hear it broadcasted later. In an attempt to influence his immediate and wide-ranging audiences, Clinton suited both his content and style to the genre of what rhetoricians call a "personal apologia," which offered him the greatest potential for rhetorical success.

The thesis must focus on one or several specific aspects of the speech. I decided to explore the genre of a personal apologia because I believe it enabled Clinton to meet certain rhetorical goals that he otherwise would not have been able to accomplish.

In this "Prayer Breakfast Speech" Clinton appears to have learned from his previous failed apology only a few weeks earlier in August of 1998. That nationally-televised speech, nicknamed the "Map Room Speech," took the form of "forensic self-defense," which argues that (1) the president had kept the oath of office, (2) the accusers had undermined the Constitution, and (3) the president is responsible to the people and the Constitution, not to the Congressional accusers (Campbell and Jamieson). As a forensic self-defense, his August apology sounded insincere. Many Americans found the formal language and distant style inconsistent with the highly personal nature of his situation. Moreover, the fact that Clinton spoke into a television camera rather than directly addressing a live audience contributed to the impersonal tone of this speech. His decision to begin a speech about such a delicate moral decision with information about his grand jury indictment seemed devoid of true emotion. He focused a large part of his content on legal issues related to the investigation, which further degraded the personal manner of this speech. Clinton ended by actually rebuking his audience, a tactic that many Americans would not have expected. In fact, Clinton even portrayed himself as the victim of ruthless privacy invasion, a rhetorical move that did not help him establish a desirable ethos throughout the speech. By the end of the speech, Clinton seemed to be saying that his audience should apologize to him, an understandably awkward situation considering the fact that this speech was supposed to be Clinton's apology to them. Self-defense, at this point, was futile. His supporters did not need to hear an apology because they already approved of his leadership despite his moral weaknesses. His enemies used the speech to further accuse Clinton of placing blame on external factors outside his control rather than taking personal responsibility for the situation. The nature of his speech as a self-defense rather than an apology likely left many moderate Americans still wondering about the authenticity of Clinton's remorse. His personal apologia at the Prayer Breakfast, on the other hand, provided him with the tools necessary to develop a persona that proved more rhetorically effective for his diverse audiences.

Campbell and Jamieson point out the various factors that comprise a personal apologia: (1) a shift in focus from the accuser to the defender, (2) a favorable presentation of the defender's personal character, (3) a personal tone, (4) an argument that the actions do not merit impeachment, and (5) an argument that the actions do not call executive leadership into question. Given that Clinton delivered this speech at a prayer breakfast, his decision to share a personal apologia was an appropriate strategy. The apology's personal nature and emphasis allow Clinton to display a greater degree of sincerity and humility, values that the clergymen in his audience would have anticipated and appreciated. These qualities also enable Clinton to discuss his personal journey of repentance—again, another ideal highly esteemed among his audience members. Furthermore, the very fact that a live audience is listening to his address strengthens the personal nature of his speech. The personal apologia also proves effective for Clinton's broader audience of the American people. Clinton often referred to religious themes in his speech, a tactic that could have alienated some members of his more broad audience. However, once again, the personal nature of the apology, and the humble persona that it allowed Clinton to embody,

The element of surprise, whether or not it helps a speaker, always gains audience attention. Therefore, it is worth exploring how this surprising element of Clinton's speech ultimately worked against him in this situation.

Because we know that Clinton was trying to appeal to a very broad audience, it helps to examine particular parts of that audience. Knowing how specific groups of Americans might have reacted to this speech furthers our understanding of the speech's purpose and overall effect.

Here I refer directly to a text we read in class so that my professor can see that I am fulfilling the requirement to analyze a speech using the knowledge I gained in the class.

enabled his message to resonate with many Americans. Most people appreciate a humble and repentant spirit in a sincere apology.

> With background established, here's where I begin my analysis of the speech.

Contrasting the defiant nature of his Map Room Speech, Clinton focuses attention away from his accusers and instead directs it toward himself: "First, I want to say to all of you that, as you might imagine, I have been on quite a journey these last few weeks." When he does address his enemies, he approaches their accusations in a gracious and humble manner by paradoxically noting that the invasion of his privacy, although a painful experience, may ultimately produce a stronger man and country. Therefore, instead of attacking his opponents, he smartly

> This is an example of when I speculate about why Clinton crafted his speech as he did.

uses their accusations to further strengthen his personal appeal. He employs a classic and effective rhetorical strategy by establishing common ground with and goodwill towards his critics: he mentions near the beginning that he agrees with their criticisms of his past apologies ("I agree with those who have said . . . I was not contrite enough"). Furthermore, he fashions various aspects of his content in such a way that could particularly resonate with his immediate audience. When he states, " . . . hope that with a broken spirit and a still strong heart I can be used for greater good," he suggests the principles of grace and mercy. The clergymen in attendance would have predominantly valued these ideals and appreciated Clinton's intention to use the lessons learned through this ordeal for "greater good" in the future.

> Clinton indirectly suggests rather than explicitly states his legal innocence. Depending on how one views Clinton's personal character and intentions, it could either help or hinder his credibility at this point in the speech.

Since Clinton's moral failures had resulted in legal action against him, he naturally needed to address this issue in his speech. However, his previous speech met with disastrous results when he focused too heavily on this particular aspect. In his Prayer Breakfast speech, however, Clinton wisely establishes the point that his actions did not merit impeachment, "I will instruct my lawyers to mount a vigorous defense, using all available appropriate arguments," and then he quickly moves on to the spiritual implications of his actions. Obviously, his immediate audience would find this emphasis appropriate, and it also helps further establish his ethos among his audience of the American public. Additionally, Clinton suggests that his mistakes have not permanently damaged his leadership abilities by noting his continuing goals for leading America ("I will intensify my efforts to lead our country and the world toward peace and freedom"). He builds on this idea with a touching story about a little Florida boy who told President Clinton that he wanted to grow up to be the President.

> It is very important that Clinton makes this distinction about his position as a role model, considering that his immediate audience valued moral uprightness. If he had simply said that children should grow up to be like him, without distinguishing which aspects of his character were worth imitating, his audience could have been offended.

By mentioning that children can still look up to him as a role model, not necessarily because of his moral actions but because of his repentance and ability to learn from mistakes, Clinton effectively points out, albeit indirectly, that he is still a legitimate leader. Granted, some members of his audience would disagree with this point; nevertheless, Clinton includes this argument to strengthen his credibility among audience members who are willing to support his leadership.

Since a personal apologia, by its very nature, must be sincere, Clinton's stylistic choices prove equally as important as his content. Mending broken trust is a nearly impossible task. We often find it difficult to forgive others based solely on their words. While the apology may sound good, how can we be sure that this individual isn't still lying to us? Therefore, however convincing the content of Clinton's personal apologia, it would have been a complete loss without a convincing presentation of the content. In other words, Clinton's language delivery was necessary to the effectiveness of his message. His style both reiterated and enabled his content. Primarily, his decision to write the speech himself signified the profound personal nature of this speech. His continual use of the personal pronoun *I* emphasizes this point. Very early in the speech Clinton admits uncertainty regarding his personal message: "I may not be quite as easy with my words today as I have been in years past." Although that admission violates a basic guideline of public speaking, it works in this situation to further demonstrate the authenticity of his apology and develop his humble persona.

Sensitive to his immediate audience, Clinton often speaks in religious terms. Toward the beginning of his address, he invokes clerical vocabulary by using phrases such as "repentance," "a broken spirit," and "forgiveness." All of these phrases helped him build his credibility with his immediate audience. Acknowledging the fact that repentance takes time, Clinton asks for prayer in helping him and the country move forward; naturally, the religious leaders in his audience would have appreciated his request for God's help in healing the emotional scars of this experience. Clinton further reaches out to his immediate audience by quoting a passage from the Yom Kippur liturgy, appealing to the Jewish members of his audience. Finally, Clinton ends his speech by combining phrases from the Prayer of Saint Francis and the Bible, leaving his religiously-minded immediate audience with spiritual themes.

On a more general level, the speech's simple and direct style helps Clinton's overall message. Whereas a more formal and polished speaking style normally befits a president, the highly personal nature of this speech demanded that Clinton present himself in the most genuine way possible. Therefore, he strategically avoids using complicated words or phrases and instead delivers his speech in a way that emphasizes his humanity. When he confesses, "I don't think there is a fancy way to say that I have sinned," it sounds like a heartfelt apology.

At this point, an important rhetorical situation appears. Although the speech itself displays many rhetorical strengths, the context in which Clinton delivered it also proves fundamentally significant. His humility and remorse appear genuine in this speech, which strengthens his credibility with the audience; however, one cannot forget that he had already

Rhetoric never occurs in a vacuum; the historical, social, and political context in which a speech is delivered always affects the speech itself and the audience's response in some way. This speech is a somewhat extreme example of the context's effect on an audience.

As Clinton spoke to multiple audiences, I wrote this paper for multiple audiences: my professor and students who would read this textbook. Knowing that some students may read this paper with little to no understanding of communication theory, I explained this idea in a more detailed manner than I may have if I was only writing for my professor.

severely damaged his credibility before the speech took place. By the time he delivered this address, his audience had been following this sad saga for nearly nine months and had likely already judged his behavior and personal character. Naturally, some members of both audiences were hesitant to forgive Clinton or were downright opposed to accepting his apology from the onset. No matter how effectively he presented his personal character in this speech, his audience's diversity made it nearly impossible for him to completely repair his reputation and trustworthiness in a single rhetorical act. This demonstrates the important rhetorical phenomenon of the audience: speakers do not simply act upon passive audience members nor persuade by injecting them with information or arguments. Audience members use their own perceptions and beliefs to critically interpret all speeches within their contexts. Clinton's personal apologia is an extreme example of the context retaining just as much rhetorical influence as the speech itself.

Because we can't get inside the head of each audience member, it is ultimately impossible to finally assess the overall "effectiveness" of the speech, because individuals interpreted its message differently. Therefore, the concluding paragraph provides me with a place to merely speculate why Clinton chose certain rhetorical strategies and how those choices most likely affected his audience members.

Given the context, the speech itself contained appropriate content and a meaningful delivery style that allowed Clinton to develop the most appealing persona possible. Though we cannot measure the overall effect of this speech, his intentional rhetorical choices strengthened the impact of his personal apologia. Where this speech lacked the formality and finesse of typical presidential addresses, it contained vulnerable and humble pleas for forgiveness. In so doing, Clinton made the most of a challenging rhetorical situation.

Work Cited

Campbell, Karlyn Kohrs and Kathleen Hall Jamieson. *Deeds Done in Words: Presidential Rhetoric and the Genres of Governance*. Chicago: The University of Chicago Press, 1994. 127–43.

Reading Responses

1. Which two parts of McGiness's analysis do you find most persuasive? For each part, list the features that McGiness uses to persuade you.

2. In her introduction, McGiness describes how her own feelings about Clinton's actions shaped her analysis of his speech and her claim about that speech. Note places in her essay that seem affected by McGiness's feelings. For each place, describe how you see her feelings shaping the essay.

3. When she presents her analysis of Clinton's speech, McGiness focuses first on the content of the speech and then on the style. Analyze the style of McGiness's essay, paying special attention to her word choice, her sentence structures, and her sentence subjects. What changes would you recommend if she were delivering the paper as an oral presentation?

PUBLIC WRITING

INTRODUCTION

Place yourself in President Bush's position soon after Hurricane Katrina devastated New Orleans and other parts of the Gulf Coast: A growing number of citizens angrily accuse the administration of incompetence in providing relief to the disaster area and injustice toward New Orleans' poor black population. The number of critical voices grows. President Bush and his administration decide that he must speak to the nation, but should he apologize for the poor disaster preparation and relief? How does a speaker face a skeptical—maybe even hostile—audience?

In this speech, President Bush tries to gain the audience's trust, acknowledging the victims' desperation ("grieving for the dead, and looking for meaning in a tragedy that seems so blind and random") and their bravery ("a powerful American determination to clear the ruins and build better than before"). He also appeals to a "united country," which both names his ideal audience and challenges his audience to become united. In his seventh paragraph, Bush also lists the recovery that has happened (electric power and river shipments restored, levee breaks repaired, among others), and then outlines his plan for further action.

Bush does not acknowledge responsibility for the poor response until much later in the speech, yet he does not apologize. He states, "I, as President, am responsible for the problem, and for the solution." He does not let the audience doubt his position of authority, nor does he cast himself as weak. But he does not apologize until he has fully described the action that federal agencies are currently planning, and then only implicitly.

Did President Bush make the right choices when he addressed an upset nation? The day after his speech, the *New York Times* reported that evacuees, Governor Kathleen Babineaux Blanco (Democrat), and Senator Mary L. Landrieu (Democrat) responded positively, with Landrieu claiming that the ideas were "innovative and bold." President Bush's head speech writer, Michael Gerson, has said that he took special pride in this speech because it addressed issues of race and poverty. As time passes, historians and other critics will judge Bush's ability to reframe his work after this natural disaster.

Post-Katrina Speech from Jackson Square, New Orleans, September 15, 2005

President George W. Bush

Good evening. I'm speaking to you from the city of New Orleans—nearly empty, still partly under water, and waiting for life and hope to return. Eastward from Lake Pontchartrain, across the Mississippi coast, to Alabama into Florida, millions of lives were changed in a day by a cruel and wasteful storm.

In the aftermath, we have seen fellow citizens left stunned and uprooted, searching for loved ones, and grieving for the dead, and looking for meaning in a tragedy that seems so blind and random. We've also witnessed the kind of desperation no citizen of this great and generous nation should ever have to know—fellow Americans calling out for food and water, vulnerable people left at the mercy of criminals who had no mercy, and the bodies of the dead lying uncovered and untended in the street.

These days of sorrow and outrage have also been marked by acts of courage and kindness that make all Americans proud. Coast Guard and other personnel rescued tens of thousands of people from flooded neighborhoods. Religious congregations and families have welcomed strangers as brothers and sisters and neighbors. In the community of Chalmette, when two men tried to break into a home, the owner invited them to stay—and took in 15 other people who had no place to go. At Tulane Hospital for Children, doctors and nurses did not eat for days so patients could have food, and eventually carried the patients on their backs up eight flights of stairs to helicopters.

Many first responders were victims themselves, wounded healers, with a sense of duty greater than their own suffering. When I met Steve Scott of the Biloxi Fire Department, he and his colleagues were conducting a house-to-house search for survivors. Steve told me this: "I lost my house and I lost my cars, but I still got my family . . . and I still got my spirit."

Across the Gulf Coast, among people who have lost much, and suffered much, and given to the limit of their power, we are seeing that same spirit—a core of strength that survives all hurt, a faith in God no storm can take away, and a powerful American determination to clear the ruins and build better than before.

Tonight so many victims of the hurricane and the flood are far from home and friends and familiar things. You need to know that our whole nation cares about you, and in the journey ahead you're not alone. To all who carry a burden of loss, I extend the deepest sympathy of our country. To every person who has served and sacrificed in this emergency, I offer the gratitude of our country. And tonight I also offer this pledge of the American people: Throughout the area hit by the hurricane, we will do what it takes, we will stay as long as it takes, to help citizens rebuild their communities and their lives. And all who question the future of the Crescent City need to know there is no way to imagine America without New Orleans, and this great city will rise again.

The work of rescue is largely finished; the work of recovery is moving forward. In nearly all of Mississippi, electric power has been restored. Trade is starting to return to the Port of New Orleans, and agricultural shipments are moving down the Mississippi River. All major gasoline pipelines are now in operation, preventing the supply disruptions that many feared. The breaks in the levees have been closed, the pumps are running, and the water here in New Orleans is receding by the hour. Environmental officials are on the ground, taking water samples, identifying and dealing with hazardous debris, and working to get drinking water and waste water treatment systems operating again. And some very sad duties are being carried out by professionals who gather the dead, treat them with respect, and prepare them for their rest.

In the task of recovery and rebuilding, some of the hardest work is still ahead, and it will require the creative skill and generosity of a united country.

Our first commitment is to meet the immediate needs of those who had to flee their homes and leave all their possessions behind. For these Americans, every night brings uncertainty, every day requires new courage, and in the months to come will bring more than their fair share of struggles.

The Department of Homeland Security is registering evacuees who are now in shelters and churches, or private homes, whether in the Gulf region or far away. I have signed an order providing immediate assistance to people from the disaster area. As of today, more than 500,000 evacuee families have gotten emergency help to pay for food, clothing, and other essentials. Evacuees who have not yet registered should contact FEMA or the Red Cross. We need to know who you are, because many of you will be eligible for broader assistance in the future. Many families were separated during the evacuation, and we are working to help you reunite. Please call this number: 1–877–568–3317—that's 1–877–568–3317—and we will work to bring your family back together, and pay for your travel to reach them.

In addition, we're taking steps to ensure that evacuees do not have to travel great distances or navigate bureaucracies to get the benefits that are there for them. The Department of Health and Human Services has sent more than 1,500 health professionals, along with over 50 tons of medical supplies—including vaccines and antibiotics and medicines for people with chronic conditions such as diabetes. The Social Security Administration is delivering checks. The Department of Labor is helping displaced persons apply for temporary jobs and unemployment benefits. And the Postal Service is registering new addresses so that people can get their mail.

To carry out the first stages of the relief effort and begin rebuilding at once, I have asked for, and the Congress has provided, more than $60 billion. This is an unprecedented response to an unprecedented crisis, which demonstrates the compassion and resolve of our nation.

Our second commitment is to help the citizens of the Gulf Coast to overcome this disaster, put their lives back together, and rebuild their communities. Along this coast, for mile after mile, the wind and water swept the land clean. In Mississippi, many thousands of houses were damaged or destroyed. In New Orleans and surrounding parishes, more than a quarter-million houses are no longer safe to live in. Hundreds of thousands of people from across this region will need to find longer-term housing.

Our goal is to get people out of the shelters by the middle of October. So we're providing direct assistance to evacuees that allows them to rent apartments, and many already are moving into places of their own. A number of states have taken in evacuees and shown them great compassion—admitting children to school, and providing health care. So I will work with the Congress to ensure that states are reimbursed for these extra expenses.

In the disaster area, and in cities that have received huge numbers of displaced people, we're beginning to bring in mobile homes and trailers for temporary use. To relieve the burden on local health care facilities in the region, we're sending extra doctors and nurses to these areas. We're also providing money that can be used to cover overtime pay for police and fire departments while the cities and towns rebuild.

Near New Orleans, and Biloxi, and other cities, housing is urgently needed for police and firefighters, other service providers, and the many workers who are going to rebuild these cities. Right now, many are sleeping on ships we have brought to the Port of New Orleans—and more ships are on their way to the region. And we'll provide mobile homes, and supply them with basic services, as close to construction areas as possible, so the rebuilding process can go forward as quickly as possible.

And the federal government will undertake a close partnership with the states of Louisiana and Mississippi, the city of New Orleans, and other Gulf Coast cities, so they can rebuild in a sensible, well-planned way. Federal funds will cover the great majority of the costs of repairing public infrastructure in the disaster zone, from roads and bridges to schools and water systems. Our goal is to get the work done quickly. And taxpayers expect this work to be done honestly and wisely—so we'll have a team of inspectors general reviewing all expenditures.

In the rebuilding process, there will be many important decisions and many details to resolve, yet we're moving forward according to some clear principles. The federal government will be fully engaged in the mission, but Governor Barbour, Governor Blanco, Mayor Nagin, and other state and local leaders will have the primary role in planning for their own future. Clearly, communities will need to move decisively to change zoning laws and building codes, in order to avoid a repeat of what we've seen. And in the work of rebuilding, as many jobs as possible should go to the men and women who live in Louisiana, Mississippi, and Alabama.

Our third commitment is this: When communities are rebuilt, they must be even better and stronger than before the storm. Within the Gulf region are some of the most beautiful and historic places in America. As all of us saw on television, there's also some deep, persistent poverty in this region, as well. That poverty has roots in a history of racial discrimination, which cut off generations from the opportunity of America. We have a duty to confront this poverty with bold action. So let us restore all that we have cherished from yesterday, and let us rise above the legacy of inequality. When the streets are rebuilt, there should be many new businesses, including minority-owned businesses, along those streets. When the houses are rebuilt, more families should own, not rent, those houses. When the regional economy revives, local people should be prepared for the jobs being created.

Americans want the Gulf Coast not just to survive, but to thrive; not just to cope, but to overcome. We want evacuees to come home, for the best of reasons—because they have a real chance at a better life in a place they love.

When one resident of this city who lost his home was asked by a reporter if he would relocate, he said, "Naw, I will rebuild—but I will build higher." That is our vision for the future, in this city and beyond: We'll not just rebuild, we'll build higher and better. To meet this goal, I will listen to good ideas from Congress, and state and local officials, and the private sector. I believe we should start with three initiatives that the Congress should pass.

Tonight I propose the creation of a Gulf Opportunity Zone, encompassing the region of the disaster in Louisiana and Mississippi and Alabama. Within this zone, we should provide immediate incentives for job-creating investment, tax relief for small businesses, incentives to companies that create jobs, and loans and loan guarantees for small businesses, including minority-owned enterprises, to get them up and running again. It is entrepreneurship that creates jobs and opportunity; it is entrepreneurship that helps break the cycle of poverty; and we will take the side of entrepreneurs as they lead the economic revival of the Gulf region.

I propose the creation of Worker Recovery Accounts to help those evacuees who need extra help finding work. Under this plan, the federal government would provide accounts of up to $5,000, which these evacuees could draw upon for job training and education to help them get a good job, and for child care expenses during their job search.

And to help lower-income citizens in the hurricane region build new and better lives, I also propose that Congress pass an Urban Homesteading Act. Under this approach, we will identify property in the region owned by the federal government, and provide building sites to low-income citizens free of charge, through a lottery. In return, they would pledge to build on the lot, with either a mortgage or help from a charitable organization like Habitat for Humanity. Home ownership is one of the great strengths of any community, and it must be a central part of our vision for the revival of this region.

In the long run, the New Orleans area has a particular challenge, because much of the city lies below sea level. The people who call it home need to have reassurance that their lives will be safer in the years to come. Protecting a city that sits lower than the water around it is not easy, but it can, and has been done. City and parish officials in New Orleans, and state officials in Louisiana will have a large part in the engineering decisions to come. And the Army Corps of Engineers will work at their side to make the flood protection system stronger than it has ever been.

The work that has begun in the Gulf Coast region will be one of the largest reconstruction efforts the world has ever seen. When that job is done, all Americans will have something to be very proud of—and all Americans are needed in this common effort. It is the armies of compassion—charities and houses of worship, and idealistic men and women—that give our reconstruction effort its humanity. They offer to those who hurt a friendly face, an arm around the shoulder, and the reassurance that in hard times, they can count on someone who cares. By land, by sea, and by air, good people wanting to make a difference deployed to the Gulf Coast, and they've been working around the clock ever since.

The cash needed to support the armies of compassion is great, and Americans have given generously. For example, the private fundraising effort led by former Presidents Bush and Clinton has already received pledges of more than $100 million. Some of that money is going to the Governors to be used for immediate needs within their states. A portion will also be sent to local houses of worship to help reimburse them for the expense of helping others. This evening the need is still urgent, and I ask the American people to continue donating to the Salvation Army, the Red Cross, other good charities, and religious congregations in the region.

It's also essential for the many organizations of our country to reach out to your fellow citizens in the Gulf area. So I've asked USA Freedom Corps to create an information clearinghouse, available at usafreedomcorps.gov, so that families anywhere in the country can find opportunities to help families in the region, or a school can support a school. And I challenge existing organizations—churches, and Scout troops, or labor union locals to get in touch with their counterparts in Mississippi, Louisiana, or Alabama, and learn what they can do to help. In this great national enterprise, important work can be done by everyone, and everyone should find their role and do their part.

The government of this nation will do its part, as well. Our cities must have clear and up-to-date plans for responding to natural disasters, and disease outbreaks, or a terrorist attack, for evacuating large numbers of people in an emergency, and for providing the food and water and security they would need. In a time of terror threats and weapons of mass destruction, the danger to our citizens reaches much wider than a fault line or a flood plain. I consider detailed emergency planning to be a national security priority, and therefore, I've ordered the Department of Homeland Security to undertake an immediate review, in cooperation with local counterparts, of emergency plans in every major city in America.

I also want to know all the facts about the government response to Hurricane Katrina. The storm involved a massive flood, a major supply and security operation, and an evacuation order affecting more than a million people. It was not a normal hurricane—and the normal disaster relief system was not equal to it. Many of the men and women of the Coast Guard, the Federal Emergency Management Agency, the United States military, the National Guard, Homeland Security, and state and local governments performed skillfully under the worst conditions. Yet the system, at every level of government, was not well-coordinated, and was overwhelmed in the first few days. It is now clear that a challenge on this scale requires greater federal authority and a broader role for the armed forces—the institution of our government most capable of massive logistical operations on a moment's notice.

Four years after the frightening experience of September the 11th, Americans have every right to expect a more effective response in a time of emergency. When the federal government fails to meet such an obligation, I, as President, am responsible for the problem, and for the solution. So I've ordered every Cabinet Secretary to participate in a comprehensive review of the government response to the hurricane. This government will learn the lessons of Hurricane Katrina. We're going to review every action and make necessary changes, so that we are better prepared for any challenge of nature, or act of evil men, that could threaten our people.

The United States Congress also has an important oversight function to perform. Congress is preparing an investigation, and I will work with members of both parties to make sure this effort is thorough.

In the life of this nation, we have often been reminded that nature is an awesome force, and that all life is fragile. We're the heirs of men and women who lived through those first terrible winters at Jamestown and Plymouth, who rebuilt Chicago after a great fire, and San Francisco after a great earthquake, who reclaimed the prairie from the Dust Bowl of the 1930s. Every time, the people of this land have come back from fire, flood, and storm to build anew—and to build better than what we had before. Americans have never left our destiny to the whims of nature—and we will not start now.

These trials have also reminded us that we are often stronger than we know—with the help of grace and one another. They remind us of a hope beyond all pain and death, a God who welcomes the lost to a house not made with hands. And they remind us that we're tied together in this life, in this nation—and that the despair of any touches us all.

I know that when you sit on the steps of a porch where a home once stood, or sleep on a cot in a crowded shelter, it is hard to imagine a bright future. But that future will come. The streets of Biloxi and Gulfport will again be filled with lovely homes and the sound of children playing. The churches of Alabama will have their broken steeples mended and their congregations whole. And here in New Orleans, the street cars will once again rumble down St. Charles, and the passionate soul of a great city will return.

In this place, there's a custom for the funerals of jazz musicians. The funeral procession parades slowly through the streets, followed by a band playing a mournful dirge as it moves to the cemetery. Once the casket has been laid in place, the band breaks into a joyful "second line"—symbolizing the triumph of the spirit over death. Tonight the Gulf Coast is still coming through the dirge—yet we will live to see the second line.

Thank you, and may God bless America.

Reading Responses

1. President Bush ends his speech with an image of New Orleans funeral bands playing first sad music and then joyful. List the "sad" sections of this speech and then the "joyful" ones. How do they relate to each other?

2. Prior to this speech, many had criticized the federal government for responding too slowly to the needs of the victims of Hurricane Katrina. Note the places where President Bush responds to those criticisms. How would you describe his responses? How are they like/unlike an apology?

3. President Bush devotes much of his speech to listing the actions of specific federal agencies. How do you think employees of those agencies responded? How did those who were affected by the hurricane respond? How do you think President Bush hoped Americans in general would respond?

MORE WRITING IN SPEECH COMMUNICATION

INTRODUCTION

You've now read a speech by President Obama on the Gulf oil spill (which some have called "Obama's Katrina"), and you've read a speech that President George W. Bush delivered in the wake of Katrina. The following essay analyzes the rhetoric that then-Senator Obama used in 2005 in public comments about President Bush's handling of the Katrina crisis.

The authors of the essay were both professors of communication when they wrote the essay that follows (Waymer is at Virginia Tech, and Heath is now retired from the University of Houston). They did not know, of course, that Senator Obama would go on to become president and have his own environmental crisis to deal with. The focus of Waymer and Heath's argument is on the ways that two senators—Obama and Landrieu (Louisiana)—effectively used rhetoric that drew into the public conversation the voices of those groups who were most affected by Hurricane Katrina but who had the least power to do anything. Waymer and Heath care less about the two senators than they do about how politicians can affect ideas and actions when dealing with crises like Katrina.

The excerpt from the essay gives you the main points of Waymer and Heath's argument (summarized in the Abstract), as it is supported by examples of Senator Obama's public comments. (We deleted the sections on Senator Landrieu's rhetoric.)

Emergent Agents: The Forgotten Publics in Crisis Communication and Issue Management Research

Damion Waymer and Robert L. Heath

Journal of Applied Communication Research, Vol. 35. 1, February 2007, pp. 88–108

[Abstract] *Crisis communication research rarely highlights the voices of marginalized publics or their advocates whose interests are affected by crisis situations. We take a different approach by using a response to a natural disaster to expand our theorizing about crisis situations beyond those that hurt the bottom line. Using official statements from Senators Landrieu and Obama about events surrounding Hurricane Katrina as texts for analysis, we demonstrate how they used transcendence, rhetorically, and appropriated the Bush administration's key term—security—to garner more support for their positions, Katrina sufferers, and relief efforts. Implications of this strategy serve to broaden crisis communication theorizing, and to provide insights into ways to strengthen the quality of crisis emergency response planning and response protocols.*

Keywords: Crisis Communication; Hurricane Katrina; Emergent Agents; Transcendence; Issues Management; Public Relations; Security. . . . .

Displaying Transcendence During a Crisis: A Means of Combating the Narratives of Continuity and Control

. . . In times of crisis, organizations use public relations tools, such as press conferences, press releases, and other forms of mediated communication, as the primary means to reach the goal of minimizing or reversing damage to relationships. They also make statements to enact control in the face of uncertainty and to frame crisis events by demonstrating that they influence their destinies (Heath, 1997). Although the narrative frame of an organization's being in control of its destiny is the one we often hear in crisis situations, there are other frames, at times competing ones, that support or circumvent a responsible party's story.

The very nature of crisis situations provides publics with the opportunity to challenge the frame that the organization is, in fact, in control of its destiny. Crises can provide individuals and publics that are not directly affected by a crisis situation with a platform from which to speak, and can possibly empower otherwise marginalized stakeholders and publics by equipping them with negotiation tools to enter into a dialogue. . . .

Through analysis of discourse of this sort, we believe that we can demonstrate how, in crisis planning and response, key voices not ordinarily considered can be heard, and why they need to be. If not, they might be heard at some other point; or they might be totally ignored to the detriment of developing a full and honest sense of the crisis into public scrutiny. These voices help frame the crisis, the quality of response to it, and the lessons learned that can mitigate future crises of similar kinds. If the voices are not heard during the crisis, they are likely to be stronger and more condemning after the fact. This realization can inform and enhance crisis communication research and best practices while also strengthening the quality of emergency response planning and response protocols.

Below, we turn to Senators Landrieu and Obama, who sagely displayed transcendence and featured "security" in such a manner that the term resonated with public sentiments about the government's responsibility to its citizens. More specifically, Senator Obama took advantage of the outpouring of public sympathy for those affected by Hurricane Katrina and the floods by stretching the favored term "security" to make these events a matter of national concern just like the Bush administration did for 9/11 (which could have remained regional, New York and Pentagon problems) and for the Iraq war (which could have been regarded as a regionalized, overseas skirmish). By using the rhetoric of security—just as had been done in the two previous instances before Katrina—Obama appropriated the technique of the Bush administration to transcend the discourse of Katrina from a regional, localized concern to a national concern.

According to Hearit (1997), to transcend means to "go beyond" or "cross over"; moreover, in the terms of external "organizational communication, transcendence is a form of symbolic action whereby a corporation [or other organization] redefines its acts so that they are viewed from a larger context, one that customarily features an ethical dimension" (pp. 219–220). Hearit's (1997) use of transcendence featured the organization's point of view rather than that of the victims; however, in the current case, transcendence was used by emergent agents on behalf of marginalized stakeholders. Senators Landrieu and Obama refused to allow for the events surrounding Katrina to stop at the level of race or class, which could be perceived as intolerable. Instead they found a way to remedy the problem by appealing to a broader, unifying concept of security. This strategy was a clever form of rhetorical invention, as few U.S. citizens would question the ethicality of ensuring the safety and security of all citizens. Moreover, since at least 9/11, and including the 2004 campaign that launched Obama into national prominence, the term "security" has been the hallmark of the Bush administration.

Stretching the Rhetoric of National Security

Senators Landrieu and Obama used the rhetorical invention of transcendence based on the term "security" to interpret and criticize the planning and preparation for and response of government agencies to the Hurricane Katrina crisis. . . .

Although we cannot attribute motives with complete accuracy, by closely analyzing the rhetorical strategies the Senators employed, we can develop useful insights into the meaning of and possible motivation for their statements, as well as the meaning and motivations that these statements might have induced in others. Undeniably, Hurricane Katrina shed light on the important issues of race and class; however, the Senators responded to this national disaster through transcendence; in doing so, they cleverly appropriated the administration's favored term, "security," along the way. The Senators used the term in the following ways: (1) security is national, not bi-partisan; (2) security must do more than plan for the "haves and cans"—it must also encompass planning for the "have nots," the "have nothings," and the "can'ts"; (3) security additionally must strike a strategic balance between, as opposed to a bifurcation of, free market solutions and government intervention as viable ways to address this crisis situation; (4) security further entails making such organizations as FEMA more reflective and responsible, as well as creating oversight and appointing a CFO to assure responsiveness to the issues and needs instead of profit maximization for those who might seek to profit unjustly from the crisis; and (5) finally, security involves being accountable to all citizens, especially those who are most vulnerable.

Throughout our analysis, we further develop these five notions and demonstrate how the Senators used them rhetorically to transcend the dividing lines of race and class. We have collapsed these five notions into three overarching themes. Thus, we have separated the Senators' remarks into three parts: (1) "We failed our citizens so badly"; (2) "Ineptitude is colorblind"; and (3) "We need to be pragmatic instead of ideological."

We Failed Our Citizens So Badly   . . . Senator Obama's argument is . . . clear; we failed as a nation (and are failing in other ways, such as energy policy) to make our nation—especially its most vulnerable citizens—secure. When emergency response and crisis prevention measures in times of natural disasters seem predicated on an "SUV" (sports utility vehicle) evacuation model instead of one that acknowledges a non-SUV population, a lack of national security is present. Senator Obama (2005c) illustrated this point in stating:

> [W]hat must be said is that whoever was in charge of planning and preparing for the worst case scenario appeared to assume that every American has the capacity to load up their family in an SUV, fill it up with $100 worth of gasoline, stick some bottled water in the trunk, and use a credit card to check in to a hotel on safe ground. (para. 11)

This clearly was not the case in New Orleans, where the overwhelming majority of the citizens who were left behind did not have such means. . . .

Obama (2005c), in addition to asking, "How we could have failed our fellow citizens so badly?" evoked the memory of 9/11 to show the unity of the nation, as well as to show the nation that by failing to plan adequately for and evacuate citizens of New Orleans the nation was vulnerable to both natural and terrorists attacks:

> One of the heartening things about this crisis has been the degree to which the outrage has come from across the political spectrum; across races; across income. The degree to which the American people sense that we can and must do better, and a recognition that if we cannot cope with a crisis that has been predicted for decades—a crisis in which we're given four or five days notice—how can we ever hope to respond to a serious terrorist attack in a major American city in which there is no notice, and in which the death toll and panic and disruptions may be far greater? (para. 9)

Obama sagely made the connection between preparing for a natural disaster and preparing for a terrorist attack by using a trifecta of invocations of "national security": (1) The Bush administration deemed 9/11 a matter of national security; (2) The Bush administration deemed the situation in Iraq a matter of national security; and (3) Senator Obama deemed Hurricane Katrina a matter of national security. Although Mayor Nagin made this point well in his public statements, this point did not seem to be widely accepted until Senator Obama connected the pieces of this trifecta and articulated them. Therefore, if preparation for a natural disaster is on a par with terrorism, then it is a matter of national security; failure to prepare adequately constitutes a national crisis. Thus Obama, by showing us the interconnectedness of the failings in the Katrina crisis and the failings of 9/11, as well as the threats associated with both, forces us to give serious thought to his question: "How we will prevent such a failure from ever occurring again?"(para. 8).

Ineptitude is Colorblind   Obama (2005c) noted:

> There's been much attention in the press about the fact that those who were left behind in New Orleans were disproportionately poor and African American. I've said publicly that I do not subscribe to the notion that the painfully slow response of FEMA and the Department of Homeland Security was racially-based. The ineptitude was colorblind. (para. 10)

The crisis situation that Katrina created was not an issue of race, but rather one of neglect and disparity in income and opportunities. The Senator further illustrated this point in stating:

> [It] is the deeper shame of this past week—that it has taken a crisis like this one to awaken us to the great divide that continues to fester in our midst. That's what all Americans are truly ashamed about, and the fact that we're ashamed about it is a good sign. (para. 13)

The Senator, in taking the position that the issue was not a racial issue and reassuring the audience that all Americans were ashamed by what they had witnessed, was able to transcend local white-versus-black conflicts and position the crisis as a national concern and, in doing so, brought the interconnectedness of society to the fore. In this society, like all others, we need, rely on, and are dependent on one another for survival; however, the Senator reminds his audience that U.S. citizens have neglected this all-important precept:

And so I hope that out of this crisis we all begin to reflect—Democrat and Republican—on not only our individual responsibilities to ourselves and our families, but to our mutual responsibilities to our fellow Americans. I hope we realize that the people of New Orleans weren't just abandoned during the Hurricane. They were abandoned long ago—to murder and mayhem in their streets; to substandard schools; to dilapidated housing; to inadequate health care; to a pervasive sense of hopelessness. (Obama, 2005c, para. 12)

By framing this issue as a threat to national security, the Senator was able to span partisan lines.

Usually, during the onset of wars and times of domestic discord, such as terrorist attacks, the nation is united. There is no time for bi-partisan politics. Only after a situation has lingered do bi-partisan politics begin to enter the discussion. In framing the Katrina crisis as a threat to national security, Obama likens it to other non-partisan concerns. In short, this crisis spans party lines and political orientation.

Senator Obama exhibited non-partisanship, both in terms of what he said in his public utterances and in his actions. He openly spoke about his association with Presidents Clinton and Bush, Sr., as well as joint sponsorship of federal legislation. He used these associations and the transcendent security frame to induce unity among U.S. citizens as it pertained to this national crisis. As the Senator stated, "Indeed, if there's any bright light that has come out of this disaster, it's the degree to which ordinary Americans have responded with speed and determination even as their government has responded with unconscionable ineptitude" (Obama, 2005c, para. 7).

Obama (2005c) acknowledged that ineptitude is colorblind, but he refused to dismiss it. In fact, he brings it to the fore in noting its unacceptability: "We're gonna have to do some hard thinking about how we could have failed our fellow citizens so badly, and how we will prevent such a failure from ever occurring again" (para. 8). . . .

We Need to be Pragmatic Instead of Ideological.   The Senators, through discourse, established the following: being ideological about Katrina largely contributed to this crisis situation. . . .

Senator Obama (2005b) stated that, in recent times, the Democratic Party has often been considered one that looks "for government for the first answer to every problem," whereas the Republican Party has often been seen as preferring to rely on free market forces as solutions to crisis; he quickly tried to move away from the philosophical differences and became pragmatic: "I think that what we are going to have to figure out is how do we do both and as opposed to either/or" (para. 5).

Senator Obama furthered his point through the following example:

All of us recognize that jobs are the best anti-poverty program and . . . we should ask the market to create those jobs and create the framework in which entrepreneurship and business development can occur . . . [; however,] we also have to recognize that there are communities that may not have access to capital and they may need government to help initially seed their entrepreneurial efforts. (para. 5)

The Senator (2005a) concluded his comments by observing that ideally everyone would recognize that individuals "have to take responsibility and that the market solution, where possible, is potentially the more efficient and preferable one, but also recognizing government has a role. That's the kind of practical, common sense, pragmatic America that I think works best" (para. 5).

Part of ensuring security is to be sure that individuals and organizations do not misappropriate or mismanage funds that are intended to help those in need. The Senator recognized that there would be individuals and organizations attempting to profit from the crisis. In two of his presentations, he drew attention to "no-bid" and "cost-plus" contracts that the government used in Iraq (Obama, 2005a, 2005b). He did not want the funds allotted for the Katrina recovery efforts to be squandered. Thus, the Senator paired up with Republican Senator Tom Coburn to "create a Chief Financial Officer (CFO) to oversee all expenditures associated with the Hurricane Katrina relief and reconstruction effort" (Obama, 2005a, para. 4).

In this bill, the Senators specifically laid out the details concerning the duties of the CFO. The bill required the President to appoint this officer, this appointment had to be confirmed by the Senate, and this officer was to oversee and manage any agency using federal funds for the Hurricane Katrina relief effort. In addition, he or she was to oversee the dispersing of the funds to determine whether the people most in need were receiving the aid and to determine whether companies that hired local workers were receiving the funds. Ultimately, the Senator was prodding the federal government and federal agencies to be reflective, responsible, and above all accountable. This is evident in the following comment: "As we look towards the massive Gulf Coast rebuilding efforts ahead, we must demand accountability over how the billions of dollars we've given to FEMA are spent" (Obama, 2005a, para. 5). In his rhetoric, however, Senator Obama was holding the federal government and agencies accountable for a great deal more.

Conclusion

Hearit (1997) has suggested that successful use of a transcendent strategy requires two components: redefinition and an appeal to higher values. The Senators, by redefining what Mayor Ray Nagin, Kanye West, and others deemed issues of race and class and positioning the events surrounding Hurricane Katrina more broadly as relating to a national security promise that was going unfulfilled, were successful in garnering more support for their positions and Katrina sufferers. By stretching the rhetoric of security, the Senators were able to equate preparation for a national disaster with preparation for a terrorist attack. They also emphasized that both are matters of national security, and failure to prepare adequately for a natural disaster—just as failure to prepare for terrorist attacks—as grounds for a national crisis. . . .

Senators Landrieu and Obama's comments, as well as the positioning and the accuracy of their positions, helped give other alternative frames power that probably forced government agencies into positions they would have preferred to avoid. We believe, for instance, that the Senators' voices helped to secure more financial assistance for Katrina victims and restoration efforts from the Bush administration. Simply put, the Senators' discourse and actions help us to explain how during a crisis an alternative frame can emerge and acquire legitimacy when expressed in ways that give voice to a group that otherwise is likely to be marginalized by the crisis—and is silent because it is marginalized. In this case, transcending issues of race and class by using the Bush administration's key term of "security" enabled the Senators to add strength and credibility to their positions, as well as empower other marginalized publics' frames. . . .

References

[We include only the references cited in the excerpted portion of the article.]

Hearit, K. M. (1997). On the use of transcendence as an apologia strategy: The case of Johnson controls and its fetal protection policy. *Public Relations Review, 23,* 217–231.

Heath, R. L. (1997). *Strategic issues management: Organizations and public policy challenges.* Thousand Oaks, CA: Sage.

Obama, B. (2005a, September 14). *Obama, Coburn to introduce Hurricane Katrina oversight legislation.* Retrieved January 5, 2006, from http://obama.senate.gov/press/050914-obama_coburn_to_introduce_hurricane_katrina_oversight_legislation/index.html

Obama, B. (2005b, September 21). *Poverty in America and opposing photo ID requirement for voting.* Retrieved January 5, 2006 from, http://obama.senate.gov/podcast/050921-poverty_in_america_and_opposing_a_photo_id_requirement_for_voting/index.html

Obama, B. (2005c, September 6). *Statement of Senator Barack Obama on Hurricane Katrina relief efforts.* Retrieved January 5, 2006, from http://obama.senate.gov/statement/050906-statement_of_senator_barack_obama_on_hurricane_katrina_relief_efforts/index.html

Reading Responses

1. Use the examples from this essay to compare Barack Obama's rhetoric in 2005, when he was a U.S. senator, to his BP Oil Spill remarks. How have his appeals to multiple audiences changed? How have they remained the same?

2. What evidence from Waymer and Heath's essay would support an argument that a president must appeal to more audiences than a senator must? What evidence would support an argument that senators and presidents have similar audiences?

3. Summarize Waymer and Heath's argument that Senator Obama used rhetoric of "transcendence" effectively. Identify evidence that President Obama used "transcendence" and "security" to appeal to his audiences in his BP Oil Spill remarks.

WRITING ASSIGNMENTS

Assignment 1

On February 24, 2009, President Obama delivered his first State of the Union address, and, as is common practice, a spokesperson for the opposing political party responded to the president's speech in nationally televised remarks. The Republican Party selected Louisiana

Governor Bobby Jindal to complete this task. It seemed like a wise selection: Governor Jindal enjoyed enormous voter approval and seemed destined for future political success, perhaps even a run for the presidency himself. But Jindal's speech, entitled "Americans Can Do Anything," was criticized as ineffective by political analysts and even members of the Republican Party (you can find text of the speech at http://www.gov.louisiana.gov/index.cfm?md=newsroom &tmp=detail&catID=3&articleID=1032. Search online to watch video of the speech). In the days after that speech, it was difficult to imagine that Bobby Jindal could ever overcome that bad performance and regain the trust of his political party.

Your task for this assignment is to write a speech that Governor Jindal could give that would help him put to rest lingering doubts about his potential for national political leadership. Decide whether Jindal should apologize, defend his performance, or combine apology with defense. Determine how specific you will be about the weaknesses of Jindal's performance and how directly you will address the criticism he earned for that speech. Craft a speech that will address multiple audiences—political analysts, members of the Republican Party, and Americans who may some day decide about voting Jindal into a national office.

Assignment 2

Although few of us will ever speak before an international audience as President Obama did, academics regularly defend their ideas from critique. They do so in "exchange" sections of major research journals, before governmental bodies, and in subsequent articles that they publish. Your task for this assignment is to analyze how academics in an academic discipline (perhaps your major) respond to the critique of others. Interview a professor to determine where critique occurs in her academic discipline. Locate an exchange between two or more authors in which they critique the work of others. Analyze that exchange to determine how authors describe not only the ideas they are critiquing but also how they address the authors of those ideas. If the original author has a chance to respond, how does that author respond to the critique?

As you begin drafting, consider who would be interested in your findings and what they could do with the information that you provide. How comfortable are you with the uses to which others might put your research? What uses would you like to encourage, and how can you encourage readers to do those? What uses would you like to discourage, and how can you discourage readers from doing those?

Assignment 3

Nearly every college and university has a policy on plagiarism. In fact, the National Council of Writing Program Administrators has drafted a position statement on plagiarism found online at http://wpacouncil.org/node/9. These policies usually include a description of plagiarism and the consequences that result when students plagiarize.

Your task for this assignment is to collect data and write a report that either justifies your school's plagiarism policy or suggests future revisions to the policy. To begin, determine the kind of information you want to gather about plagiarism at your institution and how you will gather that information. Are you interested in how students think about plagiarism? How much and what kinds of plagiarism occur? How teachers detect plagiarism? How they train students to avoid plagiarism? How attitudes about plagiarism at your school fit with those nationwide?

As you begin drafting, consider the audiences of your report carefully. If you justify the policy, your primary audience will be students. But others will be interested, too: teachers and administrators rely on documents such as yours as they talk about plagiarism with students. If you recommend revisions to the plagiarism policy, your primary audience will be school administrators who must approve such changes, but you can expect that teachers and students will read the document carefully, too. Decide on the central message of the report, its organization, and its tone. Determine the type and amount of evidence you will include in the report and how you will present that evidence.

14

SOCIOLOGY

In the comic above, what looks to be an empty ocean is actually full of drama—you just need to know where to look for it.

Human society is full of drama, too, if you know where to look and what to look for. Choose a public place where you can unobtrusively observe couples who appear to be married. Malls, parks, and restaurants are likely places. In a paragraph for each, describe three or four couples, including specifics that you observe.

What evidence makes you believe that the couple is married? Does the couple seem happy together? What is the physical distance between the couple? How affectionate is the couple?

Are they talking together? If so, who does most of the talking? What is the mood of the conversation? At the end of each paragraph, write out a specific question you have about this couple.

PORTABLE RHETORICAL LESSON: LIMITING A RESEARCH TOPIC

Did you find it difficult to write out a different question about each of the couples you observed? You likely felt some frustration because you didn't know the couples well enough to ask specific questions. You may have hesitated to ask a single specific question because you know that marriage is a complicated social relationship. These are the frustrations and worries that sociologists—and all researchers, really—must manage.

To begin to manage the complexity of their research, sociologists have developed methods for narrowing a research topic to a manageable size. The following outline highlights the basic steps.

1. After you identify the general topic of your research, read previous research on the topic to help you identify the problems or questions that deserve further research and the methods that have proven effective for other researchers.

2. Narrow your focus to one aspect of the topic or one specific problem.

3. Develop a theoretical framework—a model that describes the situation, the people involved, and the lens through which you view the situation. A theoretical framework uses precedents from previous scholarship as the foundation for the new framework. By using previous research to help you understand what questions can be answered and are worth answering, the theoretical framework helps to limit the scope of the research questions and hypotheses.

4. Develop one or more hypotheses—possible explanations—that you will test in your research. The hypothesis provides a very clear focus, helping readers to see exactly how the research topic is limited.

5. Develop a research design, using methods to test the hypotheses that have proven effective for other researchers.

6. Assess the research data collected to determine if it does or does not support the hypotheses.

You will notice that these steps drive toward the goal of making a **point** (through refinement of a hypothesis) and work very hard to design **research methods** and collect **evidence** (data) that support the point.

But the special emphasis that propels the steps—and the readings to follow—is the need to limit the scope of the topic. Without limiting the topic, it would be impossible to conduct research in sociology; the variables involved in any human social interactions are far too complex. In the last paragraph of Professor Brandsen's introduction to the first reading, she explains how the reading gets more and more specific about the initial hypothesis. In other words, she shows how sociologists are experts at the **Portable Rhetorical Lesson** of the chapter: limiting a topic. And you will be wise to apply this practice in all your courses.

WRITING IN THE DISCIPLINE

INTRODUCTION

by Cheryl Brandsen, Professor of Sociology

As social scientists, sociologists attempt to research human communities as objectively as possible. To achieve anything like scientific objectivity, sociologists must address two related problems: (1) even seemingly simple human interactions are exceedingly complex, and (2) sociologists' own life experiences affect how they look at human interactions.

Sociologist C. W. Mills argues that if researchers want to understand human behavior and social interaction, they must cultivate a "sociological imagination," a way of thinking about the world that relies on creative thought, careful review of previously published research, and objective scientific practices for their own research. This kind of imagination, says Mills, focuses on the relationship between "private troubles" and "public issues," between what might look like individual, personal problems and the larger structures of society. Sociological imagination helps researchers see how decisions or problems that seem to be solely personal and intimate—unemployment, suicide, or family relationships, for instance—are shaped by larger social, economic, historical, and political forces. And sociological imagination enables researchers to see past cultural stereotypes. When faced with the question from the final reading in this chapter (Why do young women have babies and yet remain unmarried?), for example, cultural stereotypes provide easy answers. But a sociological imagination compels researchers to think more creatively, looking for more complex answers that have greater explanatory power. Those potential answers form hypotheses that can be tested by reliable social science research.

Most people think about divorce, for example, in personal terms. A woman wonders where she "went wrong" or ruminates about her partner's bad habits. To prevent a subsequent divorce, the woman will focus on individual adjustments: "I will work fewer hours," "I will choose more wisely," or "I will manage money more effectively." That nearly 50 percent of marriages end in divorce, however, suggests that divorce might be more than an individual trouble. A sociological imagination pushes sociologists to wonder whether something in society influences the stability of marriages: high rates of unemployment, geographic mobility, changing gender roles and sexual norms, or unrealistic ideals about romantic love.

The authors of "Parenting as a 'Package Deal': Relationships, Fertility, and Nonresident Father Involvement Among Unmarried Parents," are highly respected sociologists (Ronald Mincy is a professor at Columbia University, Kathryn Edin a professor at Harvard, and Laura Tach, at the time of this study, was a graduate student at Harvard). They begin their essay by narrowing their research focus to unmarried couples who have a child together. In the last sentence of the first paragraph (immediately following the Abstract), the researchers narrow their focus even further to the relationship between the father and child after the father's romantic relationship with the child's mother has ended. And they identify a single measureable factor in that relationship: the amount of contact between nonresident fathers (fathers who do not live with the child and mother) and the child.

They conclude their introduction (the last paragraph before the section titled "Background") by presenting hypotheses. Formally defined, a hypothesis is a provisional explanation for a particular phenomenon that can be empirically tested. Informally defined, hypotheses in sociology offer specific answers to the questions that emerge from a sociological imagination. But they are answers that can be tested. Rather than merely accept a cultural stereotype of "deadbeat dad," these authors begin with a previously proven hypothesis: that fathers' involvement with their children lessens after a breakup between parents. This is the "package deal hypothesis"; the "package" is the connection between the relationship between the parents and the fathers' involvement with the children.

The authors then (in the same paragraph) "extend" the established hypothesis to argue that what causes fathers' involvement to lessen after a breakup is more than simply the breakup. Rather, fathers' involvement also depends on whether fathers and mothers move into new romantic relationships and have new children after breaking up. And they restate this hypothesis in the first sentence of the last paragraph of the "Background" section (the restated hypothesis is identified by a marginal note).

In the section entitled "Background," the authors construct the theoretical framework for their study. A useful theoretical framework provides a road map to guide research; more formally, a theoretical framework offers a set of interrelated, logical statements that describe, explain, or predict social events. In sociology, a theoretical framework provides an image of society that guides thinking and research. It includes a summary of previous research on the topic (often called a "literature review") and leads to a clearly defined problem to be investigated. The theoretical framework and the defined problem then shape what research methods are selected.

Regardless of the particular research methods chosen, sociologists work to ensure that the research is reliable, valid, and generalizable. *Reliable* means that the researcher has controlled for personal bias—that there is a high likelihood that other researchers would get the results if they duplicated the study; *valid* means that the results are very likely to represent something true about the social situation; and *generalizable* means that the truth of the results can be applied to situations beyond those of the experiment.

In the "Discussion" section, the authors consider how well their results support and specify their hypothesis. As you read, pay attention to the author's process of narrowing their focus: Step 1: the established "package deal hypothesis" that fathers' involvement with children lessens after a breakup. Step 2: the "extended" hypothesis that fathers' involvement also depends on whether either parent moves into a new relationship and has additional children. Step 3: the finding that mothers' movement into a new relationship and having new children is the most significant factor in lessening fathers' involvement. So the authors arrive at a conclusion that can stand as the starting point, the hypothesis to be extended, in future research.

✓ Reading Tips

Because sociologists achieve objectivity by carefully limiting the focus of their study to a testable hypothesis and by painstakingly describing their research (testing) methods and results, their writing can seem exceedingly complex.

To manage the complexity:

- First, look for the social problem that the authors study. In this article, you find that described in the "Abstract" and again in the "Discussion" section; also note the very last paragraph of the article. Jot down a summary of the problem and keep that handy as you read through the article.

- Next, find the places where the authors limit the topic (for example, the third paragraph after the "abstract"). Be sure that you understand the exact limits of the study.

- Next find the hypothesis that the authors actually test. Look in the section called "The 'Package Deal' and Nonmarital Father Involvement," and follow the marginal comments.

- Try to understand how the findings (look in the first paragraph of the "Discussion" section) do or do not fit in the theoretical framework—the model with which the authors begin their study (again, look for marginal annotations to help identify the relevant information).

Parenting as a "Package Deal": Relationships, Fertility, and Nonresident Father Involvement among Married Parents

Laura Tach, Ronald Mincy, and Kathryn Edin

Demography 47.1 2010

For a more complete description of this study of "fragile families," check out this link: http://www.fragilefamilies.princeton.edu/.

A longitudinal survey is one that takes place over time with the same participants surveyed during each wave of the study.

[Abstract]

Fatherhood has traditionally been viewed as part of a "package deal" in which a father's relationship with his child is contingent on his relationship with the mother. We evaluate the accuracy of this hypothesis in light of the high rates of multiple-partner fertility among unmarried parents using the Fragile Families and Child Wellbeing Study, a recent longitudinal survey of nonmarital births in large cities. We examine whether unmarried mothers' and fathers' subsequent relationship and parenting transitions are associated with declines in fathers' contact with their nonresident biological children. We contend that father involvement drops sharply after relationships between unmarried parents end. Mothers' transitions into new romantic partnerships and new parenting roles are associated with larger declines in involvement than fathers' transitions. Declines in fathers' involvement following a mother's relationship or parenting transition are largest when children are young. We discuss the implications of our results for the well-being of nonmarital children and the quality of nonmarital relationships faced with high levels of relationship instability and multiple-partner fertility.

In the late 1990s, over 80% of nonmarital births in the United States were to couples who were romantically involved. Forty percent of all unmarried parents and over half of urban unmarried parents were living together at the time of the birth (Bumpass and Lu 2000; McLanahan et al. 2003). Even though these parents express a desire to stay together and eventually marry each other, their romantic relationships dissolve rapidly in the first few years after the child's birth. Over 40% of nonmarital relationships end by the child's birthday, and by the time the child is 5 years old, over 60% of parents are no longer romantically involved with each other (Center for Research on Child Wellbeing 2003, 2007). The fragility of nonmarital unions has led to concern about whether fathers will remain in contact with their children after their relationships with mothers end.

> This is an example of the authors using sociological imagination, seeing a social situation clearly enough to be able to ask reasonable questions about it.

There is reason to be skeptical. In the American context, fatherhood has traditionally been viewed as part of a "package deal" (Furstenberg and Cherlin 1991; Townsend 2004) in which fatherhood is contingent on the relationship between the father and the child's mother. In this view, men attempting to father outside the context of a marriage or a coresidential union will have difficulty staying involved with their children. Fatherhood roles may be even more difficult to fulfill if fathers have competing familial obligations, a challenge that is particularly salient for unmarried parents, who have high rates of multiple-partner fertility. Almost 60% of children born to unmarried parents have at least one half-sibling already, despite the fact that their parents are, on average, only in their mid-20s (Carlson and Furstenberg 2006).

> a couple who lives together

> notable or important

In this article, we extend the "package deal" hypothesis, arguing that it predicts not only that fathers' involvement with children will decline after a breakup but also that subsequent transitions into new partner and parenting roles pose significant added barriers to involvement. As the father and mother of a nonmarital child enter into new family-like relationships, they may feel considerable pressure to recreate the "package deal" with the new family, without the interference of prior partners or children from past relationships. Although this may

> The "package" is made up of (1) a romantic relationship to a child's mother and (2) a father–child relationship.

> The hole in the scholarship that their research will fill.

occur among both married and unmarried parents as they transition from one partner to another, we focus on the latter group, which has received less scholarly attention. And while there are many dimensions of father involvement—including contact, shared activities, communication, emotional closeness, and financial contributions (Hawkins, Amato, and King 2007)—we focus on the amount of contact between father and child here because the level of involvement, rather than financial support (which is often adjudicated by law and collected and disbursed by the state) or the quality and content of involvement, is more closely linked to the concept of the "package deal."

> Here the focus of the research is limited to a very specific variable, the amount of contact between father and child.

Background

The image of unwed fathers as uninvolved parents plays a dominant role in public discourse about poverty, family structure, and race. A growing body of evidence from the social sciences, however, suggests that unmarried fathers with young children are usually quite involved. Two panel studies—the National Longitudinal Survey of Youth, which began to follow a sample of youth aged 14–19 in 1979, and the National Survey of Families and Households, a national probability sample of all U.S. households launched in 1981—provided the first nationally representative portraits of unmarried fathers (Lerman 1993; Mott 1990; Seltzer 1991). Mott (1990), for example, found that in the mid-1980s, almost 40% of children under age 4 had contact with their nonresident fathers at least once a week. A number of in-depth qualitative studies have also found that among unmarried fathers, the salience of the father role and engagement in fathering activities is high (Hamer 2001; Sullivan 1993; Waller 2002; Young 2003) and that mothers may serve as gatekeepers, controlling fathers' access to their nonresident children (Classens 2007).

> In qualitative research, words, rather than numbers, are used to study social relationships. Qualitative research is used when the problem being investigated is looking at how or why something exists. This contrasts with quantitative research which uses statistical analyses to answer questions.

This body of work also demonstrated that involvement declined quite dramatically as the children got older (Lerman 1993; Seltzer 2000). Additional surveys conducted in the 1990s showed consistent evidence of a downward trend in involvement as the children aged, though the rates differed considerably across the studies (Argys et al. 2007). One study, using adolescents' reports from the National Longitudinal Study of Adolescent Health, found that by the time nonmarital children reach adolescence, their chances of having a regularly involved father are quite low, with only 20% of fathers still involved by the time the children were 15 years old (Argys and Peters 2001).

This decline in father involvement seems surprising given the evidence from the baseline wave of the Fragile Families and Child Wellbeing Study, a representative survey of nonmarital children in large cities that began following families between 1998 and 2000, which found that the vast majority of fathers who had a nonmarital birth were present at the time of the birth and said that they wished to play an active role in their child's life. When the surveyors interviewed the mothers of these children just after the birth, 8 in 10 said the father had been supportive during the pregnancy. Furthermore, nearly all the fathers interviewed said they intended to stay involved (McLanahan et al. 2003).

> In this paragraph the authors list all the factors that have been previously studied before they direct the reader's attention to the ones that they will study.

The degree of father involvement, measured along a variety of dimensions, varies depending on the particular subgroup being examined. Studies that considered all nonresidential children, both marital and nonmarital, found lower rates of father involvement with nonmarital children. Father involvement also varies by race and ethnicity: typically, rates for African Americans are higher and rates for Hispanics are lower than for the average American father, all else being equal (Danziger and Radin 1990; Huang 2006; King 1994; King, Harris, and Heard 2004; Mott 1990; Seltzer 1991; but see Seltzer and Bianchi 1988). Additional factors associated with father involvement include parental education (Argys and Peters 2001; Huang 2006; King et al. 2004), father's age (Lerman and Sorenson 2000), earnings (Lerman and Sorensen 2000; Seltzer 1991), work status (Danziger and Radin 1990), child gender (King et al. 2004; Manning and Smock 1999; but see Cooksey and Craig 1998), the presence of additional children, the father's current marital status, the number of years since the father left the home (Argys and Peters 2001), the payment of child support (Seltzer 1991), and the quality of the coparenting relationship (Sobolewski and King 2005; but see Amato and Rezac 1994). Waller and Swisher (2006) focused solely on unmarried fathers and found that a wide array of risk behaviors, such as physical abuse, drug and alcohol use, and incarceration, were associated with lower odds of father–child contact.

The "Package Deal" and Nonmarital Father Involvement

Fatherhood has been viewed as a relationship that is not independent of, but largely flows through and is contingent on, the relationship between the father and the child's mother. This explanation is often used to account for the surprisingly low levels of father–child contact and child support payment following a divorce (Furstenberg and Cherlin 1991). To the extent that notions of the "package deal" are still strongly institutionalized within American society, men attempting to father outside the context of a marriage, a coresidential union, or a romantic relationship will have more difficulty staying involved with their children.

> These are examples of "transaction costs."

On a practical level, fathers must pay additional transaction costs to retain contact with children after a coresidential or romantic partnership ends, such as planning for visitation time, traveling to the mother's house and picking up the child, and having to bargain with the custodial parent for access to the child. Never-married fathers' costs may be particularly high because no automatic legal procedure exists for adjudicating conflicts or granting visitation rights to unmarried fathers. Thus, while both formerly married and unmarried couples may enact the "package deal," unmarried fathers may have greater difficulty staying in contact with their children outside of a coresidential union.

The authors use the theoretical model for their hypothesis by noting how their hypothesis relates to the hypothesis in Furstenberg (1995). This shows the relationship between the old "package deal" hypothesis and the new hypothesis being tested in this study. The rest of this paragraph also explains why the research is important.

Following Furstenberg (1995), we extend the application of the "package deal" hypothesis, arguing not only that it predicts declines in involvement after breakup but also that subsequent transitions into new partner and parenting roles pose significant added barriers to involvement. These processes are especially relevant for couples who bear children outside of marriage because such transitions are far more common among them (Graefe and Lichter 2007). The impact of these subsequent transitions is also particularly important in the U.S. context: Andersson (2002) has shown that both married and cohabiting American couples with children are significantly more likely to break up and are far more likely to repartner than comparable couples in other industrialized countries. Unmarried couples in the United States also lack the legal, institutional, and normative supports that unmarried couples in many other industrialized countries enjoy.

Here is a restatement of the authors' hypothesis. It contains two things to be tested: "subsequent relationships" and "subsequent fertility" of father and mothers.

For the large and growing subset of parents who have children outside of marriage and who experience exceptionally high rates of subsequent partner and parenting transitions, we expect that transitions into subsequent relationships, and subsequent fertility within those relationships, are key mechanisms through which nonresidential father involvement declines over time. As fathers move on to subsequent partners and parental roles, the demands inherent in maintaining these new relationships could crowd out obligations to children from prior relationships. Mothers' transitions into subsequent partnerships might also prompt them to play a gatekeeper role, excluding the biological father in favor of the new father figure in the home, especially if the new father figure becomes the biological father of a subsequent child.

Methods . . .

Measurement

A dependent variable is the behavior or attitude that can be explained or predicted by the independent variable. Here the dependent variable is father involvement.

Dependent variables. The main dependent variable in our study is father involvement, measured by two dimensions of father–child contact.[3] Fathers were coded as having *no contact with child* if the mother reported that the father had not seen the child since the previous interview. This measure captures one extreme of father–child contact. We also use a more intensive measure of father involvement, the *number of days in the past month* the father saw the child, given that the father had

The authors tell us the two ways (dimensions) that they will measure the dependent variable.

contact with the child since the previous interview. This is a continuous variable ranging from 0 to 30 days. . . .

An independent variable is a condition that is relatively stable, understood to be the cause of the relationship between variables.

Independent variables. We use several measures to capture the subsequent relationship characteristics of unmarried mothers and fathers in our sample. We measure the *time since parents stopped coresiding* as an ordinal variable that indexes the number of survey waves the parents have not lived together. For example, in the fourth survey wave, parents were coded as 0 if they still lived together, 1 if they were living together at the third wave but were not living together at the fourth, 2 if they were living together at the second wave, but not in the third or fourth wave, and 3 if they were living together at the first wave but not any of the subsequent waves. Parents who never lived together during the study period (since the child was born) were coded as 4. This indexing was repeated for each of the survey waves.

Variables can be measured in a number of ways and with varying degrees of precision. When something is an "ordinal variable," it means that there is an order to the possible responses one can make (0 = still living together vs. 4 = never having lived together). This contrasts with nominal variables, which are often thought to have one clear response (e.g., in which state do you live?).

We also measure at each wave whether the *father has a new partner*, the *mother has a new partner*, the *father has subsequent children with a different partner*, and the *mother has subsequent children with a different partner*. At each follow-up survey wave, mothers and fathers were asked whether they were currently involved in a romantic relationship with someone other than the father/mother. Mothers were also asked whether the father was living with or married to another woman at each follow-up survey wave. Each parent was also asked whether s/he had children with someone other than the father/mother, and mothers were asked whether the father had children with someone other than her.

Time-varying controls. The parents' relationship status was categorized as *married, cohabiting, romantically involved,* or *no relationship* based upon the mothers' reports at each wave. Parents' residential status was defined as *living together* if mothers reported they lived together all or most of the time and as *not living together* otherwise. Fathers were coded as *employed* if they reported doing any regular work for pay during the week prior to the interview. Father's *annual earnings* were measured in thousands of dollars, derived from their reports of wages and weeks worked in the past year.

Results

While fathers' behavioral and economic characteristics remain relatively stable across the follow-up survey waves, Table 2 shows that their romantic and cohabiting relationships with mothers quickly dissolve. By the five-year follow-up, about 16% of unmarried mothers were married to the father, about 18% remained together in cohabiting unions, 5% were still romantically involved but did not live together, and over 60% were no longer in a relationship with each other. This does not mean

The first four rows of the table show the characteristics that remain stable over time: father's employment, earnings, prison time, and drug use.	**Table 2 Behavioral and Relationship Characteristics After a Nonmarital Birth**		

Variable	One-Year Follow-up	Three-Year Follow-up	Five-Year Follow-up
All Unmarried Fathers			
Father employed	74	71	76
Father's earnings ($)	19,507	20,669	22,758
Father ever in jail or prison	39	50	53
Father used drugs	10	12	15
Relationship status with biological mother			
Married	11	15	16
Cohabiting	37	26	18
Romantically involved	12	6	5
No relationship	40	53	61
Resident fathers	52	44	36
Nonresident fathers	48	56	65
Nonresident Fathers			
Mother new partner	26	41	51
Married to new partner	9	10	17
Cohabiting with new partner	40	56	69
Father new partner	23	44	51
Married to new partner	13	14	16
Cohabiting with new partner	43	70	60
Mother new child by new partner	2	18	24
Father new child by new partner	3	9	26
Saw child since previous survey	87	73	66
Saw child in past month	63	49	46
Mean number of days father saw child	9.9	8.9	8.7
N	3,243	3,123	3,050

Notes: Weighted by national sampling weights for each survey year. All values are percentages unless otherwise indicated.

that the parents remained single, because transitions out of relationships were followed by rapid transitions into new romantic relationships for both mothers and fathers. Around one year after the child's birth, one quarter of unmarried mothers who did not coreside with the father had new romantic partners. Over half of these new partnerships were cohabiting or marital unions. After five years, about half of unmarried, nonresident parents had a new romantic partner, and over a quarter had a subsequent child with a new partner. Of these new partnerships, 16%–17% were marital unions for both mothers and fathers, and another 60%–69% were cohabiting unions.

Table 2 also details the proportions of nonmarital children who had contact with their biological fathers at one, three, and five years. Both coresidence and involvement rates among unmarried fathers began high but declined throughout the first five years of a child's life. Almost half of nonmarital children resided with their fathers around the time of their first birthday, but this figure declined to only 36% by their fifth birthday. At their first birthday, 63% of nonresident children had seen their fathers in the past month. By the child's third birthday, only half had seen their fathers in the past month. Overall, by the time they reached age 5, nonresident children who had any contact with their fathers (since the prior survey) saw them an average of nine days per month, or about two times per week, on average.

Next, we examine nonresident father involvement at the five-year follow-up by parents' subsequent relationship and fertility statuses. Table 3 shows that mothers' repartnering and subsequent children are strongly associated with lower levels of father involvement. When mothers had no new partners or children, 77% of nonresident fathers had contact with the child in the past year, and 58% in the past month; when mothers had new partners and new children, these percentages decline to 45% and 27%, respectively. In contrast, nonresident fathers' subsequent transitions are not as strongly associated with their involvement. When they had no new partners or children, 71% of fathers had contact with their children since the last survey and 51% had contact in the past month; when they had a new partner and new child, 63% of fathers had contact with their child since the last survey wave, and 40% had contact in the past month. We compared these associations with other factors known to influence father involvement. The lower involvement rates associated with subsequent partners and children for mothers are comparable in magnitude to the lower involvement rates among fathers who have been in jail, have abused drugs, or are unemployed.[6]

. . .

> The authors state their main finding as the concluding sentence of the paragraph.

Table 3 Nonresident Father Involvement by Economic, Behavioral, and Subsequent Relationship Characteristics at the Five-Year Follow-up

Variable	Past Year	Past Month	Number of Days in Past Month	% of Nonresident Fathers
All Nonresident Fathers	66	46	8.7	100
Mother's Subsequent Relationships				
No partner or child	77	58	11.2	45
Partner but no child	67	44	6.5	33
Child but no partner	44	28	7.5	7
Partner and biological child	45	27	5.6	15
Father's Subsequent Relationships				
No partner or child	71	51	10.4	44
Partner but no child	60	41	7.8	30
Child but no partner	75	56	10.5	9
Partner and biological child	63	40	6.6	17
Father's Characteristics				
No drugs in past year	69	50	9.7	80
Drugs in past year	54	30	4.5	20
Never been in jail or prison	69	54	10.4	36
Ever been in jail or prison	64	41	7.6	64
Employed at prior survey wave	70	52	9.6	68
Not employed at prior survey wave	60	32	6.4	32
Earned more than $15,000	65	43	7.9	62
Earned $15,000 or less	68	50	9.9	38

Notes: N = 2,019. Figures are weighted by national sampling weights. ~e sample is restricted to couples who were unmarried at child's birth and in which the father was nonresident at the five-year follow-up. Number of days in past month is calculated based on the subsample of fathers who saw their nonresident child in the past year.

Discussion

Our analysis shows that transitions to subsequent partner and parental roles among unmarried parents, especially those of the mother, may be a driving force behind the large declines in father involvement that occur over time. Mothers' subsequent partners and children are strongly associated with increases in the probability that the biological father will have no contact with his child, but the association between fathers' own subsequent partners and children and their involvement is not nearly as large as mothers'. Second, both mothers' and fathers' subsequent romantic partnerships are associated with declines in the intensity of father involvement in the past month, although mothers' subsequent relationships are still nearly twice as strong as fathers'. Changes in a mother's romantic and parental status are strongly related to declines in paternal involvement and are at least as great in magnitude as changes in a father's economic characteristics or other personal characteristics. Changes in a father's status are not predictive of whether the father has contact with the child but are related to the intensity of his involvement, suggesting a "crowding out" effect.

These results are somewhat surprising given that research related to the "package deal" hypothesis has focused primarily on the impact of fathers' subsequent partnerships and parenting roles on ongoing father involvement, even though the theory itself is gender-neutral. Readers should also note the contrast between the small body of work on marriage transitions among divorced *mothers,* which have found only a modest effect, and the rather large associations we report here. It is possible that given the unique constraints and pressures unmarried mothers and fathers face, especially the lack of formal visitation agreements and the much greater frequency of partner transitions and multiple-partner fertility, father involvement is more contingent on cultural norms that regard fatherhood as part of a "package deal."

In all, the evidence points more strongly to the role of mothers "swapping daddies" than it does to the role of fathers "swapping kids." Why might the impacts for mothers' transitions be so large? One possibility is that the sharp difference in the legal context within which divorcing and unmarried fathers must operate matters. Divorcing fathers' custody, financial obligations, and visitation rights are all adjudicated together at the time of the divorce. Conversely, in the nonmarital context, fathers are less frequently involved in the legal process by which child support orders are made and visitation is assigned. Under these circumstances, mothers who wish to "swap daddies" can far more easily do so. A second possibility is that for mothers who are unmarried at the time of their child's birth, subsequent partnerships may be especially

---

Sidebar notes (left margin):

Their findings support the "extended" hypothesis that is more specific than the "package deal" hypothesis. The data suggest that father involvement is affected more by mothers' subsequent romantic relationships and children than it is by fathers' subsequent relationships and children.

The authors note that their results are inconsistent with research that forms part of their theoretical framework.

The findings allow the authors to state, in memorable terms, a more specific conclusion than their hypothesis suggested. The hypothesis tested effects of both fathers and mothers; the findings support a more important role for mothers. This finding can in turn become the starting point hypothesis for future research.

fragile (as their past partnerships were) and thus especially vulnerable to the threat of ongoing involvement of a former partner, even if only for the purposes of seeing the child. Third, unmarried mothers who repartner typically do so with men who have more human capital and fewer behavioral problems than did their prior partners (Bzostek, Carlson, and McLanahan 2007; Graefe and Lichter 2007). It is quite possible that unmarried fathers' own very low human capital and high degree of other serious problems make their past partners less likely to cooperate in visitation than would otherwise be the case. Finally, the fact that mothers' transitions are more consequential does not necessarily mean that mothers are primarily responsible for the decline in father involvement. Our results are also consistent with fathers choosing to become less involved when mothers repartner than when they repartner themselves.

The impact of mothers' relationship transitions on intensive father involvement weakens as children get older, however, suggesting that relationship transitions may be less predictive of declines in father involvement after fathers have had sufficient time to cement their role as the primary father figure in their children's lives. The children themselves may also play a greater role in deciding the level of contact, thus limiting the mother's ability to be a gatekeeper. Additionally, qualitative evidence suggests that mothers' new partners do not tend to be active as social fathers unless the child is very young (Nelson and Edin forthcoming).

Because fatherhood is generally enacted in the most meaningful way within the context of a conjugal union, because the fragility of these unions is high, and because repartnering and subsequent childbearing are common, children born to unmarried parents are likely to experience multiple father figures who represent a series of temporary commitments rather than a lifelong obligation. Since stability is critical for child well-being, the shifting cast of fathers and father figures in children's lives is likely to detract from, not add to, their well-being.

> sexual relationship

Notes

3. In a comparison of mothers' and fathers' reports of father involvement at the one-year follow-up (when missing data are least for both mothers and fathers), we found that mothers and fathers agreed on reports of yearly contact in 94% of cases for which we had information reported by both the mother and father, and in 91 % of cases for whether the father saw the child in the past month.

6. Of course lack of biological father involvement does not mean that there is no involvement on the part of the asocial father, and we discuss the role of fathers in greater detail at the end of the article.

References

Allison, P. 2001. *Missing Data*. Thousand Oaks, CA: Russell Sage Foundation.

Amato, P. and S. J. Rezac. 1994. "Contact with Nonresident Parents: Interparental Conflict and Children's Behavior." *Journal of Family Issues* 15:191–207.

Amato, P. and J. M. Sobolewski. 2004. "The Effects of Divorce on Fathers and Children: Nonresidential Fathers and Stepfathers." Pp. 341–67 in *The Role of the Father in Child Development*, 4th ed., edited by M. E. Lamb. Hoboken, NJ: John Wiley and Sons.

Andersson, G. 2002. "Children's Experience of Family Disruption and Family Formation: Evidence From 16 FFS Countries." *Demographic Research* 7:343–64.

Argys, L. M. and H. E. Peters. 2001. "Patterns of Nonresident Father Involvement." Pp. 49–78 in *Social Awakenings: Adolescent Behavior as Adulthood Approaches*, edited by R. T. Michael. New York: Russell Sage Foundation.

Argys, L. M., E. Peters, S. Cook, S. Garasky, L. Nepomnyaschy, and E. Sorenson. 2007. "Measuring Contact Between Children and Nonresident Fathers." Pp. 375–98 in *Handbook of Measurement Issues in Family Research*, edited by S. L. Hofferth and L. M. Casper. Mahwah, NJ: Erlbaum.

Bumpass, L. and H.-H. Lu. 2000. "Trends in Cohabitation and Implications for Children's Family Contexts in the United States." *Population Studies* 54:29–41.

Bzostek, S. 2008. "Social Fathers and Child Wellbeing." *Journal of Marriage and Family* 70:950–61.

Bzostek, S., M. J. Carlson, and S. McLanahan. 2007. "Repartnering After a Nonmarital Birth: Does Mother Know Best?" Working Paper #2006-27-FF. Center for Research on Child Wellbeing, Princeton University, Princeton, NJ.

Carlson, M. and F. Furstenberg. 2006. "The Prevalence and Correlates of Multipartnered Fertility Among Urban U.S. Parents." *Journal of Marriage and Family* 68:718–32.

Center for Research on Child Wellbeing. 2003. "Union Formation and Dissolution in Fragile Families." Fragile Families Research Brief No. 14. Princeton University, Princeton, NJ.

———. 2007. "Parents' Relationship Status Five Years After a Non-Marital Birth." Fragile Families Research Brief No. 39. Princeton University.

———. 2008. "Introduction to the Fragile Families Public Use Data." Princeton University, Princeton, NJ.

Cherlin, A. 1978. "Remarriage as an Incomplete Institution." *American Journal of Sociology* 84:634–50.

———. 2004. "The Deinstitutionalization of American Marriage." *Journal of Marriage and Family* 66:848–61.

Claasens, A. 2007. "Gatekeeper Moms and (Un)Involved Dads: What Happens After a Breakup?" Pp. 204–27 in *Unmarried Couples With Children*, edited by P. England and K. Edin. New York: Russell Sage Foundation.

Coleman, M., L. Ganong, and M. Fine. 2000. "Reinvestigating Remarriage: Another Decade of Progress." *Journal of Marriage and the Family* 62:1288–307.

Cooksey, E. C. and P. H. Craig. 1998. "Parenting From a Distance: The Effects of Parent Characteristics on Contact Between Nonresidential Fathers and Their Children." *Demography* 35:187–200.

Furstenberg, F. F. and A. J. Cherlin. 1991. *Divided Families: What Happens to Children When Parents Part*. Cambridge, MA: Harvard University Press.

Graefe, D. R. and D. T. Lichter. 2007. "When Unwed Mothers Marry: The Marital and Cohabiting Partners of Midlife Women." *Journal of Family Issues* 28:595–622.

Halaby, C. N. 2004. "Panel Models in Sociological Research: Theory Into Practice." *Annual Review of Sociology* 30:507–44.

Hamer, J. F. 2001. *What It Means To Be a Daddy: Fatherhood Among Black Men Living Away From Their Children*. New York: Columbia University Press.

Hausman, J. A. 1978. "Specification Tests in Econometrics." *Econometrica* 46:1251–72.

Hawkins, D., P. Amato, and V. King. 2007. "Nonresident Father Involvement and Adolescent Well-being: Father Effects or Child Effects?" *American Sociological Review* 72:990–1010.

Hofferth, S. L. 2006. "Residential Father Family Type and Child Well-being: Investment Versus Selection." *Demography* 43:53–77.

Hofferth, S. L., J. Pleck, J. L. Stueve, S. Bianchi, and L. Sayer. 2002. "The Demography of What Fathers Do." Pp. 63–90 in *Handbook of Father Involvement,* edited by C. S. Tamis-LeMonda and N. Cabrera. Mahwah, NJ: Lawrence Erlbaum Associates.

Huang, C. C. 2006. "Child Support Enforcement and Father Involvement for Children in Never-Married Mother Families." *Fathering* 4:97–111.

Juby, H., J. M. Billette, B. Laplante, and C. Le Bourdais. 2007. "Nonresident Fathers and Children: Parents' New Unions and Frequency of Contact." *Journal of Family Issues* 28:1220–45.

King, V. 1994. "Variation in the Consequences of Nonresident Father Involvement for Children's Wellbeing." *Journal of Marriage and the Family* 56:963–72.

King, V., K. M. Harris, and H. E. Heard. 2004. "Racial and Ethnic Differences in Nonresident Father Involvement." *Journal of Marriage and Family* 66:1–21.

Lerman, R. I. 1993. "A National Prolem of Young Unwed Fathers." Pp. 27–51 in *Young Unwed Fathers: Changing Roles and Emerging Policies,* edited by R. I. Lerman and T. J. Ooms. Philadelphia: Temple University Press.

Lerman, R. I. and E. Sorensen. 2000. "Father Involvement With Their Nonmarital Children: Patterns, Determinants and Effects on Their Earnings." Pp. 137–59 in *Fatherhood: Research, Interventions, and Policies,* edited by H. E. Peters, G. W. Peterson, S. K. Steinmetz, and R. D. Day. New York: The Haworth Press.

Lichter, D. T., Z. Qian, and M. L. Crowley. 2005. "Child Poverty Among Racial Minorities and Immigrants: Explaining Trends and Differentials." *Social Science Quarterly* 86:1037–59.

Manning, W. D. and K. Lamb. 2003. "Adolescent Well-being in Cohabiting, Married, and Single Parent Families." *Journal of Marriage and Family* 65:876–93.

Manning, W. D. and P. J. Smock. 1999. "New Families and Nonresident Father-Child Visitation." *Social Forces* 78:87–116.

———. 2000. "'Swapping' Families: Serial Parenting and Economic Support for Children." *Journal of Marriage and the Family* 62:111–22.

Manning, W. D., S. D. Stewart, and P. J. Smock. 2003. "The Complexities of Fathers' Parenting Responsibilities and Involvement With Nonresident Children." *Journal of Family Issues* 24: 645–67.

McLanahan, S., I. Garfinkel, N. Reichman, J. Teitler, M. Carlson, and C.N. Audigier. 2003. "The Fragile Families and Child Wellbeing Study: Baseline National Report." Center for Research on Child Wellbeing, Princeton University, Princeton, NJ.

Mincy, R. B. 2001. "Who Should Marry Whom? Multiple Partner Fertility Among New Parents." Paper presented at the annual meeting of the Association for Public Policy and Management, Washington, DC.

Mincy, R. B. and C.-C. Huang. 2002. "Determinants of Multiple-Partner Fertility." Paper presented at the annual meeting of the Population Association of America, Atlanta, GA.

Mincy, R. B. and H. Pouncy. 2007. "Baby Fathers and American Family Formation." Essay, *Future of the Black Family Series.* Center for Marriage and Families at the Institute for American Values, New York.

Mott, F. L. 1990. "When Is a Father Really Gone? Paternal-Child Contact in Father-Absent Homes." *Demography* 27:499–517.

Nelson, T. and K. Edin. Forthcoming. *Fragile Fatherhood.* New York: Russell Sage Foundation.

Osborne, C. and S. McLanahan. 2007. "Partnership Instability and Child Wellbeing." *Journal of Marriage and Family* 64:1065–83.

Seltzer, J. A. 1991. "Relationships Between Fathers and Children Who Live Apart: The Father's Role After Separation." *Journal of Marriage and the Family* 53:79–101.

———. 2000. "Child Support and Child Access: The Experiences of Marital and Non-Marital Families." Pp. 69–87 in *Child Support: The Next Frontier*, edited by T. Oldham and M. Melli. Ann Arbor, MI: University of Michigan Press.

Seltzer, J. A. and S. M. Bianchi. 1988. "Children's Contact With Absent Parents." *Journal of Marriage and the Family* 50:663–67.

Sobolewski, J. M. and V. King. 2005. "The Importance of the Coparental Relationship for Nonresident Fathers' Ties to Children." *Journal of Marriage and Family* 67:1196–212.

Stephens, L. S. 1996. "Will Johnny See Daddy This Week? An Empirical Test of Three Theoretical Perspectives of Postdivorce Contact." *Journal of Family Issues* 17:466–94.

Stewart, S. D. 1999. "Nonresident Mothers' and Fathers' Social Contact With Children." *Journal of Marriage and the Family* 61:894–907.

Sullivan, M. L. 1993. "Young Fathers and Parenting in Two Inner City Neighborhoods." Pp. 52–73 in *Young Unwed Fathers: Changing Roles and Emerging Policies*. Philadelphia: Temple University Press.

Townsend, N. W. 2004. *The Package Deal: Marriage, Work, and Fatherhood in Men's Lives*. Philadelphia PA: Temple University Press.

Waller, M. R. 2002. *My Baby's Father: Unwed Parents and Paternal Responsibilities*. Ithaca, NY: Cornell University Press.

Waller, M. R. and R. Swisher. 2006. "Fathers' Risk Factors in Fragile Families: Implications for 'Healthy' Relationships and Father Involvement." *Social Problems* 53:392–420.

Young, A. 2003. *The Minds of Marginalized Black Men: Making Sense of Mobility, Opportunity, and Future Life Chances*. Princeton, NJ: Princeton University Press.

Yuan, A. S. and H. A. Hamilton. 2006. "Stepfather Involvement and Adolescent Wellbeing: Do Mothers and Nonresident Fathers Matter?" *Journal of Family Issues* 27:1191–213.

Reading Responses

1. Review the "Background" section, and list all the prior research findings that shape the authors' hypothesis. Create a visual representation of the relationship between this previous research and the authors' hypothesis.

2. Prior to reading this research, would you have blamed these fathers for not spending much time with their children? Using research described in this study, write a short letter to a nonresident father in which you help him see the factors that affect the time he spends with his child. Decide whether or not you will encourage him to overcome these factors.

3. Describe a study that could follow this one. What factors should the researchers' focus on? Frame your answer as a hypothesis. Sketch out a theoretical framework for your hypothesis, using the research that Tach, Mincy, and Edin present in their essay.

Notes on Grammar, Style, and Rhetoric:
Noun Phrases

Laura Tach, Ronald Mincy, and Kathryn Edin's "Parenting as a 'Package Deal': Relationships, Fertility, and Nonresident Father Involvement among Unmarried Parents" is a striking mix of sentences that are quite easy to read and those that are more challenging.

Consider some sentences that seem quite easy. Here is one from the first paragraph: "Forty percent of all unmarried parents and over half of urban unmarried parents were living together at the time of the birth" (114). And here is one from later in the article: "By the child's third birthday, only half had seen their fathers in the past month" (120).

Many writing teachers say that such sentences are good examples of the clausal style. That is, they generally use clauses to depict persons existing in a certain state or doing something to someone or something else: some of the parents were living together and only some of the children had seen their fathers in the past month. The core of the meaning is spread across a clause.

These sample sentences contrast to some others in the article. Consider, for example: "Next, we examine nonresident father involvement at the five-year follow-up by parents' subsequent relationship and fertility statuses" (120). This sentence is not markedly longer than the earlier two examples, yet many readers will have to read it more than once to figure out the meaning.

What lies at the heart of the challenge in reading this and similar sentences? Long and densely informative noun phrases, especially noun phrases that contain one or more nominalizations. I'll explain the grammatical terms as I talk about their use.

The main ingredient of a noun phrase is a noun, often preceded by *a, an,* or *the: the involvement.* Such noun phrases can have one or more modifiers before the noun: *the markedly lower involvement.* They can have one or more modifiers after the noun: *the involvement of fathers in parenting activities.* And they can have one or more modifiers both before and after the noun: *the markedly lower involvement of fathers in parenting activities.*

Because writers can include several modifiers both before and after a noun, they can produce phrases that carry a great deal of information. Here is an example from the abstract: "Declines in fathers' involvement following a mother's relationship or parenting transition. . . ." And later in the article we read: "The lower involvement rates associated with subsequent partners and children for mothers . . . ." (120).

Further, since a long noun phrase can appear wherever a single noun can appear (for example, as the subject or the direct object of a sentence), it is possible to construct sentences that are made up almost entirely of noun phrases. Here is a slightly modified version of the first sentence in the Discussion section; in it the subject (underlined) and the direct object (underlined) are each a long noun phrase: *Transitions to subsequent partner and parental roles among unmarried parents may cause the large declines in father involvement that occur over time.*

But there is more to the story of why some sentences in this article can be challenging to understand. Many of the noun phrases contain nominalizations, and most nominalizations pack a lot of information in one word. A nominalization is a noun derived from a verb or an adjective. From the verb *involve,* for example, we have derived the nominalization *involvement.* And from the adjective *salient* we have derived *salience.*

Now consider how writers can use nominalizations to pack up a great deal of information. Without a nominalization, they could describe a situation with a series of sentences: *Sometimes unmarried people have children. In those cases, often the father participates in lots of activities with the children. But sometimes the father and mother of those children decide not to stay together. When that happens, the father and mother can both move on to new relationships. And after that happens, the father frequently does not participate in as many activities with the children.* Or those writers could pack up all this information with nominalizations in a long noun phrase: *the decline in father involvement in parenting activities after a relationship transition.*

For those who are experts in the area of studying fathers' involvement with children born out of wedlock, the noun phrase can actually be economical to use. They don't have to write all those sentences each time they want to write about these ideas; after they present the material with sentences the first time, they can use the noun phrase to refer back to it. However, we often do not write only to experts, and when we do not, we need to remember that if we use such noun phrases as *the decline in father involvement in parenting activities after a relationship transition,* we run the risk of making our readers work too hard to unpack our meaning. And we might even risk looking as if we are trying to show off. Those are risks we should be very cautious about taking.

In Your Own Writing . . .

How do you know when to use long and dense noun phrases and when to avoid them?

- Use long noun phrases when you need a shorthand way of referring to a complex idea. You might want to describe the complex idea first using sentences. After that, you can refer to the complex idea with a noun phrase.
- Use long noun phrases to refer to information that your reader already understands.
- Avoid long noun phrases when your reader is unfamiliar with the subject matter in general or the long complex idea that the noun phrase specifically refers to.
- Avoid long noun phrases when you do not know how well your reader can read. Long noun phrases pose significant challenges for weaker readers.

STUDENT WRITING

INTRODUCTION

by Joy Van Marion, sociology major

The Assignment. In my Introduction to Sociology class, our professor often encouraged us to imagine possible human social relationships. When we conducted our own sociological research, we tested one of those potential relationships with a hypothesis-driven study. Because we were amateur social science researchers, our professor gave us a list of narrow topics with well-established theoretical frameworks. I picked "acceptance of cohabitation" (basically, whether or not people approve of unmarried people in a sexual relationship living together).

The Content. Because I was also taking a political science course that semester, I was doing a lot of thinking about how people identify with a particular political party. I began to wonder if these two aspects of human society related to each other, so I decided to research how students' political views related to their views about cohabitation. This gave me an independent variable (a person's established, chosen political views) and a dependent variable (a person's views on cohabitation). To break these independent and dependent variables down further, I created categories for both variables. For example, I categorized political views as liberal, moderate, and conservative. I categorized reasons to cohabitate as economics, safety, and sex.

From there, I used surveys to gather information from a sample of college students. The survey method was ideal because the surveys didn't take long to fill out, and that left me time to interview students. Once I collected all the student surveys, my professor ran statistical tests through the computer on the data, and I discovered if my hypothesis was right.

Learning to Write in Sociology. Sociologists use the structure of their report to emphasize their objectivity. The first part of my sociology report, the abstract, provided a short summary of the whole project. Then I included my problem statement, which includes my questions and why they are important. In this section, I tried to grab the reader's interest and show why the questions I asked were good ones. Next, in the "Literature Review," I laid out my theoretical framework. I described what I had found in the scholarship on cohabitation and, in particular, how people's political perspectives relate to their views on cohabitation. In this way, I fit my research into a bigger scholarly conversation on the subject.

In "Research Design," I show the reader how I tested my hypothesis—with a survey. A section of my report called "Sampling and Data Collection" describes the characteristics of the people we studied and the strengths and weaknesses of my research design. In the "Data Analysis" (results) section I used tables to show the relationship between my independent variables and dependent variables. For social scientists, tables are like pictures in a story; they present everything at a glance. In my conclusion, I described what I had learned and what my study can offer to other scholars.

[This student essay follows APA guidelines for formatting and documentation.]

The Politics of Cohabitation
Joy Van Marion

Abstract

The purpose of this research project is to survey a sample of the student body at a small, Midwestern college to determine their views on cohabitation. Students were given the opportunity to relay personal information such as political identification and opinions on cohabitation. The data were then reviewed and patterns noted. The following paper specifically analyzes survey data regarding students' political associations and their feelings about cohabitation.

Problem Statement

The problem statement explains the need or purpose for the study, offering some background context, and sparking interest in the subject.

Cohabitation is reshaping the structure of family life and society on the whole. Statistics show that this specific relationship is on the rise. In 1970, 523 thousand American couples cohabitated. In 1993 that number rose to 3.5 million (Wilhelm, 1998). Two questions might be

I learned the importance of proper citation to verify statistics and give the author credit. Many of the social sciences use the American Psychological Association's formatting method (APA) to cite sources, and that is what was required for this course.

asked: "For what reasons do people choose to cohabitate?" and "How do their political views correlate to their willingness to cohabitate?" To answer these questions, researchers must explore the reasons people choose to cohabitate rather than form another relationship such as marriage. Furthermore, they must study the attitudes that members of American society hold toward the social practice of cohabitation. This study attends to possible connections between people's political views and their attitudes toward the practice of cohabitation. By researching the relationship between people's political stances and their acceptance of cohabitation, we may start to better understand people's attitudes toward cohabitation.

Literature Review

The literature review explores what other studies have been done on and/or relate to your research subject. This helps you decide where your study fits into the research, what it might verify or disprove that other studies have already looked at, or what it might accomplish that other studies have not yet set out to do. The literature review is therefore the theoretical foundation for my research design.

Cohabitation is a popular and growing development in social relationships across the United States. Cohabitation in this study specifically refers to a mutual relationship of emotional and/or physical intimacy between two members of the opposite sex who, though not married, share the same residency. This social relationship appeals to heterosexual couples for economic, safety, and physical reasons. Yet cohabitation remains controversial, as evidenced by two articles on this topic that appeared in magazines for the general public.

According to Carin Gorrell, "about half of American couples today live together before marrying" (2000, p. 16). In her article Gorrell describes the relationships of couples who cohabitate prior to marriage and those who do not. Gorrell summarizes a study by Catherine Cohan, Ph.D., to suggest that couples who cohabitate before marriage face more difficulties in marriage than those who don't. According to Cohan's research, cohabitating couples do not problem-solve or communicate as well as other couples (as cited in Gorrell, 2000). Cohan speculates that perhaps the people who choose to cohabit before marriage have weak communication skills prior to cohabitation, and thus their weaker communication skills are not a result of cohabitation. Cohan also suggests that possibly the lack of commitment in a cohabitating relationship weakens a couple's investment in the relationship and diminishes their attempts to improve their communication patterns (2000). Gorrell's attitude toward cohabitation become clear when she concludes with this statement from Cohan: "There is no evidence that living together before marriage benefits couples" (as cited in Gorrell, 2000, p. 16).

On the other hand, Gunnell argues in favor of cohabitation, claiming that individuals should not be required to limit themselves to marital relationships alone. Furthermore, according to Gunnell, social relationships like cohabitation will evolve to meet society's needs; since social relationships evolve, people should be free to live and love as they like. While Gunnell expresses concern that the children resulting from male/female relationships are cared for in a healthy environment, she argues that all other decisions regarding the characteristics of the relationship should be left to the adults involved (Gunnell, 2000).

These two views appear to suggest a population divided over cohabitation. Lye and Waldron (1997) offer four main hypotheses as to why people hold the beliefs that they do about cohabitating. First, they offer the Consumerism Hypothesis that focuses on people's lifetime goals as a factor that shapes their attitudes about cohabitation. According to this hypothesis, "high aspirations for material goods and living standards contributes to non-traditional family and gender role behavior and attitudes" (p. 201). In other words, people who want to prosper financially would tend to cohabitate and would, as a result, have positive attitudes regarding cohabitation.

> Hypotheses mark the research method of many social sciences. It all begins with potential answers to a question about human society.

Second, Lye and Waldron (1997) describe the Higher Order Needs Hypothesis. This hypothesis focuses on a pattern of human reasoning as the source for people's attitudes toward the social practice of cohabitation. This hypothesis suggests that people's desire for "personal fulfillment, self-actualization and individual autonomy" (p. 201) could cause them to choose a type of relationship (such as cohabitation) that satisfies their sexual needs but does not limit their personal freedom. Thus, the hypothesis predicts that people who focus more intensely on their personal needs and goals are more likely to cohabitate and, in turn, to accept cohabitation as an acceptable (perhaps even preferable) social practice.

Next, Lye and Waldron describe the Political Ideology Hypothesis. This hypothesis proposes a correlation between people's political views and their acceptance or rejection of cohabitation as a social practice. The hypothesis suggests that people who hold liberal views about political issues would be inclined to approve of cohabitation. People who hold more conservative views about political issues would be negatively disposed toward this relationship.

Fourth, Lye and Waldron discuss the Social Concerns Hypothesis. This explanation suggests that a combination of "traditional" and "non-traditional" views shape a person's social interactions, and consequently, their attitudes toward cohabitation.

Interestingly, the results of Lye and Waldron's research most closely supported the Political Ideology Hypothesis. Their research seems to suggest that people's political beliefs strongly correlate to their attitudes regarding cohabitation (Lye and Waldron, 1997). Wilhelm (1998) offers supporting data for the relationship between people's political beliefs and their attitudes toward cohabitation. She concludes, "Participation in left-oriented activism strongly affects the likelihood of cohabitation" (p. 310).

For college students in particular, three central factors seem to influence their attitudes toward cohabitation. Knox (1999) outlines these: age, hedonistic sexual values, and interracial dating experiences. He argues that the evidence suggests those students who are older, believe in hedonist practices, and do or would date people of different ethnicities are more likely to enter a cohabitating relationship (Knox, 1999).

In the following report, cohabitation will be studied from the perspective of students enrolled in a small, Midwestern college. The data that were collected for this study are meant to confirm the young adult's attitude toward cohabitation and determine who favors it, who objects to it, and whether the political views of the individual correlates with her or his attitude toward cohabitation.

Hypothesis

> This section on my hypothesis is where I get to make a statement about what I think the answers to my questions will be, where I put my theory to the test.

There is a significant correlation between an individual's political views and his/her stance on cohabitation. People who hold conservative political views are more likely to disapprove of cohabitation. Persons who have liberal political ideologies are more likely to approve of cohabitation. People with "middle-of-the-road" political ideologies are more likely to approve of cohabitation in some circumstances and disapprove of it in others. The independent variable is the political identity of each individual. The dependent variable is the individual's response toward cohabitation. The assumption is that the independent variable affects the dependent variable.

Research Design

> This is my methods section.

Surveys were used to collect data on cohabitation. The advantages of this research method include its time efficiency, cost efficiency, and ability to examine a wide range of subjects. Surveys study a representative sample of the population in a relatively small amount of time (Tischler, 2000). People are asked direct questions and given the opportunity to respond in short answers. However, the answers received from the population are not always accurate. People may not be truthful in their

> Here I explain some research limitations to help the reader know how to interpret the study's findings.

responses if they are uncomfortable with the questions or feel threatened by them. Also, if the respondents misinterpret a question's meaning, their answers may not be accurate reflections of what they really think or believe. Consequently, the results will be skewed. Researchers must recognize the potential for error in a survey (Tischler, 2000).

Sampling and Data Collection

The target for study was the student body of a small, Midwestern college. The sample of subjects drawn from the population at this college included 478 students. Of the 478 respondents, 237 were males and

241 were females. The total number consisted of 143 freshmen, 143 sophomores, 101 juniors, and 91 seniors. Participants ranged from 17 years of age to 24 years of age. The population size was small enough to study carefully and large enough to monitor for results and significant patterns. The surveys were distributed to specific individuals in an attempt to gather data from an equal number of first, second, third, and fourth year students as well as an equal number of male and female students. Though the final sample of students did not match the original outline for the sample, the sample obtained is still valid for study.

Certain limitations of the sampling and data collection did occur. An equal number of first, second, third, and fourth year students were not contacted. It is important to note, too, that the actual respondents could only choose between the answers provided for them and may not have been able to provide the fullest explanations. Furthermore, participants may have been confused about the meaning of questions and been unable to provide the most accurate information. Those who answered the questions may have purposely given a false reply if they felt ashamed or were offended by a question. In short, the survey did not reach equal populations of the student body and could not extract the most honest or complete data.

> These explanations help show how the data are skewed. Later, I learned that some student subjects were confused about the definition of cohabitation. This confusion may have affected their answers.

Data Analysis

> The results section.

> Cross-tabs are statistical tests.

The cross-tabs necessary to test this hypothesis address the political views and the social views on cohabitation of 478 college students. In Table 1, the data establish a foundation of political ideologies, distinguishing between liberal, middle-of-the-road, and conservative participants. Tables 2, 3, and 4 show which respondents approved of cohabitation for economic reasons, safety reasons, and the satisfaction of sexual desires. Finally, the data in Tables 2, 3, and 4 also depict the individuals' political views next to their estimation of whether or not there is a chance that they would cohabitate before marriage.

Table 1   Frequency Count Percentage Table

	Frequency	Percent
Liberal	85	17.8
Middle-of-the-road	215	45.0
Conservative	177	36.8
No Response	2	0.4
Total	$n = 478$	100.0

n = number of respondents

Based on survey data, the 478 respondents are divided into three categories: liberal, middle-of-the-road, and conservative as shown in Table 1.

> Looking back, I think I might give a bit more of an explanation about Table 2 by summarizing the test results in words instead of relying on the table alone to illustrate the findings.

Table 2 identifies student views on cohabitation for economic reasons. Of the 85 liberal respondents, 76.5% approve of cohabitation for economic reasons and 23.5% disapprove. Of the 214 middle-of-the-road respondents, 71.5% approve of cohabitation and 28.5% disapprove. Of the 174 conservative respondents, 37.5% approved of cohabitation and 62.5% disapproved. The numbers suggest that for economic benefits the liberal students are more approving of cohabitation and the conservatives are less approving.

Table 2   Cross-Tabs Correlating Political Affiliation with Views on Cohabitation for Economic Reasons

	Yes, I agree with cohabitation for economic reasons	No, I do not agree with cohabitation for economic reasons	Total
Liberal	76.5%	23.5%	100%
Middle-of-the-road	71.5%	28.5%	100%
Conservative	37.5%	62.5%	100%

Regarding cohabitation for security purposes (Table 3), of the 85 liberal respondents, again, 76.5% agree with cohabitation and 23.5% disagree. Of the 214 middle-of-the-road respondents, 70.1% agree and 29.9% disagree. And of the 174 conservative respondents, 39.1% agree while 60.9% disagree. Here, too, there is a decreasing amount of support for cohabitation as the political status of an individual shifts from liberal to conservative.

Table 3   Cross-Tabs Correlating Political Affiliation with Views on Cohabitation for Safety Purposes

	Yes, I agree with cohabitation for safety purposes	No, I do not agree with cohabitation for safety purposes	Total
Liberal	76.5%	23.5%	100%
Middle-of-the-road	70.1%	29.9%	100%
Conservative	39.1%	60.9%	100%

In response to cohabitation for sexual desires as outlined in Table 4, 8.5% of the 85 liberal respondents approve while 91.5% disapprove. Of the 214 middle-of-the-road respondents, 2.8% approve while 97.2% disapprove. Of the 174 conservative respondents, 1.2% approve and 98.8% disapprove. In this case, too, the liberals were more supportive of cohabitation for sexual purposes than were conservatives.

Finally, respondents were asked to indicate whether there is a chance they might cohabitate before marriage, based on their personal experience. Among liberal students, 63.9% said yes and 36.1% said no. Among middle-of-the-road students, 45.1% of the middle-of-the-road respondents said yes and 54.9% said no. Among conservative students, 19.3% of the conservatives said yes while 80.7% said no.

Table 4   Cross-Tabs Correlating Political Affiliation with Views on Cohabitation to Satisfy Sexual Desires

	Yes, I agree with cohabitation to satisfy sexual desires	No, I do not agree with cohabitation to satisfy sexual desires	Total
Liberal	8.5%	91.5%	100%
Middle-of-the-road	2.8%	97.2%	100%
Conservative	1.2%	98.8%	100%

The results were as expected and the hypothesis made at the beginning of this study is supported. There appears to be a connection between people's political ideals and their views on cohabitation. The liberals strongly favored cohabitation in more circumstances than the conservatives did. Interestingly, the middle-of-the-road respondents were very supportive of cohabitation for economic or safety reasons while they were almost completely disapproving of it for sexual purposes. And overall the liberals were the most likely to cohabitate before marriage, followed by the middle-of-the-road participants, with the conservatives least likely to cohabitate of them all.

The information provided here is valid and reliable for the purposes of a research analysis in an introductory course in sociology. It evaluates a sample of the student body as they understood the questions concerning cohabitation and then reacted from personal opinion. The data are unreliable to the extent that participants may have misinterpreted questions and consequently responded incorrectly, intentionally lied, or chosen not to answer at all. The results of this survey cannot be generalized to all college student populations.

Conclusions

In summary, the findings are consistent with the original hypothesis. If these patterns are representative of the college's student body, researchers may begin making predictions about the future social relationships within this local society based on the connections drawn here between the political ideals of students and their views on cohabitation. A greater number of liberals in the community may indicate the potential for a rise in the practice of cohabitation; whereas a greater number of conservatives may suggest the potential for a decline in cohabitating relationships.

On a broader scale, political identification may be taken as an indicator of one's standing on cohabitation. Liberals tend to embrace tolerance of new and developing social relationships that appear appropriate to the present-day culture. If a relationship is financially and physically satisfying, then they tend to approve. Conservatives tend to cling to traditional family structures and reject changes to these relationships. They are strongly tied to their historical and often religious roots, which make little or no room for relationships of cohabitation.

Out of the collective knowledge base come creative and resourceful applications.

In closing, it is impossible to state from the evidence found here that an individual's political standing will confirm their position on cohabitation. However, the data strongly suggest that there is some association between political ideology and one's stand on cohabiting. The research and findings from this study form a base of empirical evidence on which to build future sociological studies.

References

Gorrell, C. (2000, Nov/Dec). Live-in and learn. *Psychology Today*, 33, 16.

Gunnell, B. (2000, Aug 28). "I do"—But not for long, thanks. *New Statesman*, 129, 13.

Knox, D. (1999, Dec). Characteristics of college students who cohabit. *College Student Journal*, 129 (4), 510–12.

Lye, D. N. and Waldron, I. (1997). Attitudes toward cohabitation, family, and gender roles: Relationships to values and political ideology. *Sociological Perspectives*, 40 (2), 199–225.

Tischler, H. L. (2001). *Introduction to sociology* (7th ed.). New York: Harcourt.

Wilhelm, B. (1998, Sept). Changes in cohabitation across cohorts: The influence of political activism. *Social Forces*, 77 (1), 289–313.

Reading Responses

1. Review the research by Lye and Waldron on page 325–326. Prior to reading Van Marion's results, which did you believe to be the most influential factor on people's attitudes toward cohabitation? Did her study change your mind? If not, why not?

2. In her review of literature, Van Marion does more than present all the scholarly research on cohabitation; she builds the theoretical framework for her own study. Analyze how Van Marion builds this framework: What research does she begin with? What research does she end with? And recommend revisions: Which additional topics should she have researched? Which topics could she have eliminated from her review of the literature?

3. Working from Lye and Waldron, Van Marion looks only for a correlation between political affiliation and attitudes toward cohabitation, not for all the causes of students' attitudes toward cohabitation. Using sociological imagination, list possible factors that account for the correlation between students' political affiliation and their attitudes toward cohabitation. Then, rank-order your list from what you suspect to be the most significant to least significant factor.

PUBLIC WRITING

INTRODUCTION

Stephanie Coontz teaches history and women's studies at Evergreen State University. She has appeared before Congress and many television audiences, and she has published several books and many scholarly articles on the history of marriage, global perspectives on marriage, and the nature of modern, Western marriages. In her writing for general audiences (as in this piece, written for the *New York Times*), Coontz encourages her readers to engage in sociological imagination by describing multiple factors that affect personal relationships like happiness in marriage. She does so to encourage her readers to follow the advice she provides in the main point of her article: that couples should invest time into maintaining their romantic relationship, even when they are busy raising children.

Even though she is writing for nonspecialists, Coontz develops a theoretical model from previous scholarship to narrow the focus of her claim. She limits her topic by identifying a cultural stereotype from long ago, describes the effect of parenting on different types of couples, and then focuses on the effects of parenting on one of those types: "collaborative couples."

Till Children Do Us Part
Stephanie Coontz

The New York Times, February 5, 2009

Half a century ago, the conventional wisdom was that having a child was the surest way to build a happy marriage. Women's magazines of that era promised that almost any marital problem could be resolved by embarking on parenthood. Once a child arrives, "we don't worry about this couple any more," an editor at *Better Homes and Gardens* enthused in 1944. "There are three in that family now. . . . Perhaps there is not much more needed in a recipe for happiness."

Over the past two decades, however, many researchers have concluded that three's a crowd when it comes to marital satisfaction. More than 25 separate studies have established that marital quality drops, often quite steeply, after the transition to parenthood. And forget the "empty nest" syndrome: when the children leave home, couples report an increase in marital happiness.

But does the arrival of children doom couples to a less satisfying marriage? Not necessarily. Two researchers at the University of California at Berkeley, Philip and Carolyn Cowan, report in a forthcoming briefing paper for the Council on Contemporary Families that most studies finding a large drop in marital quality after childbirth do not consider the very different routes that couples travel toward parenthood.

Some couples plan the conception and discuss how they want to conduct their relationship after the baby is born. Others disagree about whether or when to conceive, with one partner giving in for the sake of the relationship. And sometimes, both partners are ambivalent.

The Cowans found that the average drop in marital satisfaction was almost entirely accounted for by the couples who slid into being parents, disagreed over it or were ambivalent about it. Couples who planned or equally welcomed the conception were likely to maintain or even increase their marital satisfaction after the child was born.

Marital quality also tends to decline when parents backslide into more traditional gender roles. Once a child arrives, lack of paid parental leave often leads the wife to quit her job and the husband to work more. This produces discontent on both sides. The wife resents her husband's lack of involvement in child care and housework. The husband resents his wife's ingratitude for the long hours he works to support the family.

When the Cowans designed programs to help couples resolve these differences, they had fewer conflicts and higher marital quality. And the children did better socially and academically because their parents were happier.

But keeping a marriage vibrant is a never-ending job. Deciding together to have a child and sharing in child-rearing do not immunize a marriage. Indeed, collaborative couples can face other problems. They often embark on such an intense style of parenting that they end up paying less attention to each other.

Parents today spend much more time with their children than they did 40 years ago. The sociologists Suzanne Bianchi, John Robinson and Melissa Milkie report that married mothers in 2000 spent 20 percent more time with their children than in 1965. Married fathers spent more than twice as much time.

A study by John Sandberg and Sandra Hofferth at the University of Michigan showed that by 1997 children in two-parent families were getting six more hours a week with Mom and four more hours with Dad than in 1981. And these increases occurred even as more mothers entered the labor force.

Couples found some of these extra hours by cutting back on time spent in activities where children were not present—when they were alone as a couple, visiting with friends and kin, or involved in clubs. But in the long run, shortchanging such adult-oriented activities for the sake of the children is not good for a marriage. Indeed, the researcher

Ellen Galinsky has found that most children don't want to spend as much time with their parents as parents assume; they just want their parents to be more relaxed when they are together.

Couples need time alone to renew their relationship. They also need to sustain supportive networks of friends and family. Couples who don't, investing too much in their children and not enough in their marriage, may find that when the demands of child-rearing cease to organize their lives, they cannot recover the relationship that made them want to have children together in the first place.

As the psychologist Joshua Coleman suggests, the airline warning to put on your own oxygen mask before you place one on your child also holds true for marriage.

Reading Responses

1. Describe a family portrayed on a television show or in a movie, paying special attention to how the parents interact with the children and each other. What factors from Coontz's article are evident in the television show?

2. What is the purpose of the final line of Coontz's article? How does that line encourage the reader to engage in sociological imagination? How does that line reinforce Coontz's point?

3. Writers for general audience magazines like *Time*, *Newsweek*, or the *New Yorker* regularly include references to scholarly research. List the reasons that writers might have for including that research.

MORE WRITING IN SOCIOLOGY

INTRODUCTION

Many people are surprised by the number of poor women who become mothers when they are very young, some as early as 14 or 15. Some policy makers have proposed that fewer young women will get pregnant if these women have access to good sex education and effective birth control. Others seem to blame the girls themselves, pointing to lax morals or the breakdown of the nuclear family. Rather than rely on speculation, two professors of sociology, Kathryn Edin (Harvard Univeristy) and Maria Kefalas (St. Joseph's Univeristy), writing in a journal for sociologists, examine the sociological factors behind the number of poor, young mothers by asking two questions: Why do poor women have children when they are very young? Wouldn't it be wiser for them to wait until marriage to have children?

It might seem that previous research has already answered that last question. In the 1990s social scientists discovered a number of negative outcomes for children raised in mother-only families. Relying in part on these studies, some politicians reformed welfare in 1996 (The Personal Responsibility and Work Opportunity Reconciliation Act) and, even more to the point, politicians authorized nearly two billion dollars in 2003 to encourage welfare recipients to marry.

Edin and Kefalas find it striking that in the midst of these policy discussions the voices of young, unwed mothers—those most affected by poverty and early childbearing—are seldom heard. So they interviewed single mothers from low-income communities in Philadelphia. Edin and Kefalas focus on the answers from one of their interviewees, Jen Burke. Through rich description and Jen's own words, they paint a full picture of Jen's life as a young, poor, single mother. As readers come to understand Jen's life and perspective more fully, they are better able to imagine how Jen's social setting within a larger political and economic context, shapes the complicated choices she makes. Through this informal case study, Edin and Kefalas let readers hear Jen's story for themselves.

Unmarried with Children
Kathryn Edin and Maria Kefalas

Contexts: Understanding People in Their Social Worlds, 2005, 4(2):16–22.

Jen Burke, a white tenth-grade dropout who is 17 years old, lives with her stepmother, her sister, and her 16-month-old son in a cramped but tidy row home in Philadelphia's beleaguered Kensington neighborhood. She is broke, on welfare, and struggling to complete her GED. Wouldn't she and her son have been better off if she had finished high school, found a job, and married her son's father first?

In 1950, when Jen's grandmother came of age, only 1 in 20 American children was born to an unmarried mother. Today, that rate is 1 in 3—and they are usually born to those least likely to be able to support a child on their own. In our book, *Promises I Can Keep: Why Poor Women Put Motherhood Before Marriage,* we discuss the lives of 162 white, African American, and Puerto Rican low-income single mothers living in eight destitute neighborhoods across Philadelphia and its poorest industrial suburb, Camden. We spent five years chatting over kitchen tables and on front stoops, giving mothers like Jen the opportunity to speak to the question so many affluent Americans ask about them: Why do they have children while still young and unmarried when they will face such an uphill struggle to support them?

Romance at Lightning Speed

Jen started having sex with her 20-year-old boyfriend Rick just before her 15th birthday. A month and a half later, she was pregnant. "I didn't want to get pregnant," she claims. "*He* wanted me to get pregnant. As soon as he met me, he wanted to have a kid with me," she explains. Though Jen's college-bound suburban peers would be appalled by such a declaration, on the streets of Jen's neighborhood, it is something of a badge of honor. "All those other girls he was with, he didn't want to have a baby with any of them," Jen boasts. "I asked him, 'Why did you choose me to have a kid when you could have a kid with any one of them?' He was like, 'I want to have a kid with *you*'." Looking back, Jen says she now believes that the reason "he wanted me to have a kid that early is so that I didn't leave him."

In inner-city neighborhoods like Kensington, where child-bearing within marriage has become rare, romantic relationships like Jen and Rick's proceed at lightning speed.

A young man's avowal, "I want to have a baby by you," is often part of the courtship ritual from the beginning. This is more than idle talk, as their first child is typically conceived within a year from the time a couple begins "kicking it." Yet while poor couples'
pillow talk often revolves around dreams of shared children, the news of a pregnancy—
the first indelible sign of the huge changes to come—puts these still-new relationships
into overdrive. Suddenly, the would-be mother begins to scrutinize her mate as never
before, wondering whether he can "get himself together"—find a job, settle down, and
become a family man—in time. . . .

Most poor, unmarried mothers and fathers readily admit that bearing children while
poor and unmarried is not the ideal way to do things. Jen believes the best time to become
a mother is "after you're out of school and you got a job, at least, when you're like
21. . . . When you're ready to have kids, you should have everything ready, have your house,
have a job, so when that baby comes, the baby can have its own room." Yet given their
already limited economic prospects, the poor have little motivation to time their births as
precisely as their middle-class counterparts do. The dreams of young people like Jen and
Rick center on children at a time of life when their more affluent peers plan for college and
careers. Poor girls coming of age in the inner city value children highly, anticipate them
eagerly, and believe strongly that they are up to the job of mothering—even in difficult circumstances. Jen, for example, tells us, "People outside the neighborhood, they're like,
'You're 15! You're pregnant?' I'm like, it's not none of their business. I'm gonna be able
to take care of my kid. They have nothing to worry about." Jen says she has concluded that
"some people . . . are better at having kids at a younger age. . . . I think it's better for some
people to have kids younger."

When I Became a Mom

When we asked mothers like Jen what their lives would be like if they had not had children, we expected them to express regret over foregone opportunities for school and
careers. Instead, most believe their children "saved" them. They describe their lives as
spinning out of control before becoming pregnant—struggles with parents and peers,
"wild," risky behavior, depression, and school failure. Jen speaks to this poignantly. "I was
just real bad. I hung with a real bad crowd. I was doing pills. I was really depressed. . . . I
was drinking. That was before I was pregnant." "I think," she reflects, "if I never had a
baby or anything . . . , I would still be doing the things I was doing. I would probably still
be doing drugs. I'd probably still be drinking." Jen admits that when she first became
pregnant, she was angry that she "couldn't be out no more. Couldn't be out with my
friends. Couldn't do nothing." Now, though, she says, "I'm glad I have a son . . . because
I would still be doing all that stuff."

Children offer poor youth like Jen a compelling sense of purpose. Jen paints a before-
and-after picture of her life that was common among the mothers we interviewed.
"Before, I didn't have nobody to take care of. I didn't have nothing left to go home
for. . . . Now I have my son to take care of. I have him to go home for. . . . I don't have
to go buy weed or drugs with my money. I could buy my son stuff with my money! . . .
I have something to look up to now." Children also are a crucial source of relational intimacy, a self-made community of care. After a nasty fight with Rick, Jen recalls, "I was crying.

My son came in the room. He was hugging me. He's 16 months and he was hugging me with his little arms. He was really cute and happy, so I got happy. That's one of the good things. When you're sad, the baby's always gonna be there for you no matter what." Lately she has been thinking a lot about what her life was like back then, before the baby. "I thought about the stuff before I became a mom, what my life was like back then. I used to see pictures of me, and I would hide in every picture. This baby did so much for me. My son did a lot for me. He helped me a lot. I'm thankful that I had my baby."

Around the time of the birth, most unmarried parents claim they plan to get married eventually. Rick did not propose marriage when Jen's first child was born, but when she conceived a second time, at 17, Rick informed his dad, "It's time for me to get married. It's time for me to straighten up. This is the one I wanna be with. I had a baby with her, I'm gonna have another baby with her." Yet despite their intentions, few of these couples actually marry. Indeed, most break up well before their child enters preschool.

I'd Like to Get Married, But . . .

The sharp decline in marriage in impoverished urban areas has led some to charge that the poor have abandoned the marriage norm. Yet we found few who had given up on the idea of marriage. But like their elite counterparts, disadvantaged women set a high financial bar for marriage. For the poor, marriage has become an elusive goal—one they feel ought to be reserved for those who can support a "white picket fence" lifestyle: a mortgage on a modest row home, a car and some furniture, some savings in the bank, and enough money left over to pay for a "decent" wedding. Jen's views on marriage provide a perfect case in point. "If I was gonna get married, I would want to be married like my Aunt Nancy and my Uncle Pat. They live in the mountains. She has a job. My Uncle Pat is a state trooper; he has lots of money. They live in the [Poconos]. It's real nice out there. Her kids go to Catholic school. . . . That's the kind of life I would want to have. If I get married, I would have a life like [theirs]." She adds, "And I would wanna have a big wedding, a real nice wedding."

Unlike the women of their mothers' and grandmothers' generations, young women like Jen are not merely content to rely on a man's earnings. Instead, they insist on being economically "set" in their own right before taking marriage vows. This is partly because they want a partnership of equals, and they believe money buys say-so in a relationship. Jen explains, "I'm not gonna just get into marrying him and not have my own house! Not have a job! I still wanna do a lot of things before I get married. He [already] tells me I can't do nothing. I can't go out. What's gonna happen when I marry him? He's gonna say he owns me!"

Why is Jen, who describes Rick as "the love of my life," so insistent on planning an exit strategy before she is willing to take the vows she firmly believes ought to last "forever"? If love is so sure, why does mistrust seem so palpable and strong? In relationships among poor couples like Jen and Rick, mistrust is often spawned by chronic violence and infidelity, drug and alcohol abuse, criminal activity, and the threat of imprisonment. . . .

Trust has been an enormous issue in Jen's relationship with Rick. "My son was born December 23rd, and [Rick] started cheating on me again . . . in March. . . . " Things finally came to a head when Rick got another girl pregnant. "For a while, I forgave him for everything. Now, I don't forgive him for nothing." Now we begin to understand the source of Jen's hesitancy. "He wants me to marry him, [but] I'm not really sure. . . . If I can't trust him, I can't marry him, 'cause we would get a divorce. If you're gonna get married, you're supposed to be faithful!" she insists. To Jen and her peers, the worst thing that could happen is "to get married just to get divorced." . . .

These Are Cards I Dealt Myself

. . . Jen clearly sees how her life has improved since Rick's dramatic exit from the scene. "That's when I really started [to get better] because I didn't have to worry about what he was doing, didn't have to worry about him cheating on me, all this stuff. [It was] then I realized that I had to do what I had to do to take care of my son. . . . When he was there, I think that my whole life revolved around him, you know, so I always messed up somehow because I was so busy worrying about what he was doing. Like I would leave the [GED] programs I was in just to go home and see what he was doing. My mind was never concentrating." Now, she says, "a lot of people in my family look up to me now, because all my sisters dropped out from school, you know, nobody went back to school. I went back to school, you know? . . . I went back to school, and I plan to go to college, and a lot of people look up to me for that, you know? So that makes me happy . . . because five years ago nobody looked up to me. I was just like everybody else."

Yet the journey has not been easy. "Being a young mom being 15, it's hard, hard, hard, you know." She says, "I have no life. . . . I work from 6:30 in the morning until 5:00 at night I leave here at 5:30 in the morning. I don't get home until about 6:00 at night." Yet she measures her worth as a mother by the fact that she has managed to provide for her son largely on her own. "I don't depend on nobody. I might live with my dad and them, but I don't depend on them, you know." She continues, "There [used to] be days when I'd be so stressed out, like, 'I can't do this!' And I would just cry and cry and cry. . . . Then I look at Colin, and he'll be sleeping, and I'll just look at him and think I don't have no [reason to feel sorry for myself]. The cards I have I've dealt myself so I have to deal with it now. I'm older. I can't change anything. He's my responsibility—he's nobody else's but mine—so I have to deal with that."

Becoming a mother transformed Jen's point of view on just about everything. She says, "I thought hanging on the corner drinking, getting high—I thought that was a good life, and I thought I could live that way for eternity, like sitting out with my friends. But it's not as fun once you have your own kid. . . . I think it changes [you]. I think, 'Would I want Colin to do that? Would I want my son to be like that . . . ?' It was fun to me but it's not fun anymore. Half the people I hung with are either. . . . Some have died from drug overdoses, some are in jail, and some people are just out there living the same life that they always lived, and they don't look really good. They look really bad." In the end, Jen believes, Colin's birth has brought far more good into her life than bad. "I know I could have waited [to have a child], but in a way I think Colin's the best thing that could have happened to me. . . . So I think I had my son for a purpose because I think Colin changed my life. He saved my life, really. My whole life revolves around Colin!"

Promises I Can Keep

There are unique themes in Jen's story—most fathers are only one or two, not five years older than the mothers of their children, and few fathers have as many glaring problems as Rick—but we heard most of these themes repeatedly in the stories of the 161 other poor, single mothers we came to know. Notably, poor women do not reject marriage; they revere it. Indeed, it is the conviction that marriage is forever that makes them think that divorce is worse than having a baby outside of marriage. Their children, far from being liabilities, provide crucial social-psychological resources—a strong sense of purpose and a profound source of intimacy. Jen and the other mothers we came to know are coming of age in an America that is profoundly unequal—where the gap between rich and poor continues to grow. This economic reality has convinced them that they have little to lose and, perhaps, something to gain by a seemingly "ill-timed" birth.

The lesson one draws from stories like Jen's is quite simple: Until poor young women have more access to jobs that lead to financial independence—until there is reason to hope for the rewarding life pathways that their privileged peers pursue—the poor will continue to have children far sooner than most Americans think they should, while still deferring marriage. Marital standards have risen for all Americans, and the poor want the same things that everyone now wants out of marriage. The poor want to marry too, but they insist on marrying well. This, in their view, is the only way to avoid an almost certain divorce. Like Jen, they are simply not willing to make promises they are not sure they can keep.

Reading Responses

1. Did Edin and Kefalas offer you a new way of understanding why young, poor women have children? What surprised you most?

2. Because they use a case study methodology, the authors never state their theoretical framework explicitly. How would you describe their theoretical framework?

3. What in Jen's story most sparked your own curiosity? What aspect of Jen's story would you research in greater depth, if you had the opportunity?

WRITING ASSIGNMENTS

Assignment 1

Your task for this assignment is to create a theoretical framework for a hypothesis about a specific factor affecting marriages in the United States.

To begin, use the readings in this chapter to brainstorm about possible factors. Extend your brainstorming by researching previous scholarship (consult a reference librarian for help) to help you locate a single factor. Do additional research to identify how previous scholars have investigated this factor.

Once you have chosen the factor that you will research, free-write about your personal experience with this factor. Create one list of your own assumptions about this factor, attempting as best you can to identify your biases. Create a second list of common cultural assumptions about this factor.

Now draft a short article in which you present a common cultural assumption about the factor, a hypothesis about that factor, and a theoretical framework of research for your hypothesis.

Assignment 2

Because of the complexity of human relationships, sociologists are careful to detail their theoretical frameworks. But our focus on theoretical framework in this chapter should not imply that researchers in other disciplines do not root their research in theory; it may be that in their published work they do not make those roots as obvious as sociologists do.

Your task for this assignment is to show the theoretical roots in a piece of academic scholarship from religious studies, biotechnology, or nursing.

- "Civil Religion in America" by Robert Bellah
- "Feeding the World in the Twenty-first Century" by Gordon Conway and Gary Toenniessen (Chapter 16)
- "A Phenomenologic Study of Chronic Pain" by Sandra P. Thomas (Chapter 18)

To begin, read the piece carefully and describe as specifically as possible what it is that the researcher is curious about. You may find it helpful to formulate this as a research question or a hypothesis. Then, describe for yourself the theoretical frame for this research. You may need to do some careful analysis because the researcher may have left this somewhat or nearly completely unstated. Note the research (if any) that grounds the theoretical frame. Finally, list the conclusions that result from the research as well as the limitations of the research—both those the researcher notes and additional limitations that you note.

In the first part of your report, describe what serves as an equivalent for the sociological imagination—the focus of the researcher's curiosity and the researcher's main point. In the second part of your report, describe the theoretical framework that supports the researcher's point. Then evaluate the researcher's use of that theoretical framework, noting how the researcher helps and hinders the reader's understanding of the main point.

Assignment 3

This assignment requires you to engage your sociological imagination as Joy Van Marion did when she researched attitudes regarding cohabitation. Your task for this assignment is to report on a sociological study that you have conducted, paying special attention to the relationship between your theoretical model and your hypothesis. If your teacher allows it, consider collaborating with a partner on this project.

To begin, propose a list of possible answers to the following question: What sociological factors correspond to a person's ideas about the ideal relationship of parents to children? Once you have isolated one or two factors that you suspect to be especially important, do some library research to build a theoretical model for your study. The most efficient way to conduct this research is to ask for help from a reference librarian.

As you review this research, pay attention to research studies that relate to each other, noting studies that build on other research as well as those that contradict the findings of previous research. As you describe your theoretical model in your research report, be sure to help your reader see these relationships. Cite your sources in APA style.

Choose one of the sociological factors you researched, and draft a hypothesis about the relationship between this factor and people's ideas about ideal parents. Simplify your hypothesis as much as possible, and be sure that you will be able to gather information about your hypothesis through a simple methodology. Design a methodology to test your hypothesis, conduct your study, and analyze the results.

In your report, describe the theoretical model that supports your hypothesis, your methodology, and your results. When you discuss your results, be sure to (1) show the relationship between your study and those that comprise your theoretical model, (2) note the limitations of your study, and (3) describe future research that could provide more information about your hypothesis.

POLITICAL SCIENCE

Where do you draw the line?

Ever heard of Koguryo? Most Americans haven't, but most people in China and South Korea have. Some of the territory that was once ancient Koguryo is now in China; the rest is in North Korea. According to Korean history, Koguryo was one of the three ancient kingdoms of Korea and the site of a famous battle. Thus, modern Koreans claim this ancient region and its history as their own. But China claims it, too. The Chinese *English People's Daily Online* describes Koguryo as "the ancient Koguryo Kingdom of China" and quotes the Chinese scholar Wei Cuncheng: "Koguryo was a regime established by ethnic groups in northern China some 2,000 years ago, representing an important part of Chinese culture."*

But this is ancient history. Why are the Chinese or Koreans passionate about it now? Two reasons: first, tombs in the region are now World Heritage sites. Prestige and tourism dollars are sure to follow. Second, some experts in international politics speculate that China is looking to the future. If North and South Korea ever re-unify, Koreans might claim the ancient Koguryo territory for this new, powerful Korea.

- If you were Korean, what types of evidence could you use to claim Koguryo as a part of your national history? Create a list of at least five different types of evidence, ordering the list from most persuasive type of evidence at the top to least effective evidence at the bottom. You might find it helpful to do an Internet search on the word "Koguryo" to see what kinds of evidence political scientists have used.

*"China's ancient Koguryo Kingdom site added to World heritage List," http://english.peopledaily.com.cn/200407/01/eng20040701_148209.html

PORTABLE RHETORICAL LESSON: BUILDING CREDIBILITY AS AN AUTHOR

As you worked through the Koguryo exercise, you did two things that acquainted you with primary rhetorical experiences of writers in political science. First, you conducted **research** to find **evidence.** When writing about international politics, the experts do thorough research, and they cite that research frequently. The first reading in this chapter, for example, contains a staggering 150 citations. Even the student writing in this chapter uses 29 footnotes in an essay of less than 3,000 words—pretty impressive.

Why would you do such thorough research? The second part of your experience in the Koguryo exercise suggests an explanation.

You imagined being a Korean, arguing that part of your ancient land should be restored to you. In that context, your research was deeply important to your personal sense of national pride and patriotism. And if you had the time to carry on through research into publication, what you wrote might help your country make decisions about exerting political pressure or maybe even going to war to regain your land. It is the sense of potential consequences that creates such strong personal commitment—and that makes people who write about international politics deeply aware of the second Key Rhetorical Concept: their role as an **author.**

If you hope to inspire readers to take action because you believe that values such as equality, economic stability, or justice are at stake, your arguments will breathe with passion for the topic. You see that zeal, for example, in some of the language choices of the authors in this chapter. Christopher Layne, in the first reading, describes "democratic peace theory" (which he argues against) as a "myth" in his title and as "wishful thinking" in his conclusion. And James King, the chapter's student writer, takes an impassioned stand, using language such as: "the economic depravity of Israel's Arab population" and "The popular opinion of Jews in Israel regarding their fellow Arab citizens . . . shows an obvious lack of democratic value. . . ."

When writers combine an arsenal of knowledge about their subject with personal commitment to and understanding of the potentially world-changing consequences of international political actions, they achieve this chapter's **Portable Rhetorical Lesson:** a credible authorial voice. You can improve your credibility as an author by

1. Convincing your audience that you know what you're talking about, and
2. Demonstrating that what you're talking about is important.

To achieve those two goals,

1. Do enough research so that you really do know what you're talking about (confident enough even to discuss what your opponents believe), and
2. Write about topics that you really believe are important.

The readings in this chapter provide models that help you to see how you can make use of these rhetorical skills of political scientists in your own writing.

WRITING IN THE DISCIPLINE

INTRODUCTION

by Simona Goi,
Professor of Political Science

Generally speaking, political scientists write to accomplish three goals: to explain why something happened in the past, to predict what might happen in the future, or to influence/change what might happen in the future. Christopher Layne's essay explicitly addresses the first goal, but he does so because he hopes to lead people to see how to accomplish the other two: if we understand why some states chose not to go to war, we might be able to prevent war in the future. This is a source of the passion that drives Layne's research. In this light, we can see that Layne is motivated not just by academic interest, but also by a belief that what he writes can help prevent future wars.

Layne is an international relations theorist who is a professor at Texas A&M. His article reproduced here, one of the truly influential pieces of his distinguished career, is part of the scholarly research on the relationship between a country's type of government and that country's willingness to go to war. Political analysts have noted that democracies do not normally fight other democracies, even though they *do* go to war against nondemocratic states. But *why* won't democracies go to war with other democracies? Are democratic governments inherently more moral than their nondemocratic counterparts, and therefore less likely to use war to accomplish political ends? Or do democratic governments listen more carefully to their citizens who hope to avoid the human and financial costs of a war? One answer to these research questions is "democratic peace theory," the dominant theory regarding the relationships between democratic states. Layne addresses the topic in two ways: first, he summarizes scholarly explanations for why democratic states do not go to war against other democratic states, and then he tests those explanations against an alternative hypothesis that he proposes.

Layne's essay is an excellent example of how political scientists develop complex logical arguments. First, Layne introduces the topic and notes its importance. Democratic peace theory is important, according to Layne, because it shapes American foreign policy in crucial ways: American politicians "who have embraced democratic peace theory see a crucial link between America's security and the spread of democracy" (220). Next he reviews two prominent versions of democratic peace theory, and he introduces a competing theory to explain how nations get along with each other: a theory that he calls "realism." Then, Layne tests democratic peace theory and realism by applying them to case studies of historical events with known outcomes. Using four historical conflicts (only one appears in this abridged version of his essay) as case studies, Layne analyzes how well democratic peace theory and realism each explain the actions of these combating democratic states. Layne concludes that democratic peace theory cannot account for the historical evidence. Instead, realism better explains why these democratic countries avoided war with each other.

When political scientists write, they make good use of the passion that propels them to choose a particular research topic and sustains them through the hard work of collecting and analyzing large amounts of historical and analytical evidence. They write knowing that other scholars, using different evidence or a different method for analyzing the evidence, will likely come to different conclusions. Their various explanations compete with one another. In fact, the same journal issue in which Layne's article appears includes an article entitled "How Liberalism Produces Democratic Peace." It analyzes the same historical period that Layne does, but looks at it from a different perspective and produces different conclusions. But both writers try to convince others to see this topic as they do because they believe that their research will improve the chances for peace in the world.

✓ Reading Tips

Because the writing of political scientists is often long and complex, you'll read more efficiently if you map out the logical progression of ideas. So,

1. List the features of both "democratic peace theory" and "realism."

2. Match those features to the historical events that Layne describes in the Trent affair.

3. Find the three ways that Layne states the point of his essay:
   - Thesis statement (which recognizes that his point is arguable)
   - Hypothesis (which Layne tests by analyzing case studies)
   - Recommendations (which outline ways Layne wants readers to respond)

Compare and combine the different expressions of the point to help you understand what's most important to Layne.

Finally, this essay is very complex. To follow the argument, highlight key ideas, jot down notes in the margins, and refer back to the headings of each section as you read the section. Note how each individual paragraph contributes to the core idea identified by the heading.

> Democratic peace theory is based on the philosophy of Immanuel Kant. The title lets you know that Layne doesn't believe in the theory.

Kant or Cant:
The Myth of the Democratic Peace

Christopher Layne

International Security, 1994 19(2): 5–49

Policymakers who have embraced democratic peace theory[1] see a crucial link between America's security and the spread of democracy, which is viewed as the antidote that will prevent future wars. . . . Because of its theoretical claims and policy implications, the democratic peace theory merits careful examination.[3] In this article, I focus primarily on a critique of the persuasiveness of democratic peace theory's causal logic and ask whether democratic peace theory or realism is a better predictor of international outcomes. I then briefly assess the robustness of democratic peace theory's empirical evidence in light of my conclusions about the strength of its explanatory power.

I begin by reviewing the explanations of the Democratic Peace advanced by democratic peace theorists. There are two strands to the theory's causal logic. One attributes the absence of war between democracies to institutional constraints: the restraining effects of public opinion, or of the checks and balances embedded in a democratic state's domestic political structure. The other posits that it is democratic norms and culture—a shared commitment to the peaceful adjudication of political disputes—that accounts for the absence of war between democratic states. As I demonstrate, the institutional-constraints argument fails to provide a compelling explanation for the absence of war between democracies. Thus, democratic peace theory's explanatory power rests on the persuasiveness of the contention that democratic norms and culture explain why, although democratic states fight with non-democracies, they do not go to war with each other.

This article's centerpiece is a test of the competing explanations of international outcomes offered by democratic peace theory and by realism. This test is based on case studies of four "near misses"—crises where two democratic states almost went to war with each other. These four cases are well-documented instances of democratic great powers going to the brink of war without going over it. As such, they present an opportunity to determine which of the competing hypotheses advanced respectively by democratic peace theory and realism best account for international political outcome. . . .

I conclude that realism is superior to democratic peace theory as a predictor of international outcomes. Indeed, democratic peace theory appears to have extremely little explanatory power in the cases studied. Doubts about the validity of its causal logic suggest that the empirical evidence purporting to support democratic peace theory should also be revisited. Democratic peace theorists contend that the theory is validated by a large number of cases. However, a powerful argument can be made that the universe of cases from which it can be tested is actually quite small. This is a crucial issue, because if the theory's empirical support is based on a small-N universe, this magnifies the importance of possible exceptions to the rule that democracies do not fight each other (for example, World War I, the War between the States, the War of 1812). I conclude by discussing democratic peace theory's troublesome implications for post–Cold War American foreign policy.

The Case for a Democratic Peace: Its Claims and Its Logic

Democratic peace theory does not contend that democratic states are less war-prone than non-democracies; they are not. The theory does,

---

Sidebar annotations:

In the first four paragraphs, Layne summarizes his entire article. Because this is a summary, these paragraphs are difficult to read. Consider rereading these four paragraphs after you finish the entire essay.

Layne states his reason for writing—to test which theory better predicts known, historical outcomes.

In an article as long and complex as this, it is a rhetorical advantage for Layne to be bold and up-front about his point.

A small N means that there are very few cases to study. With too few numbers a statistical study may yield questionable results. So Layne chooses a "case-study" method, looking very closely at a small number of key cases.

however, make two important claims, first, that democracies never (or rarely; there is a good deal of variation about this) go to war with other democracies.[5] As Jack S. Levy observes, the "absence of war between democracies comes as close as anything we have to an empirical law in international relations."[6] Second, when democracies come into conflict with one another, they only rarely threaten to use force, because it is "illegitimate" to do so. Democratic peace theory explicitly holds that it is the very nature of democratic political systems that accounts for the fact that democracies do not fight or threaten other democracies.

> An empirical law is a law that all observable evidence supports—like the law of gravity.

The Causal Logic

> Causal logic refers to the relationship between an event, its causes, and its effects.

Democratic peace theory must explain an anomaly: democracies are no less war-prone than non-democratic states. Yet, while they will readily threaten and fight non-democracies, they do not threaten or fight other democracies. The key challenge for the theory, then, is to identify the special characteristics of democratic states that restrain them from using coercive threats against, or actually going to war with, other democracies. The theory advances two alternative explanations: 1) institutional constraints; and 2) democratic norms and cultures.[8]

There are two major variants of the institutional constraints argument. Michael Doyle, building on Immanuel Kant, explains that democratic governments are reluctant to go to war because they must answer to their citizens.[9] Citizens pay the price for war in blood and treasure; if the price of conflict is high, democratic governments may fall victim to electoral retribution. Moreover, in democratic states, foreign policy decisions carrying the risk of war are debated openly and not made behind closed doors, which means that both the public and policymakers are sensitized to costs of fighting. A second version of the institutional constraints argument focuses on "checks and balances"; it looks at three specific features of a state's domestic political structure: executive selection, political competition, and the pluralism of the foreign policy decision making process.[10] States with executives answerable to a selection body, with institutionalized political competition, and with decision making responsibility spread among multiple institutions or individuals, should be more highly constrained and hence less likely to go to war.

> The U.S. fits this description: the president is elected by the people, we have political parties that compete with each other, and the power of the government is distributed among three branches: the executive, the legislative, and the judicial.

> In other words, the same things that promote peace within a country will promote peace between that country and others.

The democratic norms explanation holds that "the *culture, perceptions, and practices* that permit compromise and the peaceful resolution of conflicts without the threat of violence *within countries* come to apply across national boundaries toward other democratic countries."[11] Democratic states assume both that other democracies also subscribe to pacific methods of regulating political competition and resolving disputes, and that others will apply these norms in their external relations with fellow democracies. In other words, democratic states develop positive perceptions of other democracies. Consequently, Doyle says, democracies, "which rest on consent, presume foreign republics to be also consensual, just and therefore deserving of accommodation."[12] Relations between democratic states are based on mutual respect rooted in the fact that democracies perceive each other as dovish (that is, negotiation or the status quo are the only possible outcomes in a dispute). This perception, it is argued, is based on a form of learning. Democratic states benefit from cooperative relations with one another and they want to expand their positive interactions. In turn, this desire predisposes them to be responsive to the needs of other democratic states, and ultimately leads to creation of a community of interests. As democracies move towards community, they renounce the option to use (or even to threaten to use) force in their mutual interactions.[13]

The democratic ethos—based on "peaceful competition, persuasion and compromise"—explains the absence of war and war-like threats in relations between democratic states.[14] Conversely, the absence of these norms in relations between democracies and non-democracies, it is said, explains the paradox that democracies do not fight each other even though in general they are as war-prone as non-democracies: "When a democracy comes into conflict with a nondemocracy, it will not expect the nondemocratic state to be restrained by those norms [of mutual respect based on democratic culture]. It may feel obliged to adapt to the harsher norms of international conduct of the latter, lest it be exploited or eliminated by the nondemocratic state that takes advantage of the inherent moderation of democracies."[15] Thus it is a fundamental postulate of democratic peace theory that democracies behave in a qualitatively different manner in their relations with each other than they do in their relations with non-democracies.

The Realist Case: The Same Things Over and Over Again

In this section, Layne describes realism, an alternative way of explaining how countries get along with each other.

If history is "just one damn thing after another," then for realists international politics is the same damn things over and over again: war, great power security and economic competitions, the rise and fall of great powers, and the formation and dissolution of alliances. International political behavior is characterized by continuity, regularity, and repetition because states are constrained by the international system's unchanging (and probably unchangeable) structure.

The realist paradigm explains why this is so.[16] International politics is an anarchic, self-help realm. "Anarchy," rather than denoting chaos or rampant disorder, refers in international politics to the fact that there is no central authority capable of making and enforcing rules of behavior on the international system's units (states). The absence of a rule-making and enforcing authority means that each unit in the system is responsible for ensuring its own survival and also that each is free to define its own interests and to employ means of its own choice in pursuing them. In this sense, international politics is fundamentally competitive. And it is competitive in a manner that differs crucially from domestic politics in liberal societies, where the losers can accept an adverse outcome because they live to fight another day and can, therefore, ultimately hope to prevail. In international politics, states that come out on the short end of political competition face potentially more extreme outcomes, ranging from constraints on autonomy to occupation to extinction.

> In other words, if a politician loses one battle, she can regroup and try again. If a country loses a battle to another country, it is less likely to remain autonomous.

It is anarchy that gives international politics its distinctive flavor. In an anarchic system, a state's first goal is to survive. To attain security, states engage in both internal and external balancing for the purpose of deterring aggressors, and of defeating them should deterrence fail. In a realist world, cooperation is possible but is hard to sustain in the face of the competitive pressures that are built into the international political system's structure. The imperative of survival in a threatening environment forces states to focus on strategies that maximize their power relative to their rivals. States have powerful incentives both to seek the upper hand over their rivals militarily and to use their edge not only for self-defense but also to take advantage of others. . . .

In the international system, fear and distrust of other states is the normal state of affairs. . . .

Testing Democratic Peace Theory

Institutional constraints do not explain the democratic peace. If democratic public opinion really had the effect ascribed to it, democracies would be peaceful in their relations with all states, whether democratic or not. If citizens and policymakers of a democracy were especially sensitive to the human and material costs of war, that sensitivity should be evident whenever their state is on the verge of war, regardless of whether the adversary is democratic: the lives lost and money spent will be the same. Nor is democratic public opinion, *per se*, an inhibitor of war. For example, in 1898 it was public opinion that impelled the reluctant McKinley administration into war with Spain; in 1914 war was enthusiastically embraced by public opinion in Britain and France. Domestic political structure—"checks and balances"—does not explain the democratic peace either. "This argument," as Morgan and Schwebach state, "does not say anything directly about the war-proneness of democracies," because it focuses on an independent variable—decisional constraints embedded in a state's domestic political structure—that is associated with, but not exclusive to, democracies.

> "Institutional constraints" explanations

> Now Layne takes on the second claim of democratic peace theory: norms and culture.

Because these explanations fall short, the democratic norms and culture explanation must bear the weight of the democratic peace theory's causal logic. It is there we must look to find that "something in the internal makeup of democratic states" that explains the democratic peace.[18]

Democratic peace theory not only predicts a specific outcome—no war between democracies—but also purports to explain why that outcome will occur. It is thus suited to being tested by the case study method, a detailed look at a small number of examples to determine if events unfold and actors act as the theory predicts. The case study method also affords the opportunity to test the competing explanations of international political outcomes offered by democratic peace theory and by realism. To test the robustness of democratic peace theory's causal logic, the focus here is on "near misses," specific cases in which democratic states had both opportunity and reason to fight each other, but did not. . . .

Democratic peace theory, if valid, should account powerfully for the fact that serious crises between democratic states ended in near misses rather than in war. If democratic norms and culture explain the democratic peace, in a near-war crisis, certain indicators of the democratic peace theory should be in evidence: First, public opinion should be strongly pacific. Public opinion is important not because it is an institutional constraint, but because it is an indirect measure of the mutual respect that democracies are said to have for each other. Second, policymaking elites should refrain from making military threats against other democracies and should refrain from making preparations to carry out threats. Democratic peace theorists waffle on this point by suggesting that the absence of war between democracies is more important than the absence of threats. But this sets the threshold of proof too low. Because the crux of the theory is that democracies externalize their internal norms of peaceful dispute resolution, then especially in a crisis, one should not see democracies threatening other democracies. And if threats are made, they should be a last-resort option rather than an early one. Third, democracies should bend over backwards to accommodate each other in a crisis. Ultimata, unbending hard lines, and big-stick diplomacy are the stuff of Realpolitik, not the democratic peace.

A realist explanation of near misses would look at a very different set of indicators. First, realism postulates a ratio of national interest to democratic respect: in a crisis, the more important the interests a democracy perceives to be at stake, the more likely that its policy will be shaped by realist imperatives rather than by democratic norms and culture. When vital interests are on the line, democracies should not be inhibited from using threats, ultimata, and big-stick diplomacy against another democracy. Second, even in a crisis involving democracies, states should be very attentive to strategic concerns, and the relative distribution of military capabilities between them should crucially—perhaps decisively—affect their diplomacy. Third, broader geopolitical

> Social scientists, like natural scientists, always identify their methods for testing their hypotheses.

> "Ultimata" is the plural of "ultimatum"—an all-or-nothing demand that offers no room for negotiation. In "big-stick diplomacy," a country threatens to use its superior military power as a way to coerce another country to do something. *Realpolitik* focuses on self-interest and what is practical over what is moral.

considerations pertaining to a state's position in international politics should, if implicated, account significantly for the crisis's outcome. Key here is what Geoffrey Blainey calls the "fighting waterbirds' dilemma," involving concerns that others watching from the sidelines will take advantage of a state's involvement in war; that war will leave a state weakened and in an inferior relative power position vis-a-vis possible future rivals; and that failure to propitiate the opposing state in a crisis will cause it to ally with one's other adversaries or rivals.[21]

> Because of space limitations, we have included only the first case study.

I have chosen to study four modern historical instances in which democratic great powers almost came to blows: 1) the United States and Great Britain in 1861 ("the Trent affair"); 2) the United States and Great Britain in 1895–96 (the Venezuela crisis); 3) France and Great Britain in 1898 (the Fashoda crisis); and 4) France and Germany in 1923 (the Ruhr crisis).[22]

Anglo-American Crisis I: The *Trent* Affair, 1861

> The Civil War. A rhetorical advantage of the case-study method is that people like to read stories. Beginning this story in the context of what may be America's most captivating story—the Civil War—is smart rhetoric.

In 1861, tensions arising from the War Between the States brought the Union and Britain to the brink of war. The most important causes of Anglo-American friction stemmed from the Northern blockade of Confederate ports and the consequent loss to Britain of the cotton upon which its textile industry depended. The immediate precipitating cause of the Anglo-American crisis, however, was action of the USS *San Jacinto* which, acting without express orders from Washington, intercepted the British mail ship *Trent* on November 8, 1861. The *Trent* was transporting James M. Mason and John Slidell, the Confederacy's commissioners-designate to Great Britain and France; they had boarded the *Trent,* a neutral vessel, in Havana, Cuba, a neutral port. A boarding party from the *San Jacinto,* after searching the *Trent,* placed Mason and Slidell under arrest. The *Trent* was allowed to complete its voyage while the *San Jacinto* transported Mason and Slidell to Fort Warren in Boston harbor, where they were incarcerated.

When word was received in Britain, the public was overcome with war fever. "The first explosion of the Press, on receipt of the news of the *Trent,* had been a terrific one."[28] An American citizen residing in England reported to Secretary of State William H. Seward, "The people are frantic with rage, and were the country polled I fear 999 men out of 1000 would declare for war."[29] From Edinburgh, another American wrote, "I have never seen so intense a feeling of indignation in my life."[30]

The British government was hardly less bellicose than the public and the press. Fortified by legal opinions holding that Mason and Slidell had been removed from the *Trent* in contravention of international law, the Cabinet adopted a hard-line policy that mirrored the public mood. Prime Minister Lord Palmerston's first reaction to the news of the

Trent incident was to write to the Secretary of State for War that, because of Britain's "precarious" relations with the United States, the government reconsider cuts in military expenditures planned to take effect in 1862.[31] At the November 29 Cabinet meeting, Palmerston reportedly began by flinging his hat on the table and declaring to his colleagues, "I don't know whether you are going to stand this, but I'll be damned if I do!"[32]

The Cabinet adopted a dual-track approach towards Washington: London used military threats to coerce the United States into surrendering diplomatically, while on the diplomatic side, Foreign Secretary Lord John Russell drafted a note to the Union government in which, while holding firm to the demand that Mason and Slidell be released, he offered Washington an avenue of graceful retreat by indicating that London would accept, as tantamount to an apology, a declaration that the *San Jacinto* had acted without official sanction. Nevertheless, the note that was actually transmitted to Washington was an ultimatum. Although the British minister in Washington, Lord Lyons, was instructed to present the communication in a fashion calculated to maximize the chances of American compliance, his charge was clear: unless within seven days of receipt the Union government unconditionally accepted Britain's demands, Lyons was to ask for his passports and depart the United States. As Russell wrote to Lyons: "What we want is a plain Yes or a plain No to our very simple demands, and we want that plain Yes or No within seven days of the communication of the despatch."[33]

Although some, notably including Russell, hoped that the crisis could be resolved peacefully, the entire Cabinet recognized that its decision to present an ultimatum to Washington could lead to war. The British believed that there was one hope for peace: that Washington, overawed by Britain's military power and its readiness to go to war, would bow to London's demands rather than resisting them.[34] As the Undersecretary of State for Foreign Affairs stated, "Our only chance of peace is to be found in working on the fears of the Government and people of the United States."[35]

Driven by the belief that Washington would give in only to the threat of force, London's diplomacy was backed up by ostentatious military and naval preparations. Anticipating a possible conflict, the Cabinet embargoed the export to the United States of saltpeter (November 30) and of arms and ammunition (December 4). Underscoring the gravity of the crisis, for only the fourth time in history the Cabinet created a special war committee to oversee strategic planning and war preparations. Urgent steps were taken to reinforce Britain's naval and military contingents in North America. Beginning in mid-December, a hastily organized sealift increased the number of

an ingredient in gunpowder

regular British army troops in Canada from 5,000 to 17,658, and Royal Navy forces in North American waters swelled from 25 to forty warships, with 1,273 guns (compared to just 500 before the crisis).[36] These measures served two purposes: they bolstered London's diplomacy and, in the event diplomacy failed, they positioned Britain to prevail in a conflict.

London employed big-stick diplomacy because it believed that a too-conciliatory policy would simply embolden the Americans to mount increasingly serious challenges to British interests.[37] Moreover, British policymakers believed that England's resolve, credibility, and reputation were at stake internationally, not just in its relations with the United States. The comments of once and future Foreign Secretary Lord Clarendon were typical: a figure . . . we shall cut in the eyes of the world, if we lamely submit to this outrage when all mankind will know that we should unhesitatingly have poured our indignation and our broadsides into any weak nation . . . and what an additional proof it will be of the universal . . . belief that we have two sets of weights and measures to be used according to the power or weakness of our adversary."[38] Thus "the British were prepared to accept the cost of an Anglo-American war . . . rather than sacrifice their prestige as a great power by headlong diplomatic defeat."[39]

London's hard-line policy was fortified by its "general optimism about the ultimate outcome" of an Anglo-American war.[40] Queen Victoria said a war would result in "utter destruction to the North Americans" and Secretary of State for War George Cornewall Lewis said "we shall soon iron the smile out of their face."[41] Palmerston was therefore untroubled by the discomfiture imposed on the Union by London's uncompromising policy. In his view, regardless of whether the crisis was resolved peacefully or resulted in war, Britain's interests would be upheld. He wrote to Queen Victoria:

If the Federal Government comply with the demands it will be honorable to England and humiliating to the United States. If the Federal Government refuse compliance, Great Britain is in a better state than at any former time to inflict a severe blow upon, and to read a lesson to the United States which will not soon be forgotten.[42]

In late 1861, the war against the Confederacy was not going well for Washington and the one major engagement, the first Battle of Manassas, had resulted in a humiliating setback for the Union army. Whipped up by Secretary of State Seward, who was a master at "twisting the lion's tail" for maximum domestic political effect, Northern opinion was hostile in London and resented especially Queen Victoria's May 1861 neutrality proclamation, which Northerners interpreted as *de facto* British recognition of Southern independence. News of the seizure of Mason

(in actual fact)

and Slidell had a double effect on Northern public opinion. First, it was a tonic for sagging Northern morale. Second, it was seen as a warning to Britain to refrain from interfering with the Union's prosecution of the war against the Confederacy. Thus, although some papers (notably the *New York Times* and the *New York Daily Tribune*) urged that Washington should placate the British, public opinion strongly favored a policy of standing up to London and refusing to release Mason and Slidell.[43] In response to Britain's hard line, "a raging war cry reverberated across the Northern states in America."[44] Charles Francis Adams, Jr., whose father was U.S. minister in London at the time, wrote later of the affair: "I do not remember in the whole course of the half-century's retrospect . . . any occurrence in which the American people were so completely swept off their feet, for the moment losing possession of their senses, as during the weeks which immediately followed the seizure of Mason and Slidell."[45]

The Lincoln administration was aware of the strength of anti-British sentiment among the public and in Congress (indeed, in early December, Congress passed a resolution commending the *San Jacinto's* captain for his action). There is some evidence that in order to placate public opinion, President Lincoln was inclined toward holding on to Mason and Slidell, notwithstanding the obvious risks of doing so.[46] Nevertheless, after first toying with the idea of offering London arbitration in an attempt to avoid the extremes of war or a humiliating climbdown, the United States elected to submit to Britain's demands. Given that Washington "could not back down easily," it is important to understand why it chose to do so.

The United States bowed to London because, already fully occupied militarily trying to subdue the Confederacy, the North could not also afford a simultaneous war with England, which effectively would have brought Britain into the War Between the States on the South's side.[47] This was clearly recognized by the Lincoln administration when the cabinet met for two days at Christmas to decide on the American response to the British note. The cabinet had before it two critical pieces of information. First, Washington had just been informed that France supported London's demands (ending American hopes that Britain would be restrained by its own "waterbird" worries that France would take advantage of an Anglo-American war).[48] Second, Washington had abundant information about the depth of the pro-war sentiment of the British public. . . .

Facing the choice of defying London or surrendering to its demands, Washington was compelled to recognize both that Britain was serious about going to war and that such a war almost certainly would result in the Union's permanent dissolution. During the cabinet discussions, Attorney General Edward Bates suggested that Britain was seeking a war with the United States in order to break the Northern blockade of

Southern cotton ports and he worried that London would recognize the Confederacy. The United States, he said, "cannot afford such a war." He went on to observe, "In such a crisis, with such a civil war upon our hands, we cannot hope for success in a . . . war with England, backed by the assent and countenance of France. We must evade it—with as little damage to our own honor and pride as possible."[51] Secretary of State Seward concurred, stating that it was "no time to be diverted from the cares of the Union into controversies with other powers, even if just causes for them could be found."[52] When the United States realized that Britain's threat to go to war was not a bluff, strategic and national interest considerations—the "waterbird dilemma"—dictated that Washington yield to Britain.

The *Trent* affair's outcome is explained by realism, not democratic peace theory. Contrary to democratic peace theory's expectations, the mutual respect between democracies rooted in democratic norms and culture had no influence on British policy. Believing that vital reputational interests affecting its global strategic posture were at stake, London played diplomatic hardball, employed military threats, and was prepared to go to war if necessary. Both the public and the elites in Britain preferred war to conciliation. Across the Atlantic, public and governmental opinion in the North was equally bellicose. An Anglo-American conflict was avoided only because the Lincoln administration came to understand that diplomatic humiliation was preferable to a war that would have arrayed Britain with the Confederacy and thus probably have secured the South's independence. . . .

Policy Conclusions: Why It Matters

The validity of democratic peace theory is not a mere academic concern. Democratic peace theory has been widely embraced by policymakers and foreign policy analysts alike and it has become a lodestar that guides America's post-Cold War foreign policy. Michael Doyle's 1983 conception of a democratic "zone of peace" is now routinely used in both official and unofficial U.S. foreign policy pronouncements. Following the Cold War, a host of commentators have suggested that the export or promotion of democracy abroad should become the central focus of American's post-Cold War foreign policy.[140] From Haiti to Russia, America's interests and its security have been identified with democracy's success or failure. National Security Adviser Anthony Lake said that America's post-Cold War goal must be to expand the zone of democratic peace and prosperity because, "to the extent democracy and market economics hold sway in other nations, our own nation will be more secure, prosperous and influential."[141]

Those who want to base American foreign policy on the extension of democracy abroad invariably disclaim any intention to embark on a

> A guiding star. Layne uses the term to indicate that democratic peace theory directs U.S. foreign policy. He then considers the problems that result from the U.S. using this flawed theory as a guide.

"crusade," and profess to recognize the dangers of allowing policy to be based on excessive ideological zeal."[142] These reassurances are the foreign-policy version of "trust me." Because it links American security to the nature of other states' internal political systems, democratic peace theory's logic inevitably pushes the United States to adopt an interventionist strategic posture. If democracies are peaceful but non-democratic states are "troublemakers" the conclusion is inescapable: the former will be truly secure only when the latter have been transformed into democracies, too.

That is, following democratic peace theory, the U.S. intervenes in the internal affairs of other countries to press them to adopt a democratic form of government.

Indeed, American statesmen have frequently expressed this view. During World War I, Elihu Root said that, "To be safe democracy must kill its enemy when it can and where it can. The world cannot be half democratic and half autocratic."[143] During the Vietnam War, Secretary of State Dean Rusk claimed that the "United States cannot be secure until the total international environment is ideologically safe." These are not isolated comments; these views reflect the historic American propensity to seek absolute security and to define security primarily in ideological (and economic) terms. The political culture of American foreign policy has long regarded the United States, because of its domestic political system, as a singular nation. As a consequence, American policymakers have been affected by a "deep sense of being alone" and *they* have regarded the United States as "perpetually beleaguered." Consequently, America's foreign and defense policies have been shaped by the belief that the United States must create a favorable ideological climate abroad if its domestic institutions are to survive and flourish. . . ."[145]

That is, the U.S. must create democracies abroad so that its own democracy will flourish.

Democratic peace theory is dangerous in another respect, as well: it is an integral component of a new (or more correctly, recycled) outlook on international politics. It is now widely believed that the spread of democracy and economic interdependence have effected a "qualitative change" in international politics, and that war and serious security competitions between or among democratic great powers are now impossible.[147] There is therefore, it is said, no need to worry about future great power challenges from states like Japan and Germany, or to worry about the relative distribution of power between the United States and those states, unless Japan or Germany were to slide back into authoritarianism.[148] The reason the United States need not be concerned with the great-power emergence of Japan and Germany is said to be simple: they are democracies and democracies do not fight democracies. . . .

a change in the nature, character, or degree of something

If American policymakers allow themselves to be mesmerized by democratic peace theory's seductive—but false—vision of the future, the United States will be ill prepared to formulate a grand strategy that will advance its interests in the emerging world of multipolar great power competition. Indeed, as long as the Wilsonian worldview underpins

A belief typical of President Woodrow Wilson, who thought that the U.S. should promote democracy in other countries and peace among nations.

American foreign policy, policymakers will be blind to the need to have such a grand strategy, because the liberal theory of international politics defines out of existence (except with respect to non-democracies) the very phenomena that are at the core of strategy: war, the formation of power balances, and concerns about the relative distribution of power among the great powers. But in the end, as its most articulate proponents admit, liberal international relations theory is based on hope, not on fact.[150] In the final analysis, the world remains what it always has been: international politics continues to occur in an anarchic, competitive, self-help realm. This reality must be confronted, because it cannot be transcended. Given the stakes, the United States in coming years cannot afford to have either its foreign policy, or the intellectual discourse that underpins that policy, shaped by theoretical approaches that are based on wishful thinking.

Notes

1. I use the term "democratic peace theory" because it is a convenient shorthand term. However, strictly speaking, the claim that democracies do not fight democracies is a proposition, or hypothesis, rather than a theory. Democratic peace "theory" proposes a causal relationship between an independent variable (democratic political structures at the unit level) and the dependent variable (the asserted absence of war between democratic states). However, it is not a true theory because the causal relationship between the independent and dependent variables is neither proven nor, as I demonstrate in this article, adequately explained. See Stephen Van Evera, "Hypotheses, Laws and Theories: A User's Guide," unpub. memo, Department of Political Science, MIT.

3. In this article, I build upon and expand the criticisms of democratic peace theory found in John J. Mearsheimer, "Back to the Future: Instability in Europe After the Cold War," *International Security,* Vol. 15, No. 1 (Summer 1990), pp. 5–56; and Kenneth N. Waltz, "America as Model for the World? A Foreign Policy Perspective," *PS* (December 1991), pp. 667–670.

4. Other cases of crises between democratic great powers that might be studied include Anglo-French relations during the Liberal entente cordiale of 1832–48, Franco-Italian relations during the Late 1880s and early 1890s and, if Wilhelmine Germany is classified as a democracy, the Moroccan crises of 1905–06 and 1911 and the Samoan crises of 1889 and 1899. These cases would support my conclusions. For example, from 1832 to 1843, the Foxite legacy disposed England's Whigs to feel a strong commitment to France based on a shared liberal ideology. Yet Anglo-French relations during this period were marked by intense geopolitical rivalry over Belgium, Spain, and the Near East, and the threat of war was always a factor in the calculations of policymakers in both London and Paris. Foreign Minister Lord Palmerston profoundly distrusted French ambitions and constantly urged that England maintain sufficient naval power to defend its interests against a French challenge. See Kenneth Bourne, *Palmerston: The Early Years, 1784–1841* (New York: Macmillan, 1982), p. 613. Also see Roger Buller, *Palmerston, Guizat and the Collapse of the Entente Cordiale* (London: Athlone Press, 1974); and Sir Charles Webster, *The Foreign Policy Palmerston, Vol. I: 1830–1841, Britain, The Liberal Movement and The Eastern Question* (London: Bell & Sons, 1951). Italy challenged France for Mediterranean ascendancy although the two nations were bound by liberalism, democracy, and a common culture. The two states engaged in a trade war

and came close to a real wax. France apparently was dissuaded from attacking Italy in 1888 when the British Channel Fleet was sent to the Italian naval base of La Spezia. Italy was prevented from attacking France by its military and economic weakness. See C.J. Lowe and F. Marzari, *Italian Foreign Policy, 1870–1940* (London: Routledge & Kegan Paul, 1975), chap. 4; C.J. Lowe, *The Reluctant Imperialists: British Foreign Policy 1879–1902* (London: Routledge & Kegan Paul, 1974), Vol. I, pp. 147–150; John A.C. Conybeare, *Trade Wars: The Theory and Practice of International Commercial Rivalry* (New York: Columbia University Press, 1987), pp. 183–188.

5. Melvin Small and J. David Singer first observed the pattern of democracies not fighting democracies in a 1976 article: Small and Singer, "The War-proneness of Democratic Regimes, 1816–1865," *Jerusalem Journal of International Relations,* Vol. 1, No. 4 (Summer 1976), pp. 50–69. Their finding has been the subject of extensive further empirical testing which has produced a consensus around the propositions stated in the text. See Stuart A. Bremer, "Dangerous Dyads: Conditions Affecting the Likelihood of Interstate War, 1816–1865," *Journal of Conflict Resolution,* Vol. 36, No. 2 (June 1992), pp. 309–441; Steve Chan, "Mirror, Mirror on the Wal . . . Are the Freer Countries More Pacific?" *Journal of Conflict Resolution,* Vol. 28, No. 4 (December 1984), pp. 617–648; Zeev Maoz and Nasrin Abdolali, "Regime and International Conflict," *Journal of Conflict Resolution,* Vol. 33, No. 1 (March 1989), pp. 3–35; R.J. Rummel, "Libertarianism and International Violence," *Journal of Conflict Resolution,* Vol. 27, No. 1 (March 1983), pp. 27–71; Erich Weede, "Democracy and War Involvement," *Journal of Conflict Resolution,* Vol. 28, No. 4 (December 1984), pp. 649–664.

6. Jack S. Levy, "Domestic Politics and War," in. Robert I. Rotberg and Theodore K. Rabb, eds., *The Origin and Prevention of Major Wars* (Cambridge: Cambridge University Press, 1989), p. 88.

7. Russett, *Grasping the Democratic Peace,* p. 33; Michael W. Doyle, "Kant, Liberal Legacies and Foreign Affairs," Part I, *Philosophy and Public Affairs,* Vol. 12, No. 3 (Summer 1983), p. 213.

8. This is the terminology employed by Russett, *Grasping the Democratic Peace;* also see Bruce Russett and Zeev Maoz, "Normative and Structural Causes of Democratic Peace," *American Political Science Review,* Vol. 87, No. 3 (September 1993), pp. 624–638. Russett points out (pp. 40–42) that, although analytically distinct, these two explanations are intertwined.

9. Doyle, "Kant, Liberal Legacies, and Foreign Affairs," pp. 205–235. See also Doyle, "Liberalism and World Politics," *Antedate Political Science Ravine,* Vol. 80, No. 4 (December 198b), pp. 1151–1169; Russett, *Grasping the Democratic Peace,* pp. 38–40.

10. T. Clifton Morgan and Sally N. Campbell, "Domestic Structure, Decisional Constraints and War: So Why Kant Democracies Fight?" *Journal of Conflict Resolution,* Vol. 35, No. 2 (June 1991), pp. 187–211; and T. Clifton Morgan and Valerie L. Schwebach, "Take Two Democracies and Call Me in the Morning: A Prescription for Peace?" *International Interactions.* Vol. 17, No. 4 (Summer 1992), pp. 305–420.

11. Russett, *Grasping the Democratic Peace,* p. 31 (second emphasis added).

12. Doyle, "Kant, Liberal Legacies, and Foreign Affairs," p. 230. It is also argued that the predisposition of democratic states to regard other democracies favorably is reinforced by the fact that liberal democratic states are linked by mutually beneficial ties of economic interdependence. Democracies thus have strong incentives to act towards each other in a manner that enhances cooperation and to refrain from acting in a manner that threatens their stake in mutually beneficial cooperation. Ibid., pp. 230–232; Rummel, "Libertarianism and International Violence,"

pp. 27–28. For the "interdependence promotes peace" argument see Richard Rosecrance, *The Rise of the Trading State* (New York: Basic Books, 1986). In fact, however, for great powers economic interdependence, rather than promoting peace, creates seemingly important interests that may be defended by overseas military commitments. . . .

13. Doyle, "Kant, Liberal Legacies, and Foreign Affairs"; and Harvey Starr, "Democracy and War. Choke, Learning and Security Communities," *Journal of Peace Research,* Vol. 29, No. 2 (1992), pp. 207–213.

14. Maoz and Russett, "A Statistical Artifact?" p. 246.

15. Russett, *Grasping the Democratic Peace,* p. 33.

16. Classic explications of realism are Kenneth N. Waltz, *Theory of International Politics* (Reading, Mass.: Addison-Wesley, 1979) and Hans J. Morgenthau, rev. by Kenneth W. Thompson, *Politics Among Nations: The Struggle for Power and Peace,* 6th ed. (New York: Knopf, 1985).

18. Manz and Russett, "Normative and Structural Causes," p. 624.

21. Geoffrey Blainey, *The Causes of War,* 3rd ed. (South Melbourne: Macmillan Co. of Australia, 1988), pp. 57–67. As the parable goes, while the waterbirds fight over the catch, the fisherman spreads his net.

22. My classification of the United States in 1861 and 1895 and of Germany in 1923 as great powers might be challenged. By the mid-nineteenth century British policy-makers viewed the United States, because of its size, population, wealth, and growing industrial strength (and latent military power), as "a great world power," notwithstanding the fact that it was not an active participant in the European state system. Ephraim Douglass Adams, *Great Britain and the American Civil War* (New York: Russell and Russell, 1924), Vol. I, p. 10. In 1895 the perception of American power had heightened in Britain and in other leading European powers. In 1923, Germany, although substantially disarmed pursuant to Versailles, remained Europe's most economically powerful state. As most statesmen realized, it was, because of its population and industry, a latent continental hegemony. Democratic peace theorists have classified all eight states as having been democracies at the time of their involvement in the crises under discussion. See Doyle, "Kant, Liberal Legacies, and Foreign Affairs," part I, pp. 214–215. Russett, *Grasping the Democratic Peace,* pp. 5–9, briefly discusses the Venezuela and Fashoda crises, but his bibliography has few historical references to these two crises (and related issues), and omits most standard sources.

28. Adams, *Britain and the Civil War,* Vol. I, p. 216.

29. Quoted in Gordon H. Warren, *Fountain of Discontent: The Trent Affair and Freedom of the Seas* (Boston: Northeastern University Press, 1981), p. 105.

30. Quoted in Adams, *Britain and the Civil War,* Vol. I, p. 217.

31. Quoted in Norman B. Ferris, *The Trent Affair: A Diplomatic Crisis* (Knoxville: University of Tennessee Press, 1977), p. 44.

32. Ibid., p. 109; Howard Jones, *Union in Peril: Tice Crisis Over British Intervention in the Civil War* (Chapel Hill: University of North Carolina Press, 1992), pp. 84–85.

33. Quoted in Jones, *Union in Peril,* p. 85.

34. Jenkins, *War for the Union,* p. 214.

35. Quoted in Kenneth Bourne, *Britain and the Balance of Power in North America, 1815–1908* (Berkeley: University of California Press, 1967), p. 219.

36. The figures are from Warren, *Fountain of Discontent,* pp. 130, 136. For an overview of British military and naval activities during the Trent crisis see Kenneth Bourne, "British Preparations for War with the North, 1861–1862," *English Historical Review,* Vol. 76, No. 301 (October 1961), pp. 600–632.

37. Ferris, *Trent Affair,* p. 56; Wilbur Devereux Jones, *The American Problem in British Diplomacy,* 2841–2861 (London: Macmillan, 1974), p. 203. In international

relations theory terms, London's view of Anglo-American relations was based on a deterrence model rather than a spiral model. See Robert Jervis, *Perception and Misperception in International Politics* (Princeton: Princeton University Press, 1976), pp. 58–111. Coexisting uneasily with the positive view of an Anglo-American community was the British image of the United States as a vulgar "mobocracy" that, unless firmly resisted, would pursue a rapacious and bullying foreign policy. Warren, *Fountain of Discontent,* pp. 47–51.

38. Quoted in Bourne, *Balance of Power,* p. 247.

39. Bourne, "British Preparations," p. 631.

40. Bourne, *Balance of Power,* p. 247.

41. Quoted in ibid., pp. 245–246, emphasis in original.

42. Quoted in Jenkins, *War for the Union,* p. 216.

43. Ferris, *Trent Affair,* pp. 111–113.

44. Norman B. Ferris, *Desperate Diplomacy: William H. Seward's Foreign Policy, 1861* (Knoxville: University of Tennessee, 1976), p. 194.

45. Quoted in Adams, *Britain and the Civil War,* Vol. I, p. 218.

46. Warren, *Fountain of Discontent,* pp. 184–185; Adams, *Britain and the Civil War,* p. 231. Howard Jones, however, suggests that Lincoln probably intended to give up Mason and Slidell and that he may have been posturing in order to shift to other members of his cabinet the onus of advancing the argument for surrendering them. Jones, *Union in Peril,* pp. 91–92.

47. Ferris, *Trent Affair,* pp. 177–182; Jenkins, *War for the Union,* pp. 223–226; Warren, *Fountain of Discontent,* pp. 181–182.

48. See Jenkins, *War for the Union,* pp. 225–226.

51. Quoted in ibid., p. 182.

52. Quoted in Jenkins, *War for the Union,* p. 224.

140. See for example Joshua Muravchik, *Exporting Democracy: Fulfilling America's Destiny* (Washington, D.C.: AEI Press, 1991); and Larry Diamond, "Promoting Democracy," *Foreign Policy,* No. 87 (Summer 1992), pp. 25–46.

141. "Remarks of Anthony Lake," Johns Hopkins School of Advanced International Studies, Washington, D.C., September 21, 1993 (Washington, D.C.: National Security Council Press Office).

142. Lake stated that the Clinton administration does not propose to embark on a "democratic crusade." Both Doyle and Russett acknowledge that democratic peace theory could encourage democratic states to pursue aggressive policies toward non-democracies, and both express worry at this. Doyle, "Kant, Liberal Legacies, and Foreign Affairs," part II; Russett, *Grasping the Democratic Peace,* p. 136.

143. Quoted in Russett, *Grasping the Democratic Peace,* p. 33.

145. Lloyd C. Gardner, *A Covenant With Power: America and World Order from Wilson to Reagan* (New York Oxford University Press, 1984), p. 27. For an excellent critique of the notion that America's domestic ideology must be validated by its foreign policy, see Michael H. Hunt, *Ideology and U.S. Foreign Policy* (New Haven: Yale University Press, 1987).

147. Robert Jervis, "The Future of World Politics: Will It Resemble the Past?" *International Security,* Vol. 16, No. 3 (Winter 1991–92), pp. 39–73.

148. For an example of this argument see James M. Goldgeier and Michael McFaul, "A Tale of Two Worlds: Core and Periphery in the Post-Cold War," *International Organization,* Vol 46, No. 3 (Spring 1992), pp. 467–491.

150. Russett, *Grasping the Democratic Peace,* p. 156, argues that, "understanding the sources of democratic peace can have the effect of a self-fulfilling prophecy. Social scientists sometimes create reality as well as analyze it. Insofar as norms do guide behavior, repeating those norms helps to make them effective. *Repeating the norms as descriptive principles can help to make them true.*" (Emphasis added.)

Reading Responses

1. Summarize the central claim of democratic peace theory and the logic that supports it. In other words, what's the chain of reasoning that supports democratic peace theory?

2. Assess Layne's use of the case-study method to test democratic peace theory. Did you find his analysis of the Trent Affair persuasive? Would you have found statistics more effective? What are the limitations of case-study evidence?

3. Near the end of his essay, Layne describes democratic peace theory as "dangerous." What in his article would most persuade you to agree with him— what evidence? What logical reasoning? Why do you think that some readers would respond passionately to this description of democratic peace theory?

NOTES ON GRAMMAR, STYLE, AND RHETORIC:
TEXTUAL COHERENCE

One striking aspect of the introductory paragraphs of Christopher Layne's "Kant or Cant: The Myth of the Democratic Peace" is that they include several prominent text connectives. Text connectives help show readers how the parts of a text relate to one another, how the overall text is organized, and sometimes how the text relates to its context. Specific examples of text connectives are elements that indicate sequences (*first, in the third place, finally*) as well as those that indicate logical or temporal relationships (*consequently, at the same time*). Other text connectives are reminders about material presented earlier (*as I demonstrated in Chapter Two*) and previews of forthcoming material (*as I will show in the next section*).

In his early paragraphs, Layne uses several statements to preview how his essay will unfold. These preview statements begin already at the end of the first paragraph. There he uses two general statements to give an overview of much of his article. One of these begins with "In this article, I focus primarily on . . . ," and the other begins with "I then briefly assess. . . ."

Then he moves to previews of the specific steps he will take in his essay. At the start of the second paragraph he writes, "I begin by reviewing. . . ." Shortly thereafter he adds, "As I demonstrate. . . ." And then in the third and fourth paragraphs, he adds still other preview statements, introduced as follows: "I deduce . . . ," "Using a process-tracing approach, I examine . . . ," "I conclude . . . ," and finally "I conclude by discussing. . . ."

Because all these preview statements occur within a handful of lines of one another, you might be inclined to ask, "Why does Layne spend so much time telling readers what he is going to do? Why doesn't he just go ahead and start his presentation?" Speculating about how Layne might respond to these questions is instructive. He could, for instance, appeal to aspects of his rhetorical situation and formulate a defense that would include several points.

First, he could note that in the United States we generally place much responsibility on the writer for signaling how texts are organized. Probably all of us, at some point in school, have been advised to use transitions, especially as we begin paragraphs. Our print culture tells us that we should take care to mark the way clearly for readers as they move through our texts. Not all cultures convey this message. In the print culture of some European countries—Germany and Finland, for example—writers are encouraged to let readers discover organizational patterns of texts on their own.

Second, he might note that his essay is long. What is reprinted of Layne's essay in this textbook is only a portion of his overall piece. To make his essay fit within the scope of a chapter in this book, the editors have had to cut several of his case studies. Similarly, Layne's argument is quite complex. He is rejecting a popular view of the democratic peace and offering a different view in its place. To lay out the essence of the view he opposes as well as of the view that he supports involves some careful explaining. In this process he gives the details of several case studies and shows how those details support his view and work against the popular one.

When writers have long and complex presentations, they have good reason to use preview statements to help readers see where they are headed. Similarly, when readers have little knowledge about the writer's subject matter, writers have good reason to use preview statements to keep them from getting lost.

In Your Own Writing . . .

- When your writing is long and complex, consider using preview statements.
- When your topic is new to your reader, consider using preview statements.
- When you write in a new discipline or a new culture, try to determine the level of text connectives that your reader expects.

STUDENT WRITING

INTRODUCTION

by James R. King,
political science major

The Assignment. I wrote the following essay as the final project for a political science class on the topic of democracy—theories about democracy as well as political states, worldwide, that follow democratic principles. My professor asked us to write a research paper that analyzed one country's attempts at democratic consolidation. Prior to this project, I had developed an interest in the Arab–Israeli conflict. I was certain that I wanted to write a paper on the status of Arab citizens of Israel, but I was unsure where that would lead.

The Content. Although it may seem obvious, the key to writing a quality political science paper is to become knowledgeable about your topic. When you become aware of the range of opinions that people have about your topic, you can more easily spot the bias of the researcher, and you can better sort out fact from opinion. I had to be well-versed on the subject of Israeli democracy. As I read a number of online and journal articles and books and spoke with my professors, I started to figure out exactly what I wanted to argue. I developed my thesis that because of Israel's heavy emphasis on its Jewish character, it cannot be considered a fully consolidated democracy. As I wrote, I continued to do research, allowing my thesis to evolve, leaving myself open to its possible changes. But, building this initial foundation was essential to the completion of this kind of controversial piece.

Learning to Write about Political Issues. Although writers in all fields must think about the audience for their essays, I think that political scientists—because everyone argues about politics—have to pay especially careful attention to their readers. I decided that I would like to publish this essay to convince people (in addition to my professor) to pay attention to the plight of Israeli-Palestinians, so I kept a secondary audience in mind as I wrote—those potential readers in an academic journal or an online publication.

Appealing to this secondary audience, I knew, would be much more difficult than writing for my professor. In my experience, most people bring strongly held opinions to the issues surrounding Israel and the Middle East; very few people come to an essay on this topic eager to be persuaded. I was aware that regardless of what I said, many of the readers of my paper would not change their views. Therefore, throughout the actual writing process, I chose to focus on the readers who, although perhaps initially uncomfortable with criticism of the state of Israel, might accept my thesis if I provided convincing evidence. I felt that if I could persuade them, then I could certainly convince any readers who were neutral on this issue.

So I set for myself the goal of convincing a slightly biased yet relatively uninformed reader. To reach out to this audience, I relied on three methods most heavily: First, in doing my research, I looked at a wide variety of sources, both in terms of the type of sources (whether a book, academic journal, news source, think tank report, etc.) and especially the political leanings of the author. I knew that it was especially critical that my research not be perceived as (or actually be) biased or one-sided. For example, I cited such well-respected sources as the *New York Times* and the BBC, and I employed quotes and statistics from the former mayor of Jerusalem, a nonpartisan Israeli research institute, and official Israeli government studies.

Second, I sought to incorporate some of the obvious objections to my thesis into the paper. I knew that the uninformed, slightly biased reader would certainly have a number of reservations about my thesis, so I included specific questions readers might have about the paper. By asking—and answering—the imagined audience's questions, I proved that I had thought deeply about the topic and that I had proposed a strong, well-supported thesis, a thesis I hoped they would accept as their own.

Finally, I used a blend of theoretical and factual analysis when I argued for my thesis. The theory helps the reader understand the overall significance of the given idea, while the facts and statistics effectively display the significance. I had to demonstrate that Israel's theory of "ethnic democracy" does not fit the definition of democracy. While certainly some people will disagree with my interpretations of facts, by using statistical evidence, I tried to illuminate tensions within Israeli democracy. After reading this combination of theoretical and factual analysis, my readers ought to have a more complete understanding of the problems facing Arab citizens of Israel and Israeli democracy; as a result, they should be more willing to agree with my thesis.

Being able to argue for an issue that you're passionate about is an important skill for any citizen in a democracy. A single political act, such as declaring war, can affect the lives of millions of people; it is vital that political leaders—and citizens in a democracy—are able to argue effectively about political acts. Perhaps my research will inspire some of my readers to investigate this issue further, or even to take action. Maybe it will inspire you.

Democratic Consolidation in Israel?: The Situation of Arab Citizens of Israel and the Implications for Larger Israeli Democracy

James R. King

In 2003, the Israeli Democracy Institute (IDI), an Israeli non-partisan research institute that analyzes the status of Israeli democracy, presented its Democracy Index to Israeli President Moshe Katsav. The report stated that "Protection of human rights in Israel is poor; there is serious political and economic discrimination against the Arab minority; there is much less freedom of religion than in other democracies; and the socioeconomic inequality indicator is amongst the highest in the sample."[1] Ori Nir, the Washington Bureau Chief for *The Forward*, and former correspondent to *Ha'aretz* newspaper, provided a number of disturbing statistics to a conference sponsored by the Foundation for Middle East Peace and the Middle East Institute:

> I used statistics to convince the reader that Arab-Israelis do not receive equal treatment.

- On a per capita basis, the Government [of Israel] spends two-thirds as much for Arabs as for Jews.
- Most [Israeli government] ministries have less than 5% Arabs on their payroll, and mostly in minor positions. The Ministries of Housing, Transportation, and Trade and Industry all had representation of less than 1% of Arabs in their workforce.
- The budget for the Ministry of Religious Affairs for 2000 only allocated 2.9% of its resources to the non-Jewish sector, although Muslims, Christians, and Druze constituted approximately 20% of the population.
- Between 1975 and 2000, only 0.3% of public construction initiated and subsidized by the Israeli government was for Arabs.
- No Arab community has been created since 1948, except for seven towns created for Bedouins in the Negev, whereas something like 1,000 towns have been created for Israeli Jews.
- Only 30% of Arab communities have an adequate sewage system (approximately 95% of the communities in the Jewish sector do).[2]

Nevertheless, Israel is considered by many Americans to be the only functioning democracy in the Middle East.[3] In a troubled region where democracy has largely failed to develop, this statement certainly has some merit. In the first part of this essay, I will analyze Israeli democracy generally, especially how and why it functions well, despite its relatively recent establishment and the difficult circumstances it has faced throughout its brief history. After this important recognition, however, the majority of the essay will examine areas in which Israeli democracy has failed to consolidate. I will contend that Israel, in fact, is not nearly as democratic as is often purported.

> It's common in political science writing to describe the organization of the essay first and then introduce the claim.

This essay will focus primarily on the explicit and inherent Jewish character of the Israeli state and how that affects the minority Arab citizens of Israel, the Israeli-Palestinians.[4] Does the fact that Israel, both as a state and in the beliefs of its Jewish citizens, sees itself ideologically (as well as in law and practice) as an ethnic state, a state for Jews worldwide, necessarily present problems for its non-Jewish citizens? Does Israel's emphasis on its "Jewishness" over its functioning as a democratic state for all its citizens, render it undemocratic, or lacking and in need of democratic transition? Or, is Israel's situation merely the result of unique circumstances? I argue that the Israeli situation is certainly unique, thus requiring different and probably more generous analysis; nonetheless, to better consolidate its democracy, Israel must move from its fundamental and all-pervasive Zionist ideology, one based on security, domination, and ethnic exclusivism, to a post-Zionist statehood that strives for a peaceful, pluralist society that is democratic before it is ethnic.

> Rhetoric in political science calls for directly stating the point of your argument—even if it is controversial. Almost any political argument is going to be controversial, so it helps to be humble but straightforward.

On the surface and certainly for its Jewish citizens, Israel does sustain a thriving democracy. Israel's bicameral parliament, the Knesset, is comprised of not only two main parties but also a large number of smaller parties, including Arab parties. The current Knesset, elected in 2003, contains eight Arabs, out of 120 total members. All Israeli citizens have voting rights, including women and Israeli-Palestinians.[5] Israeli law guarantees civil liberties for both individuals and groups, including minorities. Certainly, much of Israeli democracy is impressive, especially when one considers Israel's relatively recent establishment (1948) and the instability that results from war with its neighbors and the continued military presence in the Occupied Territories. However, I maintain that many aspects of Israeli government and society, both in structures and attitudes, in fact the very foundation of the state, demonstrate a lack of democratic consolidation. The most obvious manifestation of this failure is the condition of the Israeli-Palestinian, a complicated and under-analyzed situation.

> I begin with evidence that seems to contradict my thesis.

> Bicameral means having two chambers, houses, or branches.

Israeli-Palestinians, representing roughly twenty percent of the total Israeli population, are both Arab-Palestinians and Israeli citizens. They are those Palestinians (or descendents of those) who remained within the post-1948 borders of the newly created state of Israel and were granted Israeli citizenship. Common scholarship tends to view this Israeli-Palestinian minority as parallel to other minority groups in Western liberal democracies. According to this sort of "normal development model,"

Israeli-Palestinians are moving along in a gradual process of development and normalization in Israeli society.[6]

Although there is some validity in this model, it fails to recognize the fundamental and inescapable tension between the values of an *ethnic* state and the principles of a *democratic* one. While democratic process should promote equality by negating the ascendancy of one group or the state's identification with it,[7] Israel, as an ethnic state, "sets its goals with no thought for nationalities other than the dominant group and its members in all sorts of legally-sanctioned ways. The discrimination against other ethnic groups derives from the state's refusal to respond to demands for equality, affiliation, and identification."[8] As opposed to the model of a liberal democracy, where equal citizens compete to collectively determine the "common good,"[9] the commitments of Israeli democracy are first and foremost to its Jewish citizens, even if the policy in question is detrimental to the Arab minority.

> In this paragraph the history of Israel seems to support a claim that contradicts my thesis. But I focus on aspects of that history that support my claim.

Because Israel was founded as a safe haven for Jews worldwide, it became, necessarily, a Jewish state. Beginning in the 1870s, Jews from all over the world immigrated to Israel, with the explicit intention of establishing a Jewish state. After the horrific events of the Holocaust, this immigration project became a priority of the Western states. Finally, in 1948 Israel was founded as a Jewish democracy. From Israel's founding until now, Arabs have been isolated from the project of Israeli statehood; in fact, many within the Palestinian population (and arguably the Palestinians as a collective group) have been unwillingly forced to sacrifice their homes, their land, and their rights for this cause of a Jewish state. Foundational Israeli law, especially the legal definition of the state as the "state of the Jewish people," has also reflected the ethnically exclusive nature of the Israeli state. For example, the Law of Return and the Citizenship Law grant any Jew from anywhere in the world automatic citizenship into the state of Israel, while a Palestinian refugee cannot claim that automatic citizenship.

The current exclusion of Arabs from full democratic participation is rooted in Israel's refusal to acknowledge Arab culture. The former mayor of Jerusalem, Meron Benvenisti, in his book *Sacred Landscape: The Buried History of the Holy Land Since 1948*, argues that Israel established the distinctly Jewish character of the newly established homeland by attempting to disguise its former Arab identity. According to Benvenisti, after 1948 the Jewish state suppressed Arab history by creating a new, Hebrew map of the region. On the map, Israel altered the place names of virtually all Arab villages and geographical features, officially changing them to Hebrew names or to names that were particularly meaningful to Jews. Benvenisti maintains that by changing the long-standing Arabic names, the Jewish state was essentially declaring a war on Arab culture, announcing that it was no longer interested in living side-by-side in a bilingual or bicultural state.[10]

Unfortunately for the Palestinian-Israelis and for Israeli democracy, the unwillingness to integrate the Palestinian population and their culture into the new state certainly continued after Israel's establishment. By appealing almost entirely to this Zionist cultural, religious, and historical heritage, a heritage that Palestinians often associate with war, displacement, and exclusion, modern Israeli symbols such as the national anthem, state flag, and official state holidays[11] have made it painfully clear to Palestinian-Israelis that Israel remains a Jewish state. Eliezer Ben-Rafael and Stephen Sharot, in their book *Ethnicity, Religion, and Class in Israeli Society* recognize the dual nature of the Palestinian-Israeli's situation: "On the one hand, Arabs are granted full citizenship and legal equality. On the other hand, the Jewish-Zionist character of the state has led to the exclusion of Arabs at a number of symbolic and material levels."[12] Ghanem argues that Israel relies on two key policies to maintain this Jewish character. First, the state supports policies that reinforce Jewish superiority in all spheres. Second, the state limits the democratic character of the state and thereby minimizes Arab incorporation. Because this latter policy encourages democracy at some level, it often gives the false appearance of true democracy.[13]

It is obvious, then, that Palestinian-Israelis are isolated from their state in a number of critically important ways, in many cases as a direct result of state intentions to exclude them. Of course, this intentional exclusion results in tangible experiences of discrimination for Palestinian-Israelis. Although a number of areas could be analyzed (remember some of the statistics listed at the beginning of the essay), the remainder of this essay will look to the unequal treatment of Palestinian-Israelis in terms of land expropriation, political involvement, economics, and the popular sentiment of Jewish-Israelis. In these four areas, it will be further demonstrated that Israel has failed to develop the workings of a consolidated democracy.

Founding a Jewish state on a land that was occupied primarily by Palestinians was an extremely formidable task, one that, according to Benvenisti, did not end when the state of Israel was established in 1948. Israel continues to expropriate Arab land for state and Jewish use. Much of the land has been used to enable immigrant Jews (from under the Law of Return and the Citizenship Law) to acquire land in Israel. The Jewish Agency and the Jewish National Fund have largely succeeded in turning much of Israel into state land, or at least land distributed by the state, land that is designed to benefit only Jews. In fact, over 93% of Israeli land is state owned; Arabs own only approximately 3.5% of the land in Israel.[14]

Despite the fact that they constitute roughly twenty percent of the total Israeli population, Palestinian-Israelis are greatly underrepresented in the Israeli government. While Palestinian-Israelis do have full voting rights and some Arabs serve in the Knesset, Arab parties tend to play the permanent role of opposition. A *New York Times* article on Arab involvement in Israeli government states that "No Israeli prime minister has ever given leaders of the Arab parties significant positions of power."[15] This has been a common pattern in Israeli politics. Palestinian-Israelis are systematically excluded from the most important Knesset committees, like Finance, Defense, and Foreign Affairs.[16] Many Israeli government ministries have special departments dealing with matters of the Arab minority, but with a Jewish head.[17]

Amendment 9 to the Basic Law also excludes Arabs from full participation in Israeli government. In January of 2003, Israel's Central Election Committee disqualified two of the most prominent Arab members of the Knesset, Ahmad al-Tibi and Azmi Bisharah, from running in the election. The committee justified their decision based on al-Tibi's and Bisharah's opposition to the existence of a Jewish state (an opposition which is illegal under Amendment 9), and their promotion of an Israeli state for all citizens, regardless of ethnicity. The committee reviewed the candidacy of another controversial figure, Jewish politician Baruch Marzel, because of his open anti-Arab racism; but, amidst assurances that he no longer promoted racist policies (despite his open support for transferring Palestinians out of the West Bank and Gaza), the committee allowed Marzel to run. Eventually, this decision was overturned by the Israeli High Court of Justice.[18] According to a *New York Times* article, however, the message to Palestinian-Israelis was clear: "If you are a Jewish extremist, you can go on the campaign trail. But if you belong to the Arab minority and do not openly toe the government line, you cannot be part of the election game."[19]

The economic situation of Palestinian-Israelis remains quite dire as well, reflecting both their lack of integration into Israeli society and the Israeli government's apathy towards their plight. Statistics provide the best indicator of the difficult economic situation of the Palestinian-Israelis. These statistics were provided by the International Crisis Group, an international advocacy group, in its report entitled "Identity Crisis: Israel and its Arab Citizens"[20]:

- In 2003, some 44.7% of Arab-Israeli families lived in poverty, as opposed to roughly 20% of Israeli Jewish families;[21]
- 27 of the 30 communities in Israel with the highest unemployment rates are Arab, including the top fourteen;[22]
- The average gross hourly income of an Arab wage earner is 60% that of a Jewish counterpart.[23]

According to Sarah Kreimer, co-director of The Center for Jewish-Arab Economic Development, the Israeli Ministry of Education spends nearly twice as much per Jewish child as per Arab child. This has led to an infant mortality in the Arab sector that is nearly double that among Jews.[24]

Certainly, statistics cannot tell the entire story of the current situation of the Palestinian-Israelis. The economic depravity of Israel's Arab population cannot be attributed wholly to government discrimination, as a number of factors have contributed to their poor economic situation. It is clear, however, that the Israeli government has discriminated against this minority group, and it is also clear that this discrimination is supported by a majority of Israel's population. The popular opinion of Jews in Israel regarding their fellow Arab citizens might, in fact, be the most disturbing aspect of Israeli democracy, as it shows an obvious lack of democratic value within the population.

A number of popular opinion surveys have recorded attitudes of Israel's Jewish population toward their fellow Arab-Palestinian citizens. These surveys indicate that a large majority of Jews in Israel emphasize Israel's Jewish identity before and often times against its democratic identity. In a survey conducted in 1995 by Jewish scholar Sammy Smooha of the University of Haifa eighty-five percent of Jews surveyed said that they were opposed to any change to the Israeli state symbols to make them less offensive to the Arab minority, and seventy-four percent believed that the state should manifest great or some preference to Jews over Arab citizens. Ninety-five percent of the Jewish Israelis opposed the idea of Israel as a liberal democratic state in which Arabs can compete freely and live wherever they wish. In fact, fifty-one percent said that the term "Israeli" applies only to Jews and not Arabs.[25] The 2003 Israel Democracy Index revealed that fifty-three percent of Jewish-Israelis are openly against full equality for the Arabs, only thirty-one percent support having Arab parties in the government, and fifty-seven percent agree that Arabs should be encouraged to emigrate.[26] The popular opinions of Israelis indicate that many of the core values of a liberal democracy have failed to take hold, undoubtedly a sign of incomplete democratic consolidation.[27]

In this essay, I have shown how Israeli democracy has largely failed to consolidate in relation to its ethnic minority, the Palestinian-Israelis. In nearly all areas of Israeli society, including land distribution, political participation, the economic sphere, and general attitudes of Israeli's dominant Jewish population, Palestinian-Israelis remain marginalized and discriminated against. However, even if their status in these areas improves, Palestinian-Israelis will remain isolated from their fellow citizens in Israel. Because Israel has established itself in law, symbol, and practice as an inherently and explicitly Jewish state, Palestinian-Israelis will always face the fundamental tension of being Arab and living in a Jewish state.[28] They will remain what Dan Rabinowitz terms a "trapped minority," both Arab and Israeli, accepted by neither world.

To transition to a functioning, fully consolidated democracy, Israel must shift its focus away from its ethnic statehood. In his article, "Israel in Transition from Zionism to Post-Zionism," Herbert C. Kelman argues that Israel must begin to see itself as a state for *all* its citizens, not a state for Jews worldwide. Israel has successfully become a safe haven for persecuted Jews around the world; the Zionist project has largely been completed. Now, he argues, "The primary feature of a post-Zionist state must be to protect and advance the interests and well-being of its citizens, regardless of ethnicity."[29] Israel must regard itself as a democratic state, a state that treats all citizens equally. Only when Israel shifts away from an exclusively Jewish ethnic state to that of a liberal democracy, one that includes both Jews and Arabs, can it be considered a fully transitioned democracy.

Notes

1. "The State of Israeli Democracy," *The Democracy Index*. Israel Democracy Institute. <http://www.idi.org.il/english/article.php?id=1466>. (18 September 2004).
2. Ori Nir, "Israel's Arab Minority," The Foundation for Middle East Peace, Current Analysis, Speech given on April 30, 2003, <http://www.fmep.org/analysis/ori_nir_israels_arab_minority.html>, (25 April 2004).
3. It should be noted that the definition of what states comprise the Middle East is its own topic of debate. Many, for example, would include Turkey and Iran as a part of the Middle East. These states are certainly democratic on a number of levels.
4. "Israeli-Palestinian" is the preferred name for Arabs who are citizens of the state of Israel. They are also known as Arab-Israelis, although this name is not preferred.
5. "Political Parties and Platforms," *Israeli Democracy in Action,* <http://www.israelvotes2003.com/>, (22 April 2004).
6. As'ad Ghanem, *The Palestinian-Arab Minority in Israel, 1948–2000,* (Albany, NY: State University of New York Press, 2001), 5–7.
7. As'ad Ghanem, "State and minority in Israel: the case of ethnic state and the predicament of its minority," *Ethnic and Racial Studies,* Volume 21, No. 3 (May 1998), 429.
8. Ibid., 439.
9. Ghanem, *The Palestinian-Arab Minority in Israel,* 7.
10. Meron Benvenisti, *Sacred Landscape: The Buried History of the Holy Land Since 1948,* (Berkeley, CA: University of California Press, 2000.)
11. Ghanem, "State and Minority in Israel," 432.
12. Eliezer Ben-Rafael and Stephen Sharot, *Ethnicity, religion, and class in Israeli society,* (Cambridge, England: Cambridge University Press, 1991), 233.
13. Ghanem, *The Palestinian-Arab Minority in Israel,* 9.
14. "Identity Crisis: Israel and its Arab Citizens," The International Crisis Group, *ICG Middle East Report,* Number 25 (4 March 2004), <http://www.crisisweb.org/ /library/documents/middle_east__north_africa/arab_israeli_conflict/25_identity_crisis_israel_arab_citz.pdf>, (26 April 2004), 14.
15. David Newman, "A Decision That Hurts Israeli Democracy," *The New York Times,* January 6, 2003, (A, 21).
16. Ghanem, "State and Minority in Israel," 433.
17. Eliezer Ben-Rafael and Stephen Sharot, 235.
18. "Israeli Arabs urged to vote after disqualifications overruled," *BBC News Online,* 10 January 2003, (8 March 2004).
19. Newman, *New York Times.*

20. The full report can be found at <http://www.crisisweb.org//library/documents/middle_east__north_africa/arab_israeli_conflict/25_identity_crisis_israel_arabcitz.pdf>.

21. From "Identity Crisis: Israel and its Arab Citizens," (Mossawa Center, "Socio-Economic Report on Arab Citizens and Local Councils." <www.mossawacenter.org/eng/reports/summaryeng.htm>).

22. Ibid., (National Security Council, "The Arab Citizens of Israel—Organising Ideas for Addressing the Issue").

23. Ibid., (Central Bureau of Statistics, op. cit.).

24. Sarah Kreimer, The Center for Jewish-Arab Economic Development, <http://www.cjaed.org.il/news_161000_b.html>. (26 April 2004).

25. Ghanem, *The Palestinian-Arab Minority in Israel,* 160–163.

26. "The State of Israeli Democracy."

27. This could also include the public's relative apathy to government corruption, the lack of rule of law in the Occupied Territories, and the frequent undemocratic measures carried out even within Israel, among other things.

28. Mark Tessler and Audra K. Grant, "Israel's Arab Citizens: The Continuing Struggle," *The Annals of the American Academy of Political Science,* Volume 555 (January 1998), 97–113.

29. Herbert C Kelman, "Israel in Transition from Zionism to Post-Zionism," *The Annals of the American Academy of Political and Social Science,* Volume 555 (January 1998), 46–61.

Reading Responses

1. In his introduction, James King notes that he intentionally included objections to his thesis. Review King's essay and list the objections that he includes. Do you have additional objections to King's thesis? What are they?

2. Both Professor Goi and James King emphasize the passion that political scientists bring to their topics. Where in the essay can you detect King's passion for this topic? Is his use of emotion-laden discourse appropriate?

3. What strategies does King use to "map" his argument for his reader? Note the kind of preview statements he uses and record their location. Where in his essay do these most commonly appear?

PUBLIC WRITING

INTRODUCTION

Hassina Sherjan left Afghanistan as a refugee in 1979. She became a successful businessperson, and in 1996 she founded the nonprofit group Aid Afghanistan for Education, which she continues to direct (www.aidafghanistan.net). She first returned to Afghanistan in 1999 and established several girls' schools, which brought her into grave danger with Taliban forces. When the Taliban was defeated, Sherjan returned to Afghanistan to work for the rebuilding of her country.

Sherjan has been frequently interviewed and has published articles on Afghan affairs. Along with her frequent collaborator, Michael O'Hanlon (director of research and a senior foreign policy fellow at the prestigious Washington think-tank, the Brookings Institution), she coauthored the book *Toughing It Out in Afghanistan,* published in 2010.

Sherjan's expertise is thus a product of her decades of work for and personal experience in her home country. The opinion editorial reprinted here, in keeping with the other readings in this chapter, takes up the issues of peace and democracy, asking how Afghanistan can become more democratic when its most educated citizens choose not to participate in elections. Sherjan's piece appeared just two days before the national presidential election that took place in 2009; she was accurate in her prediction of low voter turnout. The election was so tainted with corruption that the U.S. pressured the ruling government to hold a second vote (between Afghan President Karzai, and his closest opponent), but the opponent pulled out of the process before the vote could take place.

Given Hassina Sherjan's lifelong work for social justice and the ongoing political chaos in Afghanistan, it is not surprising that her passion sizzles behind her words about the relationship of peace and democracy.

Apathy Among the Educated

Hassina Sherjan

The New York Times, August 18, 2009

A "fair and transparent election," even if one were possible, would not be enough to set Afghanistan on a path toward stability. Only when democracy is combined with a legitimate process of truth and justice will we achieve peace.

Most educated Afghans, a small but important minority of the population, will not vote because they believe there is no candidate worth voting for. The other day the marketing manager for my company's factory in Kabul told me that he and 10 friends had discussed it and decided not to vote.

"All the development has been done by private companies and nongovernmental groups," he explained. "Government has not done much. We are protesting. They should have created jobs. Youths are suffering. If the youths were busy working, there would be no war or corruption. The candidates say they will fix the roads or create jobs, but how? Talk is cheap."

It's not only the present government that he finds lacking. He pointedly criticized two of President Hamid Karzai's challengers—Ashraf Ghani, a former finance minister, and Abdul Jabar Sabit, a former attorney general. "They say, 'We will bring foreign investors'— but how will they improve security?" he asked. "The election is a mere formality."

Another colleague added: "The candidates talk about donors' funding as if everything is dependent on funding or they won't be able to do it. We have lots of resources in Afghanistan, like gas and oil in Sheberghan Province. These things can put many people to work so we don't have to be dependent on donor's funding, but no one has any solid plan."

Another problem with this "free" election is that the votes of Afghan refugees in Pakistan and Iran will be lost. Five years ago, in our first presidential vote, most Afghans in neighboring countries were able to vote, but this year there is no such mechanism in place. It is unfair to say that there haven't been obvious improvements since 2001. Our currency is stronger. We did not have any real telecommunications system, and there were only the government-controlled TV and radio stations, which were not even functioning. Today we have five phone companies, and around a dozen each of TV and radio stations. Thousands of miles of roads have been built, millions of children are going to school, thousands of Afghans are joining the Army and police forces daily and, most important, we finally have electricity around the clock.

But the big question is why, despite all this development, has the insurgency increased and faith in the government deteriorated?

In part it stems from too much "cosmetic development" and a lack of employment and basic services, like garbage collection. But the main cause is that people lost trust in the government for lack of a proper and transparent justice system. Out of desperation, many young Afghans either leave the country for Iran or Pakistan to seek employment or join the extremists.

Thus, in addition to democracy and accountability, Afghans need a truth and justice process like that of South Africa. Afghan leaders, through all our wars, need to admit their errors and atrocities, and apologize to the Afghan people. War criminals need to withdraw from politics. We also need to protect and empower Afghan women, and prosecute those who have abused and betrayed them.

Afghanistan's collective psyche is scarred, and when emotional traumas are not dealt with properly, they inevitably lead to violence. Even a free and fair election is no substitute for justice.

Reading Responses

1. List the social, economic, and technological advances that Hassina Sherjan describes, and then list the lingering problems she notes. Google Hassina Sherjan to look for evidence of changes since the 2009 election in her more recent writing. How have things changed? How have they stayed the same?

2. Sherjan suggests that Afghanistan needs a "truth and justice process" like that of South Africa. Do the research to learn about South Africa's truth and reconciliation process. Write a short summary of how the process works, the kinds of problems it addresses, and the solutions it provides. Could it work for Afghanistan? Explain your reasoning.

3. Sherjan says that educated Afghanis boycotted the democratic election because they did not trust the candidates. What do you think of their decision to opt out of participating in a democracy? What do they gain and lose? What does the country gain and lose?

MORE WRITING IN POLITICAL SCIENCE

INTRODUCTION

People sometimes say that professors "live in an ivory tower," by which they mean that professors focus on abstract questions and ignore real-world problems. In this brief essay, John Owen (a professor of politics and international relations at the University of Virginia) reviews *Electing to Fight: Why Emerging Democracies Go to War*, a scholarly book published by two well-known political scientists—Edward Mansfield and Jack Snyder. Owen uses his review to persuade his readers not only that *Electing to Fight* is an important book but also that "ivory-tower" research in political science can speak to real-world political problems like U.S. policy in the Middle East.

Owen begins by describing a profound irony: political scientists usually fume that American presidents pay no attention to academic research when they forge foreign policy, but President George W. Bush relied on a prominent theory—democratic peace theory—to justify the war with Iraq, a war that made most academics fume. The problem, according to Owen, is that President Bush, like most politicians, relied on an oversimplified version of democratic peace theory, namely the presumption that democracies go to war less frequently than other forms of government. Applied to the Middle East, the simplified thinking goes like this: if Iraq becomes a democracy it will no longer fight with its neighbors; it will begin to stabilize this politically troubled region. Such thinking is flawed, according to Owen, because it does not pay attention to nuances in what counts as a "democracy," nuances that profoundly affect a democracy's appetite for war. In essence, Owen reminds politicians that "the devil is in the details."

Owen builds his argument that politicians should pay attention to the complexity by describing one in-depth study of democratic peace theory, *Electing to Fight*. Authors Mansfield and Snyder categorize democracies and then examine the war-lust among the different types of democracies. They conclude that "incomplete democracies," countries that have some but not all features of a democracy, are actually more likely to go to war than authoritarian states. Young democracies are also highly likely to instigate war. Because Iraq is both a young and an incomplete democracy, Mansfield and Snyder's research suggests that it will likely retain its appetite for war. Rather than stabilize the region, a democratized Iraq is likely to continue to cause trouble for its neighbors and for the United States.

In this review, Owen does not merely summarize Mansfield and Snyder's book; he uses the book to make his own case. He argues that U.S. presidents should take the time to understand the complexities of political science research before they use it as the basis for going to war.

Iraq and the Democratic Peace:
Who Says Democracies Don't Fight?
John M. Owen IV

Foreign Affairs 2005 84(6): 122–7. Review of *Electing to Fight: Why Emerging Democracies Go to War.* By Edward D. Mansfield and Jack Snyder. MIT Press, 2005.

Seldom if ever has the hostility between academics and the U.S. president been so pronounced. Of course, political scientists always seem to complain about the occupant of the White House, and Republicans fare worse than Democrats: Herbert Hoover was called callous, Dwight Eisenhower a dunce, Richard Nixon evil, Ronald Reagan dangerous, and George H.W. Bush out of touch. But professors have consigned George W. Bush to a special circle of their presidential hell. And the White House seems to return the sentiment.

According to the academics, Bush's chief transgressions have had to do with foreign policy, especially the Iraq war—a mess that could have been avoided if only the president and his advisers had paid more attention to those who devote their lives to studying international relations.

The irony of this argument is that few other presidents—certainly none since Woodrow Wilson, a former president of the American Political Science Association, scribbled away in the Oval Office—have tied their foreign policies more explicitly to the work of social science. The defining act of Bush's presidency was grounded in a theory that the political scientist Jack Levy once declared was "as close as anything we have to an empirical law in international relations," namely, that democracies do not fight one another.

The theory, which originated in the work of the eighteenth-century philosopher Immanuel Kant and was refined in the 1970s and 1980s by several researchers working independently, has, since the 1990s, been one of the hottest research areas in international relations. Although some skeptics remain and no one agrees about why exactly it works, most academics now share the belief that democracies have indeed made a separate peace. What is more, much research suggests that they are also unusually likely to sign and honor international agreements and to become economically interdependent.

The administrations of Presidents George H.W. Bush and Bill Clinton made frequent appeals to the theory in public, and it seems to have informed their support for democratization in former communist lands and in Haiti. The current Bush administration, however, has gone much further in its faith in the idea, betting the farm that the theory holds and will help Washington achieve a peaceful, stable, and prosperous Muslim world as, over time, Iraq's neighbors, following Iraq's example, democratize. The United States' real motives for attacking Iraq may have been complex, but "regime change"—the replacement of Saddam Hussein's gruesome tyranny with a democracy—was central to Washington's rhetoric by the time it began bombing Baghdad in March 2003.

Why has a president who set his defining policy around one of political science's crown jewels come in for so much venom from the same academics who endorse the idea? After all, a host of peer-reviewed journal articles have implicitly supported the president's claim that a democratic Iraq would not threaten the United States or Israel, develop weapons of mass destruction, or sponsor terrorism. Are professors simply perpetual critics who refuse to take responsibility for the consequences of their ideas? Or does Bush hatred trump social science?

The Bush administration's desire to break with its predecessors and alter the authoritarian status quo in the Middle East was admirable. But the White House got its science wrong, or at least not completely right: the democratic peace theory does not dictate that the United States can or should remake Iraq into a democracy. In *Electing to Fight: Why Emerging Democracies Go to War*, the veteran political scientists Edward Mansfield and Jack Snyder make two critical points. Not only is turning authoritarian countries into democracies extremely difficult, much more so than the administration seems to have anticipated. The Middle East could also become a much more dangerous place if Washington and the rest of the world settle for a merely semi-democratic regime in Baghdad. Such an Iraq, Mansfield and Snyder imply, would be uncommonly likely to start wars—a bull in the Middle Eastern china shop. Unfortunately, such an Iraq may also be just what we are likely to end up with.

Illiberal Democracies

At first glance, the realists' critique of the Iraq war is easier to understand than that of the democratic peace theorists. Indeed, realism—which holds that a country's type of government has no systematic effects on its foreign policy—is enjoying a revival in Washington these days, precisely because of the war. According to the realists, the best way to have dealt with Saddam would have been not to overthrow him but to use coercive bargaining: to have threatened him with annihilation, for example, if he ever used nuclear weapons.

Even the democratic peace theory, however, does not necessarily prescribe the use of force to transform despotisms such as Iraq into democracies. Indeed, by itself, the argument that democracies do not fight one another does not have any practical implications for the foreign policymaker. It needs an additional or minor premise, such as "the United States can make Iraq into a democracy at an acceptable cost." And it is precisely this minor premise about which the academy has been skeptical. No scholarly consensus exists on how countries become democratic, and the literature is equally murky on the costs to the United States of trying to force them to be free.

This last part of the puzzle is even more complicated than it first appears. Enter Mansfield and Snyder, who have been contributing to the democratic peace debate for a decade. Their thesis, first published in 1995, is that although mature democracies do not fight one another, democratizing states—those in transition from authoritarianism to democracy—do, and are even more prone to war than authoritarian regimes. Now, in *Electing to Fight,* the authors have refined their argument. As they outline in the book, not only are "incomplete democratizing" states—those that develop democratic institutions in the wrong order—unlikely ever to complete the transition to democracy; they are also especially bellicose.

According to Mansfield and Snyder, in countries that have recently started to hold free elections but that lack the proper mechanisms for accountability (institutions such as an independent judiciary, civilian control of the military, and protections for opposition parties and the press), politicians have incentives to pursue policies that make it more likely that their countries will start wars. In such places, politicians know they can mobilize support by demanding territory or other spoils from foreign countries and by nurturing grievances against outsiders. As a result, they push for extraordinarily belligerent policies. Even states that develop democratic institutions in the right order—adopting the rule of law before holding elections—are very aggressive in the early years of their transitions, although they are less so than the first group and more likely to eventually turn into full democracies.

Of course, politicians in mature democracies are also often tempted to use nationalism and xenophobic rhetoric to buttress their domestic power. In such cases, however, they are usually restrained by institutionalized mechanisms of accountability. Knowing that if they lead the country into a military defeat or quagmire they may be punished at the next election, politicians in such states are less likely to advocate a risky war. In democratizing states, by contrast, politicians know that they are insulated from the impact of bad policies: if a war goes badly, for example, they can declare a state of emergency, suspend elections, censor the press, and so on. Politicians in such states also tend to fear their militaries, which often crave foreign enemies and will overthrow civilian governments that do not share their goals. Combined, these factors can make the temptation to attack another state irresistible.

Mansfield and Snyder present both quantitative and case-study support for their theory. Using rigorous statistical methods, the authors show that since 1815, democratizing states have indeed been more prone to start wars than either democracies or authoritarian regimes. Categorizing transitions according to whether they ended in full democracies (as in the U.S. case) or in partial ones (as in Germany in 1871–1938 or Pakistan throughout its history), the authors find that in the early years of democratic transitions, partial democracies—especially those that get their institutions in the wrong order—are indeed significantly more likely to initiate wars. . . . In most of these cases, the authors find what they expect: in these democratizing states, domestic political competition was intense. Politicians, vying for power, appeased domestic hard-liners by resorting to nationalistic appeals that vilified foreigners, and these policies often led to wars that were not in the countries' strategic interests.

Although their argument would have been strengthened by a few comparative studies of democratizing states avoiding war and of full democracies and authoritarian states starting wars, Mansfield and Snyder are persuasive. In part this is because they carefully circumscribe their claims. They acknowledge that some cases are "false positives," that is, wars started by states that have wrongly been classified as democratizing, such as the

Iran–Iraq War, started by Iraq in 1980. They also answer the most likely objections to their argument. Some skeptics, for example, might counter that Mansfield and Snyder get the causality reversed: it is war or the threat of it that prevents states from becoming mature democracies. Others might argue that democratizing states become involved in more wars simply because their internal instability tempts foreign states to attack them—in other words, that democratizers are more sinned against than sinning. Analyzing data from 1816 through 1992, Mansfield and Snyder put paid to these alternative explanations. Bad domestic institutions usually precede wars, rather than vice versa, and democratizing states usually do the attacking. . . .

The authors' conclusions for foreign policy are straightforward. The United States and other international actors should continue to promote democracy, but they must strive to help democratizing states implement reforms in the correct order. In particular, popular elections ought not to precede the building of institutions that will check the baleful incentives for politicians to call for war. Mansfield and Snyder are unsparing toward well-intentioned organizations that have pressured authoritarian governments to rush to elections in the past—often with disastrous consequences. As the authors show, for example, it was organizations such as the World Bank and the National Democratic Institute that pushed Burundi and Rwanda to increase popular sovereignty in the early 1990s—pressure that, as Mansfield and Snyder argue, helped set off a chain of events that led to genocide. Acknowledging their intellectual debt to writers such as Samuel Huntington (particularly his 1968 book *Political Order in Changing Societies*) and Fareed Zakaria, Mansfield and Snyder have written a deeply conservative book. Sounding like Edmund Burke on the French Revolution but substituting statistics and measured prose for rhetorical power, the authors counsel against abruptly empowering people, since premature elections may well usher in domestic upheavals that thrust the state outward against its neighbors.

Back in Baghdad

This brings the conversation back to Iraq, and in particular the notion that the United States can turn it into a democracy at an acceptable cost. In effect, Mansfield and Snyder have raised the estimate of these costs by pointing out one other reason this effort may fail—a reason that few seem to have thought of. Forget for a moment the harrowing possibility of a Sunni-Shiite-Kurdish civil war in Iraq. Set aside the prospect of a Shiite-dominated state aligning itself with Iran, Syria, and Lebanon's Hezbollah. What if, following the departure of U.S. troops, Iraq holds together but as an incomplete democratizer, with broad suffrage but anemic state institutions? Such an Iraq might well treat its own citizens better than the Baathist regime did. Its treatment of its neighbors, however, might be just as bad.

Although Saddam was an unusually bellicose and reckless tyrant, attacking Iran in 1980 and Kuwait in 1990 and engaging in foolish brinkmanship with the United States, as Mansfield and Snyder imply, a democratic Iraq may be no less bellicose and reckless. In the near future, intensely competitive elites there—secularists, leftists, moderates, and both Shiite and Sunni Islamists—could compete for popularity by stirring up nationalism against one or more of Iraq's neighbors. And Iraq lives in a dangerous neighborhood.

Already, Iraqi Shiite parties have been critical of Sunni-dominated Jordan; Iraqi Sunni parties, of Shiite-dominated Iran; and Iraqi Kurdish parties, of Turkey.

One hopes that the White House contemplated this scenario prior to March 2003. Whether it did or not, the possibility must be considered now, by U.S. civilian and military leaders, academics, and U.S. allies who agree with those academics. If Mansfield and Snyder are correct about the bellicose tendencies of young, incompletely democratized states, the stakes of Iraq's transition are higher than most have supposed. . . . The odds may be long that Iraq will ever turn into a mature democracy of the sort envisaged by the Bush administration. But those odds are lengthened by the refusal of those states in Europe and the Middle East that could make a difference actually to do so.

Reading Responses

1. Owen begins his review by focusing his readers' attention on the fact that President George W. Bush relied on democratic peace theory to justify going to war with Iraq. How will his audience likely respond to that claim? How passionate do you expect they will be?

2. How does Owen establish Mansfield and Snyder's credibility? How does he establish his own?

3. Did Owen persuade you? What aspects of his argument did you find persuasive? What aspects did you find less so?

WRITING ASSIGNMENTS

Assignment 1

For his research paper, James King chose a political topic that he already knew and cared about. But his passion for the topic didn't blind him to the strongly argued claims of others. While reading previous research on his topic, King made sure to read what had been written by those who might disagree with his opinions, and he included information from those sources in his essay.

Your task for this assignment is to write a research-based essay on a political topic that you already know something about. Your essay should include a thesis that you really believe in, one you'd be willing (maybe even eager) to defend in public. You might choose to use hypotheses to help you prove your thesis or a set of recommendations to sharpen the point of your thesis. Start brainstorming by creating a list of three topics that you've recently discussed with others. For your own benefit, narrow the scope of each topic as much as possible. So, for example, instead of researching "environmentalism," research "ground water contamination" or even better, "Los Angeles ground water contamination." For each of these topics, use research databases to complete the following lists. Keep track of the sources you find by listing them in a bibliography:

- List the words or search terms that research databases use to describe this topic.
- List the issues that people are currently discussing.
- List the "camps" or groups of people who share opinions about this topic. Be sure to look for a full range of scholarly groups and record their points.
- Note the kind of evidence that authors use: statistics, expert opinions, case studies, scientific experiments, quotes from authorities or authoritative texts, etc.

As you draft, revise your thesis into a point that you believe in, one you can support and defend with scholarly evidence and logic. Be sure to include scholarly research from those who might disagree with your thesis, those who will seem impartial, and those who agree with you. Provide logical reasoning that connects your research to your point. In other words, do everything you can to create a credible voice for yourself—and thereby increase your chances of actually changing your reader's mind.

Assignment 2

In Western countries people with HIV can live almost normal lives, thanks to new anti-retroviral drugs, but that is not the case for the more than 25 million AIDS/HIV-infected people who live in developing countries such as Botswana, Zimbabwe, Haiti, and Thailand. Antiretroviral drugs are rarely available to these people because the drugs are expensive, are complex to administer, and require careful supervision by trained medical personnel. Some have suggested that developing countries forget about trying to treat those infected with HIV/AIDS and, instead, concentrate on preventing new infections. What gets lost in these statistics is the patient—the person suffering the effects of this ravaging disease. The readings in Chapter 18, "Nursing," on the other hand, demonstrate the rhetorical power of personal experience to counter the potentially numbing effect of numeric evidence. When personal experience is not possible—because of geographic or historical distance— examples and case studies can produce a similar rhetorical effect.

Your task is to research the topic of HIV/AIDS in developing countries, looking for both numeric information and information about individuals who suffer the effects of HIV/AIDS. Using both numeric and case study information, write an essay that ends in a set of recommendations. You can start your research with two Web sites that provide reliable information—www.unaids.org (the U.N. Web site for HIV/AIDS) and www.who.int/hiv/en (the World Health Organization Web site for HIV/AIDS). Choose to focus on either a particular developing country or a particular aspect of the HIV/AIDS crisis in developing countries. Decide on the claim you want to make and frame that as the working draft of your thesis.

As you begin drafting, list the likely responses that readers will have to your thesis. Include some of these in your essay and answer these questions or criticisms with evidence and reasoning. Consider the relationship between your working thesis and your recommendations, and revise both to enhance the relationship.

Assignment 3

In Christopher Layne's fourth endnote, he lists political conflicts, other than the Trent conflict, between democracies that also support his claim that realism better predicts historical outcomes than democratic peace theory.

Your task for this assignment is to select one of the political conflicts that Layne lists in his fourth endnote and write a case study of the conflict that emphasizes the features of the conflict that make it good evidence for the value of realism. Consult reference librarians for help finding detailed descriptions of these historical events.

As you begin drafting, consider how you will describe the theory of realism to emphasize the features that your case study will demonstrate. Decide where in your essay you will help the reader make connections between the historical events and how realist theory accounts for them. And think about how you will document the information you include in your essay.

16

BIOTECHNOLOGY

When you're hungry for breakfast, the American Egg Board (www.aeb.org) wants you to consider an incredible, edible egg (their trademarked phrase). Cheryl Long and Tabitha Alterman encourage you to eat eggs, too, but in an article in *Mother Earth News,* they warn that some eggs are more incredible than others. Long and Alterman argue that you should avoid eggs from factory farms like those that support the American Egg Board because these farms cruelly restrict the movements of chickens and produce eggs with lower nutritional content (see "Meet Real Free-range Eggs" at motherearthnews.com).

- Go to the American Egg Board site, and watch some of the videos on the Eggs 101 page. List the information that you found most reassuring about egg production. Describe each occasion when they address concerns about the experience of the chickens or the nutritional quality of the eggs that they produce.
- Read Long and Alterman's article and list the information that would persuade you to consider paying more for eggs from free-range hens. How would you describe the way they refer to large-scale egg farmers?
- Can you see any common ground or compromises between the two groups—any goals that they agree on?

PORTABLE RHETORICAL LESSON: PERSUADING WITH BALANCED ARGUMENTS

The preceding exercise requires you to think about food in ways beyond everyday needs: the ethical, scientific, and economic aspects of food production and consumption. You had to weigh competing claims on your morals and your pocketbook, and you had to decide what evidence was most persuasive.

The authors in this chapter face three major challenges that are similar to those you faced in the opening exercise:

1. Their audience is made up of various types of people (scientists, philosophers, politicians, sociologists, and businesspeople); they have different ethical and practical assumptions and agendas, which makes them more open to some approaches to the problems than to others. A person in charge of a country's finances must be persuaded that solutions are affordable; a person who writes about ethics must believe that solutions account for long-term implications for people's health.

2. The authors are talking about highly volatile issues—all the scientific, industrial, and ethical arguments about providing healthy and affordable food. And when the stakes run high, so do emotions.

3. The pressing need to solve problems including food, energy, and health means that stalemate and inaction are not options. They have to find common ground if they hope to move forward toward consensus on solutions that people can enact.

Given those challenges, writers in biotechnology need first to invest in making two kinds of rhetorical choices. First, they make a **point** in the form of what we call an "accommodating thesis," a thesis that will appeal to the various readers who must cooperate to act. Second, they use **research methods and evidence** that their various readers will trust.

To persuade people with varied vested interests to collaborate to solve problems, writers in biotechnology devise balanced arguments—the **Portable Rhetorical Lesson** for this chapter. Balanced arguments aim to keep all the involved parties talking together, involved in the ongoing conversation about problems and solutions. To achieve such balance, biotechnologists practice three particular strategies for building trust and cooperation:

1. Use a moderate tone. They demonstrate respect for those with whom they disagree, they admit the limits of their own claims, they honestly acknowledge their opponents' worthwhile objections, and they imply that effective change will happen only if all sides can find points of agreement. The "Notes on Grammar, Style, and Rhetoric" demonstrates how "hedges" help to convey this moderate tone.

2. Present evidence that everyone respects and understands. Facts, data—gathered through effective scientific methods—provide the best basis for common ground. And the data are presented in forms (tables, graphs, figures) that all readers understand. But authors will lose their audience's ear if they present only the facts that support their proposals. So they offer data that identifies both problems as well as possible effects of solutions—positive, negative, and uncertain.

3. Provide practical solutions. The authors emphasize that their solutions are the best available options—not necessarily perfect, but the best currently available. To argue for the best available solution, authors use data to establish the urgency of the problem, describe possible solutions, and demonstrate the superiority of one solution. A thesis with these features will accommodate both supporters and opponents.

When you write papers for college classes, especially in your first or second year, you write on many different topics. When you are committed to a single topic for only as long as it takes to write one paper, you may tend to build arguments that have strong "end-of-conversation" conclusions. Any one paper could well be the last thing you ever say about the paper's topic. But that experience does not prepare you for the fact that in your professional lives you will likely work on a small number of topics for a long time. To prepare for that reality, imagine yourself in the position of biotechnologists, accommodating yourself to ongoing debates about your topic, offering balanced, reasonable contributions to progress rather than asserting final say.

WRITING IN THE DISCIPLINE

INTRODUCTION

by David Koetje,
Professor of Biology

> People on both sides of the debate are unwittingly collaborating to create a very considerable threat indeed. The threat is that the debate over the pros and cons of genetically modified crops may become so acrimonious that the sides cease speaking to each other altogether. . . . Through our rhetoric, we may erode the foundation of mutual trust apart from which democratic institutions fail.
>
> Gary Comstock, "The Threat That Biotechnology Is"

One surefire way to infuriate your critics is to call their motives into question. Consider this quote from biotechnology proponent Norman Borlaug: "I think the researchers at Cornell who fed Bt corn pollen to monarch butterflies were looking for something that would make them famous and create this big hullabaloo that's resulted."* Put-downs are another conversation buster. In response to a challenge from an environmentalist who was questioning the need for GM crops, one biotechnologist retorted, "Well, I live in the *real* world." Though cheap shots like this may be normal in national politics, they can hardly be considered good persuasive writing because they further entrench existing disagreements rather than encouraging people to work together to solve real-world problems.

"Feeding the World in the Twenty-First Century" addresses widely held concerns about genetically modified (GM) foods and other forms of agricultural biotechnology. This article became an important piece of the history of the GM food debates. The authors, Gordon Conway and Gary Toenniessen, have served, respectively, as the president and the director of the food security program at the Rockefeller Foundation, a philanthropic organization that funds scientific and social research to improve the lives of poor people. The

---

*"Billions Served: Norman Borlaug," interview by Ronald Bailey. *Reason Magazine*, April 2000.

Rockefeller Foundation has funded efforts to advance agricultural science and biotechnology throughout the world. Naturally, Conway and Toenniessen see a lot of promise in biotechnology. Yet their respect for diverse ethical concerns and accurate scientific knowledge makes their writing persuasive for all their readers.

Context and Content of the Argument. Concern about GM crops, which have a gene borrowed from some other species, has spread worldwide. Can GM crops alleviate problems of hunger and death from starvation? Biotechnology proponents claim that GM crops are more resistant to insect infestation, disease, drought, flooding, and pollution. Therefore, they can boost food production, especially in developing countries where soils tend to be poorer. Critics of biotechnologies like genetically modified crops counter that agricultural companies are more likely to benefit more from GM crops than the poor and the hungry.

Conway and Toenniessen published this article in *Nature,* a leading scientific journal headquartered in the U.K. (a country that is deeply opposed to genetically modified crops) and read by scientists and policy analysts worldwide. The authors argue that GM crops help humanity; they "ensure that the world's poorest people do not still go hungry in the twenty-first century." Of course, some readers strongly disagree. But even if they disagree, they may like, for example, the authors' proposal of a partnership between the public sector (universities and international research centers) and the private sector (industry) to ensure that GM technologies are accessible to developing countries.

Conway and Toenniessen strive to make peace by appealing first to proponents, then to critics. First they discuss the benefits of GM crops and validate proponents' passionate advocacy of them; then they validate critics' concerns and admonish the proponents of biotechnology to take these concerns seriously.

Rhetorical Strategies for Balancing Passion, Reason, and Scientific Evidence. Good persuasive writing in bioethics must carefully balance scientific knowledge and ethical considerations. Conway and Toenniessen cite numerous published essays to frame their contributions within the wider conversation. These references point the reader to what has already been written about the topic, but more importantly, they acknowledge the important contributions that others—including critics—are making to the debate. Reference #15 is one such book. Environmentalists praise it for its well-reasoned summary of the ecological risks of GM crops, particularly those with the enhanced fitness traits identified earlier. Conway and Toenniessen refer to these criticisms as "genuine concerns." They also are careful to cite primary sources. Information passed on secondhand by way of a Web site posting, or even published in a review article, is not as reliable as the original source. This general rule applies to all persuasive writing.

Conway and Toenniessen include figures to present scientific data that underscore some of their primary points: the worrisome drop in crop yields in developing countries (Figure 1) and the diversity of biotechnology research in developing countries (Table 1 and Figure 2). But keep in mind that readers may respond to the data in different ways. For example, Figure 1 assumes a type of agricultural production that makes extensive use of high-energy inputs (fertilizers and fuels) to support monocultures (fields devoted to one species). For those who support alternative methods (such as organic farming), these data may underscore their contention that modern production agriculture, and biotechnology by extension, cannot sustain agriculture in developing countries. For a scientifically sophisticated audience, the data represent important talking points.

Finally, note how Conway and Toenniessen maintain the scientific sophistication of their arguments for a very diverse audience. Although most *Nature* readers are scientists, the authors recognize that not every reader will be. So they take care to avoid excessive use of scientific jargon. Most college graduates should understand most of the scientific terms and concepts. That the authors have been considerate of their audience's diversity—both in terms of their familiarity with the science and their ethical value systems—is another earmark of a good persuasive article.

✓ Reading Tips

In some science writing, readers can go to the data in the "Results" section and learn what they need to know. In this thesis-driven essay you need to read the whole text to follow the argument.

- Use the section headings as topic markers. Jot down each heading and sketch out the argument in each section. Determine how the sections fit together.

- Keep a list of the occasions when the authors appeal to people on both sides of the issue. Note the evidence that the authors use to appeal to those in favor of using technology on food production. Note the evidence they use to attract those who are opposed.

Feeding the World in the Twenty-First Century

Gordon Conway and Gary Toenniessen

Nature 1999, 402(suppl): C55–C58

The gains in food production provided by the Green Revolution have reached their ceiling while world population continues to rise. To ensure that the world's poorest people do not still go hungry in the twenty-first century, advances in plant biotechnology must be deployed for their benefit by a strong public-sector agricultural research effort.

> This one-paragraph abstract lays out the basic premise of the paper.

The Green Revolution was one of the great technological success stories of the second half of the twentieth century. Because of the intro-

> Critics disagree strongly with this statement . . .

duction of scientifically bred, higher-yielding varieties of rice, wheat and maize beginning in the 1960s, overall food production in the developing countries kept pace with population growth, with both more than doubling. The benefits of the Green Revolution reached many of the world's poorest people. Forty years ago there were a billion people in developing countries who did not get enough to eat, equivalent to 50 per cent of the population of these countries. If this proportion had remained unchanged, the hungry would now number over two billion—more than double the current estimate of around 800 million, or around 20 per cent of the present population of the developing world. Since the 1970s, world food prices have declined in real terms by over 70 per cent. Those who benefit most are the poor, who spend the highest proportion of their family income on food.

> . . . and this one. However, proponents of agricultural biotechnology typically use this argument to justify their cause.

The Green Revolution brought benefits too for the industrialized world. The high-yielding varieties of staple crop plants bred by the international agricultural research centres of the CGIAR (the Consultative Group on International Agricultural Research) have been incorporated into the modern varieties grown in the United States and Europe. The additional wheat and rice produced in the United States alone from these improved varieties is estimated to have been worth over $3.4 billion from 1970 to 1993.[1]

Yet today, despite these demonstrable achievements, over 800 million people consume less than 2,000 calories a day, live a life of permanent or intermittent hunger and are chronically undernourished.[2] Most of the hungry are the women and young children of extremely poor families in developing countries. More than 180 million children under five years of age are severely underweight: that is, they are more than two standard deviations below the standard weight for their age. Seventeen million children under five die each year and malnourishment contributes to at least a third of these deaths.

> In other words, 97.7% of kids their age weigh more than these hungry kids.

> The authors point this out to set up their argument that biotechnology, which offers tools to address such needs, is essential.

As well as gross undernourishment, lack of protein, vitamins, minerals and other micronutrients in the diet is also widespread.[3] About 100 million children under five suffer from vitamin A deficiency, which can lead to eye damage. Half a million children become partly or totally blind each year, and many subsequently die. Recent research has shown that lack of vitamin A has an even more pervasive effect, weakening the protective barriers to infection put up by the skin, the mucous membranes and the immune system.[4] Iron deficiency is also common, leading to about 400 million women of child-bearing age (15–49 years) being afflicted by anaemia. As a result they tend to produce stillborn or underweight children and are more likely to die in childbirth. Anaemia has been identified as a contributing factor in over 20 per cent of all maternal deaths after childbirth in Asia and Africa.

If nothing new is done, the number of the poor and hungry will grow. The populations of most developing countries are increasing rapidly and by the year 2020 there will be an additional 1.5 billion mouths to feed, mostly in the developing world. What is the likelihood that they will be fed?

The End of the Green Revolution

> Supporting data lend scientific credibility to their argument. Note, however, that the root cause of this rate of deceleration is open to speculation.

The prognosis is not good. As indicated in Fig. 1, there is widespread evidence of decline in the rate of increase of crop yields.[5-7] This slowdown is due to a combination of causes. On the best lands many farmers are now obtaining yields close to those produced on experimental stations, and there has been little or no increase in the maximum possible yields of rice and maize in recent years. A second factor is the cumulative effect of environmental degradation, partly caused by agriculture itself.

> In this paragraph the authors make these claims to support their contention that biotechnology offers the best solution. Critics may contend that market intervention may offer a better approach.

Simply exporting more food from the industrialized countries is not a solution. The world already produces more than enough food to feed everyone if the food were equally distributed, but it is not. Market economies are notoriously ineffective in achieving equitable distribution of benefits. There is no reason to believe that the poor who lack access to adequate food today will be any better served by future world markets. Food aid programmes are also no solution, except in cases of specific short-term emergency. They reach only a small portion of those suffering chronic hunger and, if prolonged, create dependency and have a negative impact on local food production.

> Cheap food has come to imply "industrial agriculture," which many claim is at the heart of food security problems.

About 130 million of the poorest 20 percent of people in developing countries live in cities. For them, access to food means cheap food from any source. But 650 million of the poorest live in rural areas where agriculture is the primary economic activity, and as is the case in much of Africa, many live in regions where agricultural potential is low and natural resources are poor.[8] They are distant from markets and have limited purchasing power. For them, access means local production of food

> Local food is often touted as a remedy for the economic ills of global industrial agriculture.

that generates employment and income, and is sufficient and dependable enough to meet local needs throughout the year, including years that are unfavourable for agriculture.

All these arguments point to the need for a second Green Revolution, yet one that does not simply reflect the successes, and mistakes, of the first. In effect, we require a 'Doubly Green Revolution', an

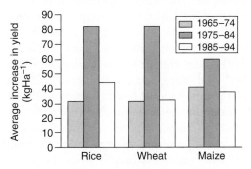

Figure 1 Average annual increase in yields of rice, wheat and maize in developing countries by periods.

Those who argue for sustainable agriculture will like these first two points. Conway and Toenniessen are probably hoping this will foster acceptance of their third component.

agricultural revolution that is both more productive and more 'green' in terms of conserving natural resources and the environment than the first. We believe that this can be achieved by a combination of: ecological approaches to sustainable agriculture; greater participation by farmers in agricultural analysis, design and research; and the application of modern biotechnology directed towards the needs of the poor in developing countries, which is the subject of the rest of this article.

The Price of Biotechnology

For many, this stretches the definition of "plant breeding." The authors are no doubt doing this to make a point: there's more to biotechnology than just genetic engineering.

The application of advances in plant breeding—including tissue culture, marker-aided selection (which uses DNA technology to detect the transmission of a desired gene to a seedling arising from a cross) and genetic engineering—are going to be essential if farmers' yields and yield ceilings are to be raised, excessive pesticide use reduced, the nutrient value of basic foods increased and farmers on less favoured lands provided with varieties better able to tolerate drought, salinity and lack of soil nutrients.

Noting this problem will gain some support among biotechnology's critics.

In the industrialized countries the new life-science companies, notably the big six multinationals—Astra-Zeneca, Aventis, Dow, Dupont, Monsanto and Novartis—dominate the application of biotechnology to agriculture. In 1998, 'genetically modified (GM)' crops, more accurately referred to as transgenic or genetically engineered crops, mostly marketed by these companies or their subsidiaries, were grown on nearly 29 million hectares worldwide (excluding China).[9] That year, 40 percent of all cotton, 35 percent of soya beans and 25 percent of maize grown in the United States were GM varieties.

1 hectare = 10,000 square meters = 2.47 acres

So far, the great majority of the commercial applications of plant genetic engineering have been for crops with single-gene alterations that confer agronomic benefits such as resistance to pests or to herbicides. These agronomic traits can reduce costs to the farmer by minimizing applications of insecticides and herbicides. However, as with many agricultural inputs, the benefits received by farmers vary from year to year.

Bt is shorthand for *Bacillis thuringiensis,* a common soil bacterium that produces Bt toxin, which kills caterpillars. It has no effect on humans and is therefore used in organic farming. Biotechnologists have placed the gene for Bt toxin in various crops to deter insect infestations. This may, however, speed insect resistance to Bt toxin.

Most of the GM crops currently being grown in developing countries are cash crops; Bt cotton, for example, has reportedly been taken up by over a million farmers in China. But despite claims to be 'feeding the world', the big life-science companies have little interest in poor farmers' food crops, because the returns are too low. National governments, the international research centres of the CGIAR, and a variety of western donors are, and will continue to be, the primary supporters of work that produces advances in biotechnology useful to poor farmers. New forms of public–private collaboration could help to ensure that all farmers and consumers benefit from the genetic revolution and, over time, this should increase the number of farmers who can afford to buy new seeds from the private sector.

The cost of accomplishing this will not be insignificant but it should not be excessive. For example, over the past 15 years, the Rockefeller Foundation has funded some US$100 million of rice biotechnology research and trained over 400 scientists from Asia, Africa and Latin America. In several places in Asia there is now a critical mass of talented scientists who are applying the new tools of biotechnology to rice improvement. To date, most of the new varieties are the result of tissue culture and marker-aided selection techniques. For example, scientists at the West Africa Rice Development Association have used anther culture to cross the high-yielding Asian rices with traditional African rices. The result is a new plant type that looks like African rice during its early stages of growth (it is able to shade out weeds, which are the most important constraint on crop production in Africa; . . .) but becomes more like Asian rice as it reaches maturity, thus giving higher yields with few inputs. Marker-aided selection is being used to breed rice containing two or more genes for resistance to the same pathogen, thereby increasing the durability of the resistance, and to accumulate several different genes contributing to drought tolerance.

> Plants can be regenerated from tissues grown in artificial media supplemented with plant growth hormones. Although such plants are typically clones, some can have new useful genetic traits.

> DNA fragments can serve as "markers" to identify plants that have certain genes even before the plant displays the trait associated with that gene. This expedites breeding.

> Anthers are the male parts of a flower.

Potential of Genetic Engineering

For some time to come, tissue culture and marker-aided selection are likely to be the most productive uses of biotechnology for cereal breeding. However, progress is being made in the production of transgenic crops for the developing countries. As in the industrialized countries, the focus has been largely on traits for disease and pest resistance, but genes that confer tolerance of high concentrations of aluminium (found in many tropical soils) have been added by Mexican scientists to rice and maize . . . , and Indian scientists have added two genes to rice which may help the plant tolerate prolonged submergence. There is also the possibility of increasing yield ceilings, through more efficient photosynthesis, for example, or by improved control of water loss from leaves through regulation of stomatal opening and closing.[10]

> That is, submergence under water during floods.

> Stomata are the specialized openings on the surfaces of leaves that allow gas and water exchange with the environment.

In addition to generating new traits that enable the plant to grow better (input traits), which are useful to poor farmers, GM technology can also generate plants with improved nutritional features (output traits) of benefit to poor consumers. One of the most exciting developments so far has been the introduction of genes into rice that result in the production of the vitamin A precursor β-carotene in the rice grain.[11] β-carotene is a pigment required for photosynthesis and is synthesized in the green tissues of all plants, including rice, but is not usually present in non-photosynthetic tissues such as those of seeds. Traditional plant breeding has given us some plants that produce β-carotene in non-photosynthetic tissue, such as the roots of carrots, but despite decades of searching no rice mutants had been found that produce β-carotene in the grain, so conventional breeding was not an option. To get the cells of the grain to produce β-carotene, genetic engineers added three genes for key enzymes for β-carotene biosynthesis to the rice genome. The grain of the transgenic rice has a light golden-yellow colour . . . and contains sufficient β-carotene

Table 1 Biotechnology research useful in developing countries

Traits now in greenhouse or field tests	Traits now in laboratory tests
Input traits	*Input traits*
Resistance to insects, nematodes, viruses, bacteria and fungi in crops such as rice, maize, potato, papaya and sweet potato	Drought and salinity tolerance in cereals
	Seedling vigour in rice
Delayed senescence, dwarfing, reduced shade avoidance and early flowering in rice	Enhanced phosphorus and nitrogen uptake in rice and maize
Tolerance of aluminium, submergence, chilling and freezing in cereals	Resistance to the parasitic weed *Striga* in maize, rice and sorghum, to viruses in cassava and banana, and to bacterial blight in cassava
Male sterility/restorer for hybrid seed production in rice, maize, oil-seed rape and wheat	Nematode resistance and resistance to the disease black sigatoka in banana
New plant types for weed control and for increased yield potential in rice	Rice with the alternative C, photosynthetic pathway and the ability to carry out nitrogen fixation
Output traits	*Output traits*
Increased β-carotene in rice and oil-seed rape	Increased β-carotene, delayed post-harvest deterioration and reduced content of toxic cyanides in cassava
Lower phytates in maize and rice to increase bioavailable iron	
Modified starch in rice, potato and maize and modified fatty-acid content in oil-seed rape	Increased vitamin E in rice
	Apomixis (asexual seed production) in maize, rice, millet and cassava
Increased bioavailable protein, essential amino acids, seed weight and sugar content in maize	Delayed ripening in banana
Lowered lignin content of forage crops	Use of genetically engineered plants such as potato and banana as vehicles for production and delivery of recombinant vaccines to humans
	Improved amino-acid content of forage crops

to meet human vitamin A requirements from rice alone. This 'golden' rice offers an opportunity to complement vitamin A supplementation programmes, particularly in rural areas that are difficult to reach. These same scientists and others have also added genes to rice that increase the grain's nutritionally available iron content by more than threefold.

Over the next decade we are likely to see much greater progress in multiple gene introductions that focus on output traits or on difficult-to-achieve input characteristics (Table 1).

That the authors are talking about the poor is implied in this comment on potential benefits.

The potential benefits of plant biotechnology are considerable, but are unlikely to be realized unless seeds are provided free or at nominal cost. This will require heavy public investment by national governments and donors, at times in collaboration with the private sector, both in the research and in the subsequent distribution of seed and technical advice. Breeding programmes will also need to include crops such as cassava, upland rice, African maize, sorghum and millet, which are the food staples and provide employment for the 650 million rural poor who need greater stability and reliability of yield as much as increased yield.

The Role of the Public Sector

In subsequent generations of the crop, these gene technologies would prevent reproduction via seeds or prevent expression of the novel genes. Some are now proposing these technologies as a strategy to reduce genetic pollution from transgenic plants.

None of this will happen through marketing by multinational seed companies, particularly if they decide to deploy gene-protection technologies, commonly referred to as terminator gene technologies, which will mean that farmers cannot save seed from the crop and sow it to get the next crop. In developing countries roughly 1.4 billion farmers still rely on saving seed for their planting materials and many gain access to new varieties through farmer-to-farmer trade. Much of the success of the Green Revolution was due to the true-breeding nature of the higher-yielding rice and wheat varieties.

Enabling technologies include methods and instruments, some of which are patented.

While terminator technology is clearly designed to prevent rather than encourage such spread of proprietary varieties among poor farmers, some argue that it will do them no harm because they can still use and replant new varieties from the public sector. But if the companies tie up enabling technologies and DNA sequences of important genes with patents, and then use terminator technologies to control the distribution of proprietary seed and restrict its use for further breeding, the public sector will be severely constrained in using biotechnology to meet the needs of the poor.

Hybrid seed is used extensively in developed countries.

Rather than using the terminator technology to protect their intellectual property in developing countries, it would be better if seed companies focused on producing hybrid seed combined with plant variety protection (PVP) to protect the commercial production of the seed. Hybrid plants do produce viable seed but it is not genetically identical to the original hybrid seed; it may lack some of the desirable characteristics.

Hence, there is still an incentive (for example, increased yield) for farmers to purchase hybrid seed for each planting. However, if such purchase is not possible, farmers can still use a portion of their harvest as seed and obtain a reasonable crop. Such recycling of hybrids is not uncommon in developing countries and is an important element of food security. And with PVP, new varieties can be protected while also becoming a resource that both the private and public sectors can use in further breeding for the benefit of all farmers.

Plant variety protection is more limited than typical biotechnology patents. It would allow farmers to grow it, but not sell it for seed.

Intellectual Property Rights

Even assuming that terminator technologies are not used, there is cause for concern about the rights of developing countries to use their own genetic resources, the freedom of their plant breeders to use new technologies to develop locally adapted varieties, and the protection of poor farmers from exploitation. In part, these concerns result from the privatization of crop genetic improvement, the rapid expansion of corporate ownership of key technologies and genetic information and materials, and the competitive pressure on these companies to capture world market share as rapidly as possible.

It is only recently that intellectual property rights (IPR) have become an important factor in plant breeding, primarily through the greater use of utility patents. Such patents have stimulated greater investment in crop improvement research in industrialized countries, but they are also creating major problems and potentially significant additional expense for the already financially constrained public-sector breeding programmes that produce seeds for poor farmers.

Utility patents confer broad rights to patent holders. They might cover, for example, any use of a certain useful gene. University scientists are pursuing these patents too.

The success of the Green Revolution was based on international collaboration which included the free exchange of genetic diversity and information. Most of the "added value" present in modern crops has been accumulated over the centuries by farmers themselves as they selected their best plants as the source of seed for the next planting. These "land races" have traditionally been provided free of charge by developing countries to the world community. The CGIAR centres add value through selective breeding, and the superior varieties they generate are widely distributed without charge, benefiting both developing and developed countries.

Another appeal from biotechnology's critics: crops are a common heritage that should be freely exchanged.

Patents on biotechnology methods and materials, and even on plant varieties, are complicating and undermining these collaborative relationships. Public-sector research institutions in industrialized countries no longer fully share new information and technology. Rather, they patent and license and have special offices charged with maximizing their financial return from licensing. Commercial production of any genetically engineered crop variety requires dozens of patents and licenses. It is only the big companies that can afford to put together the

The open exchange of ideas has historically been a critical component of the philosophy of science. This appeal is common among public sector scientists.

IPR portfolios necessary to give them the freedom to operate. And now, under the TRIPS (Trade-Related Aspects of Intellectual Property Rights) agreement of the World Trade Organization, most developing countries are required to put in place their own IPR systems, including IPR for plants. Furthermore, all of this 'ownership' of plant genetic resources is causing developing countries to rethink their policies concerning access to the national biodiversity they control, and new restrictions are likely.

So far, international negotiations relevant to agricultural biotechnology and plant genetic resources have not been effectively coordinated. There are inconsistencies, and the interests of poor farmers in developing countries have not been well represented. The days of unencumbered free exchange of plant genetic materials are no doubt over, and agreements and procedures need to be formulated to ensure that public-sector institutions have access to the technological and genetic resources needed to produce improved crop varieties for farmers in developing countries who will not be well served by the for-profit sector. If the big life-science companies wish to find a receptive and growing market in developing countries, they will need to work with the public sector to make sure this happens.

Some Solutions

While negotiations are underway, there are a number of things that should be done. With little competitive loss, seed companies could agree to use the PVP system (including provisions allowing seed saving and sharing by farmers) in developing countries in cooperation with public plant-breeding agencies, rather than using patents or terminator technologies to protect their varieties.

To speed the development of biotechnology capacity in developing countries, companies that have IPR claims over certain key techniques or materials might agree to license these for use in developing countries at no cost.

We would also like to see an agreement to share the financial rewards from IPR claims on crop varieties or crop traits of distinct national origin, such as South Asian Basmati rice or Thailand's Jasmine rice. The granting of free licenses to use such materials in breeding programmes in the country of origin of the trait might gain the appreciation of developing country researchers and governments.

Finally, the current opposition to GM crops and foods is likely to spread from Europe to the developing countries and maybe even to North America unless there is greater public reassurance. At the heart of the debate about the safety of GM crops and their food derivatives is the issue of relative benefits and risks. The debate is particularly impassioned in Europe. Some of it is motivated by anti-corporate or anti-American

---

Marginal notes:

A key question not adequately addressed here: what does it mean to "own" biodiversity?

Here, Conway and Toenniessen are proposing a big change in the way biotechnologists typically think about their enterprise. Following it up with some suggestions in the next paragraph lends practical support.

Risks and benefits are important, but here Conway and Toenniessen are at risk of oversimplifying critics' multifaceted concerns—.

North American biotechnologists typically support the view that GM crops are "substantially equivalent" to their non-GM counterparts and do not need extraordinary testing. This is lumping of a different kind, which critics strongly assail. Conway and Toenniessen imply that GM crops must be considered on a case-by-case basis. Thus, they contend that both camps have adopted the wrong strategy.

sentiment, but underlying the rhetoric are genuine concerns about lack of consumer benefits, about ethics, about the environment and about the potential impact on human health.[12–16]

Much of the opposition tends to lump together the various risks—some real, some imaginary—and to assume there are generic hazards.[17] However, GM organisms are not all the same and each provides different potential benefits to different people and different environmental and health risks. Calls for general moratoria are not appropriate. Each new transgene and each new GM crop containing it needs to be considered in its own right. Well planned field tests are crucial, particularly in the developing countries where the risks of using, or not using, a GM crop may be quite different from those in industrialized countries.

These three points will play well with critics, but cause concern among proponents. Clearly, throughout the paper Conway and Toenniessen are relying on their clout among proponents to win their support.

The multinational companies could take a number of specific decisions in this area that would improve acceptance of plant biotechnology in both the developing and the industrialized world. First, consumers have a right to choose whether to eat GM foods or not and although there are serious logistic problems in separating crops all the way from field to retail sale, the agricultural seed industry should come out immediately and strongly in favour of labelling. Second, the industry should disavow use of the terminator technology in developing countries and, third, it should phase out the use of antibiotic-resistance genes as a means of selecting transgenic plants. Alternatives exist and should be used.

The Rockefeller Foundation and other donors have invested significant sums in helping developing countries put in place biosafety regulations and the facilities necessary for biosafety testing of new crops and foods, but much more needs to be done. The big life-science companies could join forces and establish a fellowship programme for training developing country scientists in crop biotechnology, biosafety, intellectual property rights and international negotiations administered by a neutral fellowship agency.

This claim has far-reaching implications. In this paper they have tried to set the tone by identifying points of discussion from both sides of the debate. If you've been keeping tally, you know that they have placed the ball in the biotechnologists' court. Theirs is primarily a call to heed critics' concerns.

Most important of all, a new way of talking and reaching decisions is required. We believe a global public dialogue is needed which will involve everyone on an equal footing—the seed companies, consumer groups, environmental groups, independent scientists, and representatives of governments, particularly from the developing nations.

Agriculture in the twenty-first century will need to be more productive and less damaging to the environment than agriculture has been in the twentieth. An increased effort is needed to assure that the benefits of agricultural research reach the hundreds of millions of poor farmers who have benefited little from previous research. We believe that biotechnology has significant potential to help meet these objectives but that this potential is threatened by a polarized debate that grows increasingly acrimonious. We need to reverse this trend, to begin working together, to share our various concerns, and to assure the new technologies are applied to agriculture only when this can be done safely and effectively in helping to achieve future food security for our world.

Note added in proof: We commend the Monsanto Company's recent public commitment not to commercialize sterile seed technologies and encourage other companies to follow their lead.

Notes

1. Pardey, P. G. Alston, J. M., Christian, J. E. & Fan, S. *Summary of a Productive Partnership: The Benefits from U.S. Participation in the CGIAR* (International Food Policy Research Institute, Washington DC, 1996).
2. Conway, G. R. *The Doubly Green Revolution: Food for All in the 21st Century* (Penguin Books, London/Cornell University Press, Ithaca NY, 1999).
3. UNICEF. *The State of the World's Children 1998* (Oxford Univ. Press, Oxford/New York, 1998).
4. Somer, A. & West, K. P. *Vitamin A Deficiency: Health, Survival and Vision* (Oxford Univ. Press, New York and Oxford, 1966).
5. Mann, C. C. *Science* 283, 310–314 (1999).
6. Cassman. K. G. *Proc. Natl Acad. Sci. USA* 96, 5952–5959 (1999).
7. Pingali, P. L. & Heisey, P. W. *Cereal Productivity in Developing Countries: Past Trends and Future Prospects.* CIMMYT Economics Paper 99–03 (CIMMYT, Mexico, 1999).
8. Leonard, H. J. in *Environment and the Poor: Development Strategies for a Common Agenda* (ed. Leonard, H. J.) 3–45 (Overseas Development Council, Washington DC, 1989).
9. James, C. *Global Review of Commercialized Transgenic Crops: 1998.* ISAAA Briefs No. 8. (International Service for Acquisition of Agri-biotech Applications, Ithaca NY, 1998).
10. Mann, C. C. *Science* 283, 314–316 (1999).
11. Ye, X. D. et al. *Science* (submitted).
12. The Royal Society of London. *Genetically Modified Plants for Food Use* (The Royal Society, London, 1998).
13. Nuffield Council on Bioethics. *Genetically Modified Crops: The Ethical and Social Issues* (Nuffield Council on Bioethics, London, 1999).
14. UN Food and Agriculture Organization. *Biotechnology and Food Safety.* FAO Food and Nutrition Paper 61. (World Health Organization/FAO, Rome, 1996).
15. Rissler, J. & Mellon, M. *The Ecological Risks of Engineered Crops* (MIT Press, Cambridge MA/London, 1996).
16. May, R. *Genetically Modified Foods: Facts, Worries, Policies and Public Confidence* (http://www.2.dti.gov.uk/ost/ostbusiness/gen.html, 1999).
17. Pretty, J. *The Biochemist* (in the press).

Acknowledgements

We thank M. Lipton, S. Dryden, R. May and colleagues at the Rockefeller Foundation for comments on an earlier draft of this article.

Reading Responses

1. How much did you know about biotechnology before you read Conway and Toenniessen's essay? Did they persuade you that biotechnology is a safe and effective way to combat worldwide poverty? What parts of their essay did you find most convincing? What parts did you find least convincing?

2. On a scale of 1–10 (where 1 = simple and 10 = impossible) where would you plot the difficulty of reading this essay? Note specific places in the text where the authors go out of their way to help readers who know little about biotechnology.

3. In a marginal comment, Professor Koetje notes that Conway and Toenniessen direct most of their recommendations to those in favor of biotechnology solutions to world hunger. Why is this an effective persuasive strategy? How will critics of biotechnology respond to these recommendations?

NOTES ON GRAMMAR, STYLE, AND RHETORIC:
HEDGES IN PERSUASIVE WRITING

A student teacher was introducing a group of high-school seniors to the nature of persuasive writing. As she neared the end of the session, she paused briefly and said, "One last thing—what do you think you should do if you suspect that some readers will have a position opposed to yours? If you have a good idea about what their position is, should you bring it up? Or would you maybe want to soften how you state your position to avoid alienating those readers?"

A young man slouching in a desk responded immediately: "Soften it? You've got to be kidding. If some readers are opposed to your view, you've got to crush them. State your position as if any other view would be stupid." Several of his classmates turned toward him and grinned in agreement.

That teacher would do well in a future class on persuasive writing to show her students Gordon Conway and Gary Toenniessen's "Feeding the World in the Twenty-First Century." For in this persuasive essay, the authors clearly acknowledge that some readers will be opposed to their position. And they express their position in such a way that those opposed to it will probably not get angry or dismissive. In part, Conway and Toenniessen do this work through skillful uses of what linguists call *hedges*.

Hedges are linguistic elements that help us to soften positions, to be somewhat tentative about them, to pull back from expressing them as if we were certain about them. We can hedge with adverbs such as *possibly* and *perhaps*, with modal auxiliary verbs such as *may* and *might*, with main verbs such as *seem* and *suggest*, and with phrases such as *to a certain extent* and *to our knowledge*. In addition, we can hedge clauses that express parts of our position by introducing them with other clauses such as *We believe that*, *We suggest that*, and *It is possible that*.

In "Feeding the World," Conway and Toenniessen use two kinds of hedges at prominent points of their essay. At the end of their opening subsection, they include this sentence, which is the most general statement of their overall position: "We believe that this [having a "Doubly Green Revolution"] can be achieved by a combination of: ecological approaches to sustainable agriculture; greater participation by farmers in agricultural analysis, design and research; and the application of modern biotechnology directed towards the needs of the poor in developing countries, which is the subject of the rest of this article" (155). Note that this statement is introduced with the prominent hedge "We believe that," which Conway and Toenniessen also use to introduce some other clauses near the end of their essay. If you have some doubt about the hedging effect of "We believe that," read the sentence once with the

"We believe that" where it appears in the essay and once with the "We believe that" omitted. You should notice a striking difference in the force of these two sentences.

In the last section of their essay, which carries the modest title "Some Solutions," Conway and Toenniessen do quite a bit of hedging with modal verbs. For instance, here is a controversial claim that is hedged with the modal verb *might:* "To speed the development of biotechnology capacity in developing countries, companies that have IPR [intellectual property rights] claims over certain key techniques or materials might agree to license these for use in developing countries at no cost"(160). In several other sentences in this section, Conway and Toenniessen hedge with the modal verb *could.* Here is one example: "The multinational companies could take a number of specific decisions in this area that would improve acceptance of plant biotechnology in both the developing and the industrialized world" (161).

At this point, you might ask whether such obvious hedges in such prominent positions actually weaken Conway and Toenniessen's argument, making it appear hesitant or wordy. In fact, a hedged passage can be especially persuasive because its reasonable moderation invites readers to respond in kind. Hedges, in other words, can help writers communicate to readers, "We are reasonable people. Why not consider our view seriously?"

Besides, no one can accuse Conway and Toenniessen of being weak in their overall presentation. Indeed, they include many direct statements of what they clearly regard as facts, as when they introduce their final paragraph by writing that "Agriculture in the twenty-first century will need to be more productive and less damaging to the environment than agriculture has been in the twentieth" (161).

In Your Own Writing . . .

- If a claim can be shown to be based on facts, state it directly.
- If a claim cannot clearly be shown to be based on facts or if a claim is controversial, use a strategically placed hedge.
- Where it's especially important that your audience agree with you, use a hedge to create a claim that your audience is more likely to find acceptable.

STUDENT WRITING

INTRODUCTION

by Meghan Sheehan,
biotechnology major

The Assignment. What follows is a persuasive paper I wrote for a course titled "Perspectives in Biotechnology." The professor assumed that students had a strong laboratory background and thus could understand the technical terms. Interestingly, though, we also had to have completed prerequisite liberal arts classes before we enrolled in this class. The assignment for this paper asked us to describe a problem associated with biotechnology and provide a solution.

The Content. I chose one of the most troublesome issues in biotechnology—the proper use of genetic testing. Genetic testing, particularly universal genetic testing (that is, testing everyone) raises all sorts of concerns, from worries about private medical information becoming public knowledge to concerns that genetic testing will be used to discriminate against people. I narrowed the focus of my research to the function of genetic testing in the field of medical insurance. I was able to highlight the principal problems associated with the use of genetic testing by medical insurance companies, but providing a solution proved more complicated. Because health care is an issue of public concern that nonetheless involves private companies, I realized that any solution I offered would have political implications. I think that my solution is a good one, but I worry that those who disagree with my political leanings might disagree with my solution, too.

Learning to Write in Biotechnology. When I was writing my essay, I focused on two goals. First, given the controversial nature of my topic, I knew that I could expect both friendly and hostile readers, and I wanted to gain the respect of both. To gain their respect and to encourage them to consider my ideas, I had to respect not only the scholars I cited in my essay, but also my readers, those who disagree with me as well as those who see things my way. I knew that I wouldn't be able to convince every reader, but I hoped that I'd at least be able to make them consider my arguments, instead of angering them and causing them to dismiss my ideas. Additionally, I hoped to revise this essay and publish it in a journal, so reader respect became an absolute necessity. I tried to accomplish this goal primarily by using noninflammatory diction (which was hard) and by not mocking any of the views that I discussed in my essay (also hard, but not as hard as the first part).

The second goal was that my argument had to be practical; I wanted my readers to agree with me because I suggested reasonable solutions. This arose from my personality as much as from the class. We read a number of essays by many different authors for the class, and I disliked the essays that simply named and expounded on a problem without offering suggestions for fixing it. It is well and good to recognize a flaw, but I had no patience (and therefore no respect) for authors who couldn't suggest a way to mend it. Worst of all were the suggestions that were unworkable because they were either too vague or simply impractical. Because of this, I took great pains in my essay to include detailed and practical solutions for the problems I studied.

I kept both of these lessons in mind while I was writing this essay. Too often people are more eager to speak than they are to listen; more eager to win an argument than to find a solution that everyone can live with. By writing to build consensus rather than writing to win, I not only serve as a mediator between opposed groups, I also move us closer to implementing a workable solution rather than continuing an argument. I aimed for a well-reasoned argument that most readers could respect and find thought-provoking.

The Insurance Industry and Adult Preventative Genetic Screening: An Evil Beast Using Awesome Powers for Harm?

Meghan Sheehan

Abstract

In this paper, the issue of genetic screening in the insurance industry is discussed, particularly the practice of predictive screening prior to issuing health and life insurance. Predictive screening raises concerns that

WHAT?!? WHERE IS THE THESIS?!? Not every essay begins with a thesis. Ordering this essay in sections, marked with headings, allows me to describe the problem before I get to my main point—my solution. Without this background information, my audience would be less likely to accept the plan I'm proposing.

some clients will not be able to find insurance and that the use of genetic screening raises the risk of genetic determinism. To exemplify these concerns this paper considers attempts by the Association of British Insurers at self-regulation, regulation by the state of Michigan, and one ethicist's call for a system that circumvents the problems associated with genetic screening. Rather than perform genetic screening, the insurance industry should perform as any business would. Since the current insurance system is maladapted to absorb the influx of genetic information and yet insure everyone regardless of genetic condition, this paper presents a new system of insurance more able to handle the claims of *every* individual.

I broke my paper into parts, using headings to increase the overall readability of the essay. This section, "Current Issues," provides background information on the problem. The reader needs this information to understand both the nature of the problem and how my solution can fix it.

Current Issues in Genetic Screening and Insurance, an Introduction

Currently, outside of reproductive therapies, most genetic screening done on asymptomatic adults is termed predictive or presymptomatic testing. This type of screening is done to judge whether an adult with a familial history of a disease has a genotype conducive to the disease. For example, patients who have a family history of Huntington disease (HD) can have a genetic test performed to determine whether they have the excessive genetic DNA repeat that causes HD long before they show any sort of symptoms of the disease. Again, this type of test is typically performed only on patients who have an established familial history of the disease. Screening of this sort is not currently performed on the population at large.

Depending on your philosophical tradition, you could argue that fairness for society at large is irrelevant. This is an argument I did not think of at the time, so I did not address the point. In general, though, I'm trying to reach out to readers who might otherwise disagree with me by voicing their concerns in a respectful way.

Many people are concerned, though, that this sort of screening may eventually become a universal prerequisite for receiving health and life insurance.[1] These people worry that if a test reveals a person's genetic disposition towards a disease, especially a chronic disease, that person may face greatly increased insurance premiums or even find herself uninsurable. Along the same lines, some worry that universal predictive screening will produce a class of patients who are deemed genetically superior, from a medical stand point, and who would therefore pay a miniscule premium. In both supposed scenarios, the results of such a screening are unfair: in the first case those patients who have a greatly increased need for insurance would not receive it and in the second society at large does not benefit from the reduced rate of a few "lucky" individuals.

Genetic determinism can mean that your biological fate is caused by your genes and nothing you can do will change this fate.

I would argue that we should be concerned about universal predictive screening for another reason—the risk of genetic determinism. If people overly value the results of these tests, they might de-emphasize lifestyle choices that affect the length and quality of their lives. Furthermore, people might presume that if a person is genetically inclined towards a disease he is certain to develop that disease. Socioeconomic and environmental factors play a large role in whether a person actually succumbs to the potential disease. A classic example of other factors determining the onset of disease is the case of diabetes mellitus in genetically identical twins; only one-in-three times do both twins develop diabetes mellitus.[2] Two thirds of the time the second twin (with the exact same genes as the first twin) is able to avoid the disease by changing his exercise regimen and diet. Furthermore, many genetic diseases are not simple monogenic diseases. Therefore, screening for multigenic diseases must account for several factors, both genetic and non-genetic, before it can be fairly concluded, "yes/no, this patient has/does not have a high probability of disease." If an insurance company does not consider all factors, both genetic and non-genetic, when it interprets the results of genetic screening, it may unfairly charge an increased premium throughout the entire life of a person, even if he never develops the disease. The basis of these charges could lie solely in the interpretation of one test showing that he is an increased risk because of his propensity for a disease.

> Monogenic diseases are caused by a single genetic problem.

Addressing These Concerns

> I think my argument would be stronger if I used statistics from an American insurance association. These statistics would appeal more to readers throughout the U.S.

These are very valid concerns and both the insurance industry at large and the government have tried to address them. The Association of British Insurers (ABI), a non-government organization which 96% of insurance companies in the United Kingdom are part of, has drafted an extensive code outlining what the member companies may and may not do regarding genetic screening.[3] The guidelines address many topics and specifically state:

- Applicants must not be asked to undergo a screening in order to obtain insurance.
- If results from a screening are obtained, the insurer must consult a specialist for interpretation of the results.
- The screen must be ruled valid by the ABI genetics board before insurers can use it to cause premium increases.
- Informed, adult consent is required for all types of genetic screening.
- Policyholders are not required to reveal the results of a blood relative's test.
- Insurers must not offer lower than standard premiums on the basis of genetic test results.
- Insurers in the ABI are required to offer a minimum life insurance policy of £100,000 that cannot be affected by a genetic test.
- Each year the insurance company must demonstrate that they are following the Genetics Code set forth by ABI to renew membership status.

In the state of Michigan, citations SB590 and SB593 attempt to address some of the same issues that the ABI regulated in the United Kingdom.

Specifically, these laws prohibit health insurers from requiring an asymptomatic applicant or insured person to submit to genetic testing before issuing, renewing or continuing a policy. Additionally, applicants are under no obligation to discuss whether previous testing has been performed, and physicians are prohibited from performing predictive genetic tests without the written, informed consent of the adult subject.[4]

> I couldn't find evidence from an American insurance association, but I did find information on the laws pertaining to the state where my professor lives.

From these examples, we see that both industry associations and government agencies are trying to address the very real concerns discussed above. Especially admirable are the efforts of ABI to ensure that genetic screenings do not unfairly limit a person's access to life insurance and health insurance.

What about industry regulation of insurance in the United States? Will for-profit insurance agencies in corporate America regulate themselves as the ABI does? Already people have complained that some U.S. insurance companies are labeling some people as uninsurable,"[5] especially patients with chronic conditions such as Huntington disease and cystic fibrosis. Would a for-profit industry allow regulation that requires it to insure the "uninsurable"? James Peterson argues that this is unlikely. Furthermore, he calls for an undefined health care system in which all people are guaranteed basic health care.[6] A universal health care system would avoid the potential problems of the current insurance system, and would offer health care to all people, including those who most need the insurance because of their genetic conditions. He does not explain how such a system could be implemented, but he argues that universal, basic health care would ensure that everyone received treatment, regardless of their genes. In Peterson's argument, this concern for the "uninsurable" is the only reason why a system of universal health care is necessary.

> Peterson wrote one of the essays we read for class. I tried to summarize his proposed solution. In retrospect, I think I may have been too brief.

> I bring up this point here to prepare my audience to see an advantage of my solution—my plan takes into account other considerations in addition to patient need.

Realistically Addressing the Concerns in the United States—A Radical Approach

Is the insurance industry truly evil? Is a universal health care system necessary to ensure that each person, regardless of genetic status, is treated? Should genetic status be a factor, i.e., should genetic screening be required for insurance?

No, the insurance industry is not evil. But insurance companies are in business to make a profit; they exist primarily to make money for shareholders and only secondarily to benefit the insured. If industry companies do not make a profit, they will cease to exist; someone, presumably individuals, will have to pick up the tab for our health expenses. What does this mean for you and me? It means that when I buy health insurance from an agency, I buy a policy from a company that also insures hundreds or thousands of other people. All of us pay a premium to keep our policy active. This money is pooled together, and the company draws from this pool when one of us files a claim. Whatever is leftover in the pool is the company's profit. As a for-profit institution, an insurance company is always looking for ways to maximize the amount of money left in the pool—their profit ratio. Therefore, insurance companies seek to insure low-risk applicants because they are less likely to draw heavily from the pool. People who have no chronic health conditions have fewer regular health expenses, and with few exceptions for unforeseen catastrophic events, their claims take less from the pool than a high-risk applicant who takes out more money, and takes it out more often. To put it very simply, insurance is a business of risk-management—insurance companies seek to minimize their risks to maximize their profits. If they used genetic screening to evaluate potential policyholders, companies could further minimize their risks.

> This mysterious person could suffer from a range of diseases—from sickle cell anemia or genetically determined hypertension to diseases like Huntington disease or cystic fibrosis.

Rather than focusing on universal health care system, we should consider the possibilities for a universal *insurance* system. If we agree that morally and ethically *all* people should have access to affordable health care, we must create a system to make health care affordable. If we agree that businesses have a right to make a profit and that all people deserve affordable healthcare, we must create a system that allows companies to make a profit while still insuring high-risk people. The government can ill-afford to subsidize insurance companies, so we must seek another solution. Extremely large, privately operated insurance companies that operated under a stringent government oversight system and an unheard of profit distribution system could effectively insure all of us, low- and high-risk alike.

> Here I link together the two propositions I've carefully established. This lays the groundwork for my proposed solution.

Very, very large companies would be necessary, so large that there could be only a few in the entire country. Because insurance companies must be very large to efficiently absorb the costs of high-risk people, there is room in the U.S. for only a few companies. I propose a few companies rather than a monopoly or a government agency because I do not believe that a monopoly would benefit either the insured or the insurance companies. Currently, health insurance is distributed between multiple companies in the United States. For a condition such as Tay-Sachs disease, one in 250 people in the population at large is a carrier while one in 27 people in the Ashkenazi Jew population is a carrier.[7] Imagine one large company with a statistically average percentage of Ashkenazi Jews in their client pool. Only 1 in ~63,000 births will be a child with Tay-Sachs. Now imagine a small company that, through fate of location, insures primarily Ashkenazi Jews. Because 1 in ~800 births will be a child with Tay-Sachs, the company would have an at least 8x larger chance of paying out on Tay-Sachs claims for children of those they insure. Statistically speaking, it does not matter to that smaller company that Tay-Sachs is a rare disease; because they have a

> Tay-Sachs is a wasting disease of the neurological system. Babies born with it appear normal at first and seem to develop quite well. Slowly, though, they start to regress, and most die by age five.

comparatively small client pool, statistics simply do not work in their favor. However, if there was a very, very large (i.e., multi-regional) client pool, statistics would be restored to the 1 in ~63,000 births. Additionally, because there would be a large clientele, their pool of money would be quite large. Indeed, the pool would be so large that the payment on large claims would be a smaller percentage and hurt the company much less. Insurance companies with large pools can afford to insure those who are currently "medically uninsurable" because the statistics regarding genetic disorders actually work in their favor—the good news is that most people are not genetically predisposed to catastrophic diseases that require expensive medical treatment.

These large insurance companies should be privately operated because the current system of distributed power and government bureaucracy could not effectively process medical claims. Additionally, for reasons to be discussed below, these companies should be privately operated to ensure that they still turn a profit. Decisions about what is best for the company would still need to be made by the executives within the company to ensure that it remained vital. Additionally, incentives such as profit sharing and bonuses would encourage employees to work efficiently, and these incentives are unheard of from government employers.

The policy decisions of these large companies would require strict governmental oversight to ensure that the veritable monopoly of a few companies does not abuse the people that they serve. The government oversight should also include an independent panel of genetic counselors who interpret the results from genetics tests. In this way, the counselors can avoid the ethical dilemma of trying to serve two contrary masters (the people whose tests they read and the insurance company that employs them). Finally, the government should regulate profit distribution in the companies. Because the companies would operate in near-monopoly conditions, they could potentially make obscene profits. To combat this and to further the cause of benefiting people through advancements in medicine, a large percentage of the profits from the companies (perhaps as large as 50%, although this may not be realistic) should be *donated* to medical research. This would benefit society at large and also the company through more effective, cheaper treatments of their clients in the future.

Returning to the issue that opened this essay—should these companies perform genetic screening? I believe that they should perform genetic screening only for diseases where genetic tendency plays a role equal to other environmental factors and the genetic tendency can be flagged by a simple test. In the spirit of promoting better health for the client and keeping costs for the company down, this kind of testing would allow the company to provide incentives to help clients stay healthy. If, for example, through screening a client is discovered to have the CHD2 gene (the gene that can cause high cholesterol[8]), the insurance company can offer the client a lower premium if she can demonstrate that she lives a healthy lifestyle (through independently administered doctor physical results). In this case, government oversight would ensure two things: (1) the premium rates for those who do and do not live healthy lifestyles and (2) what would count as the minimum physical results for the lower premium. In the end, the first policyholder would benefit from a healthier lifestyle (even if she never developed the disease), the second policyholder would exercise personal autonomy, and the insurance company would benefit from the desire of policyholders to be healthy.

> Here, at the end, is the thesis. The insurance system I describe is the necessary context for this claim. Without the system, my claim is unworkable.

Only this type of universal insurance system offers the necessary controls on universal predictive genetic screening. In this system, selective screening for a few manageable diseases benefits all people. The use of any type of predictive genetic screening outside such an insurance system and government oversight creates the potential for unethical use of this technology.

References

1. "Genetic Testing." Genetics and Public Policy Center. 22 Jan. 2004 http://www.dnapolicy.org/genetics/testing.jhtml.
2. Peterson, James C. *Genetic Turning Points: The Ethics of Human Genetic Intervention.* Grand Rapids: Eerdmans, 2001. p 206–211.
3. Drell, Daniel. "FAQs." *Human Genome News* 9. p 4: nos 1–2. 1998.
4. "Genetic Testing–ABI Code of Practice." Association of British Insurers. 22 Jan. 2004. http://www.abi.org.uk/Display/default.asp?Menu_ID=946&Menu_All=1,946,0&Child_ID=203.
5. "Genetic Information and Health Insurance Enacted State Legislation." National Human Genome Research Institute. 22 Jan. 2004 http://www.genome.gov/page.cfm?pageID=10002338.
6. Peterson. p 210–211.
7. "Tay-Sachs Disease." Jewish Genetic Diseases MazorNet. 22 Jan. 2004 http://www.mazornet.com/genetics/tay-sachs.asp
8. "Gene Responsible for High Cholesterol." *Applied Genetics News.* (2001). Retrieved 22 Jan 2004 http://www.findarticles.com/cf_dls/m0DED/11_21/76142147/p1/article.jhtml

Reading Responses

1. Note three places in her essay where Meghan Sheehan accommodates her audience's prior knowledge and assumptions. For each place, describe the strategy she uses. Find two places where you believe Meghan should have worked harder to reach out to her audience.

2. Sheehan intentionally delays presenting her thesis until the last paragraph of her essay. In what ways does this organization treat the reader respectfully? In what ways might it be disrespectful to the reader? Do you think this is an ethical way to organize the essay? List your reasons.

3. List three adjectives to describe Sheehan's tone in this essay. For each adjective, jot down an example or two from her essay.

PUBLIC WRITING

INTRODUCTION

Different regions of the world have responded differently to the rapid increase in the availability of genetically modified crops. In the United States, for example, although there are many serious opponents, GM crops are common on grocery store shelves. In England, on the other hand, an ethicist at Durham University recently said that asking English people to feed their children GM foods would be like asking them to feed their children anthrax.

South Africa, like many African countries, faces great demand for food production—and thus great pressure to increase production with GM crops. South Africa's Department of Science and Technology has begun a program called "Public Understanding of Biotechnology," which, according to their Web site (www.pub.ac.za/about/aims.php), seeks to "ensure a clear, balanced understanding of the scientific principles, related issues and potential of biotechnology and to stimulate public debate around its applications in society."

The document that follows is a poster created for the "Public Understanding of Biotechnology" campaign. Like the other readings in this chapter, the need for this piece to appeal to an audience of varied opinions and levels of knowledge demands a balanced articulation of the point. In the bottom right corner—the "end" of the document—one finds the main character of the poster saying, "GM is here with its benefits and risks. What choices will you make about using it?" In other words, the main point of the piece is to say that people must make an educated choice about using GM crops, so they must become educated.

BIOTECHNOLOGY: GENETIC MODIFICATION OF CROPS

WHAT'S GM?

"GENETICALLY MODIFIED". THAT CEREAL IS THE PRODUCT OF GENETIC MODIFICATION IN A LABORATORY.

IT'S FROM BIOTECHNOLOGY: ADAPTING A BIOLOGICAL PROCESS TO MEET HUMAN NEEDS.

BUT DON'T I GET THE RIGHT TO CHOOSE?

OF COURSE YOU DO! DO YOU WANT CORN CRUNCH OR CORN CRACKLE?

GENETIC MODIFICATION INTRODUCES CHARACTERISTICS FROM ONE LIVING THING INTO ANOTHER.

BUT HOW IS IT DONE? AND WHY?

resurrection plant

1 TO GROW MAIZE IN A DRY AREA, FIND A PLANT THAT SURVIVES SEVERE DROUGHTS.

2 IN A LABORATORY, IDENTIFY THE GENE THAT GIVES THE PLANT ITS SPECIAL DROUGHT RESISTANCE.

A GENE IS A SECTION OF DNA, WHICH CARRIES INFORMATION ABOUT A PARTICULAR CHARACTERISTIC.

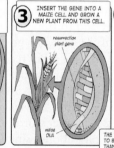

3 INSERT THE GENE INTO A MAIZE CELL, AND GROW A NEW PLANT FROM THIS CELL.

resurrection plant gene

maize DNA

4 WHEN THE MAIZE GROWS, IT IS ABLE TO SURVIVE BETTER IN DRY CONDITIONS.

THE TRANSFER OF SPECIFIC GENES IS THOUGHT TO BE MORE PRECISE AND IS MUCH FASTER THAN CONVENTIONAL BREEDING TECHNIQUES.

GM IN SOUTH AFRICA

GM CROPS HAVE BEEN GROWN COMMERCIALLY IN SOUTH AFRICA SINCE 1997. THEY CURRENTLY INCLUDE MAIZE, COTTON AND SOYA BEANS.

maize   cotton   soya beans

THE GMO ACT OF 1997 GOVERNS THE USE OF GENETICALLY MODIFIED ORGANISMS (GMO'S) IN SOUTH AFRICA.

NEW GMO'S MUST BE APPROVED BY THE DEPT. OF AGRICULTURE ADVISED BY THE GMO EXECUTIVE COUNCIL. APPROVAL INVOLVES ASSESSMENT OF IMPACT ON HUMAN HEALTH, THE ENVIRONMENT AND SOCIO-ECONOMICS.

FOOD SECURITY
FEEDING THE WORLD, NOW AND IN THE FUTURE.

WHILE GM, AMONG OTHER TECHNOLOGIES, MIGHT HELP, IT CANNOT ALONE ENSURE FOOD SECURITY. POLITICS, ECONOMICS AND POOR FARMING TECHNIQUES ARE MAJOR CONTRIBUTORS TO FOOD SHORTAGES.

TO ENSURE SUSTAINABLE FOOD PRODUCTION, SMALL-SCALE FARMERS NEED TO HAVE CONTROL OVER LAND, WATER, SEED AND ACCESS TO MARKETS.

MANY PEOPLE FEEL THAT RETAINING TRADITIONAL FARMING METHODS IS CRITICAL TO FOOD SECURITY PROVIDED ATTENTION IS GIVEN TO SUSTAINABILITY AND POVERTY ALLEVIATION.

HOW DO YOU FEEL ABOUT GENETIC MODIFICATION?

AS WITH ALL TECHNOLOGIES THERE ARE BENEFITS AND RISKS.

GM MAY SOON ALLOW US TO:

GROW MORE CROPS ON LESS LAND, AND GROW CROPS WHERE PREVIOUSLY IT WAS TOO DRY OR SALTY.

GROW CROPS FOR NEW USES, LIKE BIODEGRADABLE PLASTICS, NUTRITIONAL SUPPLEMENTS OR PHARMACEUTICALS.

BUT CONCERNS HAVE BEEN RAISED OVER HEALTH AND ENVIRONMENTAL RISKS

WILL MOVING GENES BETWEEN SPECIES PRODUCE TOXINS THAT ARE CURRENTLY NOT TESTED FOR?

WILL GM CROPS CROSS-POLLINATE WITH WILD PLANTS, TRANSFERRING UNWANTED CHARACTERISTICS THAT MAY THREATEN BIODIVERSITY?

...AS WELL AS SOCIAL AND ECONOMIC RISKS

GM PRODUCERS USE PATENTED GENES THAT CAN COST MORE AND HAVE GROWING RESTRICTIONS.

WILL THESE CROPS BE AFFORDABLE AND ACCESSIBLE TO FARMERS NOW AND IN THE FUTURE, AND WILL TRADITIONAL SEED AND TECHNIQUES BE MAINTAINED, OR LOST FOREVER?

GM SEED

GM IS HERE WITH ITS BENEFITS AND RISKS. WHAT CHOICES WILL YOU MAKE ABOUT USING IT?

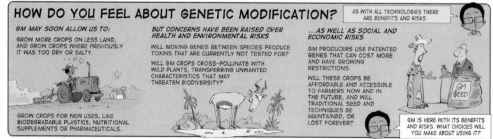

Reading Responses

1. Where does this poster present the arguments of those who support the use of GM crops? Where does it present the concerns of those who oppose GM crops?

2. Who is the audience of this poster? What role does the audience play in the debate over the use of GM crops?

3. Evaluate how this poster conveys information. How would you evaluate the visual appeal? How would you evaluate the amount, the complexity, and the sequence of information presented? Do you see any signs of an attempt to persuade the audience to favor or oppose GM crops?

MORE WRITING IN BIOTECHNOLOGY

INTRODUCTION

In this chapter we have been focusing on how biotechnologists try to create balanced, reasonable arguments. But, of course, we know that the hot-button issues that biotechnologists deal with will cause some heated and biased arguments to surface. "Science and Technology in World Agriculture" is about that very issue, discussing the ways that narratives—stories—can be used to bias or balance an argument.

The author, Pasquale Scandizzo, describes two opposing stories told by people working in biotechnology and agriculture. At one extreme, the "conservative" "conventional" story makes science and technology heroic, always creating newer and better ways for humans to produce food without harming the environment. The alternative, "radical" story is that technology serves big business and that small farmers and the environment are consequently at risk. The World Bank, says Scandizzo, offers the story that balances between these two extremes. In this excerpt we reprint one of the five examples of areas in which the World Bank narrative balances conservative and radical poles.

Scandizzo, who earned a PhD in economics at the University of California, Berkeley, is now a professor at the University of Rome. As an undergraduate he studied agricultural sciences. His knowledge of the World Bank is boosted by the fact that he was an employee of the World Bank for about ten years after he completed his Ph.D.

Science and Technology in World Agriculture: Narratives and Discourses

Pasquale Lucio Scandizzo

AgBioForum 21(1), 2009

Abstract

The narratives characterizing the current debate on world agricultural research tend to be part of a discourse that rationalizes past experience and future tendencies along the lines of extreme recounts of successes and failures. Stories of agricultural development and of accomplishments of research and science in agriculture tend to be organized according to either a conservative or a radical paradigm, which are in sharp contrast with each other and are at the origin of basic disagreements and biased information. For the neutral observer, these contrasting views—to the extent that they seem to concern facts more than opinions—cause disorientation and stress in the form of the well-known phenomenon of cognitive dissonance. Among the international institutions, the World Bank appears to have taken on the responsibility of attenuating such a phenomenon by providing, through its own narratives, stylized truths and balanced interpretations.

Key words: agriculture, research, narratives, discourse, cognitive dissonance, biotechnology, global public goods.

Narratives and Discourses on World Agriculture

According to Abell (2007), ". . . human beings frequently claim to understand events when they manage to formulate a coherent story or narrative explaining how they believe an event was caused or, more often, how the world is causally transformed from one state to another by virtue of human agency/action." The crucial nature of narratives in interpreting reality through story telling, however, goes beyond the search of causal explanations in the absence of strong statistical evidence from recurrent events. . . .

Because of their rhetorical nature, and the fact that they involve characters, plots, and color, narratives provide a more attractive cognitive framework for interpretation and search for meaning than other more descriptive or more quantitative structures of causal explanations.

On the other hand, narratives can be wildly divergent amongst one another in interpretation, meaning, and scope and cause what in psychology is known as *cognitive dissonance*. This condition may give rise to the cognitive stress of entertaining two contradictory ideas simultaneously. In fact, the theory of cognitive dissonance (Aronson, 1969) proposes that one function of narratives may also be used to reduce this dissonance by rationalizing outcomes, modifying beliefs, and justifying differences between reality and self images. . . .

The debate on world agriculture provides an interesting example of contrasting narratives along these lines, as two dominant and conflicting sets of stories confront each other. . . .

For the evolution of world agriculture, the moderate, or conservative narrative tells stories of achievements and hopeful developments with no villain and many heroes. This story is one of uninterrupted scientific progress, continuous increases of yields in the past years, even though, it is admitted, a notable slowdown has progressively occurred as the initial effects of the green revolutions have been gradually consumed and, at the same time, the expected increases from biotechnology have not yet materialized. For example, recounts of the green revolution, how it came about, how it has affected farmers' lives, etc., are common stories consistent with the conservative narrative theme.

A radical, or contrarian, set of narratives elaborates stories along a different theme: while the large farmers have benefited from yield increases, smallholders, whose yields have traditionally been far in excess (from 200 to 1000 times) of those of large farmers, have gained only marginal benefits. . . .

The contrast between the conventional and the contrarian discourse is reminiscent of the opposition between the modernist inclination to attribute scientific discoveries to unqualified social progress and the more problematic attitude of postmodernism toward the nexus between recognizable social progress and the empowerment of the elites. But it may also reflect different power positions of the parties involved, both because, as Foucault (1977, 1980) argues, science and truth are shaped by negotiating power and because discourse operates by rules of exclusion, so that power is assigned to the privileged who can speak and are listened to. . . .

The Ecological Problem

Since the publication in 1962 of Rachel Carson's "Silent Spring," environmental thinking has tended to reject altogether the traditional production paradigm [**a pattern or model**] governing the application of science to agriculture. The book persuasively argued that agricultural practices may not be sustainable because of their continuous damage to the environment and our health. While sustainability is a slippery concept, it seems clear that present agricultural practices are not sustainable, since they replace natural ecosystems with crop fields and tree farms (with accompanying loss of biodiversity and massive carbon dioxide release) and result in groundwater pollution, soil erosion, aquifer depletion, soil degradation, pesticide pollution, and other environmental stresses. Agricultural research, being guided mainly by the production paradigm, and increasingly dependent on profit-making investments of multinational companies, does not appear to be able to internalize this vision.

According to this line of thought, which represents a narrative directly challenging the story of agricultural research as an environmentally friendly activity, sustainable and multifunctional agriculture should not only be about cheap wholesome food, but also about stewardship of the land, preservation of the resource base, the health of farm workers, the preservation of the small biota [**plants and animals**] that are rich in biodiversity and are interspersed with fields, the value of rural community, and of the agricultural landscape. These objectives are especially important for climate change, where the capacity to adapt depends critically on the type of agricultural systems implemented.

The paradigm of sustainable systems does appear to be more in line with the increasing need to look at agriculture as a flexible set of opportunities rather than as a growing machinery for production. A wide variety of adaptation options has been proposed, for example, to reduce vulnerability to climate change, to help exploit the opportunities provided by increases in temperature or rainfall, or both. In general, scientists agree that agriculture can adapt to a moderate level of global warming (an increase of about 2.5° Celsius), even though adaptability would be higher for the Northern hemisphere, where climate change may provide opportunities for yield increases. Mendelsohn and Dinar (1999), for example, show that, given that adaptation occurs, increase in the average temperature would benefit US agriculture, even though, at the same time, increases of inter-annual [**year-to-year**] variations would be harmful. For the Southern hemisphere, adaptability would be lower and climate change would be a threat, rather than a potential, albeit limited source of opportunities, since temperatures are already near their maximum tolerable heat level.

The World Bank, in making a major effort to take the lead in suggesting a course of action, intervenes with a soothing message. These problems, it suggests, are a source of only passing and apparent contradictions, because

> . . . tackling climate change requires **leadership, vision, capacity, and resources beyond the development experience to date.** Yet the transformation to a more sustainable development path has already started across the world. This transformation is driven largely by higher energy costs and growing concerns about adequate access to water, land, and mineral resources to support growth and livelihoods. It is facilitated by an increasing value of a healthy and productive environment, and a stronger voice and participation of the civil society. (World Bank, 2008, p. 203)

Clearly, climate change may be creating its own set of economic tales, but the ensuing discourse suggests new boundaries of conceivable knowledge and, as such, may be pointing to a newly established frontier for thought on scientific development. The underlying narrative that the World Bank is developing in order to quench the cognitive dissonance in this regard is clear: climate change is the new prevailing force to reckon with in the field of agricultural development. It is already upon us, so that not only mitigation efforts are necessary, but also adaptation actions are inevitable. Research in agriculture, however, may be inadequate to fulfill the task of offering new choices and new solutions to the problems created by climate change because it has taken an altogether different direction: the pursuit of profit-maximizing micro-agricultural improvements within the single integrated agro-industrial enterprise in a context of thoroughly protectable property rights on innovation. A radical change is thus needed to proceed from narrowly defined, profit-oriented, short-sighted, privately dominated agricultural research to a pursuit of knowledge truly attuned to the planetary adaptation facing humanity and agriculture today. . . .

Conclusions

For agricultural research, the fact that narratives dominate the debate on scope and achievement is somewhat paradoxical, since research is committed to a rigorous methodological approach and is accountable to a scientific community, which should have little propensity to listen to the sirens of the rhetorical discourse. The highly formal nature of the scientific method and the prudence and the caveats that surround all the specific achievements of science, however, may themselves be the source of a peculiar vulnerability, when a comprehensive view of successes and failures, as well as meanings and scope are called for. The discourse about science may thus turn out to be rather un-scientific, involve prejudices, exaggerations, and controversies, and use narratives as the main vehicle of elaboration and understanding. By their very nature, these narratives will tend to dramatize the events and attempt to convey messages that may be considered extreme, either in defense of the status quo or against it.

A provocative way to interpret this state of affairs is provided by the idea that narratives are simply the side effects of technological change and this, in turn, is merely the consequence and not the cause of social change. If this is true, narratives are no more than ways by which social change anticipates and rationalizes technical change, through the predisposition of social machinery capable of engendering the innovations required. Thus, for example, the space race of the 1960s was the consequence of a heightened Cold War, and the narratives on the superiority of one or the other superpower were only part of the process of communicating this conflict to the ordinary citizen. Analogously, the biotechnological revolution, if it is indeed in the making, would be the consequence of a major re-organization of the structure of production, input provision, consumption patterns, and balance between private and public research, which is also already in the making. If this is true, the opposed narratives that are being deployed by different social groups are only the reflection of the conflict between those who feel that they are engendering the change and those who fear that they would be excluded or emarginated by it. The drama and the rhetoric of the competing narratives is due to the fact that this preventive lining up of winners and losers occurs in a transitional situation, where the impending social changes are still unclear and unclearly related to corresponding technological changes.

In this context of uncertainty and dynamic change, widely different interpretations of current events are possible, while the underlying structure of society is shifting in an unpredictable way. Different narratives summarize the attempts at explaining what happens by using a linguistic process formed by plots, heroes and anti-heroes, and, at times, pathos and drama. Because of its standing in the international community as a unique institution with financial, scientific, and moral authority, the World Bank appears to have chosen, alongside its traditional mission as a policy advocate for development, the role to provide comfort and guidance, thereby attenuating the cognitive dissonance arising from highly contradicting stories on themes such as development, research, science, climatic change, and, ultimately, human destiny.

By using . . . the influential World Development Report, . . . the World Bank provides its own set of narratives. These narratives tend to coalesce around the underlying story of the ascent of men throughout the ages by the force of their imagination and concerted efforts, but go much beyond a mere reiteration of this theme. By appealing to a wide repertoire of in-house-researched, stylized truths, they elaborate on the role and the accomplishments of large numbers of unknown and reluctant heroes: the scientists, the innovative farmers, the adapting poor. In the case of science and agriculture, they provide, in a cautious and critical way, much needed policy advice on the future course of agricultural research.

Such policy advice has to be somewhat distilled from the very complex and cautious narratives provided, but it can be summarized as a serious attempt at looking for a balance between the conventional and the radical views. Its main points are three. First, rather than concentrating on marginal innovations for a handful of commercial crops, biotechnological research in agriculture should be directed mainly at seeking a viable alternative to the present energy-intensive modes of production in agriculture. Second, it should take smallholders and local production systems as the main targets for its applications and try to build new varieties less dependent on fertilizer and insecticide inputs—and at the same time, more integrated with, rather than being alternative to—the various cultivation options (rotation, multiple cropping, use of biological pesticide control) of small farmers around the world. Third, because this challenge requires the commitment of large amounts of resources without the prospect of immediate gain, this type of research can only be undertaken by the public sector. Moreover, it can only be undertaken if the international community recognizes this conclusion as the major challenge for development and the reduction of poverty in the years ahead.

References

Abell, P. (2007). Narratives, Bayesian narratives and narrative actions. *Sociologica, 3*(2007), 1–21. Available on the World Wide Web: http://www.sociologica.mulino.it/doi/10.2383/25959.

Aronson, E. (1969). The theory of cognitive dissonance: A current perspective. In L. Berkowitz (Ed.). *Advances in experimental social psychology*, Volume 4, pp. 1–34. New York: Academic Press.

Carson, R. (1962). *Silent Spring*. New York: Houghton Mifflin.

Foucault, M. (1972). *Archeology of knowledge*. New York: Pantheon.

Foucault, M. (1977). *Discipline and punish*. New York: Pantheon.

Foucault, M. (1980). *Two lectures*. In C. Gordon (Ed.), *Power/knowledge: Selected interviews*. New York: Pantheon.

Foucault, M. (2003). *Society must be defended*. New York: Pantheon.

Mendelsohn, R., & Dinar, A. (1999). Climate change, agriculture, and developing countries: Does adaptation matter? *The World Bank Research Observer, 14*(2), 277–293.

World Bank. (2008). *Agriculture for development* (World Development Report). Washington, DC: Author.

Reading Responses

1. How does Scandizzo try to persuade you that the World Bank "intervenes with a soothing message"? Where exactly does Scandizzo try to explain why the World Bank would want to offer a balance between the two sides? Which of Scandizzo's methods of persuasion are least and most effective?

2. Summarize each of the five paragraphs of the "Conclusions" section. Then answer this question: If the World Bank, like those who argue from one of the two extremes about agricultural biotechnology, also uses its own stories, how are the World Bank stories better able to resist listening to what Scandizzo calls the "sirens of rhetorical discourse" than others?

3. Scandizzo argues that people paying attention to the global conversation about agricultural biotechnology suffer from "cognitive dissonance" not just because there are opposing sets of narratives but because both sets rely on "facts" rather than opinion for their evidence. List pieces of factual evidence (from this reading or one of the others in this chapter) that could be used to support either pro- or anti-biotechnology arguments. Can you identify any factual evidence that, depending on how it is "spun," could support either pro or anti arguments?

WRITING ASSIGNMENTS

Assignment 1

Starbucks promotes itself as a socially and environmentally responsible company. The "Responsibility" page on the company Web site (www.starbucks.com) proclaims that "We've always believed that businesses can—and should—have a positive impact on the communities that they serve," and it lists the company's good work across the globe. But Starbucks has received pointed criticism from environmental watchdog organizations like the Organic Consumers Association.

Your task is to draft a Web article for either a global food company like Starbucks or an environmental watchdog organization that describes a difficult environmental issue in a way that builds trust among those who might otherwise think of themselves as adversaries. To complete this assignment, you will have to conduct some research on the environmental issue that has polarized the adversaries. Consult a reference librarian for help with this research.

As you begin drafting, look for common ground: goals, methods, and evidence that the contending groups can agree on. Attempt to describe contentious issues in ways that all groups will accept as fair. Take advantage of strategies for writing on the Web that will help you emphasize ethical—and ultimately effective—arguments about these vital issues.

Assignment 2

Some writing teachers restrict students from writing on topics that have a reputation for dividing people, topics such as abortion, euthanasia, gun control, partisan politics, prayer in public schools, and affirmative action. These teachers claim, rightly so, that people who hold strong opinions on a controversial issue often have a difficult time assessing the validity of evidence, identifying the range of assumptions that people bring to the topic, and treating opposing arguments respectfully.

Your task is to revise an essay or speech that takes a stance on a controversial subject like those listed above so that it better acknowledges the assumptions and concerns of those who might disagree with the author. You might consider selecting a text that takes a position that you oppose. Once you've selected your text, assess how well the author addresses the concerns of those who oppose her stance. Analyze the text for issues like the following:

- What evidence does the author use? Is this evidence that a variety of people will accept?
- How does the author address the assumptions and concerns of those who oppose her?

• In what ways does the author reach out to audience members who disagree with her stance?

As you begin drafting, consider the progression of your argument carefully. What common ground can you start from? How can you address the concerns of those who will oppose point of your piece? What evidence will appeal to these readers?

Assignment 3

New advances in the field of biotechnology have sparked heated debate within the scholarly community and protests from citizens in many countries. One such advance is "Bt corn," so called because it contains *Bacillus thuringiensis* (Bt), a bacterium deadly to the caterpillars that feed on corn plants. People around the world are protesting the effects of Bt corn on the livelihoods of organic farmers, the animals who ingest the corn (and the people who eat those animals), the people who live near the Bt corn fields, and butterfly populations.

Your task is to research the one of the problems associated with Bt corn, to summarize the possible solutions to that problem, and to promote one of these solutions as the best currently available.

As you begin drafting, be sure to carefully assess the research you find, paying close attention to the credibility of the source. Because you likely do not have the expertise to develop your own solution, select a solution from your research and promote that solution in your own work. Be sure to provide citations for the research you use. Following the lead of Conway and Toenniessen, attempt to present the problem in a way that represents fairly the claims of all groups. When you present your preferred solution, emphasize how it addresses the concerns of those who might initially be inclined to disagree with it.

17

CHEMISTRY

The U.S. Environmental Protection Agency is watching the San Fernando Valley closely because the water in some of its aquifers is contaminated by industrial waste. The EPA required the cities of Los Angeles and Burbank to close wells in the San Fernando watershed and to provide clean water from other, more expensive sources. But over three million people live over those polluted aquifers; should they be afraid of their water? Should you? You may drink bottled water, but the water you use to brush your teeth, take a shower, and wash your dishes probably comes from the tap—and that water probably comes from an aquifer. One of the chief sources of public information about water quality is the EPA Web site (www.epa.gov). Search the site for information regarding water pollution in your area, keeping careful notes on the steps you take and the information you find. Review your experience and answer the following questions:

- List steps you took to get to the information about water quality in your area, including any false steps that you took. Evaluate the site: how well does it provide information that users most need to know?

- If you were to redesign the Web site, what improvements would you suggest to make information more readily available to users?

- Imagine that you have the opportunity to make an appeal to a government agency in your home area that would decide whether to take steps to improve water quality. Summarize the most important information from the site that you will use in your appeal. What additional information would you like to have?

PORTABLE RHETORICAL LESSON: SUMMARIZING TO SHAPE THE FUTURE

As you trekked through the EPA site, you might have been surprised by how much information is available. And you might also have been frustrated that the information comes in so many disconnected pieces. How do you decide what it all means? How do you find out what information is not available—or if anyone is doing research to get the information you need? Through the exercise you experienced the value of summarizing.

The first question you will need to ask yourself when you need to summarize is *why:* What is your particular **purpose** for summarizing? We all summarize to make sense of a complex topic for ourselves; for example, when you read a chapter from a textbook, you may summarize it in your notes so you understand its main ideas. But why summarize for an audience? To answer that question, think of the *effects* that a thoroughly researched and credible summary can have on an audience. A summary makes information more easily available to a reader, and it shapes readers' understanding by choosing the most important pieces and connecting the pieces into patterns.

Because summary emphasizes some information and hides other information, writers who summarize also think carefully about **organization.** In essay-long summaries, the order in which a reader ingests the parts of a summary determines the connections that the reader recognizes. The connections should form a story of what's being summarized—starting in the past, moving into the present, and suggesting a future. The actual work of summarizing is all about sorting—taking loads of information, determining which information is most important, sorting it into sets of like pieces, and then arranging the order of the sets for an audience. It's heavy-duty organizational work.

The scientific review essay, the particular genre that this chapter presents, exists for the purpose of summarizing complicated scientific research and directing the summary to call for future research—or changes in the policies of agencies such as the EPA. You may never have written a review essay; typically it's only an expert in a field that has broad enough knowledge to presume to summarize that field. But when you write an introduction to a research paper, you make the same kind of rhetorical moves that characterize review essays. You summarize enough of what other researchers have said about your topic that you can show the bigger pattern of ideas into which your work fits, and you use those patterns to move your readers toward the new ideas that you have to add.

Think of a review essay as a jigsaw puzzle. Except there's no picture on the box to tell you how the pieces should go together, and all the pieces do not come in one box; they have to be discovered separately. At any point in time, researchers on a given problem have discovered some pieces of the puzzle, but they are still looking for others. A reviewer implicitly says, "Here are the puzzle pieces that we have found so far, this is the picture they seem to be forming, so these are the pieces we need to look for next."

And it's the "what next?" part that gives the review essay its power—and that gives you the chapter's **Portable Rhetorical Lesson:** summarizing to shape the future. For example, when you read the chapter's first essay, you will see that the three-sentence Abstract forms a three-part thesis statement: the first two parts summarize what researchers know from past studies, and the third part states the problem that needs to be solved in the future. When you can use summary—your version of the emerging pattern of a puzzle—to show what's missing, what needs to be learned or done next, you can direct future study and action.

WRITING IN THE DISCIPLINE

INTRODUCTION

by Darla McCarthy, Professor of Chemistry

We all know that the pollution of our environment by toxic chemicals is a serious matter. Several types of cancer and birth defects, as well as increased incidences of miscarriage, infertility, and other physical and developmental maladies, have been linked to exposure to toxic chemicals. Leukemia and prostate cancer, for example, occur more frequently in people who have been exposed to dioxins—by-products of industrial processes such as pulp and paper bleaching, waste incineration, and pesticide manufacturing. Billions of pounds of pesticides, themselves toxic or contaminated with other toxins, are used annually in the United States; hazardous chemicals are accidentally spilled on roadways or fields; and some manufacturers and users of toxic chemicals fail to dispose of them properly. In other words, do not make the mistake of thinking that a highly specialized review in a chemistry journal has no bearing on you.

The review essay reprinted here does not take what you might think is the predictable line on environmental cleanup. Rather, author Martin Alexander (a world-renowned expert in environmental biochemistry and professor at Cornell University) argues that we might be wasting money cleaning some sites that do not pose real threats. His purpose, of course, is scientific, not political. His argument is a summary of the available scientific evidence. (And I hope you will notice how this review essay erases the line between summary and argument.)

Let me step back almost fifty years to place Alexander's work in its historical context. A review essay is, after all, a kind of history of science. Public awareness of the hazards associated with chemical pollutants was raised in the mid-1960s with the publication of *Silent Spring* (a section of which is reprinted in this chapter). In this landmark book, Rachel Carson discussed the decline of the American robin in certain regions of the United States due to its consumption of worms laden with the pesticide DDT, which was used in massive amounts to combat Dutch elm disease. Public attentiveness to chemical pollutants was further heightened in 1978, when Love Canal, a neighborhood in Niagara Falls, New York, was evacuated due to concerns regarding endemic health problems linked to soil and water contamination by toxins that had leaked from a chemical waste disposal site. Because of mounting public pressure, the U.S. Congress passed several laws regulating the production, use, and disposal of hazardous chemicals. They also passed laws that provided funding and regulations for cleaning up, or remediating, contaminated sites.

Since the publication of *Silent Spring,* billions of dollars have been spent to remediate contaminated soil and water. And it is estimated that as many as 350,000 contaminated sites will require clean-up over the next 30 years, at a cost of as much as $250 billion.* With such astronomical costs, there is currently a great deal of interest in developing more efficient, cost-effective methods for remediation. One trend is a move toward more accurate descriptions of contaminated sites.*

---

* *New Report Projects Number, Cost and Nature of Contaminated Site Cleanups in the U.S. Over Next 30 Years.* United States Environmental Protection Agency, 11 Feb. 2005. http://www.epa.gov/superfund/news/30years.htm

This is the point at which Alexander enters the story. Currently, chemists use very rigorous methods for extracting chemical pollutants from soil samples. Then they use chemical analyses to determine the amount of toxin extracted from the soil samples and determine the total amount of toxin contaminating the site. Sites with larger total amounts of contaminants are given higher priority for remediation. Scientists have recently become aware, however, that the total amount of contaminant present at a site is not necessarily a good indicator of the potential danger of that contaminant to the environment—some contaminants become so adsorbed, or stuck, to the soil that the organisms that live on or in the soil are not likely to ingest or absorb the toxin. So, even though there might be a high total amount of contaminant at a site, there may be little danger. Alexander summarizes those scientific findings and argues that they call for improved methods for characterizing contaminated sites.

Alexander, like any author of a scientific review essay, has two main goals: to summarize all the pertinent literature related to his topic, and to suggest an answer to the question "what next?" The most effective way to accomplish these goals is to craft the review as a thesis-based essay in which the main emphasis is placed on data, as if the data inevitably leads to the author's conclusions. We scientists pride ourselves on our objectivity, and the best way to remain objective is to stay focused on the data. To write a review confidently, a scientist must know the material, the research data, thoroughly. Notice that Alexander has seventy-five references in his bibliography. That's actually not much for a review essay—I've read some with more than 300 references!

The author of a review gains additional credibility by showing that he or she has been a participant in the area of science that is under review. Reviewers almost universally refer to their own published work. In other words, one earns the right to review a field of science only through building expertise in the field. Alexander cites his own publications twenty-two times.

With expertise and data in the spotlight, Alexander's review hoped to change both remediation practice and the further study of bioremediation.

✓ Reading Tips

Remember that this review essay is based on a thesis (see the first sentence after the abstract), is data-based, and concludes with a suggested course of action (the sentence just before the "Relevance" section). That means:

- First, that you should read to find the support for a thesis, which is an argument and not a proven fact or set of facts.
- Second, because the paper is data based (and not, for example, driven by emotion or personal appeal), the support for the thesis comes in the facts. Make sure that you judge the effectiveness of the paper by its fair and clear use of scientific data as grounds for the thesis.
- Finally, look for the author's suggestion of what to do next.

Each of these features should be easy for you to find; don't let yourself get bogged down in the technical information. The marginal notes should help you to understand all the science, but if you need to push past some complex chemistry to get the main points and structure of the argument, do so.

Aging, Bioavailability, and Overestimation of Risk from Environmental Pollutants

Martin Alexander

Environmental Science & Technology, 2000, *34*(20): 4259–65

Bioavailability is the ability of a chemical to be ingested or absorbed by living organisms. Bioavailability affects the toxicity of chemicals and affects their potential for biodegradation (degradation by organisms) and/or bioremediation (complete degradation or detoxification by organisms).

Organic chemicals contain carbon.

The traditional method for analyzing polluted soil is to extract, or remove, the pollutant from the soil and then to identify and quantify the pollutant by various chemical procedures. Chemists are always trying to improve their analyses either by increasing the amount of pollutant recovered from the soil in the extraction process or by increasing the sensitivity, or precision, of their chemical procedures.

The toxicological significance is a measure of how changes in the accessibility of chemicals to organisms affects the toxicity of the chemicals to the organisms.

[Abstract]

As they persist, or age, in soil, organic compounds become progressively less available for uptake by organisms, for exerting toxic effects, and for biodegradation and bioremediation by microorganisms. This declining bioavailability is not reflected by currently used methods for the chemical analysis of soils for determining concentrations of organic pollutants. As a result, such methods overestimate exposure, and thus risk, from toxic chemicals in contaminated sites.

The validity of current methods for analyzing soils to assess the risk from organic pollutants has been cast in doubt by recent research. The focus of much of the concern with analytical methods has been increasing the recovery and sensitivity of chemical procedures, and the relevancy of these procedures to living organisms has been largely ignored. However, a primary reason for performing these analyses is to provide information on the exposure of living organisms to, and hence the risk from, these pollutants. The underlying issue is one of bioavailability. . . .

In this review, information will be presented to show that the bioavailability of organic pollutants in soil declines with time and that current analytical methods, because they measure total and not bioavailable concentrations, may overestimate the magnitude of the environmental and societal problem from these pollutants. Both early and recent evidence for these changes in accessibility will be presented, and the toxicological significance of these observations will be considered. The relevance of current analytical methods will then be evaluated. Differences in bioavailability among species, environments, and compounds and the consequent need for new analytical methods will be reviewed. . . .

Many of the organic pollutants in soil were introduced years or sometimes decades ago at a time when industry and the public were not adequately aware of the scope, magnitude, and importance of soil pollution. Even early research, which has largely been forgotten, provided evidence that the availability of certain chemicals that have been in soil for some time is less than freshly added compounds, and hence the term aging (or weathering) was applied to the phenomenon. Although the early findings and their importance have been obscured with the passage of time, awareness now is growing among environmental toxicologists, risk assessors, and regulatory agencies that the total concentration of a toxicant in a contaminated environment frequently overestimates the risk of pollutants to humans, animals, and plants.

Early Evidence

Data showing the time-dependence of changes in bioavailability are now compelling. The early information came from studies of concentrations of pesticides in the field measured for long periods of time and from measurements of toxicity of pesticides to invertebrates and plants.

For example, long-term monitoring of soil revealed that DDT, aldrin and its epoxide (dieldrin), heptachlor and its epoxide, and chlordane disappeared slowly at first, but then the rate of loss fell to such an extent that further loss was either extremely slow or ceased (1). Although the initial disappearance might be partially the result of volatilization or abiotic degradation as well as biodegradation by soil microorganisms, the fact that the disappearance was almost imperceptibly slow after several years indicates that those insecticides had become poorly available to the indigenous microorganisms; otherwise, these biodegradable compounds should have continued to disappear. The results of several long- and short-term monitoring studies are presented in Figure 1, which shows that the period when little or none of the insecticides is available to soil microorganisms may occur either soon or long after the compounds were introduced into the soil. Such results also show that the percentage of the compound that is poorly or no longer bioavailable differs markedly among the several soils and sites that were examined. This failing on the part of the soil microflora cannot be attributed to low winter temperatures, periods of drought, or other adverse conditions because the monitoring often extended for several years and was done in fields or experimental plots where crops were growing. . . .

Recent Evidence

Organic compounds that have aged in the field are less bioavailable, often appreciably so, than the same compounds freshly added to samples of the same soil. In a field treated with DDT 49 years earlier, approximately 30, 12, and 34% of DDT and the DDE and DDD formed from the added insecticide were available for uptake by the earthworm *Eisenia fetida* compared to newly added chemicals, and 28 or 43% of dieldrin applied at the same time was available based on concentration in the worms or percentages assimilated, respectively. Similar reduced bioavailabilities of DDT, DDE, and DDD but not dieldrin were observed in soil from a waste disposal site in which the insecticides had aged for some 30 years (4). Field aging also diminishes the availability to microorganisms of

---

The heading reminds us that a review essay is partly history of science.

Volatilization is evaporation.

Abiotic degredation is disappearance of a chemical caused by non-biological events such as reaction with oxygen in the air or decomposition initiated by sunlight.

Microflora are populations of microscopic organisms including algae, bacteria, and fungi.

Alexander suggested in the previous section that after a certain aging period pollutants are no longer accessible to microorganisms. If that is true, then we should be able to show experimentally that pollutants are more accessible when they are first applied to soil than they are after they've aged. "Recent Evidence" shows that the accessibility of several pollutants to bacteria and earthworms decreases as the pollutants age in soil.

DDE and DDD are products of the degradation of the infamous pesticide, DDT. Interestingly it is DDE, and not DDT, that is toxic—DDE interferes with the proper incorporation of calcium into eggshells, thus weakening the shells.

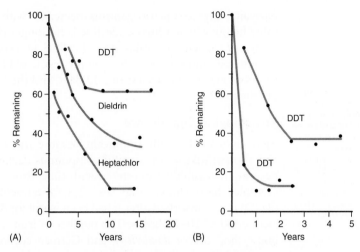

Figure 1 Changes in concentrations of three insecticides in long-term (A) and short-term (B) monitoring of several field sites. Calculated from data of Nash and Woolson and Lichtenslein et al. (1). In other field sites, the monitoring period was not sufficiently long to show the possible existence of a phase with little or no further disappearance of the insecticides.

1,2-dibromoethane that persisted for 3 years (5), simazine applied for 20 consecutive years (6), and polycyclic aromatic hydrocarbons (PAHs) in soils from a closed coking plant (7) and manufactured-gas plant (8).

Laboratory tests confirm the lesser availability to microorganisms of aged than un-aged compounds in highly dissimilar soils (Table 1). The

Table 1 Compounds Shown to Become Less Available for Microbial Degradation as a Result of Aging

Compound	Soil	Aging period (d)	Ref
naphthalene	Colwood loam	365	(73)
naphthalene	Mt. Pleasant silt loam	68	(17)
phenanthrene	Mt. Pleasant silt loam	110	(74)
phenanthrene	16 soils	200	(9)
anthracene	Lima loam	203	(18)
fluoranthene	Lima loam	140	(18)
pyrene	Lima loam	133	(18)
atrazine	Ravenna silt loam	90	(75)
atrazine	16 soils	200	(9)
4-nitrophenol	Lima loam	103	(10)
4-nitrophenol	Edwards much	103	(10)

Tables are excellent tools for summarizing large quantities of data that would otherwise be unwieldy to summarize in words. Here Alexander efficiently summarizes several experiments that illustrate that different compounds in different soil types have different aging periods.

bioavailability to microorganisms decreases with time but reaches a value below which a further decline is no longer detectable. How long it takes to reach that value and the final percentage availability vary among soils and compounds. The process may be complete in days or weeks or may take in excess of 200 days, and the loss in availability may be small or large (9, 10). . . .

Toxicological Significance

Aging is toxicologically significant because the assimilation and acute and chronic toxicity of harmful compounds decline as they persist and become increasingly sequestered with time. Studies with mammals, for example, have shown that less 2,3,7,8-tetrachlorodibenzo-p-dioxin (TCDD) was absorbed after it had been in soil for 8 days than after a contact period of 10–15 hours. The number of fruit flies (*D. melanogaster*), house flies (*Musca domestica*), and German cockroaches (*Blatella germanica*) killed by DDT and dieldrin declined markedly with increasing times of residence of these compounds in soil (13). Similar but largely forgotten data were obtained many years earlier by Peterson et al. (14), who found a marked and progressive reduction in toxicity to *D. melanogaster* as DDT persisted for 108 days in soil. An effect of aging on plants has also been noted with three herbicides: napropamide, simazine, and atrazine (3, 6, 15). In each instance, toxicity was less than that anticipated. . . . Aging also reduces the effectiveness of at least some genotoxic compounds in soil. Thus, by means of a solid-phase assay, it has been found that the genotoxicity of the carcinogens benzo(*a*)pyrene and 9,10-dimethyl-1,2-benzanthracene diminished rapidly and to a great extent within a 15-day period, although analysis following vigorous extraction showed only a slight decline in concentration after about 2 months (16). . . .

Nevertheless, a time-dependent decline in bioavailability does not always occur. This may be related to properties of the soil or of the compound. Instances in which bioavailability did not diminish include the biodegradability of simazine (6), the dermal and oral availability of TCDD and dieldrin to rodents (27, 28), and the uptake of DDE by earthworms in one soil (4). Only a small loss in bioavailability of certain compounds in sediments may occur with aging; witness that the rate of microbial dechlorination of polychlorinated biphenyls in Hudson River sediments contaminated for at least 15 years was only about 20% slower than compounds freshly added at 20 ppm (29). In addition, toxic compounds may exist in pockets or in nonaqueous-phase liquids within the soil, and after some physical disturbance, they may be released and become bioavailable. Although such compounds are aged in the sense of time, they have not been sequestered in a fashion to reduce their bioavailability to living organisms.

In the previous two sections, Alexander established that pollutants do indeed become less available for uptake by small organisms over time. In this section Alexander reviews data that show that as pollutants age in soil, their toxicity to larger plants and animals also decreases.

---

acute toxicity: causing an immediate toxic effect such as paralysis or suffocation

---

chronic toxicity: causing long-term effects such as cancer or emphysema

---

Genotoxic compounds modify DNA and thus have potential to alter genes and eventually cause cancer. Here Alexander explains that the ability of certain compounds to modify DNA decreases as the compounds age in soil. He refers to a "solid-phase assay," which is just a fancy way of saying that researchers exposed organisms to genotoxins in the soil—or on a *solid* surface—and then determined if modifications had been made to the organisms' DNA.

Carcinogens are cancer-causing substances.

Incorrect Analytical Methodologies

Here Alexander emphasizes that current methods focus only on chemical analysis—they aim to extract as much pollutant as possible out of the soil to determine the *total* amount of chemical pollutant in the soil. This type of analysis does not account for changes in the bioavailability of pollutants as they age; thus, risks are often overestimated.

The widely used protocols of federal and state regulatory agencies rely on analytical methods that entail vigorous extraction of soils and sediments with organic solvents. The aim is to remove all, or as much as possible, of the pollutant from the environmental sample. Each method is carefully evaluated to assess its accuracy, as well as its precision and sensitivity, but the accuracy is interpreted in purely chemical terms. The relevancy of such methods to the toxicity of the compound in the form in which it exists in nature is generally not considered in carrying out risk analyses, except that a default value is sometimes included to relate to the particular environmental matrix. The fact that the compound may become progressively less bioavailable as it persists, even in a single environmental matrix, is not considered in assessing risk. Thus, the regulator is not making use of information that bioavailability may decline with little or no reduction in the concentration as determined by procedures that rely on initial vigorous extractions. Hence, such methods are often not relevant for prediction of potential exposures to, and thus risks from, contaminated soils or sediments.

Environmental scientists are well aware of the fact that certain chemicals are more accessible to organisms in one type of soil (environmental matrix) than another. So, they account for the differences by including a "correction factor," or "default value."

The evidence is compelling that the quantities recovered by vigorous extraction fail to predict declining bioavailability as compounds persist in soil. For example, despite the marked diminution in effectiveness in killing three species of insects as dieldrin and DDT aged in soil, >90% of the dieldrin and ca. 85% of the DDT could still be recovered by vigorous extraction (13). . . .

If the total concentration at a polluted site is greater than the regulatory level but the bioavailable concentration is below that value, a site that might be slated for expensive cleanup might, instead, be deemed to present an acceptable risk. The public concern about a contaminated location might be allayed by the more meaningful assessment. Moreover, a site that was bioremediated but still contained concentrations of one or more contaminants above the target levels may have indeed been successfully cleaned up, even though conventional analysis suggested that the remediation was inadequate. This is true both of engineered and intrinsic bioremediation, which frequently do not destroy all of the targeted compounds. Because such bioremediation treatments act on the fraction that is bioavailable, to microorganisms at least, the accessibility of the portion that remains may be so low that the site presents little or no risk to higher organisms. . . .

New Assay Methods

The regulator is faced with a major dilemma because the magnitude of reduction in bioavailability resulting from aging is different for a single

Here Alexander addresses the key question: If bioavailability changes over time and can't be predicted, how can you predict the risk of exposure? This is his "what next?" question.

compound in different soils, for different compounds in the same soil, and for different periods of time that a compound has remained in soil. How does one predict the degree of exposure and risk from an aged compound? Bioassays are an obvious means of performing assessments, but biological measurements frequently do not have adequate precision for regulatory purposes, and they are time-consuming and expensive. An alternative is a chemical or physical assay, but the results of that assay must correlate well with the results of bioassays. . . .

Bioassays analyze the effects of pollutants on living organisms, whereas chemical and physical assays simply analyze the amounts and types of pollutants in the soil.

Several chemical and physical methods have been considered as ways to measure the bioavailability of organic compounds in soil. The results of analyses by such procedures have been correlated with bioavailability to earthworms, springtails, nematodes, and microorganisms (31, 39–43). The observation that the time-dependent decline in bioavailability is accompanied by a time-dependent decline in the quantity of compounds extracted from soil by a mild procedure (9, 10, 31, 44) suggests that a mild-extraction technique might serve as the basis for a surrogate assay for bioavailability. . . .

Here is Alexander's proposed answer to the "what next?" question—use mild extraction techniques for chemical assays. Notice that he does not overemphasize his solution; Alexander's purpose in writing the review is to highlight the issue of bioavailability, and not to solve the resulting problems. He does, however, suggest a direction that others could pursue to solve the problem.

Relevance

Because exposure to persistent compounds is overestimated by currently used chemical methods, the risk is likewise being overestimated. Inasmuch as aging appears to occur in many and possibly most contaminated soils, the bioavailability of aged chemicals probably is being overestimated very frequently. As a consequence, current approaches to evaluating sites for cleanup sometimes may alarm people in localities where the risk is small. They probably lead to choosing some sites for remediation where little such need exists and thus delay the cleanup of polluted areas where the risk is greater. They also probably result in requirements for cleanup that are unnecessarily stringent and thus lead to expenditure of funds that could be better used to decontaminate additional areas. Therefore, a more widespread recognition of bioavailability of aged compounds is necessary— among scientists, environmental engineers, regulators, and the public at large.

In his conclusion, Alexander simply summarizes his review and reminds his audience of why they should be concerned about bioavailability.

Acknowledgments

Portions of the work were supported by National Institute of Environmental Health Sciences grants ES05950 and ES07052 with partial funding from the U.S. Environmental Protection Agency, U.S. Air Force Office of Scientific Research grant F49620–95–1–0336, the U.S. Department of Agriculture, and GRI. I thank R. C. Loehr, J. W. Gillett, and E. L. Madsen for helpful comments.

Literature Cited

1. Alexander, M. In *Environmentally Acceptable Endpoints in Soil;* Linz, D. G., Nakles, D. V., Eds.; American Academy of Environmental Engineers: Annapolis, MD, 1997; 43–136.
4. Morrison, D. E.; Robertson, B. K.; Alexander, M. *Environ. Sci. Technol.* **2000,** *34,* 709.
5. Steinberg, S. M.; Pignatello, J. J.; Sawhney, B. L. *Environ. Sci. Technol.* **1987,** *21,* 1201.
6. Scribner, S. L.; Benzing, T. R.; Sun, S.; Boyd, S. A. *J. Environ. Qual.* **1992,** *21,* 115.
7. Weissenfels, W. D.; Klewer, H. J.; Langhoff, J. *Appl. Microbiol. Biotechnol.* **1992,** *36,* 689.
8. Erickson, D. C.; Loehr, R. C.; Neuhauser, E. F. *Water Res.* **1993,** *27,* 911.
9. Chung, N.; Alexander, M. *Environ. Sci. Technol.* **1998,** *32,* 855.
10. Hatzinger, P. B.; Alexander, M. *Environ. Sci. Technol.* **1995,** *29,* 537.
13. Robertson, B. K.; Alexander, M. *Environ. Toxicol. Chem.* **1998,** *17,* 1034.
14. Peterson, J. R.; Adams, R. S., Jr.; Cutkomp, L. K. *Soil Sci. Soc. Am. Proc.* **1971,** *35,* 72.
15. Bowmer, K. H. *Aust. J. Soil Res.* **1991,** *29,* 339.
16. Alexander, R. R.; Alexander, M. *Environ. Toxicol. Chem.* **1999,** *18,* 1140.
27. Shu, H.; Teitelbaum, T.; Webb, A. S.; Marple, L.; Brunck, B.; Dei Rossi, D.; Murray, F. J.; Paustenbach, D. *Fundam. Appl. Toxicol.* **1988,** *10,* 335.
28. Midwest Research Institute. *Oral Bioavailability of Soil Associated Aldrin/Dieldrin;* Project 9849-F; Midwest Research Institute: Kansas City, MO, 1991.
29. Abramowicz, D. A.; Brennan, M. J.; Van Dort, H. M.; Gallagher, E. L. Environ. *Sci. Technol.* **1993,** *27,* 1125.
31. Kelsey, J. W.; Kottler, B. D.; Alexander, M. *Environ. Sci. Technol.* **1997,** *31,* 214.
39. Loibner, A. P.; Gartner, M.; Schlegl, M.; Heutzenberger, I.; Braun, R. In *In Situ and On-Site Bioremediation;* Battelle Press: Columbus, OH, 1997; Vol. 5, 617–622.
40. Cornelissen, G.; Van Noort, P. C. M.; Parsons, J. R.; Govers, H. A. J. *Environ. Sci. Technol.* **1997,** *31,* 454.
41. Houx, N. W. H.; Aben, W. J. M. *Sci. Total Environ. Suppl.* **1993,** 387.
42. Ronday, R. *Commun. Soil. Sci. Plant Anal.* **1997,** *28,* 777.
43. Tang, J.; Robertson, B. K.; Alexander, M. *Environ. Sci. Technol.* **1999,** *33,* 4346.
44. Tang, J.; Alexander, M. *Environ. Toxicol. Chem.* **1999,** *18,* 2711.

Reading Responses

1. As Professor McCarthy notes in her introduction, Alexander summarizes a great deal of research in this review essay. How does he join it all together? To answer that question, analyze the structure of three of Alexander's paragraphs (choose paragraphs that include at least four references). For each paragraph, answer these three questions: (1) What seems to be the task of the first sentence? (2) Where in the paragraph do the references appear? (3) Why are these references in this order? Note any similarities you see in the structure of these paragraphs.

2. Alexander's thesis is "that current analytical methods, because they measure total and not bioavailable concentrations, may overestimate the magnitude of the environmental and societal problem from these pollutants." How does this thesis fit with the research he summarizes in his essay? Relying on Alexander's summary of the research, count up the number of studies he cites for two topics: the bioavailability of aging chemicals and the effectiveness of analytical procedures. Compare your

counts with Alexander's thesis, and evaluate Alexander's focus. Does all the research he cites support his thesis? If so, how does it do so? If not, what would you eliminate?

3. Professor McCarthy notes that Alexander is a well-respected scholar on the topic he reviews in this essay. How does his ethos as a respected scholar affect his review essay? As you answer that question, consider how he uses his own research and the other research he cites.

Notes on Grammar, Style, and Rhetoric:
Uses of Old Information in a Critical Review

One illuminating approach to the style of Martin Alexander's "Aging, Bioavailability, and Overestimation of Risk from Environmental Pollutants" is to examine the kinds of information his sentences convey. Most sentences can be divided into two parts, one of which conveys what linguists call old information, the other of which conveys what linguists call new information.

Old information in a sentence is information that readers know on the basis of the particular rhetorical situation, that readers with even minimal experience of the world are aware of, that appears prior to that sentence, or that can be inferred from material leading up to that sentence. For example, certain bits of information become old information after they appear once. Consider the following short text:

> Professor Alexander has written a review essay on toxic chemicals in various kinds of soil. This essay should attract some serious attention.

In the second sentence, "This essay" carries old information because it refers to information mentioned in the first sentence.

New information in a sentence is information that is not obvious from the particular rhetorical situation, that is not known to all people with even minimal experience of the world, that is not mentioned prior to that sentence, or that cannot be inferred from material leading up to that sentence.

Consider again the preceding sample text. The words "should attract some serious attention" conveys new information. If these words were blacked out, no one could guess what they are. Therefore, "This essay" makes a connection to earlier material, and "should attract some serious attention" moves the message into new territory. This sentence exemplifies what is true of the old and new information in many sentences: The old information appears early in a relatively short sentence subject, and the new information follows in a longer predicate.

Alexander's sentences use old information in at least three specific ways: (1) by using sentence subjects that package information from fairly extensive prior sections of his essay, (2) by using introductory adverbial clauses to remind readers of information presented earlier, and (3) by including entire sentences that convey only old information.

Consider first Alexander's tactic of using sentence subjects to package old information. One good example of this appears in the section labeled "Recent Evidence." Alexander begins this section with two substantial paragraphs dealing with studies of the bioavailability of organic compounds that have aged in the field. After these two paragraphs, Alexander begins a new sentence and a new paragraph with these words: "These investigations with individual compounds. . . ." This phrase is made up entirely of old information, pointing backward to remind readers of the old information summarized in the two previous paragraphs.

He does similar work with some adverbial clauses that introduce sentences. For example, in the first section of the essay, Alexander writes: "Even early research, which has largely been forgotten, provided evidence that the availability of certain chemicals that have been in soil for some time is less than freshly added chemicals . . ." (332). He then begins the next sentence with an adverbial clause: "Although the early findings and their importance have been obscured with the passage of time . . ." (332–33). This clause conveys mainly old information, referring to the "early research, which has . . . been forgotten. . . ."

Finally, at the end of this essay Alexander includes a short section that he labels "Relevance." The first sentence of this section reads as follows: "Because exposure to persistent compounds is overestimated by currently used chemical methods, the risk is likewise being overestimated" (337). Appearing where it does, this sentence is made up entirely of old information; everything in this sentence has come up earlier in the essay. In fact, most of the information in the section labeled "Relevance" is old. This section summarizes the major claims in Alexander's overall presentation.

You might worry that some readers could find these sentences repetitious, or wonder why anyone should be asked to read a sentence that doesn't add something new.

Because his argument is based on extensive and complex details, Alexander cannot afford to allow his readers to forget all the accumulated information. Readers' memory is critical for the success of the argument, so frequent reminders are necessary. And the upshot of this argument—that we might not have to invest time and money in cleaning up some toxic waste sites—is important and even startling. If he is right in his argument, then we are probably wasting time and money trying to clean up some toxic sites. If he is wrong, the results of following his advice could well be disease, deformity, and death.

In Your Own Writing . . .

- When you revise your writing, pay attention to how you use old and new information.
- Use old information in your sentence subjects to "package" information that you've already provided.
- Include old information in introductory phrases and clauses to contextualize new information.
- Put new information in the predicates of your sentences.
- When you want to help the reader make connections among topics, use entire sentences that include old information. Use entire sentences to help the reader connect new information to the argument you're building.

STUDENT WRITING

INTRODUCTION

by Arianne Folkema, chemistry major

The Assignment. My class was asked to conduct original research (in other words, no one else had previously determined the answers to the questions I was researching) and write a research report. The report was supposed to be similar to a published research report. To justify the validity of the questions I chose to research, my report's introduction had to summarize what was already known about the topic. My introduction also had to define the questions I was trying to answer. That is a lot like a review essay: first summarize what's known, then ask the "what next?" question.

The Content. My report is on the bioremediation of pentachlorophenol (PCP)—the use of live organisms to clean up ("bioremediate") sites contaminated by PCP, a toxic compound that was formerly used as an industrial wood preservative and is now a banned substance. The argument in my introduction follows this outline: (1) PCP is a toxic compound; (2) research has proven that PCP can be degraded by some microbes (bacteria and fungi) occurring naturally in the environment; (3) very little is known about PCP degradation by a microbe called *M. chlorophenolicum* PCP-1; (4) what little is known about PCP degradation by *M. chlorophenolicum* PCP-1 indicates that it degrades PCP in a different manner than do other microbes; (5) it would be beneficial to conduct further research on *M. chlorophenolicum* PCP-1 with the hope of learning if it could be more widely used to bioremediate PCP.

Learning to Write an Introduction to a Scientific Report: Lessons from Review Essays. My first exposure to original laboratory research was certainly a turning point in terms of understanding science in the "real world." I had taken many lab courses, following the protocols written in lab manuals: basic "recipe science" where the outcome is already known. I soon found out this was not the case in independent research, where the purpose is to first look at all the information available on a subject, and from there to figure out where the holes, the missing data, are . . . and to figure out ways to fill in those holes.

An introduction to a scientific report must be confident in its summary, and a scientific writer only gains confidence through thorough research, both in the lab and in published literature. So I began my project at the library. A search engine located abstracts for recently published articles containing information on everything from the metabolism of PCP by bacteria isolated from mushroom compost to observations about the degradation of pesticides by fermented sausages! The abstracts helped me to decide what publications were relevant to my project. My task was to summarize the published data clearly and use it to justify the argument that my research questions were worthwhile.

As I was drafting my paper and thinking about writing style, I took special care to be very specific and concise. One of the best ways for a scientist to be concise is to use figures, and the two figures in my introduction demonstrate the key points of the argument. Figure 1 shows a sequence of chemical changes (a pathway) that is known to break down PCP. Figure 2 shows a pathway with a question mark in the middle. That question mark was the key question for my research: How does the microbe *M. chlorophenolicum* PCP-1 break down PCP? When you see the question mark in the middle of that figure, you know just what my research is after.

When I first started reading professional research reports and reviews, I was amazed at how much research goes on, producing scientific knowledge and guiding scientists to new research. Research in science always leads to more research; scientists create change as part of the unending process of trying to understand the natural world.

Introduction to "Bioremediation of Pentachlorophenol"

Arianne Folkema

Bioremediation is the process of breaking down, or detoxifying, a toxic substance by biological organisms, in this case, the detoxification of the wood preservative, pentachlorophenol, or PCP.

Xenobiotic chemicals are foreign to biological systems, not naturally occurring.

A culture is the growth of bacteria under controlled conditions in a laboratory. The idea here is to grow large quantities of pollutant-degrading bacteria in the lab, and then to spread the bacteria on contaminated soil.

Natural bioremediation is carried out by organisms that are already present at a site prior to contamination.

Artificial bioremediation is carried out by organisms that are added to a site after it has been contaminated.

In situ means at the original site of contamination.

M. chlorophenolicum PCP-1. is the scientific name of a particular strain of bacteria.

Since the beginning of the industrial revolution, many xenobiotic chemicals have been introduced into the environment for a variety of purposes, with little attention paid to their potential long-term effects. The ecological consequences of some of these substances involve substantial damage to both aquatic and terrestrial ecosystems. In today's society, environmental, political, social and regulatory pressures demand that the use of xenobiotics be carefully monitored and that past mistakes be remedied. One technique that holds unique promise is bioremediation—the use of live organisms to clean up contaminated sites. One common technique for bioremediation is the culture of select bacteria that have the ability to break down industrial waste components. These bacteria are then added to contaminated soil.

Pentachlorophenol (PCP) is one example of a xenobiotic compound that can be bioremediated. PCP was initially produced in the 1930s for use as an industrial wood preservative and was mass-produced for this purpose, leading to the production of 45 million pounds in 1983 alone (1). The use of PCP was banned for commercial purposes in 1987 due to its extreme toxicity, which is known to damage the lungs, liver, kidney, gastrointestinal tract, nervous system, and immune system. PCP is currently listed as a priority pollutant by the US Environmental Protection Agency (EPA) (2). Fortunately, in contaminated sites where PCP had previously been used, it has been discovered that there are a number of microbes that have the unique capability to degrade PCP into less toxic substances.

There are numerous reports of the attempted bioremediation of PCP-contaminated sites. One example of natural bioremediation on an actual field site was witnessed in contaminated groundwater near sawmills in Finland, which were reported to contain up to 190mg of chlorophenols, including PCP, per liter of water. Upon study of the site, a variety of chlorophenol-degrading bacteria were isolated and characterized (3). Reports of successful artificial bioremediation (in which cultured bacteria are added to a contaminated site) are scarce, however, due to the compromised survival of bacteria *in situ*. This is illustrated by an attempt to clean up contaminated soils via the introduction of *Mycobacterium chlorophenolicum* PCP-1, a bacterium known to degrade PCP, directly to PCP-contaminated soil. In this field study, PCP degradation was observed to be 5 mg of PCP per kg of soil during the first two weeks after inoculation. However, this was only a slight improvement over the rate of PCP degradation by indigenous bacteria (2). This poor performance is possibly due to the method of inoculation, the soil properties, and/or the presence of toxic contaminants other than PCP in the soil. Additional studies have been carried out in more controlled settings such as bioreactors (vats in which microbes are grown in the presence of the compounds they metabolize), where soil properties and the presence of contaminants are not likely to be an issue. For example, the fungus *Panus tigrinus* was introduced to a mixture of chlorinated phenols at 500mg/L in a 72L bioreactor and was reported to have completely removed the PCP after three weeks (4).

Due to their potential (although often inefficient) bioremediation capabilities, research has been performed on a variety of PCP-degrading microbes. These include *Sphingobium chlorophenolicum* (4), a bacterium, and *Phanerochaete chrysosporium* (5), a fungus, on which thorough research has been done and for which the pathway of PCP degradation is known.

Figure 1 is a schematic diagram showing the chemical structures of PCP and the product of each reaction in the PCP metabolic pathways for *S. chlorophenolicum* and *P. chrysosporium*. Each of the chemical structures after PCP represents an intermediate in the pathway. The important thing to notice here is the minor differences between the structures. In the first reaction, we see that the chlorine atom (Cl) at the bottom of the molecule is removed and replaced by a hydroxyl group (OH). In the second reaction, the chlorine atom on the lower-left side of the molecule is replaced by a hydrogen atom. The last part of the pathway is not well understood, so after the fourth structure two arrows are shown to indicate multiple reactions leading to CO_2 (carbon dioxide).

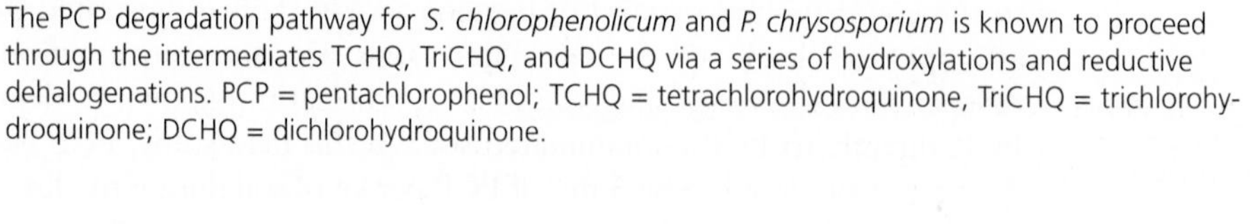

> Inoculation is the introduction of bacteria to a medium; soil, in this case.

> Indigenous means living naturally in a particular area.

> During metabolism, organisms break down compounds via a series of reactions to form the final product (often carbon dioxide). The set of reactions, with the accompanying intermediate compounds, is called a metabolic pathway. Figure 1 visualizes this concept.

Figure 1   PCP Degradation Pathway for *S. chlorophenolicum* and *P. chrysosporium*.
The PCP degradation pathway for *S. chlorophenolicum* and *P. chrysosporium* is known to proceed through the intermediates TCHQ, TriCHQ, and DCHQ via a series of hydroxylations and reductive dehalogenations. PCP = pentachlorophenol; TCHQ = tetrachlorohydroquinone, TriCHQ = trichlorohydroquinone; DCHQ = dichlorohydroquinone.

When molecules containing chlorine are degraded by microbes, generally only one chlorine atom is removed in each reaction of the pathway. So, when PCP, which contains five chlorines, is degraded, we expect there to be intermediates with four, three, two, and one chlorine atoms. The intermediate containing three chlorines in the PCP metabolic pathway utilized by *M. chlorophenolicum* PCP-1 was not identified in the experiment described here.

Look at the question mark in the third stage of the pathway; that question was the reason for my research. To understand this figure, compare each structure to the one that appears before it in the pathway. Notice that in some reactions Cl is replaced by OH, and in others Cl is replaced by H.

Less research has been conducted on another bacterium with the potential to bioremediate PCP; *Mycobacterium chlorophenolicum* PCP-1. Fewer concrete details are known about its metabolism of PCP, although it is clear that PCP metabolism by *M. chlorophenolicum* PCP-1 differs significantly from PCP metabolism by other organisms. The first step in PCP degradation by *M. chlorophenolicum* PCP-1, is the hydroxylation of PCP to form TCHQ, which is also the case for *S. chlorophenolicum* and *P. chrysosporium* (6). The identity of the second intermediate in PCP degradation by *M. chlorophenolicum* is unknown.

Fig. 2 illustrates that the second reaction in this pathway could involve either the replacement of a chlorine atom (Cl) by a hydrogen atom (H—in the top pathway) or the replacement of a chlorine atom by a hydroxyl group (OH—bottom pathway) (7).

The purpose of my research was to characterize the degradation pathway of PCP by *M. chlorophenolicum* PCP-1: to determine the identity of the second intermediate in the pathway.

The characterization of the metabolic pathway and purification of the enzymes necessary for degradation of PCP is important because it provides information that can be used to further characterize the genes encoding the enzymes involved in PCP degradation. It may then be possible to clone those genes into more robust bacteria capable of growing at more rapid rates and surviving in harsher soil environments. These genetically engineered microbes may ultimately be useful in the improved bioremediation of PCP-contaminated sites.

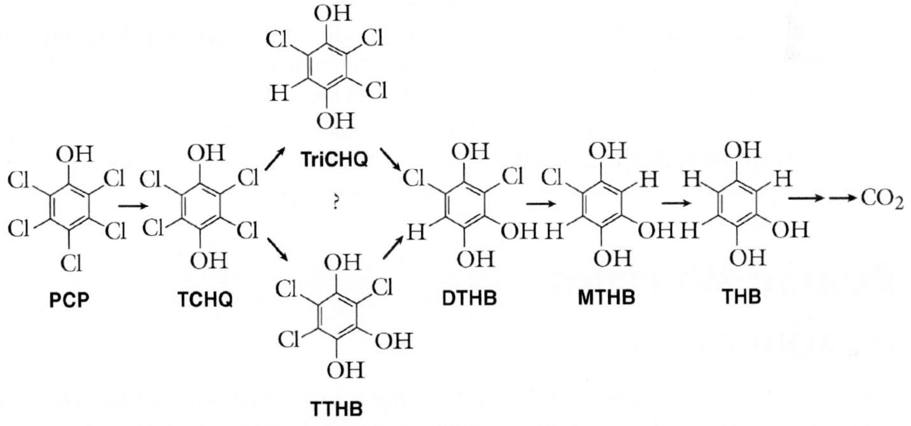

Figure 2 PCP Degradation by *Mycobacterium chlorophenolicum*

The PCP degradation pathway utilized by *M. chlorophenolicum PCP-1* is not completely defined and could either proceed through the intermediate TriCHQ or TTHB. PCP = pentachlorophenol; TCHQ = tetrachlorohydroquinone, TriCHQ = trichlorohydroquinone; TTHB = trichlorotrihydroxybenzene; DTHB = dichlorotrihydroxybenzene; MTHB = monochlorotrihydroxybenzene; THB = trihydroxybenzene.

References

1. *Pentachlorophenol Facts*. PANNA—Pesticide Action Network North America http://www.panna.org/resources/documents/factsPentachlorophenol.dv.html May, 2004.
2. Miethling, R. and U. Karlson. "Accelerated mineralization of pentachlorophenol in soil upon inoculation with *Mycobacterium chlorophenolicum* PCP1 and *Sphingomonas chlorophenolica* RA2." Appl. Environ. Microbiol. **1996**, *62:* 4361–66.
3. Mannisto, M. and M. Tiirola. "Diversity of chlorophenol-degrading bacteria isolated from contaminated boreal groundwater." *Arch. Microbiol.* **1999**, *171:* 189–197.
4. Leontievsky, A. A. and N. M. Myasoedova. "Adaptation of the white-rot basidiomycete *Panus tigrinus* for transformation of high concentrations of chlorophenols." *Appl. Microbiol. Biotechnol.* **2002**, *59:* 599–604.
5. Reddy, G. and M. Gold. "Purification and characterization of glutathione conjugate reductase: A component of the tetrachlorohydroquinone reductive dehalogenase system from *Phanerochaete chrysosporium*." *Arch. Biochem. Biophys.* **2001**, *391:* 271–77.
6. Apajalahti, J. and M. Salkinoja-Salonen. "Dechlorination and *para*-hydroxylation of polychlorinated phenols by *Rhodococcus chlorophenolicus*." *J. Bacteriol.* **1987**, *169:* 675–81.
7. Apajalahti, J. and M. Salkinoja-Salonen. "Complete dechlorination of tetrachlrohydroquinone by cell extracts of pentachlorophenol-induced *Rhodococcus chlorophenolicus*." *J. Bacteriol.* **1987**, *169:* 5125–30.

Reading Responses

1. As Arianne Folkema notes in her introduction, students find themselves in an odd position when they write summaries of research: these are usually written by an expert in a field of research, not a novice. Compare the first three paragraphs of Folkema's essay with the first three paragraphs of Alexander's review (not counting Alexander's Abstract). List the similarities and the differences. For each difference, evaluate if it results from Folkema's status as a novice researcher.

2. Folkema typically includes more information about the research she's summarizing than Alexander does. What additional information does Folkema include? Who might value this information? Why is it/isn't it worth including?

3. If you were a professor of chemistry, would you require students to include a review of literature in their research reports? Provide a set of reasons to support your answer.

PUBLIC WRITING

INTRODUCTION

The publication of Rachel Carson's *Silent Spring* is often credited with launching the environmental movement. Carson, after earning a master's degree in zoology, wrote radio scripts for the U.S. Bureau of Fisheries, later becoming an aquatic biologist and then chief editor of publications for the bureau. She turned to full-time independent writing and, after four years of research for the book, published *Silent Spring* in 1962. Chemical companies tried to prevent its publication, and Carson was threatened with lawsuits and accused of being unprofessional, an "hysterical woman," and a communist. It became, nonetheless, an international bestseller.

Silent Spring begins with a three-page chapter entitled "A Fable for Tomorrow." The chapter's opening sentence, "There once was a town in the heart of America where all life seemed to live in harmony with its surroundings" draws readers into a story of an idyllic town that is beset by unimaginable biological horrors—birds and bees disappear, vegetation withers and dies. Carson concludes the chapter by telling us that no town had suffered all the blight that she visited upon her fictional town but that "every one of these disasters has actually happened somewhere." The final paragraph of the chapter reads, "What has already silenced the voices of spring in countless towns in America? This book is an attempt to explain."

The opening chapter tells us that Carson is offering a natural history—a history of nature assaulted by humans. It is very important to recognize that history is a kind of summary, here enlivened in skin and bone and bark and root. Through this recognition Carson's "review" of the environmental record enriches our sense of the vast usefulness of summary.

There are obvious differences between this piece and a scientific review. It is grounded in thorough research, but the references sit quietly offstage so as not to "burden the text with footnotes," as Carson explains. It is also passionate and personal (note language such as "fantastic," "menace," and "endless problems").

Yet the kinship to a scientific review is evident. The first sixteen chapters of the book summarize the evidence that pesticide use is damaging nature. The last chapter, "The Other Road," answers the "what next?" question. In it she discusses the benefits of biological control over pests, identifying several particular methods, each of which has now been the subject of scientific research. In other words, *Silent Spring* follows the form and purpose of a review essay, and it brought about the field-shaping results that review writers hope for.

Realms of the Soil
Rachel Carson

Chapter 5, *Silent Spring,* 1962

. . . The problem that concerns us here is one that has received little consideration: What happens to these incredibly numerous and vitally necessary inhabitants of the soil **[worms, microbes, and all life forms that inhabit the soil]** when poisonous chemicals are carried down into their world, either introduced directly as soil "sterilants" or borne on the rain that has picked up a lethal contamination as it filters through the leaf canopy of forest and orchard and cropland? Is it reasonable to suppose that we can apply a broad-spectrum insecticide to kill the burrowing larval stages of a crop-destroying insect, for example, without also killing the "good" insects whose function may be the essential one of breaking down organic matter? Or can we use a nonspecific fungicide without also killing the fungi that inhabit the roots of many trees in a beneficial association that aids the tree in extracting nutrients from the soil?

The plain truth is that this critically important subject of the ecology of the soil has been largely neglected even by scientists and almost completely ignored by control men. Chemical control of insects seems to have proceeded on the assumption that the soil could and would sustain any amount of insult via the introduction of poisons without striking back. The very nature of the world of the soil has been largely ignored.

From the few studies that have been made, a picture of the impact of pesticides on the soil is slowly emerging. It is not surprising that the studies are not always in agreement, for soil types vary so enormously that what causes damage in one may be innocuous in another. Light sandy soils suffer far more heavily than humus types. Combinations of chemicals seem to do more harm than separate applications. Despite the varying results, enough solid evidence of harm is accumulating to cause apprehension on the part of many scientists.

Under some conditions, the chemical conversions and transformations that lie at the very heart of the living world are affected. Nitrification, which makes atmospheric nitrogen available to plants, is an example. The herbicide 2,4-D causes a temporary interruption of nitrification. In recent experiments in Florida, lindane, heptachlor, and BHC (benzene hexachloride) reduced nitrification after only two weeks in soil; BHC and DDT had significantly detrimental effects a year after treatment. In other experiments BHC, aldrin, lindane, heptachlor, and DDD all prevented nitrogen-fixing bacteria from forming the necessary root nodules on leguminous plants. A curious but beneficial relation between fungi and the roots of higher plants is seriously disrupted.

Sometimes the problem is one of upsetting that delicate balance of populations by which nature accomplishes far-reaching aims. Explosive increases in some kinds of soil organisms have occurred when others have been reduced by insecticides, disturbing the relation of predator to prey. Such changes could easily alter the metabolic activity of the soil and affect its productivity. They could also mean that potentially harmful organisms, formerly held in check, could escape from their natural controls and rise to pest status.

One of the most important things to remember about insecticides in soil is their long persistence, measured not in months but in years. Aldrin has been recovered after four years, both as traces and more abundantly as converted to dieldrin. Enough toxaphene remains in sandy soil ten years after its application to kill termites. Benzene hexachloride persists at least eleven years; heptachlor or a more toxic derived chemical, at least nine. Chlordane has been recovered twelve years after its application, in the amount of 15 per cent of the original quantity.

Seemingly moderate applications of insecticides over a period of years may build up fantastic quantities in soil. Since the chlorinated hydrocarbons are persistent and long-lasting, each application is merely added to the quantity remaining from the previous one. The old legend that "a pound of DDT to the acre is harmless" means nothing if spraying is repeated. Potato soils have been found to contain up to 15 pounds of DDT per acre, corn soils up to 19. A cranberry bog under study contained 34.5 pounds to the acre. Soils from apple orchards seem to reach the peak of contamination, with DDT accumulating at a rate that almost keeps pace with its rate of annual application. Even in a single season, with orchards sprayed four or more times, DDT residues may build up to peaks of 30 to 50 pounds to the acre; under trees, up to 113 pounds.

Arsenic provides a classic case of the virtually permanent poisoning of the soil. Although arsenic as a spray on growing tobacco has been largely replaced by the synthetic organic insecticides since the mid-'40s, *the arsenic content of cigarettes made from American-grown tobacco increased more than 300 per cent* between the years 1932 and 1952. Later studies have revealed increases of as much as 600 per cent. Dr. Henry S. Satterlee, an authority on arsenic toxicology, says that although organic insecticides have been largely substituted for arsenic, the tobacco plants continue to pick up the old poison, for the soils of tobacco plantations are now thoroughly impregnated with residues of a heavy and relatively insoluble poison, arsenate of lead. This will continue to release arsenic in soluble form. The soil of a large proportion of the land planted to tobacco has been subjected to "cumulative and well-nigh permanent poisoning," according to Dr. Satterlee. Tobacco grown in the eastern Mediterranean countries where arsenical insecticides are not used has shown no such increase in arsenic content.

We are therefore confronted with a second problem. We must not only be concerned with what is happening to the soil; we must wonder to what extent insecticides are absorbed from contaminated soils and introduced into plant tissues. Much depends on the type of soil, the crop, and the nature and concentration of the insecticides. Soil high in organic matter releases smaller quantities of poisons than others. Carrots absorb more insecticide than any other crop studied; if the chemical used happens to be lindane, carrots actually accumulate higher concentrations than are present in the soil. In the future it may become necessary to analyze soils for insecticides before planting certain food crops. Otherwise even unsprayed crops may take up enough insecticide merely from the soil to render them unfit for market.

This very sort of contamination has created endless problems for at least one leading manufacturer of baby foods who has been unwilling to buy any fruits or vegetables on which toxic insecticides have been used. The chemical that caused him the most trouble was benzene hexachloride (BHC), which is taken up by the roots and tubers of plants, advertising its presence by a musty taste and odor. Sweet potatoes grown on California fields where BHC had been used two years earlier contained residues and had to be rejected. In one year, in which the firm had contracted in South Carolina for its total requirements of sweet potatoes, so large a proportion of the acreage was found to be contaminated that the company was forced to buy in the open market at a considerable financial loss. Over the years a variety of fruits and vegetables, grown in various states, have had to be rejected. The most stubborn problems were concerned with peanuts. In the southern states peanuts are usually grown in rotation with cotton, on which BHC is extensively used. Peanuts grown later in this soil, pick up considerable amounts of the insecticide. Actually, only a trace is enough to incorporate the telltale musty odor and taste. The chemical penetrates the nuts and cannot be removed. Processing, far from removing the mustiness, sometimes accentuates it. The only course open to a manufacturer determined to exclude BHC residues is to reject all produce treated with the chemical or grown on soils contaminated with it.

Sometimes the menace is to the crop itself—a menace that remains as long as the insecticide contamination is in the soil. Some insecticides affect sensitive plants such as beans, wheat, barley, or rye, retarding root development or depressing growth of seedlings. The experience of the hop growers in Washington and Idaho is an example.

During the spring of 1955 many of these growers undertook a large-scale program to control the strawberry root weevil, whose larvae had become abundant on the roots of the hops. On the advice of agricultural experts and insecticide manufacturers, they chose heptachlor as the control agent. Within a year after the heptachlor was applied, the vines in the treated yards were wilting and dying. In the untreated fields there was no trouble; the damage stopped at the border between treated and untreated fields. The hills were replanted at great expense, but in another year the new roots, too, were found to be dead. Four years later the soil still contained heptachlor, and scientists were unable to predict how long it would remain poisonous, or to recommend any procedure for correcting the condition. The federal Department of Agriculture, which as late as March 1959 found itself in the anomalous position of declaring heptachlor to be acceptable for use on hops in the form of a soil treatment, belatedly withdrew its registration for such use. Meanwhile, the hop growers sought what redress they could in the courts.

As applications of pesticides continue and the virtually indestructible residues continue to build up in the soil, it is almost certain that we are heading for trouble. This was the consensus of a group of specialists who met at Syracuse University in 1960 to discuss the ecology of the soil. These men summed up the hazards of using "such potent and little understood tools" as chemicals and radiation: "A few false moves on the part of man may result in destruction of soil productivity and the arthropods may well take over."

Reading Responses

1. Carson opens the preceding excerpt from her chapter with three questions. Interestingly, each question serves a distinct function in her essay. Describe how each question relates to the rest of the chapter.

2. When Carson discusses particular topics, she describes first old ways of thinking and then new research. Choose one paragraph that contains both old and new information. Analyze the purpose of old information in this paragraph. What "work" does it do?

3. Carson's chapter summarizes previous scientific research just as Alexander's does. But Carson is writing to a general audience, not other experts in the field. Compare Alexander's style with Carson's. What stylistic strategies does Carson use to make her essay more readable?

MORE WRITING IN CHEMISTRY

INTRODUCTION

This reading reviews scientific data regarding the types of exposure, and the consequences of that exposure, caused by the attack on the World Trade Center. The essay is written by a large team of scientists from seven institutions. The intended audience is toxicologists and other scientists who study human exposure to toxins, and, to a lesser extent, physicians who are interested in environmental exposure to toxins. Phillip Landrigan, the lead author of the team, is an award-winning physician and scholar, a regular on TV's *Good Morning America* show, and author of over 500 scientific papers.

This review essay documents the types and amounts of toxins that were released into the atmosphere as a result of the disaster and the observed health consequences of human exposure to those toxins. Most of the scientific data regarding the types and amounts of toxins produced during the disaster has been omitted from this abridged version because it is highly technical and difficult for a nonexpert to follow. We include, however, studies of the health consequences of exposure to those toxins.

The review follows a logical argument: (1) the types and amounts of toxins released as a result of the disaster; (2) the health consequences observed; (3) the consequent need to continue monitoring the health of those exposed to the toxins. In other words, its structure is typical of a review essay, moving from a summary of what has been learned to a projection of what yet needs to be studied.

Health and Environmental Consequences of the World Trade Center Disaster

Philip J. Landrigan, Paul J. Lioy, George Thurston, Gertrud Berkowitz, L. C. Chen, Steven N. Chillrud, Stephen H. Gavett, Panos G. Georgopoulos, Alison S. Geyh, Stephen Levin, Frederica Perera, Stephen M. Rappaport, Christopher Small, and the NIEHS World Trade Center Working Group

Environmental Health Perspectives, 2004, *112*(6): 731–39

[Abstract]

The attack on the World Trade Center (WTC) created an acute environmental disaster of enormous magnitude. This study characterizes the environmental exposures resulting from destruction of the WTC and assesses their effects on health. Methods include ambient air sampling; analyses of outdoor and indoor settled dust; high-altitude imaging and modeling of the atmospheric plume; inhalation studies of WTC dust in mice; and clinical examinations, community surveys, and prospective epidemiologic studies [studies of diseases] of exposed populations. WTC dust was found to consist predominantly (95%) of coarse particles and contained pulverized cement, glass fibers, asbestos, lead, polycyclic aromatic hydrocarbons (PAHs), polychlorinated biphenyls (PCBs), and polychlorinated furans and dioxins [various poisons]. Airborne particulate levels were highest immediately after the attack and declined thereafter. Particulate levels decreased sharply with distance from the WTC. Dust pH was highly alkaline (pH 9.0–11.0). Mice exposed to WTC dust showed only moderate pulmonary inflammation but marked bronchial hyperreactivity. Evaluation of 10,116 firefighters showed exposure-related increases in cough and bronchial hyperre-activity. Evaluation of 183 cleanup workers showed new onset cough (33%), wheeze (18%), and phlegm production (24%). Increased frequency of new onset cough, wheeze, and shortness of breath were also observed in community residents. Follow-up of 182 pregnant women who were either inside or near the WTC on 11 September showed a 2-fold increase in small-for-gestational-age (SGA) infants **[that is, smaller in size than the average human fetus of the same age]**. In summary, environmental exposures after the WTC dis-aster were associated with significant adverse effects on health. The high alkalinity of WTC dust produced bronchial hyperreactivity, persistent cough, and increased risk of asthma. Plausible causes of the observed increase in SGA infants include maternal exposures to PAH and particulates. Future risk of mesothelioma **[cancer of some internal membranes, in this case lung cancer]** may be increased, particularly among workers and volunteers exposed occupationally to asbestos. Continuing follow-up of all exposed populations is required to document the long-term consequences of the disaster. *Key words:* air pollution, airway hyperresponsiveness, asbestos, occupational lung disease, PM2.5, PM10, small for gestational age (SGA).

[Introduction] The destruction of the World Trade Center (WTC) on 11 September 2001 caused the largest acute environmental disaster that ever has befallen New York City (Claudio 2001; Landrigan 2001). The combustion of more than 90,000 L of jet fuel at temperatures above 1,000°C released a dense and intensely toxic atmospheric plume containing soot, metals, volatile organic compounds (VOCs), and hydrochloric acid. The collapse of the towers pulverized cement, glass, and building contents and generated thousands of tons of particulate matter (PM) composed of cement dust, glass fibers, asbestos, lead, polycyclic aromatic hydrocarbons (PAHs), polychlorinated biphenyls (PCBs), organochlorine pesticides, and polychlorinated furans and dioxins (Clark et al. 2003; Lioy et al. 2002; McGee et al. 2003). These materials dispersed over lower Manhattan, Brooklyn, and for miles beyond. They entered nearby office, school, and residential buildings. Much remained at the site to form Ground Zero, a six-story pile of smoking rubble that burned intermittently for more than 3 months.

Populations at greatest risk of exposure included firefighters, police, paramedics, other first responders Prezant et al. 2002; Centers for Disease Control and Prevention (CDC) 2002, and construction workers and volunteers who worked initially in rescue and recov-ery and then for many months cleared rubble at Ground Zero. Others at potentially ele-vated risk included workers who cleaned WTC dust from nearby buildings, women who were pregnant on 11 September and succeeding weeks in lower Manhattan and adjacent areas of Brooklyn, and community residents, especially the 3,000 children who resided within 1 km of the towers and the 5,500 who attended school there.

Previous studies have documented the acute traumatic consequences of the attacks on the WTC, most notably the occurrence of 2,726 deaths, including 343 deaths among fire-fighters and 60 among police officers (CDC 2002). Early clinical and epidemiologic assess-ments documented a high prevalence of respiratory symptoms, particularly, persistent cough in firefighters and rescue workers exposed to WTC dust (CDC 2002; Prezant et al. 2002). The prevalence of those symptoms was related to intensity and duration of smoke and dust exposure. Studies of the mental health consequences of the disaster have documented a high prevalence of posttraumatic stress disorder (PTSD) (Galea et al. 2002b; Fairbrother et al. 2003) and other psychological sequelae **[disease consequences],** including increased rates of drug and alcohol abuse (Boscarino et al. 2002; Galea et al. 2002a; Stuber et al. 2002; Vlahov et al. 2002a, 2002b).

In this report we summarize a comprehensive assessment of the impacts on human health and the environment of the chemical contaminants generated by destruction of the WTC. The work was undertaken by a consortium of six research centers supported by the National Institute of Environmental Health Sciences (NIEHS) in collaboration with the New York City Department of Health, the U.S. Environmental Protection Agency (EPA), and the CDC. . . .

Health Risk Assessment

Overview. Health risk assessments by the NIEHS Centers began by identifying populations at high risk of exposure to WTC contaminants and then undertaking clinical and epidemiologic studies within these groups (Landrigan 2001). Future analyses will seek to relate health outcomes data to geocoded information on contaminant levels (McCurdy et al. 2000).

Firefighters. Firefighters were among the most heavily exposed populations. They also suffered the greatest loss of life of all occupational groups. In the first 24 hr after the attack on the WTC, 240 New York City firefighters sought emergency medical treatment; of these, 50 (20.8%) received treatment of acute respiratory symptoms caused by inhalation of airborne smoke and dust (Prezant et al. 2002; Spadafora 2002). Firefighters described walking through dense clouds of dust and smoke in the hours immediately after the attack, in which "the air was thick as soup" (CDC 2002).

Follow-up medical evaluation of 10,116 firefighters was conducted over the 6 months after the attack (Prezant et al. 2002). Persistent cough accompanied by other respiratory symptoms so severe as to require at least 4 weeks' leave of absence, termed "World Trade Center cough," was diagnosed in 332 firefighters (Chen and Thurston 2002; Scanlon 2002). Prevalence of WTC cough was related to intensity of smoke exposure, and occurred in 128 (8%) of 1,636 firefighters with a high level of exposure, in 187 (3%) of 6,958 with moderate exposure, and in 17 (1%) of 1,320 with low-level exposure (Figure 4). Among firefighters without WTC cough, bronchial hyperreactivity was present in 77 (23%) of those with a high level of exposure, and in 26 (8%) of those with moderate exposure (Prezant et al. 2002). One case of eosinophilic pneumonia was diagnosed in a firefighter (Beckett 2002; Rom et al. 2002). Induced sputum analysis of New York City firefighters showed increases in sputum PM **[particulate matter: dust, fibers, etc.]** levels as well as in neutrophil and eosinophil counts **[white blood cell counts].** Those abnormalities were positively correlated with levels of exposure to WTC dust and combustion products, as well as with levels of PAHs in the bodies of firefighters (Edelman et al. 2003).

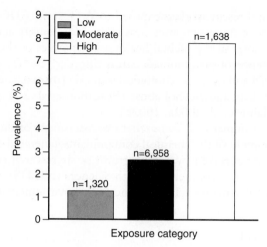

Figure 4 Prevalence of persistent cough in New York City firefighters exposed to smoke and dust from the WTC, September 2001 through March 2002.

Data from Prezant et al. (2002).

Cleanup and Recovery Workers. Many hundreds of workers were involved in clearing rubble and transporting it off-site. To assess the occupational exposures and health status of these workers, many of whom were truck drivers, a team from the Bloomberg School of Public Health at Johns Hopkins University and the Mailman School of Public Health at Columbia University undertook area air monitoring, personal exposure assessment, and health studies.

Air monitoring was conducted in October 2001 and April 2002. It focused on PM, asbestos, and VOCs. Monitoring was conducted across both day and night shifts, 7 days/week. Personal monitoring was conducted for 69 truck drivers. A total of 458 personal and area air samples were collected.

In October 2001, the highest concentrations of total dust were found at the debris pile (median, 1,603 μ_g/m^3 [**micrograms per cubic meter of air**]). Total dust levels on the pile in October were approximately five times higher than at the perimeter. By April 2002, total dust concentrations of the site had become significantly lower and were more uniformly distributed. In October 2001, median personal particulate exposure was 323.7 μ_g/m^3. By April 2002, median exposure had fallen to 137.7 μ_g/m^3. Airborne asbestos concentrations were found to be generally low. The fibers detected were mostly very short. Concentrations of VOCs were generally low. . . .

Among the 183 workers surveyed, a high proportion (32.8%) reported experiencing cough that began after the start of employment at the WTC site; 24.0% reported new onset of phlegm production; and 17.5% reported new onset of wheeze. Approximately half of all workers reported that they had experienced at least one new symptom since they had begun working at the WTC site. . . .

Community Residents. To assess prevalence of new-onset respiratory symptoms after 11 September 2001 among previously healthy persons in lower Manhattan as well as in residents with preexisting asthma, a team from NYU Medical Center in collaboration with the New York State Department of Health and the New York Academy of Medicine conducted a clinical and epidemiologic survey (Reibman et al. 2003). Symptoms were assessed by questionnaire, and pulmonary function was evaluated in a subset of the study population by standard screening spirometry [**a method for determining lung air capacity**].

A total of 2,166 residents of lower Manhattan living within a 1.6-km radius of the WTC were enrolled in this survey and compared with 200 persons living 1.6–8.0 km distant. Spirometry was performed in 52 residents. Preliminary data indicate that previously healthy persons living near Ground Zero had a greater increase in prevalence of respiratory symptoms after 11 September than did more distant residents. These symptoms were predominantly cough, wheeze, and shortness of breath. Symptoms were not associated with abnormal screening spirometry.

Preexisting asthmatic residents in the exposed area also reported a higher prevalence of respiratory symptoms after 11 September. They also reported an increased use of asthma medication relative to controls. . . .

Pregnant Women and their Offspring. Many pregnant women were either working in the WTC or working or residing in the communities of lower Manhattan on 11 September 2001. To assess pregnancy outcomes in these women and impacts on their infants, teams from the Mount Sinai School of Public Health of Columbia University established complementary prospective epidemiologic cohort studies. . . .

Pregnancy Outcomes. In the Mount Sinai cohort, no significant differences were found between the groups in mean gestational age or mean birth weight. There were no significant differences in frequency of preterm births (< 37 weeks of gestation) or in incidence of low birth weight (Table 2) (Berkowitz et al. 2003).

However, the Mount Sinai WTC cohort had a 2-fold increased risk of small-for-gestational-age (SGA) infants, defined as infants with a birth weight below the 10th percentile for gestational age in the nomogram of Brenner et al. (1976) (Table 2). This statistically significant difference was still evident after controlling for relevant covariates and potential confounders, including maternal age, parity, race/ethnicity, sex of the infant, and maternal smoking

Table 2   Pregnancy outcomes in relation to the attack on the WTC, September 2001 through June 2002

	WTC group	Control group	*p*-Value
No.	187	2,367	—
Mean gestational age (weeks)	39.1	39.0	0.55
Mean birth weight (g)	3,203	3,267	0.14
Frequency of preterm birth (%)	9.9	9.2	0.76
Frequency of low birth weight (%)	8.2	6.8	0.47
Frequency of SGA infants (%)	8.2	3.8	<0.01

Data from Berkowitz et al. (2003).

history. No significant difference in the frequency of SGA infants was observed according to the trimester of pregnancy on 11 September. No associations were evident between symptoms of posttraumatic stress, based on the PTSD Checklist (Schlenger et al. 2002), and frequency of preterm birth, low birth weight, or SGA infants.

Discussion

This report presents the most comprehensive summary to date of the environmental exposures resulting from the attack on the WTC and of their effects on human health. Our main focus was on chemical exposures. Our findings complement earlier reports describing the acute physical consequences of the disaster (CDC 2002; Prezant et al. 2002) and its psychological impacts (Boscarino et al. 2002; Fairbrother et al. 2003; Galea et al. 2002a, 2002b; Stuber et al. 2002; Vlahov et al. 2002a, 2002b).

Our assessments show that exposures to chemical contaminants were not uniform in New York after 11 September (Clark et al. 2003; Lioy et al. 2002; McGee et al. 2003; Offenberg et al. 2003). Instead, there were sharp gradients by time after the attack and by distance from Ground Zero (Table 1). **[Table 1 appears here for the first time because**

Table 1   Sequence of environmental exposures after the attack on the WTC, September through December 2001

Time period	Predominant sources of pollution	Airborne pollutants
First 12 hr after collapse (11 September 2001)	Burning jet fuel	Combustion products: gaseous and particulate
	Fires	Evaporating gases from the collapse of towers
	Collapse of the Twin Towers	Coarse particles
Days 1 and 2	Burning jet fuel	Combustion products: gaseous and particulate
	Resuspension of settled dust/smoke	Gases evaporating from piles
		Resuspended coarse particles
Days 3–13	Smoldering fires	Combustion products: gaseous and particulate
	Resuspension of settled dust/smoke	Coarse particle resuspension
		Diesel exhaust
Day 14 through 20 December 2001	Smoldering fires with occasional flareups	Combustion products: gases and particulates
	Removal of debris by trucks and other heavy equipment	Diesel exhaust

Data from Lioy et al. (2002).

in the published review it was part of a section that we deleted in this abridged version of the essay.] In the first few hours, extremely heavy exposures to high levels of dust and smoke as well as to gaseous products of combustion predominated. This pattern continued for the next 2 days, when there occurred rapid decline of smoke and dust levels and continuing decline in levels of combustion products as jet fuel and flammable building contents were consumed. A large fraction of the outdoor dust was eliminated over the first weekend after the disaster by rain that fell on Friday, 14 September, and by the U.S. EPA's cleanup of the Wall Street area. Over the next several weeks, airborne particulate levels in lower Manhattan continued to decline but rose intermittently at night and when the air was still. Transient increases were noted also when the pile was disturbed and fires flared. Diesel exhaust became an important contaminant with the arrival on site of scores of cranes, heavy trucks, and other construction equipment. For weeks, an acrid cloud hung over lower Manhattan and areas of Brooklyn until the fires were finally extinguished on 20 December.

Asbestos was of great concern to the public in New York City and to government agencies after 11 September. Asbestos, principally chrysotile, was used in the early 1970s in construction of the WTC as fireproofing up to the 40th floor of the North Tower (Nicholson et al. 1971; Reitze et al. 1972). Asbestos was not used beyond that point because of the recognition of its hazard and its replacement in the remainder of the construction with nonasbestiform fireproofing materials. Although some of this asbestos had been removed over the preceding 30 years, hundreds of tons remained on 11 September 2001 and were blasted free. Ambient air samples showed that asbestos exposures were initially elevated but fell to within U.S. EPA standards after the first few days (U.S. EPA 2004). Asbestos was found in settled dust at Ground Zero in concentrations ranging from 0.8 to 3.0% (Lioy et al. 2002). Asbestos was found in dust in nearby apartments, sometimes at higher levels than in the outside environment (Lioy et al. 2002).

Airborne lead levels were elevated in the first days after 11 September, but never highly. There is little indication that ambient air lead exposures posed substantial health risks to the population of lower Manhattan (U.S. EPA 2004).

Airborne dioxin levels were elevated substantially above normal urban background levels in the initial days after 11 September. The U.S. EPA's initial risk analysis suggests that these elevations did not result in a significant elevation in cancer or non-cancer risk (U.S. EPA 2003). Further follow-up of exposed populations will be required to evaluate the accuracy of that assessment.

Risks to health were determined by the timing, duration, and chemical composition of exposures as well as by proximity to Ground Zero. Firefighters, police, and other first responders sustained heaviest initial exposures. Studies of firefighters confirmed the presence of a positive relationship between intensity and duration of exposure and severity of pulmonary effects (Figure 4) (Prezant et al. 2002) as well as of PM levels in sputum. Prolonged exposures occurred among firefighters and other public safety personnel who remained at Ground Zero as well as among construction workers, volunteers, and workers removing rubble (Levin et al. 2002; Lippy 2002). Workers cleaning nearby buildings may also have sustained potentially serious exposures (Malievskaya et al. 2002).

Health data from the study of rubble removal workers confirm that these workers, many of whom worked at Ground Zero for many months, had sustained clinically significant exposures to airborne irritants, resulting in symptoms consistent with upper and lower airway inflammation (Levin et al. 2002). To extend these initial studies, the team at Mount Sinai has initiated the World Trade Center Worker and Volunteer Medical Screening Program. This program, supported by NIOSH, has already examined more than 10,000 workers. These workers will be followed prospectively to assess long-term and delayed effects. . . .

Airborne exposures in the residential and business communities of lower Manhattan beyond Ground Zero were much lower than those sustained by workers (U.S. EPA 2004). Daily average levels of fine particulate pollution in these communities were generally within U.S. EPA limits when averaged over a 24-hr period. Higher short-term peaks were, however, observed especially at night and could have contributed to reported health effects, especially in susceptible populations such as children, the elderly, and persons with respiratory or cardiac disease. Indoor exposures to resuspended dust may have added to total exposures (Lioy et al. 2002). Residents in these communities reported an increased frequency of new-onset pulmonary symptoms (Reibman et al. 2003) but had no abnormalities on pulmonary function testing. These findings are consistent with the observed gradient of exposures. . . .

Important questions about possible future risks to health of persons exposed to contaminants from the WTC remain unanswered:

- Will pulmonary disease persist in workers exposed to dust, especially in those who sustained very heavy exposures in the first days after 11 September and those with prolonged exposures?
- Will an increased incidence of mesothelioma result from exposures to asbestos? All types of asbestos fibers have been shown in laboratory as well as clinical studies to be capable of causing mesothelioma (Nicholson and Landrigan 1996). Pathologic studies have found short chrysotile fibers, the predominant type of fiber in WTC dust, to be the predominant fiber in mesothelioma tissue (Dodson et al. 1991; LeBouffant et al. 1973; Suzuki and Yuen 2002). Mesothelioma has been reported in persons with relatively low-dose, nonoccupational exposure to asbestos (Anderson 1982; Camus et al. 1998; Magnani et al. 2001). The greatest future risk of mesothelioma would appear to exist among first responders who were enveloped in the cloud of dust, other workers employed directly at Ground Zero, and workers employed in cleaning asbestos-laden dust from contaminated buildings. The risk of mesothelioma to residents of lower Manhattan must be considered to be extremely low but may still be elevated above background.
- Will exposure to airborne dioxin in lower Manhattan in the days and weeks after 11 September increase risk of cancer, diabetes, or other chronic disease (Kogevinas 2001)?
- Will the increased frequency of SGA observed in babies born to women who were within or near the WTC on 11 September result in long-term adverse effects on growth or development (Berkowitz et al. 2003)?

Full elucidation of these and other questions concerning the long-term and delayed health effects of exposures resulting from the attack on the WTC will require continuing, prospective, multiyear clinical and epidemiologic follow-up and further refinement of exposure assessments. That work is under way.

References

Beckett WS. 2002. A New York City firefighter overwhelmed by World Trade Center dust. *Am J Respir Crit Care Med* 166:785–6.

Berkowitz GS, Wolff MS, Janevic TM, Holzman IR, Yehuda R, Landrigan PJ. 2003. The World Trade Center disaster and intrauterine growth restriction [Letter]. *JAMA* 290:595–6.

Boscarino JA, Galea S, Ahern J, Resnick H, Vlahov D. 2002. Utilization of mental health services following the September 11th terrorist attacks in Manhattan, New York City. *Int J Emerg Ment Health* 4:143–55.

Brenner WE, Edelman DA, Hendricks CH. 1976. A standard of fetal growth for the United States of America. *Am J Obstet Gynecol* 126:55–64

CDC (Centers for Disease Control and Prevention). 2002. Injuries and illnesses among New York City Fire Department rescue workers after responding to the World Trade Center attacks. *Morbid Mortal Wkly Rep* 51(special issue):1–5.

Chen LC, Thurston G. 2002. World Trade Center cough. *Lancet* 360(suppl):S37–8.

Clark RN, Green RO, Swayze GA, Meeker G, Sutley S, Hoefen TM, et al. 2003. Environmental Studies of the World Trade Center Area after the September 11, 2001 Attack. Available: http://pubs.usgs.gov/of/2001/ofr-01-0429/ [accessed 25 March 2004].

Claudio L. 2001. Environmental aftermath. *Environ Health Perspect* 109:528–36.

Edelman P, Osterloh J, Pirkle J, Caudill SP, Grainger J, Jones R, et al. 2003. Biomonitoring of chemical exposure among New York City firefighters responding to the World Trade Center fire and collapse. *Environ Health Perspect* 111:1906–11.

Fairbrother G, Stuber J, Galea S, Fleischman AR, Pfefferbaum B. 2003. Posttraumatic stress reactions in New York City children after the September 11, 2001, terrorist attacks. *Ambul Pediatrics* 3:304–11.

Galea S, Ahern J, Resnick H, Kilpatrick D, Bucuvalas M, Gold J, et al. 2002a. Psychological sequelae of the September 11 terrorist attacks in New York City. *N Engl J Med* 346:982–7.

Galea S, Resnick H, Ahern J, Gold J, Bucuvalas M, Kilpatrick D, et al. 2002b. Posttraumatic stress disorder in Manhattan, New York City, after the September 11th terrorist attacks. *J Urban Health* 79:340–53.

Landrigan PJ. 2001. Health consequences of the 11 September 2001 attacks [Editorial]. *Environ Health Perspect* 109:A514–15.

Levin S. Herbert R, Skloot G, Szeinuk J, Teirstein A, Fischler D, et al. 2002. Health effects of World Trade Center site workers. *Am J Ind Med* 42:545–7.

Lioy PJ, Weisel CP, Millette JR, Eisenreich S, Vallero D, Offenberg J, et al. 2002. Characterization of the dust/smoke aerosol that settled east of the World Trade Center (WTC) in Lower Manhattan after the collapse of the WTC 11 September 2001. *Environ Health Perspect* 110:703–14.

Lippy BE. 2002. Safety and health of heavy equipment operators at Ground Zero. *Am J Ind Med* 42:539–42.

Malievskaya E, Rosenberg N, Markowitz S. 2002. Assessing the health of immigrant workers near Ground Zero: preliminary results of the World Trade Center Day Laborer Medical Monitoring Project. *Am J Ind Med* 42:548–9.

McGee JK, Chen LC, Cohen MD, Chee GR, Prophete CM, Haykal-Coates N, et al. 2003. Chemical analysis of World Trade Center fine particulate matter for use in toxiciological assessment. *Environ Health Perspect* 111:972–80.

Nicholson WJ, Rohl AN, Ferrand EF. 1971. Asbestos air pollution in New York City. In: *Proceedings of the Second International Clean Air Congress* (Englund HM, Beery WT, eds.) New York: Academic Press, 36–139.

Offenberg JH, Eisenreich SJ, Chen LC, Cohen MD, Chee G, Prophete C, et al. 2003. Persistent organic pollutants in the dusts that settled across lower Manhattan after September 11, 2001. *Environ Sci Technol* 37:502–8.

Prezant DJ, Weiden M, Banauch GI, McGuinness G, Rom WN, Aldrich TK. 2002. Cough and bronchial responsiveness in firefighters at the World Trade Center site. *N Engl J Med* 347:806–15.

Reibman J, Lin S, Matte T, Rogers L, Hoerning A, Hwang S, et al. 2003. Respiratory health of residents near the former World Trade Center: the WTC Residents Respiratory Health Survey [Abstract]. *Am J Respir Crit Care Med* 167:A335.

Reitze WB, Nicholson WJ, Holaday DA, Selikoff IJ. 1972. Application of sprayed inorganic fiber containing asbestos: Occupational health hazards. *Am Ind Hyg Assoc J* 33:178–91.

Rom WN, Weiden M, Garcia R, Yie TA, Vathesatogkit P, Tse DB, et al. 2002. Acute eosinophilic pneumonia in a New York City firefighter exposed to World Trade Center dust. Am *J Respir Crit Care Med* 166:797–800.

Scanlon MD. 2002. World Trade Center cough—a lingering legacy and a cautionary tale. *N Engl J Med* 347:840–2.

Schlenger WE, Caddell JM, Ebert L, Jordan BK, Rourke KM, Wilson D, et al. 2002. Psychological reactions to terrorist attacks: findings from the National Study of Americans' Reactions to September 11. *JAMA* 288:81–88.

Spadafora R. 2002. Firefighter safety and health issues at the Word Trade Center site. *Am J Ind Med* 42:532–38.

Stuber J, Fairbrother G, Galea S, Pfefferbaum B, Wilson-Genderson M, Vlahov D. 2002. Determinants of counseling for children in Manhattan after the September 11 attacks. *Psychiatr Serv* 53:815–22.

U.S. EPA. 2003. Fact Sheet: Release of Reports Related to the World Trade Center Disaster. Exposure and Human Health Evaluation of Airborne Pollution from the World Trade Center Disaster. Toxicological Effects of Fine Particulate Matter Derived from the Destruction of the World Trade Center. Washington, DC: U.S. Environmental Protection Agency.

U.S. EPA. 2004. EPA Response to September 11. Washington, DC: U.S. Environmental Protection Agency. Available: http://www.epa.gov/wtc/ [accessed 25 March 2004].

Vlahov D, Galea S, Frankel D. 2002a. New York City, 2001: reaction and response. *J Urban Health* 79:2–5.

Vlahov D, Galea S, Resnick H, Ahern J, Boscarino JA, Bucuvalas M, et al. 2002b. Increased use of cigarettes, alcohol, and marijuana among Manhattan, New York, residents after the September 11th terrorist attacks. *Am J Epidemiol* 155:988–96.

Reading Responses

1. A scientific review rarely evokes an emotional response from readers, but this review may do exactly that. Who might have an emotional response to this review? What kind of emotions might it call up? What about the review evokes emotion?

2. These researchers review the extensive effects of the WTC attacks on the environment and on human health. Which of these topics receives more attention? Develop a research method that will help you answer that question and apply it to the text. Describe your research method and display your results.

3. This research review is written by scientists for scientists, but the topic is of great concern to all Americans. Create a set of guidelines that could help these authors write about this information for a general audience. What can they keep the same? What must they change?

WRITING ASSIGNMENTS

Assignment 1

It's difficult to find the data to construct a summary of the environmental quality of your neighborhood from the EPA Web site. And yet this information is important for everyone who lives (or is considering living) in your neighborhood.

Your task is to create a summary of the environmental quality of your neighborhood. Consult the EPA's Web site as well as other sources of information: your local EPA office, other local governmental offices (city and state), nongovernmental organizations, and journalists' investigations. Introduce your summary with an overview that describes the general environmental quality for your neighborhood. Include information on several features of environmental quality as well as a list of sources of information on environmental quality in your area.

Assignment 2

Summaries matter. They do more than describe something—they set a path for future action. This is certainly true in the business world. The ad relies on summaries of research about the target audience—the people most likely to purchase the chair; and Steelcase, the company that designed the chair, considered this audience from the very beginning.

For this assignment, complete one of the following two tasks involving Scion, the line of cars that Toyota designed and marketed to appeal to the generation of most current college students—the "Millennials." Both require you to speculate about how summary information shaped Toyota's business practice. Before choosing one of these two tasks, search the Internet for summaries of "Millennials" (you can start with the terms "Millennials" and "summary"). List the features of your generation that these summaries identify.

1. Analyze the Toyota Scion's Web site, www.scion.com, looking for ways that the creators of this Web page may have tried to attract your generation. Report on your analysis, being sure to describe features of Millennials you found in the summaries as well as descriptions of specific parts of the Web page that seem to respond to these features of Millennials.

2. Analyze one of the Scion car models, looking for features of the car that designers may have included to appeal to Millennials. Report on your analysis, being sure to describe features of Millennials you found in the summaries as well as descriptions of aspects of the Scion car that seem to respond to these features of Millennials.

Assignment 3

Most academic and professional writers review previous research as part of their own writing. How they do this reviewing differs, though, across different academic disciplines and rhetorical situations. Your task for this assignment is to compare Martin Alexander's review essay with one from another discipline to create a guide for students who have to write summaries in a variety of disciplines. Select an academic discipline that is or might be your major, and ask a professor or a reference librarian for help determining the major scholarly journals in that field.

1. Locate the back issues of one of these journals in the library, and page through them, looking for a review essay. Once you have found an essay that primarily reviews previous research in an area, copy the essay.

2. Read the essay through once so that you understand its scope and the author's argument. Then, analyze how the author crafted the review. How does the author group research on similar topics? What information about the research does the author provide? How does the author arrange the essay? What is the rhetorical effect of that arrangement? What is the author's reason for reviewing this body of research?

3. Determine the most interesting or important points of similarity and contrast between the chemistry review essay and the review essay in your discipline.

As you begin drafting, consider how description and examples from both essays can help you detail the most effective strategies for writing reviews.

18

NURSING

The following is a posting on a message board for people who have chronic pain. In it, a person named Braz describes both the physical and social effects of chronic pain:

> I am just about at the end of my rope. I am so sick of being in pain, sick of having to plan my life around my med schedule, sick of having people act like I am just using my "pain" to get attention or to get out of doing things and going places. I am sitting here now, have taken my meds and my back is still on fire, left leg and arm needing to be pulled off and I am just sick of it. I did not ask for this and I do not want to be in pain until I die . . . would rather just get it over with and be done with it.
>
> I wake up every morning and swallow a handful of pills just to be able to get the day started, I grit my teeth to get thru those first agonizing hours of the day and then have to swallow handfuls of pills through-out the day to keep the day going, then a handful at night to be able to get what sleep I do get. I am so tired of being told that I am being grumpy . . . DUH . . . if those people could have my arm or leg or back for a rainy weekend I bet my last buck they would be grumpy too.
>
> SO sick of this attitude that we are addicts . . . no one calls a diabetic an addict, or an epileptic one, yet because our problem is physical pain we are treated like shit!! I wish the parts that caused our pain would glow or beep so others would see that we are not being anti-social, we are being held in the grip of the demon pain. . . . Sorry to go on so . . . just not dealing with the pain well tonight.
>
> —*Braz*

- Is Braz reasonable to wish for more sympathy from others? Justify your answer with at least a few reasons. Use the evidence you observe in the Web posting.

- List all the kinds of evidence of chronic pain that others (family members, friends, coworkers, medical personnel) can see in Braz's life. For each kind of evidence, note the expertise that others need to make an accurate observation.

PORTABLE RHETORICAL LESSON: USING PERSONAL OBSERVATION FOR RHETORICAL PURPOSE

Braz's chronic pain demands a specific response from trained medical personnel: a treatment plan. This treatment plan responds to the implied research question: How can we lessen Braz's pain? The **point** of the treatment plan is expressed as a set of recommendations to manage the chronic pain. But how can you recommend treatment without knowing how to understand the symptoms you observe? What would make up the necessary **research methods and evidence** to justify recommending treatment? If you do not have medical training, reading Braz's post may have made you feel a bit helpless. Exactly what in Braz's post tells you something important for diagnosing the source of his pain? If you have suffered chronic pain yourself, or know someone who has, you may have learned to recognize symptoms and make judgments based on some personal observations, but you would not recommend medical treatment.

The exercise with Braz's post implicitly asks: How can a writer use personal observation for a rhetorical purpose (in this case, making recommendations)? And that question takes us to this chapter's **Portable Rhetorical Lesson** on using personal observation. One of the most difficult lessons for writers is learning when—and how—to use observation effectively.

When you wonder whether to include personal observation in a piece of writing, consider two particular points from writing in nursing:

1. "You only see what you know." This piece of advice comes from the "public" reading for this chapter, a book called *Camp Nurse*. The author constantly uses personal observation to evaluate medical crises and treat patients. She can do so only because she has a trained eye—she knows what to look for and how to respond to what she sees. In the reading from *Camp Nurse* you'll see nurses spontaneously running through lists of symptoms and possible causes in the first seconds of observing a patient. Nurses develop expertise through the knowledge they gain in coursework and the experience they gain in supervised clinical work. As a writer, you increase your expertise by increasing your knowledge of the subject matter. Your readers will trust your observations only when they trust your expertise.

2. The importance of process. The readings in this chapter reveal a typical process for nurses: (1) observe symptoms and situations, (2) record observations, (3) assess the observations, (4) seek professional consultation when possible, and (5) map out—and

record—a recommended plan of action. A patient's life can depend on a nurse's ability to translate expertise into a plan of action—a recommendation for treatment. When nurses gather information systematically (note all the specific categories that must be described—and supported with observations—in the "Care Plan" on page 470), they can make effective recommendations. Clarity and reliability are key features of effective recommendations: if patients and other members of a medical team do not understand what the nurse observed or if they do not trust a nurse's expertise, they are not likely to follow through on a nurse's recommendations.

If you wish to use personal observation in your writing, prepare yourself with a well-trained eye and effective processes (for example, assessing the use of your observations by consulting with an expert) for putting your observations to good rhetorical use.

WRITING IN THE DISCIPLINE

INTRODUCTION

by Mary E. Flikkema, Professor of Nursing

As a nurse, writer, and researcher, Dr. Sandra Thomas advocates for those who may not be able to speak for themselves. She desires that health professionals and others will hear the voices of those who are living in chronic pain. Dr. Thomas describes her writing as "giving a voice to the voiceless," a practice consistent with traditions and purposes of nursing research and writing.

The practice of nursing is both an art and a science. It is necessary for nurses to have specific scientific knowledge—in this case, knowledge about the neurological basis of pain sensations, how pain travels through the body, knowledge about pain medications and alternative therapies. The factual, scientific data is part of a much larger picture of holistic care. Holistic care, the art of nursing practice, is the recognition and treatment of human beings as unique individuals with unique lives and health experiences. The art of nursing involves the application of scientific principles in a unique way for each person. The essence of nursing is the art of caring, creatively weaving holistic approaches for each individual person.

Thomas specifies the focus of the study in her abstract, writing that her findings argue against simple or idealized understandings of chronic pain. She hopes to gain insight from those who experience severe pain every day. The content of nursing papers is about interaction with clients, or interaction with health professionals, but the focus is always on improving the health experiences of those seeking care and support.

As nurse writers prepare a document, they begin with a problem or question, an inquiry about a health issue of concern. The nurse writer determines the best method to answer those questions or concerns. For credibility Thomas followed a specific method of research involving a series of carefully controlled steps to gather and report information. She selected a qualitative method of gathering information about individuals' experiences of pain, an examination of peoples' "lived experiences." This involves the process of allowing those experiencing chronic pain to tell their own stories about their lives and experiences. Listening to individuals' experiences provides the person-to-person contact that is the content of the research findings.

Thomas also follows a conventional format in nursing literature, providing an overview of chronic pain and why it is important to write about this topic. She explains the methods used and reports the findings, her interpretation of the findings, and her analysis of the findings.

But Thomas also uses words and images that are almost certain to evoke a response from others, describing how nurses talk about chronic pain sufferers as "difficult, demanding, manipulators and addicts," or the stereotyped "low back loser." Thomas's role is not simply that of the detached, objective observer. She hopes to convey the negativity that characterizes health-care professionals, those who should be the most compassionate, kind, and helpful. She creates these images so that her readers may understand, examine their own behavior, and thus provide more supportive care. The information gathered in person from the interviews of pain sufferers evokes personal response. Thomas makes a good case for the fact that chronic pain sufferers do not have the support they need to cope with chronic pain, and she argues that change must occur in treating those with chronic pain.

In many professions, as well as in community and public life, it is necessary to provide a voice for the voiceless. For the nurse who writes, changing health care for the better is both motive and goal.

✓ Reading Tips

Read this paper from two perspectives:

- as a health-care scientist (looking for concrete, technical knowledge of chronic pain—to develop expertise) and
- as a health-care practitioner (looking for ways to understand patients' experience).

Reading the abstract will give you the first clue that you need to read from both these perspectives, and the rest of the paper will reinforce that need. The section called "Gaps in Our Understanding of Chronic Pain" emphasizes the science background, and the "Findings" section emphasizes the human experience of the study subjects and of the nurses who observed them; that's where your sympathetic response will be called on.

A Phenomenologic Study of Chronic Pain

Sandra P. Thomas

Western Journal of Nursing Research, 2000, 22(6): 683–705

[Abstract]

This "phenomenologic study" is the type of research that holistically observes "lived experience" of the subjects.

Researchers have seldom invited patients with chronic pain to describe their lived experiences. This phenomenologic study involved in-depth interviews with nine women and four men with nonmalignant chronic pain. The essence of participants' experiences was unremitting torment by a force or monster that cannot be tamed. The body was altered and recalcitrant, the life world was shrunken, and the pain set up a barrier that separated them from other people. Time seemed to stop; the future was unfathomable. Findings of this study contribute to the phenomenological literature that explores the human body and its symbolic meanings and call into question the idealized positive depiction of chronic illness that is prominent in contemporary literature.

"Pain . . . teaches us how unfree, transitory, and helpless we really are, and how life is essentially capable of becoming an enemy to itself."
—*Buytendijk (1962, p. 27)*

Buytendijk's (1962) words aptly depict the helplessness of individuals with chronic pain, a disabling health problem that affects 75 to 80 million Americans (Matas, 1997). By the time they earn the diagnostic label of chronic pain, these individuals usually have tried to get relief from a variety of self-care measures as well as a host of medical interventions. As they endure the gamut of physical examinations, diagnostic tests, exploratory surgeries, and a bewildering array of remedies, chronic pain patients progressively become more discouraged, weary, and angry. Both patients and caregivers become frustrated with one another when treatments are ineffective and suffering becomes prolonged. The cryptic advice "learn to live with it" is often the final salvo of the health care provider to the departing chronic pain patient. The biomedical approach, with its focus on pathophysiology, does not address the complexity of chronic pain and does not provide adequate guidance for successfully living with it. From the perspective of nursing's holistic philosophy, extant literature has significant limitations, including the tendency to focus on discrete aspects of the chronic pain

the study of physical illness

experience ("the parts") rather than on its interrelated wholeness. Researchers seldom invite patients to describe their lived experience. A multidisciplinary panel convened at the National Institutes of Health (NIH) in 1995 stated that "qualitative research is needed to help determine patients' experiences with . . . chronic pain" (NIH, 1995, p. 18). In this article, I present the findings of a phenomenologic study designed to "give a voice to the voiceless" (Hutchinson, Wilson, & Wilson, 1994)—the men and women who live daily with chronic pain.

> "Qualitative research" in this case is a method of gathering in-depth, holistic information about a topic of interest by interviewing those who are experiencing a particular phenomenon (thus "phenomenologic study").

Gaps in Our Understanding of Chronic Pain

The chronic pain literature is voluminous, including studies of its epidemiology and socioeconomic impact as well as its association with anxiety, depression, fatigue, immature defense style, helplessness, locus of control, and substance abuse (Ackerman & Stevens, 1989; Bates & Rankin-Hill, 1994; Covington, 1991; Elton, Hanna, & Treasure, 1994; Latham & Davis, 1994; Skevington, 1983). Notable gaps in our understanding remain nonetheless. Researcher bias is evident in the use of labels such as *immature defense style,* and numerous methodologic problems lessen reader confidence in the conclusions drawn. An excellent summary of these problems may be found in a review of 21 years of research on patients' beliefs, coping strategies, and adjustment to chronic pain (Jensen, Turner, Romano, & Karoly, 1991). Another critical analysis of the literature deplored researchers' heavy reliance on pain clinic samples and failure to use commensurable measures of pain experience (Dworkin, Von Korff, & LeResche, 1992).

> Note the labels that the author has selected to use based on her review of the literature. These labels arouse the reader's sense of injustice.

Studies that illuminate the nature of interactions between pain patients and their caregivers are particularly relevant to nursing. This literature documents paternalistic staff stoicism (Edwards, 1989); labeling of patients as *difficult, demanding, manipulators,* and *addicts* (Faberhaugh & Strauss, 1977); and adversarial relationships between patients and care providers (McCaffery & Thorpe, 1989). Nurse estimations of patients' pain intensity are often erroneous, especially when they are assessing the chronic patient. For example, in a study of 268 registered nurses, the chronic pain sufferer was negatively stereotyped and judged to have less intense suffering than an individual with acute pain (Taylor, Skelton, & Butcher, 1984). Particularly pejorative views of the chronic low back pain patient were noted, perpetuating the stereotype of the "low back loser."

> Notice again the inflammatory words the author cites to arouse one's recognition of the injustice.

> Health-care professionals learn that the definition of pain is "what the person says it is." We are trained to believe what the individuals with pain say about their pain. But the author points out that those with chronic pain may not be believed.

Although modern analgesic medications may provide episodic relief of the physical pain—at least temporarily—they fail to alleviate the profound suffering of these patients, which often is psychological and spiritual, not just physical. A survey of chronic pain patients who were members of a national self-help organization revealed that 50% of them had considered suicide—a particularly disturbing finding given that this

> This startling statistic about suicide implies that effective holistic perspective is often lacking in the treatment of chronic pain.

was a select sample of well-educated and financially secure individuals who had actively sought out a group to help them manage their condition (Hitchcock, Ferrell, & McCaffery, 1994). I believe that nurses have a moral obligation to provide more skillful psychosocial care to these patients. According to Price (1996),

> The provision of skillful psychosocial care to patients suffering from chronic illnesses starts with an appreciation of what it is like to live with a chronic condition. . . . Getting inside the experience of such illness may be key to understanding patient motivation, noncompliance with therapy and altered patterns of social engagement. (p. 275)

Research shows that nurses who have personally borne intense pain are more sympathetic to the patient in pain (Holm, Cohen, Dudas, Medema, & Allen, 1989). Qualitative studies that involve in-depth interviewing of patients could permit nurses to vicariously experience the life world of the chronic pain patient.

Although "getting inside the experience" is recommended, few qualitative studies have been conducted. One exception is a British interview study involving a large sample of 75 patients (Seers & Friedli, 1996). Despite its ambitious scope, this study has several significant limitations. The interviews were not audiotaped, and there is a possibility that the researchers' field notes may be subject to selection bias (i.e., tendency to record what the researchers were interested in or wanted to hear). At best, field notes must be regarded as incomplete accounts of participants' subjective experiences. Furthermore, the data-coding scheme was superficial (e.g., psychological state, social activities), and some themes, such as desperation of doctors, were not well supported by the quotations from study participants that the authors cited. In a phenomenological study by Bowman (1991) of 15 individuals with chronic low back pain, data were not plumbed deeply by the researcher; typical themes were varied psychological reactions and related physical symptoms. Although the interpretations were plausible, they were not highly illuminating. Semistructured interviews by Henriksson (1995) with 40 fibromyalgia patients yielded a useful typology of strategies for managing activities of daily living, but the researcher did not attempt to explore the deeper meaning of having continuous muscular pain.

Purpose of Study

Therefore, the purpose of this study was to explore the deeper meaning of what it is like to live with chronic pain, using a qualitative design. The method selected was eidetic (descriptive) phenomenology derived from the Husserlian (1913/1931) tradition, as elucidated by Pollio, Henley, and Thompson (1997). Within phenomenology, particularly within the writing of Merleau-Ponty (1945/1962), the body is viewed as a fundamental

---

Sidebar note (left margin, top):

First-person statements like this "I believe" are seldom used in professional health literature. Here the author indicates her strong feelings about the need to understand and attempt to improve the care provided.

Sidebar note (left margin, lower):

Qualitative research (phenomenology) may be considered by some to be "soft" research with no "hard data" to support the findings. Those conducting qualitative research follow specified methods for sampling, data collection, and analysis. Qualitative research provides different, "rich" data, taken directly from those who are experiencing the phenomenon. The author identifies the procedure used in her study, giving others the opportunity to critique her report.

category of human existence. In fact, the world is said to exist only in and through the body. Therefore, phenomenology appeared particularly well suited for the exploration of pain phenomena.

Method

Sample

Thirteen individuals were interviewed for the study. Criteria for participants' inclusion in the study were as follows: willingness to talk about their lived experiences, older than age 18, and nonmalignant chronic pain consistent with the following North American Nursing Diagnosis Association (NANDA) definition: "Chronic pain is an unpleasant sensory and emotional experience arising from actual or potential tissue damage or described in terms of such damage . . . without a predictable end and a duration greater than 6 months" (NANDA, 1996, p. 76). Individuals were recruited for the study via a newspaper article and network sampling. No attempt was made to recruit patients with a particular diagnosis or disease trajectory. As noted by Dworkin et al. (1992, p. 7), "chronic pain conditions at different anatomical sites . . . may share common mechanisms of pain perception and appraisal, pain behavior, and social adaptation to chronic pain." Moreover, variation in experience is considered desirable for phenomenological research because it "enhances the opportunity for the thematic structure of the phenomenon to reveal itself" (Hawthorne, 1988, p. 11).

Ages of the participants ranged from 27 to 79 years. Most were white. Nine were female, and 4 were male. Of the participants, 10 were married, and the remainder were single and/or divorced. Duration of pain ranged from 7 months to 41 years. Back pain was the Number 1 type, although shoulder, arm, neck, hip, leg, jaw, and ear pain were also reported by various participants. Pain was present at multiple sites for many of them.

Procedure

In-depth, nondirective phenomenological interviews, lasting 1 to 2 hours, were conducted with each participant after informed consent was given. Participants were asked to describe what it is like for them to live with chronic pain. Following this initial question, the interviewer sought to elicit richer description and clarification of the narrative. Interviews were audiotaped and transcribed verbatim by a professional transcriptionist who signed a confidentiality pledge. Transcripts of the interviews were analyzed according to the procedure of Pollio et al. (1997), which includes independent examination of the text by the researcher (reading, reflecting, intuiting) and thematizing in an interdisciplinary phenomenology research group in which transcripts are read aloud and discussed: "The group functions in a critical, rather than consensual, capacity" (Pollio et al., 1997, p. 49). Any proffered interpretations must be supported by citation of specific lines of text. . . .

Findings

Chronic pain patients described their experiences as an individualized dialogic process between themselves and their painful condition. Their *Lebenswelt* (life world) was shrunken and their freedom greatly constricted. The pain set up a wall or barrier that separated them from other people. Pain dominated their consciousness, as shown in the following exemplars from the transcripts.

"You can't think about anything else, really." "Pain is king. Pain rules." "The pain just rides on your nerves." "Pain dominates what you can do." "Pain is a monster. All I can say is that it's tormenting." Pain was a formidable opponent with whom they fought daily: "You're drowning and you got that will to fight to get to shore . . . to live with chronic pain is a challenge every day." "I tried to outlast it. I tried to just tough it out. But it was boss." The dyadic nature of the relationship was succinctly captured as follows: "Now it's me and this pain. It's a thing. And you've just got to fight it continuously." Feelings ran the gamut from irritability, anger, helplessness, and frustration to profound depression, despair, and exhaustion. Several participants blamed themselves for causing the original injury. Fear was pervasive: fear of the unknown, further incapacitation, and becoming a burden to the family.

In the following sections, we turn to elucidation of the figural themes—that is, those that stand out most prominently against the existential grounds of body, other people, and time. Participants' narratives included little awareness of the external world, which will soon become evident to the reader.

> Qualitative researchers look for similarities in what the study participants say. These are common "figural themes," experiences that several of the participants related to the interviewer(s).

The Altered, Recalcitrant Body. . . .

Invisibility of Pain

Despite the profound changes in their bodies, study participants ruefully acknowledged that the chronic pain was not readily apparent to other people. Chronic pain was invisible, a "secret disorder" with no outward manifestations. Because their bodies looked healthy in the eyes of others, they were accustomed to hostile glances when they disembarked from vehicles parked in spaces for the handicapped. Some longed for external manifestations of disability that could provide greater societal legitimacy: "You can't look at me and say, 'I guess she has rheumatoid arthritis.' You can't tell by looking." "It's so hard for people to understand if I say I'm in pain because they don't see it; I'm not in a wheelchair or walking with a cane." Ironically, a woman whose arm was in a sling—who conceivably might have welcomed the device as a badge of legitimacy— actually resented the attention it garnered: "I just want to wear a sign that says, 'Please don't ask.'"

Separation from Other People. . . .

Isolation

Isolation was thematic in all interviews. Dialogue took place between the study participants and their nonhuman tormentor, the pain, more so than with other human beings. Participants described their pain as imprisoning them. For example, they used terms such as locked off, roped off and caged off. Pain had somehow reset their interpersonal parameters, creating separation and distance from the world and other people, even family members. They felt that they no longer had much in common with others and no longer "fit in." Relationships in which they could be honest and authentic were few or nonexistent. Exemplars of the isolation theme included the following: "Pain separates you. It's really hard to be involved with people when you're in pain." "I feel like I'm on this little island all by myself." "My life is pulled in to where I have very little contact with anybody." "I am absolutely alone."

Trust and Mistrust of Physicians

The data indicated that when pain patients do make an effort to leave their solitary "island" to have contact with others, they are most likely to be keeping an appointment with a physician. Clearly, the most prominent others in narratives of pain patients, more significant than family members or friends, were physicians. Despite repeated experiences with doctors who were impersonal, unkind, or even cruel, participants could not abandon a fantasy that there was a caring doctor out there somewhere who could provide relief for them. Therefore, they were willing to entrust their bodies to the Magnetic Resonance Imaging (MRI) machines and scalpels again and again. But their fragile trust of physicians fluctuated, with considerable disillusionment and mistrust evident in some narratives, such as the following. "He didn't even want to listen to what I said. He just wrote out a prescription." "You wonder are they really trying to help or are they just trying to take the money?" "Some of them think females are just a bunch of walking complaints." "I still go to the library and check up on something a doctor has told me. Because I had lost a lot of trust [during the years before lupus was diagnosed]." "In every state we have moved to, I try to get a book telling me those doctors who have had some type of disciplinary action."

The author emphasizes the lack of support from health-care professionals. Recognition of the need for holistic support may help to change treatment.

Lack of Support

Only two chronic pain patients cited anyone to whom they could talk freely about their experience. One mentioned a supportive spouse and the other a sister, but the remainder of the sample did not describe any support persons. Exemplars of nonsupport, such as the following, were common in the data: "My wife wouldn't give me peace if I took a day off." "My ex [husband] couldn't understand." Nurses were virtually invisible in the narratives, a curious omission given the numerous contacts of the patients with both acute care facilities and doctors' offices. One individual spoke briefly about hospital nurses and their poor management of acute pain. Another made a vague statement of admiration for nurses and doctors but described no specific incidents or interactions. No participants mentioned nurses as part of their support system, and none of them were involved in nurse-led support groups.

Moments of Time, Existential Crisis, and Thoughts of Death

The chronicity of these patients' conditions obviously implies a disease process developing and continuing across a span of time. However, the unit of time that was most consequential to study participants was the moment, a diminutive unit but paradoxically also a lengthy, heavy one that does not correspond to customary notions of clock time. The moment contains not only the pain now but also the perceived possibility of an eternity of suffering, taking "pill after pill after pill." The pain was ever present: "I haven't had 2 days pain free in 6 years" "Constant, can't never get comfortable. Can't never rest. Can't do anything." "Wake up with it, go to bed with it, every time I move, something hurts." There is no assurance that the agony of this moment will end; the future is unfathomable. Time seems to stop. Life is on hold, its rhythms disrupted. One participant used the word limbo. Another wondered if he would "ever have a life again."

Hope and Hopelessness

The meaning of life itself was called into question by some study participants. As exemplified in the following transcript segments, participants were confronted with events that had radically revised their expectations: "I was just 25 years old when it happened. I didn't think anything like that could happen to me. . . . I'll probably never be able to carry a child." "What happened to me was quite existential. It made me very aware of my age, very aware of becoming less able, in the process of growing old. Becoming aware and accepting age and dying in all things." Strategies to maintain some hope were described in terms of "holding on" and "hanging on," but exacerbations of the painful condition often shattered tenuous hopes. A rheumatoid arthritis patient related, "I just got this area fixed and now I've got another [painful] area. Is this what it's going to be like forever for me?"

After a cyclical process of seeking the solution or cure for their problems, participants sometimes came to view treatment as futile. In a world of highly touted medical miracles and dramatic organ transplantations, they expressed bitterness about the lack of a definitive solution to their own distress: "Sometimes I just want to quit taking everything 'cause it doesn't seem like anything's working." "After six surgeries, I am probably no better off than I was to start with." "We can go to the moon, but nobody can find something to change this."

Hopelessness and thoughts of death as liberating were revealed in some interviews. One participant expressed the feelings of many:

> Really don't fear death because one day I won't hurt. . . . On a day where you feel like things are hopeless, you wonder whether you want to go on . . . and whether the quality of your life is enough to keep plugging away.

Another admitted trying to imagine how his suicide could be made to look like an accident or a natural death. Another was acutely aware that a means of liberation from suffering was already available to him: "These pills are very tempting to take more than you're supposed to."

Only 3 participants mentioned any positive aspects of their chronic pain experience. One of these said, "Maybe there's a reason, maybe it's to slow me down [to] look around to see other people are in pain. I'm more and more interested and want to be involved with helping battered women."

Discussion

Most notably expressed in the powerful metaphors used by study participants, the essence of the chronic pain experience is unremitting torment by a force or monster that cannot be tamed. In contrast to popular pain management parlance, these patients say their pain cannot be managed. Data from this study call into question the idealized positive depiction of chronic illness that is prominent in contemporary literature. Thorne and Paterson (1998), having reviewed 15 years of qualitative research on chronic illness experiences, concluded that the early focus on themes of loss and burden had shifted by the mid-1990s to positive images of normality, courage, and self-transcendence. Patients were increasingly being depicted by researchers as strong, powerful, and competent. But few of my study participants with chronic pain perceived their position as one of strength or described any personal benefit of their suffering. The transformative elements within the chronic illness experience may have been overemphasized in the optimistic literature of the 1990s. On the other hand, there may be substantive differences between chronic pain and other chronic illnesses, precluding their comparison.

The grim, ongoing struggle with chronic pain is a very individual one ("Now it's me and the pain"), although the sufferer longs for a physician rescuer. Physicians are both trusted and mistrusted, with the pendulum swinging toward greater mistrust and alienation after repeated experiences of being unheard and unhealed. Not being listened to by doctors is a well-documented complaint of many types of patients but may be particularly galling to the pain patient. No electrocardiogram can reveal the pattern of the pain; only by talking can the patient describe his or her subjective sensations. But patients interviewed by Miller, Yanoshik, Crabtree, and Reymond (1994) all claimed that their physicians did not listen to them when they tried to describe pain and its impact on their daily lives. When the researchers interviewed the physicians, a different understanding of listening was discovered: It meant hearing words as diagnostic cues, not placing the words into the context of the patients' life world. This communication gap between physician and patient was the strongest theme in Miller et al.'s study and was alluded to by participants in this study as well. It logically follows that chronic pain patients begin to doubt that health professionals can help them. In one recent report, 78% of patients with chronic neuropathic pain resulting from breast cancer treatment declined an offer of free treatment in a pain center because they did not believe that treatment would alleviate the pain. Despite an average of 29 months of living with the pain and a significant decrease in quality of life, the women remained unconvinced that the pain center therapies were efficacious (Carpenter, Sloan, & Andrykowski, 1999).

Friedemann and Smith (1997) reported intense family involvement in the lives of their sample of 30 chronic pain patients. Such intense involvement was not evident in this study. However, Friedemann and Smith's interviews were conducted for the specific purpose of obtaining descriptions of family functioning, and the interviews took place after participants had completed a questionnaire about their family's stability and growth. In phenomenological interviewing, if the respondent does not volunteer information, the researcher does not probe. Participants in this study seldom mentioned family members except to deplore their lack of understanding. They concealed their discomfort from family rather than seeking sympathy or assistance. These findings are divergent from literature about the reinforcing "secondary gain" (i.e., attention and solicitude) that chronic pain patients allegedly receive from significant others.

The need to hide pain, a prominent element of study participants' narratives, has been noted by other researchers (e.g., Hitchcock et al., 1994). The culture does not offer a "natural home" for these patients, leaving them on the "amorphous frontier of nonmembership" in society (Hilbert, 1984, p. 375). The concept of internalized stigma, which Phillips (1994) examined in AIDS patients, is perhaps germane to the chronic pain patient as well. Other literature contains concepts and metaphors that are comparable to themes of this study. Existential

> Participants' doubts about the effectiveness of treatment lead some to refuse free treatment, believing the treatment for pain would not help. This appeals to readers'—nurses'—sense of professional experience and compassion.

philosopher Camus once referred to illness as a convent. If one takes his metaphor to mean closed off from the world and deprived of worldly pleasures, it seems relevant to the chronic pain patient. Participants' narratives of pain are consistent with its portrayal by philosopher Hannah Arendt as "a borderline experience between life . . . and death" (as cited in Engelbart & Vrancken, 1984). If there is no one who understands and no place where one fits, is this not a kind of living death?

Findings of this study contribute to the phenomenological literature that explores the human body and its symbolic meanings. In contrast to healthy individuals' relative lack of consciousness of their bodies, the body is the main focus of the chronic pain patient's existence: "Bodily events become the events of the day" (Merleau-Ponty, 1945/1962, p. 85). The life world, in fact, is virtually restricted to the patient's body, as described by Plugge (1967). Themes found in this study may be contrasted with a previous phenomenological study of 16 healthy adults who were interviewed about experiences when they were aware of their bodies (MacGillivray, 1986). One of the three figural themes of the lived body in that study was engagement in the world (i.e., the body as vitality and activity). Vitality involved feeling highly energetic and fully in control of the body while engaging in an absorbing project. For example, a runner spoke of the good feelings of stretching his legs and taking in breaths as he ran. Perhaps because volitional control over the body was largely absent in this sample of pain patients, there were no similar anecdotes of body as an instrument of mastery over the world. Participants' perceptions of their bodies were sharply discrepant from the "socially engaged, skilled bodies" described by Benner (1994, p. xvii) but consistent with MacGillivray's (1986) theme of body as object: "The body 'owns' the person, demands attention, and calls the person back from the world and projects" (as cited in Pollio et al., 1997, p. 79). The chronic pain patient dwells in the world of "I cannot" instead of the world of "I can," like the cancer patients who were studied by Kesselring (1990).

These findings can assist health care providers to understand the chronic pain patient and provide more empathic, supportive care. The psychological pain of being disbelieved and stigmatized is surely as devastating to these patients as their bodily pain, perhaps more so. Therapeutic benefit was obtained by some of the study participants simply by talking to a respectful listener. As one put it, "I believe there has been a release here." Research is needed on nursing interventions that could help chronic patients cope and find meaning in their suffering.

The author summarizes the world in which those with chronic pain live, a world of "I cannot." She has indeed "given a voice to the voiceless" and provided insight for health-care professionals into the needs of those whom they serve.

Note

I am grateful to a number of individuals who assisted with the literature review, interviews, and data analysis for this project: Vicki Slater, Linda Hafley, Karen Heeks, Tracey Martin, Rebecca Ledbetter, Lisa Fleming, and Pam Watson. Linda Dalton transcribed all of the audio-tapes with commendable accuracy. The contributions of my mentor Howard Pollio and the University of Tennessee Phenomenology Research Group have been invaluable. Earlier versions of this article were presented at meetings of the Southern Nursing Research Society, the American Nurses' Association, and the European Health Psychology Society.

References

Ackerman, M., & Stevens, M. (1989). Acute and chronic pain: Pain dimensions and psychological status. *Journal of Clinical Psychology, 45,* 223–228.

Bates, M., & Rankin-Hill, L. (1994). Control, culture, and chronic pain. *Social Science and Medicine, 39,* 629–645.

Benner, P. (1994). Introduction. In P. Benner (Ed.), *Interpretive phenomenology: Embodiment, caring, and ethics in health and illness* (pp. xiii-xxvii). Thousand Oaks, CA: Sage.

Bowman, J. M. (1991). The meaning of chronic low back pain. *American Association of Occupational Health Nursing Journal, 39,* 381–384.

Buytendijk, F. J. J. (1962). *Pain: Its modes and functions.* Chicago: University of Chicago Press.

Carpenter, J. S., Sloan, P., & Andrykowski, M. (1999). Anticipating barriers in pain-management research. *Image: Journal of Nursing Scholarship, 31,* 158.

Covington, E. C. (1991). Depression and chronic fatigue in the patient with chronic pain. *Primary Care, 18,* 341–358.

Dworkin, S. F., Von Korff, M. R., & LeResche, L. (1992). Epidemiological studies of chronic pain: A dynamic-ecologic perspective. *Annals of Behavioral Medicine, 14,* 3–11.

Edwards, R. B. (1989). Pain management and the values of health care providers. In C. S. Hill Jr. & W. S. Fields (Eds.), *Advances in pain research and therapy* (Vol. 11, pp. 101–112). New York: Raven.

Elton, N., Hanna, M., & Treasure, J. (1994). Coping with pain: Some patients suffer more. *British Journal of Psychiatry, 165,* 802–807.

Engelbart, H. J., & Vrancken, M. A. (1984). Chronic pain from the perspective of health: A view based on systems theory. *Social Science and Medicine, 12,* 1383–1392.

Faberhaugh, S. Y., & Strauss, A. (1977). *Politics of pain management.* Reading, MA: Addison-Wesley.

Friedemann, M. L., & Smith, A. A. (1997). A triangulation approach to testing a family instrument. *Western Journal of Nursing Research, 19,* 364–378.

Giorgi, A. (1985). Sketch of a psychological phenomenological method. In A. Giorgi (Ed.), *Phenomenology and psychological research.* Pittsburgh: Duquesne University Press.

Hawthorne, M. C. (1988). The human experience of reparation: A phenomenological investigation. Unpublished doctoral dissertation, University of Tennessee, Knoxville.

Henriksson, C. M. (1995). Living with continuous muscular pain: Patient perspectives. *Scandinavian Journal of Caring Science, 9,* 77–86.

Hilbert, R. (1984). The acultural dimension of chronic pain: Flawed reality construction and the problem of meaning. *Social Problems, 31,* 365–378.

Hitchcock, L., Ferrell, B., & McCaffery, M. (1994). The experience of chronic non-malignant pain. *Journal of Pain and Symptom Management, 9,* 312–318.

Holm, K., Cohen, F., Dudas, S., Medema, P. G., & Allen, B. L. (1989). Effect of personal pain experience on pain assessment. *Image: Journal of Nursing Scholarship,* 21(2), 72–75.

Husserl, E. (1931). *Ideas: General introduction to pure phenomenology* (W. Gibson, Trans.). New York: Collier Books. (Original work published 1913)

Hutchinson, S., Wilson, M., & Wilson, H. (1994). Benefits of participating in research interviews. *Image: Journal of Nursing Scholarship,* 26, 161–164.

Jensen, M. P., Turner, J. A., Romano, J. M., & Karoly, P. (1991). Coping with chronic pain: A critical review of the literature. *Pain,* 47, 249–283.

Kangas, S., Warren, N. A., & Byrne, M. M. (1998). Metaphor: The language of nursing researchers. *Nursing Research,* 47, 190–193.

Kesselring, A. (1990). The experienced body: When taken for-grantedness fails. Unpublished doctoral dissertation. University of California, San Francisco.

Latham, J., & Davis, B. D. (1994). The socioeconomic impact of chronic pain. *Disability and Rehabilitation,* 16, 39–44.

MacGillivray, W. (1986). Ambiguity and embodiment: A phenomenological analysis of the lived body. Unpublished doctoral dissertation, University of Tennessee, Knoxville.

Matas, K. E. (1997). Human patterning and chronic pain. *Nursing Science Quarterly,* 10(2), 88–95.

McCaffery, M., & Thorpe, D. (1989) Differences in perception of pain and the development of adversarial relationships among health care providers. In C. S. Hill & W. S. Fields (Eds.), *Advances in pain research and therapy,* 11, 113–125. New York: Raven.

Merleau-Ponty, M. (1962). *The phenomenology of perception* (C. Smith, Trans.). Boston: Routledge Kegan Paul. (Original work published 1945).

Miller, W. L., Yanoshik, M. K., Crabtree, B. F., & Reymond, W. K. (1994). Patients, family physicians, and pain: Visions from interview narratives. *Clinical Research and Methods,* 26, 179–184.

Munhall, P. L. (1994). *Revisioning phenomenology: Nursing and health science research.* New York: National League for Nursing Press.

National Institutes of Health Technology Assessment Conference Statement. (1995, October 16–18). Integration of behavioral and relaxation approaches into the treatment of chronic pain and insomnia. Bethesda, MD: U.S. Department of Health and Human Services.

North American Nursing Diagnosis Association. (1996). Nursing diagnoses: Definitions and classification 1997–1998. Philadelphia.

Phillips, K. (1994). Testing biobehavioral adaptation in persons living with AIDS using Roy's theory of the person as an adaptive system. Unpublished doctoral dissertation, University of Tennessee, Knoxville.

Plugge, H. (1967). *Der Mensch and sein Leib* (The person and human life). Tubingen: Max Neimeyer.

Pollio, H. R., Henley, T. B., & Thompson, C. J. (1997). *The phenomenology of everyday life.* New York: Cambridge University Press.

Price, B. (1996). Illness careers: The chronic illness experience. *Journal of Advanced Nursing,* 24, 275–279.

Seers, K., & Friedli, K. (1996). The patients' experiences of their chronic non-malignant pain. *Journal of Advanced Nursing,* 24, 1160–1168.

Skevington, S. M. (1983). Chronic pain and depression: Universal or personal helplessness? *Pain,* 15, 309–317.

Taylor, A. G., Skelton, J. A., & Butcher, J. (1984). Duration of pain condition and physical pathology as determinants of nurses' assessments of patients in pain. *Nursing Research,* 33, 4–8.

Thompson, C. J., Locander, W. B., & Pollio, H. R. (1989). Putting consumer experience back into consumer research: The philosophy and method of existential phenomenology. *Journal of Consumer Research*, 16, 133–146.

Thorne, S., & Paterson, B. (1998). Shifting images of chronic illness. *Image: Journal of Nursing Scholarship*, 30, 173–178.

Reading Responses

1. In her article Thomas notes, "Research shows that nurses who have personally borne intense pain are more sympathetic to the patient in pain." Do you believe that readers will be more sympathetic to people with chronic pain after they read the personal experiences Thomas includes in her article? Will her descriptions be enough to change readers' attitudes? Why or why not?

2. Thomas cites other scholarly research as well as the results of her own study. Analyze her use of other research. When does she refer to other studies? What purpose does this research serve in Thomas's essay? What is the relationship between this research and Thomas's own research?

3. What does Thomas want nurses to do differently after reading her article? That is, what is her purpose for writing? Where does she indicate that most clearly? How will the personal experiences in the essay persuade nurses to act differently?

NOTES ON GRAMMAR, STYLE, AND RHETORIC:
APPEALS TO THE GENERAL AND PARTICULAR

Many writing researchers believe that a good way to characterize texts involves determining to what extent those texts appeal to the general or the particular. Taking this approach to "A Phenomenologic Study of Chronic Pain" by Sandra P. Thomas shows it to be an interesting combination of appeals to both the general and the particular.

What do the terms *general* and *particular* mean? To answer this question, it helps to imagine a scale, with the extraordinarily general on one end and the uniquely particular on the other. As you approach the general side of the scale, you focus on generalized people, places, objects, or phenomena. For example, a writer might focus on "thousands of adults suffering from long-term pain arising from multiple causes." As you approach the particular end of the scale, you come ever closer to focusing on one individual person, place, object, or phenomenon. For example, a writer might focus on the stab of arthritic pain Aunt Margaret feels every morning in her left shoulder.

In "A Phenomenologic Study," Thomas focuses on the general by using three closely related kinds of noun phrases. First, she uses many phrases that refer to large groups. Thus we read about "nurses," "study participants," "patients and caregivers," and "men and women who live daily with chronic pain." Second, she uses phrases that refer to types; that is, a singular term represents many individuals or objects of a certain type: "the chronic low back pain patient," "the health care provider," and even "the human body." A closely related kind of phrase refers to characteristics and experiences that many of the subjects in her study have in common: "Isolation," "the chronic pain experience," and "the profound suffering of these patients, which is often psychological and spiritual, not just physical"

(187). All three of these kinds of phrases can appear in a single sentence. For example, in the following sentence, we first find a reference to a generalized experience, then a reference to a group, and finally a reference to a type: "*Therapeutic benefit* was obtained by some of the *study participants* simply by talking to *a respectful listener*" (195, italics added).

Such appeals are accompanied by numerous appeals to the particular. For example, the report includes many exact quotations from individuals. One person says, "I feel like I'm on this little island all by myself" (191). Another complains that "After six surgeries, I am probably no better off than I was to start with" (193). We even learn about some of the patients' relatives, in one case reading about "a supportive spouse" (191).

Sometimes we encounter appeals to both the very general and the uniquely particular in the same sentence. The following example refers to a generalized experience (the "grim, ongoing struggle") and to types ("the sufferer" and "a physician rescuer"), but we also find a quotation from an individual: "The grim, ongoing struggle with chronic pain is a very individual one ('Now it's me and the pain'), although the sufferer longs for a physician rescuer" (193). Further, sometimes we find both kinds of appeals appearing within larger sections of the report. For example, in the first three paragraphs under "Findings," we first see appeals to the general with phrases such as "Chronic pain patients," "their painful condition," and "their freedom" (190). Then we encounter several exact quotations. And after the quotations we move on to generalized traits such as "irritability, anger, helplessness, and frustration . . ." (190). The pattern of appeals in these three paragraphs is the same as the pattern in the report as a whole—first come appeals to the general, then appeals to the particular, and finally some additional appeals to the general.

Why might Thomas have followed this pattern? The answer relates to her overall purpose, which she explains as follows: "I believe that nurses have a moral obligation to provide more skillful psychosocial care to these patients [with chronic pain]" (188). She wants to help nurses see how to "help chronic patients cope and find meaning in their suffering" (195). In other words, she is proposing significant changes in nursing practice. And she lays out the background to and rationale for that proposal with all the appeals to the general. But she also apparently knows that people do not accept significant changes—in medical care and most other endeavors—quickly and easily. If important aspects of nursing practice are to be changed, then nurses themselves will have to feel a sense of urgency about them. As Thomas puts it, nurses will have to get "inside the experience" (188) of long-term pain; they will have to imagine feeling such pain themselves. To help them do that, she includes all the appeals to the particular.

But there is a little more to this story. A respected writer once said that people respond to generalities with their reason and to particulars with their emotions. If he was largely correct, then we can understand even better what Thomas is doing. She uses the appeals to the general to get readers to understand and consider her proposals for changes in nursing. And she uses the appeals to the particular to get readers to feel how desperately each patient in pain needs nurses to care for him or her more sensitively. For the agenda that Thomas is pursuing, her combination of appeals works well.

In Your Own Writing . . .

• Consider how genre and field affect your use of general and particular appeals. Some genres—memoir, for example—do not include a great many appeals to the general. Some fields, such as economic theory, do not include a great many appeals to the uniquely particular.

- When you want readers not just to think about but also to act on a proposal, use appeals to the general to get them thinking and evaluating, but also include appeals to the particular to grip their emotions and move them to action.
- Use general appeals as a way to introduce particular appeals and to follow up appeals to the particular.

STUDENT WRITING

INTRODUCTION

by Curt Gritters, nursing major

The two pieces of student writing in this section each represent a different perspective on nursing.

    1. *Care Plan Assignment.* The objective of the assignment was to gather information regarding various aspects of the patient's history and current condition. I then had to use the information to establish goals for this patient's recovery and formulate a plan of care to achieve those goals (see page 471–72 of the care plan). The result was to be a list-style summary of the patient's situation and a fairly precise direction for providing care.

    The Content. I had to record both objective and subjective data. Not only do nursing students need to know patients' medical or surgical diagnoses, but they must also consider family concerns or barriers to healing and how the client will take care of himself and return to his usual lifestyle. The care plan shown here describes an 82-year-old man whose recovery from open-heart surgery was complicated by fluid accumulation in his lungs ("pleural effusion"). Because his blood was still "too thin" from anticoagulants, a procedure to remove some of that fluid was postponed (to prevent serious bleeding). Meanwhile, an infection was being treated with antibiotics.

    Writing a Care Plan. To write effective care plans, I could not cut and paste portions of interest from the patient's medical record—an easy way out. Many areas in the assignment required a small amount of information, but the patient's medical record was hundreds of pages long. I knew that summarizing in a descriptive yet concise manner was going to be the key. After compiling the lab results, for example, I could write down the ones that were especially important in his current situation.

    However, not all of the information I needed was stated explicitly in the medical record. Writing as a nurse required me both to borrow some information gleaned by others and to retrieve much of the subjective or personal data on my own.

2. Reflection Paper Assignment. The assignment asked me to step back from the medical record and even from the patient, to analyze legal and ethical concerns, and to make suggestions for improved personalized care.

The Content. A fellow student wrote the reflection paper reproduced here. Her experiences in the operating room (OR) and critical care settings are surprisingly typical. Megan watched an "everyday" (in terms of the OR) back surgery and an "everyday" brain injury case. She wrote about what she saw, identified core virtues of nursing that were either utilized or violated, and suggested improvements.

Writing a Reflection Paper.   A reflection paper starts with general observations and ends by giving specific suggestions for changing the patient's care. The nursing student must be descriptive regarding the situation he or she experienced, analytical and insightful regarding the broader issues involved, and concise in making practical suggestions for improvement in patient care. Writing reflection papers is another way of developing the critical thinking process of a nurse—a way in which nurses examine ethical issues in light of their own practice related to patient's rights (dignity, autonomy, consent, etc.) and the treatment of patients as unique human beings.

Learning to Write in Nursing.   In general nursing writing is . . .

- concise, and writing concisely requires a precise summary. For example, when explaining a heart problem that is directly related to the lungs and kidneys, the nurse must summarize concisely the heart problem, then move on to explain its involvement with the lungs and kidneys. Staying focused and not diverging into unnecessary details is vital when every second counts.

- both technically objective and descriptively subjective: the discipline uniquely stakes claims both in health-care science and patients' individual well-being.

- adaptive because patient conditions are always changing. When conditions change, goals change, and the written records and plans must change as well.

Consequently, good writing assignments for nursing students require them to put critical thinking processes onto paper. Though I realize that much of what I write as a nursing student is not what I will write as a nurse, I know that everything I do on paper now must be done in practice as a nurse. Nurses do not, for example, regularly write reflection papers on their practice, but the thought process that the reflection paper simulates must be continuous in nursing practice.

Nursing writing is a fascinating interplay between professional and personal writing styles. Care plans take the objective, scientific technicalities of health care and apply them to personalize care. Reflection papers complete the cycle by transforming personal and subjective ideas into professional practice—which is again made personal in individual care plans.

Nursing Care Plan
Curt Gritters

Nursing Care Plan: Patient Data

Your Name _____ Date of Care _____

Patient Initials _____ Room Number _____ Gender _____ Age _____

Admission Date _____ Admitting Diagnosis _____

Medical/Surgical Diagnosis (current reason for hospitalization and other potential compounding problems) 1. Cellulitis of L pleural effusion (empyema) 2. . . .	**Family/Significant Other Concerns** 1. Concern re husband's infection 2. . . .
Other health concerns/past medical/surgical history/allergies: MSO₄, ASA, CAD, MI in 82, A-fib, L, TKA, ACF, angioplasty × 2	**Financial situation** retired, financially stable, excellent insurance, no concerns
Barriers/cultural considerations (e.g., deaf, indigent, illiterate, etc.) None apparent	**Activity level (why?)** BR c BRP: rest so body can fight infection
Lab tests/diagnostic imaging/procedures (list those completed during the two days you are on the unit and why) Hgb: 10.4, BUN: 32 (azotemia), BNP: 334 (not pathognomic for CHF), INR: 2.8...	
Medications (list those received by the patient during the days you are on the unit and why) 1. Nesteritide: vasodilator/diuretic for acutely decompensated CHF (watch SBP > 90 mmHg and HR) 2. Cefazolin: antibiotic for cellulitis (watch interaction with loop diuretics (Lasix), I/O, BMqd?) . . . 3–14. . . .	

All patient care plans are made in light of the specific information about a patient. An actual data form would contain more technical information than what you see here; this just gives you examples of the contents.

The patient came into the unit after heart surgery and developed some problems that are common to those who undergo heart surgery—congestion in the lungs which makes breathing difficult; the difficulty breathing causes low levels of oxygen to be delivered to the tissues which heal the surgical wound and fight infections. Patients are routinely given drugs to prevent clots from forming, which can lead to strokes or heart attacks. Unfortunately, the drugs also cause the patient to bleed more easily. The patient described in this care plan was being watched for all of the complications that can develop after an extensive surgery such as a CABG (open-heart surgery).

Nursing Care Plan
Current Plan of Care

What is the plan of care and why? _____

Maintain BP while waiting for INR [a blood test to indicate how long it will take for blood to clot] to determine whether fluid might be drained from the lung. Antibiotics until infection is relieved.

What are the most difficult issues/problems for this patient right now? _____

1. Cellulitis of sternal incision [an infection of the chest incision for his heart surgery]

2. Cellulitis of L pleural effusion [lung congestion]

3. DOE

What potential barriers with compliance or healing do you foresee after discharge? Compliance will be okay, but obesity, diabetes, high blood pressure and cholesterol will impair healing.

How will this data influence your care of this patient (including teaching)? How will you approach this patient/family? _____

Pt [patient] very teachable, so encourage continuing weight loss, watching his diabetes (diet) → include wife with this teaching, encourage deep breathing techniques (to flow) to build R lung and compensate for L; encourage rest until infection is overcome; praise his quitting of smoking; good established relationship and conversational style willl facilitate encouragement/recommendations.

Nursing Diagnoses (list and prioritize)

1. Impaired gas exchange related to fluid accumulation in lungs as evidenced by ↓'d [decreased] lung sounds throughout and dullness upon percussion [indicates fluid in chest]

3. Infection risk for (further) related to inadequate primary defenses (broken skin) chronic disease (diabetes, etc), invasive procedures. [surgery]

2. Ineffective breathing pattern related to decreased lung expansion as evidenced by dyspnea [difficulty breathing] and lung field auscultation. [lung sounds]

4. Impaired skin integrity related to infection of skin/tissues.

Risk for imbalanced fluid volume.

Current Plan of Care, continued

Discussion and Reflection on:

Textbook Picture of Patient Diagnosis	Actual Patient Picture/Condition
Discuss the patient's illness/injury including	Discuss your patient's actual condition including
• pathophysiology	• assessment findings (related to the diagnosis)
• common signs/symptoms	• diagnostic tests and results
• expected diagnostic tests and results	• medical/surgical treatments
• usual medical/surgical treatments	• nursing interventions
• usual nursing diagnoses and interventions	
• reference(s)	

Pt has L pleural effusion (empyema). [infected fluid in the lung] This is an accumulation of fluid and pus in the pleural space caused by an infection of surgical wounds of the chest. Often this is manifest by progressive difficulty breathing and decreased mov't of the chest wall on affected side. Dullness to percussion, ↓'d breath sounds over the affected area, fever, night sweats, cough, weight loss.

Diagnostic tests and results: chest x-ray show if effusion is > 250 mL; diagnostic thoracentesis to determine cause/type of fluid; therapeutic thoracentesis to relieve pressure build up from fluid (inserting needle into the lung to drain fluid.)

Tx: therapeutic thoracentesis; drain pleural space via therapeutic thoracentesis or close thoracotomy tube, appropriate antibiotic treatment.

Nursing diagnosis: Impaired gas exchange, ineffective breathing pattern, anxiety.

References: Lewis, Ackley

Pt empyema may be complicated further by his high blood pressure which may force fluid into this space rather than out. Pt did have ↓'d breath sounds over his entire L lung. Pt also had difficulty breathing and cough and dullness upon percussion [tapping on the chest] to L lung field. However he was not running a fever and was actually gaining weight.

A thoracentesis (diagnostic but esp. therapeutic was on hold until his INR dropped into range (so the high Coumadin [a blood thinner] levels did not make him bleed uncontrollably)

Pt was on appropriate antibiotic therapy

Appropriate nursing diagnosis for RK included:
  Impaired gas exchange
  Ineffective breathing pattern
  Excess fluid volume
  Potential for (further) infection

What is the correlation between the textbook pictures and your patient's actual condition? Why?
I think it fits rather well considering the thoracentesis was on hold for his INR to drop.

This part of the "plan of care" is critical because writing about the patient problems allows us to set goals for his recovery and for the health team to evaluate if those goals are met.

Nursing Care Plan
Nursing Process/Teaching Plan

Nursing Diagnosis	Plan/Outcome Criteria	Implementation	Rationale	Evaluation of Outcomes
Impaired gas exchange Related to pleural effusion as evidenced by dyspnea [difficulty breathing], irritability, somnolence [excessive sleepiness], tachycardia.	1. PaO_2 and $PaCO_2$ are maintained within patient's normal range by 9/17. [These indicate the patient's ability to exchange oxygen and carbon dioxide] 2. Normal breath sounds are maintained, and Pt remains free of signs of respiratory distress by 9/18.	1. Monitor SaO_2 for and administer as ordered to SaO_2 levels. 2. Monitor apical radial HR [heart rate] for irregular rhythm, tachy- [too fast], and brachycardia [too slow]. 3. Teach and encourage pursed-lip breathing to improve gas exchange. 4. Position Pt HOB [head of the bed], incline 30 degrees as tolerated.	1. SaO_2 under 90% indicates oxygenation problem. 2. Hypoxia may cause cardiac arrhythmias. 3. Pursed-lip breathing results in increased use of intercostal [between ribs] muscles, increased exercise performance, and ability of Pt to self-manage. 4. Semi-Fowler's [sitting] position allows lung expansion.	1. PaO_2 and $PaCO_2$ in normal range as of 9/17. "Goal met." 2. Breath sounds were improving on left side, but Pt was still experiencing DOE [difficulty breathing with activity]. "Goal partially met."

This plan teaches nursing students various elements that must become normal processes for planning and carrying out patient care.

Teaching—and encouraging—self-care is an important part of a care plan.

The numbers in this chart refer to the four "nursing diagnoses" listed at the bottom of the first page of the "Current Plan of Care."

Reflection Paper: Peri-Operative and Critical Care Experiences

Megan Nyenhuis

the time before and during surgery, and in the recovery room

This past week I had the opportunity to have my peri-operative and critical care experiences. During both of these experiences I was able to observe the role of the nurse and identify some ethical issues that exist and virtues necessary in that setting. During my peri-operative experience, I followed a 67-year-old woman through her surgical experience. I first saw her in pre-op where she was with her family, waiting to be taken back to surgery. I then watched her surgery, a lumbar laminectomy. I admit that I did not really enjoy watching the surgery and hearing the surgeon break through some of the bone in her spine, but I made it through and so did my patient. I then followed her into the recovery room where she woke up from the anesthesia, and finally, was transferred to a medical-surgical floor.

removal of tissue pressing on nerves in the spine

This experience allowed me to somewhat understand what patients go through during their surgical experience. It also allowed me to see what the role of the peri-operative nurse is. I saw the pre-op nurse being an educator, communicator, advocator, and comforter. She explained what would happen to the patient, spoke with and listened to the patient to decrease the patient's anxiety, advocated for the patient by making sure everything was in order for the surgery and making sure everything ran smoothly, and comforted the patient by reassuring her and letting her know someone would be with her at all times. The nurse served as advocate in the operating room by being the one to stop the surgeon from cracking jokes about the patient when the patient was starting to wake up.

Nursing students are asked to describe how they see the nurse providing personal as well as technical aspects of care. Reflecting and writing are good ways to organize thoughts and impressions to evaluate them.

I was also able to observe an ethical issue in the operating room. After my patient was unconscious from the anesthesia, they moved her into position for the surgery (positioned her on her stomach). She was a bigger lady, so moving her was not the easiest task. However, they really gave little attention to being careful and gentle with the patient. They just flipped her over and pushed her into the right position. Later in the surgery when the patient was just starting to come to, the surgeon make some joke about the patient. I thought that these things were not appropriate actions in the operating room. Just because a patient is unconscious does not mean that the patient should be treated any differently.

Student nurses are taught that an important principle of nursing is patient advocacy. Reflection papers allowed a forum to "recognize reality, search for solutions, and try to transform."

Some basic virtues necessary for peri-operative nursing became evident to me as well. The ones that seem most important are courage, empathy, and compassion. Courage is necessary to confront co-workers who are not treating the patient like they should be treated as in the situation described above. Empathy is necessary because many nurses cannot understand what it is like to undergo surgery. The nurse must listen carefully and use therapeutic communication to show that she is trying to understand and that she truly cares for the patient. Compassion is necessary because surgery is a scary thing, and patients need to know that they are cared about and that someone is looking out for them and putting their needs first.

> A subdural hematoma is a blood clot on the brain.

During my critical care experience in the surgical unit, I observed a nurse who was caring for a 64-year-old man who had suffered a traumatic brain injury from a 10–15 feet fall onto cement. He had suffered a left temporal subdural hematoma, rib fractures, left atelectasis, and a mediastinal hematoma. He was unconscious and showed response to very strong stimulus on his arms only. This patient had made little progress since his admission, and doctors were not too hopeful about his prognosis.

> Atelectasis is lung congestion.

> A mediastinal hematoma is a collection of blood around the area of the heart.

An ethical issue was evident during this experience as well. The wife of this patient was understandably very upset and teary-eyed. She came to visit her husband and said things to the nurse like, "When will he wake up? It might take a few weeks, right?" The nurse had told me previously that this patient's prognosis was very poor. However, she felt like it was not her place to give a prognosis especially since the prognosis was still somewhat unknown. But she told me that she also did not want to give false hope to this wife. This situation puts the nurse in a difficult position because she might either overstep her bounds and give the patient's prognosis or give false hope which could be devastating to the family. I thought that this nurse handled the situation well by hugging the wife and reassuring her that they were doing everything they could for the patient.

Virtues that seem especially important in the critical care setting are compassion and empathy. Even if the nurse cannot understand what the patient and family are going through, the nurse can listen and comfort the patient and family and show them that they are cared about.

Reading Responses

1. In reflecting on her experiences shadowing a nurse, Megan Nyenhuis focuses on the interactions that the nurses had with their patients. She does not record the times that the nurses performed clinical tasks like administering medication or recording data. Do you think some nurses would object to this focus? On what grounds? How does Megan's purpose for writing affect the personal experiences she includes in her paper?

2. If you were experiencing severe pain, how important would a nurse's concern be to you? What would be the best way for a nurse to express concern for you?

3. Consider the information that Gritters includes on the patient data sheet. Where does he include emotional or social information? What strategies does he use in writing that must be both technical and abbreviated to showcase the humanness of his patient?

PUBLIC WRITING

INTRODUCTION

Tilda Shalof is a nurse in an intensive care unit in Toronto. She's written two other popular books on being a nurse, including the best-seller, *A Nurse's Story*. In *Camp Nurse*, excerpted here, Shalof tells about several years of nursing at summer camps that her children attended. During those summers she had to respond to a more mixed bag of medical cases than she ever did in the ICU—broken bones, bug bites, a hand almost severed by a meat slicer, self-mutilation, and homesickness. The selection reprinted here recounts the story of one girl—for whom the medical diagnosis and recommendations proved especially challenging.

In the course of the story, Shalof confirms a nurse's need for expertise. In a part of her story not included here, Shalof reports advice that another health-care specialist once gave her: "You only see what you know." In other words, without the training that teaches nurses to know symptoms, they couldn't recognize symptoms *as* symptoms. Shalof's writing also shows a nurse's need for empathy, for professional consultation, and finally, for recognition that humans can sometimes be too complicated to fix.

Camp Nurse: My Adventures at Summer Camp
Tilda Shalof

Kaplan Publishing, New York, 2010

"I sound like a seal," I heard a girl say.

I was in the midst of giving out the evening meds when I heard a strange sound. It was coming from Naomi, an always-smiling, very popular fourteen-year-old who'd never come to the Health Centre for anything before but was now sitting in the waiting room, surrounded by a group of friends while she had fits of coughing. In between bouts of a high-pitched, insistent, squeaky coughing spell, she joked around and giggled. If this had been the ICU and a patient suddenly started coughing like that, I would have placed an oximeter on her finger (an instrument we used to measure a patient's oxygen concentration). Had she been a patient in the ICU, the sudden onset of a harsh cough like this would have garnered her a stat chest x-ray and maybe even a bronchoscopy, which involved a tube placed down into her trachea and lungs, but here, that wasn't necessary—at least not yet. Even without an oximeter, just looking at Naomi's rosy complexion and relaxed manner, I was fairly certain her oxygenation was normal.

I went out into the waiting room. Her friends were joking around with her, making her laugh. "This is not a party," I said, ushering them out.

"I can't breathe!" Naomi said, waving goodbye to her friends. I brought her into the examining room and listened to her chest and heard adequate and equal air entry on both sides, but she was breathing rapidly. "I can't swallow and my chest hurts." Her hands shook. "Is this a heart attack?" Off and on she gave that strange-sounding cough.

"No," I reassured her. "Probably your chest is sore from coughing so much."

Louise [another nurse] examined her thoroughly and then we went aside to speak privately. "I think it's a panic attack," she said. "You were right to throw out the friends. We want to make sure there's no acting up for an audiences' attention. For now, let's try giving her a small dose of sedation."

I gave Naomi a tiny pill under her tongue and let that take effect. After about twenty minutes, we checked on her. She's fallen asleep, and while she slept there was no cough, shakiness or fast breathing. She must have sensed we were standing at the foot of her bed because she startled awake. As soon as she did, the cough and rapid breathing started up again. "I feel like I'm going to pass out," she yelled. I stopped in my tracks. *Someone about to pass out does not have the strength to yell. Someone about to lose consciousness is too weak to speak.*

"My heart is racing," she said, trembling. "It's flip-flopping all around!" Her hands shook violently. She clutched at her chest and took big gulps of air. "I can't breathe."

Her strange cough seemed to be gone but her pulse was racing at 120 beats [normal is 60–80 per minute] per minute and her respiratory rate was also fast at forty-five breaths a minute. I gave her a paper bag to breathe into, to try to retain the carbon dioxide she was losing by hyperventilating.

"My chest hurts," she cried. "I'm going to pass out." Before we could deal with one problem, Naomi had moved on to the next. "The room is spinning. I'm going to faint!" she shouted. I took her blood pressure and it was a robust and normal 132 over 80.

Someone about to faint would have low blood pressure, I thought.

"I feel like I'm losing control of myself," Naomi said. But her words sounded false, like she was repeating lines she'd learned.

"I'm sure it must feel that way," I said quietly. I felt sympathy for her because I could see she genuinely felt upset.

"My feet are numb! They're tingling. I can't feel my feet. They're paralyzed." She suddenly closed her eyes and lay there motionless.

"Naomi?" Look at me! Open your eye," I told her, feeling slightly alarmed.

"I think I just blacked out there for a moment," she said weakly.

But she hadn't lost consciousness. She had been awake and, I was fairly confident, completely aware of everything she was doing. None of this was adding up. I found myself in the situation I've always hated: suspecting a patient was "faking it." It was an especially uncomfortable feeling to doubt a child. I knew Louise was also looking for something deeper by her line of questioning.

"Is something bothering you, Naomi? Are you homesick?"

Naomi looked at her fiercely. "I love camp. I've never been homesick, not even for a minute."

"Because, if you are," Louise continued, "that can bring on these kinds of feelings and they can be really scary when you're away from home and missing your family."

"I live for camp." She turned away from us.

Louise and I spoke privately. "I can't find anything wrong," Louise said. "I think it's pure anxiety and nothing physically abnormal, especially since her memory is intact and she can describe her symptoms perfectly . . ." Louise's voice trailed off and I caught her drift: after a true faint, a patient can't recall events immediately prior to losing consciousness. "Let's give her another dose of sedation and watch her closely. If she worsens we'll take her to the hospital," she said, and went to call Naomi's parents.

Just then, Naomi's brother Lorne, an older camper, arrived. He rushed over to her, sat at the edge of her bed, scooped her up into his arms and held her tight. As she clung to him, their two heads of dark, curly hair mixed together like a huge, luxurious wig. . . .

The next morning, Alice told me it had been a quiet night. Naomi had slept and was now smiling and making light of what had happened, even apologizing for worrying us. She was dressed and eager to return to her cabin. Louise examined her and cleared her to return to her cabin. We wrote it off as a weird inexplicable one-off episode and since she was now well and happy again we didn't give it another thought . . . (pp. 236–39).

Late one evening a few days later, I was sitting in my room reading, when a buzz and crackle came over the walkie-talkie. "Is the nurse there?" a counsellor's voice cried out. "Someone's having a seizure!" . . .

When I got [to the cabin] I found Naomi, lying stiffly on the floor beside her bed, her friends and counsellors around her. I knelt down beside her. "Where are you?" I asked. Her eyes were open and I could tell she saw me but she didn't answer. This wasn't a seizure, but something was definitely wrong. "What's your name?" I asked her.

"It's Naomi," someone said. I explained I needed Naomi to answer for herself, because I was testing her level of consciousness, to see how her brain was working.

"What made you think she was having a seizure?" I asked the counselor.

"That's what Naomi told me."

But from what the counsellor described of what she herself had witnessed, Naomi hadn't had convulsions. She was not now in a typical post-seizure state. We brought her to the Health Centre where she immediately began to flail about and breathe rapidly. Again, I gave her a paper bag to breathe into and coached her to slow down. I worried that her hyperventilation could cause her to pass out and might lead to a drop in her carbon dioxide levels so severe that it would disrupt the acid-base balance, or the "Ph," of her blood chemistry. Calcium levels would then be affected, leading to tremors and spasms, a state called tetany. I had seen the condition of "metabolic alkalosis" in my critically ill patients but never in a healthy person.

Again, Lorne, her brother, rushed in. "Naomi! Are you okay?" She stared at him blankly. "Naomi, you're going to be okay," he told her. He turned to Louise. "Is my sister okay?"

"My neck hurts," Naomi mumbled. Louise and I looked at each other grimly. Sudden neck pain was a classic indicator of meningitis, a highly infectious, deadly disease.

"Naomi, touch your chin to your chest," Louise asked her. She couldn't. It was highly unlikely she had meningitis—there were no other signs and she'd probably received the vaccine—but just in case, we closed all the doors and put on masks and gloves to protect ourselves. If it did turn out to be bacterial, or meningococcal, meningitis, it would be life-threatening for her and dangerous for us, as well as everyone at camp who'd come anywhere near her. Anyone exposed to her would have to go on antibiotics.

Naomi's counselor went with her in the ambulance and I followed in my car. In the ER Naomi had a CT scan to examine her brain and lumbar puncture, which involved putting a needle into her spinal column, to obtain fluid to test for meningitis. When these tests were done I went in to visit her. She was now fully conscious, sitting up, giggling, and playing a finger game called Chopsticks with her counselor. It was as if nothing had happened. Again, she apologized for causing us worry.

I knew all the dire things that still had to be ruled out: seizure, a cerebral bleed, a serious disease or a tumour. The ER doctor decided to keep her overnight for close monitoring and more tests. Her counselor slept beside her in a chair, her head resting on the bed, while I headed back to camp . . . (pp. 240–42).

Naomi . . . was not coming back to camp. Her parents drove from their home in Montreal to be with her. Her doctors still couldn't come up with a diagnosis but she was feeling better and kept apologizing for "causing such a fuss and making everyone worry."

"It's bizarre," Louise said, "but I've seen this syndrome before. It's called *la belle indifference*. It's rare and occurs mostly in adolescent girls, usually well-adjusted, high-achievers like Naomi who have everything going for them. It usually starts with anxiety but quickly spirals out of control, as we saw."

"In between attacks, she was perfectly fine," I said, "even laughing about it."

Louse nodded. "Patients with this syndrome typically make light of their symptoms. The other feature is that each event occurs in front of witnesses and if they fall, they manage to protect themselves, so there's rarely an injury."

"What are her parents like?" Alice asked Louise, who had met them when she'd gone to visit Naomi in the hospital.

"Absolutely lovely. Beside themselves with worry, of course. There was also a younger brother and an older sister and they seemed to be a very close and caring family."

"So, it's hard to understand why . . ." said Alice, her voice trailing off.

We backed off and let it go. We knew and accepted that fact that there weren't always answers. Some medical mysteries never get solved. Many things get better on their own, without our doing, or understanding, anything . . . (pp. 252–53).

Reading Responses

1. Do a Google search for "conversion disorder," a psychological condition that has demanded the attention of health-care professionals for hundreds of years and that Sigmund Freud wrote about as "hysteria." What problems might a nurse face when

the observable symptoms and medical tests all lead to the conclusion that there's nothing physically wrong with a patient, despite severe physical complaints?

2. In what ways does Shalof's knowing her patients personally make her a better caregiver—in what ways a worse caregiver? In what ways does her knowledge make her a better writer?

3. What details tell you the most about Shalof's professional habits? What different kinds of concrete details does she observe? When and how does she record observations? When and how does she consult others for their expertise? How does she make decisions about what to do?

More Writing in Nursing

INTRODUCTION

"The Man in White" describes the developing profession of "nurse practitioner," or NP. Health-care journalist Lisa Ricciotti followed and talked with an NP on a typical day, and her story later appeared in a journal published for nurses (*Alberta RN*).

Lloyd Tapper is an NP in emergency medicine. In the story, Tapper first appears at the ER nursing station, dressed unlike either a nurse or a doctor; so we begin to learn about the unique role of an NP. We witness Tapper's encounters with patients, observing as he checks up on people he saw the week before, offers advice on how to stop smoking to a man who came to the ER because of a twisted ankle, advises a man with a sore back to get training on proper lifting techniques and prescribes pain meds.

Given that the profession of NP is relatively new, the author of the article seems to hope to show how useful an NP can be and thus to win support and greater pressure from the medical profession to encourage more training and licensing of NPs (the story happens in Canada, but the NP profession is growing in the United States as well). The author defines the NP as a profession that fills gaps in between nurses and doctors, showing readers that an NP has authority to do things that doctors must do (like making referrals to other doctors) and the skill to do things that nurses must do (like helping patients plan for long-term health improvement).

The Man in White
Lisa Ricciotti

Alberta RN January 2009 Volume 65.1 (www.nurses.ab.ca)

"He's the guy in the white shirt," says the receptionist, pointing to the emergency area at Edmonton's Northeast Community Health Centre. That's all the direction needed to find Lloyd Tapper among the bustle of staff moving purposefully around the ER nursing station. For one thing, he's not in a brightly coloured top like the other nurses and he's not in scrubs and a mask like the doctors. In his crisp white dress shirt and black dress pants, Tapper stands out. He also stands out as the province's only nurse practitioner working in an urban emergency department. It's a position that the 38-year-old has held for nearly four years and from day one he's worked to define his role, beginning with a departure from standard medical garb.

"Initially when I introduced the role, I wanted to make sure I had an opportunity to develop it, but not based on any traditional nursing or medical models," says Tapper, "so that the added value of the role could be identified as different, but working in complete collaboration with the entire health-care team."

Nurse practitioners are still relatively new. There are only a few hundred in the entire province—men and women who are stepping beyond the scope of the traditional nursing practice and into areas usually limited to doctors. Tapper is authorized by the College and Association of Registered Nurses of Alberta through the *Health Professions Act* to assess, diagnose, treat and refer patients. Registered nurses work under the Act as well, but are not authorized to diagnose, prescribe or refer patients to medical personnel. "If I am a registered nurse, I cannot call a cardiologist and say I want to refer this patient to your clinic. With my licence, I can pick up a phone and refer that patient to be seen by that service."

For cases beyond his expertise, he consults with, or defers to, attending ER physicians or the appropriate referral service. "If you go to your family doctor and your problem is beyond him, he'll refer you to a specialist or possibly an emergency physician. If it's outside the emergency physician's area, he may also consult with a specialist. At a time when access to health-care services is limited, the focus is on matching the client's concern with the appropriate health-care provider. That's what makes me different." says Tapper. . . .

It's now 8 a.m.—time for the IV therapy clinic, a service Tapper adopted as part of his scope of practice. He personally follows every patient in the clinic to make sure their care is continuous, stable and streamlined. Every Monday he follows up with the patients who have been receiving intravenous antibiotic treatments over the weekend. Depending on the results of their blood work and his hands-on medical examination, Tapper determines whether they can be prescribed oral medication.

Since these patients have had to come to the ward three times a day, all weekend for IV antibiotics, the change is a welcome relief. So is having a scheduled appointment, instead of waiting to see an ER doctor who is rushing between critical cases.

Today, Tapper has three patients to check up on. Blair, 53, came to the emergency room after his leg swelled to three times its normal size and Mike, 44, a paraplegic athlete, is suffering from an infection caused by pressure on his legs from his wheelchair. Tapper sees them individually, greeting each with "Hi, I'm Lloyd. It's very nice to meet you." He discusses their symptoms thoroughly, gives advice, suggesting an update on tetanus shots for Blair and advising Mike to try padding his wheelchair and avoid contact sports in the short term. Both are now well enough for antibiotic pills, but before passing out prescriptions, Tapper discusses their costs and possible side-effects. "My job is about the little things," he says.

Next in line is Brad, 42, who is concerned about numbness in his foot after twisting his ankle. Tapper determines that nothing is broken, recommends ice and ibuprophen and asks whether Brad needs a note to excuse him from work while he rests. Then Tapper leans over and plucks a package of cigarettes from Brad's shirt pocket, exposed as he bent to put on his shoes. "Have you thought about quitting or cutting back?" he asks. "Because if you want to, we can help."

Brad seems surprised, but he listens. He leaves with written instructions on how to ice his ankle and a booklet on how to stop smoking with information on the tobacco reduction clinic that Tapper developed for the Northeast Community Health Centre a year ago. It's an example of how Tapper tries to go that extra mile.

"An emergency nurse practitioner is not about dealing with major trauma situations," says Tapper. "That's more the role of emergency physicians with years of specialized training. What I can offer is health promotion, illness prevention and continuity of care."

Tapper's interactions with his patients reflect that focus. He gives Shawn, a young roofer with a very sore back, instructions on proper icing techniques and a prescription for anti-inflammatories, but also advises him to ask his boss for training on proper lifting techniques. Tapper also suggests Shawn begin wearing a back support. "You only get one back. Look after it," he says.

Between patients, Tapper walks over to the mental health and addictions services clinic, also part of the Northeast Community Health Centre, to make sure counseling sessions have been set up for a woman he treated the week before, a victim of domestic abuse. "I'm there for them, right now or when they're ready. I don't judge. If they let me in, I can help." He recently linked another seriously abused victim with social workers for placement in a safe house. "She's been beaten before," Tapper says. "But it is very difficult for her to leave. The violence is rapidly escalating and if she doesn't her life may be at risk."

Tapper takes the same caring approach wherever he can, using the encounters with his patients as opportunities to provide referrals to ongoing care. That's made easier by the many clinics located within Northeast Community Health Centre, an innovative model of primary health-care services, including a diabetic clinic, a senior's clinic, services for new mothers and a children's asthma clinic.

"He wants to make sure patients don't fall between the cracks," says Carol Yeomans, an emergency nurse who's worked with Tapper for the past four years. "He always tries to link them to whatever they need to get them on track, back on the road to Wellness and responsibility for their health. He takes the extra time that an emergency physician doesn't have."

From an emergency physician's perspective, it's a big benefit to have a nurse with Tapper's training around. "He has the knowledge and he's taken on so much. He can do sutures, IVs, follow-up calls and paperwork. If he wasn't here, there'd be quite a void. We could use a couple of people like him at other hospitals," says Dr. Terry Stetsko.

It's now approaching noon and Tapper has decided to take lunch since it's not too busy—by emergency department standards anyways. This afternoon, he'll see a bit more of everything: sick kids, people with infectious diseases, abdominal pains, breathing problems and maybe this week's cardiac case. Recently, a mother rushed into the department with a newborn who was near death. After being stabilized in the emergency department, the child was transported to intensive care at the Stollery Children's Hospital, eventually making a full recovery. Whatever the day will bring, Tapper feels ready. "Nursing of any kind is a privilege. You have the chance to make an impact on people's lives. When I see a chance to make a difference, I take it. I really love what I do."

Reprinted with permission of *Your Health* magazine. Fall 2008 issue.

Reading Responses

1. What details stand out in your memory about Lloyd Tapper? How do the memorable details help the author to achieve her purposes?

2. How does Tapper identify his role in relationship to nurses and doctors? What particular sentences help to answer that question?

3. Imagine the possibility of being a health-care professional. Why might you want to become a nurse practitioner rather than a nurse or doctor?

WRITING ASSIGNMENTS

Assignment 1

In "A Phenomenologic Study of Chronic Pain," Thomas argues that doctors and nurses tend to dismiss pain because pain does not show up on X-rays, MRIs, blood tests, and other "objective" biomedical tests. To "picture" chronic pain, Thomas interviews thirteen people who are living with chronic pain. She uses quotes from those interviews as her evidence for the nature and significance of chronic pain. In this way, the personal experience of people in chronic pain bears witness to that pain in a way that medical tests often don't.

Your task for this assignment is to picture Thomas's use of personal experience by charting it. You may find it helpful to review Chapter 19, "Biology," for advice on creating effective tables and figures. Reread Thomas's essay, recording each time she uses her observations as evidence. Describe how Thomas presents what she observes: quote, paraphrase, summary, or narrative. How does Thomas introduce the observation to the reader? Does Thomas cluster observations, or does she allow them to stand alone? Once you've collected your data, analyze it. What patterns do you see? How do those patterns shape the reader's experience of Thomas's article? Based on your research and your experiences as a reader of Thomas's article, make recommendations about the use of personal experience evidence in science articles.

As you begin drafting, consider how your own personal experience reading and analyzing Thomas's article can help you explain the results of your study to your reader.

Assignment 2

Chapter 20, "English Education," contains an excerpt from *Bootstraps*, in which Victor Villanueva blends humanities scholarly research with his own experiences. Sandra Thomas, author of "A Phenomenologic Study of Chronic Pain," also blends academic research with personal observations. But she does so in very different ways.

Your task for this assignment is to create a set of recommendations for using personal experience effectively. What are the issues that writers should consider regarding when and how to use personal experience? How does the situation in which they're writing affect their use of personal experience? What purposes do personal experiences serve in academic writing? What kinds of personal experiences are appropriate in academic writing? What are inappropriate? What strategies can writers use to present personal experience? To integrate it in their writing?

As you begin drafting, try to be very clear about the ways that context shapes the answers to the questions above and the means that writers can use to determine the appropriate use of personal experience in a given context.

Assignment 3

College students hear frequent warnings to avoid the "freshman fifteen" (weight gain supposedly experienced by first-year students), but recent research indicates that this warning itself can create trouble for students, especially female students.

Your task is to research and report on the effects of the myth of the "freshman fifteen" by targeting two sources of information: published research on the topic and your observations of college students. A reference librarian can help you locate published research on the topic. To gather observations, create a set of interview questions and then interview five to ten students at your school (you might want to interview only women or only men). Record their answers carefully by taking thorough notes or using a tape recorder.

As you begin drafting, consider the relationship between the kinds of evidence that you collected—how can you present your evidence so that it all works together? Consider, too, the relationship between your evidence and the claims that you make in your report—what kind of evidence will best support a particular claim? If you found particularly compelling evidence, you might direct your report to university administrators who oversee student life and include a set of recommendations in your conclusion.

19

BIOLOGY

The National Center for Catastrophic Injury Research categorizes sports injuries as fatalities, nonfatal but permanently damaging injuries, and serious but not permanent injuries. The spring 2008 report information about injuries sustained by high school female athletes appears in three different forms: words, a table, and graphs. Read the information presented in all three forms, and answer the questions that follow.

Table 7 illustrates high school female catastrophic injuries for the past 26 years— including cheerleading. High school female sports accounted for 112 catastrophic injuries during this time period, and 73 of those injuries were to cheerleaders. Of the

Table 7   High School Female Direct Catastrophic Injuries 1982–83—2007–08

Sport	Fatality	Non-Fatal	Serious	Total
Cheerleading*	2	25	46	73
Gymnastics	0	6	3	9
Track	1	1	6	8
Swimming	0	4	1	5
Basketball	0	1	3	4
Ice Hockey	0	0	2	2
Field Hockey	0	3	0	3
Softball	1	2	1	4
Lacrosse	0	0	1	1
Soccer	0	1	1	2
Volleyball	0	1	0	1
TOTAL	**4**	**44**	**64**	**112**

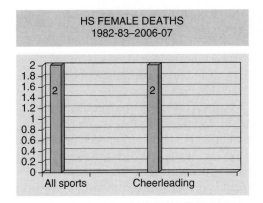

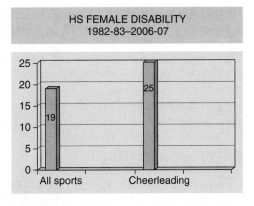

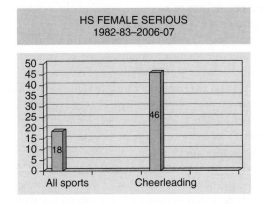

112 injuries, 4 resulted in death, 44 with permanent disability, and 64 were serious injuries with recovery. The 73 cheerleading injuries accounted for two deaths, 25 permanent disability injuries, and 46 serious injuries with recovery. High school cheerleaders accounted for 65.2% of all female sports catastrophic injuries.

- If you were going to make an argument that high school cheerleading is more dangerous than people might imagine, in what form would you present evidence for your argument? List your reasons.

- If you were making an argument to keep cheerleading as a sanctioned sport, what form would you choose for your evidence? List the advantages of the form you have chosen.

- When researchers provide data in table form, like Table 7, they usually include a verbal description like the sentences that precede Table 7. What purposes do the words serve?

PORTABLE RHETORICAL LESSON: USING VISUAL AIDS TO MAKE INFORMATION ACCESSIBLE

What was your first response to the data about catastrophic injuries in women playing high school sports? Were you surprised? Suspicious? What would make you believe the data, even though it might surprise you? Biologists respond to the challenge of suspicious readers by presenting their readers with good data. Readers accept data that has been produced by generally accepted research methods and that demonstrate a very high probability that the results are not due to chance. Consequently, research scientists are always interested in **research methods and evidence.**

Research scientists must also be concerned about **presentation.** To convince readers, scientists must provide a great deal of data, more than they can communicate in words alone. As a result, science writers have developed data-presentation strategies that accomplish two goals: (1) present information clearly so that the reader can read efficiently and (2) emphasize the most important information.

And those challenges from the opening exercise bring us to the chapter's **Portable Rhetorical Lesson:** making information visually accessible. In the introduction to the paper on rugby injuries (the first reading in this chapter), Professor Howell writes, "A scientific paper begins with data." In fact data appear somewhere in the middle of a scientific paper— in a Results section. However, when scientists actually read reports of experimental research, they begin by looking at the data.

And we use the word *looking* intentionally. Scientists have discovered that accessible information almost always appears in some visual form, typically tables and "figures" (a catch-all term for all kinds of images). Our aim in this chapter is to enable you to bring scientists' expertise to your writing tasks—expertise in choosing and creating images that convey information efficiently and that connect the images to the words in the text.

When you are choosing your visuals, remember that you have many options and that each option has its own benefits.

- *Tables* present facts—in columns and rows; they are especially useful for presenting a lot of numbers that can be categorized (into the rows and columns) for comparison.
- *Graphs* (line graphs, bar graphs, pie charts) allow the eye to detect patterns (the bar graphs in this chapter's opening exercise are good examples), and patterns are usually more important for gaining scientific knowledge than are discrete facts.
- *Illustrations* (drawings) can create simplified versions (models) of the natural world's complex systems and processes, revealing patterns in nature.
- *Photographs* are sometimes the best choice: if, for example, you want to explain how a spider can hang upside down from a glass surface, trust an electron microscope photo of the incredibly delicate hairs on a spider's foot.

Furthermore, new technology is constantly improving the presentation options available to scientists and other writers. Consider the advantages, for example, of film and audio in presenting information in electronic formats—rhetorical tools that are becoming increasingly portable.

WRITING IN THE DISCIPLINE

INTRODUCTION

by Elizabeth Howell, Professor of Biology

Imagine that you are the coach of a semiprofessional ice hockey team. Your players train for two months before competing and then play games for eight months while keeping up their training. What information might you need to make decisions about a training program that would minimize injury while maximizing wins? You could rely on your own past experience, anecdotal stories from other coaches, or a more objective source like Tim Gabbett's "Influence of Training and Match Intensity on Injuries in Rugby League." You would then read this paper with the same objectives as scientists—seeking an objective, unbiased answer to a specific research question.

Any scientific paper begins with data that answer the research question. Biologists write papers inside out by first drafting the Results section. In fact, the very first step in writing a paper doesn't involve writing at all. A scientist first designs a study to answer a specific research question; the study then yields data, and the scientist constructs a figure—typically a table or graph—to make the data easy to see and understand. In Gabbett's paper, the specific question at hand is this: How does the intensity and duration of training and play affect the injury rate of rugby players? It doesn't ask whether the players win or lose or if they get stronger as they train and play. Reading this paper explains only injury rates; scientific writing focuses narrowly on a specific research question.

Note also that the data must be quantifiable; that is, you have to be able to measure what you study. If you study the effect of a particular soil additive on plant growth, you will need to measure plant height. If you study the effect of day length on reproductive success of robins, you'll be snooping in nests to count eggs. In this study, the author explains the objective methods he used to measure injury rates, training intensity, and player exertion during matches. The figures (tables and graphs) in the Results section present an accessible summary of those measurements.

Scientists draft the Results section first because the figures represent the complete answer to the specific research question they asked. The figure (or the data it presents) is the reason that the paper exists. A scientific paper with good figures can be accepted for publication even though the text is muddy and poorly written, but even the most elegant, crystal-clear prose can't cover for bad data and confusing figures. That's why scientists write, and read, figures first.

Turn to the graphs in Figure 1 (one of the two central figures of the paper, page 268). They compare the rate of injury to the training duration, intensity, and "load" (duration plus intensity) during a season. On the X axis at the bottom of the graphs we find a spot for each month of the season. We can see at a glance that the training intensity rose over the first three months, then fell until May, and then rose again a bit, finally tapering off at the end of the season. The solid line indicates injury incidence over that same period. By following the line, we can see that as training increased, so did injury. Figure 2, which allows almost instant comparison to Figure 1, *pictures* an increase in injuries that accompanies longer and tougher games.

Having discovered the heart of the paper in the Results, a reader who finds the data potentially useful will read the rest of the paper, all of which supports and contextualizes the data figures. The Introduction provides enough *background* to allow the reader to see how it fits into a larger body of work on the subject. More subtly, by reviewing the history of previous work on the subject, the author *credentials* himself and his study. Gabbett shows his expertise by citing over twenty-five publications (many written by him) in just the first two paragraphs. Most important, the introduction moves from the broader background, to the particular system studied, and finally to the specific question, so it points directly to the results. It is easy to imagine the last sentence of the introduction posed as the central research question: "What is the influence of training and match intensity, duration and load . . . on . . . injury . . . in rugby league players?"

The Methods section describes in great detail the specific techniques used in the study. Any flaw in the methods will cast doubt on the data. (This is the section that nonexperts would be most likely to scan quickly.)

The Discussion both explains and expands on the results. In many ways it mirrors the introduction, except in reverse. Discussions start with the specific findings of a study (as in the first paragraph of Gabbett's Discussion section) and then expand outward, interpreting findings to explain their broader significance.

Once you have finished reading the paper, imagine the author asking the specific question, designing the experiment, collecting the data, generating graphs and tables, then writing the Results, Methods, Discussion, Introduction, and finally the Abstract. Do you see why many scientists write their papers inside-out? It allows them to tie everything into the story: asking an important question, using methods that produce reliable data, and presenting the data figures as the main characters of the story.

✓ Reading Tips

You probably should not read a scientific article straight through, from beginning to end. Instead, read as a scientist would.

- Start by scanning the Abstract.

- Go to the Results section, focusing first on Figures 1 and 2 and the part of the text that explains those figures—the key findings (information) in the paper.

- When you know what the main findings are, scan the Discussion section—to see why the data matter and what might be done to further the research.

- Then scan the Introduction to get the broader context, and scan the Methods only to see how carefully biologists describe methods.

- Throughout the paper, headings and visual aids—and the title assigned to each figure and table—allow you to scan and quickly pick out the information you want, so it's easy to review if you have questions.

- And anytime you need help understanding some of the science, the marginal annotations should clarify things for you. (Remember that the main point is not to learn the science but to learn how scientists think and write to achieve their purpose.)

Influence of Training and Match Intensity on Injuries in Rugby League

Tim J. Gabbett

Journal of Sports Sciences, 2004, 22: 409–17. Accepted 2 October 2003.

[Abstract]

The aim of this study was to examine the influence of perceived intensity, duration and load of matches and training on the incidence of injury in rugby league players. The incidence of injury was prospectively studied in 79 semi-professional rugby league players during the 2001 season. All injuries sustained during matches and training sessions were recorded. Training sessions were conducted from December to September, with matches played from February to September. The intensity of individual training sessions and matches was estimated using a modified rating of perceived exertion scale. Training load was calculated by multiplying the training intensity by the duration of the training session. The match load was calculated by multiplying the match intensity by the time each player participated in the match. Training load increased from December (278.3 [95% confidence interval, CI 262.2 to 294.5] units) to February (385.5 [95% CI 362.4 to 408.5] units), followed by a decline until September (98.4 [95% CI 76.5 to 120.4] units). Match load increased from February (201.0 [95% CI 186.2 to 221.8] units) to September (356.8 [95% CI 302.5 to 411.1] units). More training injuries were sustained in the first half of the season (first vs second: 69.2% vs 30.8%, $P < 0.001$), whereas match injuries occurred more frequently in the latter stages of the season (53.6% vs 46.4%, $P < 0.001$). A significant relationship ($P < 0.05$) was observed between changes in training injury incidence and changes in training intensity ($r = 0.83$), training duration ($r = 0.79$) and training load ($r = 0.86$). In addition, changes in the incidence of match injuries were significantly correlated ($P < 0.05$) with changes in match intensity ($r = 0.74$), match duration ($r = 0.86$) and match load ($r = 0.86$). These findings suggest that as the intensity, duration and load of rugby league training sessions and matches is increased, the incidence of injury is also increased.

Keywords: collision sport, football, performance, rugby league, semi-professional.

Introduction

Rugby league is an international 'collision' sport played by amateurs (Gabbett, 2000a,b), semi-professionals (Gabbett, 2002a,b,c; Courts et al., 2003) and processionals (Gissane et al., 1993; Brewer and Davis,

---

The range of numbers gives the average value and the range that most of the data fell into. CI refers to confidence interval: the researchers are 95% confident that their data falls in this range (confidence is determined by a mathematical formula). In this case, the average training load in December was 278.3 units, but there was a broader range, with the vast majority of loads being between 262.2 and 294.5 units.

P is known as the P-value; it is a measure of the quality of the statistics. These statistical results are quite good.

Scientists include keywords so that their readers can easily search the databases for related studies.

Note that the introduction gives the broader context for the research and the reasons for this particular study.

In scientific papers the references are listed in parenthesis with the authors' names and the year of the paper. The full citation will be found at the end of the article. Experts will recognize the names of other experts.

1995). The game is physically demanding, requiring players to compete in a challenging contest involving frequent bouts of high-intensity activity (e.g. running and passing, sprinting) separated by short bouts of low-intensity activity (e.g. walking, jogging) (Meir et al., 1993). During the course of a match, players are exposed to many physical collisions and tackles (Brewer and Davis, 1995; Gissane et al., 2001a,b). As a result, musculoskeletal injuries are common (Gibbs, 1993; Hodgson-Phillips et al., 1998).

Several researchers interested in rugby league have reported a higher incidence of injury as the playing level is increased (Gissane et al., 1993; Stephenson et al., 1996; Gabbett, 2000a, 2001). These findings have often been attributed to the higher intensity of elite competition (Gissane et al., 1993; Stephenson et al., 1996). It has also been shown that rugby league training injuries occur more frequently in the earlier stages of a season when training intensity and duration are high (Gabbett, 2003), while match injuries increase progressively throughout the course of a season (Gabbett, 2000a, 2003). Collectively, these results suggest that training and match intensity influence injury rates in rugby league players (Gissane et al., 1993; Stephenson et al., 1996; Gabbett, 2000a, 2003). However, no research has quantified the intensity and duration of training sessions and matches for comparison with injury rates over the course of a rugby league season.

This is the motive for the study: what is new and noteworthy about this project in relationship to previous work. Note that the motive is restated succinctly in the last sentence of this section.

The intensity, duration and overall training and match load (i.e. the product of intensity and duration) may impact to differing degrees on injury rates, and therefore warrant individual consideration for injury management throughout the season. The aim of the present study was to examine the influence of training and match intensity, duration and load on the incidence of injury over the course of a season in rugby league players.

Methods

Participants

The methods section provides precise detail of the way in which the experiments were done and how the data were collected. Other scientists who study very similar topics will read this section very carefully, partly to learn new research methods but also to critically evaluate the experiments: Note that in this paper, the methods never identify the gender of the subjects. Because you might expect men and women to get different types of injuries and react to them differently, identifying gender is pretty important and should have been done.

The incidence, site, nature, cause and severity of training and match injuries were studied prospectively in 79 semi-professional rugby league players over the 2001 season. The season lasted from December 2000 to September 2001 inclusive, with matches played from February 2001 to September 2001 inclusive. All players were registered with the same semi-professional rugby league club, and were competing in the Gold Coast Group 18 senior rugby league competition (New South Wales Country Rugby League, Australia). The players were considered to be 'semi-professional' as they were receiving moderate remuneration to play rugby league, but were also relying on additional employment to generate income. The participants in the present study could be distinguished from amateur players (who do not receive match payments) and professional players (who generate their entire income from their involvement in rugby league) (Gabbett, 2001). The playing roster for the season included 57 players, with the remaining players relegated to the amateur team affiliated with the club. Depending on age and skill, players competed in one of three teams (First Grade, Second Grade or Under 19). The Second Grade and Under 19 teams consisted of a squad of 20 players, while the First Grade team consisted of a squad of 17 players. All participants received a clear explanation of the study, including the risks and benefits involved, and written consent was obtained. The Institutional Review Board for Human Investigation approved all experimental procedures.

Matches

The players participated in 69 matches, which included trial ('friendly'), fixture and finals matches. Trial matches were 60 min in duration. Fixture and finals matches were either 60 min (Under 19), 70 min (Second Grade) or 80 min (First Grade) in duration. One finals match (Second Grade) required 2 × 10-min 'extra-time' periods (i.e. 90 min in duration) because of level scores at the end of regulation time. All matches were played under the unlimited interchange rule.

Training Sessions

Each player participated in two organized field-training sessions per week. A periodized, game-specific training programme was implemented, with training loads being progressively increased in the preparatory phase of the season (i.e. December to February) and reduced during the competitive phase of the season (i.e. March to September). The duration of training sessions was recorded, with sessions typically lasting between 60 and 100 min. Players participated in a total of 82 training sessions, which included all pre-season and in-season training sessions that corresponded with pre-season, fixture and finals matches. . . .

Results

Site of Injury

A total of 389 training injuries were recorded, with an overall incidence of injury of 105.9 [95% CI 95.4 to 116.4] per 1000 training hours. More than 35% of the training injuries sustained were to the thigh and calf. Injuries to the ankle and foot (23.9%), knee (12.1%), and thorax and abdomen (12.6%) were less common. Over the course of the season, a total of 948 match injuries were recorded, with an overall incidence of injury of 917.3 [95% CI 857.9 to 976.6] per 1000 playing hours. Approximately 19.0% of the injuries sustained during matches were to the thigh and calf. Injuries to the face (14.2%), knee (13.8%), and arm and hand (12.9%) were less common (Table 1).

Marginal notes:

First Grade are the top players.

Experiments involving human subjects must be approved by a committee of other scientists (including psychologists), and nonscientists to ensure they are safe and worthwhile. A similar board (with a veterinarian) reviews experiments involving other (nonhuman) animals.

Substitute players can enter the game to replace injured players whenever necessary.

This section describes how the intensity of the training and games were quantified. The author measures the intensity of exercise by asking the participants to rate how hard they worked using the Borg Rating of Perceived Exertion.

The Results section presents the data in the form of figures, in this case, tables and graphs. Each figure is anchored in the text. The anchor summarizes the important message of the figure, but scientists will find the figure first, look at it and analyze it, and then turn to the textual anchor to see what the author wants to emphasize.

Nature of Injury

The types of injuries sustained during training and match-play are shown in Table 2. Muscular injuries (haematomas and strains) were the most common type of training injury (45.2%), while joint injuries (22.6%) and contusions (9.8%) were less common. Muscular injuries were also the most common type of injury sustained during match-play (31.8%), while contusions (20.2%) and abrasions (17.9%) were less common.

> Tables 1–4 give the raw data in great detail; by studying them, you can see exactly what type of injury occurs when in the season, and how severe the injuries are. Note that the tables are not designed to clearly and easily answer his question: Is there a direct relationship between intensity of exertion and rate of injury?

Cause of Injury

The causes of injuries sustained during training and match-play are shown in Table 3. Overexertion was the most common cause of training injury (35.2%). The incidence of training injuries sustained while making direct contact with another player (18.8%) or falling and stumbling (13.1%) were less common. Most injuries sustained during matches were the result of tackles (38.2%). In addition, physical collisions with fixed objects (11.8%) and direct contact with another player (22.7%) were also common causes of injury.

Severity of Injury

The majority of training (97.9%) and match (92.9%) injuries were transient, resulting in no loss of playing time. Minor, moderate, and major training injuries were uncommon (Table 4).

Table 1   Site of Injury

Site of injury	Match injuries			Training injuries		
	Number	Incidence	95% CI	Number	Incidence	95% CI
Thigh and calf	160	174.2	148.7 to 199.6	142	38.6	32.3 to 45.0
Face	135	130.6	108.7 to 152.6	13	3.5	1.6 to 5.5
Arm and hand	122	118.0	97.0 to 139.1	21	5.7	3.3 to 8.2
Knee	131	126.8	105.0 to 148.5	47	12.8	9.1 to 16.5
Shoulder	90	87.1	69.1 to 105.1	13	3.5	1.6 to 5.5
Head and neck	89	86.1	68.3 to 103.9	10	2.7	1.0 to 4.4
Thorax and abdomen	100	96.8	77.8 to 115.7	49	13.3	9.6 to 17.1
Ankle and foot	91	88.1	70.1 to 106.1	93	25.3	20.2 to 30.4
Other	10	9.7	3.6 to 15.8	1	0.3	0.0 to 0.8

Note: Match injuries: incidence expressed per 1000 playing hours. Training injuries: incidence expressed per 1000 training hours. 95% CI = 95% confidence interval.

Table 2   Type of Injury

Type of injury	Match injuries			Training injuries		
	Number	Incidence	95% CI	Number	Incidence	95% CI
Contusions	191	184.8	158.6 to 211.0	38	10.3	7.0 to 13.7
Muscular strains	166	160.6	136.1 to 185.1	160	43.5	36.8 to 50.3
Joint injuries	155	150.0	126.3 to 173.7	88	24.0	18.9 to 29.0
Abrasions	170	164.5	139.8 to 189.2	31	8.4	5.4 to 11.4
Haematomas	135	130.6	108.7 to 152.6	16	4.4	2.2 to 6.5
Lacerations	32	31.0	20.1 to 41.8	4	1.1	0.0 to 2.2
Concussion	36	34.8	23.4 to 46.3	1	0.3	0.0 to 0.8
Fractures and dislocations	18	17.4	9.5 to 25.4	3	0.8	0.0 to 1.7
Unspecified medical conditions	20	19.4	10.8 to 27.9	15	4.1	2.0 to 6.2
Respiratory disorders	14	13.5	6.5 to 20.6	8	2.2	0.7 to 3.7
Blisters	9	8.7	4.7 to 14.4	20	5.4	3.1 to 7.8
Overuse	—	—	—	2	0.5	0.0 to 1.3
Other	2	1.9	0.0 to 4.6	3	0.8	0.0 to 1.7

Note: Match injuries: incidence expressed per 1000 playing hours. Training injuries: incidence expressed per 1000 training hours. 95% CI = 95% confidence interval.

Month of Injury

These are the figures (they appear on page 268) we've been waiting for (or, the ones we should have started with). In clear, direct graphics, Figure 1 demonstrates that as the training intensity and duration (training load) decreases, so does the training injury rate. In Figure 2 we see the match intensity and duration (match load) increases. The visual demonstration of the data offers instant and convincing evidence of how the experimental results add up to useful knowledge.

The frequencies of injuries sustained during training (x^2 = 121.5, d.f. = 9, $P < 0.001$) and match play (x^2 = 117.3, d.f. = 8, $P < 0.001$) were significantly different throughout different months of the season (Figs. 1, 2). At the beginning of the season (December) the incidence of training injuries was 105.2 [95% CI 55.7 to 154.8] per 1000 training hours. Training injury rates increased progressively from December to February, and then declined through to the end of the season. Expressed relative to training hours, the highest number of training injuries was recorded in February (205.6 [95% CI 162.1 to 249.0] per 1000), near the beginning of the season. When injuries at the beginning and end of the season were compared (by dividing each season in half), more training injuries occurred in the first half of the season (first vs second: 69.2% vs 30.8%; x^2 = 103.9, d.f =1, $P < 0.001$).

At the beginning of the competitive season (February), the incidence of match-play injuries was 935.5 [95% CI 721.9 to 1148.2] per 1000 playing hours. Match injury rates increased from February to

Table 3   Cause of Injury

Cause of injury	Match injuries			Training injuries		
	Number	Incidence	95% CI	Number	Incidence	95% CI
Being tackled	209	202.2	174.8 to 229.7	3	0.8	0.0 to 1.7
While tackling	153	148.0	124.5 to 171.6	2	0.5	0.0 to 1.3
Collision with fixed object	112	108.4	88.2 to 128.5	30	8.2	5.2 to 11.1
Struck by opposition player	159	153.8	130.0 to 177.8	12	3.3	1.4 to 5.1
Overexertion	75	41.6	56.0 to 89.1	137	37.3	31.1 to 43.5
Fall or stumble	66	63.9	48.5 to 79.3	51	13.9	10.1 to 17.7
Collision with player	56	54.2	40.0 to 68.4	51	13.9	10.1 to 17.7
Overuse	19	18.4	10.1 to 26.7	72	19.6	15.1 to 24.1
Temperature-related disorder	1	1.0	0.0 to 2.9	—	—	—
Twisting to pass or accelerate	2	1.9	0.0 to 4.6	—	—	—
Slip or trip	—	—	—	1	0.3	0.0 to 0.8
Scrum collapse or scrum contact	3	2.9	0.0 to 6.1	—	—	—
Struck by ball	2	1.9	0.0 to 4.6	5	1.4	0.2 to 2.5
Other	91	88.1	70.1 to 106.1	25	6.8	4.1 to 9.5

Note: Match injuries: incidence expressed per 1000 playing hours. Training injuries: incidence expressed per 1000 training hours. 95% CI = 95% confidence interval.

Table 4   Severity of Injury

Severity of injury	Match injuries			Training injuries		
	Number	Incidence	95% CI	Number	Incidence	95% CI
Transient	881	852.4	796.1 to 908.8	381	103.7	93.3 to 114.1
Minor	27	26.1	16.3 to 36.0	4	1.1	0.0 to 2.2
Moderate	30	29.0	18.6 to 39.5	4	1.1	0.0 to 2.2
Major	10	9.7	3.6 to 15.8	—	—	—

Note: Match injuries: incidence expressed per 1000 playing hours. Training injuries: incidence expressed per 1000 training hours. 95% CI = 95% confidence interval.

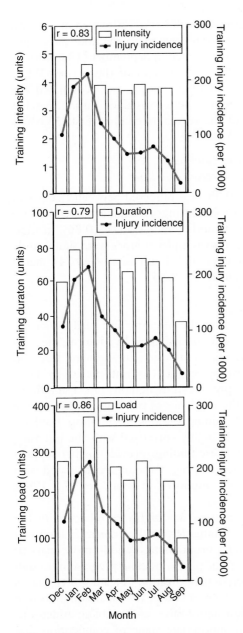

Figure 1 Influence of training intensity, duration and load on the incidence of training injuries in rugby league. Training load calculated from the product of training intensity and training duration. Units for training intensity and training load are reported as arbitrary units.

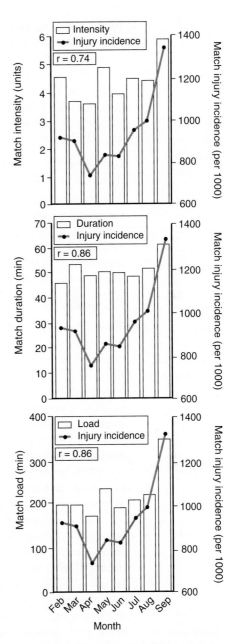

Figure 2 Influence of match intensity, duration and load on the incidence of match injuries in rugby league. Match load calculated from the product of match intensity and the time each player participated in the match. Units for match intensity and match load are reported as arbitrary units.

September. The highest number of match injuries sustained in a month was 187, recorded in July. Expressed relative to playing hours, the highest number of match injuries was recorded in September (1338.5 [95% CI 058.5 to 1618.51] per 1000), at the end of the season. When injuries at the beginning and end of the season were compared (by dividing each season in half), more injuries sustained during matches occurred in the second half of the season (second vs first: 53.6% vs 46.4%; x^2 = 16.2, d.f. = 1, P <0.001). . . .

Relationship between Incidence of Injury and Training and Match Intensity, duration and load

A significant relationship ($P < 0.05$) was observed between changes in the incidence of training injuries and changes in training intensity ($r = 0.83$), training duration ($r = 0.79$) and training load ($r = 0.86$). In addition, changes in the incidence of match-play injuries were significantly correlated ($P < 0.05$) with changes in match intensity ($r = 0.74$), match duration ($r = 0.86$) and match load ($r = 0.86$).

Discussion

> The first paragraph of this section is a nice summary of the results. It says why the study is important and how it's produced knowledge not previously available.

This is the first study to document the intensity and load associated with rugby league training sessions and matches. In addition, the relationships between training and match intensity, duration and load and the incidence of injury in rugby league has not previously been addressed. The findings of the present study demonstrate a significant positive relationship between the incidence of training injuries and the intensity, duration and load of training sessions. In addition, the incidence of match-play injuries was highly correlated with the intensity, duration and load of matches. These findings provide further support for the suggestion that injury rates in rugby league are increased with increased training and playing intensity (Gissane et al., 1993; Stephenson et al., 1996).

The incidence of training injuries was highly correlated with the intensity, duration and load of training despite the implementation of a game-specific, periodized training programme. Periodization refers to the application of sport science principles to training programme design (Bompa, 1983). The application of periodization to team sports such as rugby league is a relatively new concept (Meir, 1994), although its role in preventing unnecessarily high injury rates, and enabling athletes to reach peak performance at an appropriate stage of competition, has been well documented for individual sports (Bompa, 1983). The 38.5% increase in training load from December through to February corresponded with a 95.4% increase in the incidence of injuries sustained during training. These findings suggest that the prescribed increase in training load over the 12-week period (i.e. from December to February) was greater than was tolerable for the musculoskeletal system. Despite the

> In other words, the very program designed to get athletes in shape so they don't get injured later in the season is giving them injuries during the training itself, because it is too intense.

significant increase in injury rates in the initial phases of the training programme, the majority of injuries were transient, resulting in no significant loss of match time. In addition, given that all three teams in the present study were successful in reaching the finals series, it could be suggested that the training programme employed was successful in attaining its goal of improving player performance. However, it should be recognized that the relationship between injury incidence and training intensity, duration and load may not be applicable to other rugby league teams who use different training programmes to the present cohort of players.

The finding that injury rates increased with the applied training load raises the question of the appropriate training stimulus required to elicit improvements in physical fitness and performance. While most injuries in the present study were transient, all injuries have the potential to impact on sporting performance (Watson, 1993). It would appear that a given training load designed to elicit improvements in performance will result in a given number of injuries and, as a consequence, will inadvertently lead to some decrement in performance. However, it is unclear if the improvement in performance provided by the training stimulus is adequate to compensate for the potential reduction in performance resulting from injuries sustained while training under that same stimulus. Conversely, a poor preparation, as a result of an inadequate training stimulus, may lead to an excessive increase in match-play injuries. Therefore, the obvious challenge for rugby league conditioning coaches is to develop game-specific programmes that provide an adequate training stimulus to enhance physical fitness and performance, without unduly increasing the incidence of injury.

> One function of the Discussion section is to suggest practical application of the results.

In the present study, the incidence of match-play injuries increased from the beginning to the end of the season. In addition, the incidence of these injuries was significantly correlated with the intensity, duration and load of matches. These findings are to be expected given that the intensity of matches would be expected to increase as a 'finals' series approaches. Furthermore, the lower match intensity and load associated with early season matches most probably reflects the less competitive nature of pre-season trial matches. Rugby league teams devote a significant amount of training time to the development of defensive communication skills and cohesion in attack. It is to be expected that it may take several matches for the development of these team skills to the point where playing performance is enhanced. It is unclear if the injuries sustained in the latter stages of the season impacted significantly on the playing performance of the teams in the present study. While the present study provides important information regarding the influence of match intensity on the incidence of injury, it is equally important to determine the influence of injuries on the playing performance of rugby league players.

> Here the author mentions the limitations of his study. A Discussion section will tell the reader the significance of what was found but also what was not able to be determined. That's a characteristic of scientific ethics.

In the present study, the perceived intensity of training and matches was higher in Under 19 players than First Grade and Second Grade players. This finding may be expected given that Under 19 players have lower physiological capacities than First Grade and Second Grade players (Gabbett, 2002b) and, as a result, any absolute training stimulus would pose a higher relative physiological strain on these players. However, while perceived match intensity was higher in Under 19 players, the overall match load was highest in First Grade players, reflecting the sustained exposure to high-intensity activity for a longer duration in these players. The match injury rates also closely tracked the overall match load, with higher intensity matches resulting in the highest injury rates. These findings are consistent with previous studies that found higher rates of injury as the playing level and match intensity was increased (Gissane et al., 1993; Stephenson et. al., 1996). Although the match intensity and match injury rates of First Grade, Second Grade and Under 19 players were closely related, the training loads and training injury rates of the three teams were inversely related. First Grade players had the lowest perceived training intensity and load, but the highest training injury rates. A high training injury rate in First Grade players may have resulted in a higher number of training stoppages, thereby reducing active training time in these players.

> In other words, the matches seemed harder for the younger, less experienced players, but in fact the older, better players were working harder during their (more intense) matches.

A subjective measurement tool (i.e. RPE scale) was used in the present study to quantify training and match intensity. Although subjective RPE scales have been shown to have good agreement with other objective physiological indicators of intensity (e.g. heart rate, blood lactate concentration) (Foster et al., 1995; Foster, 1997), it is possible that the relationship between training and match intensity and injury incidence may have been different with a different measurement of intensity. Future studies could utilize heart rate, blood lactate concentration or other physiological markers to quantify the relationship between injury incidence and intensity. Alternatively, recent evidence has shown that the speed of matches may influence the incidence of injury in team sport athletes (Norton et al., 2001). The use of video analysis would permit the quantification of training and match speed, thereby providing a more objective estimate of training and match intensity.

> Researchers often critique their own methods to reveal more limitations of the study. While they did the work, they need to be objective about the strengths and weaknesses of their experiments.

In summary, the present study examined the influence of training and match intensity, duration and load on the incidence of injury over the course of a season in rugby league players. The findings suggest that as the intensity, duration and load of rugby league training sessions and matches is increased, the incidence of injury is also increased. Further studies are required to determine the appropriate training stimulus required to enhance the physical fitness and performance of rugby league players, without unduly increasing the incidence of injury.

> The suggested studies could be done by this researcher or others who are interested in the study.

References

Bompa, T. U. (1983). *Theory and Methodology of Training. The Key to Athletic Performance*. Dubuque, IA: Kendall-Hunt.

Brewer, J. and Davis, J. (1995). Applied physiology of rugby league. *Sports Medicine*, 20, 129–135.

Coutts, A., Reaburn, P. and Aht, G. (2003). Heart rate, blood lactate concentration and estimated energy expenditure in a semi-professional rugby league team during a march: a case study. *Journal of Sports Sciences*, 21, 97, 103.

Dunbar, C. C., Robertson, R.J., Baun, R. et al. (1992). The validity of regulating exercise intensity by ratings of perceived exertion. *Medicine and Science in Sports and Exercise*, 24, 94–99.

Finch, C. F., Valuri, G. and Ozanne-Smith, J. (1999). Injury surveillance during medical coverage of sporting events—development and testing of a standardised data collection form. *Journal of Science and Medicine in Sport*, 2, 42–56.

Foster, C. (1997). Monitoring training in athletes with reference to overtraining syndrome. *Medicine and Science in Sports and Exercise*, 30, 1164–1168.

Foster, C., Hector, L. L., Welsh, R. et al. (1995). Effects of specific versus cross-training on running performance. *European Journal of Applied Physiology*, 70, 367–372.

Foster, C., Florhaug, J. A., Franklin, J. et al. (2001). A new approach to monitoring exercise training. *Journal of Strength and Conditioning Research*, 15, 109–115.

Gabbett, T. J. (2000a). Incidence, site, and nature of injuries in amateur rugby league over three consecutive seasons. *British Journal of Sports Medicine*, 34, 98–103.

Gabbett, T. J. (2000b). Physiological and athropometric characteristics of amateur rugby league players. *British Journal of Sports Medicine*, 34, 303–307.

Gabbett, T. J. (2001). Severity and cost of injuries in amateur rugby league: a case study. *Journal of Sports Sciences*, 19, 311–347.

Gabbett, T. J. (2002a). Influence of physiological characteristics on selection in a semi-professional rugby league team: a case study. *Journal of Sports Sciences*, 20, 399–405.

Gabbett, T. J. (2002b). Physiological characteristics of junior and senior rugby league players. *British Journal of Sports Medicine*, 36, 334–339.

Gabbett, T. J. (2002c). Training injuries in rugby league: an evaluation of skill-based conditioning games. *Journal of Strength and Conditioning Research*, 16, 236–241.

Gabbett, T. J. (2003). Incidence of injury in semi-professional rugby league players. *British Journal of Sports Medicine*, 37, 36–43.

Gibbs, N. (1993). Injuries in professional rugby league. a three-year prospective study of the South Sydney professional rugby league club. *American Journal of Sports Medicine*, 21, 696–700.

Gissane, C., Jennings, D. C. and Standing, P. (1993). Incidence of injury in rugby league football. *Physiotherapy*, 79, 305–310.

Gissane, C., Jennings, D., Jennings, S., White, J. and Kerr, K. (2001a). Physical collisions and injury rates in professional super league rugby. *Cleveland Medical Journal*, 4, 147—155.

Gissane, C., White, J., Kerr, K. and Jennings, D. (2001b). Physical collisions in professional super league: the demands of different player positions. *Cleveland Medical Journal*, 4, 137–146.

Hodgson-Phillips, L., Standen, P.J. and Batt, M. E. (1998). Effects of seasonal change in rugby league on the incidence of injury. *British Journal of Sports Medicine*, 32, 144–148.

Meir, R. (1994). A model for the integration of macrocycle and microcycle structure in professional rugby league. *Strength and Conditioning Coach*, 2, 6–12.

Meir, R., Arthur, D. and Forrest, M. (1993). Time and motion analysis of professional rugby league: a case study. *Strength and Conditioning Coach*, 1, 24–29.

Norton, K., Schwerdt, S. and Large, K. (2001). Evidence for the aetiology of injuries in Australian football. *British Journal of Sports Medicine*, 35, 418–423.

Stephenson, S., Gissane, C. and Jennings, D. (1996). Injury in rugby league: a four year prospective study. *British Journal of Sports Medicine*, 30, 331–334.

Watson, A. S. (1993). Incidence and nature of sports injuries in Ireland: analysis of four types of sport. *American Journal of Sports Medicine*, 21, 137–143.

Reading Responses

1. When you read the Results section, which presentation of data was easiest for you to understand—the written version, the tables, or the graphs? Why?

2. In the Results section, the author presents some data in tables and some in graphs (Figures 1 and 2). Present the information in Table 1 as a bar graph and compare the two: which presentation is more effective? Now create a bar graph for the information in Table 4. Which presentation is more effective? Based on your experience, what factors would you consider when choosing a table or a bar graph for information?

3. Reread the "Nature of Injury" paragraph in the Results section and Table 2. What function do the words fulfill? What function does the table fulfill?

Notes on Grammar, Style, and Rhetoric:
Passive Verbs

One significant controversy about scientific prose centers on the question of whether scientists should use verbs in the passive voice. What kind of verbs are these? To begin, they are transitive verbs, verbs that signal the transfer of action from an agent onto some kind of recipient. When transitive verbs appear in the active voice, the agent is expressed as the subject of the sentence, and the recipient is expressed as the direct object:

The head trainer [agent] *classified* [action] *the injury* [recipient].

When these verbs appear in the passive voice, the recipient is expressed in the subject, and the agent is usually expressed after the verb in a prepositional phrase:

The injury [recipient] *was classified* [action] *by the head trainer* [agent].

Sometimes, however, writers choose to delete the reference to the agent:

The injury was classified.

When writers are deciding between the active and the passive voice of a verb, they choose whether to focus on the agent (active voice) or on the recipient (passive voice) of the action.

Writers should be cautious about using passive verbs for several reasons. First, a sentence with a passive verb will typically be longer than the corresponding sentence with an active verb (as in first two of the earlier examples).

Second, passive verbs do not depict actions as directly and energetically as active verbs do:

Active: *Reckless players sometimes break an arm or a leg.*
Passive: *An arm or a leg is sometimes broken by reckless players.*

Although both sentences depict the same activity, the passive sentence has a more static quality than does the active sentence.

Third, studies of language processing have shown that a sentence is easier to read when it presents the agent before the action and the action before the recipient. Sentences with passive verbs, you recall, move from the recipient through the action to the agent.

Finally, when writers use passive verbs and omit references to agents, they can mask responsibility:

The toxic chemicals were marketed as environmentally safe.

Who marketed the chemicals? No one can tell. In some cases, then, writers intentionally use passives to avoid revealing who the agents of actions are. And when these actions fall into the realm of the unethical, so does the use of passive verbs.

On the basis of these and related cautionary notes, the current edition of the Council of Science Editors style manual advises scientists to use active verbs. But why is this advice ignored by so many scientists? And is it possible that you could have good reasons to use some passive verbs in your own scientific writing?

You can take a significant step toward answering these questions by examining the functions of passives in the scientific report on rugby injuries, which contains over sixty verbs in the passive voice. These verbs appear in every major section of the report, but most of them appear in the Methods section. What functions do passive verbs fulfill for the author?

First, he uses passive verbs to present what he views as facts of the world of rugby. For instance, early in the report he writes, "During the course of a match, players are exposed to many physical collisions and tackles . . . " (263). The effect of this sentence is clear: Injuries occur; to whom they occur does not matter, so passive voice is the right choice.

Second, the author writes as if there were no agent at all associated with the activities of conducting and reporting on the study. For example, he uses subject–verb combinations such as these: "The intensity of individual training sessions was estimated," "Training load was calculated," "Injury rates were calculated," "A total of 389 training injuries were recorded" (264), "A subjective measurement tool (i.e., RPE scale) was used" (271), and "Further studies are required" (271). References to the author and experimenter do not occur. In fact, in the entire report the words *I* and *me* never appear. (Quotations not followed by a page reference come from parts of the paper not reproduced here.)

When scientists report on their research and leave out all or almost all references to themselves as the agents, they are usually aiming for at least two effects. For one thing, they hope to keep their readers focused on the scientific objects and processes, an effect that would be difficult to achieve if some sentences included references to agents (as in *We classified almost 400 training injuries*). For another thing, they imply that whatever preparing, experimenting, calculating, and interpreting they do would come out exactly the same way if someone else performed the tasks. The passive voice implies that the study is reproducible. In this way, passive verbs reflect and support the fundamental practices of science.

So . . . the most important style guide for biologists advises the use of active voice, but most publications in biology contain many passive voice constructions. Assume that the debate doesn't continue out of stubbornness; there are good and bad reasons for using passive voice in the sciences. It's clear that you will need to be purposeful in your choices.

In Your Own Writing . . .

- Be alert for passive verbs that mask responsibility for unethical actions. Point them out in what you read, and avoid them in your own writing.
- Determine your reader's attitude toward passive verbs and take that into consideration as you draft.
- Use passive verbs when you want to focus the reader's attention on the action or the recipient of the action rather than on the agent of the action.

STUDENT WRITING

INTRODUCTION

by Cathryn Ghena, exercise science major

The Assignment. Because research is such a vital component of the health sciences, exercise science majors take a course in research methods. The research process, the same used by all health-care scientists, involves asking a question, developing a hypothesis, designing and conducting the experiment, analyzing the data, and, of course, writing the paper. What is then done with this research? In our case, we had the opportunity to present our research in a poster format at the annual conference of the Midwest American College of Sport Medicine. This meant condensing our project on a 4′ × 8′ board and placing it among dozens of other student posters.

The Content. Our results showed a significant increase in mean levels of oxygen consumption, energy expenditure, and heart rate during *Wii* as compared to Mario Tennis. Such results show that interactive video games cause the gamer to work harder than do sedentary video games. However, the values of the interactive *Wii* games were still not intense, not high enough to be considered a replacement for aerobic training.

Learning to Write in Health Sciences. Our research group members were all intrigued by factors influencing childhood obesity. With a bit of questioning and discussion, we formed our research question: Do interactive video games, specifically the *Nintendo Wii*™, cause a greater increase in aerobic exertion than sedentary video games, specifically *Nintendo*™ Mario Tennis, and would such increased levels be comparable to that of aerobic training?

Next we had to design an experiment. We tested ten college-aged males, all regular gamers, enough to gather reliable statistical data. First, we collected base values for each subject, including maximal oxygen consumption (VO_2max), heart rate (HR) and energy expenditure (kcal/min), all of which are good measures of aerobic fitness. While we collected the oxygen consumption data, subjects played an 18-minute round of sedentary tennis doubles on Mario Tennis. After a ten-minute rest, they played an 18-minute round of interactive tennis doubles on the *Wii*.

Once we gathered all the data, we had to figure out how best to share it. First, and maybe most important, is learning to be concise. When doing research, you essentially become an expert on your topic. This makes it easy to ramble on forever. Unfortunately, such detail is rarely necessary or even appreciated, and it's impossible within the limits of a poster project. Having a long paper doesn't mean an automatic "A," nor does it prove your intelligence. At the same time, though, just because your paper is short doesn't mean it's concise; don't sacrifice essential material for the sake of length. To find a balance between these two, determine what material really is essential. Then present that as efficiently as possible, which means using figures.

Another important part of a poster is its visual effect. In a poster session, people literally stand in front of a poster and have to be able to read it from several feet away. It makes sense, then, that generally half of a poster is filled with tables, charts, and photographs of

Oxygen Consumption During Sedentary and Physically Active Video Gaming in College Males

D. Van Dyke, C. Ghena, E. Metzger, K. Kerekes, J. Walton, J. Bergsma, Calvin College, Grand Rapids, MI.

Introduction

A recent study found 85% of students admitted to playing video games regularly, with over 30% of American homes boasting at least one video game system[1]. Traditionally, gaming has been considered a sedentary activity, requiring no gross motor movements. Meanwhile, the percentage of overweight young people has tripled in the last 25 years, and sedentary lifestyles have been linked to a higher risk of CVD, hypertension and Type II Diabetes[2]. In 2006 Nintendo joined the "active" game community when it released its Wii[TM] system. Nintendo Wii[TM] uses infrared and gravity sensing components to allow gamers to control play by manipulating a remote controller in a manner which mimics a sport movement. This study examined and compared aerobic strain elicited by the Nintendo Game Club[TM] and the Nintendo Wii[TM] to determine if any aerobic training benefit may be derived from either system.

Methods

Subjects: Ten college-age male volunteers (Table 1) were recruited to serve as subjects. All gave written informed consent to participate, and the study was approved by the Institutional Review Board. All Subjects were familiar with both video games used in testing.

Video Games

Sedentary: (SED) Nintendo Game Club[TM]: Mario Tennis[TM]: Doubles
Active: (ACT) Nintendo Wii[TM]: Wii Sports[TM]: Tennis: Doubles

Experimental Design: On the first visit, subjects completed a PAR-Q form and an informed consent before undergoing maximal exercise treadmill testing to determine maximal oxygen consumption (VO_{2max}) and heart rate (HR_{max}). The test protocol employed 3-minute stages in an incremental fashion designed to induce fatigue by the 12th minute of exercise. Metabolic measures were made using a Max 1 metabolic cart system. VO_2 was measured throughout, and HR, BP, and RPE were monitored and recorded in the last 10 seconds of each stage. Subjects ran until volitional fatigue. On the second visit, subjects reported to the lab exactly one week later at the same time of day to play two bouts of video games while VO_2, HR, caloric expenditure, and RPE were measured. In each case, the SED game was played first, followed by a 10-minute rest, then the ACT game. Each game was played for 18 minutes.

Statistical Design: Mean values for VO_2, Peak VO_2, calorie expenditure and HR were compared using an ANOVA post-hoc paired t test, with significance equal to p=.05.

Results

Mean VO_2 was higher on ACT video game than on SED video game (Figure 1). This difference was significant (p = .05). Mean HR was higher during ACT game play than SED game play (Figure 2). This difference was again significant (p = .05). The ACT game elicited significantly greater kcal expenditure than did the SED game (Figure 3) (p = .05). When mean VO2 is expressed as a percent of VO_{2max} values from both ACT and SED systems fail to reach the minimum requirement for aerobic training (Figure 4). Similarly, when mean HR is expressed as a percent of HR_{max} values from both ACT and SED systems fail to reach a minimum requirement for aerobic training (Figure 5). Mean data are expressed in Table 2.

Figure 1

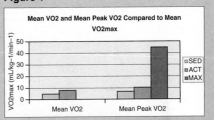

Mean VO2 and Mean Peak VO2 Compared to Mean VO2max

Figure 2

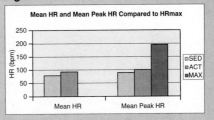

Mean HR and Mean Peak HR Compared to HRmax

Figure 3

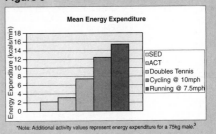

Mean Energy Expenditure

*Note: Additional activity values represent energy expenditure for a 75kg male.[3]

Table 1. Subject Characteristics

Age	Height (cm)	Weight (kg)	BMI	VO2max (mL·kg–1·min–1)	HRmax (BPM)
21.4	180.4	75	23	44.8	192.8

Figure 4

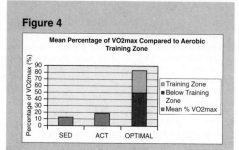

Mean Percentage of VO2max Compared to Aerobic Training Zone

Figure 5

Mean Percentage of HRmax Compared to Aerobic Training Zone

Table 2. Mean Data

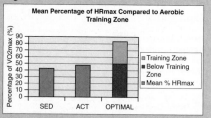

	Mean VO2 (mL·kg–1·min–1)	Mean Peak VO2 (mL·kg–1·min–1)	Mean Percent VO2max	Mean HR (bpm)	Mean Peak HR (bpm)	Mean Percent HRmax	Mean kcals/min
SED	4.88	6.51	11.22	80	91	41.57	1.88
ACT	7.6	9.86	17.25	93	102	48.31	2.99

Discussion

While the *Nintendo Wii*™ elicits significantly greater oxygen consumption, calorie expenditure, and heart rate response than the Nintendo Game Club™, these increases are not great enough to provide any aerobic training benefits. The small sample size limits the strength of this study. A larger sample size must be studied to understand the relationship between active games and aerobic training benefits more completely. Additional studies should look at the effect of active games on high BMI and or low VO2max populations, and across varied age groups, particularly in children.

References

1. Schmitt, B. D. (2006). Video Games [Electronic version]. *Clinical Reference Systems, 2006*(2). from General Reference Center Gold
2. TV-Turnoff Network. (2004). *Screened In: How Excessive Screen Time Promotes Obesity.* Washington, D.C.
3. Wilmore, Jack H., and David L. Costill. (2004). *Physiology of Sport and Exercise.* 3rd ed. Hong Kong: Human Kinetics.

Notes on the poster

1. Acronyms and abbreviations: **ACT** = active, stand-up gaming; **BP** = blood pressure; **BMI** = body mass index; **CVD** = cardiovascular disease; **kcal/min** = energy expenditure; **HR** = heart rate; **PAR-Q** = medical history and consent form; **RPE** = rating of perceived exertion, **SED** = sedentary, sit-down gaming; VO_2 **max** = maximal oxygen consumption.

2. Other definitions: **aerobic strain**: amount of oxygen uptake; the harder you're working, the greater your O_2 uptake; **aerobic training zone**: amount of exertion required for aerobic benefit; **Institutional Review Board**: an ethics review board that must grant approval to all research designs that use human or animal subjects.

3. The visual features. **Title**: the large font of the title is a necessary eye-catcher. People at poster sessions often wander around looking for topics of interest; they have to be able to see your topic at a glance. **Graphs and tables**: most of the poster is taken up with figures and tables because they offer the easiest way to quickly see the findings. **Headings**: "Introduction," "Methods," "Results," "Discussion," and "References" are the standard sections of most scientific writing, in posters, published papers, and lab reports.

4. The sections. The **Methods** section includes demographics of the people who participated, what was done, and the statistical design used to analyze the data. The **Results** section summarizes the findings. Notice that all the sentences are short and to the point. The **Discussion** wraps up the poster, in our case, with a one-sentence summary of the results. It also suggests limits of the study and recommendations for further research. Maybe people reading the poster will be intrigued enough to conduct their own study and use ideas or methods from your work.

the research data collection. A health science audience will be able to look at the figures and immediately see the research results. This gets rid of unnecessary reading, saving a lot of time. To aid in this process, you learn that your figures should have features like a title, key, and labeled axes.

A second consideration is the audience. Professionals in health sciences present to either a general audience or an audience of other scientists.

If you write for a general audience, be sure to do a good job breaking everything down. One common barrier is abbreviations like CVD, VO_2max, and BMI. Be sure to explain all abbreviations, no matter how simplistic. This goes hand in hand with the second barrier—complexity. If the audience doesn't understand what they're reading, then they won't get anything out of it. This only makes your paper frustrating and then easily forgotten. Be sure to break all the concepts down, give examples, and use charts and tables.

We presented our poster to fellow specialists. Poster sessions are a unique way of data presentation. Having a day or two at a conference to find the information you're interested in from among thousands of posters can be overwhelming. Using keywords make this possible. In the abstract, there will be different words that are specific to your research topic. The audience can search all the poster abstracts ahead of time for keywords, and they are able to choose what posters to see at the conference. For example, people who searched for VO_2max, aerobic training, or calorie expenditure, might have stumbled on our abstract, which would help them decide whether to go see the poster in person. At the poster presentation interested individuals have the opportunity to ask questions and discuss the research in more detail with the poster's authors. In that situation you can bring out some of your research that you didn't put on the poster.

Overall, writing in the health sciences means learning what's expected of you—having good content and making it really easy and quick to understand.

Reading Responses

1. Write out the sentence that most directly summarizes the main findings of the research. What section was it in? How does that sentence relate to the title of the poster? Revise the title of the poster to emphasize the main findings of the research, rather than the topic of the research.

2. Which of the graphs best supports the findings it reports? Explain your reasons for that choice. List three strategies that the authors could use to emphasize that graph.

3. Study the blocks that are mostly words. What's their function? How do they complement the graphs and tables? Make three revision recommendations to enhance the function of text in this poster.

PUBLIC WRITING

INTRODUCTION

In "The Female Hurt," Maguerite Holloway (contributing editor at *Scientific American*, professor at The Journalism School at Columbia University, and 2009 winner of a Presidential Teaching Award) uses a mixture of illustrations and figures to explain why female athletes have a different rate and pattern of injuries than male athletes. In some ways, the article looks very different than the other articles in this chapter. It begins with a "catchy" title that gives very little specific information, and it also has anatomical drawings that are "artist renderings" of the human body. In other ways, it looks a lot like the other papers in this chapter. The author quotes scientific studies that involve experimental and control subjects, cites specific numbers, and embeds three graphs in the text. The hybrid nature of the paper reflects its intended audience. *Scientific American* articles are written for nonexperts who have a general interest in news-making science.

Keeping in mind the chapter's portable rhetorical lesson, think about the figures in the article. You will notice how clearly and effectively the results are conveyed by the figures. The difference between male and female injury rate and participation in sports is made obvious, at a glance, by the bar graphs.

The figures in this paper share another characteristic with figures in journals published for experts. Although the author of this paper did not collect the data and did not design her paper around her lab work, she still would have started with these figures, as they tell the core of the story. The paper is centered on the following observation: female athletes have a higher rate of ACL injury. This fact (and the graph that conveys it) comprises what amounts to the "results" section: explanations of why the injury rate is higher are equivalent to the introduction and discussion.

The Female Hurt
Marguerite Holloway

Scientific American 2000, 11(3): 32–37.

"I don't want to hear a bunch of thuds," bellows Deborah Saint-Phard from her corner of the basketball court. Several dozen young women and girls, some barefoot, some in jeans and tank tops, some in full athletic regalia, look sheepish. They jump again, trying to keep their knees slightly bent and facing straight forward, trying to make no noise when their feet hit the floor. "I can hear you landing," Saint-Phard nonetheless admonishes, urging them into a softer touchdown. "Control your jump."

Saint-Phard is a doctor with the Women's Sports Medicine Center at the Hospital for Special Surgery in New York City. She and several colleagues have traveled to this gymnasium in Philadelphia for "Hoop City"—a National Collegiate Athletic Association (NCAA) event—to teach young women how to jump safely. Female athletes, particularly those playing basketball, volleyball and soccer, are between five and eight times more likely than men are to injure their anterior cruciate ligament, or ACL, which stabilizes the knee. Some 20,000 high school girls and 10,000 female college students suffer debilitating knee injuries each year, the majority of which are ACL-related, according to the American Orthopedic Society for Sports Medicine. Tearing the ligament can put an athlete out of the game for months, if not forever.

"This is a huge public health problem for women," says Edward M. Wojtys, an orthopedic surgeon at the University of Michigan. "Fourteen- to 18-year-olds are subjected to injuries that many of them will never recover from, that will affect whether they can walk or exercise at 40 and 50." For this reason, physicians are placing new emphasis on teaching female athletes how to jump in such a way that they strengthen their knees and protect their ACLs. "We have to get them when they are young," Saint-Phard says.

Torn ACLs are just one of the medical problems that plague female athletes. Injuries and ailments that occur with higher incidence in women than in men are garnering more attention as women enter sports in record numbers—not only as Olympians and professionals but for fitness and recreation. Today 135,110 women participate in collegiate athletics, according to the NCAA, up from 29,977 in 1972. The number of girls playing high school sports has shot up from 294,015 to 2.5 million in the same time frame. As a result,

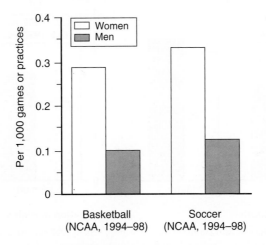

Frequency of ACL injury

Source: "Anterior Cruciate Ligament Injury Patterns" by Elizabeth Arendt et al., *Journal of Athletic Training,* June 1999.

researchers, physicians and coaches are increasingly recognizing that girls and women engaged in sports have some distinct medical concerns.

This makes perfect sense. Women's bodies are shaped differently than men's, and they are influenced by different hormones. They may be at greater risk not only for ACL tears but for other knee problems, as well as for certain shoulder injuries. Women are also uniquely threatened by a condition called the female athlete triad: disordered eating habits, menstrual dysfunction or the loss of their menstrual cycle, and, as a consequence of these two changes, premature and permanent osteoporosis. "We are seeing 25-year-olds with the bones of 70-year-olds," Saint-Phard says.

Although the passage of Title IX legislation in 1972 required that institutions receiving federal funding devote equal resources to men's and women's sports, it has taken a while for the particular needs of female athletes to emerge. As an example, Wojtys points to the ACL: "It took us 15 to 18 years to realize that this problem existed." Women entering sports even a decade and a half after Title IX received less care from coaches and physicians than male athletes did, says Saint-Phard, who competed in the 1988 Olympic shot-put event. When she was in college, she recalls, "the men's teams got a lot more resources and a different level of coaches than the women's teams."

And today even those conditions that are increasingly well recognized as more problematic for women are not fully understood, and their etiology and treatment remain controversial at times. "There is not enough awareness of the differences," says Regina M. Vidaver of the Society for Women's Health Research. For most of the people treating sports injuries, she explains, "their predominant history is with men." . . .

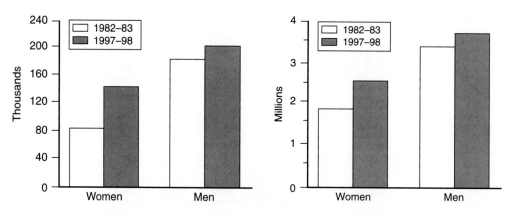

Participation in NCAA Sports   Participation in High School Sports

Sources: National Collegiate Athletic Association Participation Statistics Report, 1982–98; National Federation of State High School Associations Participation Study. Copyright NFHS 2010. Used by permission..

Tearing into ACL Injuries

The most obvious musculoskeletal difference between men and women is the breadth of their hips. Because a woman's pelvis tends to be wider, the muscles that run from the hip down to the knee pull the kneecap (the patella) out to the side more, sometimes causing what is called patellofemoral syndrome—a painful condition that appears to occur more frequently in women. In men, the muscle and bone run more directly vertically, putting less lateral pull on the patella. Some studies also indicate that women's joints and muscles may tend to be more lax than men's; although this adds to greater flexibility, it may mean that female joints and muscles are not necessarily as stable.

Increased laxity and differences in limb alignment may contribute to ACL injuries among female athletes. And yet, even though physicians and coaches first recognized in the 1980s that female athletes were more prone to this injury, there is still no resolution about the cause. "It is an area of controversy," observes Joseph Bosco, an orthopedic surgeon at New York University. . . .

Recent studies indicating that ACL injuries can be prevented by training women to jump differently and to develop their hamstring muscles suggest that inadequate training is at least a large part of the problem. "We train and condition women in the same way that we do the men," says Wojtys, who showed in a 1999 study that women tend not to bend their knees as much as men do when they land a jump, thereby increasing the pressure of the impact on the joints. "They probably need their own training programs."

The Cincinnati Sportsmedicine and Orthopaedic Center focuses on just such an approach. In 1996 Frank R. Noyes and his colleagues there followed 11 high school girl volleyball players who went through Sportsmetrics, a grueling six-week jump-training program the researchers had created. They found that all the participants improved their hamstring strength and that all but one were able to reduce their landing forces, placing less stress on their knees as a result (and achieving the "quiet landing" Saint-Phard was looking for in Philadelphia).

The investigators went on to follow two new groups of female athletes—those who did this strength training and those who did not—as well as a group of male athletes without Sportsmetrics. In an article published last year in the *American Journal of Sports Medicine,* the authors, led by Timothy E. Hewett, reported that only two of the 366 trained female athletes (and two of the 434 male athletes) suffered serious knee injuries, whereas 10 of the 463 untrained women did. They concluded that specially trained female athletes were 1.3 to 2.4 times more likely to have a serious knee injury than the male athletes were, whereas the untrained females were 4.8 to 5.8 times more likely.

The idea that better, or perhaps more, training could have a strong effect on injury rates is supported by work with another set of women: army recruits. According to a recent study by Nicole S. Bell of the Boston University School of Public Health, female recruits were twice as likely to suffer injuries during basic combat training than men were—and two and a half times more likely to have serious injuries. . . .

Noyes is also working to redress another sports medicine imbalance. Historically, men have been more likely than women to have knee surgery. Noyes believes that there are two reasons. First, knee surgery used to be a difficult procedure with often poor outcomes, so it was limited to athletes who really "needed" it—in other words, professional male athletes. Second, there has been a perception among physicians that women would not fare as well during the often painful surgery and recovery. So Noyes and his colleagues decided to examine the responses of both men and women to ACL surgery. They determined that although women took slightly longer to heal, both sexes fared equally well in the long run.

Noyes's work on surgery outcomes and the growing consensus about the importance of neuromuscular control appear to have shifted some attention away from another area of ACL injury investigation: hormonal influences. Researchers have found that the ACL has estrogen and progesterone receptors—target sites that respond to those two hormones. In studies in animals and in vitro, they have discovered that the presence of estrogen decreases the synthesis of collagen fibers, the building blocks of ligaments. It also increases the levels of another hormone, relaxin, which in turn adds to the disorganization of collagen fibers. This change in the ligaments makes the ACL more flexible and, according to the hypothesis, more vulnerable to injury.

This view seems supported by some studies, including one by Wojtys published two years ago in the *American Journal of Sports Medicine*. He and his team questioned 40 women with ACL injuries; the majority of the tears occurred during ovulation, when estrogen levels were highest. Other studies show some increased muscle laxity in ovulating women, but nothing dramatic. . . .

"Estrogen probably has some role," notes Jo A. Hannafin, orthopedic director at the Women's Sports Medicine Center. But, she says, no one is applying the studies' findings to the court—limiting, say, what time of month a player should or should not play. The hormonal result "just reinforces old stereotypes," Bosco adds. "It takes weeks and weeks for the effects [of estrogen] to be seen, so it doesn't make sense. We still strongly encourage women to participate in athletics over the whole month."

Treating the Triad

Estrogen's role in the other major health threat to female athletes is not at all controversial. Exercise or poor eating, or both, can cause an athlete's body to develop an energy deficit, become stressed and lose essential nutrients. Any or all of these changes can cause levels of follicular-stimulating and luteinizing hormones to fall and ovulation to therefore cease. Absent their menstrual cycles, young athletes do not have the requisite estrogen at precisely the time they need the hormone the most to help retain calcium and lay down bone. By the age of 17, nearly all a young woman's bone has been established, explains Melinda M. Manore, a professor of nutrition at Arizona State University. If an athlete's level of estrogen remains low, she can start to lose bone mass at a rapid rate, which can lead to stress fractures and, if the process is not curbed, premature osteoporosis.

The phrase "female athlete triad" was coined in 1992 by participants at an American College of Sports Medicine meeting. Since then, anecdotal reports have indicated that the occurrence of the triad is on the rise. "I think young women are more and more aware of their body size," Manore says. Furthermore, female athletes are especially vulnerable.

Eating disorders—such as obsessive dieting, calorie restriction or aversion to fat (all labeled disordered eating), as well as anorexia and bulimia (the so-called classic eating disorders)—are disproportionately high in girls and women who participate regularly in sports. Averaged across various sports, some 30 percent of these individuals have an eating problem, as opposed to 10 to 15 percent of the general population— although no one knows for sure,

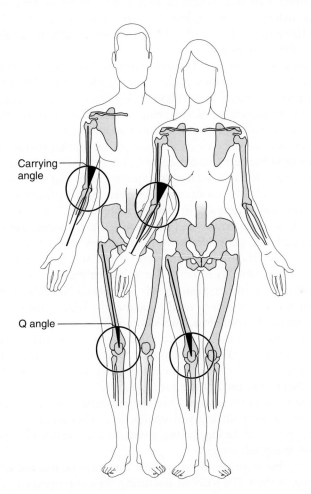

The Inside Story on Injury

The skeletons of women differ from men's most visibly in the width of the pelvis. As a result, women have a wider Q angle (a measure of bone alignment from hip to knee) and carrying angle (from upper to lower arm), which can lead, respectively, to higher rates of knee and elbow or shoulder injuries.

because no large-scale studies on prevalence have been conducted in the U.S. The proportion may be as high as 70 percent in some sports. "High achievers, perfectionists, goal setters, people who are compulsive and determined—those are the things that characterize our best athletes," says Margot Putukian, a team physician at Pennsylvania State University. Those are also the very qualities that often lead people into problem eating.

And athletic culture—particularly for swimmers, runners, skiers, rowers and gymnasts—only continues to reinforce these behaviors and expectations. Many coaches encourage their athletes to lose weight so they can be faster or have less mass to move through acrobatic maneuvers. According to a recent study, female gymnasts weigh 20 pounds less than those in the 1970s did. And many female athletes at all levels see losing their period as a badge of honor.

"They don't see it as a negative," Putukian explains. "They see it as something that happens when you get in shape, a sign that you are training adequately." What they also don't see is what is happening to their bones—until they develop stress fractures. "They fly through their adolescent years with no knowledge of why being too thin is dangerous," Saint-Phard says.

Treating the triad is challenging, and, as Putukian notes, "there is not a lot of great data to tell us what is the best thing." Researchers now recognize that female athletes experiencing these problems need the combined talents of a physician, a nutritionist and, if they have bulimia or anorexia, a psychologist—a multidisciplinary team that most schools and colleges lack. "When you have a kid who has an eating disorder, it is very frustrating," Putukian says. "It is reversible if you catch it early on, irreversible if you don't." She tells her athletes—who are all questioned about their menses and their eating habits during their initial physical—that if they haven't had their period for three months, they are in danger.

Putukian tries to get them on a birth-control pill and works with them to change their eating habits if they have a problem. But although the pill restores some hormonal activity, it does not provide the requisite levels for normal bone development. And hormone replacement therapy, which is used by some physicians, has not been extensively tested in young women. Nevertheless, Putukian notes that athletes may be easier to treat than women in the general population because there is an incentive: competition. "It is an incredible tool," she says. "You can help kids come back." Putukian has refused to let several athletes compete until they got their weight up to healthy levels; their desire to participate drove them to improve their eating habits.

Putukian, Manore and others would like to see young women better educated about the consequences of excessive dieting and amenorrhea. They admit that little can be done about the cultural pressures facing young women—the unrealistic icons of emaciated beauty that destroy many self-images.

But they believe that if girls understand that they may be jeopardizing their freedom to take a simple jog in their 30s without fracturing their osteoporotic hips or leg bones, they will change their behavior.

The investigators hope that athletes will focus on how they feel and how they perform, rather than on how much they weigh. But as with the jump-training program to prevent ACL injuries, there remains a great divide between the medical community's recommendations and the reality of the track or court or gymnasium. Only when those are fully integrated will Title IX have truly fulfilled its promise.

Reading Responses

1. The introduction to the first reading in this chapter indicates that graphics need to be "anchored" in the text. That is, the writers use words to help explain the tables, graphs, figures, etc. Note two places in this article where the author fails to do this and describe how an anchor in the text could make the image more effective.

2. In this article, the author and others make two claims that seem to be contradictory. First, female athletes have been hurt because they have been treated like male athletes. Second, female athletes have been hurt because they have not been treated like male athletes. How have they been treated like males? How have they not? Are these two claims contradictory after all?

3. Compare the introduction to this article to the introduction to "Influence of Training and Match Intensity on Injuries in Rugby League" and to Ghena's introduction to her poster. Which two are most alike? Why do you think these authors chose the rhetorical strategies they used for their introductions?

MORE WRITING IN BIOLOGY

INTRODUCTION

Our purpose for this reading is simple—to show you how an image (in this case an illustration) functions to make communication clear and efficient. Using images in this way probably goes back for as long as humans have been writing and drawing. Famous images come to mind—for example, we all recognize the double-helix model of DNA that James Watson and Francis Crick published in 1953. Without that image, understanding the structure of DNA would be next to impossible.

In the short opening parts of the article printed here, the authors, Manini and Clark (professors at, respectively, the University of Florida and Ohio University), introduce their review essay (a genre that we study in Chapter 17) on a type of exercise. To summarize what researchers at the time knew about "blood flow restricted" exercise, Manini and Clark had to explain how the technique works and its effects on the body. No scientist would imagine trying to convey that kind of information without the use of images.

The illustration in Figure 1, at a glance, shows readers the mechanism of the exercise practice—exactly how it works—and its physiological effects—the use of "up" arrows, for example, indicates four bodily effects that increase under the exercise regime.

By the way, this technique is still highly experimental and potentially very dangerous. The authors report on the available research, but they do not recommend the practice. In fact, they specifically warn, "Considering the limited data regarding the safety and clinical viability of BFR exercise, we must caution against the immediate clinical application of BFR exercise by medical professionals." In other words, they say that doctors should not let their patients use this method even in supervised settings. Please don't try this on your own.

Blood Flow Restricted Exercise
and Skeletal Muscle Health

Todd M. Manini and Brian C. Clark

Exercise and Sports Sciences Reviews (2009), 32.2: 78–85

Introduction

The most common method for increasing both muscle mass and strength is through the performance of high intensity resistance exercise, where the American College of Sports Medicine typically recommends that resistance training with loads exceeding 70% of maximal strength be used to induce optimal muscle hypertrophy [enlargement]. These recommendations are based on evidence that has accumulated over the past three decades, indicating that compensatory muscle growth results from mechanical loading of the muscle tissue and occurs in a fasting state and without insulin signaling. Therefore, tension development through either passive or active techniques by itself facilitates protein synthesis and is typically considered a fundamental determinate of skeletal tissue mass (10, 13).

Increasing evidence suggests that hypertrophy also can be induced with low-intensity exercise performed under blood flow restricted (BFR) . . . conditions (1, 21, 29). The observation that BFR exercise at low mechanical loading causes muscle growth seemingly opposes traditionally based programs. Although many questions remain regarding the efficacy, safety, and mechanisms of action of BFR exercise training, scientists are beginning to develop a better understanding of the model. This review aims to present the latest findings regarding BFR exercise and discuss the potential mechanisms of action that seem to be discordant with traditionally based theories of muscle hypertrophy.

Mechanics of Blood Flow Restricted Exercise

The concept of exercise training with BFR has been around for nearly 40 years and was popularized in Japan by Yoshiaki Sato in the mid-1980s. Today, Sato has commercialized his training method in Japan (known as KAATSU training), where it is now relatively common. Although there is no universal way in which the training is used, it uses a relatively simple approach that generally involves placing a narrow compression cuff around an appendicular limb [arm or leg], which is inflated during exercise (Fig. 1). . . . One common feature of most BFR protocols, which may play an important mechanistic role, is that the compressive cuff remains inflated throughout the exercise session, including the rest period. As such, during subsequent sets, the number of repetitions that can be performed is substantially reduced by approximately 30%-50%.

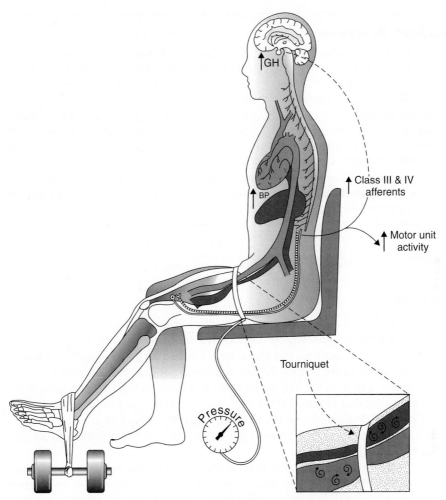

Figure 1 Conceptual model of the physiological responses to blood flow restricted exercise (BFR). GH indicates growth hormone; BP, blood pressure; . . . ["Class III and IV afferents" are nerve fibers that carry messages from the body to the brain; a "motor unit" is a single nerve cell and the muscle fiber it sends messages to, so "motor unit activity" refers to how active, or stimulated, the motor unit is.]

References [cited in excerpt]

Abe, T., Kearns, C. F., Sato, Y. Muscle size and strength are increased following walk training with restricted venous blood flow from the leg muscle, Kaatsu-walk training. *J. Appl. Physiol.* 2006; 100:1460–6.

Goldberg, A. L., Etlinger, J. D., Goldspink, D. F., Jablecki, C. Mechanism of work-induced hypertrophy of skeletal muscle. *Med. Sci. Sports.* 1975; 7: 185–98.

Hornberger, T. A., Esser, K. A. Mecahnotransduction and the regulation of protein synthesis in skeletal muscle. *Proc. Nutr. Soc.* 2004; 63: 331–5.

Ohta, H., Kurosawa, H., Ikeda, H., Iwase, Y., Satou, N., Nakamura, S. Low-load resistance muscular training with moderate restriction of blood flow after anterior cruciate ligament reconstruction. *Acta. Orthop. Scand.* 2003; 74: 62–8.

Reading Responses

1. What is the relationship between the illustration and the text? What parts of the illustration could you not fully understand without reading the text? What does the illustration add to your understanding that the text does not provide? What additional information could the illustration have provided?

2. In the introduction to this reading we mention the double-helix model of DNA. Do some research into the history of science. Describe three other models that have reformed scientific understanding. Were the models described through diagrams, equations, words, or other methods?

3. Think of a process or mechanism that you are studying for one of your classes and draw a diagram to illustrate how the process or mechanism works. Add whatever text is necessary to explain your illustration to a reader.

WRITING ASSIGNMENTS

Assignment 1

So, how much of your athletic ability results from your genetics? Australian researchers have discovered that human muscles contain a protein, alpha-actinin 3, that helps them make fast, strong contractions, like those sprinters use. In some people, a different protein substitutes for alpha-actinin 3; this abnormal protein helps muscles in sustained exercise, such as a marathon. The researchers wondered whether these muscle proteins are present in different ratios in the muscles of different types of athletes, and whether these differences could account for their Olympic success. The researchers presented their data in a paper that can be found at this site: http://www.inmr.com.au/articles/ACTN3AmJHumGenetics.pdf.

The central figure of the paper is presented earlier; just as in the rugby paper, the figure tells most of the story. For you to understand this story, you need to know that in the figure the scientists have nicknamed the normal version of apha-actinin 3 "R" and the abnormal version "X." Humans, like all complex animals and plants, have two versions of every gene. So, a person could have two versions of the normal protein ("RR"), one normal and one abnormal ("RX"), or two abnormal versions ("XX"). The graph measures what percentage of each group has each pattern of genes: RR, RX, and XX. The numbers are represented as the gray, black, or white boxes. (You can ignore the narrow lines. They show the range of high and low values for statistical purposes only.)

Your task for this assignment is to create a verbal explanation of the figure. First, describe the topic a bit so that your reader understands the context for the information that the table and figure provide. Then summarize the data in the figure, drawing your reader's attention to the most important results. Finally, help the reader understand the implications of the results—how does this research affect the reader or others in the world?

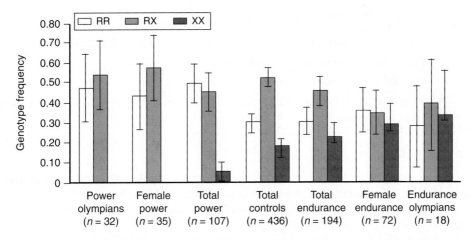

Figure 1 *ACTN3* genotype frequency in controls, elite sprint/power athletes, and endurance athletes. Compared with healthy white controls, there is a marked reduction in the frequency of the *ACTN3 S77*XX genotype (associated with αa-actinin-3 deficiency) in elite white sprint athletes; remarkably, none of the female sprint athletes or sprint athletes who had competed at the Olympic level (25 males and 7 females) were αa-actinin-3 deficient. Conversely, there is a trend toward an increase in the *S77*XX genotype in endurance athletes, although this association reaches statistical significance only in females. Error bars indicate 95% CIs.

As you begin drafting, you'll want to draw the reader's attention to how the pattern of genes in "Total Power" athletes (short-distance runners, swimmers, and cyclists, speed skaters, and judo athletes) differs from those in "Total Endurance" athletes (long-distance runners, swimmers, and cyclists, and cross-country skiers). And you'll want to help the reader understand how the pattern of genes in "Endurance Olympians" and "Power Olympians" differs from the other athletes and from the general population.

Assignment 2

On the Web site for the National Center for Catastrophic Injury Research (http://www.unc .edu/depts/nccsi/) you can find the most recent reports on sports injuries sustained by high school and college players. Each report contains much data, too much for a reader to comprehend at a glance. In marketing, a common way of presenting complex information quickly and effectively is a PowerPoint presentation because you can easily blend visual presentations of information (tables, figures, images) with verbal representations. To create an effective PowerPoint presentation, you must present data effectively so that the audience understands the information and can see the connection between the information and the author's central point.

Your task for this assignment is twofold:

A. Review the most recent NCCSI report and choose a type of athlete and/or type of sport. Create a PowerPoint presentation that supports a claim about catastrophic injuries to these athletes. Use visual and textual presentation to support your claim.

B. In a two-page report, justify your choices, focusing on four questions.

- Why did you choose to use figures to represent certain information?
- Why did you choose text for other information?
- Why did you arrange your figures and text as you did?
- What does your PowerPoint presentation emphasize about the data? What does it de-emphasize?

Assignment 3

Marguerite Holloway ("The Female Hurt") provides a valuable service by using visuals to help professionals interpret the complex biological data produced by scientific experiments. Trainers and coaches are most likely to influence the behavior of female athletes, but they can do so only if they understand the data.

Your task for this assignment is to provide the same kind of service for trainers and coaches of a sport you played as a child. Using research databases that cover biological journals, locate several research articles on your sport. Select one that includes useful information and interpret that information so that trainers, coaches, and athletes can easily understand the data contained in some of the article's tables, graphs, and figures.

As you begin drafting, review the strategies that Holloway uses to help her readers understand complex data and lay out all the options available to you (verbal, visual, design) for displaying information clearly. Think, too, about how you can use options together to achieve a common effect.

ENGLISH EDUCATION

In 1987, E. D. Hirsch published *Cultural Literacy, What Every American Needs to Know,* a book that included a list of 5,000 pieces of "basic information" that people need to know to be able to "thrive in the modern world." The book became an instant best-seller—the subject of academic scrutiny, party games, and water-cooler arguments. Some thought that the book offered educational equality, others saw it as tradition-bound elitism, and many thought that instead of focusing on lists of must-know information, educators should focus on how students learn at all.

Here are some items from Hirsch's list.

1939–1945	genocide	Realpolitik
aficionado	Hoover Dam	utilitarianism
Chernobyl	incumbent	vicious circle
the Danube River	prime the pump	xenophobia
fetish	quadratic equation	zero-sum game

- Divide Hirsch's items into three lists: (1) items you know, (2) those that sound familiar but that you couldn't explain, and (3) those you don't know. Do you know more than you don't know?

- Recommend fifteen new items for Hirsch's list. What people, places, events, terms, and brief quotations are now "basic information" that every American should know? How did you pick these?

- What strategies would you use to teach these items to students? Would you require students to memorize information about each item on a list? Would you do something more creative? Explain why you think your teaching strategy would be effective.

PORTABLE RHETORICAL LESSON: CHALLENGING CONVENTIONS PURPOSEFULLY

Most days, you see your teachers doing things that you expect: giving a lecture with Power-Point, explaining answers to a homework assignment, leading a discussion. You can probably remember times, though, when a teacher surprised you. The questions about E. D. Hirsch's *Dictionary of Cultural Literacy* ask you to think about the how you might use traditional or innovative teaching methods. To answer the questions, you probably remembered former teachers, teachers who might be memorable because they tried new methods.

As a writer, when you contemplate using unusual strategies, you need to consider yourself as an **author.** You have to know what your audience thinks and expects of you—your character, personality, values. You should wonder if your persona allows you to experiment with unconventionality. You must trust your ability to come across to readers as creative rather than confusing, or worse, or mistaken. As the student writer in this chapter observes, an author must be sure that readers will recognize breaks with convention as "*choices* rather than *mistakes.*" A sentence fragment, for example, could be read either as an effective way to add emphasis or as a grammatical error.

Challenging convention also gets writers thinking about **organization.** A writer can capture and keep a reader's attention by organizing a text so that it surprises and keeps the reader thinking about connections among parts of the writing. Victor Villanueva's writing (the first reading in this chapter) provides a good example.

In some ways, writers are also teachers; they want readers to understand and learn from them. And, like teachers, writers usually communicate by meeting readers' expectations—by following the conventions of a genre. Readers' previous experiences of genres (murder mystery, business memo, lab report, movie review, etc.) tell them what to expect. So it makes sense that writers usually take advantage of readers' expectations and follow conventions. If you fulfill enough of your readers' expectations so that they don't feel confused, you can use unconventionality to pique their curiosity. Using the **Portable Rhetorical Lesson** of this chapter—challenging conventions—catches readers' attention, helps them to remember what they've read, and propels them to mull over ideas long after they finish reading.

Challenging conventions is a powerful rhetorical tool, and you need to use it wisely. In fact, many students shy away from experimenting with conventions because they view it as too risky to their grades. But effective writers upend expectations when they have good reasons for doing so. The readings in this chapter show two different kinds of unconventionality: unconventional *content* and unconventional *form.*

Each of the readings contains unconventional content: new ideas and practices for teaching English. Ideas that create controversy. Each reading also uses minor breaks from formal written conventions. But it is the reading from Villanueva's book that combines the challenge of new ideas with challenges to formal conventions of written English: moving between first- and third-person references to the author, using sentence fragments, arranging the parts so they jump back and forth in time and topic, and so on.

The readings in this chapter show that effective writers use breaks with convention to:

- Call special attention to something—a key problem or question, the author's personal experience, a radical claim
- Jolt readers into alertness and into thinking critically about what they are reading
- Signal readers to expect unconventional ideas

One last note about breaking with convention: a little goes a long way. Most of Villanueva's sentences would escape the red pen of the pickiest of grammarians. He creates no new words or marks of punctuation, his pronouns have clear referents, and his sentences have subjects and verbs. And yet his writing is boldly innovative.

Observing the strong effects of a few breaks with formal conventions teaches you how strongly readers react to the unconventional. And that lesson should help you to decide when unconventionality might work for you.

WRITING IN THE DISCIPLINE

INTRODUCTION

by William J. Vande Kopple, Professor of English

Bootstraps: From an American Academic of Color is a scholarly argument about educational philosophy. It was written for English teachers, published by the National Council of Teachers of English. The author, Victor Villanueva, is a professor of composition and rhetoric at Washington State University and winner of several national awards for his teaching and research. *Bootstraps* was so influential that it is often assigned to students majoring in secondary English education.

Villanueva's final sentences in the section reprinted here capture well his fundamental purpose for writing: "We can do critical literacy. And what better to be critical of than the cultural norms contained in tradition? Start with what students know or have been told they ought to know. Allow and encourage a questioning of the norms. And maybe look to how things might be—and ought to be—changed." In other words, Villanueva aims to move readers to examine the social, economic, and political forces that they have always taken for granted within their culture and to ask how these forces might need to be altered in order to promote justice and equity.

You might be surprised by some aspects of the form of *Bootstraps*. Villanueva calls his book "a postmodern text." If you scan this reading, you will notice abrupt shifts in the organization. For example, Villanueva shifts from one time period to another; at one point readers learn about the autumn of 1984, while shortly thereafter they start reading about 1990. He also includes shifts in subject matter—leaping, for example, from a description of how he learned that he had been replaced as the director of a basic-writing program to some critical examination of E. D. Hirsch's *Cultural Literacy*. Further, Villanueva draws attention to his own experience in education by shifting his references to himself, sometimes referring to himself as "Victor," sometimes "he," and still other times "I"; in other parts of the book, he refers to himself as the "graduate student," the "new Teaching Assistant," "Victor the Curiosity," "Dr. V. the Deadbeat," and "Papi."

Running through the book, however, are five closely related lines of thought. In one line, Villanueva tells the story of his life, describing his successes and failures in teaching. In another line, he introduces readers to educational scholars who have affected his life. In a third line, he discusses theories of the social, economic, and political forces in the United States, especially as these forces affect persons of color. In yet another line, he connects the theoretical discussions to specific aspects of his own life. Finally, he includes several descriptions of classroom practices that he thinks will promote "critical dialogue within a cultural literacy."

I also believe that these pages from *Bootstraps* can help readers examine how they conventionally think about social, economic, and political forces. Too often, we evaluate these forces only in terms of our own experience ("Racism? Sure, when I was a kid there was a lot of trouble. But about half of the families in my neighborhood now are African-American. Racism is probably a thing of the past."). In *Bootstraps* Villanueva alerts us to how social, economic, and political forces actually affect other individuals' lives. Racism, for example, does not mean exactly the same thing for everyone. If we look closely, we will find a mosaic of responses to such forces as racism, materialism, and individualism.

In conveying this general message, Villanueva implicitly asks his readers to think like educators. We should learn humility and fight our tendency to see the entire world only in terms of our own experience. We should be eager to hear how others have been affected by powerful social forces. We should be willing to have our views of powerful social forces become more complex than we usually like them to be. And we should have the courage to evaluate theories about social forces on the basis of both our own and other individuals' experiences.

These emphases are important for everyone, not just for English teachers.

✓ Reading Tips

1. Be prepared to shift your reading speeds when Villanueva shifts his genres between narrative and analysis.
   - Narrative. You can read these sections at story pace. Underline the moments in the story that best illustrate the point Villanueva is making.
   - Analysis of theory. You will have to read these sections more slowly. Find definitions of unfamiliar terms, paraphrase complex ideas, and summarize Villanueva's main point in each analytical paragraph.

2. Find examples that show how the stories and analysis work together to forward the thesis.

3. Analyze challenges to conventions. Each time you notice Villanueva doing something unexpected, add a note in the margin that records:
   - The strategy Villanueva uses to challenge convention
   - The rhetorical purpose for that strategy
   - The way that the strategy helps you to better understand or engage his argument

Of Color, Classes, and Classrooms
Victor Villanueva

In *Bootstraps: From an American Academic of Color,* Urbana: NCTE, 1993.

Villanueva begins this chapter with a long fragment, throwing his readers into the middle of his description of a televised panel discussion. This use of a storyteller's rhetoric makes us feel personally involved from the very first sentence.

Hot, bright, stage lights blaring down on the four teachers and two parents seated in a circle before a TV camera. The six are about to speak on the cable network's public access channel.

Channing is the ring leader. He is a big man, large, round face with a shock of rumpled gray hair, a large belly pressing on a gray vest, not the rotund of the sedentary, but the large of the powerlifter. He is big, blustery, and brilliant: a polymath, well-versed in everything it seems, another who had traveled the class system: a childhood of unusual affluence, son of a government ambassador, an adulthood of unusual poverty.

There is Jolinda. She is lovely, thin, with shoulder-length auburn hair, sparse make-up. She has a quick, critical mind—decisive, un-flinching. A long-time interracial marriage and a racially mixed child to raise keeps her decidedly active politically, a hard-working Democrat for Jesse Jackson's Rainbow Coalition, a hard-working advocate for her children's school.

David Zank, goatee, beret, an administrator and a teacher at Jolinda's and Channing's and Victor's children's school. He administers an alternative public school. It's an elementary school, one not divided into traditional grades, though the students tend to group themselves into the younger, the older, the middle kids. It's a school that attracts children from all of the city's classes and races. Instead of a set curriculum, children decide on projects of interest, the teachers providing all that is necessary to carry out the projects: the mechanics, say, of building an airplane, lessons on aerodynamics, on the history of experiments in flight, and so on, though this ideal isn't always reached. Discipline is handled through "forum": students, teachers, and parents in a circle to discuss injustices. Injustices, not rules—there are no rules, really, but infringements on what is generally held to be socially acceptable behavior. Anyone can call for a forum. Issues are discussed. The school is democracy in action, not the usual contradiction of an authoritarian structure preaching democracy. Zank is an instrumental part of that school.

There are also two teachers from one of the more traditional public schools in the area. Their names are now forgotten, our being together limited to that one show. Channing had found them. Silver gray hair on both, off the neck, tastefully curled atop heads, the look of professional coiffeurs. They have stylish glasses, pleasant faces. Both are part of this discussion before the camera because they are upset by recent changes in their curriculum, changes imposed from above, from higher administration.

> Villanueva lists some of his identities in the third person—as if he is joining his readers in observing himself from a distance.

And there is Victor, graduate student, parent.

Channing opens the discussion. At issue is a new curriculum the city has purchased from a major publishing house. It's a computerized package. Depending on how they perform on a standardized pretest, students are presented with a series of hierarchically ordered mastery tests. Versions of a mastery test are taken and retaken until a certain score is attained; then students are directed to the next test, which is taken, retaken again, until a certain score is reached; then onto the next, and so on. The guarantee of the package is that there will be a city-wide improvement on national standardized scores, a guarantee that will be made good, no doubt. But the teachers protest that all curricular decisions are thereby taken from them, that they will be able to do nothing but teach to tests.

Zank's school has annually refused to administer standardized tests on the grounds that even though they measure nothing but the ability to take tests they are too easily read as matters of intellectual ability by the students themselves. He tells the teachers to do the same as his school's teachers—refuse to take part. The teachers say that though they agree with Zank on principle, they cannot afford to jeopardize their jobs. They would not have the support of their principal, would not enjoy the support of Zank's teachers. Jolinda argues that their jobs are the education of children—matters of public responsibility more than personal security. Again, there is agreement on principle, but personal security is not confined to any one individual; there are families to care for. Victor suggests not teaching to the tests, but teaching test-taking. His life would have been easier, perhaps, if he had understood standardized test-taking and knew not to take what they actually measure (test-taking) seriously. Zank nods, saying "Paulo Freire kind of stuff."

> After growing up in a poor family in Brazil, at a time when the ruling class oppressed the poor, Paulo Freire (1921–1997) was exiled. After his years in exile, he returned to Brazil to become Secretary of Education in Brazil's largest school district. His radical pedagogy, which calls for teachers and students to examine cultural practices to expose, critique, and change oppressive situations, has been adopted by numerous North American educators.

Victor had never heard of Paulo Freire before Zank's comment. He reads *Pedagogy of the Oppressed*. The things written there make sense. He sees what has been working in his children's school: children believing in their humanity, willing and able to take social responsibility, even at the age of six. He sees the problem he has had with the school, despite being pleased in the main: "laissez-faire." Here's Freire:

I cannot leave the students by themselves because I am trying to be a liberating educator. Laissez-faire! I cannot fall into laissez-faire. On the other hand, I cannot be authoritarian. I have to be radically democratic and responsible and directive. *Not* directive of the *students,* but directive of the process, the liberating teacher is not doing something to the students but with the students. (Shor and Freire 46)

> To be "laissez-faire" is to interfere in the affairs of others as little as possible.

Students cannot be left to their own devices totally, yet they cannot be handed everything.

Fall 1984. Victor is placed in charge of the English department's basic-writing program. He is the best candidate for the job in a number of ways; his fields are rhetoric and composition; he is doing research that focuses on basic writing; he is of color in a program replete with students of color; and he is willing, as were the directors of the program before him, to undertake the job at teaching-assistant pay. Administration denies the color aspect. Tokenism, stereotyping—sensitive issues.

He institutes a Freire-like dimension to the curriculum. He does away with the focus on sentence-combining, adopts the autobiography of Carolina Maria deJesus, *Child of the Dark*, the story of a woman from the *favelas* of Brazil, where Freire had spent his adolescence, the likely nurturing ground for his pedagogy. Her diary presents a view from the eyes of a barely literate woman, her political awareness and the contradictions she embodies, her understanding of social stratification, and her desire for what she believes she cannot have, the social stigma she suffers in having to provide for her children by collecting trash, and the pride she nevertheless feels, the way she is labeled a Marxist by a local politician when she complains about her living conditions in a system she somehow believes in. It's the story of an American of color and of poverty set in Brazil. It is a story that the basic-writing students might well understand. And, because she is barely literate, the writing is such that the students can be critical of her language use, can gain confidence in their own abilities with literacy.

The basic-writing teachers seem to enjoy teaching the book. But the political is downplayed. Discussions turn on the cultural: "Tell me 'bout the ghetto and I'll tell you 'bout the 'burbs." Students enjoy the dialogue. But there seems to be no dialectic, no sustained probing into the conditions that relegate certain peoples to the ghettos and others to the 'burbs in disproportionate numbers. In some sense, this is a minor problem, outweighed by the students' being heard at all.

Still there are problems, not with the material but with the relations between students and teachers, the kinds of problems discussed by Lisa Delpit. Students are being graded on their courage more than on how others at a university or elsewhere might regard their writing. Disgruntled students complain that they have been lied to, that they thought they really were "A" or "B" writers, only to find that others consider them barely literate. Irate professors say that the university is no place for remedial courses. Victor convinces the higher administration that the basic-writing program is a cultural education, not remediation. The program survives, eventually acquiring a regular, permanent administrator.

But while Victor was still there, there were still the disgruntled and the irate to contend with. He prepares a memo that quotes Louis Faraq'an, a naive move. The memo notes that Faraq'an defines black power as the ability for black people to come to the table with their own food. The point is to have teachers stop proffering academic charity, no matter how well intentioned. Victor knew the pain of charity.

If an organization were to engage in "tokenism," it would offer just enough opportunities to minorities so that it would avoid criticism and perhaps even look good.

Favela is a term used commonly in Brazil to describe slums.

Lisa Delpit grew up on the "wrong side of the tracks" in Baton Rouge, LA, where she was among the first African Americans to integrate the Catholic schools. She has devoted her life to challenging the educational system. She argues that linguistic and cultural standards must be taught to African Americans and other minorities to empower these oppressed groups. Rather than just teaching to one cultural norm, though, Delpit says that teachers need to take a critical approach to the dominant culture, while also recognizing and drawing on the cultural strengths that all of their students bring to the classroom.

Louis Farrakhan (born 1933) currently serves as a leading Muslim thinker and teacher. He organizes groups for the political empowerment of black people in the U.S. and around the world.

He goes on a job interview. He returns to find a memo announcing his replacement for the coming academic year. He had not been consulted. The rationale was that he would surely get a job. But he remembered the teachers' argument in that television show. He had gone too far.

There must be a way to go about doing our jobs in some traditional sense and meeting some of the potential inherent in our jobs, the potential for social change, without inordinately risking those jobs. Utopianism within pragmatism; tradition and change.

When I think of tradition, I think of the literary critic turned compositionist, turned social critic—E. D. Hirsch. His *Cultural Literacy* is simplistic and politically dangerous, say his critics in English studies (e.g., Bizzell, Johnson, and Scholes). There is surely the sense that he's suggesting a return to halcyon days that never were, surely not wondrous bygone days for people of color, surely not for the poor. Hirsch is among those who believe that "multilingualism is contrary to our traditions and extremely unrealistic" (93). More myth than history. It is this mythic nostalgia that permeates his book that causes him to be read as advocating teaching a literary canon. He denies it (xiv). He says that he is advocating a national-cultural set of common assumptions to be learned through an understanding of national-cultural allusions, his list of "what literate Americans know," a list, he points out, containing relatively few references to literary works (146–215; xiv). But he apparently senses the superficiality, backing up his theory with references to broad reading (109, 23). What, then, to read? Seems like we're back to a canon.

And that canon has historically favored one gender and one race. That this is the case, says Hirsch, is an accident of history (106). He seems not to regard how that particular accident has had a high casualty count over time. And it keeps recurring—like the same fender-bender with the same car at the same intersection—time and again. But Hirsch does go on to argue that national-cultural allusions are subject to change, that as more women and people of color become literate, they will affect the norms. And there is something to this. There are more women in the canon nowadays, more people of color. But the changes are not proportionate to the accomplishments or the potentials of women or people of color, surely. And those who enter the canon tend to be those who are politically safe. We read Langston Hughes's "Theme for English B" more often than Hughes's more angry "The Negro Speaks of Rivers." We read Martin Luther King, Jr. but little of W. E. B. DuBois, Richard Rodriguez instead of Ernesto Galarza, Emily Dickinson more often than Virginia Woolf (see Aiken; West "Canon Formation"). Hirsch's hopes are for better test scores and for greater access to the middle class, not for making the class system more equitable.

For all that, there *is* something to cultural literacy. One has to know how to be heard if one is to be heard. Those who rail the loudest against

A professor and educational theorist, E. D. Hirsch (born 1928) is perhaps best known for his *Cultural Literacy: What Every American Needs to Know.* He's been accused of elitism for arguing that there is a single cultural literacy every student ought to learn.

Arguments about a canon, a list of books that everyone should read, have been very common in discussions of literature in the last several decades.

Note how Villanueva here—and elsewhere—strives to give opposing arguments the credit they deserve.

A "polemic" is a controversial argument, and "dialectic" is argument through an exchange of opposing ideas, so the point is that students should stretch themselves to see things from opposing points of view.

cultural literacy can afford to. They already have it. How, then, to exploit it without being subsumed by it?

Critical literacy, like that espoused by Paulo Freire and others, will lead to change, we're told. And I agree with that too. But what are the students to be critical of? How do they come to know what to be critical of? Why not cultural literacy, the national culture? Play out the polemic; develop the dialectic.

Antonio Gramsci (1891–1937). Villanueva refers to Gramsci's belief that the ruling ideology or culture must be resisted by alternative cultural perspectives, an ideal that has been embraced by many educators and political theorists.

One theorist who has seen the necessity for both the cultural and the critical is Antonio Gramsci. His theories will provide the focus of the next chapter. For now, it's enough just to mention that he was an advocate of teaching a national culture, of teaching the classics, of something that sounds a lot like cultural literacy. Yet Gramsci also added that the classics and the national-cultural should be taught in such a way as to expose what he called the folkloristic, the commonly accepted ways of the world, the things too often accepted as if they are a part of nature—in short, the ideological. This suggests to me that it is possible to provide what's needed for the commonly accepted notions of success but with a critical dimension that might foster social action among teachers and among students. This is what sociologist Stanley Aronowitz and educational theorist Henry Giroux call "the language of possibility" (138–62). This is likely what Freire alludes to when he writes of pedagogy that pits permanence with change (Pedagogy 72). I prefer "tradition" to "permanence," given Hirsch's observation that traditions can and do change. Tradition and change for changes in traditions.

"Ideological" means based on a fixed system of beliefs

Stanley Aronowitz is a proponent of radical social change, protesting the corporate nature of many educational institutions.

Henry Giroux is a leading critical theorist who has adopted Freire's notion of education as a process of uncovering political and cultural ideologies that will lead students and teachers to social activism. Here Villanueva shifts from the theoretical to the personal and familial.

In a way, the graduate course on classical rhetoric I teach lends itself best to Gramsci's ideas. We read Plato, Aristotle, Cicero, Quintilian, and others. And we discuss and write about the ways in which some of the things they espoused are still with us—things like censorship for children's better good; things like the only meaningful language should be on abstractions rather than concretes. Plato and the rhetoric of the constitution. We find the first-century idea of proper oratorical arrangement and discover the basis for the five-paragraph theme. We find Cicero writing of writing as a mode of learning and Quintilian writing of peer-group work. We look at how the ancients are still with us and question the degree to which they ought to be. Students gather something of a classical education, a matter of some prestige, and they develop a critical perspective.

"Tradition and change for changes in traditions" forms a key to Villanueva's argument: we need to recognize both the need for change and the fact of traditions. Only when we accept tradition and change can we achieve the long-term changes that will create future traditions.

Something of the same ideas can be adapted for undergraduates, secondary students, elementary students.

1990, Flagstaff: Victor and Carol's younger children attend the public school. The school district has adopted a literacy package from a major publishing house that explicitly discourages individual instruction. All the children perform their drills in unison, do their reading together—everybody, every time, getting 100 percent on everything.

This isn't a matter of collaboration. Just recitation. No talking to neighbors seated ten inches away; no looking at neighbors. The books contain color: drawings of kids with nappy hair or slant eyes, not caricatures, done respectfully; yet there is a single cultural norm being advanced—force-fed cultural literacy.

More than hints at racism start to crop up at home. The brown-skinned, curly haired five-year-old daughter asks whether an Indian woman (the largest number of people who are of color in the community) would care for a human baby if she found one. A human baby! Another daughter, seven at the time, considerably more immersed in this literacy package than the kindergartner, mentions in passing that she doesn't care for black people. She doesn't know any. And she fails to see her own sister's features, forgets the pictures of her aunt, on whom the West African comes out clearly.

Victor and Carol don't blame the school completely. Market forces have them living in a predominately white community, making for little exposure to the kind of cultural complexity Victor and Carol's older children had known in Seattle or that Victor had known as a child in New York. But even if the school was not completely to blame for the hints at racism Victor and Carol would now have to counter, there remained the school's blind acceptance of a reductive notion of cultural literacy, a presentation that did nothing to expose and glory in difference as well as similarity.

Home schooling becomes the only short-term (and economically viable) alternative. Victor and Carol expose the national-cultural, but with an eye to multiplicity. The seven-year-old reads Cinderella, for instance. But she doesn't just stop with the Disney version. She reads translations of the Grimm Brothers' version, Poirot's seventeenth-century French version, an older Italian version, an ancient Chinese version. They're readily available. Discussion concerns how different people, with different ways and living in different times, can see some of the same things differently. She writes her own Cinderella story, which inevitably includes characters and situations from her own life. Spelling comes from the words she's trying to use in her own writing. It has a context. Grammar comes from trying to make her stories sound like she wants them to.

Other subjects take a similar tact. For history and geography, for example, she reads stories of dragons from China and dragons of the middle ages and dragons of C. S. Lewis and even dragons of Homer. She writes dragon stories.

Oral proficiency more or less takes care of itself; no need to impose doggedly the standard dialect. Victor's dialect changed without his being overtly conscious of it. The Spanish accent that Sister Rhea Marie had long ago warned his parents about disappeared, as did much of the black dialect he had acquired on the block. The more he became

C. S. Lewis (1898–1963) is perhaps best known today for his *Chronicles of Narnia.*

exposed to written discourse, the more his speaking came to reflect that exposure. And exposure to different worldviews, even if written in one standard dialect, provided the critical perspective. Reading aloud would help hone speaking skills in the prestige dialect.

I take the Cinderella idea to high school and college. The only real difference in the high school and the college is that I have the college students look up and report on literary critics who write about fairy tales. They read people like Bruno Bettelheim, who comes up with crazy interpretations of Cinderella as going through Freudian puberty rites, or others who write about fairy tales and archetypes, or Plato and his notion that fairy tales should be used to indoctrinate children into proper attitudes about life and the gods. I have the students do research about the historical or cultural conditions which existed at the time and place of the various versions. They become exposed to academics and academic discourse using a kind of literature they know intimately. They feel comfortable being critical of the great authorities. With the junior high and high school kids I've visited on short stints, I have provided the histories and selected the critical analyses; otherwise, the assignments have been the same.

> Bruno Bettelheim (1903–1990) was a developmental psychologist who taught at the University of Chicago from 1944–1973 and who directed the Orthogenic School for children with emotional problems.

Students resist being critical of fairy tales. They want to say that fairy tales are simply diversions for children. And this is okay as a jumping-off point for discussion. Resistance is a good thing, an assertion of authority, an opening for dialogue (see Giroux). So it tends that through the dialogue some begin to question what else might be contained in those simple diversions. A student writes about Rosie the Riveter during World War Two, women not just entering male-dominated jobs, like business and medicine, but performing "man's work," physical labor—and doing well. Then she wonders at Disney's Cinderella, which promotes the house wench whose only hope for the future is to marry well. She wonders if Disney's version didn't help put Rosie's daughters "back in their place." Another writes about the Chinese version, about foot binding as a way to keep women in their place. She wonders if having Cinderella wear glass is a kind of modern foot binding. Another notices how Red Riding Hood's stories become more and more sexual as they approach the Victorian era. Another student: Is Jack and the Beanstalk a promotion of laissez-faire economics, get rich however you can? Is Robin Hood a proto-socialist? Students look at fairy tales and children's stories, and, in looking, begin to question the obvious and the natural, begin to question ideology.

> Roland Barthes (1915–1980) was a French structuralist-turned-poststructuralist critic who saw a text as "a fabric of quotations, resulting from a thousand sources of cultures." His book *Mythologies* (1957) contains 54 short pieces that demonstrate the presence of ideology and power structures in a variety of cultural situations.

Another way we look at ideology is by using Roland Barthes's little book *Mythologies.* The book contains a series of articles Barthes had written for a popular French magazine in the 1950s. Here, again, the idea works for high school and for college. The college students are asked to read and work with the theoretical essay at the end of the book, where Barthes explains semiology. Others get the idea without the thick theoretical language. But I want to introduce the college students to the esoteric language of "pure" theory. They resist—vehemently. There was outright mutiny in one class.

But, generally, they do tend to respond well to the essays. In one essay, for example, Barthes explains the popularity of professional wrestling as a spectacle, as containing the elements of ancient Greek plays. Students get the notion of the spectacle. One student writes about how wrestling in the 1990s exploits stereotypes, exploits and promotes existing prejudices. A videotape of contemporary wrestling backs him up. In terms of ideological mythologies, another student, a retired policeman, writes about TV ads to help the hungry as maintaining the myth of American prosperity. The poor and hungry children are in Latin America or in Africa, never dying of hunger and disease in America's cardboard shacks. A sophisticated literary theory is introduced—traditional academic discourse—and critical questioning arises—a possibility for change.

> Here Villanueva uses the passive voice to describe this pedagogy: he avoids attributing the success of the class to the teacher, the students, or the texts. He reinforces his belief that collaborative critical engagement produces both greater understanding and the potential for change.

The basic idea is to present the cultural in such a way as to have students question worldviews, become critical. Action presupposes a need for action. Questioning what is commonly accepted makes clear the need for action. Among the things that are commonly accepted is the canon.

Literature can be set up so as to create a dialectic between differing worldviews, between the national-cultural and the critical. Students read Hemingway, for example, as male, white, middle-class as they come, skeptical, perhaps, but no radical. Then they read Buchi Emecheta's *Double Yoke*—the story of a black African woman trying to get through different value systems, cultures, different ways of viewing the world, her struggles at gaining a college degree. Men and women are at issue, black and white; the tribal ways that the main character, Nko, was raised with against the modern Western ways of the university. White students confronting the college community, women, African American students, American Indian students—all have a portion of Nko's pains, and, since the story takes place far away, the defense of bigotries does not come up immediately, as it often does in more explicitly African American or Latino or American Indian literature (though it is good to have these prejudices present themselves). Nko and Hemingway's Nick Adams handle things differently, confront different obstacles. Ideologies peep out of the classroom discussions (which usually begin with moral questions: Nick's sense of responsibility, Nko's integrity). What is it about where the characters come from that causes them to behave and believe in different ways? We can look at Steinbeck and Ayn Rand, Rodriguez and Galarza, Louis L'Amour and Leslie Marmon Silko. Students sometimes shock themselves with their own prejudice—anti-color *and* anti-white.

The students write about how they too must confront conflicts, and about the sources of those conflicts. These aren't always explained in grand cultural terms, but the cultural is always present, often coming out in discussions. They write autobiographies (or narratives if culturally uncomfortable with the autobiographic). The things they are to write about concern their own experiences, experiences that are tied to the things they are reading. Toward the end of the semester they are asked to downplay the autobiographical elements but keep them in mind. The autobiographical is an important assessment tool, even essential—always there, really. "[A]ll writing, in many different ways, is autobiographical," says Donald Murray, even "academic writing, writing to instruct, textbook writing" (67; 73). But outside the English classroom the autobiographical, the narrative, is not usually appreciated (Spellmeyer). So we look at how the personal is impersonally imparted in writing, still looking to different worldviews espoused in standard written form. We look at Booker T. Washington and W. E. B. DuBois, then find out about their backgrounds, how two African Americans living in the same time can come to polar viewpoints. Or we look at Martin Luther King, Jr. and Malcolm X. In a sense, the strategy is not much different from that proposed by David Bartholomae and Anthony Petrosky: an investing of the personal into what is read and an investigation into how what is read appears, its presentation. The difference is in the introduction of difference within convention. Throughout, there are the culturally literate and the critical, both in what they read and in what they write.

Some students—even a lot, even those who come from poor minority backgrounds—reject the critical views. This is to be expected. People are not turned around overnight. Floyd, back in Kansas City, showed that. But the goal is not necessarily to have students relinquish national-cultural myths. The goal is to expose them to differences and similarities within the literacy conventions they have to contend with, to know the traditional norms while also appraising them, looking at the norms critically. It's a directed process, not propaganda.

All of this is to say that it is possible to have our educational cake and eat it too. It is possible to do our jobs as others define them: provide *haute couture,* "high literacy," literacy skills, standardized-test-ready cultural literacy. And it is possible to do our jobs as we believe they ought to be done: with students recognizing that education should carry social responsibility. We can do critical literacy. And what better to be critical of than the cultural norms contained in tradition? Start with what students know or have been told they ought to know. Allow and encourage a questioning of the norms. And maybe look to how things might be—and ought to be—changed.

David Bartholomae and Anthony Petrosky both teach at the University of Pittsburgh. Villanueva refers to Petrosky and Bartholomae's pedagogy that combines personal experience with critical inquiry, a pedagogy made especially evident in their *Ways of Reading* (sixth edition, 2002).

Villanueva had met Floyd earlier in his life, when he had conducted some ethnographic research in the Midwest. In Villanueva's words, Floyd tried "to promote a Freire-like pedagogy in a school designed exclusively for students who had been locked out of the public schools, mainly by the court system."

Works Cited

Aiken, Susan Hardy. "Women and the Question of Canonicity." *College English* 48 (1986): 288–301.

Aranowitz, Stanley, and Henry Giroux. *Education Under Seige: The Conservative, Liberal, and Radical Debate Over Schooling.* South Hadley, MA: Bergin and Garvey, 1985.

Barthes, Roland. *Mythologies.* Trans. Annette Lavers. London: Hill and Wang, 1972.

Bartholomae, David, and Anthony Petrosky. *Facts, Artifacts, and Counterfacts: A Theory and Method for a Reading and Writing Course.* Upper Montclair, NJ: Boynton/Cook, 1986.

DeJesus, Carolina Marie. *Child of the Dark: The Diary of Carolina Marie deJesus.* Trans. David S. Clair. New York: E.P. Dutton, 1962.

Delpit, Lisa D. "The Silenced Dialogue: Power and Pedagogy in Educating Other People's Children." *Harvard Educational Review* 58 (1988): 280–98.

Emecheta, Buchi. *Double Yoke.* New York: Braziller, 1982.

Freire, Paulo. *Pedagogy of the Oppressed.* Trans. Myra Bergman Ramos. New York: Herder and Herder, 1970.

Giroux, Henry. *Theory and Resistance in Education: A Pedagogy for the Opposition.* London: Heinemann, 1983.

Hirsch, E. D., Jr. *Cultural Literacy: What Every American Needs to Know.* Boston: Houghton Mifflin, 1987.

Murray, Donald M. "All Writing is Autobiography." *College Composition and Communication* 42 (1991): 66–74.

Shor, Ira, and Paulo Freire. *A Pedagogy for Liberation: Dialogues on Transforming Education.* South Hadley, MA: Bergin & Harvey, 1987.

Spellmeyer, Kurt. "Foucault and the Freshman Writer: Considering the Self in Discourse." *College English* 51 (1989): 715–29.

West, Cornel. "Minority Discourse and the Pitfalls of Canon Formation." *Yale Journal of Criticism* 1:1 (1987): 193–201.

Reading Responses

1. Villanueva begins this chapter by describing two events from his life: his appearance on a TV show and his directing of a basic writing program at a state university. Do you think he's described things even-handedly? List the people who come off looking good in Villanueva's description. List those who come off looking bad. For each person you've listed describe how he/she views the purpose of education. How does Villanueva use autobiography to make his argument?

2. List the goals that Villanueva has for education— that is, catalog the ways Villanueva hopes education will shape students. What goals do you have for your education? How closely do they match Villanueva's?

3. Consider the "interruptions" in Villanueva's writing— those surprising shifts in content, structure, and style. List three shifts that you found to be effective and the reasons they were effective. List three that you found to be ineffective and the reasons they were ineffective.

NOTES ON GRAMMAR, STYLE, AND RHETORIC:
SENTENCE FRAGMENTS AND SPECIAL EFFECTS

In *Bootstraps* Villanueva regularly violates conventions of formal, academic writing. Here we focus on his willingness to go against the convention that forbids the use of sentence fragments.

What is a sentence fragment? The sixth edition of *The Longman Handbook for Writers and Readers* states that a sentence fragment is "[a] cluster of words punctuated as a sentence but lacking a crucial element that enables it to stand alone as a sentence . . ." (578). The *Longman Handbook* goes on to give examples of various kinds of sentence fragments:

* A fragment because it lacks a subject: "Yet also needs to establish a family counseling program" (578).
* A fragment because it lacks a verb: "The new policy to determine scholarship size on the basis of grades rather than on the basis of need" (579).
* A fragment because it begins with a subordinating word and lacks an independent clause: "Although they also consider most criticism of the test overblown" (580).
* A fragment because it includes an example and lacks an independent clause: "For example, knowledge of computer-aided design" (581).

You must take care never to leave unintentional fragments in your writing, especially your formal writing. If you leave unintentional fragments in such writing, readers might not take your ideas seriously. In fact, since the convention forbidding fragments is so strong, readers might start to question your ability to write.

But it is a fact that skilled writers sometimes use intentional fragments for special effects, even in formal writing. In the reading selection from *Bootstraps* Villanueva uses about a dozen fragments. And he uses them to try to achieve several kinds of effects. Here is a sampling:

1. At one point he uses a fragment to mark one of his abrupt shifts in topics: "Fall 1984" (368).
2. At another point he uses a fragment to make a biting comment about one of E. D. Hirsch's positions: "More myth than history" (369).
3. At the very beginning of the selection he uses a fragment to throw readers into the middle of a scene he will describe: "Hot, bright, stage lights blaring down on the four teachers and two parents seated in a circle before a TV camera" (366).
4. And in an anecdote about his family, he uses a fragment to add emphasis and drama to his reaction to a racist comment his five-year-old daughter had made: "A human baby!" (371). The use of fragments for special emphasis or drama is the most common use of intentional fragments. And this use is particularly interesting because it probably exemplifies something that Villanueva tries to accomplish throughout his book: facilitating "the reader's participation in creating the text" (quoted from a later chapter). That is, a fragment leaves room for a reader to fill in the missing parts, to help in creating the meaning and thus feel an emotional connection to the story.

In Your Own Writing . . .

* Assess your relationship with your reader and consider the context of your writing before you decide to use sentence fragments to make a point.
* Edit your final work carefully to ensure that it contains only the sentence fragments that you've used intentionally.
* Be sure that you know what you are trying to achieve with a sentence fragment and that a sentence fragment is the best way to achieve that effect.
* Check that the sentence fragment does not overly confuse the reader.
* Be sure that your reader will think that the effect justifies breaking the convention forbidding fragments.

STUDENT WRITING

INTRODUCTION

by Cherilyn Dudley, English education major

The Assignment. During my student teaching semester I taught in a remedial reading class for first- and second-year students at an inner-city high school with a lot of ethnic diversity. For the seminar we took while student teaching, we had to read Victor Villanueva's book *Bootstraps* and write an essay in which we critiqued Villanueva's perspectives on education. After writing the critique, we wrote a lesson plan (I wrote mine for my remedial reading class) that embodied our philosophy in light of Villanueva's ideas.

The Content. I feel strongly that education should raise awareness about social issues and that students should be enabled and encouraged to take action in these areas. So in my critique I focused on how and when students should be encouraged to think critically about the world around them. I also discussed the importance of writing style. Villanueva's unusual method of writing is one way to communicate a passion for social justice, but there are other media through which students may feel more comfortable voicing their opinions and beliefs: art, poetry, music, narrative, nonfiction essay, journalism, etc.

The lesson plan, "Debatable Civil Rights," was the second part of my assignment. My goal was to encourage students to think critically about society and to realize that things are not as equal as they might seem. I also wanted them to explore some civil rights Web sites so that they would become familiar with the many organizations that tackle social inequalities in our society and so they could see the many ways in which they can bring about change in their communities.

Learning to Write in English Education. As an English education major, most of the books I've read and papers I've written have consistently followed the Standard English requirements that my professors so highly esteem. For this reason, reading *Bootstraps* was an unusual experience. Were I to write a paper for an English professor in the style of Villanueva, I know I would get much corrective feedback: sentence fragments underlined, misplaced or missing punctuation circled, and innumerable remarks about fluidity and continuity. Many English professors would either not accept Villanueva-style writing from their students, or they would give it a bad grade.

I wonder about two things: (1) the writing I have done as an English education student and (2) the challenges and benefits of stepping outside those standard writing forms. To be honest, aside from an occasional introduction in which I tried to be creative, I have intentionally adhered to the conventions of academic English. Although I had some creative writing assignments in high school, only once did I take the chance to exercise such creativity in college. The professor of my English class gave us the option to write an essay in the same voice as that of the author we had read. Because the author had poured out his soul in his writing, I decided to be equally honest and vulnerable. Turning in the paper, I was terrified; I had not held back at all and had no idea how the professor would respond. When I got the paper back, I saw that the professor had made a few structural and stylistic notes and had given me an A–. But what really horrified me was the lack of comments about *what* I had written. Just like Villanueva, I had used the medium of an experimental style to communicate something that was very important to me. Although the professor had helpful things to say about my style, I felt as though the style was just a means to convey the most important part of the essay: my thoughts, beliefs, and experiences. I was satisfied with the grade, but I couldn't help feeling uncomfortable about knowing that my professor had scrutinized my deepest feelings—especially since I had no idea what his response to them had been.

I believe that Villanueva's style of writing makes people nervous because it is so genuine. Villanueva is passionate about what he writes because he has experienced it himself. These experiences shape not only the educational philosophy he recommends but also the practical suggestions he makes for teachers. Most students avoid this kind of genuine expression for several reasons: (1) we aren't passionate about every single topic we write about, (2) our life experiences don't always connect to the topics we're writing about, and (3) we don't have the same authority or confidence as Villanueva. He makes it clear that he has read and understands complex philosophies. And as an influential scholar in the field of English education, readers accept his unconventional choices as *choices* rather than as *mistakes*. He has gained enough academic respect to put unconventionality to good use. In a classroom, only one person has the final say about our writing—the professor. If the professor doesn't buy into our forms of individualistic expression, then our own grades are at stake. So most students shy away from this option and continue to adhere to Standard English expectations.

Who Cares?: Analysis and Application of Victor Villanueva's *Bootstraps*

Cherilyn Dudley

Some of the most frequently asked questions in high school include "Why does this matter?" and "Why should I care?" And many teachers can't give convincing answers. Because of these common student frustrations about a useless education, I decided to teach a unit in my student teaching classroom about the history of civil rights and the value of social action. I introduced these topics through biographies of liberation movement leaders like Martin Luther King Jr., César Chávez, Malcolm X, Fannie Lou Hamer, and Nelson Mandela.

> A unit is a set of lesson plans on a particular topic or theme.

On the first day of the unit, I asked students to complete a survey of their attitudes regarding civil rights. Students quickly completed the sheet on their own, and once we began sharing perspectives, the class erupted into debate. I hadn't expected students to respond so strongly to the statements on the sheet, but the school has a diverse student body, and many felt that their civil rights had been violated at one time

> Although this essay is a "critique," I agree with most of the philosophies Villanueva advocates. Therefore, I analyze the *Bootstraps* excerpt by extending the application of his ideas and discussing practical ways to use his philosophies in the classroom.

or another. As we further examined and discussed civil rights in class, students moved from feeling angry to making specific plans to safeguard their rights. What I experienced as a student teacher convinces me that Victor Villanueva is right to promote the challenging of social norms as a goal for education. Through individual assignments as well as larger decisions about curriculum, teachers should strive to implement Villanueva's ideas about critical cultural literacy. At each stage of education, we must encourage children to analyze how they see the world, to understand that different people perceive the world in different ways, to discuss sources and effects of these worldviews, and to put what they've learned into practice as actively engaged citizens.

> Education is a field in which the rhetoric of experience can carry weight in an argument.

As my experience proves, questioning norms and traditions can lead to controversy, so it is important that teachers consider when and how to encourage such questioning. In this endeavor, we can find guidance from child psychologist Jean Piaget. Piaget claims that children go through three main cognitive stages during the elementary and high school years. From the time they begin to talk until the age of seven, children are in a "preoperational" stage of development. During this stage, they perceive everything as "here and now" and nicely fitting what they believe about the world. Although the egocentrism of infancy influences the early years of this stage, it is during this time that young children should be exposed to the idea that not everyone lives as they do. Villanueva describes how he accomplished this in his own family: his daughters read international versions of fairy tales and identified the similarities and differences among them. Teachers can accommodate this stage in the classroom by introducing literature and art from a variety of cultures, bringing in speakers or going on fieldtrips that showcase different ways of life, and teaching cultural units in which teachers and students affirm and celebrate cultural differences. Through mere exposure to diversity, young children will begin to realize that there is more than one way of seeing the world and that not everyone thinks the way they do.

> Although the next few paragraphs are mostly about the application of Villanueva's ideas, I occasionally reference specifics from his book so my reader doesn't think I'm getting too far away from the assignment to critique *Bootstraps*.

> In my mind, critical thought processes include weighing the positives and negatives of something and making a judgment about its value.

Between first grade and early adolescence, children transition into the "concrete operational" stage of development. During this time, they develop critical thought processes and begin to make rational judgments about concrete and abstract ideas. Using the preoperational observations they made in their younger years, students in later elementary and junior high school should learn to critique world literature, politics, history, and other subject matters. As the educational focus shifts from telling to asking, students can discuss why our society does things the way it does. Under the teacher's guidance, students can begin to formulate ideas and perspectives about what literature might reveal about cultures, both foreign and familiar. In junior high, students should be exposed to literature that raises questions and concerns about society. Students can begin to make connections between other cultures and their own as they wonder why their government and society operate as they do. Through this stage of critical analysis, students begin to define who they are and what they believe, and as they begin to make judgments about their own culture, they will learn to see it in a more objective light.

During adolescence, young adults apply the critical thinking of the concrete operational stage to an active "formal operational" stage of development. In this stage, they learn to use hypothetical and deductive reasoning to make conclusions about society and suggest solutions to problems in the world around them. In high school classrooms, teachers can foster this type of thinking through interdisciplinary studies. When students bring history and politics into their English classes, they can examine different models of cultures and societies in literature, comparing these structures to those found around the world. Students can research and debate social equality, economic opportunity, political infrastructure, and other aspects of life as they begin to articulate their own worldviews. Reading books such as *Lord of the Flies, The Jungle, Utopia, Animal Farm,* and other culturally, socially, and politically critical literature will nurture students' own critical consciousness. And making connections between books such as these and current events—i.e., newspaper or magazine articles—will turn the inevitable high school question "Who cares?" back to the students: Do *they* care enough about their world to express their ideas publicly and to act on them? As adolescents prepare to establish lives separate from their parents and enter the workforce, they must become confident enough to express unconventional opinions and disagree with mainstream society. This isn't an easy mindset for teachers to teach or for students to learn. Even in his college classes, Villanueva has to encourage students to become comfortable "being critical of the great authorities" (98). Rather than accepting everything the way it is, Villanueva advocates an education that encourages questioning, engagement, and reflection. Piaget agrees, and so do I.

By making a general statement that applies both to the application I've discussed as well as to Villanueva himself, I shift the focus back to *Bootstraps* after the discussion about applying his ideas.

Unconventional critical thoughts are often best represented by experimental, unconventional ways of communication. In *Bootstraps,* Villanueva defies Standard English grammatical and syntactical rules as he aims to convey not only knowledge and philosophies, but also emotionally-charged experiences and perceptions of the world. As students develop their own philosophies and perceptions, they must discover how to best express themselves genuinely. Taking a non-traditional approach to communication can be intimidating, but so is holding culturally critical viewpoints. Villanueva chooses to express himself through a varied narrative writing style, but students might choose a different medium to convey their thoughts: poetry, journalism, research essays, or even art or music. The important decision is not necessarily *how* an individual's beliefs are communicated, but rather *that* they are communicated in a genuine and effective manner.

Although there are many benefits and strengths of authentic, unique self-expression, there are also draw-backs. Writing is only powerful when it meets the needs of its audience. Readers who want to learn about the demographics of education for minorities or the poor would seek statistics, charts, or clear organizational structure of most research articles. And Villanueva's unconventional style might encourage these readers to dismiss *Bootstraps* as unscholarly. On the other hand, Villanueva's descriptive, emotive writing style is more effective for readers who want to learn about someone's experiences with education and perspectives on educational philosophy. As students decide how to best express their developing worldviews, they must keep this tension in mind.

> Every good argument should include a counterargument, and this paper is no different. In this paragraph I point out legitimate disadvantages of Villanueva's experimental style, while also sending a cautionary message to students: they need to be discerning about how, when, and with whom to use unique, creative forms of expression.

As students discover what issues to be critical of and what stylistic means they should use to communicate those concerns, they need to make the personal decision about how this criticism should affect their life and learning. Students should learn to put their convictions into action as they find ways to get involved in their communities. Teachers should encourage students to seek out information resources and organizations that challenge them to go beyond classroom learning. Through such venues, students can live out their ideals and discover that they can influence the world around them. And as long as students find a way to get involved that matches their talents and interests, they will continue to be active in those areas even after the school year ends.

> As this critique touches on many different aspects of Villanueva's philosophy and style, the concluding paragraph is meant to summarize and bring cohesion to the different areas of the paper's focus.

Although some may perceive Villanueva's ideals of educating for cultural criticism as radical or threatening to the classroom teacher's authority, I believe that evoking a critical consciousness in students is the most powerful and effective method of educating. Students too often feel that they can get away with passively regurgitating facts in the classroom. Quite often, they don't "care" about what is being taught; they think their voice doesn't matter because they are not as educated as the teacher or lack a position of authority. However, their experiences and perceptions about the world can and should be articulated and shared. Students need to know that each of them has something valuable to contribute to the world. And while they must be stylistically aware of how to effectively communicate their worldviews, they must also find a method of communication that accurately conveys their individuality. Whether they express themselves through art or music, narrative or non-fiction, conventional Standard English or experimental Villanueva-style reflection, when students critique and question the world around them, their critical thought will often lead to active promotion of positive, much needed changes in society.

Lesson Plan: Debatable Civil Rights

Cherilyn Dudley

Objectives:

> The objectives help the teacher, as well as anyone else who looks at the lesson plan, identify the main goals of the class period. Through them, the teacher articulates what he or she wants the students to learn.

1. Students will become familiar with the three main rights listed in the Declaration of Independence.
2. Students will be able to formulate definitions of words based on their nature and function.
3. Students will be able to examine and critique their own as well as one another's perspectives on the enactment of civil rights today both in society and in politics.
4. Students will be able to identify and articulate ways they can participate in promoting social justice and equality in today's society.

Materials:

> You don't want to be standing in front of 30 expectant students before you realize you've forgotten the hand-outs and overheads you need for your lesson! The Materials section ensures that you'll be well-prepared for class.

Overhead with opening sentence of Declaration of Independence
Anticipation Guide: *Get it Right!*

Methods:

> The Methods section describes the specific activities a teacher will do in class. It includes how the material will be introduced, how it will be developed as it is further explained, and how the class will be concluded.

Introduction (10 minutes)

1. Students will share what they know about the Declaration of Independence and the three rights it lists in its introduction.
2. Teacher will put up Declaration of Independence, and a student will read the first sentence aloud to the class:

   "We hold these truths to be self-evident, that all men are created equal, that they are endowed by their Creator with certain unalienable Rights, that among these are Life, Liberty and the pursuit of Happiness."

> Anticipation Guides are a type of introductory activity designed to pique student interest in a subject before it is studied more in-depth.

3. Hand out Anticipation Guide; Students will write their own definitions for the three rights (Life, Liberty, pursuit of Happiness).
4. Student definitions for each of these rights will be listed on the board.

Development (40 minutes)

5. Students will read the Anticipation Guide statements and mark whether they agree or disagree.
6. The teacher will ask students to review the definitions they came up with for "Life, Liberty, and pursuit of Happiness." Class will discuss

what makes a definition a "good definition": how to make it specific, yet broad enough so it doesn't exclude anything. Students will revise at least one of their personal definitions of the three rights to make it stronger and more effective.

7. Students will share the conclusions they reached for each of the Anticipation Guide statements, as well as justification for these differing conclusions. The class will debate statements that were more controversial.

During the Conclusion of a lesson, class material is reviewed and the teacher gives the assignment.

Conclusion (5 minutes)

8. Class will review the Declaration of Independence sentence, and the teacher will reiterate how even in today's society, rights that may seem to be quite straight-forward and simple are not always valued and preserved.

9. Students will be assigned to use the Internet to research a specific area of Civil Rights that interests them (women's rights, minority rights, economic rights, etc.). They must write a journal describing (1) a recent event in today's news that demonstrates either respect or disrespect for others' rights, (2) how they think the rights listed in the Declaration of Independence were, or could have been, justly applied in that situation, according to their definition of those rights, and (3) what they can do to influence and/or promote the continued goal of equality (students may reference website suggestions for getting involved).

Assignment:

Journal, which will be discussed in class the next day

Assessment:

It's amazing how students can pretend they're listening but never actually hear a thing. Prompting them to list the three rights is an easy way to make sure they specifically note which three we're talking about. Defining them gives them some ownership over the material and encourages them to think about the rights more in-depth.

Class participation with Anticipation Guide and debate Journal

["Anticipation Guide"]

Get it Right!

What rights does the Declaration of Independence say everyone should have? List them here, and write your own definition of what each right means:

1.
2.
3.

I intentionally designed this activity to create some controversy and disagreement about civil rights so students would recognize the ongoing debate that occurs over this issue. Numbers 2–5 are the most controversial, and student responses will be influenced by their individual beliefs and experiences. Number 5 encourages students to think critically about their own society and its practices.

Based on what you know and believe about Civil Rights, circle AGREE or DISAGREE next to each statement. Be prepared to justify your decisions, and remember there is no one right answer!

1. AGREE   DISAGREE   Regardless of ethnicity, religion, political preference, gender, or social class, all people should have access to the same rights.

2. AGREE   DISAGREE   U.S. citizens should have more rights in the U.S. than people who are not U.S. citizens.

3. AGREE   DISAGREE   Illegal immigrants should not be given any of the rights that U.S. citizens possess.

4. AGREE   DISAGREE   Even if they are U.S. citizens, convicted criminals should not have the same rights as other citizens.

5. AGREE   DISAGREE   It is the duty of the U.S. to make sure other countries provide their citizens with the same rights as those we enjoy in our country.

6. AGREE   DISAGREE   Regardless of ethnicity, religion, political preference, gender, or social class, all people *do* have access to the same rights in our society today.

Reading Responses

1. How does Dudley's reading of *Bootstraps* compare with yours? Do you think that she has been critical enough of Villanueva in her "critique"? Why or why not?

2. Review Dudley's essay, noting each time she describes her personal experience. How do her descriptions compare with Villanueva's?

3. Consider what Dudley asks her students to reveal on the "Get It Right!" survey. Do you think that some students might be uncomfortable with this activity? Is it necessary for teachers to make students uncomfortable? What do they accomplish by doing so? What do they risk?

PUBLIC WRITING

INTRODUCTION

At several points in *Bootstraps,* Villanueva refers to E. D. Hirsch's *Cultural Literacy, What Every American Needs to Know* (1987). Now retired, Hirsch was a Professor of English at the University of Virginia when he published *Cultural Literacy,* and he had developed a reputation as an influential literary critic and theorist on the teaching of writing. His work on education includes *The Schools We Need and Why We Don't Have Them* (1996) and *The Knowledge Deficit* (2006). And his influence can be connected to a focus on "core knowledge" that is a feature of the No Child Left Behind act.

Cultural Literacy quickly became a topic of conversation among educators and noneducators alike. It is easy to imagine why it touched off such interest and conflict.

Here we reproduce a short article that Hirsch uses as part of the introduction to a different book, *The New Dictionary of Cultural Literacy,* Third Edition (2002). The dictionary lists the specific facts that Hirsch and his collaborators think people in our culture should know. In this introductory essay, Hirsch offers an abbreviated version of his famous argument for promoting cultural literacy through teaching common knowledge. Hirsch reasons that because we learn by associating something new with something we already know, learning requires "a knowledge of shared, taken-for-granted information."

Compared to Villanueva, Hirsch sounds like a thorough traditionalist. But does the larger project, the dictionary that this piece introduces, play with convention? Have you read any other books for your college courses that are made up of lists of facts—places, people, dates, slang words and phrases—that a culturally literate person should know?

The Theory Behind the Dictionary:
Cultural Literacy and Education
E. D. Hirsch Jr.

From the Introduction to *The New Dictionary of Cultural Literacy,* Third Edition (2002)

The conceptions that underlie this dictionary are outlined in my book *Cultural Literacy,* published in 1987. But in fact, the dictionary project was begun before I thought of writing a separate book, and the book itself was first conceived merely as a technical explanation of the ideas that led us to undertake the dictionary. . . . So here, in brief compass, is why this project was undertaken, and why we hope it will help improve American public education and public discourse. . . .

The novelty that my book introduced into this discussion is its argument that true literacy depends on a knowledge of the *specific* information that is taken for granted in our public discourse. My emphasis on background information makes my book an attack on all formal and technical approaches to teaching language arts. Reading and writing are not simply acts of decoding and encoding but rather acts of communication. The literal words we speak and read and write are just the tip of the iceberg in communication. An active understanding of the written word requires far more than the ability to call out words from a page or the possession of basic vocabulary, syntax, grammar, and inferencing techniques. We have learned that successful reading also requires a knowledge of shared, taken-for-granted information that is not set down on the page.

To grasp the practical importance of that point for our entire education system, we need to ask a fundamental question. Why is high national literacy the key to educational progress in all domains of learning, even in mathematics and natural sciences? We have long known that there is a high correlation between students' reading ability and their ability to learn new material in diverse fields. That sounds vaguely reasonable, even obvious, but why *exactly* should it be the case? Let's try to understand the not-so-obvious reason for the high correlation between reading ability and learning ability.

The true measure of reading ability is the ease and accuracy with which a person can understand *diverse* kinds of writing. All standardized tests of reading ability include samples from several different subject matters. But why isn't one long sample just as effective a test as several short ones? Well, if reading ability were a purely generalizable skill, one long sample would be an adequate diagnostic test. But in fact, reading ability is not a generalizable skill. If a young boy knows a lot about snakes but very little about lakes, he will make a good score on a passage about snakes, but a less good score on a passage about lakes. So to get a fairly accurate picture of his overall reading ability, we have to sample how he does on a variety of subjects.

But notice that this variability in a person's performance shows us something of utmost importance about reading ability. To have a good *general* reading ability, you need to know about a lot of things. If you know about lakes and snakes, and rakes and cakes, you will have a higher reading ability than if you just know about snakes. Aha! you might say, that simply means you will read better if you have a broad vocabulary. That is true. But remember what it means to have a broad vocabulary. Knowing a lot of words means knowing a lot of things. Words refer to things. Language arts are also knowledge arts.

We have now taken a first step in understanding the correlation between reading ability and learning ability. We have established that high reading ability is a multiplex skill that requires knowledge in a wide range of subjects. It turns out that the same is true of learning ability. A basic axiom of learning is that the easiest way to learn something new is to associate it with something we already know. Much of the art of teaching is the art of associating what kids need to learn with what they already know. The process of learning often works as metaphor does, yoking old ideas together to make something new. In the nineteenth century, when people wanted to describe the new transportation technology that went *chug-chug-chug,* they called the engine an "iron horse" and the rail system the "track way" (if they were Dutch) or "rail way" (if they were English) or "iron way" (if they were French, German, or Italian) or "narrow iron lane" (if they were Greek). All of these metaphors successfully conveyed a new concept by combining old concepts. . . .

It should now be clear why reading ability and learning ability are so closely allied. They both depend on a diversity of prior knowledge. You can easily read a range of new texts if you already know a lot; so too you can easily learn a broad range of knowledge if you already know a lot. It should not surprise us, therefore, that back in the 1950s the College Board found out that the best predictor of how well students would perform in school was their performance on a general knowledge test. "Reading, writing and arithmetic" and the general ability to learn new things all show a high correlation with broad background knowledge.

I must ask your indulgence to take another step along the path I am leading you. Reading and learning ability depend on something more definite than broad, unspecified knowledge. To a significant degree, learning and reading depend on *specific* broad knowledge. The reason for this goes back to my earlier point that reading is not just a technical skill but also an act of communication. When somebody is reading with understanding, communication is taking place between writer and reader. Conversely, if communication isn't taking place, the reader isn't accurately understanding what he or she is reading. Successful communication depends on understanding both the text's literal meanings and its implied meanings. These all-important implied meanings can only be constructed out of specific knowledge shared between writer and reader. Let me give a very brief example of why this is so. Here are the beginning words of a school textbook on chemistry:

> You are beginning your study of chemistry at a time when growing numbers of people are concerned about the declining quality of life. Chemistry can help you gain a deeper and more satisfying understanding of our environment than you have now. If you are curious and wish to know more about natural processes, minerals of the earth, water and solutions, and gases of the atmosphere, the activities in chemistry beckon to you.

That's it. As a child, I'm supposed to know before reading the passage that chemistry has to do with minerals, water, and solutions, that numbers of people are concerned about the quality of life, that quality of life has something to do with water and solutions. Understanding that passage will be easy if I already know what "chemistry," "solution," and "declining quality of life" are supposed to signify. . . .

Therefore, learning depends on communication, and effective communication depends on shared background knowledge. The optimal way to fulfill this requirement of communication is simply to insure that readers and writers, students and teachers do in fact share a broad range of specific knowledge. This makes good communication possible, which in turn makes effective learning possible, and also enables a society to work. In short, we have come round to the point of my book. An important key to solving the twin problems of learning and literacy is to attain the broadly shared background knowledge I have called "cultural literacy." My book argues that the content of this literate background knowledge is not a mystery, and that it can be taught systematically to all our students. The book further claims that if we do impart this content, we can achieve the universal literacy that is a necessary foundation for further educational, economic, and social improvements. No active reading researcher—that is to say, no one who is thoroughly conversant with the empirical data in cognitive research—has challenged this analysis. . . .

Publishers and schools need to direct their energies to enhancing the effectiveness with which core literate content is presented. They should not try to overhaul the entire content of literate culture, which cannot successfully be done in any case. Professional linguists have often remarked on the inherent conservatism of literacy. Some of its elements do not change at all. Spelling, for example is extraordinarily conservative, because so many people have learned the traditional forms, and so many books have recorded them, that successful spelling reform would require orthographical thought-police. This linguistic inertia induced by print and mass education also extends to other contents of literate culture.

But the conservatism of literate culture is far from total. New elements are constantly coming in, and the old ones falling out of use. Americans have successfully pressed for cultural reforms, including greater representation of women, minorities, and non-Western cultures. In addition, literate culture must keep up with historical and technical change. Yet the materials of literate culture that are recent introductions constitute about a fifth of its total. The disputed territory of literate culture is much smaller still—about 4 percent. Thus, 96 percent of literate culture is undisputed territory, and most striking of all, *80 percent of literate culture has been in use for more than a hundred years!*

Such cultural conservatism is fortunate and useful for the purposes of national communication. It enables grandparents to communicate with grandchildren, southerners with midwesterners, whites with blacks, Asians with Latinos, and Republicans with Democrats—no matter where they were educated. If each local school system imparts the traditional reference points of literate culture, then everybody is able to communicate with strangers. That is a good definition of literacy: the ability to communicate effectively with strangers. We help people in the underclass rise economically by teaching them how to communicate effectively beyond a narrow social sphere, and that can only be accomplished by teaching them shared, traditional literate culture. Thus the inherent conservatism of literacy leads to an unavoidable paradox: the social goals of liberalism *require* educational conservatism. We only make social and economic progress by teaching everyone to read and communicate, which means teaching myths and facts that are predominantly traditional.

Those who evade this inherent conservatism of literacy in the name of multicultural antielitism are in effect elitists of an extreme sort. Traditionally educated themselves, and highly literate, these self-appointed protectors of minority cultures have advised schools to pursue a course that has condemned minorities to illiteracy. The disadvantaged students for whom antielitist solicitude is expressed are the very ones who suffer when we fail to introduce traditional literate culture into the earliest grades. . . .

The real test of any educational idea is its usefulness. We hope this dictionary will be a useful tool. We also hope and expect that no one will be willing to stop with cultural literacy as a final educational aim. Cultural literacy is a necessary but not sufficient attainment of an educated person. Cultural literacy is shallow; true education is deep. But our analysis of reading and learning suggests the paradox that broad, shallow knowledge is the best route to deep knowledge. Because broad knowledge enables us to read and learn effectively, it is the best guarantee that we will continue to read, and read and learn, and deepen our knowledge. True literacy has always opened doors—not just to deep knowledge and economic success, but also to other people and other cultures.

Reading Responses

1. Describe times when teachers have pressed you to learn background information. How did you respond? When have you felt the need for this knowledge? When have you resisted learning this kind of information? Why did you resist?

2. Review Hirsch's argument, looking for places where he breaks with convention. Describe two places where Hirsch breaks convention and what effect each has on the reader.

3. Summarize Hirsch's argument about the conservatism of literate culture, paying special attention to the advantages Hirsch describes. What disadvantages can you imagine?

MORE WRITING IN ENGLISH EDUCATION

INTRODUCTION

James Paul Gee has won widespread attention and acclaim for his work on literacy, which includes how we "read" visual and verbal messages in complex contexts. He is a professor in the College of Education at Arizona State University.

It is very common to read reports on the effect of playing video games on a student's performance in school. Conventional thinking focuses on the negative effects of video games on students. In his book *What Video Games Have to Teach Us about Learning and Literacy*, Gee challenges those conventional ideas. He announces his challenge to the thinking that video gaming is bad in his very first sentence: "I want to talk about video games—yes, even violent video games—and say some positive things about them."

In this excerpt from the book, Gee analyzes what teachers can learn about reading from the ways that gamers use manuals and online help sites. Additional ways that Gee challenges convention in his writing are the following: using short, simple sentences; including information in multiple parentheses, addressing readers directly with "you."

Situated Meaning and Learning: What Should You Do After You Have Destroyed the Global Conspiracy?

James Paul Gee

From *What Video Games Have to Teach Us about Learning and Literacy,* Palgrave Macmillan, 2nd ed., 2007

. . . Games often come with manuals. They also sometimes come with a booklet, written as a diary, or notes, or otherwise set as part of the virtual world of the game, that gives the back story or background information for that virtual world. For example, *American McGee's Alice,* a game where Alice has gone insane and returned to a nightmarish Wonderland, comes with a booklet entitled "Rutledge Private Clinic and Asylum Casebook," which contains Alice's physician's daily notes on her treatment.

For most games, publishers offer highly colorful and detailed strategy guides that tell players all about the game (its characters, maps and geography of the world, weapons, enemies, objects to be found, fruitful strategies to follow, etc.). Such guides also give a complete walkthrough for the game. A number of Internet sites offer (usually free) a variety of different walkthroughs ("faqs") written by players themselves. These sites also offer hints from players and "cheats" for the games. (Cheats are ways to manipulate the game's programming to do things like give yourself extra life or more ammunition.)

These texts are all integrated into the appreciative systems associated with the affinity groups connected to video games. Different players and groups have different views about whether, when, and how to use these texts. For example, consider walkthroughs on a site like gamefaqs.com. These documents often run to 70 or more single-spaced pages and are written according to a tight set of rules about what they should contain and look like (including a list of each date on which the walkthrough was revised). Some players shun walkthroughs entirely, though they may write them. Others argue that walkthroughs can and should be used, but only to get a hint when one is thoroughly stuck. Indeed, the writers of the walkthroughs themselves often recommend that players use them this way. (Imagine producing a 70-page, single-spaced document and advising people to look at it only when they are stuck.)

Of course, if children had walkthroughs in school when they studied things like science, we would call it "cheating" (let alone if they had "cheat codes"). But, then, imagine what a science classroom would look like where learners wrote extensive walkthroughs according to strict norms and debated when and how to use them, debates that became part and parcel of the learners' growing appreciative systems about what it means to "do science (well)." And, indeed, in a sense, real scientists do have walkthroughs. They know (through talk with others and through texts) the case histories of how relevant related discoveries in their field were made. They also have opinions about how closely one should consult or follow these histories.

It is now a piece of folk wisdom that "young people" don't read things like manuals but just start playing games, often looking at the manual or other guides later. Yet I would argue that these young people are using print in the way it should be used when people actually understand what they read in a useful and situated way. Baby boomers—perhaps too influenced by traditional schooling—often try to do otherwise to their regret and frustration, when they insist on reading a manual before they have any embodied understanding of what the manual is about (i.e., the game).

The problem with the texts associated with video games—the instruction booklets, walkthroughs, and strategy guides—is that they do not make a lot of sense unless one has already experienced and lived in the game world for a while. Of course, this lack of lucidity can be made up for if the player has read similar texts before, but at some point these texts originally made sense because the player had an embodied world of experience with games in terms of which to situate and spell out their meanings. . . .

When I give talks on video games to teachers, I often show them a manual or strategy guide and ask them how much they understand. Very often they are frustrated. They have no experience in which to situate the words and phrases of the texts. All they get is verbal information, which they understand at some literal level, but which does not really hang together. They cannot visualize this verbal information in any way that makes sense or makes them want to read on. I tell them that that is how their students feel when confronted with a text or textbook in science or some other academic area if they have had no experiences in terms of which they can situate the meanings of the words and phrases. It's all "just words," words the "good" students can repeat on tests and the "bad" ones can't.

When you have played a video game for a while, something magical happens to the texts associated with it. All of a sudden they seem lucid and clear and readable. You can't even recall how confusing they seemed in the, first place. At that point, players can use the text in a great variety of ways for different purposes. For instance, they can look up details that enhance their play. Or such guides can fill out players' knowledge of the places, creatures, and things in the virtual world in which they are living. Players can troubleshoot problems they are having in the game, with the game, or with their computer. They can get hints or compare their play to how others have done.

Let me take the booklet that comes with *Deus Ex* as an example of what I mean by saying that texts associated with video games are not lucid unless and until one has some embodied game experience in which to "cash out" the meanings of the text. The book contains 20 small pages, printed in double columns on each page. In these pages, there are 199 bolded references that represent headings and subheadings. One small randomly chosen stretch of headings and subheadings that appears at the end of page five and the beginning of page six says: *Passive Readouts, Damage Monitor, Active Augmentation and Device Icons, Items-at-Hand, Information Screens, Note, Inventory, Inventory Management, Stacks, Nanokey ring, Ammunition.* Each of these 199 headings and subheadings is followed by text that gives information relevant to the topic and relates it to other information throughout the booklet. In addition, the booklet assigns 53 keys on the computer keyboard to some function in the game, and these 53 keys are mentioned 82 times in relation to the information contained in the 199 headings and subheadings. So, although small, the booklet is packed with relatively technical information.

Here is a typical piece of language from this booklet:

Your internal nano-processors keep a very detailed record of your condition, equipment and recent history. You can access this data at any time during play by hitting Fl to get to the Inventory screen or F2 to get to the Goals/Notes screen. Once you have accessed your information screens, you can move between the screens by clicking on the tabs at the top of the screen. You can map other information screens to hotkeys using Settings, Keyboard/Mouse.

This makes perfect sense at a literal level, but that just goes to show how worthless the literal level is. When you understand this sort of passage at only a literal level, you have only an illusion of understanding, one that quickly disappears as you try to relate this information to the hundreds of other important details in the booklet. First of all, this passage means nothing real to you if you have no situated idea about what "nano-processors," "condition," "equipment," "history," "Fl," Inventory screen," "F2," "Goals/Notes screen" (and, of course, "Goals" and "Notes"), "information screens," "clicking," "tabs," "map," "hotkeys," and "Settings, Keyboard/Mouse" mean in and for playing games like *Deus Ex*.

Second, though you know literally what each sentence means, together they raise a plethora of questions if you have no situated understandings of this game or games like it. For instance: Is the same data (condition, equipment, and history) on both the Inventory screen and the Goals/Notes screen? If so, why is it on two different screens? If not, which type of information is on which screen and why? The fact that I can move between the screens by clicking on the tabs (but what do these tabs look like; will I recognize them?) suggests that some of this information is on one screen and some on the other. But, then, is my "condition" part of my Inventory or my Goals/Notes—it doesn't seem to be either, but, then, what is my "condition" anyway? If I can map other information screens (and what are these?) to hotkeys using "Setting, Keyboard/Mouse," does this mean there is no other way to access them? How will I access them in the first place to assign them to my own chosen hotkeys? Can I click between them and the Inventory screen and the Goals/Notes screens by pressing on "tabs"? And so on—20 pages is beginning to seem like a lot; remember, there are 199 different headings under which information like this is given.

Of course, all these terms and questions can be defined and answered if you closely check and cross-check information over and over again through the little booklet. You can constantly turn the pages backward and forward. But once you have one set of links relating various items and actions in mind, another drops out just as you need it and you're back to turning pages. Is the booklet poorly written? Not at all. It is written just as well or as poorly as—just like, in fact—any of a myriad of school-based texts in the content areas. It is, outside the practices in the semiotic domain from which it comes, just as meaningless, no matter how much one could garner literal meanings from it with which to verbally repeat things or pass tests.

When I first read this booklet before playing *Deus Ex* (and having played only one other shooter game, a very different one), I was sorely tempted to put the game on a shelf and forget about it. I was simply overwhelmed with details, questions, and confusions. When I started the game, I kept trying to look up stuff. But I understood none of it well enough to find things easily without searching for the same information over and over again. In the end, you just have to actively play the game and explore and try everything. Then, at last, the booklet makes good sense, but by then you don't need it all that much. . . .

There is much discussion these days about how many children fail in school—especially children from poor homes—because they have not been taught phonics well or correctly in their early years. But the truth of the matter is that a great many more children fail in school because, while they can decode print, they cannot handle the progressively more complex demands school language makes on them as they move up in the grades and on to high school.

School requires, in respect to both oral and written language, forms or styles of language that are different from and, in some respects, more complex than everyday oral language used in informal face-to-face conversations. The forms of language used in texts and discussions in science, math, social studies classes, and other content areas go by the general name of "academic language," though different varieties of academic language are associated with different content areas in school.

Academic language, like the language in the *Deus Ex* booklet, is not really lucid or meaningful if one has no embodied experiences within which to situate its meanings in specific ways. For example, consider this academic-language quote from a high school science textbook:

> The destruction of a land surface by the combined effects of abrasion and removal
> of weathered material by transporting agents is called erosion . . . The production
> of rock waste by mechanical processes and chemical changes is called weathering.

Again, one can certainly understand this at some literal word-byword, sentence-by-sentence way. However, this is not "everyday" language. No one speaks this way at home aroundthe table or at a bar having drinks with friends. But this language is filled with all the same problems the language of the *Deus Ex* booklet held for me when I had not lived through any experiences in terms of which I could situate its meanings. Without embodied experiences with which to cash out its meanings, all the above academic text will do—as the *Deus Ex* booklet did to me initially—is fill one with questions, confusion, and, perhaps, anger.

For example: I have no idea what the difference is between "abrasion" and "removal of weathered material by transporting agents," which I would have thought was one form of abrasion. What's a "transporting agent"? What's a "mechanical process"? I am not really clear on the difference between "mechanical processes," especially in regard to weather, and "chemical changes." And what chemicals are we talking about here—stuff in rain?

Since the first sentence is about "erosion" and the second about "weathering," I suppose these two things are connected in some important way—but how? They must be two forms of "destruction of a land surface," given that this is the subject of the first sentence. But, then, I would have thought that producing "rock waste" was a way of building, not just destroying, land, since rock waste eventually turns into dirt (doesn't it?) and thus, I would have supposed, eventually into potentially fertile land. But this is a geology text, and they don't care about fertile land (or do they?). The word "land" here has a different range of possible situated meanings than I am familiar with.

Of course, I can turn the pages of the book back and forth clarifying all these points. After all, these two sentences are meant to be definitions—not of the words "erosion" and "weathering" in everyday terms but in specialist terms in a particular semiotic domain. And, of course, I do need to know that they *are* definitions, and I may not even know that if I have had little experience of specialists trying to define terms in explicit and operational ways so as to lessen the sort of ambiguity and vagueness that is more typical of everyday talk. Since they are definitions, they are linked and cross-linked to a myriad of other terms, descriptions, and explanations throughout the book, and I can follow this tangled trail across the pages, back and forth, losing bits of the connections just as I need them and page turning yet again.

However, once I have experienced the sorts of embodied images, actions, and tasks that engage geologists—including their ways of talking and debating, their reasons for doing so, their interests, norms, and values—then the text is lucid and useful. Confusion, frustration, and anger disappear. Given such understanding, everybody would pass the test and we couldn't fail half the class and reward a small set of "winners"—people who can repeat back verbal details they remember well when they don't fully understand them in any practical way.

In the end, my claim is that people have situated meanings for words when they can associate these words with images, actions, experiences, or dialogue in a real or imagined world. Otherwise they have, at best, only verbal meanings (words for words, as in a dictionary). Situated meanings lead to real understanding and the ability to apply what one knows in action. Verbal meanings **do not** (though they do sometimes lead to the ability to pass paper and pencil tests). This is why so many school children, even ones who are good at school, can pass tests but still cannot apply their knowledge to real problem solving.

More Learning Principles

Let me conclude this discussion by listing further learning principles that our discussion of learning and thinking in video games in this chapter has implicated. Once again, in this list, I intend each principle to be relevant both to learning in video games and learning in content areas in classrooms. . . .

17. **Situated Meaning Principle** The meanings of signs (words, actions, objects, artifacts, symbols, texts, etc.) are situated in embodied experience. Meanings are not general or decontextulized. Whatever generality meanings come to have is discovered bottom up via embodied experiences.

18. **Text Principle** Texts are not understood purely verbally (i.e., only in terms of the definitions of the words in the text and their text-internal relationships to each other) but are understood in terms of embodied experiences. Learners move back and forth between texts and embodied experiences. More purely verbal understanding (reading texts apart from embodied action) comes only when learners have had enough embodied experience in the domain and ample experiences with similar texts.

Reading Responses

1. Do you play video games? If you do not, interview a college student to answer the following questions. Describe the effect that playing video games has had on your performance in school. What have been the positive effects? What have been the negative effects? Have the positive effects outweighed the negative ones?

2. Which of Gee's challenges to convention is most risky? What is he risking? How significant is the risk?

3. Gee suggests that providing students with "walkthroughs" as they study science might be considered "cheating." Make a brief argument that providing this kind of help in school would be cheating. Provide reasons and examples to support your claim.

WRITING ASSIGNMENTS

Assignment 1

Your task is to take on the role of student teacher and create two different lesson plans for teaching high school students about one of the new terms you recommended for Hirsch's list. One plan should replicate the kind of education you experienced in high school classes that used conventional teaching methods. The other plan should include features that challenge conventional teaching practice. To begin, free-write about your opinions of modern high schoolers: What do they take for granted? What do you as a teacher need to wake them up to? How can you break conventions to help them understand in a new way?

As you begin drafting, use Dudley's lesson plan as a template for your own, including all the features that she has in hers. Record your thoughts and emotional responses as you create the two lesson plans: Which was easiest to craft? Which do you expect to be more effective? Which best enacts what you believe should be the goals of a high school education? Consider how you might use your experience in introducing your lesson plans or comparing them.

Assignment 2

In the years immediately after September 11, 2001, most college students could vividly describe their experiences on that day because they had been teenagers on that day. They had understood the gravity of the horrible scenes that were playing out on their television and computer screens. You are likely to have been a child in 2001, and to remember much less. In a few years, college students will know September 11, 2001, as only one more date in history.

Your task for this assignment is to describe American life—during, or soon after September 11, 2001—in a way that will help future students understand what happened and why those events were important. Be sure to combine personal experience and academic research in ways that help the reader engage your main point in the essay.

To begin, free-write about your memories of September 11, 2001, including as many details as possible. Interview others, family members if possible, about their own memories of that time in American history, and—if possible—about their memories of how you experienced that time. Do some research about September 11 and the time following that event, paying attention to how people and governments responded to those events. Consider researching your hometown and local events rather than events in distant cities.

As you begin drafting, consider what you want your reader to understand about September 11. Begin with a working idea of your main point that you will refine as you draft.

Experiment with ways you could use unconventional form, style, organization, evidence, and so on to encourage your reader to engage with your main point.

Assignment 3

For almost a decade, the U.S. educational system has been shaped by the "No Child Left Behind" act (known by the acronyms NCLB or ESEA for Elementary and Secondary Education Act). This federal law requires school districts to test students regularly to determine what they're learning and how well they're learning it. The U.S. Department of Education maintains a Web site that provides data on how students in individual school systems have performed on standardized tests and advice for teachers and parents (http://www.ed.gov/nclb/landing.jhtml?src=pbt). Not surprisingly, it describes the NCLB act in positive terms. An Internet search combining the phrases "No Child Left Behind" and "NCTE," the acronym for the National Council of Teachers of English, produces fewer than one thousand hits, but among those is NCTE's critique of the NCLB act as well as descriptions of the effects of the NCLB act from English teachers across the country.

Your tasks for this assignment are three:

1. Free-write about your experience taking standardized tests in school, including as many specific details as possible. How often did you take standardized tests? Was there a routine to test-taking days? How did you feel as you took the test? How did you and others react to your performance on the tests? How did your teachers seem to view the test? If you did not take standardized tests in school, describe who assessed your academic work, how they did so, and how you and your parents responded to that assessment.

2. Read about the NCLB (now ESEA) act on the Department of Education Web site and on other reputable Web sites such as NCTE's. Keep track of the Web sites you visit, jotting notes for yourself about the author of the Web site, the author's attitude about the NCLB act, and any information you find interesting. Free-write about your opinion of the NCLB act—overall, is it a good law or a bad one? What effects does it have on education in the United States? Which of these effects are positive? Which are negative?

3. Write a thesis-based essay in which you support your claim about the NCLB act. Develop and support your claim as Victor Villanueva does, by blending your autobiographical experience and your research. Expand your earlier autobiographical descriptions with vivid, effective specifics. Be sure to note the source of your research support. If you have good reason to do so, consider breaking conventions that readers associate with a thesis-based academic essay, conventions related to organization, type and presentation of evidence, logical structure, and grammar. Be prepared to justify your choices.

APPENDIX

The Ethnobiologist's Dilemma
Jared Diamond

Jared Mason Diamond (1937–) was born in Boston and attended Harvard and Cambridge universities. He teaches physiology at UCLA, where he specializes in evolutionary biology by studying the birds of New Guinea. He writes regularly for Natural History *and* Discover *magazines. His 1992 book,* The Third Chimpanzee, *collects his essays on human prehistory, the biology of human nature, unique human traits, and the human place in history. Diamond's book* Guns, Germs, and Steel *(1998), which argues that environment and biology explain the European conquest of the Americas, won a Pulitzer prize for nonfiction. Diamond's latest book,* Collapse: How Societies Choose to Fail or Succeed, *discusses the sets of factors that contribute to whether societies fail or succeed. "The Ethnobiologist's Dilemma," published in the scientific journal* Natural History *in June 1989, suggests that humans develop quite different systems of communication based on their cultures and environments.*

1 "Listen, I already told you. The reason I said your VW didn't start was its solenoid was no good. Like I said, what the solenoid does is. . . . OK, forget it, you don't need to understand it. All you have to know is I fixed it and you owe me $203.67 and you can drive it again."

My car mechanic must have seen my eyes glaze over, just as I had seen my physiology students' eyes glaze over when I tried to explain osmotic diuresis to them in my lecture that same morning last month. It's humiliating to feel like an ignoramus, as I do about cars. At least I feel OK in my own areas of scientific expertise. So do most other scientists in their specialty: scientists are generally the experts who know more about their subject matter than do any other people. But there's one science in which this usual directional flow of information is often stood on its head. That's the branch of cultural anthropology termed *ethnobiology*—the study of how people from different cultures perceive and classify animals and plants.

In my column in the April 1989 issue I described how many New Guinea tribesmen are walking encyclopedias of facts about locally occurring species. This month's piece is about the cruel dilemma that arises when these walking encyclopedias are quizzed by an ethnobiologist, or even by a professional ornithologist naïve about New Guinea birds, as I was when I began working in New Guinea twenty-five years ago. I'll mainly discuss birds, but similar issues arise with classifications of

"The Ethnobiologist's Dilemma" by Jared Diamond, published in Natural History, June 1989.

other species. I eventually realized that the ethnobiologist's dilemma illustrates the frustrations that all of us face in everyday life, whenever we have to a quiz experts like our doctor or car mechanic.

As you may recall from my last column, New Guineans have distinct names in their local languages for almost every bird species living in the vicinity. Their knowledge of the behavior and life history of many species far exceeds what Western scientists know. The same is true of some other "primitive" peoples living elsewhere in the world, such as Amazonian Indians. I and other biologists working in such areas want this expertise for its own sake. I would need several lifetimes of observation to discover for myself what New Guineans already know about the birds I study. By learning names for New Guinea birds in local languages, I can tap into this knowledge. Foré tribesmen wouldn't understand me if I asked about the "blue bird of paradise," but they talked for hours when I asked about the *kongonámu*, their Foré name for this species.

5   Ethnobiologists are also interested in this expertise, but for another reason. They want to know how different human cultures perceive and organize information. Nothing is as fascinating as understanding how another human being thinks. It's challenging enough to understand someone who shares your language, culture, and much of your life, like your spouse; it becomes infinitely more challenging when the person belongs to a different society. Ethnobiology offers a well-defined approach to this problem, because species possess an objective reality, and some of the same species occur in areas occupied by different human cultures. Particular goals of ethnobiologists include discovering what units people choose to name (species or other groupings?), whether tribesmen group units hierarchically as we group species into genera and families, and whether the answers to these questions vary among peoples.

The first step in an ethnobiological study is a seemingly simple one: to gather from informants a list of names of birds (or of other animals or plants) in a local language and to determine which bird each name refers to. Yet the apparent simplicity of this task is deceptive, as I gradually came to realize while gathering such lists in New Guinea, talking with ethnobiologists, reading their papers, and reinterviewing tribespeople previously studied by ethnobiologists. Anthropologists focus on theoretically interesting questions posed by naming but often fail to appreciate the pitfalls in that mundane first step of obtaining a correct list of bird names. While the goal is to understand a people whose perceptions differ from ours, those very differences make it hard for us to discern their perceptions. To compound this problem, most anthropologists know much less about the local birds than do the tribesmen they're interviewing. Let's consider three stimuli that scientists have used to gather lists of bird names: pictures in bird books, dead specimens of birds, and live birds encountered in the jungle.

To Western scientists accustomed to book learning, the most obvious approach is to show a tribesman a book with pictures of bird species likely to occur in his area, and ask him to name the birds depicted. The virtues of this method are that a compact field guide may depict hundreds of species, you don't have to find and identify birds in the jungle, and every informant is shown the same birds. Among the many anthropologists and linguists who used this method were Leonard Glick and Kenneth McElhanon in their respective studies of New Guinea's Gimi and Selepet peoples.

During my early years in New Guinea, I too used this method until I realized that the results were too variable to trust. When shown pictures of bird species that I knew occurred in the vicinity, local people sometimes gave names in agreement with the names they gave when they and I together observed the same bird species alive in the jungle. But sometimes the names disagreed. In other cases people failed even to recognize pictures of common local birds or professed to recognize bird species that could not possibly occur in the area.

A glaring error of naming on Vella Lavella Island in the Solomon archipelago finally made me understand one of the flaws in the picture method. I had spent the day bird watching with some knowledgeable old men who named and described the habits of fifty-five bird species that we encountered. In the evening I showed them bird pictures in a field guide. When we came to the picture of a lesser frigatebird, I expected my guides to apply the name *belama*, which they had used for the frigatebirds we saw soaring that day. In fact, they pronounced it to be a *pitikole*, the name they had used for the willie wagtail.

10

A more ludicrous mistake would be impossible to imagine. Frigatebirds are huge seabirds (eight-foot wingspread), have deeply forked tails, soar high in flocks, catch fish, and are usually silent. Willie wagtails are small flycatchers (eight inches long), have a fan-shaped tail that they wave incessantly, hop on the ground in villages, catch insects, and call noisily. The only feature shared by frigate-birds, and willie wagtails is that both are black and white.

10

Shocked by this gross failure of the experts, I reexamined the pictures from a fresh perspective, as if I were a Vella Lavella islander shown a bird book for the first time. On a printed page was a black-and-white pattern about four inches across. Having spent several decades reading books, I was accustomed to conjuring up a large, three-dimensional sketch. But the islanders weren't used to this leap of imagination. Instead, they saw what was really there: a flat, blackand-white, bird-shaped image, much closer in size to a real willie wagtail than to a real frigatebird.

I'm not arguing that pictures are of no value as an ethnobiological tool. It's just that, for informants from a barely literate society, identifications based on pictures are unreliable unless confirmed by a better technique. The picture method's failures illustrate the risk of using our own perceptions to devise tests for the perceptions of other peoples.

An ethnobiological technique that avoids some drawbacks of the picture method is to show people actual specimens of local birds that have been shot. Whenever I was making collections of New Guinea birds, I routinely asked local villagers to name each of my specimens, and so have many other ornithologists. Most anthropologists can't apply this method because they aren't collecting bird specimens. In Peru, however, anthropologists Brent Berlin and James Boster collaborated with ornithologist John O'Neill to test this approach rigorously. They showed locally collected specimens of 157 bird species to Aguaruna Jívaro Indians, asked each Indian to name each specimen, and did three such naming trials on twenty-eight, twenty-five, and twenty-seven Indians, respectively.

In my experience, names elicited by specimens agree better with names elicited by live birds than do names elicited by pictures. Nevertheless, problems of discrepancies and inabilities to name some locally common species still occur. A superb New Guinea informant named Mero, who lived at Kiunga on the Fly River, helped me see what was going wrong. Mero had described for me 125 local bird species, named many fruits that each frugivorous bird species ate, and guided me to one of New Guinea's rarest birds, the white-bellied pitohui. Far more abundant than the white-bellied pitohui, though, is the related rusty pitohui, one of the most conspicuous and distinctive birds of the New Guinea lowlands. It constantly gives loud calls audible hundreds of yards away, dives in and out of vine tangles, and scours the whole jungle from the understory to the canopy. In groups of up to ten, rusty pitohuis lead flocks of other bird species in their search for food (see "Strange Traveling Companions," December 1988). Thus, after Mero had named for me such rarities as the whitebellied pitohui, I was astonished when he could not decide what to name a specimen of the rusty pitohui that I handed him.

15   As I had done on Vella Lavella, I tried to see the situation from Mero's point   15 of view. Here he stood holding a dead, silent, motionless, utterly undistinctive brown bird, stripped of all the characteristics that he associated with the rusty pitohui.

Gone were the bugling calls, the shaking of the vine tangles, the excitement as the jungle came alive and as dozens of other birds swept after the pitohuis. For Mero, the rusty pitohui was that noise and excitement, not this drab carcass. Perhaps the same conclusion lay behind a remark that a Kaluli tribesman named Jubi, living barely a hundred miles east of Mero's village, made to ethnobiologist Steven Feld. After Feld had been attempting for months to decipher Kaluli bird names, Jubi suddenly lost his patience and blurted out, "Listen—to you they are birds, to me they are voices in the forest."

Berlin's, Boster's, and O'Neill's accounts of their experiments suggest that bird specimens may pose similar problems for Peruvian Indians as for Mero and Jubi. In response to specimens of the 157 bird species, Indians came up with 275 bird names, less than half of which appeared to Berlin and his colleagues to be valid names (as judged by being applied consistently to a given specimen or to several very similar species). Indians volunteered eight names of birds said to be relatives of the most distinctive local woodpecker. Yet when Indians were shown specimens of eight local woodpecker species, only one species received the same name from all informants, and only two names were confined to a single woodpecker species (but each of those species more often received a different name).

Much of this variability among Indian informants was undoubtedly due to some of them knowing more about birds than others. However, another contributing factor is surely that Indians distinguish live woodpeckers by call, drumming pattern, habitat, and perch, as well as by appearance. Dead specimens were stripped of those recognition marks, just as was the dead rusty pitohui for Mero.

The basic problem with trying to elicit bird names by pictures or specimens is that these methods fail to present birds in the way that New Guinea hunters normally perceive them. To elicit names under natural circumstances, I routinely have one or two local hunters accompany me through the jungle whenever I am bird watching in New Guinea. I ask them to name each bird that we see or hear, and I check their identifications by asking them to tell me details of the bird's habits. This method has proved to be reliable because whenever I have worked in areas where biologists of the Whitney South Seas Expedition used the same method in the 1920s and 1930s, identifications of names obtained by me and by the Whitney biologists agree closely.

20   I also ask hunters to describe and name all the birds that they know, in addi-   20
tion to the ones that we have seen or heard together. When they eventually run out of names, I prod them for any they might have forgotten by asking them to describe all nocturnal birds or all ground-dwelling birds or all birds similar to a parrot or some other type of bird that they have already described. At all costs, I avoid yes/no questions. I also avoid giving people a complete description of some bird and asking them to name it, for that would leave me no way of checking whether they really know the species in question.

It often still happens that I want to find out whether a hunter knows some particular bird species that he hasn't as yet spontaneously described to me. In that case I give a brief description of the bird. If the hunter claims to know it, I ask him to describe more about it so I can tell if he really knows that bird. But I still have to remind myself that New Guinea hunters don't experience birds as we see them—through binoculars or displayed in Peterson field guides. Hunters remember certain species by their songs, others by their behavior, still others by their plumage. It took me years to learn what features of each bird species were most salient for New Guineans and hence should be included in my brief description.

For example, when I described the moustached tree swift's white moustache and eye stripe, which are so striking as seen through my binoculars or in field guides, no New Guinean ever guessed the bird I was talking about. Instead, what impresses New Guineans is the silhouette, distinctive at a hundred yards: the bird's wings are so long that they cross behind its back as it sits perched, and the forked tail also appears crossed. In villages all over the New Guinea region, if I stand with my arms crossed behind my back and with my legs crossed and say nothing more, people immediately laugh, know that I'm referring to the moustached tree swift, and proceed to describe its habits and to give their name for it. As another example, I never got a response when I described the bush hen's chickenlike build and green bill. Instead, I learned to imitate the catlike wailing duet of the male and female foraging together. The result is always a laugh of recognition, a name and account of habits, and a story to the effect that the answering wails really don't come from two birds, but from a single bird's mouth and anus answering each other.

Thus, to elicit names successfully, one must learn how local hunters perceive each bird species. The worst risk is that hunters are likely to give you oversimplified information, or no information at all, if they sense that you yourself don't know much about the subject. This risk is illustrated by a tale of woe I heard from the late Ralph Bulmer, an ethnobiologist who was unusual in being not only an anthropologist but also a zoologist of professional caliber. Bulmer spent years with the Kalam people of the New Guinea Highlands, studying their understanding of birds, mammals, and plants. Out of those years came one of the most remarkable contributions to the ethnobiological literature: a book entitled *Birds of My Kalam Country*, which Bulmer coauthored with a Kalam tribesman/walking encyclopedia named Ian Saem Majnep. In that book, Saem recorded in his own words his knowledge of 137 out of the 140 bird species found by Western ornithologists in the Kalam area, while Bulmer added his own observations plus identifications of Saem's Kalam bird names (for example, *tbwm-kab-ket-nonm* = crested berrypecker = *Paramythia montium*).

One year, after Kalam people had already told Bulmer names and descriptions for more than 1,400 species of animals and plants known to them, Bulmer began to quiz them about rocks as well. To his great surprise, they claimed to have just one word covering all rocks. In vain did Bulmer protest that the Kalam had until recently used stone tools, and so surely they must have names for different types of rocks to identify which ones made good tools. Bulmer's Kalam friends brushed aside his protests and continued to insist that they didn't classify rocks by name.

The next year, Bulmer returned to the Kalam area with a geologist friend whom he introduced to his Kalam informants. Within an hour, the geologist gave Bulmer a long list of words that the informants had volunteered for different rocks, which they classified according to texture, color, locality, hardness, and use. At that point Bulmer exploded to his Kalam friends, "How could you lie to me? After all these years that I've been working with you! You kept insisting that you didn't bother to classify rocks, and now you've embarrassed me in front of my friend!" To which the Kalam replied, "When you asked us about birds and plants, we saw that you knew a lot about them, and that you could understand what we told you. When you began asking us about rocks, it was obvious you didn't know anything about them. Why should we waste our time telling you something you couldn't possibly understand? But your friend's questions showed that he does know about rocks."

Therein lies the root of the ethnobiologist's dilemma. You have to know almost as much about the local birds as the tribesman you're interviewing if you're to succeed in learning his names for birds. It's pointless walking with a hunter through the jungle and asking him to name bird calls, when you dont know what bird species is making each call that you hear. You can't describe a bird's salient habits if you don't know its habits and know which of them appear most salient to a local hunter. Worst of all, your informants will perceive correctly that you can't grasp all the complexities of their knowledge, so they'll tell you only as much as they think you can understand. Tribesmen in New Guinea and some other parts of the world know far more about local birds than do most anthropologists interviewing them. To approach the tribesmen's knowledge takes years even for ornithologists specializing in New Guinea birds. Thus, ethnobiologists, need to emulate Bulmer's example, invest the time required to attain professional competence in a local fauna, and learn to identify birds in the way that tribesmen do. The second-best alternative is for ethnobiologists to collaborate with biologists who already have that competence.

This piece has seemingly been about a mere problem of methodology in an arcane discipline. In fact, all of us must often ask experts to explain things to us that they understand well and we don't. We have to ask questions of our doctor, car mechanic, tax accountant, house contractor, and so forth. It's usually frustrating, because few experts have the time, patience, or ability to explain things in a way that nonexperts can understand.

For instance, the starter on my 1961, VW Beetle broke down not just last month but many times before that. One mechanic after another fixed it but would not explain the problem and how I could avoid it. The mechanics undoubtedly saw that I am as ignorant about cars as Ralph Bulmer was about rocks, and that I could not understand their explanation. The bad service that I continue to get is my own fault for not practicing what I preach to ethnobiologists: I never took the trouble to study a VW manual. Similarly, consumer advocates are now urging us that if we want to get good care from our doctors, we have to be willing to spend some time reading up on our own health problems.

Thus, I see the ethnobiologist's dilemma as a metaphor for much of modern life. To them that already understand, more knowledge will be freely given. To the rest of us dolts, it's a struggle.

STUDENT SAMPLES
1301

SUMMARY AND PARAPHRASE

Rollin Willis

SUMMARY

Jared Diamond introduces his article, "The Ethnobiologist's Dilemma," with a common source of frustration in our daily lives, which is the frustration of experts not telling us all the information we want to hear on a subject. Diamond ran into this problem while studying cultural organizational systems in New Guinea; he was trying to learn names given to local birds by New Guinean tribesmen. When photo books of birds and dead bird carcasses were shown to tribesmen, they were unable to identify the birds in question; to them these representations of birds did not represent birds in the wild. Diamond needed to ask the right questions about birds in order to be told accurate information (196–199).

To do this he had to know about the birds in question. Diamond and other scientists have found it necessary when dealing with native peoples to know the subject they are inquiring about, to be given the detailed information they want. The Tribesmen's thinking differed from western ideas. Diamond points out that this problem is not limited to his field of study, but is something we all encounter when trying to obtain information from experts, on a subject we don't know much about (199–201).

PARAPHRASE

Diamond was stunned that a native islander, who was experienced and knowledgeable, was inaccurately naming two birds in bird book. To understand why the islander was having trouble naming the birds Diamond viewed the photos from the islander's prospective, instead of as a westerner. The islander was unaccustomed to photos, seeing them only as monotone patterns, instead of translating them to three-dimensional objects as someone who was accustomed to photos would. Because of this lack of understanding of imagery, to the islander the smaller of two bird photos represented the smaller of the two birds (Diamond 198).

Diamond, Jared. "The Ethnobiologist's Dilemma." *First Year Writing in the Disciplines*. Boston: Pearson, 2012. 196–201. Print.

SUMMARY AND PARAPHRASE

Amber Rendon

SUMMARY

In Jared Diamond's article "The Ethnobiologist's Dilemma", published in Natural History, June 1989, Diamond writes about the complications that arise when professional scientists are ingenuous about New Guinea birds and how the ethnobiologist's dilemma is experienced in everyday life. Three cases that scientist use are: pictures in bird books, dead specimens, and live birds seen in the jungle.

The picture method was a failure, because the New Guinea people are far less literate than we Americans are. Therefore, the way the scientist perceives the pictures is different than the informants and is an unreliable source to test on. The dead specimen method was a lot more accurate than the picture method but still had some problems with it. The hunters were unable to identify some of the dead specimens because they identified the birds by their unique calls and their role in the jungle, not by a carcass. The dilemma with these two methods was these weren't the methods the New Guinea people used to identify the birds in everyday life. The third case, studying the live birds in the jungle, ended up being the most reliable method used. Diamond's results from this case were very similar with other biologists' results that have tested in New Guinea as well.

The main dilemma of the whole experiment was that if the scientist didn't seem well informed about the birds, the informants will not think you can understand their complex descriptions that they know. If so, they will only tell you what they think you are capable of understanding, which brings up the lesson the ethnobiologist dilemma has for the readers; for the people who understand more about the subject they are inquiring about the more they information they will be given.

PARAPHRASE (FROM –JARED DIAMOND, "THE ETHNOBIOLOGIST'S DILEMMA," (198)

Diamond reexamines the pictures from the perspective of the islanders, and realizes that on paper was a simple black-and-white drawing. For him he was used to taking something so simple as that drawing and make it into a three-dimensional life size sketch, but the islanders were not accustomed to do that. For them they saw what was really there, a small sketch of a bird that looks like a willie wagtail rather than a frigatebird.

Works cited

Diamond, Jared. "The Ethnoliogist's Dilemma." *First Year Writing in the Disciplines.* Boston: Pearson, 2012. 196–201. Print.

IDENTIFYING RHETORICAL CHOICES

Rollin Willis

Jared Diamond writes the article "The Ethnobiologist's Dilemma," revealing an overlooked perspective to his audience. That is, it takes a good amount of knowledge on a subject to be given more knowledge on that subject from an expert. Diamond says, "To them that already understand, more knowledge will be freely given. To the rest of us dolts, it's a struggle" (201). In this article Diamond is prescribing a way to avoid frustration when talking with experts. He suggests that prior to bringing a question to a professional, the novice should learn about the subject. Diamond's goal is to point this abstract perspective out to his audience.

Diamond published his article in the scholarly magazine Natural History. This magazine's subscription often goes along with museum memberships, giving Diamond access to a varied audience composed of scientists as well as the educated lay ("Natural History Magazine"). It is evident that this article is not explicitly targeting scientists, because not all museum members will be scientists, also because the article makes use of everyday language. It is clear Diamond writes with the intent to cater to an audience of those who are simply interested in the subject of ethnobiology, those who enjoy museums, and those who do academic work.

RHETORICAL CHOICES

1. Diamond opens and closes the article "The Ethnobiologist's Dilemma" with an anecdote. Diamond begins the article with a story of an interaction he had with a car mechanic. Where the mechanic told Diamond, ". . . forget it, you don't need to understand it. All you have to know is I fixed it and you owe me $203.67 and you can drive again" (196). Then at the end of the article Diamond comes back to this opening story, saying, "The bad service that I continue to get is my own fault for not practicing what I preach to ethnobiologists: I never took the trouble to study a VW manual" (201). The use of this anecdote helps the audience connect Diamond's experiences in New Guinea to experiences in their own lives; it is an example of an occurrence that is known to Diamond's whole audience. This rhetorical device causes the audience to attribute more credit to what Diamond says.

2. When Diamond uses the example of his dealings with car mechanics he is self-deprecating. Describing the situation in a humorous and humble way, Diamond says, "My car mechanic must have seen my eyes glaze over, just as I had seen my physiology students' eyes glaze over when I tried to explain osmotic diuresis to them in my lecture that same morning last month . . . At least I feel OK in my own areas of scientific expertise" (196). Opening the article with a self-deprecating tone is extremely important for capturing the audience. Any experts reading this article would quickly stop reading if they felt Diamond was pushing a view on them, the learned reader is not interested in being told how to think. Writing with humility also helps Diamond to draw in the educated lay, who potentially could feel intimidated

by an academic writer's advanced knowledge. Diamond's self-deprecation does well to make the reader feel comfortable. The example also gives Diamond credit as he has been on both sides of the dilemma, as a professor and a student. Helping the audience relate to Diamond, in turn giving them more reason to listen.

3. In the main body of the article Diamond uses an extended metaphor to relate what he has learned from dealing with New Guinean tribesmen to everyday life. Diamond writes about his own struggles as an ethnobiologist in New Guinea, as well as the struggles of other scientists attempting the tap into tribal knowledge. In one example Diamond writes about an ethnobiologist moving out of his area of expertise of animals to ask tribesmen about rocks. This ethnobiologist had little luck being told by the tribesmen, "When you asked us about birds and plants, we saw that you knew a lot about them, and that you could understand what we told you. When you began asking us about rocks, it was obvious you didn't know anything about them. Why should we waste our time telling you something you couldn't possibly understand?" (Diamond 201). This is an extended metaphor because Diamond continually circles back to these experiences with the tribesmen in order to illustrate the larger issue of it takes knowledge to be given knowledge. This is an example that Diamond wants his audience to apply to their lives. Demonstrating why it is when his readers ask a person of a particular expertise a question on a subject that they themselves are uneducated in, they receive a simple response. Through the use of this metaphor throughout the article the audience is persuaded by Diamond.

4. Diamond's word choice shows his respect for people of different areas of skill. For example Diamond refers to the New Guinean tribesmen as "experts" (198). Even going as far to describe them as ". . . walking encyclopedias of facts about locally occurring species" (Diamond 196). This is an interesting perspective of the tribesmen that often goes unrealized, tribal peoples are often seen as unskilled due to the lack of their modern knowledge. Diamond does not see them in this way. Further pointing out that often people of a particular expertise are not given proper credit for their immense amount of knowledge, due to the subject matter of that knowledge https://raiderwriter.engl.ttu.edu/writingelements/elementread.asp?keyword =fragment. This addresses a common error that says there is no need to come to a laborer with knowledge in order to converse. Diamond shows his audience his appreciation and respect for those with knowledge by his word choice. This appeals to all of Diamonds readers, demonstrating to them that he is of good character, that he does not judge a book by its cover. Diamond's goal is to influence his audience to respect those that often are not attributed to possess great knowledge.

5. In the article Diamond keeps his audience's attention through the use of vivid imagery. Diamond uses incredible imagery when describing why the tribesmen do not equate dead birds to live birds, "Gone were the bugling calls, the shaking of the vine tangles, the excitement as the jungle came alive and as dozens of other birds swept after the pitohuis" (199). This description of living birds clearly shows the difference between how living and dead birds are seen by the tribesmen, allowing the reader who has never seen birds alive in the jungle to understand the difference. Imagery keeps Diamond's whole audience drawn to the progression of the article.

To scientist used to reading plain matter of fact scientific articles, "The Ethnobiologist's Dilemma" offers colorful descriptions that make the article a pleasurable read. The educated lay will also be enticed by Diamond's powerful descriptions of his experiences in New Guinea. Diamond's imagery keeps his readers focused on his article. Persuading the readers to continue deeper into the article, all the time exposing themselves to Diamond's views.

IDENTIFYING RHETORICAL CHOICES

Marcus Anders

"The Ethnobiologist's Dilemma" by Jared Diamond is intended for current ethnobiologist and those interested in his field of work. He's also addressing those currently studying to be enthnobiologist. Diamond speaks in an academic tone, uses highly descriptive diction, historical allusions, and compares himself to much notable ethnobiologists in several instances to establish credibility. Thru credibility ethos is incorporated in the essay and his rhetorical choices strengthen Diamond's purpose. His purpose is to show current and aspiring ethnobiologist that humans develop different ways of communicating based on their culture and environment. He also shows that to truly learn from an informant and broaden your knowledge, you must first acquire the necessary knowledge in order to comprehend your informant's information. (196–201)

RHETORICAL CHOICES:

1. Imagery

   Diamond uses imagery when he explains the obvious differences of the frigate and wagtail birds, "Frigatebirds are huge seabirds . . . black and white" to show how the informants easily got them confused because of their different communications system. This really gives the reader a good example of how people of different cultures and environments perceive things differently. (198)

2. Allusion

   Diamond alludes to Ralph Bulmer's time classifying rocks in Kalam and his heated conversation with the Kalam. Because he obviously knew nothing about the Kalams' ways of rock classification, the Kalam could not explain to Bulmer their ways of classification. Diamond shares this instance to strengthen his idea for his audience that "to them that already understand, more knowledge will be freely given. To the rest of us dolts, it's a struggle". (201)

3. Credibility through Expert Comparisons

   Diamond says "This method has proved . . . Whitney biologists agreed closely". When he says this, Diamond is establishing his credibility as an ethnobiologist by telling the audience how the method of bird classification he used in New Guinea got him results that closely agreed with the experts at Whitney South Seas. This shows that he's an expert and a reliable source, and through this fact the audience will support him more and trust what he has to say. (199)

4. Analogy

Diamond uses an analogy when he compares the Ralph Bulmer incident to his time in the VW car repair shop to explain to the audience the dilemma in more general and understandable terms. "For Instance, the starter . . . I could not understand their explanation." If Diamond would have known more about his vehicle, he could probably keep it out of the repair shop. This analogy really brings out the purpose to his audience. (201)

5. Maxim

Diamond uses maxim when he states "To them that already understand, more knowledge will be freely given. To the rest of us dolts, it's a struggle". He says this in an attempt to clarify his purpose to his audience and persuade them with a strong statement. (201)

Works Cited

Diamond, Jared. "The Ethnobiologist's Dilemma." *First Year Writing, Writing: In the Disciplines.* 6 ed. Boston: Pearson, 196–201. Print.

Constructing Thesis Statements for the Rhetorical Analysis

Houston Quintanilla

"THE ETHNOBIOLOGIST'S DILEMMA" –EXPLANATION & THESIS

1. In "The Ethnobiologist's Dilemma," Jared Diamond writes this article for readers of Natural History who have a particular interest in ethnobiology, however the audience is not exclusive to just professional scientists because in the article Diamond discusses in great detail what he did while in New Guinea. Jared Diamond's purpose was to emphasize the need that the average person must have prior knowledge of a subject in order to learn from an expert. Diamond wants his audience to realize that before learning from a professional they must gain knowledge over the subject.

2. In "The Ethnobiologist's Dilemma," Jared Diamond uses analogies, metaphors, and illustration in order for his readers to understand they must have prior knowledge of a subject in order to learn from a professional.

"POLITICS AND THE ENGLISH LANGUAGE"– EXPLANATION & THESIS

1. George Orwell directed his article toward the audience of people interested in books at the end of World War II, such as established writers, up & coming writers, and the literary community of Great Britain at the time. Orwell wanted his audience to realize the relationship between bad writing and bad politics. George Orwell made his readers aware of how authors at the time were using their writing to twist the truth of what was really happening. Authors consistently turned the truth in their writing at the end of World War II because patriotism was widely popular in the allied countries and George Orwell strongly disliked how authors did this.

2. George Orwell uses the rhetorical choices formal language, rhetorical questioning, and complex diction in his article, "Politics and the English Language," to show his audience the relationship between bad writing and bad politics so the readers realize how authors of the time period used their writing to twist the truth.

"A HOMEMADE EDUCATION" –EXPLANATION & THESIS

1. The audience of "A Homemade Education," was minorities, particularly African Americans but also anyone not white. Malcolm X believed history had been "whitened" throughout the years and people who had not been properly educated actually thought history was accurate. X wrote this article because he wanted his audience to reclaim their lost history for themselves. I believe Malcolm X also wrote this article for white people involved in education, politics, or the civil rights movement so they could help to "unbleach" history and portray the truth by taking history out of the European bias.

2. Malcolm X uses statistics, hyperbole, and euphemism in his article, "A Homemade Education," to unbleach history and encourage non-white minorities to reclaim lost history for themselves.

Works Cited

Diamond, Jared. "The Ethnobiologist's Dilemma." *First-Year Writing: Writing In the Disciplines*. 6 ed. Boston, MA: Pearson, 196–201. Print.

"Natural History Magazine." Natural History Magazine. N.p., 2013. Web. 15 Feb. 2013.

Orwell, George. "Politics and the English Language." *First-Year Writing: Writing In the Disciplines*. 6 ed. Boston, MA: Pearson, 204–214. Print.

"Portfolio at NYU." Portfolio at NYU. N.p., n.d. Web. 22 Feb. 2013.

X, Malcolm. "A Homemade Education." *First-Year Writing: Writing In the Disciplines*. 6 ed. Boston, MA: Pearson, 226–233. Print.

Constructing Thesis Statements for the Rhetorical Analysis

Andrew Scibek

MALCOLM X, "A HOMEMADE EDUCATION"

X's intended audience for his piece was that of young minorities alive during the civil rights movement. X wrote this essay to show how his determination in educating himself allowed him to become a crucial component in the civil rights movement. X also explains in his essay how he was able to better understand the ways in which the white people of his time displayed ignorance towards the non-white people through the accumulation of knowledge. This ties into the theme of ignorance being the enemy.

Malcolm X's "A Homemade Education" employs personal anecdotes, colloquial diction, and careful sentence structure to teach the young minorities of the civil rights movement the significance of an education in order to evade the burden of ignorance.

DIAMOND, "THE ETHNOBIOLOGIST'S DILEMMA"

Jared Diamond's purpose behind his article is to show the many problems that confront ethnobiologists in their field of study. He also highlights how these problems parallel challenges faced in everyday life. Another point Diamond makes in his paper is that sometimes individuals need to educate themselves prior to asking a superior for assistance. Diamond's intended audience is comprised of those who work in the field of ethnobiology and those who are also interested in sciences as a whole.

In "The Ethnobiologist's Dilemma", Jared Diamond uses evidence from sources and personal anecdotes to persuade those interested in the field of ethnobiology and sciences as a whole to stress the importance of putting forth the required effort needed to comprehend what you're studying before consulting an expert.

ORWELL, "POLITICS AND THE ENGLISH LANGUAGE"

Orwell's piece appeals to modern language writers who have a general interest in political rhetoric. The purpose behind Orwell's piece is to highlight the degradation of the English language. He explains that the quality of the English language is lowering with time due to the decreasing ideals with which the language is maintained. Orwell also incorporates the theme of how political writing has suffered due to the decay of the English language. He argues that political speeches are meant to stir emotions, but do not sufficiently explain the speaker's point.

George Orwell uses direct quotes, formal diction, and political jargon in his essay "Politics and the English Language" in order to explain to modern language writers the ways in which the English language has decayed and how it has affected political rhetoric.

Works Cited

Diamond, Jared. "The Ethnobiologist's Dilemma." *First-Year Writing: Writing In the Disciplines.* 6 ed. Boston, MA: Pearson, 196–201. Print.

Orwell, George. "Politics and the English Language." *First-Year Writing: Writing In the Disciplines.* 6 ed. Boston, MA: Pearson, 204–214. Print.

X, Malcolm. "A Homemade Education." *First-Year Writing: Writing In the Disciplines.* 6 ed. Boston, MA: Pearson, 226–233. Print.

EVALUATING AND INTEGRATING QUOTATIONS

Chase Barnes

Diamond uses metaphors, professional and personable tones, and multiple anecdotes to urge the reader to research a subject before approaching an expert for knowledge about that subject.

FIRST QUOTATION:

> The first example I will be using is Diamond's extended metaphor. The metaphor is the majority of the article.

I am going to summarize the extended metaphor that Diamond uses to show how important it is to know almost as much as an expert when talking to the expert on a subject. I am summarizing this metaphor because the passage is too long to quote, but I still want to retain the original meaning. Diamond uses the metaphor of not getting help from a mechanic when he doesn't understand why his car breaks down. He compares this to Bulmer not receiving information from tribesmen when he doesn't know anything about rocks. This goes back to my point of needing to know almost as much as an expert does on a subject before the expert will give out his information. This summary will be the starting paragraph of my essay after my introduction. This will be my strongest point showing Diamond's purpose, so I chose to put it first.

SECOND QUOTATION:

> "When you began asking us about rocks, it was obvious you didn't know anything about them. Why should we waste our time telling you something you couldn't possibly understand" (Diamond 201).

This quote will be in the first body paragraph but it will follow the extended metaphor. This quote further proves the extended metaphor as well as Diamond's purpose, so putting this quote second will add more support to my essay. The quote is from a New Guinea tribes men, when he tells Ralph Bulmer why they gave him no information about rocks. Bulmer didn't have any knowledge on rocks so he received no new knowledge from the tribe's people. I'm going to use this as a quote because Diamond flat out states his purpose.

THIRD QUOTATION:

"It's humiliating to feel like an ignoramus, as I do about cars" (Diamond 196).

This quote will go be the first piece of supporting evidence for second body paragraph. The second paragraph will talk about personable and professional tones, and this quote shows something that most people can relate to. The personable tone that Diamond takes on at the beginning of the article helps laymen in the audience identify with his purpose. I will quote this sentence because the tone that Diamond uses is the rhetorical choice that I will be discussing. If I were to use a summary or a paraphrase the tone that Diamond uses would be lost.

FOURTH QUOTATION:

"In my experience, names elicited by specimens agree better with names elicited by live birds than do names elicited by pictures. Nevertheless, problems of discrepancies and inabilities to name some locally common species still occur" (Diamond 198).

This quote will also be in my second body paragraph but it will come after the quote about the personable tone. I am using this quote second because Diamond starts out with the personable tone and switches to a professional tone. I chose to use this quote because it appeals to the academics and scientists in the audience by using more technical sounding words. I will quote this line as well because the tone that Diamond uses is the most important aspect of the sentence. It is a longer sentence but that aspect only helps to make it a more professional sounding sentence.

FIFTH QUOTATION:

"I eventually realized that the ethnobiologist's dilemma illustrates the frustrations that all of us face in everyday life . . ." (Diamond 196).

This last quote will go in the last body paragraph of my analysis. I chose to use this as the last choice because I believe it is the weakest of three choices. Diamond uses this line and other instances of first person point of view to help the readers relate to his purpose. The first person point of view is more intended for the laymen in the audience, because they are used to reading novels in this point of view, while the scientists are more used to reading academic essays which are typically not in first person. I am going to quote this line because the specific diction, such as "I" and "us" dictates the point of view.

Works Cited

Diamond, Jared. "The Ethnobiologist's Dilemma." *First Year Writing: Writing in the Disciplines*. Boston: Pearson, 2012. 196–201 Print.

EVALUATING AND INTEGRATING QUOTATIONS

Taylor Martin

In Jared Diamond's article "The Ethnobiologist's Dilemma," the use of anecdotes, metaphors, and diction are used to argue the importance of having knowledge of a subject before trying to get information from an expert and hope to be able to understand what they tell you.

1. "I described how many New Guinea tribesmen are walking encyclopedias of facts about locally occurring species" (Diamond pg. 196).

   This quotation supports my claim that Diamond uses metaphors (paragraph 3) to promote is ideal of having knowledge in a subject before asking an expert for information. This specific quote I will use to show that Diamond is trying to speak to the environmental scientists because they would be able to relate to the use of the tribesmen as encyclopedias and will be able to understand why such an idea would be necessary with that situation. This quote I will not be paraphrasing due to the content already being already easy to understand.

2. "My car mechanic must have seen my eyes glaze over, just as I had seen my physiology students' eyes glaze over when I tried to explain osmotic diuresis to them in my lecture . . ." (Diamond pg. 196).

   This quotation will be used to support the claim that Diamond uses anecdotes (paragraph 2) to support his ideal. This quote will be used to show that Diamond is also reaching out to the educated laypeople along with the scientists because he is taking a situation that most people will experience in their life and show the merits of knowing a little about the subject being discussed before trying to understand what the expert is saying. I will not be paraphrasing this quote due to it being able to support my point without being edited.

3. "I expected my guides to apply the name belama, which they had used for the frigatebirds we saw soaring that day" (Diamond pg. 198).

   This quotation I will use to prove that the diction (paragraph 4) used by Diamond allows him to reach the educated laypeople who also read Natural History instead of just the environmental scientists. This quote shows this because in it he uses jargon that would only be known by people who had studied the frigatebird with the New Guinea tribesmen. But instead of just leaving the sentence with the jargon he also goes further to explain what the word meant so that the other readers could understand what he is getting at and help him promote the need become educated in subjects you will be working with experts on. Because of the way the quote is formatted and since it has jargon in it I will not paraphrase it.

4. "After Feld had been attempting for months to decipher Kaluli bird names, Jubi suddenly lost his patience and blurted out, 'Listen—to you they are birds, to me they are voices in the forest'"(Diamond pg. 199).

I will use this quotation to support that Diamond used anecdotes (paragraph 2) to promote and also show how he came about his idea to become knowledgeable in a subject before asking an expert. This quote will work perfectly for that because it explains why previous methods were flawed and also showed that to learn from the tribesmen you have to see the animals from their point of view. This quote will also work to show him reaching out to the educated laypeople because when they try and pry information they know nothing about in everyday life the expert usually also get annoyed and by showing his story and how to overcome this obstacle he hopes he can show people that they also must do the same as the scientists.

5. "Foré tribesman wouldn't understand me if I asked about the 'blue bird of paradise,' but they talked for hours when I asked about the kongonámu, their Foré name for this species" (Diamond pg. 197).

I will use this quotation in paragraph 2 to support the claim that Diamond used anecdotes to support his claim of becoming knowledgeable in a subject before talking to an expert in that field. This quote will work to support this claim because with Foré's account without knowing the name of the bird in question from the native's perspective he would be unable to gain the information he needed. This would appeal to the scientists because they would understand the need what has occurred and how they should follow in example. This would also appeal to the educated laypeople because with the use of explaining what the words he was using being defined as a name for the bird the laypeople would understand just how important it was for the scientist to know that name and be able to understand how that could relate to their lives.

Works Cited

Diamond, Jared. "The Ethnobiologist's Dilemma." *First Year Writing: Writing in the Disciplines.* Boston: Pearson, 2012. 196–201 Print

RHETORICAL ANALYSIS

Rollin Willis DRAFT 1.2

Frequently, novices who are looking for in-depth answers to their questions go to experts for solutions, only to find that their own intellectual limitations are standing between themselves and their learning. Jared Diamond realizes that the novice is not turned away because of their question, but because of a lack of knowledge on the subject in question. Diamond, an ethnobiologist, came across this problem while working with tribesmen in New Guinea to study the names of native birds, where this seemingly trivial task of eliciting local bird names from tribesmen was fraught with unforeseen problems. Diamond is not the only scientist to have come across the issue of acquiring knowledge from tribesmen; others have struggled as well to find the correct method to approach these experts. Diamond addresses the problem in an essay in a 1989 issue of Natural History, "The Ethnobiologist's Dilemma," where he brings his realization to an audience of scientists and science enthusiasts. In this article Diamond presents an entirely new perspective on how to correctly approach an expert with a question. Diamond uses an anecdote that begins and ends the text, a humorous and self-deprecating tone, and unconventional identification of natives as experts to subtly suggest that in order to effectively gain knowledge from an expert, one must first learn enough about the subject to communicate effectively. Diamond successfully persuades scientists and those interested in science to learn as much as possible about a topic before bringing their questions to a professional.

Diamond uses an anecdote that bookends his article to both cite the problem he is addressing as well as to compare the tribesmen to the types of experts the reader will more likely encounter. The first anecdote the author uses is an account of an interaction he had with a car mechanic, upon which the mechanic told Diamond, ". . . forget it, you don't need to understand it. All you have to know is I fixed it and you owe me $203.67 and you can drive again" (196). This anecdote is an example of the interaction Diamond wants to fix and that his audience of scientists and educated laypeople can relate to. By using this anecdote at the beginning of the article, the reader is reminded of how annoying this type of interaction is, which grabs their attention. Now the reader has an interest in what the author has to say. This is not the only time an anecdote aids the article. At the end of the article, Diamond comes back to this opening story, saying, "The bad service that I continue to get is my own fault for not practicing what I preach to ethnobiologists: I never took the trouble to study a VW manual" (201). The use of this anecdote again helps the audience connect Diamond's experiences in New Guinea to experiences in their own lives; it is also an example of an occurrence that is known to Diamond's whole audience, both scientists and educated laypeople. This rhetorical device causes the audience to realize the argument Diamond is suggesting is relevant to their lives, leading them to continue reading and listen to what Diamond has to say.

The anecdote aids the article in another way by creating a humorous, self-deprecating tone, which is a wise strategy because it allows both portions of his audience to feel more comfortable listening to his advice on dealing with experts. As a well-known author, scientists, and expert, Diamond could have easily opened with an anecdote that placed him as the expert, but by using the example with the mechanic, Diamond's tone is less didactic and more humorous and accessible, which works in the essay's favor. The example involving the mechanic is used by Diamond to create the desired tone. Diamond says, "My car mechanic must have seen my eyes glaze over, just as I had seen my physiology students' eyes glaze over when I tried to explain osmotic diuresis to them in my lecture that same morning last month . . . At least I feel OK in my own areas of scientific expertise" (196). The quote creates a self-deprecating tone because the author humbles himself by describing his struggles sharing his own expertise. This tone is necessary because in general, people are not receptive to being told what to do, requiring gentle counsel into new ideas. This is especially the case for Diamond's audience of scientists who are accomplished experts. Diamond's self-deprecating tone gives the scientists in the audience a feeling that they are not being told to change their ways, but rather, that they are in control of whether they follow the article's advice or not. In turn, this increases the likelihood that the scientists will listen to what Diamond is saying. Diamond's tone does far more than appeal exclusively to scientists; it also appeals to educated laypeople. These educated laypeople would feel intimidated by an academic writer's advanced knowledge, possibly causing them to stop reading. By giving this example at the beginning of the article, the author humbles himself before his audience, producing the desired effect of a sense of learning between the audience and author. However, the tone through the rest of the article is not self-deprecating. After the author makes the audience feel comfortable, he then needs to appear confident to truly gain the trust of his audience. Through the rest of the essay, Diamond presents himself as an expert in his field capable of altering established methodology with regards to acquiring knowledge from experts. Diamond's purpose is to have his audience apply his message to their own lives. The only way this is possible is if the audience reads the article, making it of the utmost importance that the audience feels comfortable while reading. Therefore, the author's use of a self-deprecating tone in the beginning of the article is effective. Now that the author has made the audience feel comfortable, he can move on to strengthening his argument.

Diamond uses unconventional word choice when describing the tribesmen he encountered in New Guinea to both strengthen his article's purpose and convey his message to his audience. Diamond's word choice shows his respect for people of different areas of skill. For example, Diamond refers to the New Guinean tribesmen as "experts" (198), even going as far to describe them as ". . . walking encyclopedias of facts about locally occurring species" (196). This is an interesting perspective of the tribesmen that often goes unrealized. Tribal peoples are often seen as unskilled due to the lack of their modern knowledge. Diamond does not see them in this way, which is proven by his use of the term "'primitive'" in quotes (196). He is showing just how incorrect it is to think there is nothing to learn from these individuals. Further, pointing out that often people of a particular expertise are not given proper credit for their immense amount of knowledge due to the subject matter of that knowledge. Diamond wants his audience to realize this critical error in thinking. This use of quotations addresses a common assumption that says there is no need to come to a laborer with knowledge in order to converse. This word choice appeals to all of Diamond's readers, demonstrating to them that he is of good character, and he does not judge a book by its cover. Diamond's goal is to influence his audience to respect those that often are not attributed to possess great knowledge, in addition to those who normally are seen as possessing great knowledge, to promote a better method of receiving knowledge from an expert.

When traveling to New Guinea, Diamond ran into the ethnobiologist's dilemma, which he sees as an example of a problem common in daily life. The effect of the article, "The Ethnobiologist's Dilemma," is to persuade its audience to bring their questions to experts only after having learned extensively about the topic in question, respecting all experts. Diamond successfully reaches his intended audience, scientists and educated laypeople, with a message that is relevant to their lives. Diamond achieves this through a combined use of a self-deprecating tone, informal word choice, and anecdotes. By following Diamond's advice, the novice will find it easier to obtain knowledge from experts.

Works Cited

Diamond, Jared. "The Ethnobiologist's Dilemma." *First-Year Writing: Writing In the Disciplines.* 6 ed. Boston, MA: Pearson, 196–201. Print.

DRAFT 1.2

Frequently, novices who are looking for in-depth answers to their questions go to experts for solutions, only to find that their own limited familiarity is standing between themselves and their learning. Jared Diamond realizes that the novice is not turned away because of their question, but because of a lack of knowledge on the subject in question. Diamond, an ethnobiologist, came across this problem while working with tribesmen in New Guinea to study the names of native birds, where this seemingly trivial task of eliciting local bird names from tribesmen was fraught with unforeseen problems. Diamond is not the only scientist to have come across the issue of acquiring knowledge from tribesmen; others have struggled as well to find the correct method to approach these experts. Diamond addresses the problem in his essay "The Ethnobiologist's Dilemma," in a 1989 issue of Natural History, where he brings his realization to an audience of scientists and science enthusiasts. In this article, Diamond presents an entirely new perspective on how to correctly approach an expert with a question. Diamond uses an anecdote that begins and ends the text, a tone that shifts between self-deprecating humor and knowledgeable confidence, and unconventional word choice when identifying natives as experts to subtly suggest that in order to effectively gain knowledge from an expert, one must first learn enough about the subject to communicate effectively. Diamond successfully persuades scientists and those interested in science to learn as much as possible about a topic before bringing their questions to a professional.

Diamond uses an anecdote that bookends his article to both cite the problem he is addressing as well as to compare the tribesmen to the types of experts the reader will more likely encounter. The first anecdote the author uses is an account of an interaction he had with a car mechanic, upon which the mechanic told Diamond, ". . . forget it, you don't need to understand it. All you have to know is I fixed it and you owe me $203.67 and you can drive again" (196). His audience of scientists and educated laypeople can relate to this anecdote because they are likely to have come across a situation similar to Diamond's in which they are the novice. Using this anecdote at the beginning of the article helps Diamond grab the readers' attention by reminding them how frustrating this type of interaction is. This is not the only time an anecdote aids the article. At the end of the article, Diamond comes back to this opening story, saying, "The bad service that I continue to get is my own fault for not practicing what I preach to ethnobiologists: I never took the trouble to study a VW manual" (201). The use of this anecdote again helps the audience connect Diamond's experiences in New Guinea to experiences in their own lives; it is also an example of an occurrence that is known to Diamond's whole audience, both scientists and educated laypeople. This rhetorical device helps the audience realize the argument Diamond is suggesting is relevant to their lives, leading them to continue reading and listen to what Diamond has to say.

The anecdote aids the article in another way by creating a humorous, self-deprecating tone, which is a wise strategy because it allows both portions of his audience to feel more comfortable listening to his advice on dealing with experts. As a well-known author, scientist, and expert, Diamond could have easily opened with an anecdote that placed him as the expert, but by using the example with the mechanic, Diamond's tone is less didactic and more humorous and accessible, which works in the essay's favor. The example involving the mechanic is used by Diamond to create the desired tone, such as when Diamond says,

"My car mechanic must have seen my eyes glaze over, just as I had seen my physiology students' eyes glaze over when I tried to explain osmotic diuresis to them in my lecture that same morning last month . . . At least I feel OK in my own areas of scientific expertise" (196). The quote creates a humorous self-deprecating tone because the author humbles himself by describing his struggles sharing his own expertise. This tone is necessary because in general, people are not receptive to being told what to do, requiring gentle counsel into new ideas. This is especially the case for Diamond's audience of scientists who are accomplished experts. Diamond's self-deprecating tone gives the scientists in the audience a feeling that they are not being told to change their ways, but rather, that they are in control of whether they follow the article's advice or not. In turn, this increases the likelihood that the scientists will listen to what Diamond is saying. Diamond's tone does far more than appeal exclusively to scientists; it also appeals to educated laypeople. These educated laypeople would feel intimidated by an academic writer's advanced knowledge, possibly causing them to stop reading. By giving this example at the beginning of the article, the author humbles himself before his audience, producing the desired effect of a sense of learning between the audience and author. However, the tone through the rest of the body of the essay is not self-deprecating.

Following the first anecdote, Diamond quickly shifts to a scholarly and more academic tone. After the author makes the audience feel comfortable, he then needs to appear confident to truly gain the trust of his audience. To establish credibility Diamond switches to a more scholarly tone which he carries through the body of the essay. Diamond presents himself as an expert in his field capable of altering established methodology with regards to acquiring knowledge from experts. For example, Diamond says, "In my experience, names elicited by specimens agree better with names elicited by live birds than do names elicited by pictures" (198). After the author has made the audience feel comfortable with the humorous tone, he can move on to strengthening his argument with a scholarly tone that highlights his experience and knowledge. These tones work together to help Diamond achieve a larger desired effect of appealing to the audience in a credible manner. This helps the audience recognize that Diamond has experience on both sides of the ethnobiologist's dilemma, both as an expert and a novice. Diamond's shifts in tone lead the audience to trust his knowledge on the issue.

Diamond uses unconventional word choice when describing the tribesmen he encountered in New Guinea to both strengthen his article's purpose and convey his message to his audience. Diamond's word choice shows his respect for people of different areas of skill. For example, Diamond refers to the New Guinean tribesmen as "experts" (198), even going as far to describe them as " . . . walking encyclopedias of facts about locally occurring species" (196). This is an interesting perspective of the tribesmen that often goes unrealized by modern societies. Tribal peoples are often seen as unskilled due to the lack of their modern knowledge. Diamond does not see them in this way, which is proven when he says "Their knowledge of the behavior and life history of many species far exceeds what Western scientists know. The same is true of some other 'primitive' peoples . . ." (196). The use of the word "primitive" in quotes highlights Diamond's view that the tribesmen are very advanced. He is showing just how incorrect it is to think there is nothing to learn from these individuals. Further, Diamond's language points out how often people of a particular expertise are not given proper credit for their immense amount of knowledge due to the subject matter of that knowledge. Diamond wants his audience to realize this critical error in thinking. This use of quotations addresses a common assumption that says there is no need to come to this situation with knowledge in order to converse. This word choice appeals to all of Diamond's readers, demonstrating to them that he is of good character, and he does not judge a book by its cover. Diamond's goal is to influence his audience to respect those that often are not attributed to possess great knowledge, in addition to those who normally are seen as possessing great knowledge, to promote a better method of receiving knowledge from an expert.

There is a common problem prevalent in daily life; it arises when a novice who is uneducated on a subject goes to an expert for advice only for the novice to be turned away. Diamond called this issue the ethnobiologist's dilemma after running into the same problem in New Guinea. The effect of the article, "The Ethnobiologist's Dilemma," is to persuade its audience to bring their questions to experts only after having learned extensively about the topic in question. It is important to realize that all experts require respect no matter their field of expertise. Diamond successfully reaches his intended audience, scientists and educated laypeople, with a message that is relevant to their lives. Diamond achieves this through a combined use of a tone that shifts between self-deprecating humor and knowledgeable confidence, unconventional word choice, and the use of anecdotes at the beginning and end of his article. By following Diamond's advice, the novice will find it easier to obtain knowledge from experts, instead of struggling to learn from experts.

Works Cited

Diamond, Jared. "The Ethnobiologist's Dilemma." *First-Year Writing: Writing In the Disciplines.* 6 ed. Boston, MA: Pearson, 196–201. Print.

Rhetorical Analysis

Chase Barnes   Draft 1.2

In "The Ethnobiologist's Dilemma," by Jared Diamond, he urges the reader to make a concerted effort at acquiring a thorough knowledge on a subject before trying to understand an expert's point of view on that subject. In the essay, Diamond suggests there is a communication barrier between experts with a lot of knowledge and people who have little knowledge on a subject. This article, published in Natural History magazine in 1989, is intended for "an educated, professional readership of scholars and scientists, but the engrossing, easy-to-understand stories and brilliant photography in Natural History hold appeal for anyone interested in the biological and natural sciences" (NaturalHistory.com). This magazine appeals to scientists in all fields, but also other academics and even people who are interested in the natural sciences or history unprofessionally. Diamond uses an anecdote that bookends the article, an extended metaphor, and a mix of personable and professional tones to urge the reader to research a subject before approaching an expert.

Diamond uses an anecdote that bookends, or begins and ends, the text in his article in order to illustrate his purpose that people need to educate themselves on a subject before talking to an expert. He begins by describing an anecdote with his mechanic "The reason I said your VW didn't start was its solenoid was no good. Like I said what the solenoid does is . . . OK, forget it, you don't need to understand it". The anecdote at the beginning of the story sets a humorous instead of didactic tone that is seen throughout the article. The slightly humorous and self deprecating tone resonates with the laymen in the audience because the article is now an easier read than a scientific journal. The tone also puts the audience in Diamond's shoes to see the purpose form his point of view. Diamond says he ". . . never took the trouble to study a VW manual", which is why he continues to not get any information from the mechanics about why his car continually breaks down (Diamond 201). When Diamond is in New Guinea, he realizes that the tribes will not give their information ". . . if they sense that you yourself don't know much about the subject" (Diamond 200). The organization Diamond uses, an anecdote at the beginning and referring back to that anecdote in his conclusion, creates a sense of completeness as Diamond wraps up his article. Using these anecdotes allows the non-academics in the audience to relate to Diamond's purpose easily by showing that a highly educated individual like himself has gone through these everyday struggles that continue to plague non experts. The scientists and professors in the audience are able to relate to another anecdote that Diamond recounts when he says ". . . just as I had seen my physiology students' eyes glaze over when I tried to explain osmotic dieresis to them. . ." (196). Not only does Diamond relate his purpose back in a way that the laymen will understand, but he also gives an anecdote that most scientists and professors have also been through.

Diamond's use of an extended metaphor illustrates a comparison between "the ethnobiologist's dilemma . . . and modern life" (Diamond 201). Diamond recalls three different methods of obtaining names of birds in New Guinea, and their effectiveness. The first method that Diamond used was to show the natives pictures of the local birds in books. Diamond soon realized that this method was ineffective as the tribesmen could not relate the small picture of the bird in the book, to the actual bird in real life when Diamond says ". . . the islanders weren't used to this leap of imagination. Instead, they saw what was really there . . ." (198). This experience with the first naming method is particularly effective at relating the professors and other experts to Diamond's purpose. Experts on any subject often have trouble explaining their knowledge to non-experts, such as the Diamond's encounter with his mechanic. Using this extended metaphor section Diamond does not only urge the non-experts to have knowledge on a subject, but also urges the experts in the audience to be patient and try different learning styles with the laymen. Diamond recounts a second method that is often used in obtaining the names of birds: that is to use dead specimens. Diamond soon realized that this method has its drawbacks as well. When he became frustrated that a native was not able to name a particular dead bird correctly, that tribesmen shouted "listen-to you they are birds, to me they are voices in the forest" (Diamond 199). The second method is one that most experts have a personal connection with. An expert or professional has a very deep connection with their work, and what may seem like just a solenoid or bird to a layman, is so much more to the mechanic or tribesmen who interacts with them daily. Diamond shows that laymen need to understand how an expert views something by gaining knowledge on that subject. The last method that Diamond describes is the most effective, not only for him in the jungles of New Guinea, but anyone looking to gain an extensive knowledge on a subject, this last method is to follow the expert and learn in their environment. For Diamond this was following the hunters through the jungles, for someone looking to learn more about their car this could be getting under the hood with a mechanic. This last method shows the laymen and the experts in the audience that in order to overcome the communication barrier they must both be willing to make a conscious effort to understand the other party. In the metaphor section, Diamond recounts an instance in which another ethnobiologist, Bulmer, attempted to classify rocks in addition to the local plants and animals. Bulmer encounters his own dilemma when the tribe's people refuse to give him any information about the rocks. When the tribesmen did give the information to a geologist, Bulmer was outraged. The tribesmen explained "When you began asking us about rocks, it was obvious you didn't know anything about them. Why should we waste our time telling you something you couldn't possibly understand" (Diamond 201). Diamond compares this to himself struggling in modern life, when trying to understand the reasons for his car continually breaking down, without having any knowledge of cars. Diamond realizes that "the mechanics undoubtedly saw that I am as ignorant about cars as Ralph Bulmer was about rocks, and that I could not understand their explanation" (201). The metaphor relates to the audience, not only with their fascination with science, but also their day to day lives.

The professional and personable tones that Diamond blends into his article make this easy to read for the scientists and academics in the audience as well as the scientifically interested individuals. Diamond starts his article with a personable tone when talking about his car breaking down. He gives an example that most people can identify with when he says "it's humiliating to feel like an ignoramus, as I do about cars" (Diamond 196). He then switches his tone to a more professional manner when speaking of past experiences in New Guinea. When talking about different naming methods, he says "in my experience, names elicited by specimens agree better with names elicited by live birds than do names elicited by pictures. Nevertheless, problems of discrepancies and inabilities to name some locally common species still occur" (Diamond 198). The personable tone that Diamond uses in the beginning of his article makes him more personable to all his readers, while the professional tone that he takes on in the middle of his piece appeals more to the academic minds in the audience. Diamond finishes his article by switching back to the personable tone he took on in the beginning of his article by concluding with, "To them that already understand, more knowledge will be freely given. To the rest of us dolts, it's a struggle" (Diamond 201). In addition to stating his purpose once again, the personable tone that arcs from the beginning to the end helps to bring his article to a close.

This essay encourages the audience to gain their own knowledge on a subject before making an attempt at talking to an expert. To successfully support his purpose, Diamond uses two anecdotes to show the dilemma of the communication barrier between experts and laymen. The use of the extended metaphor relates his trials and tribulations in New Guinea to the struggles of gaining knowledge that many face today. The varying tones also help relate his purpose to a broader audience, and keep the text enjoyable and intellectually stimulating at the same time. These three rhetorical choices combine in a very effective way to create an argument for people to gain their own knowledge before talking to an expert, and for the experts to be patient and understanding with the laymen.

Works Cited

Diamond, Jared. "The Ethnobiologist's Dilemma." *First Year Writing: Writing in the Disciplines*. Boston: Pearson, 2012. 196–201 Print.

Natural History Magazine. Web. 15 Feb, 2013 http://www.magazine-agent.com-sub.info/Natural-History/Welcome.

STUDENT SAMPLES 1302

SYNTHESIZING SOURCES

Sandi Collins

The articles, "Me Talk Pretty One Day", "Learning to Read and Write", and "A Homemade Education", written by David Sedaris, Frederick Douglass, and Malcolm X, respectively, discuss three distinct, influential educational journeys. Each describing differing experiences of educational enlightenment, the authors reveal their accounts of studying abroad to learn a foreign language, learning in secrecy to eventually break free from slavery, and self-educating to become a minister of freedom. Although the authors reflect on the differing effects of their educational environments, they all emphasize the cathartic realizations of their successes, as opposed to remaining ignorant in their once simpler worlds. A common theme that pervades all three sources is that of antagonistic inspirations and their ability to catapult the intimidated student to a level of unstoppable effort. With continuous examples of intense intimidation by his French college professor, such as her "attack" on another student (Sedaris 220), and her "unpredictability" lending toward the tendencies of a "wild animal" (Sedaris 221), Sedaris successfully demonstrates how his intense desire to learn overcame the seemingly unbeatable insecurity that he suffered as a result of the repetitive abuse from his college professor. His "fear and discomfort crept beyond the borders of the classroom" and resulted in his irrational belief that he could not speak French in any capacity (Sedaris 221). His epiphany surfaced at the end of the semester when he realized that he could finally understand everything his demeaning professor said to him. He describes the rewards as both "intoxicating" and "deceptive" and his understanding of the world had changed (Sedaris 222). In contrast to Sedaris' lengthy account of punishing rhetoric, Malcolm X's brief mention of the disparaging comments from his seventh-grade History teacher are just as successful in explaining his quiet resolve to advertise the truth about the black man's role throughout history. Through the painful memory that his teacher had elicited laughter from his classmates in response to a joke about Negroes, X demonstrates how that incident caused him to take "special pains" (Malcolm X 229) to hunt for literature with knowledge of black history. Like Sedaris, Frederick Douglass shares the profound effect of his mistresses' treatment of him as a slave. He discusses how her initial actions toward him showed a caring woman, one who intended to teach him, but upon the instruction of her husband, soon became an obstacle to his desire to learn. He explains how her temperament changed from "lamb-like" to "one of tiger-like fierceness". He recalls that she snatched a newspaper from him, showing him that she believed that "education and slavery were incompatible with each other"(Douglass 223). Douglass' experience demonstrates a liberating yet painful response to his heightened awareness. He describes that he sometimes felt that becoming educated was a "curse" because he had a new perspective of his "wretched condition" (Douglass 224). He was even jealous at times of his brethren for their "stupidity" and lack of ability to discern their degradation from being enslaved (Douglass 224). The author's defining moment is expressed in his description of wishing for death while simultaneously yearning to live because he had learned of the "hope of being free" (Douglass 225).

One of the common differences among these three accounts includes the roles of their peers, and the individual efforts that the authors took to incorporate their peers' contributions into their lives. While Sedaris perceived his peers as friends and fellow sufferers, and expresses camaraderie amongst them (Sedaris 222), Douglass discusses his relationships either as a sort of barter system that included an exchange of goods or "bread" (Douglass 224), or as a competition he manipulated in order to "beat" his rival (Douglass 226). Malcolm Xs' approach to his peers was strictly from a spectator's point of view. He mentions wanting to "emulate" his fellow inmate, Bimbi, (Malcolm X 227) and discusses with reverence the heated debates that took place among the inmates in the school building located on the prison grounds (Malcolm X 228). Although each of these experiences is unique in the differing backgrounds and time periods, Sedaris, Douglass, and Malcolm X analyze through reminiscent portrayals, the similar effects of how oppressive influences motivated them to challenge themselves and become successful in their respective areas of education.

Works Cited

First-Year Writing: Writing In the Disciplines. 6th ed. Massachusetts: Pearson, 2012. Print.
Douglass, Frederick. "Learning to Read and Write." 222–226. Print.
Malcolm X. "A Homemade Education." 226–233. Print.
Sedaris, Davis. "Me Talk Pretty One Day." 219–222. Print

SYNTHESIZING SOURCES

Charles Knight

Within the three articles: "Me Talk Pretty One Day", "Learning to Read and Write", and "A Homemade Education" written by David Sedaris, Frederick Douglass, and Malcolm X, the major focus examines the enlightenment of the mind that accompanies the learning of a new language. Although all three authors were writing in completely different contexts and time periods, they all emphasize their own experiences in which they discovered truth about learning, as well as life as a whole, through differing methods of learning new languages.

Throughout all three articles, each author presents a language barrier they each deal with that is inhibiting their daily lives. Within the Sedaris article, he presents his situation of being in a French class in Paris, where his unforgiving and unsympathetic teacher leaves him scrambling for understanding of the French language, which ultimately drives him, through mostly fear, to study exponentially harder to understand the language. Eventually, he suddenly discovers that he can understand on a higher level. He states, "understanding doesn't mean you can speak the language" (Sedaris 222). His stress-induced scrambling for meaning allowed for a more natural realization of the French language, rather than just knowing what the French words meant in English. Unlike the learning of a new spoken language, Douglass (while a young slave), as well as Malcolm X recall how their learning how to read and write allowed them to find truth in the evil world around them. Together, through their newfound appetite for learning within books, both men find that white men have been in control of much of the world for most of history. They both realize that within their illiterate ignorance, they had no understanding of the past, and therefore had no relevant position to comment on the injustices they saw in their own time periods.

Differences arise within the end product that becomes of these realizations of Malcolm X and Douglass. Douglass at first sees his newfound ability to read as "a curse rather than a blessing . . . it had opened my eyes to the horrible pit, but to no ladder upon which to get out" (Douglass 224). This depressive attitude eventually leads him to the inspiration to become an abolitionist. Conversely, Malcolm X saw "the ability to read awoke inside me some long dormant craving to be alive" (Malcolm X 232). This positive view on the avenue of learning of the plight of the white man in history then goes on to inspire his black power rationale and teachings. Less life changing that Malcolm X and Douglass, Sedaris merely finds enlightenment through true understanding of another language, as opposed to understanding of human interaction as a whole.

While each author had a differing opinion on how to react to the recently acquired knowledge about the world that surrounded him, they each discovered that through the learning of a new form of communication, the world they saw was expanded immensely and provided new opportunities for which they could alter their own life paths.

Works Cited

Douglass, Frederick. "Learning to Read and Write." *First-Year Writing: Writing In the Disciplines*. Boston: Pearson Learning Solutions, 2012. 226–33. Print.

Sedaris, David. "Me Talk Pretty One Day." *First-Year Writing: Writing In the Disciplines*. Boston: Pearson Learning Solutions, 2012. 226–33. Print.

X, Malcolm. "A Homemade Education." *First-Year Writing: Writing In the Disciplines*. Boston: Pearson Learning Solutions, 2012. 226–33. Print.

ANNOTATED BIBLIOGRAPHY

Michaela Yarbrough

Question: Does word size and line spacing in the typography of children's books allow for optimum reading comprehension and improve learning in children?

Thesis: Typography is defined as the study of text. Although often overlooked, text plays a major role in understanding and improving elementary learning. Studies have recognized that text is usually not geared towards children and may need a better format for beginning readers. In general, research has mostly focused on how line spacing, typeface, and text size affect children's reading speed. Although past research has speculated that the word grouping and typeface (font) affects children's reading, current research indicates that larger word size and line spacing are more effective in improving children's reading speed and comprehension.

Carver, Ronald P. "Effect Of A "Chunked" Typography On Reading Rate And Comprehension." *Journal of Applied Psychology* 54.3 (1970): 288–296. SocINDEX with Full Text. Web. 10 Feb. 2013.

Carver's article investigates whether spatial "chunking" has an effect on reading efficiency in adults. His findings show that chunking does not have an effect on reading. However, his studies instead demonstrate that capitalization formatting effect reading rate. This article is not completely relevant to my topic since it only discusses adults; however, it is does present a good point of discussion regarding formatting and "chunking" of words. This article also brings up the effects of capitalization and its effect on reading speed which could be a good subtopic to investigate in my review. Carver studies equal numbers of male and female college students in his paper making his research more substantial. Carver is a published author in the Journal of Applied Psychology and has written several papers on reading comprehension and reading speed. Since this article was published in 1970, it therefore would be used to discuss past studies on reading comprehension. Overall, the quality is substantial, and states clear results.

Hughes, Laura E., Wilkins, Arnold J. "Typography in children's reading schemes may be suboptimal: Evidence from measures of reading rate." *Journal of Research in Reading* 23.3 (2000): 314–325. Academic Search Complete. 5 Feb. 2013.

Hughes researches the effect of text spacing and size on children's reading speeds. Hughes finds that larger spacing and font size is beneficial to anyone and particularly takes notice of "visual stress" as a factor of affecting reading speed and could be a potential sub-topic to my discussion of typefaces. Hughes studies a survey of 120 children ages 5–8 to determine her results and uses a Rate of Reading Test to gauge the speed of each of the children. The scope is both appropriate and thorough by the use of multiple sources as well as precise experimental procedures. The quality of this article is very good in both comprehension and academic merit. Published in the Journal of Research in Reading, this article is approved as an "empirical" study and is part of a large collection of research regarding studies in literacy in children and adults.

Reynolds, Linda, Walker, Sue, Duncan, Alison. "Children's Responses to Line Spacing in Early Reading Books or 'Holes to tell which line you're on." *Visible Language* 40.3 (2006): 246–267. Art & Architecture Complete. Web. 9 Feb. 2013.

Motivation to read. This article addresses line spacing and its effect on children's reading rate. Reynolds and Walker find that wider line spacing is easier to read and is preferred over smaller spacing measurements. Reynolds consideration of reading in conjunction with motivation is a valid topic in my research because it recognizes typography's role in reading. This article creates a relationship between line spacing and encouraging kids to read. Reynolds and Walker use miscue analysis to study a large scope of children which is the study of reading using oral tests and recording the data. This method is appropriate for their study, but only because they control their variables carefully. Reynolds and walker have investigated this topic in the past, but have improved and elaborated their previous study by considering spacing and word size over serifs and infant characters. Their research can be found in the Journal of Visible Language which is a series of articles that provide scholarly information on the role and importance of graphic arts in the world.

Walker, Sue, Reynolds, Linda. "Serifs, sans serifs and infant characters in children's reading books." *Information Design Journal & Document Design* 11.2/3 (2002/2003): 106–122. Communication & Mass Media Complete. Web. 5 Feb. 2013.

Walker studies serifs, infant characters, and typefaces' effects on children's reading rate. Although she does not find a significant effect in serif fonts have on children's reading, Walker offers examples of good typefaces for beginning readers. The topic of infant characters is a good topic to address and would be beneficial to consider in my review since these characters are frequently used in children's books. I found this source to be very thorough in its research. Walker's research is published as an academic journal and is based on a combination of miscue analysis and children's comments. Miscue analysis uses oral reading to identify mistakes and make interpretations on those observations. Walker surveys a very small number of 24 students in her research in order to control their research, but limits the potential variability of her results. Walker recognizes this limitation along with the need for a further study on other elements of typography like line spacing in addition to her current study. Overall the quality is well written and researched. Sue Walker has written several articles concerning reading rate including a follow up journal a few years later investigating line spacing in children's books.

Weiss, David S. "<u>Effects of text segmentation on children's reading comprehension</u>" *Discourse Process* 6.1 (1983): 77–89. Web. 10 Feb. 2013.

Weiss investigates text segmentation and its effect on children. Weiss finds that this segmentation helps differentiate good readers from bad readers rather than reading speed. This article is a great example of early research on text segmentation in typography and its relationship to children's reading. By using this source, I can compare it to Carver's article under early research on typography's influence on children. This article also adds a discussion of line length and its effect on children's reading speed. Although this source was published in 1983, the research is good and presents some early insight into not only the studies of typography but also the research methods used in the past. The article comes from the Discourse Process journal which investigates discourse comprehension and aims to investigate different fields. Therefore as an investigative paper, this article samples a wide scope of children, but comes to moderate conclusions as an early study. These conclusions are very limited and rely on further evidence to make concrete statements given the limited research on the typography at the time. The article can get wordy at times, but overall it gives an introduction to typography research in the past.

Wilkins, Arnold, Cleave, Roanna, Grayson, Nicola, Wilson, Louise. "<u>Typography for children may be inappropriately designed.</u>" *Journal for Research in Reading* 32.4 (2009): 402–412. Academic Search Complete. Web. 5 Feb. 2013.

Wilkins expands on previous studies by focusing on text size and typeface as factors that affect reading speed and comprehension. This article adds insights including specified studies on certain typefaces, and exact spacing measurements. This article also extends its research to consider text color and its visual effect on children's reading. This article would be a great bridge to my conclusion because it begins to introduce new evidence that could use further research like color in text. This study is much more controlled than previous studies concerning text size by providing exact text measurements and structured experiments. Although the procedures can get a bit wordy and exact, the results push previous studies by concluding that veranda was easiest to read and larger sizes were preferred. This article comes from the Journal for Research in Reading which specializes in scholarly studies on literacy and comprehension in adults and children. Wilkins has assisted in writing several academic journals and has been working and publishing research regarding children's literacy for the past several years.

ANNOTATED BIBLIOGRAPHY

Charles Knight

European University Institute. "The Economic Viability of Renewables." Article. European University Institute. N.p., 26 June 2012. Web. 3 Feb. 2013.

This article examines the economic viability of wind energy in Europe. Currently in Europe, the increasing rate of unemployment has made the wind energy proposition a tough sale. The author's main source, Dr. Michael Pollitt, states that this notion is "misguided". He also goes on to argue against the idea that the increase of wind energy will create a smaller carbon footprint. He simply states that the only real argument that has merit in today's economy is the fact that electricity generated form wind is cheap, and eventually could compete on the same level as fossil fuels. The article does a good job focusing on the economic reasons why wind energy is a viable option. However, the article focuses on why wind could be viable in the future, and doesn't say anything about the economic data on current wind projects.

Most of the article's information comes from commentary of Dr. Michael Pollitt, who speaks on behalf of the Florence School of Regulation Energy Policy and European Union Law Dept. The article was published by the European University Institute.

Herzog, Antonia, Timothy Lipman, and Jennifer Edwards. "Renewable Energy: A Viable Choice." Environment 43.10 (2001): n. pag. Web. 4 Feb. 2013.

This article focuses on the shifting of the need for renewable energy sources due to the fact that new technologies that have been implemented in the past 10–15 years have made long term use possible, as well as making renewable energy competitively efficient. The article then goes on to discuss the climate benefits that would be realizable in the long term, and the fact that fossil fuel will be on the decline within the next century. Lastly, the article discusses the policy options that could be implemented if renewable energy was the focus of the US energy funding.

While no commentary is made on the author's credentials or background, the fact that this article was published in the scholarly journal, Environment, goes to show that the authors have reputable credibility. Furthermore, the extensive research and document length leave little doubt regarding the author's level of expertise.

Marvel, Kate, Ben Kravitz, and Ken Caldeira. "Geophysical Limits to Global Wind Power." Nature Climate Change 3 (2012): 118–21. Web. 2 Feb. 2013.

This article chooses to discuss the potential amount of energy that could be gathered on Earth. The article goes into much detail about the ultra-efficient, high altitude wind turbines that have the highest level of average power density. This highly technical research was done in order to explain that the current system of wind turbines on Earth is not performing as well as they could be. The article then goes on to explain how the Earth has the potential to create four times more energy (if using the high altitude turbines) than if using current style low level turbines. Near the conclusion however, the articles discusses that the information contained doesn't count for much because the future of wind energy will most likely rely on the rules and regulation in place for economic and political reasons.

The article was posted by a national scientific journal, so the credibility of the article is present. The article contains three authors, which show that any outlying opinion or theory would be counteracted by the other, so no irrational biased is present. The only fact that detracts from the level of credibility of the authors is the lack of background knowledge on them. Inclusion of this information would allow a completely scholarly level of credibility.

Reily, Scott. "Economic Viability of Renewable Energy." Article. Green Chip Stocks. N.p., 7 Apr. 2012. Web. 3 Feb. 2013. .

This article begins by discussing the finite amount of oil that is on the Earth. Since oil is the world's primary energy source this presents a dilemma where wind energy could step in. The article then discusses the fact that federal spending on jobs in the renewable energy department produce more that 4 times more jobs than in the petroleum department. This leads the reader to assume that renewable energy is a more viable solution to the energy crisis than petroleum. The author leaves the argument at that, and his argument seems quite short and lacking substance. He only discusses one statistic to which he bases his whole argument on. If he had included other studies or statistics to back up his claim, his argument would be well researched and more believable. This article begins by discussing the finite amount of oil that is on the Earth. Since oil is the world's primary energy source this presents a dilemma where wind energy could step in. The article then discusses the fact that federal spending on jobs in the renewable energy department produce more that 4 times more jobs than in the petroleum department. This leads the reader to assume that renewable energy is a more viable solution to the energy crisis than petroleum. The author leaves the argument at that, and his argument seems quite short and lacking substance. He only discusses one statistic to which he bases his whole argument on. If he had included other studies or statistics to back up his claim, his argument would be well researched and more believable.

The author, Scott Reily, provides the reader with no previous data for which to assess his expertise in the subject. Furthermore, his credibility is hindered by his lack of education credentials. The location of the article is a website titled "Green Chip Stocks" which focuses mainly on the financial and economic sector of green living.

Trevitt, Sophie. "The Viability of Renewable Energy." Vibewire. Australian Climate Coalition, 26 Mar. 2012. Web. 8 Feb. 2013. .

This article's main discussion is the potential for the presence of solar energy in Australia. The author goes on to discuss how many major countries in Europe have substantially more advanced solar programs in their respective homelands. The author makes a call for action in Australia for realize their own energy capacity, given that they are the sunniest country in the world. The author is clearly for solar usage, and doesn't discuss any of the problems associated with infrastructure or ease of use. Secondly, the author chooses not to discuss the political prerequisites that large-scale solar use would require.

The author has fairly good credibility, given that she is the director of the Australian Climate Coalition (ACC). The ACC is funded by the Australian government, which adds to the credibility to the article. The only downfall is that no mention to the background of the author herself, and she has no educational clues or titles.

USA. Office of Indian Energy and Economic Development. US Department of the Interior. "Wind Energy Development." A discussion of wind energy, environmental impacts associated with wind energy development, and mitigation measures to avoid or reduce wind energy development impacts. Tribal Energy and Environmental Information. N.p., 24 Aug. 2011. Web. 6 Feb. 2013.

This article has sections that are divided into a basic analysis of the resources and technology in use in the wind energy industry. Since this is a government article, there is no opinion or bias expressed, just the information about the industry. This article lays out a basic overview on the uses for wind energy, how the US can benefit from wind, and how the infrastructure of getting electricity form the wind works. Overall, the message of this article helps one understand the logistics and protocol that goes into the wind industry.

The writer(s) of this article have a great amount of credibility due to the fact that this is a government published article. They don't present any sort of bias, just the facts about the existing wind industry.

SENTENCE-LEVEL REVISIONS

Michaela Yarbrough

THESIS

While past research has speculated that word grouping affects children's reading, current research concentrates on the impact that line spacing, word size, and typeface (font) have on children's reading.

ORIGINAL

Line Spacing

Current research regarding word spacing has focused mainly on line spacing's effect on children's word recognition. In Reynolds and Walker's article "Children's Responses to Line Spacing in Early Reading Books," they find that increased and decreased line spacing does not significantly improve children's reading. However, the researchers found that children noticed these differences and identified the wider spaced lines easier to read than the reduced spacing (246). Reynolds and Walker also suggest that additional space allows for an "accurate return sweep of the eyes" allowing for better comprehension and familiarity of words (248). Similarly, Walker's study "Describing the Design of Children's Books" suggests that double the amount of line space should be allotted for young children as well as a "thick space" for older children (197). With this said, Walker's studies revolve around books published in the early 1900's; however, her research still makes important observations regarding space for readers alike. In contrast to Walker, Reynolds points out that too much space can be bad for children (248). Compared to Walker, Reynolds also goes on to consider children's opinions during her study and also considers how space effects children's motivation to read (265). Nevertheless, Reynolds and Walker agree that that more space is better for children. Additionally, Hughes's article "Reading at a distance," analyzes the effect of spacing, but considers the effects of distance unlike Reynolds and Walker. Hughes finds that space in text is crucial for legibility and is more important than increasing the letter size (213). Thus all authors agree that more space between lines is beneficial and perhaps most effective in improving children's' reading.

REVISED

Line Spacing

Current research regarding text spacing has focused line spacing's effect on children's ease to read. Reynolds, Walker, and Duncan find that changing the line spacing does not significantly improve children's reading due to minimal changes in results (264). However, they found that children recognized these differences and perceived the wider spaced lines were easier to read than the reduced spacing because it allowed for an "accurate return sweep of the eyes" giving better comprehension and familiarity of words (Reynolds, Walker, and Duncan 248). Reynolds, Walker, and Duncan also believe wider spacing could have an effect on children's motivation to read based on children's comments in their research. They found that if children perceived the "appearance of the text" to be difficult it could reduce the "appeal" of the book and "discourage" attempts to read the text (265). Compared to Walker, Reynolds, and Duncan's research, Sue Walker's later individual research simply focuses on the attributes of design in children's books from the early 1900s and does not regard spacing in relationship to children's motivation. She mainly draws evidence from observation to create checklists of common characteristics in these children's books (Walker Describing 185). In terms of spacing, Walker finds that larger spacing is "desirable" for younger children and a "thick space" is promoted for older children (Describing 197). Walker's observations provide early insight into the design of books and suggest that children of today could benefit from trends of the past. In contrast, Hughes and Wilkins also consider the effects of spacing but look at its effect in relationship to distance (Reading 213). They find that space in text is crucial for legibility and also consider it is more important than increasing the letter size (Reading 213). For example, more children found it easier to understand words that had larger spacing than larger word size (Reading 223). As a result, although Hughes and Wilkins resolve spacing affects reading acuity and fluency rather than motivation or word recognition, Hughes and Wilkins agree with Reynolds, Walker, and Duncan that line spacing has effects on children's reading. Thus despite differing concentrations, all authors agree that more space between lines affects children's reading.

EVALUATION

After reading my "Line Spacing" paragraph I found I needed revision in clarifying citation and synthesis. Since I have multiple articles whose authors overlap, I realized I needed to be clearer which article I was referring to in my synthesis. When introducing a new piece of research, I made sure to include the first word of the article in parenthesis instead of writing out the whole title in my paragraph. For instance, writing "(Reading 213)" instead of "In Hughes and Wilkins's article "Reading..."" clarifies which article by Hughes and Wilkins I am talking about without making my paragraph wordy and confusing to the reader. In addition, I also realized I was not completely citing all of the authors from each article. In my revisions I made sure to include all authors as they appear in my works cited instead of mentioning just the first author on the list. This change not only gives credit to all authors from the research, but it also helps show a relationship between the articles and differentiates which article I am talking about.

In addition to clarifying my citations, I worked on being more specific in my research to improve my synthesis. By omitting unnecessary words that made my meaning confusing, I was able to make my sentence structures more concise and clear. For example, I condensed "increased and decreased line spacing" to "changing the line spacing" to make my message less wordy, but still understandable to the reader. By also providing specific evidence from my research, I was able to elaborate why the author's research is relevant to my topic which helped make my synthesis stronger. To improve my synthesis, I also tried to clarify the chronology of articles that had similar authors. For instance by mentioning, "Sue Walker's later individual research" after introducing Reynolds, Walker, and Duncan's study helps differentiate the two articles Walker wrote and show their relationship to the reader.

In addition, I worked on word choice in my paragraph. I worked to make sure each source was coherent in content by changing words to stress different ideas especially when considering my topic sentence. By tweaking my topic sentence to focus on the "ease of children's reading" I am able to better relate all of my sources together since not all focus on "word recognition."

SENTENCE-LEVEL REVISIONS

Amy Werdenberg

Thesis: Researchers around the world hold varying opinions on what the root of the problem is and what steps need to be taken to resolve the conflict.

ORIGINAL PARAGRAPH:

Some have suggested that China should allow Tibet the system of autonomy which is currently in place in Hong Kong, another self-ruled Chinese territory. In "The Future of Tibet: A Chinese Dilemma" Michael Davis explains that this system allows regional control of currency, citizenship, border patrol, commerce, and liberal rights. This system may not work as well in Tibet though, for several reasons. To begin with, Hong Kong was a British colony for one hundred years, borrowed from China from 1897 to 1997. Throughout the twentieth century the people of Hong Kong essentially ruled themselves and had economic, education, tourist, transportation, healthcare, and technology systems already in place when China regained control in 1997. Hong Kong is also an urban setting. The people of Tibet are primarily nomadic and have never had much of a government. Barry Sautman quotes the Dalai Lama's Taiwan envoy, Dawa Tsering, as stating that "before 1951, Tibetans were not a unified people and had no concept of living in a sovereign State" (127). Davis further explains that the Hong Kong model would not work in Tibet because Tibet is lacking several vital institutions. "In the absence of local [democratic] institutions for the exercise of control over the local government, including . . . multi-party elections and protection of the basic freedoms of association and the press, there is little likelihood the community will be able to exercise true autonomy" (11). He also explains China's "top-down" system of autonomy, in which Beijing selects the officials for the highest authority positions. These leaders then select the officials below them, and so on, until all positions are filled with Beijing-approved authorities. Davis points out that, despite being well prepared for self-rule, even Hong Kong has difficulty "resisting encroachment on its autonomy" (12). He argues that this system, though it seems ideal, will ultimately fail in Tibet.

I read chapters 40–43 in the handbook and, working through each "Quick Help" box, I read through and revised my paragraph about half a dozen times. I tried to edit to be more concise but I found there was not a lot of unnecessary wording. I also felt that I already had good sentence variety and length. I did make some changes, however, that I think helped the paragraph to flow better. I rearranged the order of the strings of ideas (sentences five and eight) so they would flow from least to greatest importance. I changed the "Some" in the first sentence to be more specific, "The Dalai Lama." I realized I had used the words "in" and "system" several times in the first few sentences, so I changed some of the vocabulary. I moved the portion about "top-down" autonomy to the beginning, where it makes more sense, explaining first the current system followed by the desired system. Finally, I checked all the quotations for mechanical correctness. This was pointed out to me by both graders and, though I thought I understood proper citation, there were still a few errors to correct. I also added a sentence at the end that was my own as opposed to concluding with

Davis's ideas. This was also suggested by one of the graders. I need to do this with all my paragraphs, in order to keep the literature review my own synthesis and not simply a summary of the writings of others.

REVISED PARAGRAPH:

The Dalai Lama has shown some interest in the type of autonomy currently active in Hong Kong, another self-ruled Chinese territory. In "The Future of Tibet: A Chinese Dilemma" Michael Davis explains Tibet's current "top-down" system of autonomy, in which Beijing selects the officials for the highest authority positions. These leaders then select the officials below them, and so on, until all positions are filled with Beijing-approved authorities (11). This structure is not actually autonomous at all. Davis also explains Hong Kong's current system, which allows regional control of currency, commerce, citizenship, border patrol, and liberal rights. There are several reasons why this structure may not work as well in Tibet. To begin with, Hong Kong was a British colony from 1897 to 1997. Throughout the twentieth century the people primarily ruled themselves and had economic, transportation, education, healthcare, and technology systems already in place when China regained control in 1997. Hong Kong is also an urban setting. Tibetans are primarily nomadic and they are not used to thinking as a nation. Barry Sautman quotes the Dalai Lama's Taiwan envoy, Dawa Tsering, as stating that "before 1951, Tibetans were not a unified people and had no concept of living in a sovereign State" (127). Davis further explains that the Hong Kong model would not work in Tibet because Tibet is lacking basic governmental institutions (11–12). "In the absence of local [democratic] institutions for the exercise of control over the local government, including . . . multi-party elections and protection of the basic freedoms of association and the press, there is little likelihood the community will be able to exercise true autonomy" (11). Davis points out that, despite being well prepared for self-rule, even Hong Kong has difficulty "resisting encroachment on its autonomy" (12). He concludes that, though it seems ideal, this system will ultimately fail in Tibet. Perhaps this is one reason why China has not offered this structure of autonomy to Tibetans.

Davis, Michael C. "The Future Of Tibet: A Chinese Dilemma." Human Rights Review 2.2 (2001): 7. Academic Search Complete. Web. 12 Feb. 2013.

Sautman, Barry. "Tibet's Putative Statehood and International Law." Chinese Journal Of International Law 9.1 (2010): 127–142. Academic Search Complete. Web. 14 Feb. 2013.

ANALYSIS OF LOGICAL SUPPORT

Michaela Yarbrough

In the article "Till Children Do Us Part," Stephanie Coontz informs married couples that it is possible to maintain a happy relationship. By first denouncing early theories, then pinpointing problems in marriages after parenthood, and finally focusing to encourage "collaborative couples" to work to continue a healthy relationship while raising children, Coontz maintains an effective argument through factual evidence and theoretical support.

Coontz first uses factual evidence to counter early beliefs and to encourage the success of a marriage. By offering evidence that marriages are actually happier without children, Coontz appeals to married couples who want to improve their marriage (268). After introducing a quote from an article in 1944 that encourages kids as a solution to happiness, Coontz emphasizes "25 separate studies" to argue its irrelevance today by showing parenthood actually decreases "marital quality" (Coontz 268). As a professor of Women's studies and a researcher on marriage, Coontz uses the numerical value of research to convince her audience that she knows and understands the results that show how to achieve a happy marriage. Her comment stating a relationship is not completely "doomed" also offers hope for her audience and shows she believes there is more to a successful marriage than just parenthood (268).

Coontz also suggests educated theories to pinpoint initial problems in marriages and warns struggling couples that parenthood can worsen a relationship. By stating challenges like disagreements of when to conceive and the potential of increased gender roles after birth, Coontz warns couples how a relationship can suffer in the process of having children and therefore uses her relationship categories to assess her audience's readiness of parenthood as well as the stability of their current relationship. She assumes couples in her audience may be having marital problems and may see children as a solution. We know this because she mentions that "sharing in child-rearing do not immunize a marriage" to show she believes it still takes effort in the relationship to make it continue to succeed on its own in the midst of children. Her argument remains effective since her understanding of marital problems is insightful by showing a typical sequence of life after children, so most couples in her audience can relate to this reasoning. However, her argument fails to address nontraditional couples and assumes a relationship is between a man and a woman, so the problems of gender roles are not completely applicable to homosexual couples.

After observing possible factors parenthood brings to a marriage, Coontz offers a solution to "collaborative marriages." Coontz recognizes that collaborative couples do not have initial problems with parenthood, but rather simply lose sight of each other during parenthood known as "intense style parenting" (269). Therefore, Coontz provides evidence from Ellen Galinsky to show couples that they do not need to worry about their kids as much as they think (269). By doing so, Coontz aims to encourage couples to worry more about their strengthening relationship than their kids in order to achieve a happy marriage. This evidence is moreover effective since Coontz draws from her educational background to report her theories as valid advice. Although she could still include more statistical evidence to show the success of a relationship, Coontz is writing to a general non-specialist audience and must paraphrases her evidence to engage more people. Therefore, Coontz is effective in offering advice to everyday couples.

After looking at Coontz's use of factual and theoretical support, she proves to be successful in maintaining an informative argument to married couples. Although Coontz simply encourages personal efforts by couples to achieve a healthy marriage, she ultimately believes it is possible to achieve while raising children.

Works Cited

Coontz, Stephanie. "Till Children Do Us Part." *First-Year Writing: Writing in the Disciplines.* Ed. Texas Tech University. Boston: Pearson Learning Solutions, 2012. 267–269. Print.

ANALYSIS OF LOGICAL SUPPORT

Jamie Waldo

In "Till Children Do Us Part," Coontz utilizes both recent and past research completed on the subject of marital relationships after conception. Since Coontz is not addressing a professional audience who may have had much more experience in this area of research, this variety of research is useful in making the information more convincing for the general public. Coontz also uses many common sense approaches to her analysis of this research. When analyzing different types of relationships – those who agreed on being parents, who conceived by coincidence, were ambivalent about conception, and couples who did not both agree on conceiving, but one gives in to save the relationship – is able to explain why each struggle after having a child. She uses each of these examples to highlight the importance of maintaining different aspects of adult social life in order to sustain the marriage. Coontz takes the stance that without taking time out to have some one-on-one time, or time in social circles with peers, the marriage is much more likely to thrive throughout the child's life and after they leave home. Overall, Coontz focuses mainly on the research that has been done on the topic of marriage before and after conception, focusing on the strength and overall happiness of the couple.

The author assumes that the audience has some sort of background in marriage and childbearing. Coontz does not, however, assume that the audience understands all the jargon of the field. She explains certain terms in order to enhance the understanding of the reader, including terms like "empty nest syndrome." As a reader, it is obvious that Coontz is not writing to an audience of experts. She tends to use more common diction, as opposed to a more complex sentence structure with hard-to-understand terminology. Also, being written for The New York Times is another indication as to who the audience is that Coontz is writing to. Certain aspects of the article are appealing to parents of children because they will be able to relate to the information being presented. They will more than likely fit into one of the aforementioned categories. On the other hand, this also neglects a large section of society who do not have children, or are not married.

Coontz assumes that all members of society fit into one of these categories. She is writing this article about American society as a whole, saying that all members of society fit into each of the categories that she has presented. Also, when presenting the information about the statistical changes that have occurred over the past 50 years, she specifies that there is twice as much father involvement in the child's life since 1965. Coontz also makes the assumption that children do not want this much interaction with their parents, but want them to be more relaxed when they are spending time together. This is an assumption that she puts as an umbrella over all of our society. There is no proof given that this holds true in a research-based study. Since she bases her assumptions on what she assumes is the majority of people in the United States, those in the minority groups, it is more likely that these people will not identify, or agree with the information being presented in the study. Coontz's background in marriage studies has made her more biased in one direction than any other researcher would be. This makes the reader approach the article more cautiously. The argument does make sense logically, but it is too broad for it to be completely effective and convincing for the entirety of our society.

ANALYSIS OF LOGICAL SUPPORT

Amy Werdenberg

Stephanie Coontz's article, "Till Children Do Us Part," seeks to inform readers of the changes in parenting theory over the past fifty years. Written for the New York Times in early 2009, her article is written for a very broad, "average" audience and her language is simple, easy to understand. She begins by explaining the primary thought of half a century ago, including a direct quote from a popular women's magazine- one that is still popular today. Coontz then shifts promptly into research of the past twenty years and the theme of the article: marriage satisfaction drops significantly with the addition of children. She then goes on to explain some of the potential factors of this unhappiness, research and studies done on various aspects of that theory, and she concludes with some simple possible solutions to avoiding the problem.

Coontz's primary assumption is that couples want happy marriages, which is a practical assumption as no one wants a bad or stressed marriage. She also assumes that perhaps couples do not know the best ways to keep their marriage strong after the addition of children. This, too, is reasonable. It is fairly well known that the divorce rate today hovers around fifty percent. There is also another assumption which appears about halfway through the article, when she mentions that ". . . children did better socially and academically because their parents were happier," (269). This assumption that parents care about their children's social and academic success is also rather obvious, and practically everyone would agree that a good parent would care about those things. She does not need to spend any time explaining these points of view or arguing for them, as they are deemed obvious and universal.

In the article, Coontz employs only studies and research, with no personal stories, anecdotes or interviews. When writing for a broad audience, like the New York Times, it is often effective to use statistics and facts, which more readers will accept over personal stories. Though the theme is the change in parenting theory over the past fifty years, most of the studies cover only the last 20–25 years. This is strategic because Coontz is essentially comparing the way her readers were raised versus how they should be raising their own children. A few readers may have a problem with Coontz's findings, arguing that they were raised "fine," that they "turned out great," or that their parents are still happily married. However the article does not seek to cause dissension or begin a debate, but rather to present the facts of research and help couples who may be struggling in their marriages. The author assumes that her subject is one that people care about and, because it has changed so much, needs to be addressed.

Coontz's first source is that of two researchers at the University of California at Berkeley, Philip and Carolyn Cowan. Their report was for a paper for the Council on Contemporary Families, and it addresses some of the different factors to be considered when looking at unhappiness in marriage. Their programs, designed to help couples resolve differences, saw positive results. This was Coontz's primary source, and given their background and actions taken, they are solidified as reliable. The next three sources mentioned provide very little detail or background information. Coontz does not explain the factors of the studies, nor the stipulations of the research, only the results discovered. Early in the article she also mentions "more than 25 separate studies," (268). Readers could question the quality of these sources, but it is likely that the average reader is not as interested in the resume of the source as the outcome of the study and the solutions suggested. This is especially true when the outcomes of so many different studies are in agreement. Had Coontz been writing to a more specific audience, such as a group of psychologists, she would have had to include more detail. Writing for the New York Times she was limited on space and she included only that which she felt was important to the average reader.

One potential issue is that Coontz covers a lot of different thoughts in this short article. She could have gone into much more detail, explanations, and examples of one or two ideas, but instead she chose to briefly mention many different aspects. While this can be effective when trying to cover a broad topic for a broad audience in just a short article, it could leave her readers wanting more information. She does, however, do an effective job reporting the facts of her research without overpowering the article with opinion. She presents the problem, reported research, and potential solution to a problem that many Americans struggle with every day.

Works Cited

Coontz, Stephanie. "Till Children Do Us Part." *First Year Writing: Writing in the Disciplines.* Boston: Pearson, 2012. 268–69. Print.

REVISION FOR SOURCES

Jamie Waldo

While working through and evaluating the sources used throughout the draft, it became increasingly evident that I had too much reliance on sources in some sections and not enough support in other sections. I found several instances in which there was a claim that had no support, or a direct quotation left to stand on it's own without any explanation as to the importance of its presence in the paper. Overall, the sources used exemplify the benefits of developmentally appropriate practice, but do not necessarily focus as much on the financial/funding aspect of the education as was stated in the thesis. Since the revisions are a stronger, more appropriate use of the sources, and the paper focuses primarily on developmentally appropriate practice, before the final draft is submitted, the thesis will be changed. Overall, in order to better the paper, more sources were integrated into the paragraphs to support the claims being made. Secondly, more explanation of the quotes was added, allowing for further understanding of the paper. Also, it was very useful to consult the quick help box in the handbook for transitional phrases. Many of these phrases were incorporated into the edited editions of the selections. Lastly, when reading through the edited paragraphs, the direct quotations were edited in order to assist in fluency of the paper. This will allow further comprehension of the topic presented.

ORIGINALS:

Passage 1:

What is developmentally appropriate practice? According to David Elkind, "the curriculum should be matched to the child's level of mental ability" (113). It is not hard for the average individual to understand that you cannot give a kindergarten student a worksheet full of calculus problems and expect the child to be able to answer the questions appropriately. It becomes a more fine-tuned idea that certain tasks can be achieved at specific milestones in a child's life, and when the teacher is incapable of understanding these milestones, he or she will not be able to appropriately educate the children in the classroom. The idea behind this type of program is that the students are directing their own learning with assistance from their teacher. They are learning problem-solving abilities and proper interaction skills with other students (Frede 117). The type of knowledge necessary to facilitate these interactions comes from not only experience, but also from specialized degrees that train teachers to notice and act upon the smallest of cues that a child gives.

Passage 2:

Opponents to this idea pose arguments regarding validity of the reliability of these programs. They also oppose governmental funding of these programs and argue that these are actions that should only be addressed in the child's home. Developmentally appropriate programs demand that teachers be more educated, having at least an associate's degree, and that each teacher be trained in proper classroom management and teaching skills for these young children (Frede 119). Between the smaller class size and the higher education of the teacher, a developmentally appropriate classroom is the best place in which a young child can be educated. This requires state and federal funding. When the belief is that a child receives the best education possible from his or her parents, the consensus is typically the same. When attending to the concept, though, it must be taken into account that many mothers and fathers are in the workforce and cannot afford time off to educate their children through the preschool years. In this case, a developmentally appropriate classroom is the only feasible place to take children. Placing students in a daycare setting before their first birthday actually increases their reading recognition and math abilities (Caughy). Many times when students are placed in a non-developmentally appropriate daycare, only to be left alone to play with the same toy all day long with no attention given, it leads to higher levels of cortisol in children, which is directly linked to high levels of stress (Geoffroy). This does not occur in a developmentally appropriate classroom because the class size is so small that that the teacher can attend to each child's needs to ensure they are being met.

Passage 3:

Another element to consider when addressing the funding of developmentally appropriate practice is the long-term effects it will have on the students educated in this manner. According to David Weikart's study, the students who are enrolled in developmentally appropriate programs are much more likely to succeed socially (234). "By age 27, only one-fifth as many program group members as nonprogram group members have been arrested five or more times (7% vs 35%)" in very low socioeconomic areas (234). It has also been measured that with the use of this program, the students, when reaching adulthood, are more likely to remain married, earn four times as much money per month, and obtain higher academic degrees. (234) With results like this, it only makes sense that this program be made readily available for all children. Overall, according to the study conducted by Reynolds, Temple, Robertson, and Mann, students who are enrolled in preschool programs that are developmentally appropriate are more likely to have greater academic achievement throughout their lives, fewer instances of grade retention, and higher cognitive processing skills when entering school (2340). With so much proof of success, it is hard to imagine why anyone would consider not using program such as these. In 1992, statistics proved that for every one child, $12,358 was given for schooling per year versus $57,585 per prison inmate per year (Weikart 235). When reducing the number of criminal offenses in a child's future, further reducing the possibility of their incarceration, it is only logical that the government set aside enough money per year for children to go through these programs instead of jail time later in life.

REVISIONS

Revision 1:

What is developmentally appropriate practice? In a study conducted by Huffman and Speer, the authors define a developmentally appropriate environment as being one in which "children can observe and participate in ongoing patters of progressively more complex activity guided by persons with whom the child has developed a positive emotional relationship where children have opportunity, resources, and encouragement to engage in the activities on their own" (168). Overall, a developmentally appropriate classroom is one in which the students feel safe and cared for, have the opportunity to learn at their own pace, and have much diversity in resources to facilitate their learning activities. David Elkind asserts that in order for a school to be developmentally appropriate, curriculum must be on the children's developmental level (113). Ideally, the major premise of education is that the children grow up to become adults who are capable of thinking critically and creatively (Elkind 115). It is not hard to understand that you cannot give a kindergarten student a worksheet full of calculus problems and expect him or her to be able to answer the questions correctly, but educating young children is much more precise than this. Education and training provide highly specialized skills that allow teachers to observe and assist in certain tasks and act upon the smallest of cues that a child gives each day in the classroom. Frede declares, "the best teachers provide support for the child" throughout his or her time in the classroom (125). Also, it is stated that those with more "formal" education and "specialized training" are better able to work with these children (Frede 119). When the teacher is incapable of recognizing indicators and is unable to support the children, he or she will not be able to appropriately educate the students in the classroom.

Revision 2:

Opponents to this idea pose arguments regarding validity of the reliability of the implementation of these programs, whether or not a developmentally based curriculum is the best option for young children, and questions have been posed as to the measurable long-term effects this type of program has on students (Huffman 169). By proxy, these people are also adversaries of the funding of such programs. This group of people is justified in their worry of the implementation of developmentally appropriate programs. Huffman also states that in one state only "20% met even minimal standards for developmentally appropriateness" (169). Giving more funding to these types of programs, however, can amend this issue. Most often, it is the result of a lack of funding that leads to developmentally inappropriate classrooms. Developmentally appropriate programs demand that teachers be more highly educated, having at least an associate's degree, and that each teacher be trained in proper classroom management and teaching skills for these young children (Frede 119). The higher level of education demanded in a developmentally appropriate program makes the implementation of these practices more feasible. Between the smaller class size and the higher education of the teacher, a developmentally appropriate classroom is the best place in which a young child can be educated. Placing students in a daycare setting before their first birthday actually increases their reading recognition and math abilities (Caughy). This requires more state and federal funding. Attending to the issue of whether a developmental or didactic approach is more beneficial for the students, Frede concludes that the students who are enrolled in a developmentally appropriate program tend to score higher on achievement tests, and have lower levels of grade retention (484). On the contrary, it is noted that the more didactic environments have results of lower test scores and measurably less academic success by grade four (Huffman 169). Many times when students are placed in a non-developmentally appropriate daycare, only to be unstimulated throughout the course of a day, the child tends to have higher levels of cortisol, which is directly linked to high levels of stress (Geoffroy). This does not occur in a developmentally appropriate classroom because smaller class sizes allow the teacher to attend to each child's needs to ensure they are being met.

Revision 3:

Another element to consider when addressing the funding of developmentally appropriate practice is the long-term effects it will have on the students educated in this manner. David Elkind maintains that teaching students coping skills early on, and teaching them to self-regulate will "automatically" transfer these abilities to other areas of their lives (114). Reynolds concludes that students who are enrolled in preschool programs that are developmentally appropriate are more likely to have greater academic achievement throughout their lives, fewer instances of grade retention, and higher cognitive processing skills when entering school (2340). Overall, "preschool participation was associated with significantly higher rates of school completion" meaning that developmentally appropriate programs have significant impacts on students' lives (Reynolds 2344). According to Weikart's study, the students who are enrolled in developmentally appropriate programs are much more likely to succeed socially, remain married, and earn four times more money per month, and obtain higher academic degrees (234). "By age 27, only one-fifth as many program group members as non-program group members have been arrested five or more times (7% vs 35%)" in very low socioeconomic areas (234). These results emphasize the importance that developmentally appropriate programs be made readily available for all children, lowering the possibility of future costs of incarceration. In 1992, statistics proved that for every one child, $12,358 was given for schooling per year versus $57,585 per prison inmate per year (Weikart 235). When reducing the likelihood of criminal offenses in a child's future, further reducing the possibility of their incarceration, it is only logical that the government set aside enough money per year for children to go through these programs instead of jail time later in life.

Revisions for Sources

Amy Werdenberg

1. ORIGINAL:

In addition to concerns about the preservation of Tibetan culture, many sources also agree that the bulk of development and urban jobs are enjoyed not by native Tibetans, but instead by the Han immigrants, who are more skilled and better educated. The word "progress," used by Chen (45) and many others when describing changes made toward modernization, indicates steps taken in the right direction, but some natives are actually living in greater poverty than they had been previously. The Chinese government has forced nomadic shepherds to settle, has strongly discouraged the system of bartering (Karan 9), and has forced farmers to plant wheat instead of the more durable barley (Dhussa 3). In a study from the Shigatse area Goldstein, Childs, and Wangdui agree that changes have benefitted Han Chinese more than native Tibetans (58). Though Beijing has finally begun to address some of these problems in recent years, it has caused hardship for many for too long. Meanwhile, in urban centers the Han take advantage of the new amenities and they have a near monopoly on the tourism industry. "Tibetan" souvenirs are manufactured by Chinese businesses, and formerly sacred temples of worship have been turned into pit stops along tourist routes (Karan 12). Just like the segregation in the United States up until the 1960s, job priority is given to the Han population, and Tibetans are suffering as a result. When one cannot find a job in the country in which he used to enjoy freedom, or when a farmer is no longer permitted to work in the longstanding tradition of his family, regression has occurred and overall improvements have not been made.

I realized that the order of this paragraph was not fluent. It began with the idea of the Han dominating the job market, then moved on to new problems for Tibetans, and then picked back up on the topic of the Han. Since the subject of the paragraph was supposed to be about the Han taking over jobs, I deleted a large portion that went off on a tangent. In doing so, I erased small portions of paraphrase by two sources (Karan and Dhussa), but both were used elsewhere in the paper. I also edited the introduction information on the Goldstein, Childs, and Wangdui study, to present more pertinent information. The whole paragraph now flows better and stays on topic.

Revision:

In addition to concerns about the preservation of Tibetan culture, many sources also agree that the bulk of development and urban jobs are enjoyed not by native Tibetans, but instead by the Han immigrants, who are more skilled and better educated. In a study concerning the government's development initiative, Goldstein, Childs, and Wangdui agree that changes have benefitted Han Chinese more than native Tibetans (58). Particularly in urban centers the Han take advantage of the new amenities and they have a near monopoly on the tourism industry. "Tibetan" souvenirs are being manufactured by Chinese businesses, and formerly sacred temples of worship have been turned into pit stops along tourist routes (Karan 12). Just like the segregation in the United States up until the 1960s, job priority is given to the Han population, and Tibetans are suffering as a result. When one cannot find a job in the country in which he used to enjoy freedom, or when a farmer is no longer permitted to work in the longstanding tradition of his family, regression has occurred and overall improvements have not been made.

2. ORIGINAL:

China has also instituted a free education program throughout the region. Guo Longyan explains the strategy of the Beijing government, in which they choose ethnic Tibetans, send them to Chinese universities for study, and then return them to Tibet to teach others (74). Naturally, as they attend the Chinese schools these Tibetans will be taught the socialist and nationalist agendas. They will then bring the ideas home, where their fellow countrymen will learn from those they trust. Though not exactly "brainwashing," this strategy will be very effective in spreading the Chinese agenda.

I realize now that I made an error with this source that I am usually careful to avoid: I paraphrased a source without properly introducing the writer. My audience has no idea who Guo Longyan is, what he wrote, where I found the source, or whether or not he is reputable and trustworthy. Though I included him in the "Works Cited" portion, an audience should not have to interrupt their reading in order to look up this information. I still felt that he was an important source to use in this paragraph about education, so I rewrote the portion to provide a bit of a background.

Revision:

China has also instituted a free education program throughout the region. An employee of the Lhasa Teachers' College in Tibet, Guo Longyan describes the government's strategy in his study for Chinese Education and Society. He explains that Beijing chooses promising ethnic Tibetans and sends them to Chinese universities for study, and then returns them to Tibet to teach others (74). Naturally, as they attend Chinese schools these Tibetans will be taught the socialist and nationalist agendas. They will then bring the ideas home, where their fellow countrymen will learn from those they trust. Though not exactly brainwashing, this strategy will be very effective in spreading the Chinese agenda and promoting the loyalty of Tibetans.

3. ORIGINAL:

Though modernization has improved the health, literacy, and life expectancy of the people, the changes were forced upon them and significantly altered their simple way of living. Regardless of what happens politically in the future, it is safe to say that Tibet is changed forever. The simple way of life is no more; it has been replaced by concerns of the modern world. The peaceful nation that was once hidden on the roof of the world is now irrevocably connected with it. The Dalai Lama, in his book My Land and My People (1962), and quoted by Dhussa, wrote, ". . . we had to learn the bitter lesson that the world has grown too small for any people to live in harmless isolation" (3).

I thought this quote by the Dalai Lama was a fitting way to end my paper so I originally included it as my last sentence. However, the more I read it, the choppier it seemed; the flow of the paragraph was interrupted by all the background information. I decided to rearrange the sentences and end with my own thoughts instead of his. I still feel that there is a lot of citation information, but I did not want to cut any of it for fear of not representing it properly. Feedback on this issue would be appreciated, but I believe the revision is an improvement over the original.

Revision:

Though modernization has improved the health, literacy, and life expectancy of the people, the changes were forced upon them and have significantly altered their simple way of living. The peaceful nation that was once hidden on the roof of the world is now irrevocably connected with it. The Dalai Lama, in his book My Land and My People (quoted by Dhussa), wrote, ". . . we had to learn the bitter lesson that the world has grown too small for any people to live in harmless isolation" (3). Simplicity has been replaced by concerns of the modern world; regardless of what happens politically in the future, it is safe to say that Tibet is changed forever.

Works Cited

Dhussa, Ramesh Chandra. "Tibet: A Nation In Exile." American Geographical Society's Focus On Geography 52.2 (2009): 1–6. MasterFILE Premier. Web. 06 Apr. 2013.

Goldstein, Melvyn C., Geoff Childs, and Puchung Wangdui. "Beijing's "People First" Development Initiative For The Tibet Autonomous Region's Rural Sector—A Case Study From The Shigatse Area." China Journal. (2010): 57–75. Web. 06 Apr. 2013.

Guo, Longyan. "Cross-Cultural Socialization At Tibetan Classes (Schools) In The Interior." Chinese Education & Society 43.3 (2010): 73–96. MasterFILE Premier. Web. 09 Apr. 2013.

Karan, Pradyunna P. "The New Tibet." American Geographical Society's Focus On Geography 52.2 (2009): 7–13. Science & Technology Collection. Web. 19 Feb. 2013.

REVISIONS FOR SOURCES

Wayne Swink

PASSAGE 1

The purpose of these sources from Nayak et al., is to show that GM crops themselves are not a scapegoat for an increased use in pesticides. I feel some readers believe a GM crop's natural insecticide expression directly contributes to the pollution in our environment. This passage is intended to show the reader that the natural expressed protein gene in a GM crop can actually help reduce the use of insecticides, which reduces pollution. It is shown from the source material that the developing country of India, and the world, has benefited from the proper use of the GM crops' expressions. While the US had somewhat abused the GM crops' expressions and used more pesticides rather than less.

I relied heavily on this source to make my point in the following passage. I feel the two pieces of source material were valuable to my argument and needed to be presented. I used the material for evidence to highlight my claim that GM crops benefit the environment. The paraphrased material for my source, regarding insecticide use in the US, is to show the counterclaim that GM crops are harmful to the environment. I placed both pieces of material into individual passages as I continue to argue that GM crop treatments are safer than chemical treatments. I did this to show the importance of both statements, but I am not sure if this information would be better presented in a summary.

The only significant change I have made to this passage was to introduce the Researchers by name and added the institution they are associated with to add more authority to my source material. Again, I feel this passage flows well, but I would change the passage to more of a summary.

Original

Also, according to Nayak et al., a field test in India was conducted from 2004 to 2006 on a Bt variety of eggplant. The test showed an 80 percent reduction of pesticide use on the Bt eggplant crops compared to non-Bt controlled eggplant crops. With India being the second largest producer of eggplant in the world, this accounted for a 42 percent reduction of total insecticide use on worldwide commercially available eggplants (113). GM insecticide crops are a passively natural treatment that is rapidly replacing the manmade chemical treatments known to be harmful to the environment. However, these genetic modifications may not encourage all producers to use less chemical pesticides on their crops. For example, research shows from 1996 to 2004 pesticide use on GM crops, here in the US, increased by 122 million pound in the nine year period (Nayak et al. 115). It is clear that much of the hazards are in the application of pesticide rather than the GM crop itself.

Revised

Also, according to researchers Nayak et al., from the National Institute of Jute and Allied Firbe Technology in India, a field test was conducted from 2004 to 2006 on a Bt variety of eggplant grown in that country. The field test showed an 80 percent reduction of pesticide use on the Bt genetically modified eggplant crops compared to non-Bt controlled egg-plant crops. With India being the second largest producer of eggplant in the world, this accounted for a 42 percent reduction of total insecticide use on worldwide commercially available eggplants during that time period (113). GM insecticide crops are a passively natural treatment that is rapidly replacing the manmade chemical treatments known to be harmful to the environment. However, these genetic modifications may not encourage all producers to use less chemical pesticides on their crops. For example, further research conducted by Nayak et al. has show from 1996 to 2004 pesticide use on GM crops, here in the US, increased by 122 million pound in the nine year period (115). It is clear that much of the hazards exist with the producers' application of pesticide rather than the GM crop itself.

PASSAGE 2

The role of the following passage is to show that there are specific modifications made to gene proteins in GM crops to only target families of insects that feed off of the crop, while they do not affect additional wildlife. My point is that certain protein expressions only affect specific insects. In this passage I have used two sources from the same research as evidence to argue this point.

I relied on these two sources from the same research to make a single point. The purpose of the sources is to show a specific protein expression and its target insect. This is meant to give my readers a couple of explanations to my claim.

But, I did not present these sources appropriately by separating them into two different paraphrases. After some review, I feel these sources are better presented in a summary. By placing the sources in a summary, I cut out the redundancy of citing two sources and allowed the idea to flow better.

Original

This is a valid concern, but biotechnical selection of modified genes typically prevents this from occurring. Bioengineers genetically alter specific proteins in the DNA of the crop to target specific family groups of insects. For example, Cryl protein (insecticide) is effective at dispatching moth and butterfly larvae, while Cry3 protein is effective against beetles (Srivastava et al. 136). Furthermore, the toxicity level of all Cry proteins to mammals, birds, and fish are extremely low (Srivastava et al. 136). Non-target insects are not directly or indirectly affected by these proteins, and are not susceptible to the insecticide.

Revised

This is a valid concern, but biotechnical selection of modified genes typically prevents this from occurring. Bioengineers genetically alter specific proteins in the DNA of the crop to target specific family groups of insects. Several biotechnological researchers, Srivastava et al., observed that Cryl protein (insecticide) is effective at dispatching moth and butterfly larvae, while Cry3 protein is effective against beetles. Furthermore, the researchers assert the toxicity level of all Cry proteins to mammals, birds, and fish are extremely low (136). Non-target insects are not directly or indirectly affected by these proteins, and are not susceptible to the insecticide.

PASSAGE 3

The purpose of this source is to show a specific negative effect herbicide resistant GM crops may cause on plant biodiversity. Based on my research, I believe this is a public concern amongst my audience and it needs to be addressed in my argument. This particular passage discusses the existence of the "super weed". Even though adaptation is a natural process, some of my readers may fear GM crops have sped up this process in some invasive plants. I have only used one source to make this point in my argument. It is because I had a tough time finding any specific instances where invasive plants were becoming a problem due to GM crops. Most of the researchers are only speculating on this issue. Still, it is important issue to my argument.

The purpose of this source for my readers is to show that "superweeds" are a real issue, but it has not rapidly occurred as most people speculate. I used the specific example of the mustard plant as my evidence. I believe this is a good example, but I need to revise my presentation of the material. Just like the previous passages, I have not used any signal verbs in this source material. I noticed a trend in my argument. I had been excluding signal verbs which poorly sets up my source material.

To effectively revise this passage, I had to include a signal phrase to set up my source material. Instead of having a single sentence paraphrase, I had to include the material in two sentences. I believe this has set up my material better and with a smoother transition into the source.

Original

When this happens with invasive plants or "superweeds", it will require producers to use stronger herbicides, or use more hazardous chemicals to get rid of them. Also, it is important to note that the first "super weed" already exists due to GM crop properties. GM modified canola crops have been known to spread their herbicide resistant traits to the wild mustard plant creating the first "super weed" (Nayak et al. 116). Still, plant adaptation is a natural evolutionary process. After twenty years of planting and globalization of GM crops, "super weeds", like the wild mustard plant, have not been observed at a detrimental level or seem to have negatively affected biodiversity in a region.

Revised

When this happens with invasive plants or "superweeds", it will require producers to use stronger herbicides, or use more hazardous chemicals to get rid of them. Also, it is important to note that the first "super weed" already exists. Researchers Nayak et al. have confirmed that properties from GM modified canola crops have affected the wild mustard plant. These researchers report that the GM canola crops have been known to spread their herbicide resistant traits to the wild mustard plant creating the first, and only, "super weed" (116). Still, plant adaptation is a natural evolutionary process. After twenty years of planting and globalization of GM crops, "super weeds", like the wild mustard plant, have not been observed at a detrimental level or seem to have negatively affected biodiversity in a region.

Essay Drafts

Michaela Yarbrough

LITERATURE REVIEW: DRAFT 1.1

Introduction

Typography is defined as the study of visual text and its formatting and design. The purpose of this literature review is to synthesize the studies of typographical elements regarding text grouping, spacing, word size, and typeface in children's reading material. Although most research was inconclusive since it was limited in its field of study, all authors add understanding to typography's role in children's learning. While past research has speculated that word grouping affects children's reading, current research indicates that line spacing, word size, and typeface (font) are more effective in improving children's reading.

Terminology

In order to understand the context of this study, some background information is necessary. In typography, "typeface" is a group of characters that share a similar style, like Arial or Comic Sans. Media files that describe how typefaces are displayed are called Font. Serif fonts, such as Times New Roman, are fonts that have small lines at the ends of the letters. Sans Serif fonts, or "without" serif, such as Arial do not have the small lines on the bottom. Infant characters are simplified letters that are thought to be less confusing for children. Infant characters replace complex letters like the double-bowled "g" to a single bowl, and the curved stem "a" to a straight line stem in infant form. "Point" is the size of the font while letter spacing is the distance between text lines.

Early Studies About Grouping/Text Segmenting

Early research has been inconclusive in the effects text grouping has on children's reading, but all show early investigations of typography. Carver's research shows that "chunking" does not have an effect on reading (288). However, Carver's research is not completely relevant to this topic since he studies adult readers' comprehension and speed rather than children's reading. Yet, Carver's research still demonstrates early attempts to experiment with text spacing and its effects on reading and education. In contrast, Weiss observes a different form of "chunking" by looking at the effects of test segmentation. He finds that the "pausal phrase format" increases reading level by one level, that is, "poor readers" read as well as "average readers," and average readers read as well as advanced readers (Weiss 77). Although Weiss' results showed positive effects on children, they were not easily transferrable to the classroom since teacher's assistance could intervene with positive results (87). In their research, both Weiss and Carver used a "Latin square" testing method that helps isolate text grouping changes. However, Weiss is much more detailed in his research by giving his test subjects optimum time allotments, while Carver prolongs his testing time and may have skewed his results due to reading fatigue. While Weiss and Carver investigate text segmentation in depth, later researchers, like Walker in "Serifs, Sans serifs and infant characters in children's reading books," see text grouping as a minor factor and only briefly addresses it in her essay. Walker considers text grouping is mainly used by advanced readers, and suggests further grouping studies are based on the "Gestalt Principle of proximity" which means words close to each other form groups to create a stronger meaning (Walker 109). All authors demonstrate an early interest in text spacing's significance in children's reading, but due to weak results, the attention to word grouping diminishes in later studies.

Line Spacing

Current research regarding word spacing has focused mainly on line spacing's effect on children's word recognition. In Reynolds and Walker's article "Children's Responses to Line Spacing in Early Reading Books," they find that increased and decreased line spacing does not significantly improve children's reading. However, the researchers found that children noticed these differences and identified the wider spaced lines easier to read than the reduced spacing (246). Reynolds and Walker also suggest that additional space allows for an "accurate return sweep of the eyes" allowing for better comprehension and familiarity of words (248). Similarly, Walker's study "Describing the Design of Children's Books" suggests that double the amount of line space should be allotted for young children as well as a "thick space" for older children (197). With this said, Walker's studies revolve around books published in the early 1900's; however, her research still makes important observations regarding space for readers alike. In contrast to Walker, Reynolds points out that too much space can be bad for children (248). Compared to Walker, Reynolds also goes on to consider children's opinions during her study and also considers how space effects children's motivation to read (265). Nevertheless, Reynolds and Walker agree that that more space is better for children. Additionally, Hughes's article "Reading at a distance," analyzes the effect of spacing, but considers the effects of distance unlike Reynolds and Walker. Hughes finds that space in text is crucial for legibility and is more important than increasing the letter size (213). Thus all authors agree that more space between lines is beneficial and perhaps most effective in improving children's' reading.

Word Size

Research agrees in addition to line spacing, bigger text size is beneficial for child readers. In Walker's article "Describing the design of Children's books: An Analytical Approach," she strongly states that "size of typeface" is the "most important factor in the influence of books upon vision" (196). Walker's studies are not completely relevant since they revolve around children's books from the early 1900s, but her reports still consider the needs of beginning learners and their perceptions of words. Likewise, Hughes encourages larger word size since he believes type may be too small for effective reading comprehension (410). Hughes agrees with Walker by stating that size usually gets smaller as age increases, but then goes further by considering "visual stress" as a result of smaller lettering and could create confusion and frustration in students (314). Hughes is also more urgent than Walker by calling for a change in books by educators. Similarly, Wilkins observes reading speed, but unlike Hughes does not focus on comprehension. He finds that larger font is beneficial and for even older children. In addition, both Hughes and Wilkins found that larger word size designed for younger children was usually read faster by older children and thus larger type size was beneficial to all ages of children. All Walker, Hughes and Wilkins recognize that word size is an important factor of consideration and as size is adjusted it can affect the way children learn to read.

Typefaces

While most studies usually generalize specific named typefaces to general serif categories, combined research agrees that sans serif typefaces are more suitable and preferred for children's reading. Moret-Tatay investigates typeface in terms of serifs by looking at how they affect "lexical access" i.e. vocabulary recognition (619). Despite the fact he tested college students rather than children, Moret-Tatay's findings indicate sans serif fonts were more effective. He states these results could still be transferrable to children since sans serifs were very beneficial for older students (Moret-Tatay 623). Walker and Reynolds's add to Moret-Tatay research in their article "Serifs, sans serifs and infant characters in children's reading books" by testing the legibility of serif and sans serif typefaces (Gill and Century fonts) in children. Although Walker and Reynolds's results were not as conclusive as Moret-Tatay's results, they found that Gill Schoolbook, a sans serif font, was more preferred by children and provided an idea of an "appropriate" type of font for use in teaching young readers (119). In contrast, Walker and Reynolds point out that some teachers may underestimate children's "adaptability" to understand serif fonts; however, preference shows that even children prefer infant characters over serif fonts despite their capability to read serif fonts (107, 119). In addition, Wilkins had similar results showing different typefaces made minimal effects on children's reading, but revealed Verdana, a sans serif font, as the preferred font over Sassoon (serif font) (408). Like Moret-Tatay, Wilkins identifies the continuation of strokes to help children read faster unlike Walker who mainly focuses a little more on comprehension. Yet, all agree that serifs have minor effects on reading and that preference from both teachers and children lean towards sans serif fonts.

Conclusion

After looking at past and current studies regarding typography and the main elements that affect children's reading, research leans towards word size and line spacing as the most effective elements on children's reading. Typeface was found to be less important, but was still considered as a relevant factor in terms of legibility and preference. While other variables could be considered such as visual text disabilities and color, this paper focuses on basic typographic elements initially speculated. More research is necessary in order to further understand what specifically effects children's reading rates and comprehension today. However, these studies have enabled researchers to think about not only the layout of children's books, but also learn more about how typography overall affects children's learning. Understanding the elements in typography and studying its impact on children's reading will thus help improve text formats in children's reading material and ultimately the learning experience of today's youth.

Works Cited

Carver, Ronald P. "Effect Of A "Chunked" Typography On Reading Rate And Comprehension." *Journal of Applied Psychology* 54.3 (1970): 288-296. SocINDEX with Full Text. Web. 10 Feb. 2013.

Hughes, Laura E., and Arnold J. Wilkins. "Reading At A Distance: Implications For The Design Of Text In Children's Big Books." *British Journal of Educational Psychology* 72.2 (2002): 213. Academic Search Complete. Web. 22 Feb. 2013.

Hughes, Laura E., Wilkins, Arnold J. "Typography in children's reading schemes may be Suboptimal: Evidence from measures of reading rate." *Journal of Research in Reading* 23.3 (2000): 314–325. Academic Search Complete. 5 Feb. 2013.

Moret-Tatay, Carmen, and Manuel Perea. "Do Serifs Provide An Advantage In The Recognition Of Written Words?." *Journal of Cognitive Psychology* 23.5 (2011): 619–624. Academic Search Complete. Web. 21 Feb. 2013.

Reynolds, Linda, Sue Walker, and Alison Duncan. "Children's Responses to Line Spacing in Early Reading Books or 'Holes to tell which line you're on." *Visible Language* 40.3 (2006): 246–267. Art & Architecture Complete. Web. 9 Feb. 2013.

Walker, Sue. "Describing the Design of Children's Books: An Analytical Approach." *Visible Language* 46.3 (2012): 180-199. Art Full Text (H.W. Wilson). Web. 5 Feb 2013.

Walker, Sue, and Linda Reynolds. "Serifs, sans serifs and infant characters in children's reading books." *Information Design Journal & Document Design* 11.2/3 (2002/2003): 106–122. Communication & Mass Media Complete. Web. 5 Feb. 2013.

Weiss, David S. "Effects of text segmentation on children's reading comprehension" *Discourse Process* 6.1 (1983): 77-89. Web. 10 Feb. 2013.

Wilkins, Arnold, et al. "Typography for children may be inappropriately designed." *Journal for Research in Reading* 32.4 (2009): 402–412. Academic Search Complete. Web. 5 Feb. 2013.

Michaela Yarbrough

LITERATURE REVIEW: DRAFT 1.2

Introduction

Typography is defined as the study of visual text and its formatting and design. The purpose of this literature review is to synthesize the studies of typographical elements regarding text grouping, spacing, word size, and typeface in children's reading material. Although most research was inconclusive due to a limited exploration of typography and children, all authors add understanding to typography's role in children's learning. While past research has speculated that word grouping improves children's reading, current research indicates that line spacing, word size, and typeface (font) are more noticeably effective factors in improving children's reading.

TERMINOLOGY

In order to understand the context of this study, some background information is necessary. In typography, "typeface" is a group of characters that share a similar style, like Arial or Comic Sans. Media files that describe how typefaces are displayed are called Font. Serif fonts, such as Times New Roman, are fonts that have small lines at the ends of the letters. Sans Serif fonts, or "without" serif, such as Arial do not have the small lines on the bottom.

Infant characters are simplified letters that are thought to be less confusing for children. Infant characters replace complex letters like the double-bowled "g" to a single bowl, and the curved stem "a" to a straight line stem in infant form. "Point" is the size of the font while letter spacing is the distance between text lines.

Early Studies About Grouping/Text Segmenting

Early research has been inconclusive in the effects text grouping has on children's reading, but all show early investigations of typography. Ronald P. Carver's research shows that "chunking" does not have an effect on reading (296). However, Carver's research is not completely relevant to this topic since he studies adult readers' comprehension and speed rather than children's reading. Yet, Carver's research still demonstrates early attempts to experiment with text spacing and its effects on reading and education. In contrast, David S. Weiss observes a different form of "chunking" by looking at the effects of test segmentation. He finds that the "pausal phrase format" increases reading by one level, that is, "poor readers" read as well as "average readers," and average readers read as well as advanced readers (Weiss 77). Although Weiss' results showed positive effects on children, they were not easily transferrable to the classroom since teacher's assistance could intervene with positive results (87). Despite these differences, both studies find that reading is affected. In their research, Weiss and Carver use a "Latin square" testing method that helps isolate text-grouping changes. However, Weiss is much more detailed in his research by giving his test subjects optimum time allotments, while Carver prolongs his testing time and may have skewed his results due to reading fatigue. While Weiss and Carver investigate text segmentation in depth, later studies by Sue Walker and Linda Reynolds see text grouping as a minor factor and only briefly address its relevance (Serifs 109). Walker and Reynolds believe text grouping is mainly used by advanced readers, and suggest further grouping studies could be investigated through the "Gestalt Principle of proximity" which means words close to each other form groups to create a stronger meaning (Walker 109). All of these authors demonstrate an early interest in text spacing's significance in children's reading, but due to weak results, the attention to word grouping diminishes in recent studies.

Line Spacing

Current research regarding text spacing has focused on line spacing's effect on children's ease to read. Linda Reynolds, Sue Walker, and Alison Duncan find that changing the line spacing does not significantly improve children's reading due to minimal changes in results (264). However, they found that children recognized these differences and perceived the wider spaced lines were easier to read than the reduced spacing because it allowed for an "accurate return sweep of the eyes" giving better comprehension and familiarity of words (Reynolds, Walker, and Duncan 248). Reynolds, Walker, and Duncan also believe wider spacing could have an effect on children's motivation to read based on children's comments in their research. They found that if children perceived the "appearance of the text" to be difficult it could reduce the "appeal" of the book and "discourage" attempts to read the text (265). Compared to Walker, Reynolds, and Duncan's research, Sue Walker's later individual research simply focuses on the attributes of design in children's books from the early 1900s and does not regard spacing in relationship to children's motivation. She mainly draws evidence from observation to create checklists of common characteristics in these children's books (Walker Describing 185). In terms of spacing, Walker finds that larger spacing is "desirable" for younger children and a "thick space" is promoted for older children (Describing 197). Walker's observations provide early insight into the design of books and suggest that children of today could benefit from trends of the past. In contrast, Hughes and Wilkins also consider the effects of spacing but look at its effect in relationship to distance (Reading 213). They find that space in text is crucial for legibility and also consider it is more important than increasing the letter size (Reading 213). For example, more children found it easier to understand words that had larger spacing than larger word size (Reading 223). As a result, although Hughes and Wilkins resolve spacing affects reading acuity and fluency rather than motivation or word recognition, Hughes and Wilkins agree with Reynolds, Walker, and Duncan that line spacing has effects on children's reading. Thus despite differing concentrations, all authors agree that more space between lines affects children's reading.

Word Size

Research agrees in addition to line spacing, bigger text size is beneficial for child readers. Sue Walker strongly states that "size of typeface" is the "most important factor in the influence of books upon vision" (Describing 196). However, Walker's studies are not completely relevant since they revolve around children's books from the early 1900s, but her reports still consider the importance of design and the needs of beginning learners and their perceptions of words. Likewise, Laura E. Hughes and Arnold J. Wilkins encourage larger word size since they believe type may be too small for effective reading comprehension (Typography 410). They agree with Walker by stating that font size usually gets smaller as age increases. However, Hughes and Wilkins go further by considering "visual stress" as a result of smaller lettering and state it could hinder performance and slow speed (Typography 315). Hughes and Wilkins are also more urgent than Walker by calling for a change in books by educators. In a more recent article, Arnold J. Wilkins observes reading speed in relationship to word size, but unlike his earlier study with Hughes he does not focus on comprehension. He finds that larger font is beneficial for both younger and older children. In addition, both studies also agree that larger word size designed for younger children was read faster by older children, thus larger type size was beneficial to all ages. When comparing Wilkins and Walker, Wilkins is more detailed in field research by testing children, while Walker focuses more on the general effectiveness of word size in the design of children's books. Nonetheless, Walker, Hughes and Wilkins recognize that adjusting word size is an important factor to consider and can affect the way children learn to read.

Typefaces

While most studies have found the effects of specific typefaces inconclusive, combined research agrees that generalized sans serif typefaces are more suitable and preferred for children's reading. Carmen Moret-Tatay and Manuel Perea investigate typeface in terms of serifs by looking at how they affect "lexical access" i.e. vocabulary recognition (619). Although

Moret-Tatay and Perea tested college students rather than children, their findings indicate sans serif fonts were more effective and call for further study as their results could be applied to younger children based on beneficial results on older students (Moret-Tatay and Perea 623). Sue Walker and Linda Reynolds's add to Moret-Tatay and Perea's research by testing the legibility of serif and sans serif typefaces (Gill and Century fonts) for children (Serifs 108). Although Walker and Reynolds's results were not as clear as Moret-Tatay and Perea's results, they found that Gill Schoolbook, a sans serif font, was more preferred by children and provided an idea of an "appropriate" typeface for use in teaching young readers (119). While some researchers like Moret-Tatay try to identify specific typefaces that affect children's reading, Walker and Reynolds suggest teachers may underestimate children's "adaptability" to understand serif fonts; they found that serif fonts have a minimal affect on children's reading (107). However, Walker and Reynolds find that children prefer infant characters over serif fonts despite their capability to read serif fonts (107, 119). In addition, Wilkins found that showing different typefaces made minimal effects on children's reading, but revealed Verdana, a sans serif font, as the preferred font over Sassoon (serif font) (408). Like Moret-Tatay, Wilkins identifies the continuation of strokes to help children read faster, unlike Walker who mainly focuses on comprehension. Yet, the majority agrees that serifs have minor effects on reading and both teachers and children prefer sans serif fonts.

Conclusion

After looking at past and current studies regarding typography and the main elements that affect children's reading, research leans towards word size and line spacing as the most effective elements on children's reading. Typeface was found to be less important, but was still considered as a relevant factor in terms of legibility and preference. While other variables could be considered such as visual text disabilities and color, this paper focuses on basic typographic elements initially speculated. More research is necessary in order to further understand what specifically effects children's reading rates and comprehension today. However, these studies have enabled researchers to think about not only the layout of children's books, but also learn more about how typography overall affects children's learning. Understanding the elements in typography and studying its impact on children's reading will thus help improve text formats in children's reading material and ultimately the learning experience of today's youth.

Works Cited

Carver, Ronald P. "Effect Of A "Chunked" Typography On Reading Rate And Comprehension." *Journal of Applied Psychology* 54.3 (1970): 288-296. SocINDEX with Full Text. Web. 10 Feb. 2013.

Hughes, Laura E., and Arnold J. Wilkins. "Reading At A Distance: Implications For The Design Of Text In Children's Big Books." *British Journal of Educational Psychology* 72.2 (2002): 213. Academic Search Complete. Web. 22 Feb. 2013.

Hughes, Laura E., Wilkins, Arnold J. "Typography in children's reading schemes may be Suboptimal: Evidence from measures of reading rate." *Journal of Research in Reading* 23.3 (2000): 314–325. Academic Search Complete. 5 Feb. 2013.

Moret-Tatay, Carmen, and Manuel Perea. "Do Serifs Provide An Advantage In The Recognition Of Written Words?." *Journal of Cognitive Psychology* 23.5 (2011): 619–624. Academic Search Complete. Web. 21 Feb. 2013.

Reynolds, Linda, Sue Walker, and Alison Duncan. "Children's Responses to Line Spacing in Early Reading Books or 'Holes to tell which line you're on." *Visible Language* 40.3 (2006): 246–267. Art & Architecture Complete. Web. 9 Feb. 2013.

Walker, Sue. "Describing the Design of Children's Books: An Analytical Approach." *Visible Language* 46.3 (2012): 180–199. Art Full Text (H.W. Wilson). Web. 5 Feb 2013.

Walker, Sue, and Linda Reynolds. "Serifs, sans serifs and infant characters in children's reading books." *Information Design Journal & Document Design* 11.2/3 (2002/2003): 106–122. Communication & Mass Media Complete. Web. 5 Feb. 2013.

Weiss, David S. "Effects of text segmentation on children's reading comprehension" *Discourse Process* 6.1 (1983): 77–89. Web. 10 Feb. 2013.

Wilkins, Arnold, et al. "Typography for children may be inappropriately designed." *Journal for Research in Reading* 32.4 (2009): 402–412. Academic Search Complete. Web. 5 Feb. 2013.

Daniel Marquez

LITERATURE REVIEW: DRAFT 1.1

Recreational fishing is one of the dominant pastimes of the American people, and for that matter, people worldwide (Cook and Cowx, 2004). With the creation of dams in both the eastern and western river systems of North America, and the subsequent habitat destruction, native anadromous salmonid populations have suffered great declines over the past century (Brown and Day 2002). Recently a contentious issue has arisen among fisheries biologists concerning the methods for conserving of our wild salmonid fisheries. Although previously little was known about its effects on wild populations, fish hatchery stocking has been a key tool in the management of recreational fish stocks and has been practiced at a massive global scale (Araki and Schmid 2010). Recent research has indicated that the current methods of fish hatchery stocking may have negative impacts on wild salmonid populations, and should be altered or in some cases discontinued in order to preserve our native anadromous salmonid stocks.

Much of the research on this subject concerns the fitness and survival rates of the hatchery fish that are being released. In their study "Fitness of Hatchery-Reared Salmonids in the Wild", Araki et al look at both Pacific and Atlantic salmon, as well as in steelhead trout from hatcheries and examine links between brood stock origin and fitness. They compare fourteen previous studies and conclude that in all cases fitness is lower in hatchery-reared fish as compared to their wild counterparts, but that among the hatchery-reared fish, fitness was higher in stocks that used local wild brood stock as compared to domesticated brood stock. They also found that fitness diminished in hatchery-reared stocks in generations removed from the local wild brood stock. So while this study did show a big difference in fitness between hatchery-reared and wild salmonids, it did offer some suggestions of how hatchery methods could be improved to increase the fitness in hatchery-reared fish.

Another study that looks at the fitness of hatchery fish is entitled "Comparative Performance of Genetically Similar Hatchery and Naturally Reared Coho Salmon in Streams" by Rhodes and Quinn. This study looks at the survival, movement, and growth of a population of hatchery coho salmon that were separated at an early stage of life. One group of fry was released into a natural stream, while the other was raised totally within a hatchery. After three months, the stream-reared fish were inventoried and marked. The hatchery-reared fish were then marked and released in the same abundance as the marked stream fish. A year later the stream was sampled to compare the survival rates between the hatchery and naturally reared fish. At the end they found that there was little difference in the survival rates between the two groups, but that the hatchery-reared fish did show a slightly larger body mass. This would suggest that even though the rearing methods for the two groups were very different, there was little change in survival rates. Because the study included no comparison to the survival rates of a wild-born population, it's hard to make a conclusion of the efficacy of hatchery fish in general based on this study. It can however be concluded that rearing methods have little impact on the fitness of hatchery fish.

Reproductive success is another aspect of fitness that has been studied in hatchery-influenced salmonid populations. In the 2006 study, "Reproductive Success of Captive-Bred Steelhead Trout in the Wild: Evaluation of Three Hatchery Programs in the Hood River", Araki et al compare the reproductive success between wild fish, traditional hatchery fish (fish from hatcheries that use domesticated, non-local brood stock), and supplemental hatchery fish (fish from hatcheries that use wild, local brood stock). They were able to determine the parentage of returning fish through genetic pedigree analysis of the first two run-years after stocking began due to the fact that the spawning grounds were disconnected from the main stream so every returning fish had to be passed above a dam by hand. The researchers found that supplemental hatchery fish had a comparable reproductive success rate to that of wild fish, but hatchery fish had a much lower reproductive success rate when compared to the other two types. They also found that the progeny of supplemental hatchery fish breeding with wild fish had a similar reproductive success rate to that of wild fish, but the progeny of either type of hatchery fish breeding with other hatchery fish had significantly lower reproductive success. The researchers concluded that supplemental hatchery programs could in fact boost population levels in the first two years after introduction, while traditional hatchery fish have an immediate drag on total population levels. The researchers do admit though that because their study was only conducted over two years, there very well could be long-term effects of supplemental hatchery fish that they were not seeing.

Luckily, in the study, "Effective Size of a Wild Salmonid Population is Greatly Reduced by Hatchery Supplementation" by Christie et al, the researchers conduct a very similar study to that of the 2006 study by Araki et al except theirs takes place over seventeen years instead of two years. In this study, which was also conducted in Hood River system, the researchers looked at a population of steelhead trout that was not influenced by tradition hatchery stocking, but was undergoing hatchery supplementation. They did similar genetic pedigree analysis on returning fish and were able to determine lineages over the years. The researchers found that while indeed the supplementation program increased the total population of steelhead trout, over the years the effective population (the fish that reproduced and whose progeny then also reproduced) went into decline. As mentioned in the conclusion of this paper and further discussed in the paper "Effective Population Size of Steelhead Trout: Influence of Variance in Reproductive Success, Hatchery Programs, and Genetic Compensation Between Life‐History Forms" by Araki et al, the researchers note that this concept of effective population versus total population represents the main trade-off involved with hatchery supplementation. Although total population may be increased through hatchery supplementation, if the effective population decreases, so does genetic diversity and thus resilience, making a population more vulnerable to future disturbance.

Another important effect of the use of hatchery stocking is described in the paper "Hatcheries and Endangered Salmon" by Meyers et al. The authors of this paper talk about the legal implication of hatchery stocking. In 2001, a U.S. district judge ruled that coho salmon in Oregon had to be removed from the endangered species list because "hatchery fish were included in the same population segment with which they were genetically associated" (Meyers et al 2004). This ruling has major implications for the wild coho salmon population because while listed as an endangered species, they were highly protected, but when removed from the list, their habitat becomes much more susceptible to development resulting in degradation. The authors describe this as another trade off concerning hatchery stocking because while hatchery supplementation may be an effective way of reviving a damaged population, the fact that it is being supplemented could damage it further. The authors conclude that the goal for fisheries should be to have a naturally self-sustaining population and that the use of hatcheries should be avoided.

With all this new research coming to light, there may need to be changes made to the way anadromous salmonid populations are managed. The research seems to indicate that the choices that will need to be made are marked by a series of trade-offs that really come down to the values of what we want our fish stocks to look like. Hopefully there will be further research that makes it clear as to what should done to preserve our native anadromous salmonid population properly.

References

Araki, H., Waples, R. S., Ardren, W. R., Cooper, B., & Blouin, M. S. (2007). Effective population size of steelhead trout: influence of variance in reproductive success, hatchery programs, and genetic compensation between life‐history forms. Molecular Ecology, 16(5), 953–966.Araki,

Araki, H., Berejikian, B. A., Ford, M. J., & Blouin, M. S. (2008). Fitness of hatchery-reared salmonids in the wild. Evolutionary Applications, 1(2), 342–355.

Araki, H., Ardren, W. R., Olsen, E., Cooper, B., & Blouin, M. S. (2006). Reproductive Success of Captive‐Bred Steelhead Trout in the Wild: Evaluation of Three Hatchery Programs in the Hood River. Conservation Biology, 21(1), 181–190.

Araki, H., & Schmid, C. (2010). Is hatchery stocking a help or harm?: evidence, limitations and future directions in ecological and genetic surveys. Aquaculture, 308, S2–S11.

Brown, C., & Day, R. L. (2002). The future of stock enhancements: lessons for hatchery practice from conservation biology. Fish and Fisheries, 3(2), 79–94.

Christie, M. R., Marine, M. L., French, R. A., Waples, R. S., & Blouin, M. S. (2012). Effective size of a wild salmonid population is greatly reduced by hatchery supplementation. Heredity.

Cooke, S. J., & Cowx, I. G. (2004). The role of recreational fishing in global fish crises. BioScience, 54(9), 857–859.

Myers, R. A., Levin, S. A., Lande, R., James, F. C., Murdoch, W. W., & Paine, R. T. (2004). Hatcheries and endangered salmon. Science, 303(5666), 1980–1980.

Rhodes, J. S., & Quinn, T. P. (1999). Comparative performance of genetically similar hatchery and naturally reared juvenile coho salmon in streams. North American Journal of Fisheries Management, 19(3), 670–677.

Daniel Marquez

LITERATURE REVIEW DRAFT: 1.2

Recreational fishing is one of the dominant pastimes of the American people, and for that matter, people worldwide (Cook and Cowx 2004). With the creation of dams in both the eastern and western river systems of North America, and the subsequent habitat destruction, native anadromous salmonid populations have suffered great declines over the past century (Brown and Day 2002). Recently a contentious issue has arisen among fisheries biologists concerning the methods for conserving of our wild salmonid fisheries. Although previously little was known about its effects on wild populations, fish hatchery stocking has been a key tool in the management of recreational fish stocks and has been practiced at a massive global scale (Araki and Schmid 2010). Recent research has indicated that the current methods of fish hatchery stocking may have negative impacts on wild salmonid populations, and should be altered or in some cases discontinued in order to preserve our native anadromous salmonid stocks.

Much of the research on this subject concerns the fitness and survival rates of the hatchery fish that are being released. In their study "Fitness of Hatchery-Reared Salmonids in the Wild", Araki et al look at both Pacific and Atlantic salmon, as well as in steelhead trout from hatcheries and examine links between brood stock origin and fitness. They compare fourteen previous studies and conclude that in all cases fitness is lower in hatchery-reared fish as compared to their wild counterparts, but that among the hatchery-reared fish, fitness was higher in stocks that used local wild brood stock as compared to domesticated brood stock. They also found that fitness diminished in hatchery-reared stocks in generations removed from the local wild brood stock. So while this study did show a big difference in fitness between hatchery-reared and wild salmonids, it did offer some suggestions of how hatchery methods could be improved to increase the fitness in hatchery-reared fish.

Another study that looks at the fitness of hatchery fish is entitled "Comparative Performance of Genetically Similar Hatchery and Naturally Reared Coho Salmon in Streams" by Rhodes and Quinn. This study looks at the survival, movement, and growth of a population of hatchery coho salmon that were separated at an early stage of life. One group of fry was released into a natural stream, while the other was raised totally within a hatchery. After three months, the stream-reared fish were inventoried and marked. The hatchery-reared fish were then marked and released in the same abundance as the marked stream fish. A year later the stream was sampled to compare the survival rates between the hatchery and naturally reared fish. At the end they found that there was little difference in the survival rates between the two groups, but that the hatchery-reared fish did show a slightly larger body mass. This would suggest that even though the rearing methods for the two groups were very different, there was little change in survival rates. Because the study included no comparison to the survival rates of a wild-born population, it's hard to make a conclusion of the efficacy of hatchery fish in general based on this study. It can however be concluded that rearing methods have little impact on the fitness of hatchery fish.

Reproductive success is an aspect of fitness that has been studied in great detail in hatchery-influenced salmonid populations. In the 2006 study, "Reproductive Success of Captive-Bred Steelhead Trout in the Wild: Evaluation of Three Hatchery Programs in the Hood River", Araki et al compare reproductive success in wild fish, traditional hatchery fish (fish from hatcheries that use domesticated, non-local brood stock), and supplemental hatchery fish, (fish from hatcheries that use wild, local brood stock). The researchers determined the parentage of returning fish through genetic pedigree analysis, allowing them to calculate reproductive success. Due to the fact that the spawning grounds were disconnected from the main stream by a dam, each returning fish had to be passed above the dam by hand, which allowed them to sample the entire population. The researchers found that supplemental hatchery fish had comparable reproductive success to wild fish while traditional hatchery fish had much lower reproductive success than the other two types. They also found that the progeny of supplemental hatchery fish when breeding with wild fish had a similar reproductive success to wild fish, but the progeny of either type of hatchery fish breeding with other hatchery fish had significantly lower reproductive success. The researchers concluded that supplemental hatchery programs could in fact boost population levels in the first two years after introduction, while traditional hatchery fish have an immediate drag on total population levels. The results of this study argue that while the use of traditional hatchery fish should probably be discontinued for the purposes of conservation, there are some practical uses for hatchery supplementation for this purpose. The researchers do admit though that because their study was only conducted over two years, there very well could be long-term effects of supplemental hatchery fish that they were not seeing.

Luckily, in the study, "Effective Size of a Wild Salmonid Population is Greatly Reduced by Hatchery Supplementation" by Christie et al, the researchers conduct a very similar study to that of the 2006 study by Araki et al except theirs takes place over seventeen years instead of two years. In this study, which was also conducted in Hood River system, the researchers looked at a population of steelhead trout that was not influenced by tradition hatchery stocking, but was undergoing hatchery supplementation. They did similar genetic pedigree analysis on returning fish and were able to determine lineages over the years. The researchers found that while indeed the supplementation program increased the total population of steelhead trout, over the years the effective population (the fish that reproduced and whose progeny then also reproduced) went into decline. As mentioned in the conclusion of this paper and further discussed in the paper "Effective Population Size of Steelhead Trout: Influence of Variance in Reproductive Success, Hatchery Programs, and Genetic Compensation Between Life-History Forms" by Araki et al, the researchers note that this concept of effective population versus total population represents the main trade-off involved with hatchery supplementation. Although total population may be increased through hatchery supplementation, if the effective population decreases, so does genetic diversity and thus resilience, making a population more vulnerable to future disturbance.

Another important effect of the use of hatchery stocking is described in the paper "Hatcheries and Endangered Salmon" by Meyers et al. The authors of this paper talk about the legal implication of hatchery stocking. In 2001, a U.S. district judge ruled that coho salmon in Oregon had to be removed from the endangered species list because "hatchery fish were included in the same population segment with which they were genetically associated" (Meyers et al 2004). This ruling has major implications for the wild coho salmon population because while listed as an endangered species, they were highly protected, but when removed from the list, their habitat becomes much more susceptible to development resulting in degradation. The authors describe this as another trade off concerning hatchery stocking because while hatchery supplementation may be an effective way of reviving a damaged population, the fact that it is being supplemented could damage it further. The authors conclude that the goal for fisheries should be to have a naturally self-sustaining population and that the use of hatcheries should be avoided.

This new research seems to have a common theme: Hatchery programs, no matter how well the genetic integrity of the stock is accounted for, will have some negative long term effects on the natural population. This newly discovered fact could have a very deep impact on the science of fisheries management and fisheries policy in general. Today, there are hundreds of fish hatcheries that currently operate around the United States and these issues could bring their status in to question (Araki and Schmid 2010). Research needs to continue so that we can know the best way forward in conserving our native salmonid populations.

References

Araki, H., Waples, R. S., Ardren, W. R., Cooper, B., & Blouin, M. S. (2007). Effective population size of steelhead trout: influence of variance in reproductive success, hatchery programs, and genetic compensation between life-history forms. Molecular Ecology, 16(5), 953–966.

Araki, H., Berejikian, B. A., Ford, M. J., & Blouin, M. S. (2008). Fitness of hatchery-reared salmonids in the wild. Evolutionary Applications, 1(2), 342–355.

Araki, H., Ardren, W. R., Olsen, E., Cooper, B., & Blouin, M. S. (2006). Reproductive Success of Captive‐Bred Steelhead Trout in the Wild: Evaluation of Three Hatchery Programs in the Hood River. Conservation Biology, 21(1), 181–190.

Araki, H., & Schmid, C. (2010). Is hatchery stocking a help or harm?: evidence, limitations and future directions in ecological and genetic surveys. Aquaculture, 308, S2–S11.

Brown, C., & Day, R. L. (2002). The future of stock enhancements: lessons for hatchery practice from conservation biology. Fish and Fisheries, 3(2), 79–94.

Christie, M. R., Marine, M. L., French, R. A., Waples, R. S., & Blouin, M. S. (2012). Effective size of a wild salmonid population is greatly reduced by hatchery supplementation. Heredity.

Cooke, S. J., & Cowx, I. G. (2004). The role of recreational fishing in global fish crises. BioScience, 54(9), 857–859.

Myers, R. A., Levin, S. A., Lande, R., James, F. C., Murdoch, W. W., & Paine, R. T. (2004). Hatcheries and endangered salmon. Science, 303(5666), 1980–1980.

Rhodes, J. S., & Quinn, T. P. (1999). Comparative performance of genetically similar hatchery and naturally reared juvenile coho salmon in streams. North American Journal of Fisheries Management, 19(3), 670–677.

ARGUMENT

Wayne Swink

DRAFT 1.1

Genetically Modified crops are the future of agriculture. But, the future of GM crops seems cloudy amongst the public concerns of consumers, politicians, and activist groups. Researchers believe GM crops have received a poor public reputation simply because the process of creating GM crops is unfamiliar and scary to the consumers (Schmidt 530). However, there are genuine concerns GM crops bring to the table like negative effects on biodiversity, the surrounding environment, non target insects, and the evolution of "super weed" plants. There is the very real possibility that GM crops could be unintentionally introduced to a negative environmental chain of events. To date, there has not been any catastrophic event involving GM crops, but with the rapid pace GM crops have been embraced, it is a fathomable scenario. Despite all the negative possibilities and public resistance, GM crops around the world have mostly benefited the environment and negative effects have created minimal impact. The following will bring to light the global reduction of pesticide use that GM insecticide and herbicide crops have provided, and how this environmental benefit outweighs the minimal negative impacts GM crops have created since its inception.

There have proven to be several environmental benefits to GM insecticide crops. The most notable benefit is the drastic reduction of pesticide use. GM insecticide crops are created to simply enhance a plant's natural defense mechanism against pest insects. This makes the natural insecticide biodegradable and not a hazard to the environment. Over 80 percent of major crops in the US are genetically modified (Maghari and Ardekani 110). Many of the predominant crops such as corn, cotton, and canola have pest resistant genes, which have resulted in a significant drop in pesticide use in the US (Singh et al. 602). Furthermore, a 2005 case study of Bt (Bacillus Thuringiensis) genetically modified rice, grown in China, has shown a reduction of half the number of chemical pesticide poisonings among the rice farmers (Schmidt 533). Also, according to Nayak et al., a field test in India was conducted from 2004 to 2006 on a Bt variety of eggplant. The test showed an 80 percent reduction of pesticide use on the Bt eggplant crops compared to non-Bt controlled eggplant crops. With India being the second largest producer of eggplant in the world, this accounted for a 42 percent reduction of total insecticide use on worldwide commercially available eggplants (113). GM insecticide crops are a passively natural treatment that is rapidly replacing the manmade chemical treatments known to be harmful to the environment. However, these genetic modifications may not encourage all producers to use less chemical pesticides on their crops. For example, research shows from 1996 to 2004 pesticide use on GM crops, here in the US, increased by 122 million pound in the nine year period (Nayak et al. 115). It is clear that much of the hazards are in the application of pesticide rather than the GM crop itself.

A valid social concern regarding GM insecticide crops is the possibility of inadvertently dispatching non-target, beneficial, insects like bees (pollinators) or ladybugs (predators). This is a valid concern, but biotechnical selection of modified genes typically prevents this from occurring. Bioengineers genetically alter specific proteins in the DNA of the crop to target specific family groups of insects. For example, Cryl protein (insecticide) is effective at dispatching moth and butterfly larvae, while Cry3 protein is effective against beetles (Srivastava et al. 136). Furthermore, the toxicity level of all Cry proteins to mammals, birds, and fish are extremely low (Srivastava et al. 136). Non-target insects are not directly or indirectly affected by these proteins, and are not susceptible to the insecticide. However, there are certainly isolated cases where non-target insects may have been affected indirectly by a GM crop. Research has shown lacewing larvae, which feed on caterpillars affected by GM insecticide (Cry 1 Ab) corn, had a higher mortality rate than the lacewing larvae, which fed on non-GM corn feeding caterpillars (Singh et al. 603). Still, this problem may be directly related to the application of chemical toxins and not due to the GM crop carrying the gene; as evident from the studies of the effects of spraying non-target insects, like lacewings, with the (Cry 1 Ab) insecticides (Singh et al. 603). Thus far, there have been no significant reported losses of a non-target species due to GM crops.

With many insecticide GM crops, there are herbicide modifications made to these plants as well. Herbicide GM crops are the most successful of all biotechnological crops so far. In 2003, the US alone had produced 81 percent of soybean, 59 percent of cotton, and 15 percent of corn crops that were herbicide tolerant (Srivastava et al. 140). The US is not the only country to embrace these crops. Argentinean farmers have embraced GM soybeans, specifically, and their crop accounts for 95 percent of the market (Srivastava et al. 140). The Environmental Defense Fund considers GM herbicide crops as one of the most environmentally benign herbicides ever developed (Conko and Miller 80). Nayak et al. agrees herbicide resistance crops have the ability to decrease the overall use of herbicides and is a more environmentally friendly approach (113). GM herbicide crops are typically expressed to resist the broad spectrum glyphosate herbicide. It is the most widely used herbicide, worldwide, because of its low environmental impact and effectiveness. This is a nonspecific chemical herbicide designed to kill most plants. After it is applied, the chemical is broken down by microorganisms and does not persist long in the soil (Srivastava et al. 139). The benefit of using glyphosate resistant crops is that it reduces the need to use other harmful chemicals which leads to lower toxicity level in the soil, water, and air. This also enables farmers to use a more environmentally friendly no tilling process. This prevents topsoil erosion, reduces runoff to rivers, streams, and lakes, and releases less carbon dioxide into the atmosphere from mechanical equipment (Conko and Miller 79). Typically, predominant crops like soybeans, cotton, corn, and canola have been genetically modified to express this resistance. For example, GM (Round Up) soybeans express the nontoxic herbicide that deactivates, degrades in the soil, and is substantially equivalent to conventional commercial soybeans (Nayak et al. 113). However, with all these environmental benefits there are genuine negative effects. Specifically, the genuine possibility of invasive plants adapting to resist herbicides.

All plants have the biological ability to adapt and become resistant to herbicides like glyphosate. It is inevitable that most species of plants will eventually adapt to survive. Essentially, a GM herbicide crops is modified to skip several generational and evolutionary steps to express this adaptation. When this happens with invasive plants or "superweeds", it will require producers to use stronger herbicides, or use more hazardous chemicals to get rid of them. Also, it is important to note that the first "super weed" already exists due to GM crop properties. GM modified canola crops have been known to spread their herbicide resistant traits to the wild mustard plant creating the first "super weed" (Nayak et al. 116). Still, plant adaptation is a natural evolutionary process. After twenty years of planting and globalization of GM crops, "super weeds", like the wild mustard plant, have not been observed at a detrimental level or seem to have negatively affected biodiversity in a region. However, the inevitability of "super weeds" also raises public concerns regarding biodiversity. The most notable concern of biodiversity is if crosspollination of GM and conventional crops could be a possibility. Research shows this was an issue raised by environmentalist groups in Oaxaca, Mexico. The environmentalist groups speculated that GM corn, planted next to native corn in Oaxaca, would cross-pollinate and threaten the diversity of the native species. However, a large scale, systematic, survey showed no evidence of any invasion by the GM corn on the native species (Singh et al. 603). Again, this is a valid public concern, but in this case, cross-pollination of GM crops and conventional crops did not appear to have a significant impact on biodiversity.

With the minimal negative impact on worldwide biodiversity, its surrounding environment, and non target insects, GM crops are not the bane it is perceived to be by the public. There still stands a genuine possibility GM crops may create a catastrophic event in the future. However, based on the past twenty years of applying this technology, this is unlikely to occur. The reduction of pesticide use alone has benefited the environment tremendously, and this accomplishment is noteworthy enough to be considered the future technology of agriculture. It is predicted that, by 2015, more than 200 million hectares of land will be planted with GM crops in over 40 countries (Maghari and Ardekani 110). These crops are the future of food whether they are embraced by society or not. After all, GM crops are based off of traditional breeding practices, and gene-splicing is simply used to skip several evolutionary steps. This biotechnology has become so effective that crops are even being designed to enhance nutrition. For example, The Danford Center has created GM grains enriched with vitamin E and vegetables with enhanced folic levels (Schmidt 530). It is clear GM crops do not negatively effect the environment, rather the environment has benefited from GM crops. Once the clouds of negative perspectives have been cleared, GM crops will be embraced by society.

Works Cited

Conko, Gregory, and Henry Miller. "The Rush to Condemn Genetically Modified Crops." Policy Review 165 (2011): 69–82. EBSCOhost. Web. 15 Feb. 2013.

Maghari, Behrokh, and Ali Ardekani. "Genetically Modified Foods and Social Concerns." Avicenna Journal of Medical Biotechnology 3.3 (2011): 109–117. EBSCOhost. Web. 15 Feb. 2013.

Nayak, Laxmikanta, et al. "Genetically Modified Crops." Agricultural Reviews 32.2 (2011): 112–119. EBSCOhost. Web. 15 Feb. 2013.

Schmidt, Charles. "Genetically Modified Foods Breeding Uncertainty." Environmental Health Perspectives 113.8 (2005): 526–533. EBSCOhost. Web. 15 Feb. 2013.

Singh, Om, et al. "Genetically Modified Crops: Success, Safety Assessment, and Public Concern." Applied Microbiology & Biotechnology 71.5 (2006): 598–607. EBSCOhost. Web. 15 Feb. 2013.

Srivastava, Navin, et al. "Genetically Modified Crops: An Overview." Biotechnology 10.2 (2011): 136–148. EBSCOhost. Web. 15 Feb. 2013.

DRAFT 1.2

Genetically Modified crops are the future of agriculture. But, the future of GM crops seems cloudy amongst the public concerns of consumers, politicians, and activist groups. Researchers believe GM crops have received a poor public reputation simply because the process of creating these plants is unfamiliar and scary to the consumer (Schmidt 530). What may not be understood by some critics is that genetically modified plants are based off of traditional breeding practices, and gene-splicing is simply used to skip several evolutionary steps. However, there are genuine concerns modified plants bring to the table, like negative effects on biodiversity, the environment, non-target insects, and the evolution of "super weed" plants. To date there has not been any catastrophic events involving these crops. Nevertheless, at the rapid pace in which farmers have implemented these modified crops, it is a fathomable scenario. Despite all the negative possibilities and public resistance, GM crops around the world have mostly benefited the environment and its negative effects have created minimal impact. Specifically, GM insecticide and herbicide crops have proven to reduce the global use of pesticides. The overall reduction of pesticide use alone outweighs the minimal negative impacts of these plants. In spite of the poor reputation of genetically modified crops, they will continue to be the future of agriculture because of their environmentally friendly effects, and for their enhanced nutritional value.

There have proven to be several environmental benefits to GM insecticide crops. The most notable benefit is the drastic reduction of pesticide use. These genetic modifications are created to simply enhance a plant's natural defense mechanism against pest insects. This makes the natural insecticide biodegradable and not a hazard to the environment. Over 80 percent of major crops in the US are genetically modified (Maghari and Ardekani 110). Many of the predominant crops such as corn, cotton, and canola have pest resistant genes, which have resulted in a significant drop in pesticide use in the US (Singh et al. 602). Furthermore, a 2005 case study of Bt (Bacillus Thuringiensis) genetically modified rice, grown in China, has shown a reduction of half the number of chemical pesticide poisonings among the rice farmers (Schmidt 533). Also, according to researchers Nayak et al., from the National Institute of Jute and Allied Firbe Technology in India, a field test was conducted from 2004 to 2006 on a Bt variety of eggplant grown in that country. The test showed an 80 percent reduction of pesticide use on the Bt genetically modified eggplant crops compared to non-Bt controlled eggplant crops. With India being the second largest producer of eggplant in the world, this accounted for a 42 percent reduction of total insecticide use on worldwide commercially available eggplants during that time period (113). GM insecticide crops are a passively natural treatment that is rapidly replacing the manmade chemical treatments known to be harmful to the environment. However, these genetic modifications may not encourage all producers to use less chemical pesticides on their crops. For example, further research conducted by Nayak et al. has shown from 1996 to 2004 pesticide use on GM crops, here in the US, increased by 122 million pound in the nine year period (115). It is clear that much of the hazards exist with the producers' application of pesticide rather than the modified plants themselves.

Some critics believe that there is a possibility of GM insecticide crops to inadvertently dispatch non-target, beneficial, insects like bees (pollinators) or ladybugs (predators). This is a valid concern, but biotechnical selection of modified genes typically prevents this from occurring. Bioengineers genetically alter specific proteins in the DNA of the crop to target specific family groups of insects. Several biotechnological researchers, Srivastava et al., observed that Cryl protein (insecticide) is effective at dispatching moth and butterfly larvae, while Cry3 protein is effective against beetles. Furthermore, the researchers assert the toxicity level of all Cry proteins to mammals, birds, and fish are extremely low (136). Non-target insects are not directly or indirectly affected by these proteins, and are not susceptible to the insecticide. However, there are certainly isolated cases where non-target insects may have been affected indirectly by a GM crop. Research has shown lacewing larvae, which feed on caterpillars affected by GM insecticide (Cry 1 Ab) corn, had a higher mortality rate than the lacewing larvae, which fed on non-GM corn feeding caterpillars (Singh et al. 603). Still, this problem may be directly related to the application of chemical toxins and not due to the GM crop carrying the gene as evident from the studies of the effects of spraying non-target insects, like lacewings, with the (Cry 1 Ab) insecticides (Singh et al. 603). Thus far, there have been no significant reported losses of a non-target species due to genetically modified crops.

There are herbicide modifications made to plants as well. Herbicide GM crops are the most successful of all biotechnological crops so far. In 2003, the US alone has produced 81 percent of soybean, 59 percent of cotton, and 15 percent of corn crops that were herbicide tolerant (Srivastava et al. 140). The US is not the only country to support growing these crops. Argentinean farmers have embraced GM soybeans and their crop accounts for 95 percent of the market (Srivastava et al. 140). The Environmental Defense Fund considers GM herbicide crops one of the most environmentally benign herbicides ever developed (Conko and Miller 80). Nayak et al. agrees herbicide resistance crops have the ability to decrease the overall use of herbicides and is a more environmentally friendly approach (113). These plants are typically modified to resist the broad spectrum glyphosate herbicide. It is the most widely used herbicide worldwide because of its low environmental impact and effectiveness. This is a nonspecific chemical herbicide designed to kill most plants. After it is applied the chemical is broken down by microorganisms and does not persist long in the soil (Srivastava et al. 139). The benefit of using glyphosate resistant crops is that it reduces the need to use other harmful chemicals which leads to lower toxicity levels in the soil, water, and air. This also enables farmers to use a more environmentally friendly no-tilling process. This prevents topsoil erosion, reduces runoff to rivers, streams, and lakes, and releases less carbon dioxide into the atmosphere from mechanical equipment (Conko and Miller 79). Typically, predominant crops like soybeans, cotton, corn, and canola have been genetically modified to express this resistance. For example, GM (Round Up) soybeans express the nontoxic herbicide that deactivates, degrades in the soil, and is substantially equivalent to conventional commercial soybeans (Nayak et al. 113).

Critics believe even with all of these environmental benefits, there are substantial negative effects associated with GM crops as well. One particular negative aspect they argue is that there is a possibility for invasive plants to evolve and adapt to resist synthetic herbicides and become "super weeds" (Nayak et al. 116). All plants have the biological ability to adapt and become resistant to herbicides like glyphosate. It is inevitable that most species of plants will eventually adapt to survive. Essentially, a GM herbicide crop is modified to skip several generational and evolutionary steps to express this adaptation. When this happens with invasive plants or "superweeds", it will require producers to use stronger herbicides, or use more hazardous chemicals to get rid of them. Furthermore, it is important to note that the first "super weed" already exists. Researchers Nayak et al. have confirmed that properties from GM modified canola crops have affected the wild mustard plant. These researchers report that the GM canola crops have been known to spread their herbicide resistant traits to the wild mustard plant creating the first, and only, "super weed" (116). Still, plant adaptation is a natural evolutionary process. After twenty years of planting and globalization of GM crops, "super weeds", like the wild mustard plant, have not been observed at a detrimental level or seem to have negatively affected biodiversity in a region.

The inevitability of "super weeds" also raises public concerns regarding biodiversity. The most notable concern of biodiversity is if cross-pollination of GM and conventional crops could be a possibility. Research shows this was an issue raised by environmentalist groups in Oaxaca, Mexico. The environmentalist groups speculated that GM corn, planted next to native corn in Oaxaca, would cross-pollinate and threaten the diversity of the native species. However, a large scale, systematic, survey showed no evidence of any invasion by the GM corn on the native species (Singh et al. 603). Cross-pollination is a valid public concern, but in this case, planting GM crops next to conventional crops did not appear to have a significant impact on biodiversity.

With the minimal negative impact on worldwide biodiversity, its surrounding environment, and non target insects, GM crops are not the bane they are perceived to be by the public. There still stands a genuine possibility that these crops may create a catastrophic event in the future. However, based on the past twenty years of applying this technology, this is unlikely to occur. The reduction of pesticide use alone has benefited the environment tremendously, and this accomplishment is noteworthy enough for this technology be considered the future of agriculture. It is predicted that, by 2015, more than 200 million hectares of land will be planted with genetically modified crops in over 40 countries (Maghari and Ardekani 110). These crops are the future of agriculture whether they are embraced by society or not. After all, these plants are based off of traditional breeding practices, and gene-splicing is simply used to skip several evolutionary steps. This biotechnology has become so effective that crops are even being designed to enhance nutrition. For example, The Danford Center has created GM grains enriched with vitamin E and vegetables with enhanced folic levels (Schmidt 530). It is clear GM crops have not negatively impacted the environment. Instead, the environment has benefited from these plants. Once the clouds of negative perspectives have been cleared, these genetically modified crops will be embraced by society as the future of agriculture.

Works Cited

Conko, Gregory, and Henry Miller. "The Rush to Condemn Genetically Modified Crops." Policy Review 165 (2011): 69–82. EBSCOhost. Web. 15 Feb. 2013.

Maghari, Behrokh, and Ali Ardekani. "Genetically Modified Foods and Social Concerns." Avicenna Journal of Medical Biotechnology 3.3 (2011): 109–117. EBSCOhost. Web. 15 Feb. 2013.

Nayak, Laxmikanta, et al. "Genetically Modified Crops." Agricultural Reviews 32.2 (2011): 112–119. EBSCOhost. Web. 15 Feb. 2013.

Schmidt, Charles. "Genetically Modified Foods Breeding Uncertainty." Environmental Health Perspectives 113.8 (2005): 526–533. EBSCOhost. Web. 15 Feb. 2013.

Singh, Om, et al. "Genetically Modified Crops: Success, Safety Assessment, and Public Concern." Applied Microbiology & Biotechnology 71.5 (2006): 598–607. EBSCOhost. Web. 15 Feb. 2013.

Srivastava, Navin, et al. "Genetically Modified Crops: An Overview." Biotechnology 10.2 (2011): 136–148. EBSCOhost. Web. 15 Feb. 2013.

INDEX